W9-BZN-696

ENCYCLOPEDIA
OF
THE REFORMED FAITH

ENCYCLOPEDIA OF THE REFORMED FAITH

Donald K. McKim, Editor

David F. Wright, Consulting Editor

Westminster/John Knox Press
Louisville, Kentucky

Saint Andrew Press
Edinburgh

First published in 1992 by
Westminster/John Knox Press
Louisville, Kentucky, U.S.A.

First published in the UK by
Saint Andrew Press
121 George Street, Edinburgh EH2 4YN

First edition

This book is printed on acid-free paper that meets the American National Standards Institute Z39.48 standard. ♾

PRINTED IN THE UNITED STATES OF AMERICA
9 8 7 6 5 4 3 2 1

Library of Congress Cataloging-in-Publication Data

Encyclopedia of the Reformed faith / Donald K. McKim, editor — 1st ed.
p. cm.
Includes bibliographical references.
ISBN 0-664-21882-2

1. Reformed Church—Encyclopedias. 2. Presbyterian Church—Encyclopedias. I. McKim, Donald K.
BX9406.E56 1992
284′.2′03—dc20 91-37540

British Library Cataloguing in Publication Data

A catalogue record for this book
is available from the British Library

ISBN 0-7152-0660-5

Printed and bound by
R. R. Donnelley & Sons Co.
Crawfordsville, Indiana

PREFACE

The Reformed faith is the faith of Christian people. It is a living, vital stream of faith providing a basis for the lives of millions throughout the world. This faith has a historical tradition, contemporary expressions, and prospects of continuing to grow and develop by God's grace in the years ahead.

The following encyclopedia pays particular attention to the historical development of the Reformed faith and its current-day expressions. It considers events, persons, and theological issues that have special importance for the Reformed tradition. It is an encyclopedia of the Reformed faith to voice the conviction that history has meaning, that persons make contributions, and that theological doctrines and questions have critical impacts on human existence. This means that there is an essential connection among the past, present, and future elements of the faith. The aliveness of the faith is witnessed to by the events and persons who have shaped it as well as by the dynamic expressions of Reformed theology that have emerged.

This *Encyclopedia of the Reformed Faith* speaks too of the persuasion that the faith can be articulated and that at points its distinctiveness from other streams of Christian tradition can be perceived. Theologians varied in perspectives and orientations have claimed the name "Reformed." They have developed theological expressions portraying their understandings of Christian faith and God's revelation in Jesus Christ known through Holy Scripture. The plurality of these expressions—both by theologians and by church bodies through confessions of faith—show the varied nature of Reformed faith and Reformed theology. No single definition of "Reformed" faith has emerged from a consensus. Yet those who claim this name as their own do so with some common allegiances to past theological articulations.

The Reformed faith means most broadly the perception of Christian faith rooted in the sixteenth-century Protestant Reformation and expressed by John Calvin (1509–64). This thought and its attendant expressions took shape in Reformed confessions and other theological writings as well as in ecclesiastical forms from that time to the present. Calvin's thought has been formative. His extensive writings, particularly his *Institutes of the Christian Religion* (editions 1536–60), have provided the bedrock for much Reformed thought. His influence in the city of Geneva and involvement in many areas of that city's life ensured that his theological views took concrete and practical expression. His tireless preaching and public lecturing were the forums by which his views spread. Calvin's letters of spiritual counsel to people throughout Europe, many of whom were facing persecution, provided a living expression of his faith. His biblical commentaries and theological treatises furnished significant expression of distinctive understandings of Scripture and Christian doctrines.

Calvin's identification with the Reformed theological tradition has been such that the faith and the tradition are often referred to as "Calvinist" or "Calvinism." Calvin's successors built on his work in theirs. An important intramural scholarly debate has been about the extent to which Calvin's own insights and thought were extended and modified by later Calvinists. The development took place soon after Calvin's death and extended into the period of Reformed orthodoxy or scholasticism in the seventeenth century.

Yet Calvin's voice was not alone in setting the course for Reformed thought. Huldrych Zwingli's (1484–1531) in Zurich was earlier. Besides providing an important theological legacy, Zwingli applied the developing Protestant message to the social and political contexts of his day. Other prominent sixteenth-century theologians include Martin Bucer (1491–1551), Peter Martyr Vermigli (1500–62), Heinrich Bullinger (1504–75), Theodore Beza (1519–1605), and Girolamo Zanchi (1516–90).

The general designation "Reformed" refers to the emphasis of the Swiss Reformation—in both Zurich and Geneva—on reform of the church according to the Word of God. Most broadly, all Protestant churches are "reformed" in that they look to Scripture as their primary source of authority. In the sixteenth century, "reformed" was used as a synonym for "Protestant" and "evangelical" over against the Roman Catholic Church. In England, Queen Elizabeth commented once in a letter that non-Lutheran churches were "more reformed" in their orientations.

The Genevan Reformation began with William Farel (1489–1565), who was trained as a Christian humanist and who enlisted Calvin in the work of reform. Calvin's own training as a humanist was to have important and lasting effects on his work as a Christian theologian. His leadership in many phases of Genevan life, including the establishment of the Geneva Academy for the education and training of ministers, made Geneva an influential hub of activity as Reformed churches developed throughout Europe.

The history of Reformed churches in Europe is intertwined with national histories as Reformed Christians were persecuted, exiled, and faced the hardships of establishing churches in various countries. In many locations, Reformed churches produced confessions of faith to express their theological convictions. Early theses emerged in Zurich (1523), Bern (1528), Rive (1535), and Lausanne (1536). Among major confessional statements are the Confession of Basel (1534), the First Helvetic Confession (1536), the Second Helvetic Confession (1566), and confessions of Geneva, France, and the Netherlands: the Confession of Geneva (1537); the Consensus of Geneva (1552); the French Confession (1559); and the Belgic Confession (1561). In the Rhineland, the Tetrapolitan Confession (1530) and the Heidelberg Catechism (1563) are outstanding. Other European confessions include the Confession of Czenger (Hungary; 1557 or 1558), the Consensus of Sendomir (1570), and the Confession of Sigismund (1614). In the English language, the Scots Confession (1560), the Thirty-nine Articles (1563), the Irish Articles of Religion (1615), and the

Westminster Confession and Catechisms (1647) stand out. Important seventeenth-century theological statements are the Canons of Dort (1618) and the Helvetic Consensus Formula (1675). Whereas the Lutheran tradition selected certain theological standards as the perpetual expression of Lutheran faith, the Reformed tradition has produced a profusion of confessional statements.

Reformed churches spread through the European continent and into the Americas by emigration. Missionary expansion in the eighteenth and nineteenth centuries led to establishment of significant Reformed bodies on the African continent, particularly in South Africa, and in Australasia. Reformed bodies also grew in Latin America and in South America, in Asia, and in the Near East. Indigenization of churches with Reformed roots has now taken place and continues to do so throughout the world. The World Alliance of Reformed Churches (Presbyterian and Congregational), formed in 1970, has nineteenth-century predecessor groups that sought to provide a way for Reformed bodies to signify a sense of unity. In 1990 the World Alliance had 173 member church communions.

This *Encyclopedia of the Reformed Faith* provides a picture of major events, persons, and theological understandings of the Reformed faith. It is "encyclopedic" not in the sense that it can exhaustively treat all aspects of the Reformed faith in a comprehensive manner. It is not a history or taxonomy of "Reformed" churches. Rather, it seeks to provide a circle of knowledge (from "Accommodation" to "Zwingli") indicating how events, persons, and concepts have been particularly significant in the Reformed heritage. This orientation sets the following work apart from other general dictionaries and encyclopedias of church history and theology. The focus has been on the special importance of each component for the Reformed faith.

The work has also devoted most attention to the streams of the Reformed tradition found in Europe and in North America. A much longer story needs to be told, however, of important persons, events, and understandings emerging from Reformed contexts beyond these historic centers and on other continents. Future encyclopedias can also give more attention to contributions of laity, women, and nonwhite Reformed people. My own limitations of vision in determining the scope of this work within the necessary confines of space will be apparent. While this book can lay no claim to comprehensiveness, it does hope to make a start as a resource for painting some vital aspects of the Reformed faith. Larger reference works will supplement what is done here. For now, the purpose has been modest: to cover significant Reformed topics and to put this information within the reach and means of scholars, churches, and theological students.

The writers for this endeavor are virtually all Reformed scholars. They have lived and worked in the context of Reformed thought as a special area of professional expertise. They are themselves personally representatives of the Reformed faith by ecclesiastical commitment. I would like to express my thanks to all of them for their help with this project, for seeking to honor deadlines, and for doing the enormous job of condensing years and volumes of research into the necessary constraints of their articles. Without this cooperation, the project would not have been possible. A wide array of scholars from many traditions has been enlisted. In this regard, the encyclopedia may represent the largest cooperative Reformed venture on a single volume in history.

Besides the contributors, many persons have helped with the project. John G. Gibbs, Acquisitions Editor, encouraged this idea through a number of years until the "fullness of time" arrived. I greatly appreciate his friendship and sustained support. Robert McIntyre, Publisher, and Davis Perkins, Editorial Director of Westminster/John Knox Press, have been helpful as have been Danielle Alexander and Carl Helmich. Careful copyediting has been done by Marian Noecker. Cynthia Thompson, Associate Editorial Director, guided the process skillfully in all phases and deserves special thanks.

A great delight of this labor has been my association with David F. Wright, Dean of the Faculty of Divinity in New College, the University of Edinburgh, Scotland. As Consulting Editor, David has been thorough in suggesting articles and contributors as well as writing much himself. He persisted through all stages and supplied invaluable help with many important details. Beyond that, however, I am greatly pleased for the joy of our friendship.

Other good friends have helped in more ways than they know. Without their touch, the warmth of life would be much less. My family—LindaJo, Stephen, and Karl—endured my "computer time" and supported me with their love.

This book is dedicated to the congregation of Trinity Presbyterian Church of Berwyn, Pennsylvania. I was Interim Pastor for this wonderful people of God while the work was progressing. Their care for me, sensitivity to needs for time and "space" have made ministry in their midst a true blessing in every way. The volume is offered to them as part of the "Reformed family" in the Presbyterian Church (U.S.A.) with deep appreciation for their ongoing witness to Jesus Christ.

Donald K. McKim

Berwyn, Pennsylvania
Lent 1991

Selected Resources

The resources listed below supplement the perspectives of the preceding discussion.

Cochrane, Arthur C., ed. *Reformed Confessions of the 16th Century* (1966).
Gerrish, Brian A. *Tradition and the Modern World: Reformed Theology in the Nineteenth Century* (1978).
Leith, John H. *An Introduction to the Reformed Tradition,* rev. ed. (1981).
McGrath, Alister E. *A Life of John Calvin* (1990).
McKim, Donald K., ed. *Readings in Calvin's Theology* (1984).
———, ed. *Major Themes in the Reformed Tradition* (1991).
McNeill, John T. *The History and Character of Calvinism* (1954).

Muller, Richard A. *Christ and the Decree: Christology and Predestination in Reformed Theology from Calvin to Perkins* (1986).
———. *Post-Reformation Reformed Dogmatics,* vol. 1: *Prolegomena to Theology* (1987).
Osterhaven, M. Eugene. *The Spirit of the Reformed Tradition* (1971).
Prestwich, Menna, ed. *International Calvinism, 1541–1715* (1985).
Sell, Alan P. F. *A Reformed, Evangelical, Catholic Theology: The Contribution of the World Alliance of Reformed Churches, 1875–1982* (1991).
Vischer, Lukas, ed. *Reformed Witness Today: A Collection of Confessions and Statements of Faith Issued by Reformed Churches* (1982).

CONTRIBUTORS

P. Mark Achtemeier
Doctoral candidate
Duke University
Divinity School
Durham, North Carolina

Brett Armstrong
Doctoral candidate
Georgia State University
Atlanta, Georgia

Brian G. Armstrong
Professor of History
Georgia State University
Atlanta, Georgia

William V. Arnold
Professor of Pastoral Care
Union Theological Seminary
Richmond, Virginia

J. Wayne Baker
Professor of History
University of Akron
Akron, Ohio

E. Beatrice Batson
Professor of English
Wheaton College
Wheaton, Illinois

Robert Benedetto
Associate Librarian
Union Theological Seminary
Richmond, Virginia

Hendrikus Berkhof
Professor of Theology Emeritus
University of Leiden
Leiden, Netherlands

Lyle D. Bierma
Professor of Theology
Reformed Bible College
Grand Rapids, Michigan

Robert S. Bilheimer
Formerly Executive Director
Institute for Ecumenical Research
Cold Spring, Minnesota

Donald G. Bloesch
Professor of Theology
University of Dubuque
Theological Seminary
Dubuque, Iowa

William G. Bodamer
Professor and Chair
of Religion Department
Millikin University
Decatur, Illinois

Fred O. Bonkovsky
Professor of Christian Ethics
Columbia Theological Seminary
Decatur, Georgia

Lois A. Boyd
Assistant to the Vice-President
for Academic Affairs
Trinity University
San Antonio, Texas

R. Douglas Brackenridge
Professor of History
Trinity University
San Antonio, Texas

James D. Bratt
Associate Professor of History
Calvin College
Grand Rapids, Michigan

James L. Breed
Pastor, First Presbyterian Church
Kewanee, Illinois

R. H. Bremmer
Professor of Theology Emeritus
Enschede, Netherlands

Ian Breward
Professor, Uniting Church
Theological Hall
Ormond College
Parkville, Victoria, Australia

Geoffrey W. Bromiley
Professor Emeritus
of Church History
Fuller Theological Seminary
Pasadena, California

Robert McAfee Brown
Professor Emeritus
of Theology and Ethics
Pacific School of Religion
Berkeley, California

Stewart J. Brown
Professor of Ecclesiastical History
New College
University of Edinburgh
Edinburgh, Scotland

Donald J. Bruggink
Professor of Church History
Western Theological Seminary
Holland, Michigan

John E. Burkhart
Professor of Systematic Theology
McCormick Theological Seminary
Chicago, Illinois

Eberhard Busch
Professor of Reformed Theology
University of Göttingen
Göttingen, Germany

Philip W. Butin
Pastor, Oxford Presbyterian Church
Oxford, North Carolina

David G. Buttrick
Professor of Homiletics and Liturgics
Vanderbilt Divinity School
Nashville, Tennessee

Carnegie Samuel Calian
President and Professor of Theology
Pittsburgh Theological Seminary
Pittsburgh, Pennsylvania

Euan Cameron
Lecturer in History
University of Newcastle upon Tyne
Newcastle upon Tyne, England

Cynthia M. Campbell
Pastor, First Presbyterian Church
Salina, Kansas

Anna Case-Winters
Associate Professor
of Theology and Church
McCormick Theological Seminary
Chicago, Illinois

Alec C. Cheyne
Emeritus Professor
of Ecclesiastical History
University of Edinburgh
Edinburgh, Scotland

Milton J Coalter, Jr.
Librarian and Professor
of Bibliography
Louisville Theological Seminary
Louisville, Kentucky

Arthur C. Cochrane
Emeritus Professor of Theology
University of Dubuque
Theological Seminary
Dubuque, Iowa

Harvie M. Conn
Professor of Missions
Westminster Theological Seminary
Philadelphia, Pennsylvania

Stephen D. Crocco
Director of the Library
Pittsburgh Theological Seminary
Pittsburgh, Pennsylvania

Dan G. Danner
Professor of Theology
University of Portland
Portland, Oregon

Jane Dawson
Honorary Lecturer
in Modern History
University of St. Andrews
St. Andrews, Scotland

John W. de Gruchy
Professor of Christian Studies
University of Cape Town
Cape Town, South Africa

James A. De Jong
President and Professor
of Historical Theology
Calvin Theological Seminary
Grand Rapids, Michigan

Dawn De Vries
Assistant Professor
of Church History
McCormick Theological Seminary
Chicago, Illinois

Edward A. Dowey, Jr.
Professor of the History
of Christian Doctrine Emeritus
Princeton Theological Seminary
Princeton, New Jersey

Richard H. Drummond
Professor of the History
of Religion Emeritus
University of Dubuque Theological Seminary
Dubuque, Iowa

Nancy J. Duff
Assistant Professor
of Christian Ethics
Princeton Theological Seminary
Princeton, New Jersey

Carlos M. N. Eire
Associate Professor
of Religious Studies
University of Virginia
Charlottesville, Virginia

Gabriel Fackre
Professor of Christian Theology
Andover Newton Theological School
Newton Centre, Massachusetts

Benjamin Wirt Farley
Professor of Bible
Erskine College
Due West, South Carolina

John L. Farthing
Associate Professor of Religion
Hendrix College
Conway, Arkansas

Nathan P. Feldmeth
Adjunct Professor
Fuller Theological Seminary
Pasadena, California

Ronald Ferguson
Minister, St. Magnus Cathedral
Kirkwall
Orkney, Scotland

Janet E. Fishburn
Professor of American Church History
Drew University Graduate School
Madison, New Jersey

Duncan B. Forrester
Professor of Christian Ethics
and Practical Theology
New College
University of Edinburgh
Edinburgh, Scotland

David Foxgrover
Pastor, Congregational Church
Batavia, Illinois

John M. Frame
Professor of Theology
Westminster Theological Seminary
Escondido, California

Albert H. Freundt, Jr.
Professor of Church History
Reformed Theological Seminary
Jackson, Mississippi

Paul R. Fries
Dean and Professor of Theology
New Brunswick Theological Seminary
New Brunswick, New Jersey

Mary McClintock Fulkerson
Assistant Professor of Theology
Duke University Divinity School
Durham, North Carolina

Richard B. Gaffin, Jr.
Professor of New Testament
Westminster Theological Seminary
Philadelphia, Pennsylvania

Richard C. Gamble
Director, Henry Meeter Center for Calvin Studies
Calvin College and Seminary
Grand Rapids, Michigan

Timothy George
Dean and Professor of Divinity
Samford University Divinity School
Birmingham, Alabama

John H. Gerstner
Professor Emeritus of Church History
Pittsburgh Theological Seminary
Pittsburgh, Pennsylvania

Catherine Gunsalus González
Professor of Church History
Columbia Theological Seminary
Decatur, Georgia

W. Fred Graham
Professor of Religious Studies
Michigan State University
East Lansing, Michigan

Thomas M. Gregory
Emeritus Professor of Religion and Philosophy
New Wilmington, Pennsylvania

Donald D. Grohman
Professor of Religion and Philosophy
Knoxville College
Knoxville, Tennessee

Allen C. Guelzo
Associate Professor of American History
Eastern College
St. Davids, Pennsylvania

Shirley C. Guthrie, Jr.
Professor of Systematic Theology
Columbia Theological Seminary
Decatur, Georgia

Howard G. Hageman
President Emeritus
New Brunswick Theological Seminary
New Brunswick, New Jersey

Donald A. Hagner
Professor of New Testament
Fuller Theological Seminary
Pasadena, California

Elizabeth Bess Haile
Southhampton, New York

Michael A. Hakkenberg
Assistant Professor of History
Roanoke College
Salem, Virginia

Douglas John Hall
Professor of Christian Theology
McGill University
Montreal, Canada

Charles E. Hambrick-Stowe
Adjunct Professor
Lancaster Theological Seminary
Lancaster, Pennsylvania

Hendrik Hart
Professor of Philosophical Theology
Institute of Christian Studies
Toronto, Ontario, Canada

Trevor A. Hart
Lecturer in Systematic Theology
University of Aberdeen
Aberdeen, Scotland

W. Ian A. Hazlett
Lecturer in Ecclesiastical History
University of Glasgow
Glasgow, Scotland

Robert M. Healey
Professor of Church History
University of Dubuque Theological Seminary
Dubuque, Iowa

Alasdair I. C. Heron
Professor of Theology
University of Erlangen
Erlangen, Germany

I. John Hesselink
Professor of Systematic Theology
Western Theological Seminary
Holland, Michigan

J. David Hoeveler, Jr.
Professor of History
University of Wisconsin
Milwaukee, Wisconsin

Philip C. Holtrop
Professor of Religion
Calvin College
Grand Rapids, Michigan

Richard Hörcsik
Dean of the Reformed College
Sarospatak
Member, Hungarian Parliament
Sarospatak, Hungary

Edward M. Huenemann
Staff, Theology in Global Context Association
Closter, New Jersey

Philip E. Hughes†
Formerly Professor, Westminster Theological Seminary
Philadelphia, Pennsylvania

W. Michael Jinkins
Pastor, Brenham Presbyterian Church
Brenham, Texas

Merwyn S. Johnson
Professor of Historical and Systematic Theology
Erskine Theological Seminary
Due West, South Carolina

R. Tudur Jones
Honorary Professor of Church History
University College of North Wales
Bangor, Wales

Christopher B. Kaiser
Associate Professor of Historical and Systematic Theology
Western Theological Seminary
Holland, Michigan

Douglas F. Kelly
Assistant Professor of Theology
Reformed Theological Seminary
Jackson, Mississippi

Earl Wm. Kennedy
Professor of Religion
Northwestern College
Orange City, Iowa

Robert M. Kingdon
Professor of History
University of Wisconsin
Madison, Wisconsin

James Kirk
Senior Lecturer in Scottish History
University of Glasgow
Glasgow, Scotland

William Klempa
Principal, Presbyterian College
Montreal, Canada

R. Buick Knox
Formerly Professor
of Ecclesiastical History
Westminster College
Cambridge University
Cambridge, England

Richard G. Kyle
Professor of History
Tabor College
Hillsboro, Kansas

David C. Lachman
Editor, *The Presbyterian Advocate*
Wyncote, Pennsylvania

John H. Leith
Professor of Theology Emeritus
Union Theological Seminary
Richmond, Virginia

Robert Letham
Pastor, Emmanuel Presbyterian Church
Wilmington, Delaware

Alan E. Lewis
Professor of Constructive Theology
Austin Presbyterian Theological Seminary
Austin, Texas

Robert D. Linder
Professor of History
Kansas State University
Manhattan, Kansas

David Little
Senior Scholar
U.S. Institute of Peace
Washington, D.C.

Bradley J. Longfield
Visiting Assistant Professor
of American Christianity
Duke University Divinity School
Durham, North Carolina

A. T. B. McGowan
Minister, Trinity Possil
and Henry Drummond Church
Glasgow
Glasgow, Scotland

Barbara J. MacHaffie
Assistant Professor of Religion
Marietta College
Marietta, Ohio

C. T. McIntire
Associate Professor of History
University of Toronto
Toronto, Ontario, Canada

Elsie Anne McKee
Associate Professor
of the History of Worship
Princeton Theological Seminary
Princeton, New Jersey

Alexander J. McKelway
Professor of Religion
Davidson College
Davidson, North Carolina

Donald K. McKim
Minister, Presbyterian Church (U.S.A.)
Berwyn, Pennsylvania

LindaJo H. McKim
Editor, *The Presbyterian Hymnal*
Berwyn, Pennsylvania

Joseph C. McLelland
Professor of Religion
McGill University
Montreal, Canada

Jack P. Maddex, Jr.
Professor of History
University of Oregon
Eugene, Oregon

P. C. Matheson
Dean of the Faculty of Theology
University of Otago
Knox College
Dunedin, New Zealand

M. Douglas Meeks
Dean and Professor of Theology
Wesley Theological Seminary
Washington, D.C.

Julius Melton
Executive Director
of Institutional Advancement
Davidson College
Davidson, North Carolina

Bruce M. Metzger
Professor of New Testament
Language and Literature Emeritus
Princeton Theological Seminary
Princeton, New Jersey

Daniel L. Migliore
Professor of Systematic Theology
Princeton Theological Seminary
Princeton, New Jersey

Donald G. Miller
Formerly President, Pittsburgh
Theological Seminary
Pittsburgh, Pennsylvania

Glenn T. Miller
Professor of Church History
Southeastern Baptist
Theological Seminary
Wake Forest, North Carolina

Kenneth P. Minkema
Associate Research Editor
of Edwards' Works
Yale Divinity School
New Haven, Connecticut

Samuel Hugh Moffett
Professor of Ecumenics
and Mission Emeritus
Princeton Theological Seminary
Princeton, New Jersey

James H. Moorhead
Professor of American Church
History
Princeton Theological Seminary
Princeton, New Jersey

Lewis S. Mudge
Dean and Professor of Theology
San Francisco Theological Seminary
San Anselmo, California

John M. Mulder
President and Professor
of Historical Theology
Louisville Theological Seminary
Louisville, Kentucky

Richard A. Muller
Professor of Historical Theology
Calvin Theological Seminary
Grand Rapids, Michigan

N. R. Needham
Librarian, Rutherford House
Edinburgh, Scotland

Roger Nicole
Professor of Theology
Reformed Theological Seminary
Maitland, Florida

Rick Nutt
Assistant Professor of Religion
Muskingum College
New Concord, Ohio

Hughes Oliphant Old
Center of Theological Inquiry
Princeton, New Jersey

Jeannine E. Olson
Assistant Professor of History
Rhode Island College
Providence, Rhode Island

Richard R. Osmer
Associate Professor
of Christian Education
Princeton Theological Seminary
Princeton, New Jersey

M. Eugene Osterhaven
Emeritus Professor
of Systematic Theology
Western Theological Seminary
Holland, Michigan

Douglas F. Ottati
Professor of Theology
Union Theological Seminary
Richmond, Virginia

James I. Packer
Professor of Theology
Regent College
Vancouver, B.C., Canada

Robert J. Palma
Professor of Religion
Hope College
Holland, Michigan

Thomas D. Parker
Professor of Theology
McCormick Theological Seminary
Chicago, Illinois

Charles Partee
Professor of Church History
Pittsburgh Theological Seminary
Pittsburgh, Pennsylvania

Andrew Pettegree
Lecturer in Modern History
University of St. Andrews
St. Andrews, Scotland

John H. Primus
Professor of History
Calvin College
Grand Rapids, Michigan

Barbara A. Pursey
Adjunct Assistant Professor
University of Dubuque
Theological Seminary
Dubuque, Iowa

Andrew Purves
Associate Professor
of Pastoral Theology
Pittsburgh Theological Seminary
Pittsburgh, Pennsylvania

Ralph W. Quere
Professor of the History
of Doctrine
Wartburg Theological Seminary
Dubuque, Iowa

Robert R. Redman, Jr.
Director, Doctor of Ministry
Program
Fuller Theological Seminary
Pasadena, California

W. Stanford Reid
Professor of History Emeritus
University of Guelph
Guelph, Ontario, Canada

Ian S. Rennie
Dean and Professor of Church
History
Ontario Theological Seminary
Willowdale, Ontario, Canada

Jack B. Rogers
Vice-President
for Southern California
and Professor of Theology
Presbyterian Seminary of the West
Pasadena, California

John B. Roney
Assistant Professor of History
Sacred Heart University
Fairfield, Connecticut

Andrew C. Ross
Senior Lecturer
in Ecclesiastical History
New College
University of Edinburgh
Edinburgh, Scotland

H. Martin Rumscheidt
Professor of Theology
Atlantic School of Theology
Halifax, Nova Scotia, Canada

Letty M. Russell
Professor of Theology
Yale University Divinity School
New Haven, Conncctiut

Leland Ryken
Professor of English
Wheaton College
Wheaton, Illinois

Jean-Loup Seban
Assistant Professor of Church
History
Princeton Theological Seminary
Princeton, New Jersey

Henry R. Sefton
Senior Lecturer in Church History
Divinity School
University of Aberdeen
Aberdeen, Scotland

Alan P. F. Sell
Professor of Religious Studies
University of Calgary
Calgary, Alberta, Canada

M. Richard Shaull
Professor of Ecumenics Emeritus
Princeton Theological Seminary
Princeton, New Jersey

Donald W. Shriver, Jr.
President
Union Theological Seminary
New York, New York

Donald Sinnema
Associate Professor of Theology
Trinity Christian College
Palos Heights, Illinois

Elwyn A. Smith
St. Petersburg, Florida

Holly Haile Smith
Southampton, New York

James C. Spalding
Formerly Professor of Religion
University of Iowa
Iowa City, Iowa

Wayne R. Spear
Professor of Theology
Reformed Presbyterian Theological
Seminary
Wilkinsburg, Pennsylvania

Stephen R. Spencer
Associate Professor
of Systematic Theology
Dallas Theological Seminary
Dallas, Texas

Gordon J. Spykman
Professor of Theology
Calvin College
Grand Rapids, Michigan

John W. Stewart
Lecturer in American Church
History
Yale University Divinity School
New Haven, Connecticut

K. J. Stewart
Research Student
Faculty of Divinity
New College
University of Edinburgh
Edinburgh, Scotland

Jack L. Stotts
President and Professor
of Christian Ethics
Austin Presbyterian Theological
Seminary
Austin, Texas

George W. Stroup
Professor of Theology
Columbia Theological Seminary
Decatur, Georgia

N. M. Sutherland
Professor of Early Modern
European History Emeritus
Little Milton, Oxfordshire, England

Charles M. Swezey
Dean and Professor of Christian
Ethics
Union Theological Seminary
Richmond, Virginia

L. Gordon Tait
Professor of Religion
College of Wooster
Wooster, Ohio

J. Randolph Taylor
President
San Francisco Theological Seminary
San Anselmo, California

Eugene TeSelle
Professor of Church History
and Theology
Vanderbilt Divinity School
Nashville, Tennessee

Jack Thompson
Lecturer in Mission
Selly Oak Colleges
Birmingham, England

Peter Toon
Professor of Systematic Theology
Nashotah House
Nashotah, Wisconsin

Jay M. Van Hook
Professor of Philosophy
Northwestern College
Orange City, Iowa

John C. Vander Stelt
Assistant Professor
of Philosophy and Theology
Dordt College
Sioux Center, Iowa

Ronald J. VanderMolen
Professor of History
California State University
Turlock, California

Kenneth Vaux
Professor of Ethics
University of Illinois Medical Center
Riverside, Illinois

Lukas Vischer
Office protestant
pour l'oecuménisme en Suisse
Evangelische Arbeitsstelle
Oekumene Schweiz
Bern, Switzerland

Derk Visser
Professor of History
Ursinus College
Collegeville, Pennsylvania

Arvin Vos
Professor of Philosophy
Western Kentucky University
Bowling Green, Kentucky

Dennis N. Voskuil
Professor of Religion
Hope College
Holland, Michigan

John R. Walchenbach
Pastor, Preston Hollow Presbyterian
Church
Dallas, Texas

Dewey D. Wallace, Jr.
Professor of Religion
George Washington University
Washington, D.C.

Andrew F. Walls
Director, Centre for the Study of Christianity in the Non-Western World
New College
University of Edinburgh
Edinburgh, Scotland

Robert C. Walton
Direktor für Neue Kirchen- und Theologiegeschichte
Westfälische Wilhelms Universität
Münster, Germany

Louis B. Weeks
Dean and Professor of Historical Theology
Louisville Theological Seminary
Louisville, Kentucky

Charles C. West
Emeritus Professor of Christian Ethics
Princeton Theological Seminary
Princeton, New Jersey

James A. Whyte
Emeritus Professor of Christian Ethics and Practical Theology
St. Mary's College
University of St. Andrews
St. Andrews, Scotland

Preston N. Williams
Professor of Theology and Contemporary Change
Harvard Divinity School
Cambridge, Massachusetts

David Willis-Watkins
Professor of Systematic Theology
Princeton Theological Seminary
Princeton, New Jersey

John E. Wilson
Professor of Church History
Pittsburgh Theological Seminary
Pittsburgh, Pennsylvania

Marianne L. Wolfe
Stated Clerk, Pittsburgh Presbytery
Pittsburgh, Pennsylvania

John Wolffe
History Department
University of York
York, England

David F. Wright
Senior Lecturer in Ecclesiastical History
Dean of the Faculty of Divinity
New College
University of Edinburgh
Edinburgh, Scotland

Henry Zwaanstra
Professor of Historical Theology
Calvin Theological Seminary
Grand Rapids, Michigan

ABBREVIATIONS

AIB — Jack Rogers and Donald McKim, *The Authority and Interpretation of the Bible* (San Francisco: Harper & Row, 1979)
AP — *American Presbyterians*
ARG — *Archiv für Reformationsgeschichte*
ARH — *Archive for Reformation History*
BC — *Book of Confessions*
BCP — *Book of Common Prayer*
CD — Karl Barth, *Church Dogmatics* (Edinburgh: T. & T. Clark, 1936–69)
CF — Friedrich Schleiermacher, *The Christian Faith* (1821–22; 2nd ed. 1830–31; ET 1928)
CFI — Hendrikus Berkhof, *Christian Faith: An Introduction to the Study of the Faith,* rev. ed. (Grand Rapids: Wm. B. Eerdmans Publishing Co., 1986)
CH — *Church History*
CO — *Ioannis Calvini Opera qui supersunt omnia,* ed. W. Baum, E. Cunitz, and E. Reuss, 58 vols. (Brunswick and Berlin: Schwetschke, 1865–1900)
CR — *Corpus Reformatorum* (Berlin and Leipzig, 1834–)
Creeds — *The Creeds of Christendom,* ed. Philip Schaff, 3 vols. (1877)
CTJ — *Calvin Theological Journal*
DD — Alan P. F. Sell, *Defending and Declaring the Faith: Some Scottish Examples, 1860–1920* (Colorado Springs, Colo.: Helmers Howard Publishers, 1987)
DNB — *Dictionary of National Biography,* and supplements (London, 1885–)
EPM — Patrick Collinson, *The Elizabethan Puritan Movement* (1967; repr. New York: Routledge, Chapman & Hall, 1982)
ET — English translation
FD — Otto Weber, *The Foundations of Dogmatics,* 2 vols. (ET Grand Rapids: Wm. B. Eerdmans Publishing Co., 1982–83)
Gr. — Greek
HC — Heidelberg Catechism
HCC — Philip Schaff, *History of the Christian Church,* 12 vols. (1883–93)
Inst. — John Calvin, *Institutes of the Christian Religion*
JPH — *Journal of Presbyterian History*
LCC — Library of Christian Classics, 26 vols.
NIV — New International Version

NSH	*The New Schaff-Herzog Encyclopedia of Religious Knowledge,* 13 vols. (New York, 1908–1912; repr. Grand Rapids: Baker Book House, 1949–50); supplement, *Twentieth Century Encyclopedia of Religious Knowledge,* 2 vols. (1955)
NT	New Testament
OT	Old Testament
PCUS	Presbyterian Church in the United States
PCUSA	Presbyterian Church in the United States of America
PC(USA)	Presbyterian Church (U.S.A.)
RCA	Reformed Church in America
RD	Heinrich Heppe, *Reformed Dogmatics,* ed. Ernst Bizer (ET 1950; repr. Grand Rapids: Baker Book House, 1978)
RGG	*Die Religion in Geschichte und Gegenwart,* 2nd ed., 5 vols. (1927–31); 3rd ed., 6 vols. (1957–65)
RSV	Revised Standard Version
SCJ	*Sixteenth Century Journal*
SJT	*Scottish Journal of Theology*
TEV	Today's English Version
TRE	*Theologische Realenzyklopädie,* ed. G. Krause and G. Müller (Berlin, 1977–)
TZ	*Theologische Zeitschrift*
UPCNA	United Presbyterian Church of North America
UPCUSA	United Presbyterian Church in the U.S.A.
WARC	World Alliance of Reformed Churches
WCC	World Council of Churches
WCF	Westminster Confession of Faith
WLC	Westminster Larger Catechism
WSC	Westminster Shorter Catechism
WTJ	*Westminster Theological Journal*

Accommodation

Latin rhetoricians and jurists used "accommodation" (Lat. *accommodatio*) for the process of adapting, fitting, and adjusting language to the needs and capacities of their hearers. This meant accounting for an audience's situation, character, intelligence, and emotional state.

Rhetorically trained early church theologians such as Origen, Chrysostom, and Augustine* used the concept when dealing with difficulties in the Bible. Calvin,* a classicist, expanded this and used accommodation to explain every relationship between God* and humanity.* Given the great gulf between God and humankind, by virtue of God's transcendence and human finiteness, God's holiness and human sinfulness, for God to communicate with humanity and God's revelation* to occur God must condescend to communicate in ways humans can understand, according to the limits of human capacities. This method of revelation of God's speaking and acting in human forms is God's accommodation.

Calvin saw accommodation as grounded in scriptural portrayals of God as Father, teacher, and physician. Three specific scriptural uses of accommodation are the law* (*Inst.* 2.11.13), the Lord's Prayer (*Inst.* 3.20.34), and the sacraments* (*Inst.* 4.1.1). Through these, the divine message of salvation* is conveyed, just as, more generally, in the language of Scripture* itself. God "lisps" in speaking of who God is to "accommodate the knowledge of [God] to our slight capacity" (*Inst.* 1.13.1). Using parental imagery, Calvin quoted Augustine: "We can safely follow Scripture, which proceeds at the pace of a mother stooping to her child, so to speak, so as not to leave us behind in our weakness" (*Inst.* 3.21.4). Calvin used accommodation to deal with God's nature (*Inst.* 1.13.1); creation (*Inst.* 1.14.3) and function of angels (*Inst.* 1.14.11); fate (*Inst.* 1.16.9); and God's ways with humans (*Inst.* 1.17.12–13). The supreme instance of accommodation, however, is Jesus Christ. In Christ, God has fully entered into the human by becoming a person. Calvin commented: "In Christ God so to speak makes himself little (*quodammodo parvum facit*), in order to lower himself to our capacity" (*ut se ad captum nostrum submittat*; *Commentary* on 1 Peter 1:20). For Calvin, human limitations were not barriers to hearing and understanding God's revelation and message of salvation, since God used humans to express the written Word of God* in Scripture.

F. L. Battles, "God Was Accommodating Himself to Human Capacity," *Interpretation* 31, no. 1 (January 1977): 19–38; Rogers and McKim, *AIB*.

DONALD K. MCKIM

Accommodation Plan

A plan of union between the Presbyterian Synod of Albany and the Congregational Middle Association of New York (1808). It enabled the Congregational Middle Association to be received "as a constituent branch of this [Presbyterian] Synod . . . retaining their own name and usages in the administration of the government of their churches." Thus the plan enabled Congregationalists and Presbyterians to become voting members of a united synod.

The Accommodation Plan supplemented the historic Plan of Union between the Presbyterian General Assembly and the Congregational General Association of Connecticut (1801). The Plan of Union instructed Congregational and Presbyterian missionaries to cooperate in the organization of new churches in frontier areas and allowed these churches to call ministers from either body. While the purpose of the Accommodation Plan was to facilitate the broad cooperation outlined in the union agreement (1801), it also set an organizational precedent by enabling Congregational churches to enter Presbyterian structures.

The plan helped spread the Congregational Awakening to Presbyterian churches and contributed to the formation of the great interdenominational benevolent and missionary societies, especially the American Board of Commissioners for Foreign Missions* and the American Home Missionary Society.* Gradually a number of theological and organizational problems arose, and the plan finally proved to be impractical as a model of church government. From the mid-1830s through the 1840s the Plan of Union unraveled as both Presbyterians and Congregationalists formed separate denominational and mission structures.

R. H. Nichols, *Presbyterianism in New York State* (1963).

ROBERT BENEDETTO

Adherents

A term used in many churches that follow the presbyterian* order. It denotes regular and committed adult church attenders who are not communicant members. In some places adherents are allowed to vote in the election of ministers and play a full part in the life of the congregation but are not allowed to become elders.* In parts of the Highlands of Scotland the number of adherents substantially exceeds the number of communicants because of an exaggerated reverence for the Lord's Supper,* which persuades people that only the aged and the markedly holy are qualified to approach the Lord's Table.

DUNCAN B. FORRESTER

Admonitions to Parliament

Two manifestoes to the English Parliament (1572; 1573) citing practical abuses and calling for reform in the Church of England. The First Admonition, written by two young representatives of the early Puritan wing of Elizabethan clergy, John Field* and Thomas Wilcox,* signals an important new development in early English Puritanism.* Frustrated by their failure (1560s) to secure reform of "popish abuses," the Puritan party began to direct its attack against the authority structure itself, that is, the episcopal government of the church, calling for a system of Reformed or Presbyterian polity.* The First Admonition, in harsh and cynical tones, condemns the establishment for abuses in church practice, contrasting the Church of England with the apostolic, NT church. To strengthen the argument, two letters from continental Reformed theologians, Rudolph Gualter and Theodore Beza,* were appended.

The Second Admonition, often ascribed to Thomas Cartwright,* outlines in more detail the presbyterian form of government to restore true discipline and result in genuine church reform. The Admonitions were hotly debated and were the opening salvo in the battle between presbyterian Puritans and the establishment in the Church of England, a struggle that continued throughout most of the rest of the century.

W. H. Frere and C. E. Douglas, eds., *Puritan Manifestoes* (1907; repr. 1972); D. J. McGinn, *The Admonition Controversy* (1949).

JOHN H. PRIMUS

Adopting Act

An action by the Synod of Philadelphia of the American Presbyterian Church (1729) requiring ministers to subscribe to the Westminster Confession* and the Westminster Larger and Shorter Catechisms. A compromise, the Adopting Act attempted to resolve the dispute between strict subscriptionists and non-subscriptionists who argued that the Bible alone should be all-sufficient for all necessary doctrines and practices.

The act required ministers to "declare their agreement in and approbation of" the Westminster Standards. However, it was recognized that there were essential as well as nonessential articles in these standards and also that an arriving minister or a ministerial candidate might have scruples about accepting everything in the Westminster documents. When this was the case, the person was to inform the presbytery or the synod, which would then decide whether his scruple applied to an essential point of doctrine, worship, or government. If it did, the minister was expected to leave the Presbyterian ministry; if it did not, he was admitted. Thus the principle established that the ordaining body had some flexibility in judging the correctness of a minister's subscription.

The controversy lingered after 1729. While the act was challenged by the strict subscriptionists, it was eventually reaffirmed by the new Synod of New York and Philadelphia (1758) as part of the agreement ending the Old Side–New Side division.

G. S. Klett, ed., *Minutes of the Presbyte-*

rian Church in America 1706–1788 (1976); L. J. Trinterud, *The Forming of an American Tradition* (1949).

L. GORDON TAIT

Adoption

The theologoumenon of adoption (or filiation) is that biblical understanding of the ultimate divine purpose in redemption which sees human persons as drawn into a peculiar relationship with God* as Father, through a relationship with God as Son and as Holy Spirit.* As such, it is a soteriological motif inseparable from the doctrines of the incarnation* and the Trinity.*

Biblical. Properly speaking, the language of adoption (Gr. *huiothesia*) is found only in the Pauline corpus (esp. Rom. 8; Gal. 4), though the idea of Christians as "sons" of *Abba* (God the Father) lies at the heart of Jesus' own message and ministry. The precedent for Paul's language can be discovered in the Jewish belief that Israel, through its election and rescue from Egypt by Yahweh, progressed from a status of slavery to one of "sonship" (a transition paralleled in the Christian's experience of redemption from sin). But it is equally clear that, for Paul, the "adoption" proper to Christian experience is rooted ontologically in the decision of God to send God's own Son into the world as a human being and is no mere metaphor. It is through union with Christ* and living "in him" that Christian existence consists in adoption, since it is precisely being given to share in the hitherto unique filial relation of love with the Father in the Spirit.

Patristic. Among the early Christian theologians, several took this central biblical theme and developed it theologically, being careful to distinguish the "adopted" sonship of Christians from the "natural" Sonship of him who is "consubstantial" with the Father, yet seeing the two as inseparably linked. It is within this context, as the christological thinking of the church developed, that the term "deification" (Gr. *theopoiēsis*) was introduced as a radical statement of the ultimate meaning of adoption, or filiation, clarifying the implication that human beings are given to share or participate in the very inner life of the Trinity as "sons" of the Father. It was precisely to safeguard this soteriological insight that the early theologians insisted that if Christ is thus to save us, he must be fully God as well as fully human.

Reformed. Reformed theology has often presented the God-human relationship in primarily judicial rather than filial categories, perhaps because it has traditionally focused rather more on that which human persons have been saved "from" by God than that which they have been saved "for." Yet, from John Calvin* onward, there has always been a recognition of the importance of the theme of adoption and of the ultimately prospective purpose of God in Christ in "bringing many sons to glory." Even the Westminster Confession,* the overall framework of which is unmistakably judicial, contains a separate chapter on adoption. What has sometimes been lacking, however, is clear recognition that the Trinitarian and filial understanding of God must, if it is taken seriously, provide the proper context for understanding the judicial side of God's activity rather than vice versa.

TREVOR A. HART

Advertisements, Book of

A set of ecclesiastical orders by Archbishop Matthew Parker (March 1566) to secure more uniformity in the worship* and discipline* of the Church of England. They dealt with doctrine and preaching,* prayer* and sacraments,* ecclesiastical polity, and apparel of ecclesiastics. They were met with fierce resistance from the "puritan" wing of the English clergy, particularly on the apparel issue. Their legality was challenged, for though Queen Elizabeth encouraged Parker to secure more uniformity, he was unable to achieve royal sanction of the orders.

E. Cardwell, *Documentary Annals*, 1:321–31; H. Gee and W. J. Hardy, *Documents Illustrative of English Church History* (1921).

JOHN H. PRIMUS

Africa

During the twentieth century, the part of Africa south of the Sahara has seen one of the most dramatic growth rates in the history of the church. This has affected the whole range of Christian communities—Roman Catholic, Protestant, and African Independent. Simultaneously there has been a dramatic indigenization of Christianity in Africa, so that in the last decade of the twentieth century African Christianity is both an African religion and a challenge to traditional Christian thinking in Europe and North America.

Among the Reformed family of churches a clear example of this indigenous dynamic is the development of the hymnody of the Church of Central Africa, Presbyerian, in Malawi. Encouraged by Donald Fraser (1870–1933) and Alexander Hetherwick (1860–1939), a very lively and beautiful indigenous hymnody developed. It was deeply suspect by the other missions in Central Africa for a long time because of its "Africanness." Yet it has been one of the factors in the tremendous growth of the Presbyterian Church which, by mid-century, constituted one-third of the Malawi population and at the time of independence provided the majority of the key cadres in the Congress Party.

On the other side of the continent, the Reformed Church in the Cameroons is a powerful institution within that republic. Its roots lie in the initiative of Jamaican Baptists who came to Cameroon (1845). German colonialism forced them to turn their work over to the Basel Mission (1886).

Later the development of the church was aided by American Presbyterians and the Paris Mission. The Theological Faculty of the Reformed Church at Yaoundé has provided a dynamic and creative center of thought, not only for Francophone Protestantism but for all African Christianity.

The neighboring Presbyterian Church of Nigeria is restricted in effect to the southeastern quarter of this most populous African country. The work was begun, as in the Cameroon, by the initiative of Jamaican Christians, this time the Presbyterian minority in Jamaica. With the help of the United Presbyterian Church of Scotland, the first missionaries arrived in 1846. The church has grown and produced many talented persons but has remained a regional church.

In Ghana and neighboring Togo, the Reformed tradition was introduced by the Bremen and Basel Mission Societies.* World War I led to the forced withdrawal of both societies for a time. The two churches they left became autonomous and were aided by the Scots Presbyterians and the Paris Mission. However, less happily, they were then cut into three by the Allied Powers, who gave part of the old German colony to the British and the rest to the French. Thus there came into existence two Reformed churches in what was then the British colony of the Gold Coast—the Presbyterian Church and, in the new territory, the Evangelical Presbyterian Church. In French Togo, the remainder of the church created by the Bremen Mission became L'Eglise Evangélique du Togo. All three churches, however, have flourished despite these enforced changes. They have continued to reach out evangelistically to the north and helped their nations develop.

In Zambia and Zaire the Presbyterian and Reformed churches have contributed to the United Churches. The PCUS began work in Kasai (1890). The powerful church that grew up there is now part of the Evangelical Church of Zaire which has united the whole range of Protestant denominations. In Zambia the United Church is essentially a union of the Reformed churches produced by the work of the Paris Mission, the London Missionary Society,* and Malawi and Scots missionaries from what was then Nyasaland. One of the Malawi missionaries was Rev. David Kaunda, father of Zambia's first president, Kenneth Kaunda.

In Kenya the Presbyterian Church of East Africa developed from the Church of Scotland Mission at Kikuyu, which grew from a privately funded mission at Kibwezi (1891). This church, despite its title, has been until recently a Gikuyu Church. It has used the Gikuyu language in contrast with the other churches which have used the East African common language, Swahili. Scots missionaries who made the first translation of the Bible into Gikuyu had the active help of a young teacher before he left to study in

Britain—Jomo Kenyatta, later first president of Kenya.

The Reformed and Presbyterian family of churches in Africa is now so significant that a separate division of the WARC* was established there (1989).

ANDREW C. ROSS

Afrikaners

Descendants of Dutch, and some French Huguenot* and German, settlers in South Africa. Afrikaners now constitute about 55 percent of the white population. Over 90 percent are members of three Dutch Reformed churches: the Nederduitse Gereformeerde Kerk, the Gereformeerde Kerk van Suid-Afrika, and the Nederduitse Hervormde Kerk, with the great majority belonging to the first. Though their theological heritage is Calvinist, the development of a common Afrikaans language and literature has given them a distinctive cultural bond. Their history has evolved a strong nationalist spirit and ideology, taking the political form of apartheid.* This political ideology has largely captivated major sections of the church and became governmental policy when the Nationalist Party came to power (1948).

EDWARD M. HUENEMANN

Alexander, Archibald (1772–1851)

Founding professor of Princeton Theological Seminary and "founder" of the Princeton Theology.* Alexander was tutored by William Graham, a student of John Witherspoon's* from whom he imbibed the common sense philosophy* of Scottish realism. His theological interests were awakened, and after exposure to the revivalism* of the Virginia Blue Ridge region, he professed his Christian faith (1789). He read important Reformed theologians and assumed the presidency of Hampden-Sydney College before his pastorate at Philadelphia's Third (Pine Street) Presbyterian Church. He preached to the Presbyterian General Assembly (1808) urging creation of a theological seminary and became Princeton's first professor (1812).

Studies centered on the works of Francis Turretin* and common sense philosophy. To counter Deism, Alexander taught that true knowledge came both from reason* and from religious experience.* He wrote *Evidences of the Christian Religion* (1825) and *Thoughts on Religious Experience* (1841). Alexander's doctrine of Scripture was developed by his followers, but he taught three kinds of inspiration (superintendence, suggestion, elevation) and gradually sought more objective external criteria to prove Scripture's authority. Emphases on religious experience and the witness of the Holy Spirit,* however, remained strong.

A. Alexander, *A Brief Compend of Bible Truth* (1846); L. A. Loetscher, *The Broadening Church* (1954); and *Facing the Enlightenment and Pietism* (1983); Rogers and McKim, *AIB*.

DONALD K. MCKIM

American Board of Commissioners for Foreign Missions

Organized in Massachusetts, the interdenominational ABCFM (1810–1961) was the first American foreign missionary society. Though it was predominantly Congregationalist, the Presbyterian, Dutch, German, and Associate Reformed churches also participated. Known for its work among the Georgia Cherokees (1817) and the Choctaws in Mississippi (1818), the ABCFM also operated missions in India (1813), Hawaii (1819), Syria (Beirut, 1823), China (1829), Greece (1831), Africa (1833), and Japan (1869). By 1894, it had reported 557 missionaries, 444 churches (41,522 members), and 1,022 schools (50,000 students). Its personnel conducted scientific research, translated the Bible, introduced the printing press, and provided medical services.

ROBERT BENEDETTO

American Home Missionary Society

Founded by New York Congregationalists, the American Home Missionary Society (1826–93) was an interdenominational organization of Presbyterian, Dutch Reformed, and Associate Reformed churches. These churches had withdrawn by 1861. In 1893 the Society became the Congregational Home Missionary Society. Its personnel worked in almost every state and territory. By 1893 the Society had supported 2,002 pastors and missionaries who served 3,841 congregations and funded construction of 2,444 churches and 432 parsonages. It organized churches and schools, provided grants encouraging church development, employed pastors and missionaries, and ministered to immigrants.

ROBERT BENEDETTO

Ames, William (1576–1633)

Highly influential Puritan theologian who was assistant to the president of the Synod of Dort* and whose *A Marrow of Sacred Theology* (1623) was a major Puritan theological work.

Ames was converted by William Perkins's* preaching at Christ's College, Cambridge, where he became a Fellow (1601–10). He was "a radical Puritan of the rigidest sort" and would not conform to the established church. He went to the Netherlands and became professor of theology at the University of Franeker (1622).

Ames provided a *technometria* (in *Philosophemata* [1643]), a way of defining and delineating the arts according to their nature and use, which functioned as a prolegomena to theology. He became "the foremost seventeenth-century Puritan Ramist" who imbibed his Ramism* from Perkins and believed Ramist theology made God's* revelation* intelligible.

Ames's *Marrow* was constructed Ramistically. He defined theology as "the doctrine or teaching of living to God." In this, he drew "faith" and "works" together. He divided theology (Ramistically) into "faith" and "observance," saying these "two parts are always joined together in use and exercise," yet distinguished in nature and by the rules that govern them. Ames saw theology not as a "speculative discipline but a practical one." His *De conscientia* (1622; 1630; ET *Conscience with the Power and Cases Thereof* [1639]) expanded the second part of his *Marrow*.

W. Ames, *The Marrow of Theology*, trans. from 3rd Latin ed. (1629) and ed. J. D. Eusden (1968); and *Technometry*, trans. L. W. Gibbs (1979); D. K. McKim, *Ramism in William Perkins' Theology* (1987); K. L. Sprunger, *The Learned Doctor William Ames* (1972).

DONALD K. MCKIM

Amyraut (Amyraldus), Moïse (1596–1664)

French Protestant pastor and theologian at Saumur. Trained in law (at Poitiers), Amyraut changed to theology after reading Calvin's* *Institutes*.* His moderate *Brief Treatise of Predestination* (1634) precipitated a bitter controversy in Reformed Protestantism. His covenantal theology, tied to a doctrine of universal atonement,* was its focal point, though it was fundamentally a conflict of mind-sets and types of theology—of the role in theology of the humanist* learning of the "Republic of Letters," as well as "pride of place" in Reformed Protestantism.

Heavily dependent upon Calvin and John Cameron* (his mentor), Amyraut taught an economic (or historical/linear) view of the Trinity.* The Father sent Christ to redeem the entire world, but this universal redemption was "hypothetical"; that is, it was effectual only when faith* was engendered in the heart through the Spirit.* This teaching frightened proponents of the decretal theology of most Reformed theological academies, especially since it reminded them of Arminianism.* Amyraut was tried for heresy at the National Synod of Alençon (1637) and, though exonerated, was charged not to publish his distinctive ideas further. That being impossible unless he forsook his entire covenantal understanding, the controversy plagued him until his death and tragically consumed the energies of the French Church.

B. G. Armstrong, *Calvinism and the Amyraut Heresy* (1969); F. Laplanche, *Orthodoxie et prédication: L'oeuvre d'Amyraut . . .* (1965); and *L' écriture, le sacré et l'histoire . . .* (1986); F. P. Van Stam, *The Controversy Over the Theology of Saumur . . .* (1988).

BRIAN G. ARMSTRONG

Analogy

Designation for a type of predication between univocal ("having the same meaning") and equivocal ("having different meanings") predication. A term is analogous when it names a quality that is partly the same and partly different in two or more subjects. Its theological significance is to explain how language that is derived from creatures can be applied to God.*

In John Calvin,* as in the church fathers, there is no systematic treatment of analogy as a type of predication. Yet it is implied in Calvin's doctrine of the knowledge of God* (*Inst.* 1.5–6). God's essence is incomprehensible, but there are innumerable evidences of God in creation.* So God is known from similarities in creatures which are dissimilar to God. After the fall, no true knowledge of God is possible from nature but only through revelation.*

In later Reformed theologians such as A. Quenstedt, one discerns the influence of Thomas Cajetan, a commentator on Aquinas. Essence, substance, spirit, and the like are terms predicated of both God and creatures by an analogy of intrinsic attribution. In other words, "essence" belongs to both God and creature but in different ways and because the creature has its essence from God.

In the twentieth century, Karl Barth* asserted that the only means for understanding God is by the analogy of faith (*analogia fidei*), not by any human, philosophical category (*analogia entis*). A word applied to creature and then to God has similarity in its meaning, partial correspondence and agreement, only because it has been chosen by God.

Barth, *CD* II/1; B. Mondin, *The Principle of Analogy in Protestant and Catholic Theology* (1963).

ARVIN VOS

Antiburghers

A party in the dispute among the seceded churches of Scotland over the acceptability of the burgess oath required of certain civil officeholders (1747). Fearing that the oath implied agreement with the established church, Antiburghers excommunicated those who accepted it. The two communions were split again around 1800 over the civil magistracy's role in upholding religion. Old Lights in each camp accepted this; New Lights urged total voluntarism. Though these divisions had mostly been healed by the nineteenth century, their issues, together with the original secession's complaint against patronage, demonstrate the perennial vexation of church-state issues in Scots Presbyterian history.

JAMES D. BRATT

Antirevolutionary Party

The political arm of the Netherlands neo-Calvinist movement arose in the 1870s inspired by the teachings of Guillaume Groen van Prinsterer and was long led by Abraham Kuyper.* The party sought to develop from scriptural principles and national experience a consistent political philosophy and comprehensive system of policy to counteract the secular liberalism stemming from the French Revolution. Kuyper's democratic accent alienated many conservatives (1890s). Yet the party has since then regularly served in ruling coalitions of the Dutch Parliament, most often with the Roman Catholic party, with which it merged in the late 1970s.

JAMES D. BRATT

Apartheid

This Afrikaans word for "separateness" has come to mean the fundamental philosophy that dominated the policy of the government of South Africa* (1948–89). It held that God made "nationality," ethnically defined, one of the immutable "orders of creation." South Africa had therefore to be divided among its separate "nations," with Sotho separate from Xhosa, Zulu, and others but with all "whites" defined as one nation. Since whites, with only 18 percent of the population, received 87 percent of the land, injustice was built into the system from the beginning. The so-called Coloured (Afrikaans-speaking) People and those of Asian ancestry had to live in racially segregated areas but could have no "homeland" as did whites or various "black" nations. The latter ceased to be South Africans, though the vast majority of their citizens lived and worked in "white" South Africa. Though the original theorists of apartheid had good intentions, the state that emerged after 1948 was, in practice, a ruthless, authoritarian, and unjust regime.

This philosophy has insisted on its essential Christian roots and was developed by devout members of the Nederduitse Gereformeerde Kerk (NGK; Dutch Reformed Church). The NGK was so closely related to the Nationalist Party that J. H. P. Serfontein could write (1982): "Church, state and Broederbond [Afrikaner secret society] are so interlocked that it is difficult to ascertain which wing of Afrikanerdom is actually responsible for a specific policy or plan of action" (*Apartheid Changes and the NG Kerk* [1982]).

The vast majority of "liberal" historians have explained this situation in terms of the NGK's Calvinism,* and Afrikaner leaders have done the same. The former did so while condemning apartheid, the latter in giving it divine justification. In the 1980s this interpretation has been challenged, and by 1990 an alternative explanation, at least in outline, emerged.

Afrikaner self-consciousness was formed by the experience of the moving frontier of the old Cape and the Great Trek. Throughout this period of more than 150 years, many Afrikaners were cut off from anything resembling traditional Calvinist church life with its regular preaching* from an educated ministry. In this situation, daily worship with Bible-reading by the family head was the norm and a "Boer" folk religion emerged. This echoed its Calvinist past but was shaped essentially by the trek experience and a naive bibliolatry.

The last decade of the nineteenth century saw church life become much more organized. Many young ministers were influenced by two decisive factors which, when added to the folk religion tradition, created the philosophy of apartheid. The first was a misapplication of Abraham Kuyper's* teaching on autonomy. The second was the profound impact of the missionary theory associated with Christian Keysser, which insisted that the gospel was most successfully planted when ethnic and cultural identity was preserved.

The WARC* declared apartheid a heresy (1982), and the NGK itself declared that apartheid was not in keeping with God's Word (1989).

J. de Gruchy and C. Villa-Vicencio, *Apartheid Is a Heresy* (1983).

ANDREW C. ROSS

Apologetics

Christianity has always had its cultural despisers. In every age Christian apologists have attempted to rebut objections or restate and refine Christian belief to make clearer its claims of knowledge of God.* Apologetics seeks to benefit the criticized and the critic by preserving the integrity of God who has been revealed in human thought forms as Supreme Truth.

Before and after the Reformation, apologetics often built a defense of Christianity on the same philosophy used by the unbeliever. When philosophy* was willing to be a servant to faith, the result was frequently a clearer reformulation of the faith, as seen in Augustine* and Thomas Aquinas. The Reformation, however, brought a crisis in apologetics as well as in theology. The prevailing method of defending the faith, scholasticism,* became an uncomfortable option for the Reformers. They perceived that it had been diverted from its proper objective of safeguarding the truth of God to the purpose of bolstering an organization that made itself the judge of truth. They recognized that philosophy was no longer willing to be a "handmaiden" to theology and could not be used to defend Christianity without excessive qualification of the faith.

Reformed thought thus introduced a paradigmatic change in apologetics. Shifting from a philosophy that stressed the priority of metaphysics and being, it embraced an outlook that put epistemology and truth first in preserving the authority of God in God's objective self-revelation. John Calvin* was a conscious exponent of this new approach with his stress on knowledge (*Inst.* 1). He observed that a knowledge of ourselves is mutually connected with the knowledge of God because self-knowledge arouses us to seek God. The epistemological connection is firmly seen when Calvin points out that the clarity and the truthfulness of self-knowledge, which stimulates us to seek God, are dependent upon knowing God's majesty and our own sinful pride and recognizing that God is the sole standard by which we know ourselves. Further indication of this paradigm shift is in Calvin's distinction of a twofold knowledge of God which became the definitive ordering principle of the structure of his *Institutes.*

At the heart of the Reformed apologetic stressing the reception of truth from God was a new conception of the place of the Bible. Scripture* was projected to purvey a comprehensive view of the world and life in it given by God, powerful enough to accommodate scientific and cultural change without being negatively shaped by it. Because of sin,* Scripture was necessary, and because it was from God it was authoritative and sufficient as a source of faith and life. Proclamation and exposition of the Word of God* became the apologetic, because there could be no knowledge of God that is not basically conceptual.

The Bible was viewed as "properly basic," as self-authenticating. The task of reason was not to validate such acclaim but to provide insight for biblical interpretation or application. Self-authentication meant that the Bible contains truths that are patent and can persuade to belief without supplementary aid. Thus the aim of apologetics was to set forth in a winsome fashion the promises of God and God's redemptive action in Christ. God had accommodated* his truth to human capacity in order to meet human need. Scripture gives rise to distinctive beliefs that satisfy human hopes and fears. The judgments of Scripture are believed, not because philosophy or a church council validates them, nor simply because they are helpful, but because they are accepted as truths from God. Assenting to them as true is the mediate cause of their power to arouse and satisfy religious need, and the Holy Spirit is the immediate cause of the believing.

Though centered in promulgating the biblical message, this apologetic may employ external reasons, or evidences, to achieve its purpose. Arguments that the Bible was an ancient book wonderfully preserved and coherent, and that nature, human culture, and science display amazing complexities inconceivable without divine wisdom as their source, may bring assurances. But they are not the essence of the matter; knowledge of God is the crucial issue.

Under the pressure of Deism and rationalism in the seventeenth and eighteenth centuries many Reformed apologists exploited external evidence or reverted to the use of postulates common to Deism and rationalism in attempting to defend Christianity. For a consistent Reformed apologetics, however, these indices cannot be the ground for accepting the claims of the Bible as true, since the defensibility of these supporting reasons would reappear in one's conception of God and would not be serving God, or God's Word, as the Supreme Truth.

Reformed apologetics may also use reasons integral to humanity's internal consciousness to enhance faith. Here assumptions about human nature which are found in Scripture are drawn upon. Calvin speaks of an understanding of the divine majesty implanted in all persons, and Augustine holds that there are innate principles that even the skeptic cannot deny. But while this internal illumination may be very helpful in providing fortification for the faithful in the face of atheism, it is not the ground for the individual's believing the truth of God's Word. The apologetic witness does not arise out of, or appeal for ultimate justification to, internal phenomena. It is dependent upon the appeal of truth itself as from God and vouchsafed by the Holy Spirit.*

External and internal evidence for believing the Christian message in the Scriptures can and should be provided as circumstances require, but lack of them does not invalidate the testimony of God revealed in the Bible. Hebrews 4:12 shows the apologetic thrust of God's Word: "For the word of God is living and active. Sharper than any double-edged sword, it penetrates even to dividing soul and spirit . . . ; it judges the thoughts and attitudes of the heart" (NIV). Reformed apologists need only to realize that their method is not irrational and is honoring to the God whose being is truth.

G. Clark, *Three Types of Religious Philosophy* (1989); T. Halyburton, *An Essay Concerning the Nature of Faith* (1798); P. Helm, *Varieties of Belief* (1973); J. Owen, *The Reason of Faith* (1677); A. Plantinga, "Advice to Christian Philosophers," in *Faith and Philosophy*, ed. A. Plantinga (1964).

THOMAS M. GREGORY

Architecture, Church

Reformed churches underwent architectural change commensurate with changes in their theology: in brief, pulpit rather than altar became the visual focus of the church, even as proclamation of the Word took priority over celebration of the Mass. Baptism* into the body of Christ took place during worship,* where the congregation could hear the sacrament* explained. The "priesthood of all believers" eliminated distinction between nave and chancel. Congregational participation in hymnody* as an act of prayer* and gratitude placed organs not with the means of grace but with the congregation. As the theology of the Mass as a transubstantiated sacrifice was rejected, stone altars were demolished and replaced with temporary, and only later permanent, wooden tables.

Initially, existing churches were adapted for Reformed worship. In the Zurich Münster and St. Peter's, the stone altar was torn down, a pulpit placed atop the center of the rood screen separating nave from chancel, and the Lord's Supper* was served on wooden plates and cups. In Geneva, at St. Pierre, choir stalls were removed, along with the stone altar, and the pulpit was moved from a central nave pillar to one at the crossing where the greater number of people could gather in close proximity to hear the Word. In England, stone altars became illegal under the impact of the Reformation. In the Netherlands, the conversion of large churches to Reformed worship was often accomplished by removing the stone altar and using the chancel as a place to set up long tables and benches around which the congregation would sit to partake of the Lord's Supper. The pulpit was left near the center of the nave but surrounded on all sides with seating for the congregation's comfort. In Scotland, the practice of sitting at tables for the Lord's Supper was common. Reform also touched Baptism. The private ceremony became a part of the Sunday service and was moved from a separate baptistry to the front of the church, where the sacrament might be explained to, and done in the presence of, the congregation—the body of Christ into which the person was baptized. In some churches the font was moved, in others baptism was done from a basin on the Communion table, and in others a wooden cover was placed on a stone font, to serve as both font and table. The Scots often bracketed a baptismal basin to the pulpit.

Needs for new houses of worship for the Reformed faith occurred first in France, where Huguenots* existed uneasily with a Roman Catholic majority. Invariably, theological considerations determined architecture. A Huguenot temple at Lyons (1564) was circular, with a balcony around the entire wall, a pulpit brought out to the edge of the balcony, and a Communion table on the floor in front of the pulpit. Circular or hexagonal churches were common out of consideration for the auditory nature of worship. The famous Huguenot temple of Charenton (1623) was rectangular, but large numbers of people were able to hear the preaching of the Word through the use of two levels of balconies on all four sides of the building, with the pulpit set forward of the balcony on a narrow side of the rectangle.

In the Netherlands, growing cities required new churches, and the Westerkerk was built in Amsterdam (1620–32), a very large rectangular structure, supported by pillars, with the pulpit attached to a pillar central to the long side of the building. The circular Marekerk was built in Leiden (1639). One of the most interesting solutions to the liturgical/theological problem of bringing a large number of seated parishioners into proximity, visually and audibly, with the pulpit was the double polygon of the Nieuwe Kerk in The Hague (1656).

In Switzerland, new churches at

Wädenswil (rectangular, 1764) and Horgen (a double ellipse, 1780) encompassed very large spaces without supports through the use of a newly developed bridge beam to support roof and ceiling. In each, the pulpit was affixed to the middle of the long wall. On the other three walls were balconies, with the organ facing the pulpit. In the middle of the pews was a stone font which, with the wooden cover, doubled as the Lord's Table.

In France, Switzerland, the Netherlands, and Scotland, new Reformed churches came in rectangles, squares, and circles as well as polygons and ellipses. In these churches all traces of the medieval separation of chancel and nave have disappeared. All were controlled by the primary Reformation concern for preaching* and hearing the Word. Since all were part of Christ's royal priesthood, there was no division within this large worship room. The entire church was the sanctuary where the Lord's Supper was celebrated with people seated at the table. Smaller churches left a wide central aisle for the table(s) and benches, while large churches frequently filled the large central section with chairs, supplemented by long tables for the sacrament. In St. Stephen's, Edinburgh, provision was made for six thirty-foot tables with benches on each side in the midst of a diamond-shaped church.

Organs were invariably placed somewhere other than near the pulpit. In pre-Reformation churches they were usually on the back wall, opposite the altar, or, in very large churches, alongside the chancel. As Reformed churches were built, organs were placed with the people, to assist them in their prayers (psalms and hymns). The organ was not confused with the means of grace but was to assist the people in their expressions of gratitude.

Much confusion among churches of Reformed heritage in the United States results from the waves of evangelism* of the nineteenth century. The evangelist's hired concert hall, with platform and ascending tiers for massed choirs and organ, proved to be a powerful model for local congregations. The resulting loss of theological principles, plus fads in styles, from Egyptian to modern, ushered Reformed churches into the second half of the twentieth century. They are rescued as the insights of the liturgical movement are applied to architecture.

A. Biéler, *Architecture in Worship* (1965); D. G. Bruggink and C. H. Droppers, *Christ and Architecture: Building Presbyterian/Reformed Churches* (1965); E. A. Sovik, *Architecture for Worship* (1973); H. W. Turner, *From Temple to Meeting House* (1979); J. F. and S. J. White, *Church Architecture* (1988).

DONALD J. BRUGGINK

Arminianism

Emerging from the influence of the Dutch theologian Jacobus Arminius (1560–1609), Arminianism proposed a substantial revision of the Reformed doctrines of predestination* and grace.* The five Remonstrant* Articles (1610) developed Arminius's ideas, only to meet emphatic repudiation at the Synod of Dort* (1618–19).

Reacting against the lack of Christocentricity in the supralapsarianism* of his erstwhile teacher Theodore Beza,* Arminius argued that election was subsequent to grace. God* determines to save all whom God foresees will repent* and trust Christ. Election is thus conditional on God's foreknowledge* of a person's response. Moreover, the fallen will remains free. Humans can believe or resist grace. Thus, saving grace is sufficient but not irresistible. Humans cooperate. The possibility of a true believer falling from grace totally or finally Arminius left open.

The Remonstrant Articles affirmed these claims. Election is seen as conditional on God's foreknowledge, Christ died for all but only believers are saved, grace is necessary to salvation* but is resistible, while further investigation is needed into whether all the regenerate will persevere.

The Synod of Dort condemned the articles, removing and exiling the Remonstrant ministers. It appeared to the contra-Remonstrants that Arminianism threatened to destroy the doctrine of assurance* by questioning perseverance,* that it introduced a semi-Pelagian doctrine of grace and a conditional gospel that would undermine the atonement* and justification.*

The atonement demonstrates a substantive difference between Arminianism and orthodoxy. While some form of penal substitution was at least implicit in the limited atonement taught by the Synod of Dort, Arminianism held that Christ suffered for all but did not actually pay the penalty for their sins, since all are not saved. Rather, Christ's death permits the Father to forgive all who repent and believe. Hugo Grotius, a Dutch jurist, soon developed the governmental theory of the atonement, teaching that the cross was necessary as a wise means of upholding God's moral administration of the universe and was not required by virtue of anything inherent in God's nature.

Despite suppression, Arminianism eventually spread widely throughout the world, pervading many fundamentalist* circles in North America. Methodism has been a particular base since the impetus provided by John Wesley. While holding to total depravity, Wesley taught the universality of Christ's work, the sufficiency of grace, and the ability of humanity to cooperate in appropriating it, expressly accepting the possibility of falling from grace.

The Arminian challenge posed questions for the Reformed church. Further debate on the nature of predestination and God's grace followed the controversy. Moïse Amyraut* (1596–1664) and the French Reformed theological school at Saumur developed a modified predestinarianism that met with much resistance. Arminius's reconstruction of election with Christ as foundation resulted in particular problems. Hitherto, election and Christology* had frequently been integrated in Reformed theology. Now there was a reluctance to integrate them. Arminius had stolen the idea. Reformed predestinarianism was to move in a more speculative direction.

J. Arminius, *Works*, 3 vols. (1825); C. Bangs, *Arminius* (rev. ed. 1985); A. W. Harrison, *Arminianism* (1937).

ROBERT LETHAM

Ascension

The entry into heaven of the Lord Jesus Christ in his resurrection body in order to sit at the right hand of God the Father as the Mediator who is to us king, priest, and prophet. There are three views of when this ascension occurred.

1. On Easter morning. The resurrection* was the first part of the one act of God exalting Jesus to heaven from the grave. Thus Jesus ascended when he was resurrected. In this view, all the resurrection appearances are of Jesus from heaven, and the last (Acts 1:11) is a dramatic symbolic presentation of what has happened to Jesus already.

2. On Easter evening. This view is based on John 20:17 and Luke 24:50ff. Jesus rose from the dead on Easter morning, and after appearing to his disciples he ascended from Bethany in the evening. Later resurrection appearances are from heaven, and the last (Acts 1) is symbolic (as in view 1).

3. On the fortieth day after his resurrection, the day the church has celebrated as Ascension Day. This, the traditional view, does not indicate where Jesus was when he was not with his disciples. It takes the appearance and departure recorded in Acts 1 as the actual account of the ascension of Jesus into heaven (symbolized by the Shekinah cloud of glory) as witnessed by the disciples and angels.

There is, of course, a major element of mystery in this event, for we are dealing with what is unique and supernatural. Most modern Reformed theologians favor the first view in one or another form, expounding it in relation to the resurrection and heavenly session of our Lord.

J. G. Davies, *He Ascended Into Heaven* (1958); P. Toon, *The Ascension of Our Lord* (1984).

PETER TOON

Assurance of Salvation

One of the great benefits of the Reformation was the recovery of the doctrine of the Christian believer's assurance of eternal security in Christ.

The developed Roman Catholic system opposed this doctrine. (1) It taught that the blood of Jesus availed only for the purging of sins* committed before baptism;* hence the need for the performance of penitential deeds and, after this life, purgatorial fire to deal with postbaptismal sin. (2) It distinguished between venial and mortal sins, according to which the committing of mortal sin resulted in the loss of the grace of salvation.* (3) It conceived of justifying grace* as infused grace rather than as the grace of Christ's righteousness imputed to the believer, so a person was regarded as either totally holy or, through the forfeiting of infused grace, totally unholy before God. (4) It held that a person's justification* depended not only on the work of Christ but also on one's own good works performed before and after justification as meritoriously contributing to and also increasing one's justification (semi-Pelagianism).

From this teaching no one could be sure that the grace possessed today might not be lost tomorrow or that one would not die in a graceless state of mortal sin. Because of the finite fallibility and fallenness of the human creature, for salvation to depend in part on the merit of one's own good works and not wholly on the merit of Christ's work of redemption left everything in uncertainty. In the sixteenth century the Roman Catholic Council of Trent asserted the uncertainty of salvation inherent in its teaching, declaring that "each person, when he regards himself and his own indisposition, may entertain fear and apprehension concerning his own grace, inasmuch as no one can know with a certainty of faith, which cannot be subject to mistake, that he has obtained the grace of God" (Sess. 6, canon 2), and also anathematizing any person who taught that the sinner is justified by faith* alone, apart from the cooperating merit of good works (Sess. 6, canon 9).

The Reformers contended Scripture teaches that the blood of Jesus Christ cleanses from all sin, not just from sin committed before baptism (1 John 1:7); that the believer's security is based solely on the atoning work of Christ, which, since it is the work of God on our behalf, cannot fail or come to nothing (2 Cor. 5:17–21; Phil. 1:6); that Christ himself promised that no one could pluck those who are his out of his hand (John 10: 28); and that the biblical doctrine of the election of the redeemed in Christ also ensured the final perseverance* and glorification of those who are called and justified by God (Rom. 8:29–30). In short, the redemption of sinners is, from beginning to end, the work of God by virtue of the saving grace that freely flows to the believer from the cross of Jesus (*sola gratia*). This is the sole and solid ground for the Christian assurance of the believer's security in Christ for all eternity.

PHILIP E. HUGHES

Atonement

As the work of reconciliation wrought by God in Christ, atonement has been central in the Reformed tradition. Interpretations of this saving deed have ranged from an encompassing at-one-ment of God and the world accomplished by a manifold ministry of Christ (the threefold office) to a delimited focus on a penal substitution carried out on Calvary to render the sinner acceptable to God. Whether broad or narrow in scope, the Reformed understanding of the atonement has always stressed the "cruciality of the cross" (P. T. Forsyth*).

The term "atonement" is English in origin, appearing in Elizabethan literature as the bringing of concord between persons or groups. In the Geneva Bible* (1560) the word is used interchangeably with "reconciliation" in association with the root *kpr* (Lev. 23:28; Num. 15:28), though the latter is more often translated in its cultic context as "expiation." In both the Genevan and the King James (1611) version its single NT appearance is in Rom. 5:10–11 (*katallassō*; *katallagē*), where "atonement" and "reconciliation" are used synonymously. In theological discourse its equivalents in both non-English and English traditions are "the work of Christ," "the office of Mediator," "the work of reconciliation (redemption, salvation*)," and "objective soteriology."

Over the centuries, Reformed commentary on the doctrine of atonement was marked by accents on the radical character of sin* as judged by the holiness of God;* divine sovereignty as source of the work executed; OT prefiguration of the ways of reconciliation; ethical implications of atonement; and interconnections of Christ's life and teachings, suffering and death, resurrection* and ascension.*

The Anselmic portrayal of Christ's redeeming work as satisfaction of God's offended honor was recast by the Reformers in forensic terms. Christ stood in our place to receive punishment meted out on sin by a just judge. John Calvin* notably describes Christ's vicarious work blending priestly imagery (Heb. 9:14, 25–26) with law court metaphors (Gal. 3:13):

> Because a deserved curse obstructs the entrance, and God in his character of judge is hostile to us, expiation must necessarily intervene, that as a priest employed to appease the wrath of God, he may reinstate us in his favor. Wherefore, in order that Christ might fulfill this office, it behooves Him to appear with a sacrifice. . . . God could not be propitiated without the expiation of sin. . . . By the sacrifice of his death He wiped away our guilt and made satisfaction for our sin. (*Inst.* 2.15.6)

Sacrifice and penal substitution become refrains in Reformed confessions* and catechisms.*

> The Lord Jesus, by his perfect obedience and sacrifice of himself, which he through the eternal Spirit once offered up unto God, hath fully satisfied the justice of his Father; and purchased not only reconciliation, but an everlasting inheritance in the kingdom of heaven, for all those whom the Father hath given unto him. (WCF, 8.5)

> Q. 37. What do you understand by the word "suffered"?
>
> A. That throughout his life on earth, but especially at the end of it, he bore in body and soul the wrath of God against the sin of the whole human race, so that by his suffering, as the only expiatory sacrifice, he might redeem our body and soul from everlasting damnation, and might obtain for us God's grace, righteousness, and eternal life. (HC)

Calvin, and the confessional tradition after him, followed the trajectory of sacrifice into the lower regions, interpreting the descent into hell* of the Apostles' Creed as Christ's experience of the torments that befit human sin.

The "finished work" of passion, death, and descent is succeeded in Reformed teaching by a "continuing work" of the resurrected and ascended Lord whose intercession before the Father secures for the elect the benefits of oblation. In Reformed theology, substitution is active as well as passive, the fulfillment of the law's requirements as well as acceptance of the penalty for its violations. Hence Christ "removed the enmity between God and us . . . through the whole course of his obedience" (*Inst.* 2.16.5). The merit of Christ transferred to the elect therefore is twofold: a righteousness of life exhibited in perfect holiness through his "active obedience" and a righteousness in death in which Christ suffers the consequences of our sin through his "passive obedience."

The extended range of Christ's mediatorial work to "the whole course of his obedience" is also expressed through Calvin's imaginative development of the *munus triplex**: "Therefore that faith might find a solid ground of salvation, and so rest in him, we must set out this principle, that the office which he received from the Father consists of three parts" (*Inst.* 2.15.1). Christ, the Anointed One, fulfills the promise of reconciliation embodied in the OT types of prophet, priest, and king, each called by unction into their respective offices. Thus the prophetic teacher and herald and the royal ascended Lord join the priestly Savior of Calvary in a total saving deed. Following Calvin, atonement has been conceived in these encompassing terms in Reformed confessions and catechisms (WCF, 8.1; HC, qq. 31–32; WSC, qq. 23–26) and by its theologians from the post-Reformation scholastics to Karl Barth.*

While Zwingli* cannot rank with Calvin in either influence or profundity, he sought to give systematic expression to the work of Christ. In doing so, he voiced an aspect of the doctrine of atonement often neglected in traditional formulations but taken up in the nineteenth century by the Mercersburg Theology* (John Williamson Nevin* and Philip Schaff*) and also in more recent Reformed thought. Zwingli wrote:

Wishing at length, then, to help this desperate case of ours, our Creator sent one to satisfy His justice by offering Himself for us—not an angel, nor a man, but His own Son, and clothed in flesh in order that neither His majesty might deter us from intercourse with Him, nor His lowliness deprive us of hope. For being God and the Son of God, He that was sent as deputy and mediator gives support to hope. For what cannot He do or have who is God? (*Commentary on True and False Religion*, 6)

Here the incarnational presupposition of the atonement—the affirmation that "God was *in* Christ, reconciling the world" (2 Cor. 5:19)—is forcefully stated, calling into question popular portrayals of a retributive deity punishing a loving Jesus.

Subsequent Reformed theology continued the Reformers' themes, drawing out implications and making applications according to contemporary issues. The accent on the divine sovereignty soon came to prominence in Socinian and Arminian controversies. It took form as the assertion of a *pactum salutis* between the Father and the Son in which by inscrutable decree* the Second Person is sent to execute in the human nature of Christ a "limited atonement" for the elect, with the others, the reprobate, passed over. This position is sometimes described by use of the acronym TULIP: Total depravity, Unconditional election, Limited atonement, Irresistible grace, and Perseverance of the saints—five points made at the Synod of Dort* (1618–19) against the Remonstrants* who defended human choice against Calvinist interpretations of divine sovereignty. More recently, the double decree and vicarious sacrifice have been restated by Barth* as the election and rejection of Jesus Christ, with all of humanity, de jure, a participant in the "humiliation of the Son of God" and the "exaltation of the Son of Man."

Early Reformed thought gave considerable attention to the equivalency of punishment for fallen humanity's offense against the law* of God, executed on the cross. This "penal substitutionary theory" came to the fore in the debate with exemplarist and Abelardian notions that ignored both the gravity of sin and the rigor of God. Included in the attack on the latter were "four point Calvinists" and others who held that the redemption won was sufficient for all but applied only to some.

The Reformed inheritance includes an activist emphasis on the *response* to the mandates of the divine majesty rather than its initiatives, turning away from the objectivity of both election and penal substitution and toward an obediential subjectivity. It found expression, variously, in the seventeenth-century "governmental theory" of Hugo Grotius (influential also in the New England Theology*) that views Jesus' sacrifice as upholding the sanctity of the law by exhibiting the consequences of its breach by a sinful humanity rather than execution of an equivalent punishment; the "moral influence theory" (expressed in nineteenth-century theology in the early Bushnell*) in which the life and the death of Christ are viewed as an exemplification of the divine love, the incentive required to change us rather than a suffering undergone to alter God's relationship to a sinful world.

Reformed accents on either the indicatives or the imperatives of divine sovereignty have been regularly assailed by critics for, on the one hand, the "horrible decree" of double predestination* in which speculation on the majesty of God overwhelms the biblical witness to the love of God or for, on the other hand, a preoccupation with the call to obedience that obscures both the impossibilities of human sin and the possibilities of divine grace. Challenges to the Reformed tradition continue, as in a "hermeneutics of suspicion" which charges that the historic emphasis on atonement for individual sin by a personal savior overlooks the struggle against oppression and the work of Jesus the liberator or asserts that the centrality of the cross entails the picture of a wrathful Father punishing an innocent Son and must be rejected as "child abuse theology."

Under the banner of *semper reformanda*, Reformed response has acknowledged reductionist tendencies in its tradition, both speculative excesses and subjectivistic lapses. In an attempt to be faithful to both its "world-formative" (N. Wolterstorff) character and sobriety about sin, and striving to learn from the suspicionist critique, it holds the full work of redemption to include the rule of Christ over, and our call to resist, oppressive political, economic, and social powers and principalities (see contemporary statements and confessions of Reformed churches in Vischer, ed., *Reformed Witness Today*, and statements of the WARC*). And it seeks to recover its own classical teaching about the unity of person and work, asserting that God does not inflict suffering on another but receives into the divine heart the painful consequences of human sin.

Calvin's threefold office returns time and again to provide a vehicle for integrating the various accents of the Reformed tradition and for developing a more ecumenical framework for understanding the atonement. In this inclusive rendering, Christ the prophet engages ignorance and error by the disclosure and embodiment of truth; Christ the priest meets sin and guilt by vicarious sacrifice; and Christ the king conquers suffering and death* by his liberating power. The partnership of roles invites the correction of reductionist tendencies: the exacting punishments of the penal theory are reconceived in terms of a *holy* love; the naïvetés of exemplarism are challenged by the *tough* love of accountability to the divine holiness; the militant metaphors of ransom, victory, and liberation learn from the *tender* love of Galilean *agapē* and from the realism of Calvary's sacrifice about the sin that persists in the champions of justice as well as its foes. Inclusivity also joins incarnation* and atonement and affirms the trinitarian life together, precluding the temptation to distribute what is done between a punitive deity and a perfect human sacrifice or between a wrathful Father and a loving Son.

While Reformed theology has given attention to the narrative sequence of the offices—a prophetic ministry in Jesus' life, teachings, and healings; a priestly ministry in passion and death; and a royal ministry in resurrection and ascension—it has also stressed their coinherence: the priestly and royal character of Christ's prophetic work in its vulnerable and victorious love; a prophetic and royal priesthood—the king who reigns and the Word that is proclaimed from the cross; and the royal rule of a suffering servant. The theme of mutuality persists in the concurrence of the offices in the continuing work of Christ as it applies the benefits of this finished work: the prophetic proclamation of the Word to us, the priestly intercession for us, and the royal rule over us.

R. S. Franks declared that Calvin's articulation of the threefold office is one of the lasting contributions of the Reformation. Its continuing significance is demonstrated by such twentieth-century expositions as Barth's magisterial restatement and application of prophetic, priestly, and royal roles to the ministry of the laity in both Protestant and Roman Catholic* theology. So might a doctrine of atonement, catholic and reformed, contribute to the reconciliation about which it speaks and for which it hopes.

Barth, *CD* IV/1–3; R. S. Franks, *The Work of Christ* (1918; repr. 1962); Heppe, *RD*; A. E. McGrath, *Iustitia Dei: A History of the Christian Doctrine of Justification*, vol. 2 (1986); R. S. Paul, *The Atonement and the Sacraments* (1960); L. Vischer, ed., *Reformed Witness Today* (1982).

GABRIEL FACKRE

Auburn Affirmation

As the fundamentalist/modernist controversy* escalated, the conservative majority of the 1923 General Assembly of the Presbyterian Church in the U.S.A. reaffirmed a previous (1910) "doctrinal deliverance" (Portland Deliverance) requiring ministerial candidates to accept as "essential and necessary articles of faith": biblical inerrancy, the virgin birth, the death of Christ as a sacrifice to satisfy divine justice, the physical resurrection* of Jesus, and Christ's showing his power and love by working miracles.

In opposition to this requirement, the Auburn Affirmation was circulated (1924). Ultimately it carried 1,274 signatures. A high proportion were Presbyterian ministers from New York, and most were educated at Auburn, Union (N.Y.), or McCormick seminaries.

The Affirmation opposed elevation of the stated doctrines "to the position of tests for ordination or for good standing in our church." Though worded to avoid implicating its signers in any specific opposition to the points of the Deliverance, it sought to identify as the historic policy of Presbyterianism the practice of "accepting theological differences within its bounds and subordinating them to recognized loyalty to Jesus Christ and united work for the kingdom of God." Traditional Presbyterian reluctance to allow ecclesiastical assemblies the right of authoritative interpretation of the Westminster Confession* or of Scripture* was cited.

The argument centered in a controversial distinction between the "great facts and doctrines" to which the five-point statement referred and "certain theories" concerning interpretation of these facts which it considered embedded in the particular formulations of the 1923 Deliverance.

In the interests of Christian unity and mission, it insisted, "all who hold to these facts and doctrines, whatever theories they may employ to explain them, are worthy of all confidence and fellowship."

By 1926 sympathy for doctrinal exclusivism was rapidly waning in the larger culture. That year's General Assembly reflected the influence of the Auburn Affirmation when it articulated a "principle of tolerance" according to which Presbyterianism* was defined not only as a body of belief but also as a tradition and "a controlling sentiment," which "admits of diversity of view where the core of truth is identical."

L. A. Loetscher, *The Broadening Church* (1954); C. E. Quirk, *Auburn Affirmation* (1967); PCUSA General Assembly *Minutes* (1910–26).

PHILIP W. BUTIN

Augustine and Augustinianism

Augustine (354–430), a major influence on Catholic and Protestant theology and doctrine, was born and educated in North Africa. After teaching in Rome and Milan, where he was converted to Catholic Christianity (386) through the influence of Ambrose, he returned to Africa, where he became a presbyter and then bishop in Hippo. The *Confessions* interpret his life up to his conversion* and baptism* and the death of his mother, Monica. His sermons (about 750 survive) and his controversial, expository, and theological writings (chief among which are *The Trinity* and *The City of God*) were widely used during the Middle Ages.

As Adolf von Harnack suggested, there are three "circles of thought" in Augustine's theology, successively elaborated: (1) a Neoplatonist quest for direct contemplation of God,* which enabled Christians to affirm both human reason* and the spiritual aspirations of non-Christians; (2) a Catholic insistence on revelation,* the authority of the church,* and indispensability of the sacraments,* reflected in the controversy against the Donatists' claims of personal holiness; and (3) a Pauline emphasis on the bondage of the will,* the need for grace,* and the role of predestination* in salvation,* all elaborated against the Pelagians' defense of freedom* and merit. In the practical realm, we should not overlook Augustine's influence in extending the monastic life to the clergy, who lived "the common life" under a rule. *The City of God* offered a Christian perspective not only on human history* but on political life; it was variously interpreted through the centuries to support clericalism, "political realism," or a quest for secular justice.*

Augustine's writings, edited by Johannes Amerbach and Erasmus and printed in Basel, became a major influence after 1500. Luther,* Zwingli,* and Calvin* all ascribed their "conversions" to their reading of Augustine. But tensions among the different emphases in Augustine's thought also emerged. The humanism* of the "Northern Renaissance" looked to Augustine's interest in rational and religious quests, sometimes in isolation from Christian or churchly concerns; Roman Catholicism to his affirmation of authority, the church, and the sacraments; and Protestantism to the more individualistic themes of predestination and grace. None followed Augustine uncritically. Calvin, who made much use of Augustine's writings in thinking about predestination, grace, the unity of OT and NT, the church, and the sacraments, judged him to be in error about purgatory and celibacy and took more radical positions on predestination, original sin,* and justification;* Calvin also disliked Augustine's use of allegory and numerology in exegesis, preferring Chrysostom's more literal method of interpretation.

The "Scripture principle" limited Protestant loyalty to Augustine. Post-Tridentine Catholicism nourished a more vigorous development of Augustinian anthropology, which also became the focus of major doctrinal debates within the Catholic Church. One concerned nature and grace. Against those who tended to superimpose grace upon nature, the Augustinians stressed their interpenetration, affirming both a human "desire for God" and the freedom or "gratuity" of God's invitation. Another concerned free will* and grace. Against the Thomists, who asserted that grace moves the will "physically"—that is, without its own action—the Jesuits, following Augustine, saw it acting "morally," through suggestion, inclination, and consent. A third debate concerned predestination. While assuming that predestination is based in God's will rather than human merit, Luis de Molina argued that God takes into account what human beings "would do" if offered grace, and Francisco Suárez suggested that God gives grace in a way "congruous" to their inclinations—both on the basis of passages in Augustine. The refined concepts that were introduced during these debates influenced Protestant as well as Catholic theology after 1600.

Jansenism, a more extreme form of Augustinianism in seventeenth-century France, was similar to Calvinism* in its insistence on the unconditional necessity of predestining grace; it is often blamed for a grim and pessimistic strand in French Catholicism. The more authentic Augustinian tradition is the other one, which developed in Catholic and then Protestant theology, anticipating many themes in the theology of Moïse Amyraut* and Jonathan Edwards,* liberalism, and twentieth century Catholicism.

M. Bendischioli, "L'agostinismo dei riformatori protestanti," *Revue des études augustiniennes* 1 (1955): 203–24; C. Boyer, "Jean Calvin et Saint Augustin," *Augustinian Studies* 3 (1972): 15–34; P. Brown, *Augustine of Hippo* (1967); J. Cadier, "Calvin et Saint Augustin," in *Augustinus Magister. Actes du Congrès international augustinien* (1954–55), 2:1033–56; J. Fitzer, "The Augustinian Roots of Calvin's Eucharistic Thought," *Augustinian Studies* 7 (1976): 69–98; A. von Harnack, *History of Dogma*, vol. 5 (1891); H. de Lubac, *Augustinianism and Modern Theology* (1969); and *The Mystery of the Supernatural* (1967); O. J.-B. du Roy, "Augustine, St.," *New Catholic Encyclopedia* (1967), 1:1041–58; R. P. Russell, "Augustinianism," *New Catholic Encyclopedia*, 1:1063–71; L. Smits, *Saint Augustin dans l'oeuvre de Jean Calvin*, vol. 1: *Etude de critique littéraire*, vol. 2: *Tables des références augustiniennes* (1957–58); E. TeSelle, *Augustine the Theologian* (1970); B. B. Warfield, *Calvin and Augustine* (1956); and *Studies in Tertullian and Augustine* (1930); F. Wendel, *Calvin* (1965).

EUGENE TESELLE

Australasia

The Reformed tradition is represented in Australia and New Zealand and neighboring Pacific islands by a variety of churches. The dominant strands are Evangelical Anglicanism in Sydney, the offshoots of Scots-Irish Presbyterianism and small groups of Dutch and Hungarian migrants. The Calvinist* heritage among Baptists and Congregationalists* has not had any significant survivals into the twentieth century. Migration patterns during the last century make the eastern states of Australia and the south of New Zealand the strongholds of Presbyterian churches. There is also a strong Presbyterian Church in Vanuatu stemming from the work of Scottish, Canadian, Australian, and New Zealand missionaries which began (1848) after the pioneering work of the London Missionary Society.*

A notable Presbyterian in New South Wales was the Rev. Dr. J. D. Lang. He arrived in 1823 and speedily made his mark by his journalistic gifts and acerbic temper. He had a noble vision of a free and Protestant Australia and devoted large sums to bringing migrants, as well as skillfully publicizing the advantages of the colonies, alongside his pastoral ministry. As a radical politician he was a merciless foe of Church of England privilege and moved from being a supporter of state aid and establishment to a voluntarist position. Despite being very divisive, he brought many able ministers to the Australian colonies and helped establish an evangelical Calvinism,* which was reinforced by the Disruption* in Scotland (1843) and migration of many Free Church ministers to Victoria. Notable Presbyterians in New South Wales (1867) gave considerable resources to meet the influx of gold seekers, and they speedily made significant contributions to education, the professions, journalism, and politics as well as creating a network of parishes, schools, and important universities and colleges.

There was no notable theologian in the Calvinist tradition in the nineteenth-century Australian colonies, though there was an attempt to try Rev. C. Strong of Scots Church, Melbourne, for heresy (1883) because of his alleged departures from Westminster orthodoxy. In New Zealand, James McGregor of Oamaru was a formidable exponent of confessional Calvinism, but there were also very able critics like Professor William Salmond and Principal John Dickie, both of the Theological Hall in Dunedin. Professors Rentoul and Adam in Melbourne similarly gave Calvinism a more liberal ethos, though the sharpest and most notorious opponent of the Westminster Confession* was Professor Samuel Angus of Sydney, whose studies in Princeton took him away from his Irish Calvinist heritage. Attempts to try him for heresy in a series of General Assemblies were ended by his death (1942).

By then it was clear there were broadly three approaches to the Reformed heritage—bold liberalism, liberal evangelicalism, and confessional Calvinism. The influence of Karl Barth* and Emil Brunner* brought a fresh approach, mediated by Professors John McIntyre of Sydney and Davis McCaughey and George Yule of Melbourne, which was enormously important in restating the Reformed heritage in negotiations that led to the formation of the Uniting Church (1977). Its Basis of Union is a most interesting example of Reformed theology in modern idiom, and scholars and ministers like Frank Nichol, Michael Owen, and Gordon Watson have eloquently expounded this tradition on both sides of the Tasman.

There has also been a revival of confessional Calvinism through a succession of theologians like Klaas Runia at the Reformed Theological College, Geelong, and at Moore College, Sydney, where Anglican clergy are educated. Principals T. C. Hammond and D. B. Knox have reminded generations of Evangelical Anglicans of the importance of the heritage of Calvin* and transformed the theological ethos of the largest Anglican diocese in Australia. As yet the continuing Presbyterian Church has not made any significant scholarly contributions to this revival, but many of its ministers and elders* are strongly sympathetic to the tradition of the Free Church of Scotland and some of the conservative American Presbyterian churches. There are some elements of the Reformed vision of partnership between church and state in the political ethos of Australasia, but they have been most clearly seen in the politics of Vanuatu, where a succession of former Presbyterian ministers have held office.

J. Harrison, *Baptism of Fire* (1987); S. Judd and K. J. Cable, *Sydney Anglicans* (1987); J. Jupp, *The Australian People* (1988); W. Lini, *Beyond Pandemonium* (1980); R. D. McEldowney, *Presbyterians in Aotearoa* (1990); J. G. Miller, *Live* (1975-[6 vols. currently]); J. M. Owen, *Witness of Faith* (1984); R. S. Ward, *The Bush Still Burns* (1989).

IAN BREWARD

Authority

In Reformed thought, Christian belief is not based on a rational philosophy devised by the human mind but on divine revelation,* which is the Scriptures* of the OT and the NT. The biblical writers were divinely inspired when they wrote their history, songs and psalms, and theological expositions. Consequently their writings are the recorded Word of God. The message of the Bible is that God is the sovereign creator, judge, and redeemer of the world and its inhabitants.

While the Bible is quite explicit in stating that it is the Word of God,* no one comes to a recognition of this unless enlightened by the Holy Spirit,* who opens one's eyes to the Bible's character. In Reformed thought, no one is able to understand the meaning and teaching of the Scriptures unless and until the Holy Spirit enlightens one's mind. When this happens, the reader of the Scriptures recognizes their authority and also comes to an understanding of how their teachings should be applied to one's view of the world and life in it.

From this belief in Scripture's inspiration and the enlightenment by the Holy Spirit has developed the Reformed tradition, based largely on the work of ancient church leaders such as Augustine,* medieval thinkers such as Bernard of Clairvaux, but especially the early modern theologian John Calvin,* who set forth the doctrinal position of what became known as the Reformed churches. However, over the years there have been modifications in some areas of Calvin's doctrines. Consequently, while there have been variations in Reformed points of view, the requirement is always to go back to the Scriptures as a check on the "Reformed" doctrines.

This raises the question of the nature and place of human reason.* Some even in the Reformed tradition have tended to refuse to give any credence to the use of reason, but generally most have held that God by grace has given humans the power to use their reason in a limited sense but not to be able to give an ultimate explanation of reality apart from the teachings of the Bible. Thus in the fields of science, economics, and so forth, one does have a certain freedom to use reason, but without the guidance of the Scriptures one is doomed to misuse or misapply much of its rationally gained knowledge. Reason enlightened by the Holy Spirit, however, has a true understanding, although always limited because no human has reached perfection in this life.

W. STANFORD REID

Baillie, Donald MacPherson (1887–1954)

Preacher, theologian, and ecumenical statesman, Baillie taught systematic theology at St. Andrews, Scotland (from 1934). His *God Was in Christ* (1948) won international acclaim, particularly for its imaginative use of the Pauline "paradox of grace" (1 Cor. 15:10) to illuminate christological* affirmations. While deeply indebted to the Calvinist faith and piety of his Highland upbringing, he was also a friend of the Student Christian Movement and the Iona Community and played a prominent part in Faith and Order conferences at Edinburgh (1937) and Lund (1952).

D. M. Baillie, *Theology of the Sacraments* (1957).

ALEC C. CHEYNE

Baillie, John (1886–1960)

The outstanding Scottish theologian and churchman-academic of his generation (Moderator of General Assembly;* WCC* president; Gifford Lecturer), Baillie taught in North America and Scotland, becoming dean of divinity and principal of New College,* Edinburgh. True to the substance of historic Christianity, if uneasy with some of its traditional formulations, he avoided theological or philosophical extremes, welcomed Barthianism with critical reserve, and disclosed his deepest concerns in the eloquent apologetic of *Invitation to Pilgrimage* (1942) and the piety* of *A Diary of Private Prayer* (1936).

J. Baillie, *Our Knowledge of God* (1939); and *The Idea of Revelation* (1956).

ALEC C. CHEYNE

Baillie, Robert (1599–1662)

A leader of the second reformation in Scottish Presbyterianism, typified by the National Covenant* (1638). Congenitally averse to extremism, Baillie accepted ordination in the quasi-episcopal system which James (first Stuart monarch) introduced to the Church of Scotland. But when Charles I attempted further to alter the Kirk in a non-Reformed direction, Baillie led those who reaffirmed Reformed faith and practice by the National Covenant. He was a framer of the Covenant, a member of the reconstituted General Assembly at Glasgow (1638). He filled the office of chaplain in the covenanting army which forced Charles to recognize the Covenant and was one of the influential Scottish representatives at the Westminster Assembly* where an attempt was made to extend the Covenant to England and Ireland by means of the Solemn League and Covenant.* He became professor of theology in the University of Glasgow and subsequently principal. He remained a Calvinist* theologically, a Puritan* in spirituality, and a Presbyterian* in church life, while opposing full-blown episcopacy, independency,* and the extreme Covenanters. He maintained wide correspondence and a comprehensive journal, which has been a major source of seventeenth-century Scottish church history.

Letters and Journals of Robert Baillie, 3 vols. (1841–42); G. Donaldson, *Scotland, James V to James VI* (1971); J. D. Douglas, *Light in the North: The Story of the Scottish Covenanters* (1964); F. N. McCoy, *Robert Baillie and the Second Scots Reformation* (1974); A. Smellie, *Men of the Covenant* (1909).

IAN S. RENNIE

Baird, Charles Washington (1828–1888)

Born in Princeton and raised in France, Baird returned to the United States to study at Union Seminary (N.Y.). He became pastor of an American church in Rome, but poor health forced him to return to New York. While recuperating, he wrote his pioneering study of the origins of Reformed worship,* *Eutaxia, or the Presbyterian Liturgies* (1855). After serving a Dutch Reformed Church in Brooklyn, he began a long pastorate at the Presbyterian Church of Rye, New York.

H. O. Old, "*Eutaxia* by Charles W. Baird," *AP* 66 (1988): 260–63.

HUGHES OLIPHANT OLD

Baptism

Reformed churches have understood Baptism as a covenant* sign whereby the washing of water in the name of the Father, and of the Son, and of the Holy Spirit* seals to those who receive it the promises of the gospel (cf. HC,* qq. 65–74; Second Helvetic Confession, ch. 20; WSC, qq. 92, 94).

Baptism in Scripture. Since Reformed theology affirms that the worship* of the church* must be according to Scripture,* the manner in which certain Scripture passages regarding baptism have been understood is the key to its teachings on the subject. At the beginning of all four Gospels we read of the baptism of Jesus, who, bearing the name Joshua, was baptized in the Jordan, leading the new covenant people of God* into the promised kingdom. This baptism as John the Baptist preached it was a baptism of repentance,* a washing away of sin,* leaving it behind, and an entering into the new life of the kingdom of God.* At his baptism Jesus received the Holy Spirit, for only by the power of the Spirit can one live the Christian life. Christ's baptism, as the Reformers understood it, is the pattern of Christian baptism. Huldrych Zwingli* made this point early in the Reformation, and though it was a radical departure from scholastic* theology, which understood John's baptism as being quite different from the apostles' baptism, Zwingli's approach was followed by Reformed theology rather generally. Martin Bucer* made the point that baptism stands at the beginning of the Christian life, just as it stands at the beginning of the Gospel, a prophetic sign of what that life will be, namely, a turning away from the ways of this world and an entering into the life of the Spirit, a sign and seal of our conversion.* One often asks where John the Baptist got this rite and why he used it in his ministry. Most recent scholarship has tended to dismiss the idea that it was borrowed from the Hellenistic mystery religions and favors the idea that John saw his rite in terms of Jewish proselyte baptism. This would explain why John's baptism was such a scandal to the Jews; it implied that even Jews needed to be converted to enter the messianic kingdom.

Before his ascension,* Jesus gave his disciples the commission to open up his kingdom to all the peoples of the earth by baptizing them in the name of the Father, and of the Son, and of the Holy Spirit, teaching them to observe all things he had commanded, and with this commission he gave the covenant promise that in their doing this he would be with them (Matt. 28:18–20). They were to baptize in the name of the Father, that all peoples might be received into the household of faith; in the name of the Son, that they be joined to Christ in his death and resurrection;* and finally in the name of the Holy Spirit, that they receive the gift of the Holy Spirit.

In the book of Acts, the apostles do just this. Peter preached the gospel to all nations, offering them baptism with the assurance that the promises of the new covenant were not only for the children of Israel but for the Gentiles and their children as well (Acts 2:38–39; cf. Calvin's* commentary here). Throughout Acts, it is carefully noted that Gentiles were baptized and therefore made part of the covenant community: a group of Samaritans (Acts 8:4–11); an Ethiopian (8:26–40); a Roman centurion and his household (ch. 10); Lydia, a Greek businesswoman (16:14–15); and the Philippian jailer and his household (16:29–34). In Luke's various accounts, the sign was given rather quickly. One does not hear of long preparations or of waiting until conversion has become profound. Baptism marks a beginning. Often Paul found it necessary to point out to his Gentile converts that Christian baptism was not to be confused with the initiation rites of different Hellenistic mystery religions. In Rom. 6:1–14 he makes it clear that the rite of Baptism does not confer salvation* simply by the performing of a ceremony in such a way that one's moral behavior is irrelevant to one's salvation. Baptism joins us to Christ in his death and his resurrection, not by means of a dramatic reenactment of his burial and resurrection, but by faith* in Christ expressed in the living of the Christian life. The apostles obviously understood baptism as a covenant sign and because baptism is a covenant sign it commits us to the Christian life. The ceremonial view of salvation fostered by the mystery religions is likewise attacked in 1 Cor. 10:1–13, where Paul is clear that even those who had been baptized in the sea and in the cloud during the exodus were not automatically saved.

At the core of the NT understanding of baptism are the OT types of the sacrament.* The Reformers sensed that the early church thought of the sacraments in terms of OT imagery (Bullinger,* *Decades*, 5:6–8; Calvin, *Inst.* 4.14.20–26; 4.15.9). Paul presents crossing through the Red Sea as a type of baptism (1 Cor. 10:1–2). Baptism sets us on the pilgrimage that leaves behind the land of sin and heads out toward the land of promise. In 1 Peter 3:20–21 the flood is presented as a type of baptism. This type emphasizes God's sovereign demand for justice* and righteousness among all the peoples of the earth as well as God's gracious gift of a new beginning. Reformed theology from the very beginning has found circumcision to be a particularly important type of baptism (HC, q. 74). Circumcision is, like many of the liturgical usages of the OT, a shadow of things to come (Col. 2:17). In Rom. 4:11 Paul speaks of the relation of circumcision to faith. This passage has encouraged Reformed theologians to understand the sacraments generally as covenantal signs. In Rev. 1:5–6 the various rites involving washing with water and sprinkling of blood, particularly in the ordination of the Levitical priesthood, are seen as types of baptism that set Christians apart to the service of God under the new covenant.

Rite of Baptism. In Reformed worship the rite of Baptism is understood to have four parts.

The washing of water with the Word (Eph. 5:26). This is the core of the rite. The Reformers, as the medieval schoolmen and the church fathers before them, gave great importance to following the institution of Jesus, baptizing in the name of the Father, and of the Son, and of the Holy Spirit (Matt. 28:19). These words of institution are read in the course of the rite to make clear that the church is acting at the bidding of Christ. The washing may be administered by immersion, pouring, or sprinkling, but it is understood primarily as a sign of washing and only secondarily as a sign of birth (Titus 3:5), illumination (Heb. 6:4), or burial (Rom. 6:4). A fundamental concern of Reformed churches has been that the sign of washing not be confused or obscured by additional symbolic acts such as exorcism, anointing with oil, renunciation of Satan, or the consecration of the font. With this giving of the sign, the sacrament is complete. But it entails the remaining three parts of the rite.

Prayers. First there are prayers of confession and repentance in which we cry out to God for our salvation. The prayers of confession found in the regular worship service begin the rite of Baptism, and indeed such prayers of lamentation whenever we pray them throughout the whole of our earthly life are part of the baptismal dimension of the Christian life. Then there is the baptismal invocation at the time of the administration of the sacrament in which we ask that the outward sign be fulfilled by the inward work of the Holy Spirit. Finally, the rite is concluded by the giving of a benediction to the newly baptized.

Teaching what Christ commanded. This is understood both in terms of formal catechetical instruction and in terms of lifelong study and discipleship. In the Netherlands* there is a tradition of catechetical preaching on Sunday evenings for the whole congregation.

Vows of faith. These are formally made before the church and maintained by a constant Christian witness. The Apostles' Creed traditionally expresses these vows, though a simple statement such as "Jesus Christ is my Lord and Savior" is sufficient. The Reformed understanding of Baptism sees the sacrament as a sign at the beginning of the Christian life which unfolds throughout the whole of life.

Baptismal controversies. Through the centuries certain problems have arisen in regard to the theology and administration of Baptism to which Reformed churches have given fairly consistent answers.

Baptismal regeneration. The NT assumes that one must be baptized to be counted a Christian (Acts 2:41), yet the story of the thief on the cross would indicate that necessity of baptism is not so absolute as to imply that God cannot save anyone without it. We are saved by grace* through faith (Eph. 2:8), not by going through some religious ceremony (1 Cor. 10:1–13; 1 Peter 3:21). If Reformed theology does not teach baptismal regeneration* neither does it teach decisional regeneration (John 1:13; Rom. 9:16). Salvation is God's work of grace abundantly poured out upon us through the Holy Spirit working faith in our hearts and uniting us to Christ in his death and resurrection.

Infant baptism. Beginning with Zwingli, Reformed theologians have found good reason for believing that infants were baptized in the NT church. If it is true that this is not specifically stated, it is also true that the NT does not record the baptism of anyone raised in the church. The question of how the second generation became Christian is not addressed. Throughout Scripture, covenant signs were given to children with their parents. Circumcision, which the NT clearly regards as a type of baptism, was normally administered to infants. In Jewish proselyte baptism the infants of converts were baptized because it was a well-established principle that children belong with their parents to the covenant community (cf. 1 Cor. 7:14). Jesus healed children as well as adults and at least once on the basis of the faith of a parent (John 4:50). The New England Puritans* were even willing to admit the children of the larger Christian community to the sacrament, though this so-called "half-way covenant"* was a problem for later generations. Following the Cane Ridge revival, the question was raised again and vigorously debated by Alexander Campbell and Nathan Rice. Horace Bushnell* made a significant defense of infant baptism in *Christian Nurture* (1847). During the Nazi ascendancy, Karl Barth* recommended that with the weakening of the state-supported Protestant churches of Europe, infant baptism be discontinued, though he never denied its validity. While at first his suggestion was followed in certain circles, his position elicited significant rebuttals by Oscar Cullmann and Joachim Jeremias, with the result that both European and American Reformed churches have continued infant baptism, finding it a significant witness to the sovereignty of grace.

Minister of baptism. Essential to the nature of the baptismal sign is that one is baptized by another; one does not baptize oneself. Far more than a symbolic profession of faith whereby the believer indicates his or her decision for Christ, baptism is, above all, a sign and seal of Christ's washing us from our sin and is therefore given us by a minister of the gospel acting in the name and under the authority of Christ (Matt. 28:18–19; Acts 2:38; 10:48). For this reason, "emergency baptisms" by persons other than ministers are not recognized by Reformed churches. Likewise, since it is what Christ does which is crucial, baptism is not invalidated through the unworthiness of the minister.

Mode of baptism. Whether baptism should be administered by immersion or sprinkling has aggravated American Protestantism unduly. If it is true that in classical Greek the word for baptism means to submerge, it is also true that in the popular Greek of NT times, the same word was used to refer to a number of different Jewish rites of purification involving washing (cf. the Gk. text of Mark 7:3–4; Luke 11:38; Heb. 6:2). Whatever mode of baptism is used, the sign of washing should be clear.

Rebaptism. In the ancient church, persons who committed grave sins after baptism or who under pressure of persecution had apostasized often asked to be rebaptized and received back into the fellowship of the church. While the church gradually developed disciplines of penance and readmission to regular Communion, it decided against rebaptism. Likewise, Reformed churches have taught that baptism is to be administered but once. Because Reformed churches have an abiding faith in God's faithfulness to the promises made in the sacrament itself, they regard rebaptism as constituting a sacrilege, implying that God had been unfaithful. The covenantal promises of God are not compromised by our confusion about the true nature of the sacrament, the immaturity of our faith, or our unfaithfulness to God. In the same way, baptism is not invalidated by liturgical faux pas. Reformed churches have usually been rather generous in recognizing baptisms administered by other Christian churches.

Water and Spirit. Baptism with water is an outward sign of an inward reality, namely, the baptism of the Holy Spirit. To imagine that some Christians have received only water baptism, while more advanced Christians have been baptized by the Holy Spirit is quite alien to the NT. Ephesians 4:5 teaches that there is but one baptism, and Reformed theologians therefore have always guarded against dividing water and Spirit. Water signifies the giving of the Spirit, just as much as it does the washing away of sin (Ezek. 36:25–27). To add to the sign of washing some sort of anointing or to regard confirmation* as a sacrament for the conferring of the Holy Spirit is to rob the original baptismal sign of half its meaning.

Barth, *CD* IV/4; O. Cullmann, *Baptism in the New Testament* (ET1950); E. B. Holifield, *The Covenant Sealed* (1974); J. Jeremias, *Infant Baptism in the First Four Centuries* (1960); G. W. H. Lampe, *Seal of the Spirit* (1967); H. O. Old, *The Shaping of the Reformed Baptismal Rite* (1991); R. Schnackenburg, *Baptism in the Thought of St. Paul* (1964); U. Zwingli, *Refutation of the Tricks of the Catabaptists*, ed. E. Peters (1972).

HUGHES OLIPHANT OLD

Baptists, Particular

The second of two groups of Baptist churches that in the seventeenth century emerged from Congregationalist* Puritanism.* Their name indicates their affirmation of "particular redemption" instead of the "general redemption" view of the earlier Baptists. The first congregation gathered in London by 1638 (perhaps 1633). John Gill* (1697–1771) and Andrew Fuller* (1754–1815) were prominent leaders. What came to be known as the Baptist Missionary Society was organized (1792) and sent William Carey* (1761–1834) to India. Some Particular Baptist churches formed (1831) what was later called the Baptist Union which united with the "New Connection" General Baptists (1891).

The First (1644) and Second (1677;

1689) London Confessions were the principal theological statements. The earlier confession, heavily christological,* emphasized their common affirmation of Calvinistic Puritanism, to counteract associations of Arminianism* with Baptists. The eternality of election in Christ and preterition, the particular intention and efficacy of Christ's priestly work, the effectual work of the Spirit,* and perseverance* of the elect were affirmed. The Second London Confession, explicitly modeled after the WCF* in organization and in working, continued emphasis on continuity with the Reformed faith, including the covenants* of grace* and redemption.

A recurring dispute over hyper-Calvinism* concerned the propriety of "calling" or "inviting" the unsaved to Christ (e.g., Gill) or "offering" grace and Christ or both (e.g., Fuller) or neither (e.g., Joseph Hussey).

H. L. McBeth, *The Baptist Heritage* (1987); T. J. Nettles, *By His Grace and for His Glory* (1986).

STEPHEN R. SPENCER

Barclay, William (1907–1978)

Known best for his seventeen-volume Daily Study Bible (New Testament), Barclay was primarily a popularizer who mediated the best of biblical scholarship to the broader public. He was born in the north of Scotland, studied classics at the University of Glasgow and theology at Trinity College, and was ordained to the ministry of the Church of Scotland (1933). After fourteen years of parish ministry, he became lecturer in NT language and literature at Glasgow and later professor of divinity and biblical criticism (1963). The demands on Barclay as a preacher and popular writer continued throughout his career, and here rather than in technical scholarship he made his greatest contribution to the church.

W. Barclay, *A Spiritual Autobiography* (1975); C. Rawlins, *William Barclay* (1984).

DONALD A. HAGNER

Barmen, Theological Declaration of

Representatives of Lutheran, Reformed, and United churches constituted the first Confessional Synod of the German Evangelical Church in Wuppertal-Barmen (May 29–31, 1934). The Roman Catholic Church and the so-called Free Churches (Baptist and Methodist churches) did not participate, because they were not members of the Evangelical Church in Germany.

The Barmen Declaration was unanimously adopted to withstand the errors of "German Christians" and attempts of the Reich church government "to establish the unity of the German Evangelical Church by means of false doctrine, by the use of force, and insincere practices." It became the theological basis of the true evangelical church, commonly called the Confessing Church. It was the point of departure for subsequent synods held in Dahlem (1934), Augsburg (1935), and Bad-Oeynhausen (1936). It was binding upon the church's Council of Brethren and administration in the conduct of the struggle against the Reich church bishop and church committees appointed by the government. It was adopted by the Second Free Reformed Synod, in Siegen (March 26–28, 1935), and is numbered among the historic confessions of the Reformed Church in Germany. Most constitutions of the Lutheran and United Churches in Germany have incorporated Barmen with varying degrees of authority. The United Presbyterian Church in the U.S.A. included the Barmen Declaration in its *Book of Confessions* (1967).

The "Faith Movement of the 'German Christians'" wanted to unite the twenty-nine regional churches into a state church after the pattern of the Church of England, with a bishop at its head. Claiming to stand on "Positive Christianity," the "German Christians" castigated godless Marxism, the Catholic Center Party, a mission to the Jews, intermarriage between Jews and Germans, pacifism, internationalism, and Free Masonry. All was based on the belief that "race, nationality and the nation [are] orders of life granted and entrusted to us by God." The German Christian Movement represented a syncretism of Christianity and the ideology of national socialism or Hitlerism.

The Nazi state was well aware the Confessing Church was opposed to its totalitarian claims and neo-paganism. The Confessing Church was an illegal, minority church inasmuch as the "German Christians" had won an overwhelming victory—with the aid of the Nazi propaganda machine—in the church elections (July 26, 1933). L. Müller had been elected Reich bishop at a National Synod of the German Evangelical Church that met in Wittenberg.

The Synod of Barmen did not call its six articles a confession of faith but a theological explanation of the present situation in the church. It explicitly stated, "It was not our intention to found a new church or to form a union." On the contrary, "precisely because we want to be and to remain faithful to our various confessions, we may not keep silent."

On the other hand, Barmen did say, "We are bound together by the confession of the one Lord of the one, holy, catholic and apostolic church" and "we confess the following truths." Thus Barmen confessed with its intention of declaring the right understanding of the Reformation confessions in a concrete situation. It confronted a decision concerning the ground, nature, and task of the church and of the state.

As Hans Asmussen said in his address on the Barmen Declaration: "We are raising a protest against the same phenomenon that has been slowly preparing the way for the devastation of the Church for more than two hundred years. For it is only a relative difference whether—beside Holy Scripture in the Church—historical events or reason, culture, aesthetic feelings, progress, or other powers and figures are said to be binding claims upon the Church" (Cochrane, p. 255).

A. C. Cochrane, *The Church's Confession Under Hitler* (1962).

ARTHUR C. COCHRANE

Barnes, Albert (1798–1870)

Minister, author, and leader of New School Presbyterianism. Barnes was born in New York; he graduated from Hamilton College (1820) and Princeton Seminary (1823). After ordination (1825), he became pastor of Philadelphia's First Presbyterian Church (1830) but was received only after debate over his published sermon, "The Way of Salvation" (1830). Conservatives claimed that it was influenced by New England moderate Calvinism* and appealed to the General Assembly* (1831), which censured the sermon for unguarded and objectionable passages. In 1835 it was alleged that Barnes's commentary on Romans departed from the Westminster Confession* on original sin,* human inability, justification* by faith,* and the imputation of Adam's guilt and Christ's righteousness. Barnes was acquitted by presbytery. On appeal, the synod suspended him, but the 1836 Assembly restored him. In 1837 the Old School party secured a majority and ejected its opponents.

Barnes served as a pastor until his retirement (1868) and saw the reunion of the two Presbyterian denominations (1870). He was an influential preacher, a prolific writer, an advocate of revivalism* and social reform, and an opponent of slavery. He wrote a popular eleven-volume NT commentary and an autobiography.

A. Barnes, *Life at Three-Score and Ten* (1871); S. J. Baird, *History of the New School* (1868); E. B. Davis, "Albert Barnes 1798–1870: An Exponent of New School Presbyterianism" (diss., Princeton Seminary, 1961); G. Junkin, *The Vindication, Containing a History of the Trial of the Rev. Albert Barnes* (1836); B. M. Kirkland, "Albert Barnes and Doctrinal Freedom," *JPH* 29 (March 1951): 97–106.

ALBERT H. FREUNDT, JR.

Barot, Madeleine (1909–)

A member of the Eglise Reformée de France, she began her eminent ecumenical career in the French Student Christian Movement, was a leader at the First World Conference of Christian Youth (Amsterdam, 1939), and was an early participant in the wartime French Resistance, notably as the founder-leader of the Conité Inter-Mouvement auprès des Evacués (CIMADE). She participated in WCC* meetings from 1946, and in 1953 she became director of the WCC's Department on the Cooperation of Men and Women in Church and Society. An indefatigable traveler and networker, she was an exponent of God's calling to churches worldwide to manifest the true qualities of Christ's church, particularly as these bear on men-women relationships.

ROBERT S. BILHEIMER

Barth, Karl (1886–1968)

Born on May 10, 1886, in Basel, Switzerland, the son of Fritz Barth and Anna Sartorius, Barth spent his youth in Bern and attended the Free Gymnasium, showing a keen interest in historical and military matters. Encouraged by the minister under whom he was confirmed, Barth studied evangelical theology in Bern, then in Berlin, Tübingen, and Marburg, where he was influenced by the liberal theology of Adolf von Harnack and Wilhelm Herrmann.

Barth was an assistant pastor in Geneva (1909–11) and served as pastor in Safenwil (Aargau; 1911–21). In 1913 he married Nelly Hoffmann, with whom he had five children. His son Christoph became an Old Testament scholar, and his son Markus a New Testament scholar. Barth worked closely with his lifelong friend, Pastor Eduard Thurneysen. Shocked by the silence of his theological teachers in the face of World War I, Barth joined the "religious socialists" (Hermann Kutter, Leonhard Ragaz). As a "red" clergyman, he sought to organize the workers in his congregation. However, it was his commentary on Paul's letter to the Romans (1919), a completely revised edition (1922), and an English translation (1935) that established Barth as a renowned theologian. He proclaimed the "wholly otherness" of God* and reflected the influence of Søren Kierkegaard. He insisted that "there is an infinite qualitative distinction between God and man." God is the "wholly other."

Barth's commentary on Romans led to a call to the chair of Reformed theology at Göttingen and to the rise of the so-called dialectical theology* of Eduard Thurneysen, Rudolf Bultmann, Friedrich Gogarten, and Emil Brunner.* Its journal was *Between the Times*. In 1925 Barth assumed the chair of systematic theology at Münster and in 1930 at Bonn. In these years he went his own way. This resulted in a new discovery of the Reformation and the apostasy of later Protestantism. Meanwhile his friends of the circle of dialectical theology began to go their own ways. With the rise of Hitler, Barth was from the first a passionate opponent of national socialism at a time when the church was silent. Through his pamphlet "Theological Existence Today" he created clear fronts in a confused situation. With Martin Niemöller and others he founded and led the Confessing Church which formed the opposition to the "German Christians" and the national socialist state. It adopted the famous Theological Declaration of Barmen,* drawn up by a committee of three, with Barth as the principal author. This Declaration became a doctrinal standard of many churches in Germany and other countries, including the Presbyterian Church (U.S.A.).

In the summer of 1935 Barth was dismissed from his theological chair in Bonn because he refused to take an unconditional oath of allegiance to Hitler. This resulted in his banishment from Germany and appointment to a chair of systematic theology in Basel. He continued his opposition to the Nazi regime in the periodicals *Between the Times* and *Evangelical Theology* and in pamphlets and letters. Moreover, he continued writing his major work, *Church Dogmatics*, which he began in Bonn. Through the years it grew to thirteen volumes of over nine thousand pages, rivaled in size only by the *Summa Theologica* of Thomas Aquinas.

The *CD*, though composed by a Reformed theologian, is an ecumenical work, full of new insights, and a fountain of exegetical, historical, philosophical, dogmatic, and practical ideas. Many evangelical and Roman Catholic scholars consider it the classic theological work of the twentieth century.

Though Barth championed the cause of the Allies in World War II against the Nazis, he was among the first to call for friendship toward defeated Germany. A sign of such friendship were the lectures he delivered amidst the ruins of the University of Bonn (1946–47). When the East-West conflict broke out, he refused to lump communism with nazism—not out of love for communism but as a sharp recognition of the Phariseeism of anti-communism. He continued to lecture in Basel until age seventy-five (1962). He traveled to France, Italy, Holland, England and Scotland, Hungary, and Czechoslovakia to deliver lectures. In the United States he lectured in Princeton, Chicago, and Dubuque, Iowa.

In 1948 Barth delivered the opening address at the first meeting of the WCC* in Amsterdam. After his writings had found acceptance within the Roman Catholic Church and when he retired from Basel, Barth was invited to visit Rome. He did so in September 1966 at the invitation of Pope Paul VI. On his return he published *Ad Limina Apostolorum: An Appraisal of Vatican II* (ET 1968).

Of all Barth's publications, the one that gave him greatest satisfaction was *Fides Quarens Intellectum: Anselm's Proof of the Existence of God in the Context of His Theological Scheme* (ET 1960). Yet, of all his books this has received the least attention from scholars. Fortunately two volumes of sermons (most of which he preached in prison) have been translated: *Deliverance to the Captives* (ET 1961) and *Call for God* (ET 1967). Barth wrote, "The prayers I gave [before and after the sermons] were to my mind as essential as the sermons themselves."

The question has been raised whether Karl Barth was a Reformed theologian. The answer depends on how one understands the word "Reformed." Certainly Barth was confirmed and ordained within the Reformed Church of Switzerland. But his understanding of "Reformed" is that of a church which is in the process of being continually reformed by God's Word attested in Holy Scripture. Hence no one can boast of being "reformed" except as one allows God's Word to reform God's church.

Since the days of John Calvin,* the Reformed and Presbyterian churches have been identified with the doctrines of predestination* and election. Barth offers a christological* correction to the doctrines: Jesus Christ is at once the electing God and the elected man in whom Israel and the church are elected and in whom individuals are elected and rejected.

No sketch of Barth's life and work would be complete without a reference to his hearing in Mozart's music an echo of the goodness of creation in both its positive and its negative aspects. "A thing of beauty is a joy forever" (Keats).

G. W. Bromiley, *An Introduction to the Theology of Karl Barth* (1979); E. Busch, *Karl Barth: His Life from Letters and Autobiographical Texts* (1976).

ARTHUR C. COCHRANE

Bartholomew's Day Massacres

Beginning in Paris on August 24, 1572, the St. Bartholomew's Day massacres were one of the most horrifying episodes of violence that accompanied the early stages of the Calvinist Reformation. They occurred during celebrations of a wedding designed to seal an alliance to end wars between French Protestant and Catholic factions by uniting the sister of the Catholic king of France, Charles IX, with her Protestant cousin, Henry of Navarre. They began with the assassinations, ordered by the royal privy council, of Admiral Gaspard de Coligny, political and military leader of the Protestant faction, and several other Protestant leaders. These were followed by the killing of thousands of Protestants from other walks of life by Parisian mobs, in turn followed by massacres in about a dozen French provincial cities. The widespread bloodshed profoundly shocked the international Reformed community. Many French Protestants converted to Catholicism, but others defied the royal government and returned to religious war.* Some were so disillusioned they attacked the very form of monarchic government that had permitted these atrocities and called for armed resistance in defense of basic human rights. The massacres remain a traumatic reminder of the depths of confessional hatreds during the Reformation period.

R. M. Kingdon, *Myths About the St. Bartholomew's Day Massacres, 1572–1576* (1988).

ROBERT M. KINGDON

Basel Confession

Also called the First Confession of Basel (1534) to distinguish it from the Second Confession of Basel (1536; or First Helvetic Confession*). Both documents belong to early Reformed history influenced by the theology of Zwingli* rather than that of Calvin,* a second-generation reformer.

The Basel Confession was drafted by John Oecolampadius,* principal Basel reformer, and was finalized by his successor, Oswald Myconius.* It has twelve articles: (art. 1) God,* (art. 2) the fall, (art. 3) divine providence,* (art. 4) the natures and person of Jesus Christ, (art. 5) church* and sacraments,* (art. 6) the Lord's Supper,* (art. 7) church discipline,* (art. 8) civil authority, (art. 9) faith* and works, (art. 10) judgment, (art. 11) of things forbidden and permitted, and (art. 12) against the errors of Anabaptists.

CHARLES PARTEE

Basel Mission

Founded as one of the many works of the pietist German Christian Fellowship of southern Germany and Switzerland, centered in Basel (1815). The organizational pattern is of independent Protestant nondenominational societies for mission in the English-speaking world. Its clergy are ordained by their respective parent churches, principally Reformed and Lutheran. The polity of the missionary churches is Reformed.

Concise Dictionary of the Christian World Mission (1971); *The Encyclopedia of Missions* (1904); W. Schlatter, *Geschichte der Basler Mission*, 4 vols. (1815–1919).

JOHN E. WILSON

Bavinck, Herman (1854–1921)

One of the most important Reformed theologians from the turn of the century who, together with Abraham Kuyper,* effected a revival of Dutch Reformed theology. Even outside Holland, Bavinck's four-volume dogmatics is still influential. Additionally, Bavinck published many other theological, philosophical, and educational treatises. Dogmatically and spiritually he felt congenial with the American theologians Charles Hodge* and B. B. Warfield.*

Bavinck was the son of a minister in the Dutch Reformed Secessed Church, Jan Bavinck. He studied theology at the State University of Leiden, where he received his doctorate with *De ethiek van Ulrich Zwingli* (1880). He was appointed professor at the Theological Seminary of the Secessed Church at Kampen (1883) and became professor at the Free University of Amsterdam* (1902) after an attempt to merge Kampen with Amsterdam failed.

In Kampen, Bavinck gave his inaugural lecture, *De wetenschap van de H. Godgeleerdheid* ("The Science of Holy Theology"), which laid the basis for his later dogmatics and proclaimed his solidarity with Reformed theology. God,* he said, is the object of theology,* and Holy Scripture* is its source of knowledge. God laid down a system of knowledge of God* in the Bible, and theology's duty is to find this.

As professor at Kampen, Bavinck published his four-volume dogmatics and continued to elaborate on it in Amsterdam. There he published *Gereformeerde Dogmatiek*, vols. 1–4 (1895–1901), his magnum opus, reprinted often without changes. Here he brought the old Reformed theology in line with modern times.

Bavinck's innovation in the doctrine of the inspiration of Holy Scripture* is especially striking. By introducing the notion of *organical* inspiration, he accounted for the personality, experience, and historical background of biblical authors to a larger extent than in earlier dogmatics. Equally important is his thesis that the whole of the Bible is *theopneustos*, inspired by God's Spirit. That is why Holy Scripture is the instrument of the Holy Spirit* in bringing faith* and rebirth.

In his doctrine of creation,* Bavinck opposed evolutionism, which he discussed extensively. He advanced the doctrine of election by refusing to choose between supralapsarianism* and infralapsarianism.* Both are insufficient in explaining God's election, for God's decisions know no specific order. Together they form God's eternal plan in which there is neither "before" nor "after."

Bavinck also strongly opposed Pelagianism and Arminianism.*

In his rectoral oration, *Modernisme en orthodoxie* (1911), Bavinck maintained God's existence, continuing revelation,* and recognizability against the agnostic wing of liberal theology. He gave the Stone Lectures at Princeton (1908; *Wijsbegeerte der Openbaring;* ET *Philosophy of Revelation*), in which he attempted a synthesis among great thinkers such as Augustine,* Schleiermacher,* and Kant. Bavinck wanted to prove that Christian faith does not oppose modern culture as such but only modern culture's rejection of the supernatural.

Bavinck made an important contribution to the consolidation and prospering of the Reformed churches in Holland. His integrity was undisputed.

R. H. Bremmer, *Herman Bavinck als Dogmaticus* (1961); and *Herman Bavinck en zijn tijdgenoten* (1966); Rogers and McKim, *AIB* (1979); J. Veenhof, *Revelatie en inspiratie* (1968).

R. H. BREMMER

Bavinck, Johan H. (1895–1964)

Leading missiologist among the Netherlands' conservative Reformed (Gereformeerde) church circles in the mid-twentieth century. A nephew of theologian Herman Bavinck,* he shared his uncle's irenic temperament and mystical interests. Bavinck spent most of the 1920 and 1930s in Indonesia as a minister and teacher, chiefly in native missions agencies. From 1939 he taught missions and practical theology at the Free University of Amsterdam.* Modeling empathy, keen intellect, love for human variety, and deep immersion in the receiving culture, he pushed Reformed missions away from paternalism toward mutual interchange and indigenization.

JAMES D. BRATT

Baxter, Richard (1615–1691)

Reformed pastor who was perhaps the most prolific writer in the English language. Terming himself a "mere Catholic," or a "mere nonconformist," Baxter sought the "true moderate healing terms" bringing parties together under a comprehensive English national church in which basic unity tolerated diversity.

Baxter was theologically in the mainstream of English Protestant tradition as established through the reign of James I. In discussion among pastors in Bridgnorth, where he was an assistant, he questioned the Laudians concerning the "et cetera oath" enjoined in 1640. He then wore the designation "Puritan" lightly, remembering that when his father became active in church after reading Roman Catholic devotional literature, neighbors termed *him* a "Puritan."

Called to Kidderminster (April 1641), Baxter served until the Restoration. His work, described in *The Reformed Pastor* (1656), was exemplary. As a chaplain in the army of Oliver Cromwell* he opposed antinomians. *Aphorisms of Justification* (1649) and *The Saints' Everlasting Rest* (1650) arose from this experience.

Refusing a bishopric in the Restoration, Baxter joined the ejected ministers as their chief apologist. Both under persecution and with toleration he worked for a church comprehending features of the Episcopal, Presbyterian, Independent, and Erastian positions. He urged reading even theologians with whom he did not agree as he followed the middle ground between antinomianism and Arminianism* and bridged Reformed confessional orthodoxy with the theology of the Age of Reason.

N. H. Keeble, *Richard Baxter* (1982).

JAMES C. SPALDING

Bay Psalm Book

The first book printed in North America, *The Whole Booke of Psalmes Faithfully Translated Into English Metre*, commonly known as the Bay Psalm Book, appeared in Cambridge, Massachusetts (1640). Designed for public and private worship,* this metrical version of the Psalms became extremely popular and by 1773 had gone through about seventy editions. Early editions contained no music, though an "admonition" at the end recommended tunes to which psalms in the several meters could be sung. The third, definitive edition (1651) contained more polished translations and thirty-six other "scripture-songs" and bore the popular title *New England Psalm Book.* The ninth edition (1698) was the first to include tunes, thirteen of them in two parts, melody and bass, inserted in a section at the end, reputedly the first music printed in America.

L. GORDON TAIT

Beecher, Henry Ward (1813–1887)

America's most prominent preacher (1840–70) and son of Lyman Beecher,* Beecher preached a mixture of civil religion and Christianized Social Darwinism. He largely ignored the theological substance of his Calvinist upbringing to popularize a romantic view of God* superintending a natural evolution toward ever greater heights of human unity, order, and freedom. He believed that the United States led the world as the pinnacle of human development. His liberal theology matched a social conservatism allowing for mild reforms based on the duty of the more fortunate to lift up the less advanced under God.

W. G. McLoughlin, *The Meaning of Henry Ward Beecher* (1970).

MILTON J COALTER, JR.

Beecher, Lyman (1775–1863)

Congregationalist, later a Presbyterian minister, Beecher maintained a pragmatic indifference to creedal definitions of orthodoxy. He preached human ability to respond to God's grace* despite his Calvinist allegiances. After initial opposition, he eventually embraced the manipulative "new measures" revivalism* of Charles G. Finney.* Like Jonathan Edwards,* he expected the millennium's commencement in America. As president of Cincinnati's Lane Seminary, Beecher foresaw the world's hope not in New England but in the American West's advance toward moral and political emancipation. Beecher's prediction was mixed with nativist fears of the burgeoning numbers of European Catholic immigration which in his view lacked knowledge of democratic responsibilities or true Christianity.

S. C. Henry, *Unvanquished Puritan* (1973).

MILTON J COALTER, JR.

Belgic Confession

The oldest creed of the Reformed Church of the Netherlands and its daughter churches, the confession (1561) was written by French-speaking Guido de Brès (d. 1567) from what is now Belgium. It was to show Spanish authorities that Reformed people were not rebels but law-abiding Christians. The confession sets itself against both Roman Catholic and Anabaptist doctrinal errors. It exemplifies Reformed confessional writing after the earlier creed of the Reformed Church of France.

The Belgic Confession was translated into Dutch (1562) and adopted by synods of Antwerp (1566), Wesel (1568), and Dort (1619). It was translated into English by John W. Livingston of the Reformed Church in America (1768).

The topical order is traditional: God and how God is known (arts. 1–11); creation and providence (arts. 12–13); fall and election (arts. 14–16); salvation in Christ (arts. 17–21); justification and sanctification (arts. 22–26); the church (arts. 27–29); church order (arts. 30–32); sacraments (arts. 33–35); church and state (art. 36); and last things (art. 37). Distinctive Reformed emphases are: Scripture* as normative; the sovereignty of God* and God's grace;* sin;* salvation* in Christ alone, including sanctification* and good works; the law* of God as a help in Christian living; Calvin's* view of the sacraments;* and the state as instrument of God and vehicle of God's grace.

P. J. Los, *Tekst en Toelichting van de Geloofsbelijdenis der Nederlandsche Hervormde Kerk* (1929); M. E. Osterhaven, *Our Confession of Faith* (1964).

M. EUGENE OSTERHAVEN

Bellamy, Joseph (1719–1790)

A dynamic Congregationalist* evangelist during the Great Awakening* and associate of Jonathan Edwards,* though later departing from Edwards's Reformed theology in several significant ways.

After graduating from Yale, Bellamy studied with Edwards before going to the Congregational Church in Bethlehem, Connecticut, where he served the rest of his life. He founded one of the first "Sabbath schools" in America, and his home became a training ground for theological students.

Bellamy's theological innovations sought to explain why God* permitted sin* and the fall, which, he said, were necessary in achieving the greatest good. Humans become sinful because they sin. God must punish sin, not because of divine wrath, but to maintain the integrity of divine justice. Christ died for all people, not just for the elect, as the Calvinists taught. This atonement* was the outworking of God's love, not a need for divine "satisfaction."

S. E. Ahlstrom, ed., *Theology in America* (1967).

NATHAN P. FELDMETH

Benson, Louis Fitzgerald (1855–1930)

Presbyterian minister and hymnologist. Educated at the University of Pennsylvania in law, Benson abandoned that career after seven years to enter Princeton Seminary and was ordained (1886). After a six-year pastorate in the Germantown section of Philadelphia, Pennsylvania, he became editor of several hymnals authorized by the General Assembly of the Presbyterian Church in the U.S.A., including *The Hymnal* (1895). He served on the committee that prepared the *Book of Common Worship** (1905) and on its revision committee.

Benson lectured in liturgics at Auburn Seminary and hymnology* at Princeton and wrote several books on hymnody. *The English Hymn: Its Development and Use in Worship* (1915) remains a standard in the field. His hymnological library, one of the world's most valuable private collections, was given to Princeton Seminary when he died.

LINDAJO H. MCKIM

Berkhof, Hendrikus (1914–)

Theologian of the Dutch Reformed Church (Hervormde Kerk) and ecumenical leader. Berkhof studied in Amsterdam, Leiden, and Berlin. After pastorates, five years as a part-time instructor in dogmatics and church history at the Institute "Church and World," and ten years as first director of the practical theological seminary of the Reformed Church in Driebergen, he became professor of dogmatics and biblical theology (1960) at the University of Leiden, where he served until his retirement (1981).

Berkhof has been active in the Council of Churches in the Netherlands (chairman, 1974–83), the WARC, and the WCC* (Central Committee, 1954–75).

He has written approximately twenty books, most of which have been translated into English and several into German, Japanese, and other languages. He is best known for his *Christian Faith* (1979; rev. ed. 1986); *The Doctrine of the Holy Spirit* (1964; 1976); *Christ and the Powers* (1962; 2nd ed. 1977); *Christ the Meaning of History* (1966; 1979); *Well-founded Hope* (1969); and *Introduction to the Study of Dogmatics* (1985). His most recent work is *Two Hundred Years of Theology* (1989).

Berkhof was an early proponent of dialectical* or neo-orthodox* theology, especially that of Karl Barth.* He has moved beyond Barth, especially in his Christology, which he does "from below." The influence of Friedrich Schleiermacher,* Hans Küng, and other progressive Dutch and Catholic theologians is evident in his later writings. The impact of Barth and the Reformed tradition, however, is still very prominent in Berkhof's thought.

I. JOHN HESSELINK

Berkhof, Louis (1873–1957)

A major systematic theologian of the Christian Reformed Church and first president of Calvin Seminary. Born in the Netherlands, Berkhof was profoundly influenced by the Reformed tradition of the 1834 Secession and the Dutch neo-Calvinist movement of Abraham Kuyper.* He graduated from the Theological School of the Christian Reformed Church (1900) and Princeton Seminary (1904) where he studied under B. B. Warfield* and Geerhardus Vos. Berkhof taught exegetical theology and NT at Calvin Seminary (1906–26). His *Principles of Biblical Interpretation* (1937) and *Introduction to the New Testament* (1915) belong to this period. Having distinguished himself in theological controversy, he was appointed professor of systematic theology (1926–44). Concurrently he served (from 1931) as seminary president.

A man of many talents and broad interests, Berkhof addressed contemporary theological issues and problems, most notably those concerning church and society. His reputation as a Reformed theologian rests almost entirely on his *Systematic Theology* (1941). Initially published for students, the work became a textbook. Not an original thinker, Berkhof was dependent on the Dutch dogmatician, Johan Bavinck,* for the structure and content of his theology. He was elected president of the first assembly of the Reformed Ecumenical Synod (1946).

H. Zwaanstra, "Louis Berkhof," in *Reformed Theology in America*, ed. D. F. Wells (1985), 153–71.

HENRY ZWAANSTRA

Berkouwer, Gerrit C. (1903–)

Developer of a twentieth-century confessional theology in the Dutch Reformed tradition presenting a creative evangelical alternative to liberalism, scholasticism,* and neo-orthodoxy.*

Berkouwer was born on June 8, 1903. He studied theology (1922–1927) at the Free University of Amsterdam,* founded by Abraham Kuyper.* The reigning Dutch Reformed theology was that of Herman Bavinck* which Berkouwer brought into dialogue with the new German dialectical theology on which he published his dissertation (1934). Following two pastorates, Berkouwer lectured on contemporary theology at the Free University (1940–45) and became professor of systematic theology, retiring in 1973.

Berkouwer's theological method has been described as functional or relational. The function or purpose of Scripture* is to reveal how God* is related to us. In his fourteen-volume *Studies in Dogmatics*, Berkouwer set forth his methodology: "Theology is . . . occupied in continuous attentive and obedient listening to the Word of God" (*Faith and Justification* [1954], p. 9). Berkouwer opposed all speculation that imposed logical systems or went beyond the data of Scripture. He defined theology as scholarly reflection on the normativity of revelation for faith.

While deeply rooted in Scripture, in his church, and in the Reformed confessional tradition, Berkouwer brought fresh understanding to each by his open and honest listening to other sources. He wrote three books on Karl Barth,* the last of which, *The Triumph of Grace in the Theology of Karl Barth* (ET 1956), elicited Barth's praise. After World War II, Berkouwer began to meet regularly with Roman Catholic scholars. His initial emphasis on conflict with Rome was followed by his *The Second Vatican Council and the New Catholicism* (ET 1965). A Roman Catholic theologian described it as "written from the inside out," due to his genuine entering as an official observer into the wrestling of the Council.

Rather than insisting on literal adherence to the Reformed confessions* of his church, Berkouwer sought the deepest "intent" of these documents, showing their relevance for the twentieth century. His first book on Scripture (1938) he later viewed as being based too much on a priori judgments. In *Holy Scripture* (1975), Berkouwer emphasized the Reformed principle that Scripture is its own interpreter. The clarity of Scripture is directed to its message of salvation* in Jesus Christ to whom we are called in personal relationship. The human literary form of Scripture can be understood in all its time and culture-related limitations without damaging reverence for its universally valid message. Knowledge in any field can offer an "occasion" for reexamining traditional exegesis without fear. Berkouwer concluded: "It may seem like a roundabout way to go from the message of Scripture to its unique authority. In reality, it is the true and only way to obedience" (p. 366).

Since retirement, Berkouwer has written two volumes of reflections on the theology of his period: *A Half Century of Theology: Movements and Motives* (1977) and *Zoeken en vinden: Herinneringen en ervaringen* (1989; "Seeking and Finding: Remembrances and Experiences").

JACK B. ROGERS

Beza, Theodore (1519–1605)

John Calvin's* successor at Geneva, first headmaster of the Geneva Academy,* early counselor of the French Reformation,* and a main figure in the transition to early Reformed scholasticism.*

Life. Beza learned Greek and Latin from Melchior Wolmar (also Calvin's teacher and inclined to the Reformation). As a humanist* he wrote *Juvenalia* (1548), a compilation of poems containing erotic verses which later embarrassed him. He married secretly to avoid scandal and retain the benefices for those preparing for the priesthood. By 1548 he renounced the Roman Church. He taught at Lausanne and published two more humanist works: *Abraham sacrifiant* (1550) and *Alphabetum graecum* (1554). His first theological treatise (*Tabula praedestinationis*, or *The Sum of All Christianity* [1555]) grew out of the Bolsec* controversy and was designed as a defense of Calvin's doctrine of predestination* (though he knew it was more "logical" and "methodical" than Calvin's work). His *Annotations on the New Testament* and another work on predestination (against Sebastian Castellio) both appeared in 1558. His *Confession de la foi chrestienne* for his Catholic father came out in 1558 and his first *Life of Calvin* in 1564 (later eds. 1565, 1574).

Beza wrote on heresy* and discipline,* and turned to various aspects of Christian living. He was increasingly involved in ecclesiastical matters and polemics on the sacraments* and predestination. He wrote commentaries and sermons (Eccl.; Job; the passion and resurrection of Christ) and took diplomatic trips to gain support among German princes for French Protestants. He attended colloquies with Lutherans on (especially) the Lord's Supper.*

Beza moved to Geneva (1558) and began working in the Academy (1559). His responsibilities increased when Calvin died (1564). He was moderator of the Company of Pastors* until 1580 and main pastor until a few years before his own death.

Influence. In the forty years after Calvin, Beza was mainly responsible for consolidating Genevan orthodoxy. He built on Calvin's scholastic accents but never wrote a "formal theology." His *Confession* and *Book(s) of Christian Questions and Answers* (1570; 1575) were the most complete statements of his thinking. Again he rooted predestination in God's* being—as the One who *is* eternally, immutably, and supremely just and merciful. He distinguished sharply the decree and its execution in history,* and saw Christ and the Spirit as "instruments" to accomplish God's purpose (supralapsarianism*). Finally, all other parts of his theology (church,* sacraments, etc.) were expressions of the actualizing of the decree.

Beza is also known for biblical, literary, and other activities. He discovered the fifth-century Codex Bezae, and his *Annotations* led to the Geneva Bible* (1558). His *Abraham* was the "first French tragedy," and his Psalter translations have been influential in Reformed circles. His *Du droit des magistrats* (*De jure magistratum,* 1573) is important in the history of modern political texts. Jacobus Arminius was one of his students (1580s). Indeed, the Arminian* controversy (and Synod of Dort,* 1618–19) can only be viewed against the background of Bezan decretalism.

Present scholarship. Current discussions center on how to interpret Beza's scholastic tendencies. Walter Kickel (with E. Bizer and H. Heppe) has exaggerated the discontinuities between Calvin and Beza, while Richard Muller (with Ian McPhee) has underscored the continuities. Brian Armstrong and John Bray tend toward the former, and Jill Raitt and Tadataka Maruyama toward the latter. Directly or indirectly, all are concerned with the role of predestination in Beza and later Reformed orthodoxy.* No one denies, however, that Beza was a "primary shaper of the Reformed tradition" (Raitt, *Shapers*, p. 104).

J. S. Bray, *Theodore Beza's Doctrine of Predestination* (1976); F. Gardy, *Bib-*

liographie (1960); and *Correspondance* (1962–); P.-F. Geisendorf, *Théodore de Bèze* (1949); P. C. Holtrop, *The Bolsec Controversy* (1991); W. Kickel, *Vernunft und Offenbarung bei Theodor Beza* (1967); T. Maruyama, *The Ecclesiology of Theodore Beza* (1978); R. A. Muller, *Christ and the Decree* (1986); J. Raitt, *The Eucharistic Theology of Theodore Beza* (1972); and ed., *Shapers of Religious Traditions* (1981).

PHILIP C. HOLTROP

Blake, Eugene Carson (1906–1984)

Presbyterian clergyman, denominational executive, and ecumenical leader. Blake graduated from Princeton Seminary (1932) and was pastor in Albany, New York, and in Pasadena, California. He was Stated Clerk (1951–66) of the United Presbyterian Church in the U.S.A. during the McCarthy era, civil rights struggles, and protests against America's Vietnam involvement. Blake's commitments to personal freedom, social justice, and world peace made him one of the most recognizable and controversial figures in American Protestantism. His arrest for attempting to integrate a Baltimore amusement park (1963) and his vocal opposition to the Vietnam war typified his social involvements. He was equally visible for his ecumenicity. Blake made national headlines (1960) when he proposed the merger of four mainline Protestant denominations: Episcopal, Methodist, Presbyterian, and United Church of Christ. His speech marked the beginning of the Consultation on Church Union and ushered in extended efforts to effect an organic union of major Protestant denominations. Blake became General Secretary of the WCC* in Geneva (1966) and served until his retirement in 1972. He directed the Fourth WCC Assembly (1968) in Uppsala, Sweden, implemented programs to combat racism, and promoted increased participation of third-world churches and staff in the World Council.

R. D. Brackenridge, *Eugene Carson Blake: Prophet with Portfolio* (1978).

R. DOUGLAS BRACKENRIDGE

Blumhardt, Johann Christoph (1805–1880)

Pastor in Möttlingen, Germany, Blumhardt, because of his "Kampf," was led to establish a healing community at Bad Boll. The "objective pietism" of his tradition and his influence on Karl Barth* are significant for Reformed theology. Barth said he studied Blumhardt when he became disillusioned with the theology of his teachers.

Blumhardt studied at the University of Tübingen and entered the pastorate. His inspiration, experiences, and writings came from the parish. His encounter with a troubled woman named Gottlieben Dittus was formative. She was "demon"-possessed, but by prayer and counseling she received relief. The last cry of the demon was significant. It said, "Jesus is Victor." This became the motto for Blumhardt's ministry.

He settled in Bad Boll, where people came to him for a regimen of prayer,* counseling, and Bible study. He thought the church* should be a healing society. People claimed healings, but Blumhardt focused on God's power in Christ.

His views of the name of God and the outpouring of the Spirit are remarkable. God's name was not the "I am" of Exodus but "the Lord, merciful and gracious." The "Kampf" signed that God was pouring out the Holy Spirit.

Blumhardt influenced Barth's theological revolution. One hears echoes of Blumhardt's "Jesus is Victor" in Barth's "triumph of grace."

K. Barth, *Protestant Theology in the Nineteenth Century* (1972); E. Gangler, *Johann Christoph Blumhardt: Sein Leben und seine Botschaft* (1945).

WILLIAM G. BODAMER

Boegner, Marc (1881–1968)

Eminent French ecumenical leader. As pastor in Paris and as radio preacher, Boegner gained national prominence, serving as president of the Reformed Church of France and the French Protestant Federation. During World War II, he courageously defended Jews, assisted refugees, and represented church concerns to the Vichy government; his services were recognized by election to the

Académie Française. He was a participant in various aspects of the ecumenical movement: the missionary (1910), Life and Work (1925; 1937), and Faith and Order (1937). Boegner was influential in forming the WCC* (1938–48) and served on its Presidium and Central Committee.

M. Boegner, *The Long Road to Unity* (1970).

ROBERT S. BILHEIMER

Boesak, Alan Aubrey (1946–)

Theologian, pastor, and prominent public figure in South Africa,* Boesak has become a world leader in the struggle against apartheid* and injustice. He is a world-renowned preacher, lecturer and writer, and frequent consultant to religious and political leaders. He has been the most widely recognized Calvinist or Reformed leader in the world today.

Boesak was born in Kakemas, Cape, South Africa, and classified by the South African government as "colored," growing up under all the restrictions such classification implies. Yet he excelled as a student and graduated from the University of the Western Cape and the Theological Seminary of the Nederduitse Gereformeerde Sendingkerk (NGSK). He also studied at the Theologische Hogeschool der Gereformeerde Kerken, Kampen (doctorate), the Free University of Amsterdam,* and Union Seminary (N.Y.).

Boesak has been pastor of the Bellville NGSK, moderator of the NGSK, senior vice-president of the South African Council of Churches, and a founder and patron of the United Democratic Front (a leading resistance movement in South Africa). He has received many awards and honorary degrees.

His scholarly work in the Reformed tradition, black theology, and biblical studies has given him a significant place in theological circles. But his pastoral concern, courage, and commitment to justice* have placed him close to the center of the political and social struggles of history in and beyond South Africa. The WARC* elected him president in Ottawa, Canada (1982), after he led the effort to have it declare apartheid a heresy and suspend membership of leading South African white Reformed churches. Since, he has been threatened, physically attacked, arrested, and frequently jailed (including over three weeks in solitary confinement).

Boesak's understanding and demonstration of Christian faith not only as private personal devotion to God but disciplined public response in and beyond the church* to God's sovereignty and glory are a challenge both to the Reformed tradition in the church and to powers and authorities in the world. The groundwork for such a decisive stance is most systematically spelled out in *Farewell to Innocence* (1976). Here he attacked the pseudo-innocence by which Christians have allowed the church's accommodation to the state and the state's accommodation to the church to corrupt the faith while permitting and even encouraging the practice of injustice without challenge. This critical stance makes him a conspicuous Calvinist. His writings have been translated into nine languages.

A. A. Boesak, *Black and Reformed* (1984); *If This Is Treason, I Am Guilty* (1987); and *Comfort and Protest* (1987).

EDWARD M. HUENEMANN

Bolsec, Jerome (c. 1524–1584)

A former Carmelite monk who converted to Reformed Christianity but attacked Calvin's* view of eternal reprobation within the Genevan church. The ensuing controversy (1551–55), in a sense, continues to the present. It occasioned the close relation between Calvin and Theodore Beza* as well as the rise of early Reformed scholasticism.*

Though he said he agreed with Calvin at every point except the eternal "cause" of perdition, Bolsec was imprisoned and tried (October 16–December 23, 1551). He would probably have been put to death had he not been supported by the majority of Reformed ministers in Basel, Zurich, and Bern—including Calvin's friend Heinrich Bullinger.* In general, the Reformed churches outside Geneva, Lausanne (Beza), and Neuchâtel (Farel*) thought Bolsec was not a "bad man," and not "Pelagian," "heretical," and "good for nothing" (as Calvin and Beza charged).

Bolsec pleaded for "biblical simplicity"; for relating reprobation to faith* and history;* for the "universality" and "equality" of grace;* for a strong doctrine of "election in Christ"; and for an accent on God's* initiative and humanity's* freedom.* He focused on God's address in Christ and human responses *now*, instead of on a "double predestination" rooted in a "pretemporal" *eternity* which would seem to require the fall (Lat. *lapsus*) for God to realize God's essential attributes of mercy and justice. In contrast, Calvin and the Genevan ministers (with Beza and Farel) said the decree of (double) predestination* was the "foundation" of the Reformation and that therefore the other Reformed churches should agree with them. Here are the beginnings of supralapsarianism* and infralapsarianism.*

These discussions should not be removed from the Genevan political tensions of the early 1550s between native "blue bloods" ("libertines"), who favored freedom of conscience,* and French immigrants ("refugees"), who wanted Calvin's discipline. Calvin stressed the implied metaphysics that led from eternity to time to sharpen—for the magistrates—the incompatibility of his thinking and Bolsec's. But finally the verdict of perpetual exile was more a political than a theological necessity. If the magistrates were going to keep Calvin and most of their ministers, they had to get rid of the "unknown" Jerome. They were more concerned about social "scandal" than theological "heresy."*

Bolsec found sanctuary in Bern. For political reasons he was also exiled twice from there but was restored on both occasions. He gathered a coterie of Reformed ministers and others who attacked Calvin—personally and theologically. Meanwhile, Beza wrote his *Life of Calvin*, which included the charge (3rd ed. 1575) that Bolsec's second wife allowed herself to be a prostitute for some noblemen. By then Bolsec had returned to Catholicism—though there is no evidence that he ever embraced its most distinctive tenets. Incensed at Beza's "lies," he published his scurrilous *Vie de Calvin* (1577), followed by an equally scathing life of Beza. Ironically, perhaps the majority of Reformed theologians today would be closer to Bolsec's views on predestination than to Calvin's.

For Bolsec's life, see E. Haag, *La France protestante* (1846–59); the main Latin and French texts on the controversy are in the *CO* (vols. 8, 14, 15) and in J.-F. Bergler, ed., *Registres de la compagnie des pasteurs de Genève, 1546–1553* (1964), vol. 1 (the "trial," trans. P. E. Hughes). An analysis of the controversy is found in P. C. Holtrop, *The Bolsec Controversy* (1991); for the theology in the *Vie*, see F. Pfeilschifter, *Das Calvinbild bei Bolsec* (1983).

PHILIP C. HOLTROP

Bomberger, John Henry Augustus (1817–1890)

German Reformed pastor and teacher educated at Franklin and Marshall College and Mercersburg Seminary. After Pennsylvania pastorates Bomberger became the first president of Ursinus College. Suspicious of ritualism and an incarnationalism that he believed neglected the cross, Bomberger opposed the Mercersburg Theology.* He edited the opposition, *The Reformed Church Monthly* (1868–77). Along with translations, he published *Our Position* (1856); *Infant Salvation* (1859); *Five Years' Ministry . . . in Race Street* (1860); *The Revised Liturgy* (1867); and *Reformed Not Ritualistic: A Reply to Dr. Nevin's "Vindication"* (1867).

Ursinus College Bulletin, vol. 7, no. 1 (1890); *The Rev. J. H. A. Bomberger* (1917); C. D. Yost, *Ursinus College* (1985).

ALAN P. F. SELL

Bonar, Andrew (1810–1892)

Scottish evangelical writer, educated at the University of Edinburgh and influenced by Thomas Chalmers.* He was the brother of Horatius Bonar.* He served Collace, Perthshire (1838; Church of Scotland), but joined the Free Church (1843; Disruption). He moved to Finnieston Free Church, Glasgow (1856–92), and was Moderator of the General Assembly* (1878). Bonar was the biographer of Robert Murray McCheyne* and editor of the letters of Samuel Rutherford* (1863). His *Diary* (publ. 1895) reflects his godliness.

M. Bonar, ed., *Reminiscences* (1895); F. Ferguson, *The Life of the Rev. Dr. Andrew A. Bonar* (1893).

A. T. B. MCGOWAN

Bonar, Horatius (1808–1889)

Scottish hymn writer, educated at the University of Edinburgh and ordained in the Church of Scotland (1837). He was the brother of Andrew Bonar.* He became minister at Kelso. He joined the Free Church of Scotland at the Disruption (1843) and remained in Kelso. He served the Chalmers Memorial Church, Edinburgh (1866–89), and was Moderator of the General Assembly* of the Free Church (1883).

Perhaps the greatest Scottish hymn writer, Bonar had pronounced premillennial views, mainly through the influence of Edward Irving.*

W. R. Nicoll, *Princes of the Church* (1921); W. E., ed., *Memories of Dr. Horatius Bonar* (1909); *Horatius Bonar . . . A Memorial* (1889).

A. T. B. MCGOWAN

Boston, Thomas (1676–1732)

Church of Scotland minister who served his entire ministry in the Borders, mainly in Ettrick. Boston's significance is twofold:

1. His writings. Boston's *The Fourfold State of Human Nature* (1720) became a minor classic of Scottish Calvinist theology, almost as influential with some as John Bunyan's* *The Pilgrim's Progress.* Boston's volumes on the covenant* of works and covenant of grace* rate alongside better-known continental expositions. His *Works* form twelve volumes.

2. The Marrow Controversy.* *The Marrow of Modern Divinity* (of uncertain authorship) was a compilation of writings of Reformers and Puritans.* Boston discovered it, found that it expressed his own position, promoted it, and issued an important edition with detailed notes.

The Church of Scotland, however, under the influence of a neonomian party, condemned the book as heretical and contrary to the teachings of the Westminster Confession.* Yet Joseph Caryl, specifically appointed by the Westminster Assembly* to approve books for the press, had given it his imprimatur.

The ensuing controversy was complex and bitter, and most of the principal figures on Boston's side ultimately left the Church of Scotland in the First Secession (1733), though Boston himself had died.

Boston was an orthodox federal* Calvinist committed to the theology of the Westminster Confession. His federal theology* was neither legalistic nor conditional in its understanding of grace.

See biographies by W. Addison (1936), A. Thomson (1895), and J. L. Watson (1883); A. T. B. McGowan, "The Federal Theology of Thomas Boston" (diss., University of Aberdeen, 1990).

A. T. B. MCGOWAN

Bourgeois, Louis (c. 1510–1561)

Writer of hymn tunes that gave spirit to Reformed worship. "Old Hundredth," with the Doxology, is one of his best known. By 1541 Bourgeois was in Geneva, where John Calvin* asked him to provide tunes for metrical psalms by Clément Marot* and Theodore Beza.* Music in early Calvinist circles operated under two constraints: biblical psalms alone, though in meter and the vernacular, and no instrumental accompaniment. Bourgeois increased the Genevan Psalter from 30 to 85 tunes, composing and editing for several editions over fifteen years. There was risk: his unauthorized alteration of one familiar tune led Geneva's Council to jail him briefly (1551). Locally influential was his teaching of psalm singing to the people. He hoped to introduce part singing into worship* but found Calvin and the Council opposed. This controversy may have led to his departure for Paris (1557). Nothing is known of him after 1561.

Congregational psalm singing gave excitement to Reformation Christians. Reformed leaders in other lands were clearly influenced by contact with Bourgeois's psalmody, including his collection of 50 psalms in four-part harmony (Lyons, 1547). His tunes remain prominent. After four hundred years, Switzerland's French-speaking Reformed churches included 72 in their book of 422 hymns (*Psautier romand* [1955]). France's Reformed Church used 55 (*Louange et prière* [1948]). In the American Presbyterian *Hymnbook* (1955) his contributions were outnumbered only by those of two composers who wrote for nineteenth-century American and English congregations.

JULIUS MELTON

Brainerd, David (1718–1747)

Presbyterian missionary to native American Delaware, Iroquois, Seneca, and Tutela tribes in New Jersey, New York, Connecticut, and Pennsylvania. Brainerd is known for his journal, spiritual diary, and autobiography edited by his mentor, Jonathan Edwards.* Born in Connecticut, he was educated at Yale College but was expelled in 1739. After ordination (1744), he worked for the Scottish Society for Promoting Christian Knowledge for which he kept his missionary journals. He died of tuberculosis in Southampton, Massachusetts, at Edwards's home.

J. Edwards, *Life and Diary of David Brainerd* (1765).

JAMES L. BREED

Brief Statement of Faith

"A Brief Statement of Faith: Presbyterian Church (U.S.A.)" is the eleventh and most recent (1991) confession in the *Book of Confessions* of that denomination. It developed from the reunion of the PCUS and the UPCUSA (1983). The Articles of Agreement stipulated that former confessional standards of the denomination should be combined and augmented by a fresh statement of the new church's convictions.

The Brief Statement stands firmly within the Reformed heritage. One of the tradition's characteristics is its commitment to the importance of confessing its faith anew upon occasions of moment. The reunion of churches was a gift of God* testifying to the partial recovery of the oneness of the church* for which Christ prayed. When Reformed churches unite or reunite they seek a common voice to confess their common faith.* The drive rises from the Reformed claim that the church is under obligation to state its faith in contemporary terms as well as hold firmly to the historic affirmation of the ecumenical creeds.* But it also derives from the present need to assure the uniting churches that their coming together has a theological integrity at its core. Union between churches cannot be reduced in meaning to a merger based solely on the values of efficiency and cost effectiveness. A "new" church in the Reformed tradition articulates its foundational beliefs as and when it adopts a new statement of faith.

The Brief Statement is Reformed in confessing the one faith of the one church. Thus, the Trinitarian character of faith is affirmed explicitly: "We trust in the one triune God." The Trinity* also provides the structure of the Statement with the apostolic benediction ordering its flow. The Statement follows the Confession of 1967* and the Barmen* Declaration in beginning with the Second Person of the Trinity and subsequently taking up the First Person and Third Person, before concluding with the traditional formula of the Gloria Patri.

A Reformed confession addresses the contemporary situation. The Brief Statement does so in its contemporary idiom. Gender-inclusive language about humans is incorporated. Gender-inclusive language about God is addressed. The introduction of male and female images of God enriches the confessional heritage. A line that affirms that women and men are called to all the ministries of the church locates the ordination of women in the confessional standards of the church for the first time.

The Brief Statement's contemporaneity is noted in its urgent recognition of the possibility of humans' inflicting, through nuclear holocaust or ecological assault, death to life as we know it on this planet. The positive inference from one of its lines, "We threaten death to the planet entrusted to our care," is a transformed understanding of what is required for stewardship* of the planet.

The Brief Statement was written in a form to make sections readily usable in worship.* Its evocative, semi-narrative style makes it a useful educational tool, inviting discussion and development of more complete meanings. Only as the Brief Statement lives its way into the church's life through these and other methods will it play an identity-forming and -reforming role in the church and thus be truly a Reformed creed.

J. L. Stotts and J. D. Douglass, eds., *To Confess the Faith Today* (1990).

JACK L. STOTTS

Briggs, Charles Augustus (1841–1913)

Internationally renowned as a biblical scholar, Briggs was the subject of a heresy* trial testing the openness of the Presbyterian Church in the U.S.A. to higher criticism. After theological study at Union Seminary (N.Y.) and Berlin, Briggs served briefly in a pastorate and returned to Union as a professor (1874). He was elevated to a newly created chair of biblical theology (1890). In his inaugural address, "The Authority of Holy Scripture," Briggs vigorously championed biblical criticism, attacked the notion of biblical inerrancy, and thus unleashed a major controversy within the Presbyterian Church. The General Assembly* vetoed his election to the chair of biblical theology; to keep him in that position, the seminary severed its connection to the church. Briggs was tried for heresy and ultimately suspended from the Presbyterian ministry (1895). Some years later he took Episcopal orders. In addition to his other voluminous publications, Briggs edited the International Critical Commentary series and the International Theological Library. Resigning his chair (1904), Briggs devoted his last ten years to teaching symbolics and irenics at Union—a shift underscoring his desire to foster unity among all branches of Christianity.

M. S. Massa, *Charles Augustus Briggs and the Crisis of Historical Criticism* (1990).

JAMES H. MOORHEAD

Brown, John (1722–87)

Scottish divine born in Haddington. Brown came from humble Perthshire stock. Though largely self-taught, he acquired great learning, especially in ancient and modern languages. He became minister (1751) of the Secession congregation (Associate Synod, Burgher) at Haddington, where he served until his death. He was also the Synod's divinity professor (from 1768). Among his thirty-odd publications, his renowned *Self-Interpreting Bible* (1778)—an expansive study Bible—and *Dictionary of the Holy Bible* (1769) proved lasting.

Brown's progeny was numerous and distinguished, in the ministry, theology, sciences, and literature. They long remained self-consciously his "dynasty," and some traveled the Atlantic to honor his memory (1987).

R. Mackenzie, *John Brown of Haddington* (1918).

DAVID F. WRIGHT

Brown, William Adams (1865–1943)

American Presbyterian theologian, educator, ecumenist, and leading religious liberal; professor of systematic theology at Union Seminary (N.Y.; from 1898). Brown was educated at Yale and Union before studying in Berlin, where he was influenced directly by Adolf von Harnack and indirectly by Albrecht Ritschl. Following Harnack, Brown promulgated a form of Christomatic liberalism to reconcile traditional Reformed doctrines with the scientific modes of modern thought. An immanent God was revealed most fully through Jesus Christ but also through cultural progress. Following Ritschl, Brown stressed Christian ethics and the church's role in reforming the social order. His *Christian Theology in Outline* (1906) became a virtual textbook of American religious liberalism.

W. A. Brown, *A Teacher and His Times* (1940); S. McC. Cavert, in *The Church Through Half a Century*, ed. S. McC. Cavert and H. P. Van Dusen (1936), 5–38.

DENNIS N. VOSKUIL

Browne, Robert (c. 1550–c. 1633)

Separatist harbinger of congregationalism,* educated at Corpus Christi College, Cambridge. After leaving Cambridge,

Browne taught for a while; refused ordination on the ground that the hierarchy was incompetent to bestow it; renewed his friendship with Robert Harrison and began to itinerate in the Norwich district. He led a covenanted independent church (1581). Imprisoned as a schismatic, on his release he fled with his church to Middleburg, Holland. There he published *A Book which sheweth the life and manners of all true Christians* (1582) and *A Treatise of Reformation without tarying for anie* (1582). Following quarrels with his followers, Browne left for Scotland, where he found fault with the prevailing church order and was soon in custody. Back in England, he returned to the Church of England, became master of St. Olave's School, Southwark (1586), and was subsequently ordained rector of Achurch (1591). For assaulting an officer of the law during an argument over the nonpayment of rates, Browne was committed to Northampton Gaol, where he died.

To this impetuous, erratic character we owe some of the clearest statements concerning the nature of the church qua gathered, regenerate saints. Browne believed that "the Kingdom of God* was not to be begun by whole parishes, but rather of the worthiest, were they never so few" (Peel and Carlson, p. 404); and that "the Church planted or gathered, is a company or number of Christians or believers, which by a willing covenant made with their God, are under the government of God and Christ, and keep his laws in one holy communion" (Peel and Carlson, p. 253). Here is the basis of congregational catholicity, and, consistently with it, Browne advocated advisory synods comprising whole churches, not representatives therefrom.

DNB [theologically inept]; C. Burrage, *The True Story of Robert Browne* (1906); A. Peel and L. H. Carlson, *The Writings of . . . Robert Browne* (1953); F. J. Powicke, "Brownism," *Encyclopedia of Religion and Ethics*, ed. J. Hastings.

ALAN P. F. SELL

Bruce, Robert (c. 1554–1631)

Leading Scottish Presbyterian churchman identified with the opposition to the church policy of James VI. As tough-minded minister of the High Kirk (St. Giles), Edinburgh, and twice Moderator of the General Assembly,* Bruce was one of the main stumbling blocks to the royal episcopalian policy. He was condemned to internal exile (1605) until his death, but his national power base did not diminish. It was founded on his aristocratic connections and his popular open-air preaching in Scots. He embodied the link in the Presbyterian cause between the era of Andrew Melville* and the Covenanting era, and as representing the Calvinist tradition of church autonomy.

W. Cunningham, ed., *The Sermons of Robert Bruce* (1843; with "Life"); D. C. Macnicol, *Master Robert Bruce* (1907); T. F. Torrance, ed., *Mystery of the Lord's Supper*, by R. Bruce (1958).

W. IAN A. HAZLETT

Brunner, H. Emil (1889–1966)

As pastor of the Swiss Reformed Church and professor at the University of Zurich, Brunner was one of the most influential twentieth-century Reformed theologians. His books often served as basic texts in Presbyterian and Reformed seminaries, so his views of the centrality of Christ, the authority of Scripture,* and divine truth as an "I/Thou encounter" became normative for several generations of pastors and teachers.

Brunner's name is often linked to Barth's* and his work seen as under the shadow of Barth's massive *Church Dogmatics.* Brunner said he himself was one of the first to recognize the importance of Barth's commentary on Romans, and he soon became an articulate exponent of "the theology of crisis." Like Barth, Brunner found early inspiration in Søren Kierkegaard's (1813–55) warning against any cultural absorption of Christian faith. Thus he joined the theologians of crisis in attacking nineteenth-century liberalism's tendency to view human nature optimistically, identify historical progress with the will and action of God, and interpret Christ as merely a heroic representative of modern humanity.

Brunner and Barth were identified with the so-called neo-orthodox* (or neo-Reformation) movement because it brought to bear on modern theology fundamental insights of sixteenth-century Protestantism. Certainly Brunner's insistence on the primacy of biblical revelation,* his allegiance to Nicene and Chalcedonian Christology,* and strong emphasis on the sovereignty of God*—who is always the initiator of every divine-human encounter—place his thought squarely in the Calvinist* tradition.

Barth and Brunner broke over the issue of the exclusivity of revelation (1934). For Barth, faith encounters revelation only in the written Word of Scripture as it testifies to the living Word, Jesus Christ. In an essay, "Nature and Grace," Brunner insisted that the will of God could also be perceived in the life of the church* and in human history generally. For Barth, human beings possess no natural capacity for receiving revelation. God must create the conditions for the hearing of God's Word. Brunner held that there exists even in fallen humanity a "point of contact" seen in the human ability to hear and respond to God's revelation. To this, Barth responded with *Nein!* (published with Brunner's essay as *Nature and Grace* [1946]).

Here, Barth's position may be judged closer to that of Calvin,* who in his *Institutes* introduces the possibility of general revelation only to deny its actuality. On the other hand, Brunner's openness to some natural knowledge of God is perhaps more consistent with later developments in Reformed theology—as, for example, in Scottish realism,* the nineteenth-century Princeton Theology,* and Abraham Kuyper's* doctrine of "common grace."

Brunner's extensive treatment of the Christian life also reflects a characteristic emphasis of Reformed theology, as does his passion for the ecumenical movement. He was uniquely an international theologian, holding distinguished lectureships in England, the United States, and Japan. His three-volume *Dogmatics* (1946–60) and a score of other books constitute a legacy of clear, reasonable, and open-minded theology in the Reformed tradition.

E. Brunner, *The Mediator* (1927; ET 1934); *The Divine Imperative* (1932; ET 1937); *Man in Revolt* (1937; ET 1939); *The Divine-Human Encounter* (1938; ET 1943); *The Christian Doctrine of God* (1946; ET 1950); *The Christian Doctrine of Creation and Redemption* (1950; ET 1952); and *The Christian Doctrine of the Church, Faith and the Consummation* (1960; ET 1962); C. W. Kegley, ed., *The Theology of Emil Brunner* (1962).

ALEXANDER J. MCKELWAY

Bryan, William Jennings (1860–1925)

Attorney, three-time candidate for the U.S. presidency, populist, secretary of state under Woodrow Wilson,* and elder in the Presbyterian Church in the U.S.A., Bryan was the best-known Presbyterian of his day. He worked diligently for peace through international arbitration, resigning his cabinet position over Wilson's response to the sinking of the steamship *Lusitania.*

Bryan is remembered as a leader of fundamentalist* Presbyterians committed to biblical inerrancy and opposed to the theory of evolution. He believed that evolution made humans just one more animal and removed the basis for moral and social betterment. He often propounded the adage: "It is better to know the Rock of Ages than the age of rocks."

With Clarence Darrow, Bryan was the center of controversy at the Scopes* "monkey trial" (1925) in Dayton, Tennessee. John Scopes tested the Tennessee law prohibiting the teaching of evolution in public schools. Darrow was defense attorney. He called Bryan, who was assisting with the prosecution, to the stand and argued faith and science vigorously. Bryan died soon after the trial, and fundamentalism lost its most famous and charismatic (if not always diplomatic) leader.

W. J. Bryan, *In His Image* (1922); L. Levine, *Defender of the Faith* (1965); L. G. Tait, "Evolution: Wishart, Wooster, and William Jennings Bryan," *JPH* 62 (Winter 1984): 306–21.

RICK NUTT

Bucer (Butzer), Martin (1491–1551)

Strassburg reformer and a creative influence on the shaping of the Reformed tradition. Bucer's roots lay in Sélestat in Alsace. He became a Dominican but warmed to Erasmus* and was won to reform by Martin Luther* at Heidelberg (1518). He left the order and soon married. He came to Strassburg (1523), excommunicated and penniless, together with Wolfgang Capito* and others, but quickly assumed leadership of the city's Protestant Reformation.

Bucer became eminent as a theological and ecclesiastical mediator. He labored tirelessly to overcome the Lutheran-Swiss divide on the Lord's Supper,* achieving some success in the Wittenberg Concord of 1536. The Tetrapolitan Confession* (1530) reflected the mediating position of the South German reform movement led by Strassburg. The city's reputation for toleration attracted numerous exponents of reforming radicalism, whose disruptive presence provoked (1533–34) a tightening of the Reformed church's doctrine and polity. But Bucer's stress on discipline (in part a positive response to the radicals) was never allowed full scope by the city council. He helped in the ordering of reform elsewhere (e.g., in Hesse) and was widely active as a Protestant "ecumenical" statesman. With Philipp Melanchthon he led the Protestant-Catholic colloquies in Germany (1539–41), attaining a remarkable agreement on justification at Regensburg.

John Calvin* shared in this ecumenism during his three highly formative years in Strassburg (1538–41). He learned much from Bucer (whose scholarly biblical commentaries he greatly prized) on subjects such as predestination and the Eucharist but most especially in the areas of worship* (Strassburg is the ultimate source of the Reformed tradition's *Book of Common Order**), the ministry (the four offices, and particularly the eldership*), discipline and the importance of church order in general, and education (Strassburg's Gymnasium foreshadowed the Geneva Academy). Thus it was beyond Strassburg, and chiefly through Geneva, that Bucer's pattern of a reformed church and vision of a Christian society found fullest implementation. Confirmation* was another of his contributions to reformed religion.

Opposition to the Augsburg Interim (1548) resulted in Bucer's exile from Strassburg and his move to England at Thomas Cranmer's invitation. He became Regius Professor of Divinity at Cambridge (1549), where he left his mark on Anglican Protestantism, especially in the Ordinal (1550) and the *BCP** (1552). He presented to Edward VI a blueprint of national reform entitled *The Kingdom of Christ* (1557).

Bucer's contributions to the Reformation were many and major. His versatility in seeking reconciliation sometimes made him seem unprincipled, but he had a particularly rich sense of communion and community in Christ.

H. Eells, *Martin Bucer* (1931); W. Pauck, *Melanchthon and Bucer* (1969); W. P. Stephens, *The Holy Spirit in the Theology of Martin Bucer* (1970); D. F. Wright, *Common Places of Martin Bucer* (1972).

DAVID F. WRIGHT

Buchanan, George (1506–1582)

Eminent Scottish Reformed scholar. Buchanan's studies at St. Andrews, Paris, and elsewhere on the Continent (where his Protestant sympathies took him to flight and the Portuguese inquisition imprisoned him for a year) made him perhaps the most outstanding British humanist of his day (he even spoke Gaelic and discovered the common origin of the Celtic languages). Though tutor to both Mary Queen of Scots and James VI/I, Buchanan powerfully opposed the divine right of monarchs—as did Huguenot* writers and later Samuel Rutherford*—in his *De jure regni apud Scotos* (1579). He wrote poems, plays, and a perceptive history of Scotland. He was principal of St. Leonard's College, St. Andrews, and Moderator of the General Assembly* (1567).

P. H. Brown, *George Buchanan, Humanist and Reformer* (1890); and *George Buchanan and His Times* (1906); I. D. McFarlane, *George Buchanan* (1981).

DAVID F. WRIGHT

Bullinger, Heinrich (1504–1575)

Swiss-German Protestant reformer, chief pastor of the Zurich church from Zwingli's death (1531) until the end of his life. Bullinger wrote more than one hundred published titles on exegetical, theological, historical, and ecclesiastical subjects, some of which went through twenty-five to thirty editions in the major European languages by the end of the century. He preached approximately seventy-five hundred sermons, of which around six hundred were published widely, including his best-known work, the *Decades* (1549), a complete theology in the form of fifty sermons. Bullinger was the sole author of the Second Helvetic Confession* (1566), the most comprehensive and influential of early Reformed confessions, and, jointly with Calvin, of the Zurich Agreement (Consensus Tigurinus)* on the Lord's Supper (1549), which held together the French and German Reformed traditions at a critical point. Literary remains also include more than twelve thousand manuscript letters exchanged with church and political leaders all over Europe. These have caused Bullinger to be designated "the patriarch of Reformed Protestantism." He was particularly influential in eastern Europe, Germany, and the Low Countries, and highly significant for the state church form of the Elizabethan Settlement* in Britain.

Bullinger's thought combined humanist* learning, theological interests comprehending all major doctrines* of Christian theology, and learned (and sometimes fanciful) historical apologetics,* with a dominant pastoral concern that stamped everything he taught. His most distinctive and influential theological treatise is "The One and Eternal Testament or Covenant" (1534) which is at the root of later federal theology.* Corollary convictions were the antiquity and identity of the Christian faith from "our first Christian parents, Adam and Eve" (Gen. 3:15), to the present (*The Old Faith* [1537; ET 1541]). The Reformation was the recovery of the most ancient, catholic, and orthodox teachings from the Word of God*—of which the center is God's free grace* through Christ, received through the gift of faith* alone—held against all pagan, Judaic, and Roman novelties.

Bullinger's extensive polemic on the Lord's Supper* stemmed from a Christology* emphasizing the integrity of the body of the ascended* Christ, hence attacking both Roman Catholic transubstantiation and the Lutheran doctrine of ubiquity.* He never separated gospel from law* so completely as Luther,* and held to a "third use" of the law as a guide to the faithful. This implemented a strong ethical motif throughout his works. His doctrine of predestination* led to some discord with his younger friend Calvin* and is still disputed among interpreters. His published one hundred sermons on the book of Revelation were especially influential, since other classical Protestant Reformers did not comment extensively on this part of Scripture.* Diminution of Bullinger's influence, by which he has become the least known of the major reformers, is not as yet fully understood.

H. Bullinger, *Werke* (1972ff.); and *The Decades of Henry Bullinger* (1849); J. W. Baker, *Heinrich Bullinger and the Covenant* (1980).

EDWARD A. DOWEY, JR.

Bunyan, John (1628–1688)

Bunyan, of Elstow and Bedford, is important to the Reformed tradition, since his famous allegory is one of the chief avenues by which the Puritan* spirit entered the mainstream of the English Reformation.* With Calvinism* as foundational, Bunyan's prolific writings and fervent preaching embodied a vibrant awareness of Reformed theological thought and its implication for Christian living. The author of more than sixty books, he gained a unique place in history through *Grace Abounding* (1666), *The Pilgrim's Progress* (pt. 1, 1678; pt. 2, 1684), *The Life and Death of Mr. Badman* (1680), and *The Holy War* (1682). Other works were primarily expository, doctrinal, and practical.

Bunyan joined the Bedford Baptist Church (1654) and soon began preaching in nearby villages. Prosecuted under an Elizabethan act against nonconformity, he was imprisoned for three months, which was extended to twelve years, with a brief respite during the sixth year.

Bunyan emphasized the centrality of the Bible as the foundation for belief and conduct, stressing the grace* of God as the basis of predestination,* the focal point of eternal salvation.* Initiative in the salvation of sinners belonged to God, since God elected, within God's purpose and framework of grace, certain individuals to eternal life. Subscribing to the doctrine of "effectual calling," Bunyan believed it was impossible to resist the call because of the power with which the Holy Spirit* accompanied and illuminated the sinner's understanding. None of the elect could fall from grace.

Though Bunyan was primarily an adherent of the Calvinist tradition, his view of God as Savior, providing salvation from divine wrath rather than God as sovereign ruler, and his belief in the necessity of justification* through grace alone showed influence of Luther.* The separatist tradition shaped his view of the sacraments.* He strongly opposed teachings of the Quakers and the Arminians.*

The Miscellaneous Works of John Bunyan (1976–); 12 vols. projected.

E. BEATRICE BATSON

Bushnell, Horace (1802–1876)

A prominent Congregationalist pastor and theologian whose thought exerted a profound influence during his own day and also shaped the course of Protestant theology in the twentieth century. In his youth, Bushnell planned to enter the ministry, but a period of doubt led him to study law. He was converted during a Yale revival (1831) and studied theology under N. W. Taylor.* He was also heavily influenced by Samuel Taylor Coleridge.

At the heart of his theology was a theory of language that argued that all language was poetic rather than literal. Doctrine,* therefore, represented only approximate or symbolic efforts to describe the mystery of spiritual realities. Bushnell stood against the prevailing revivalism* and argued for the power of the family in shaping Christian faith. He opposed the idea of substitutionary atonement* in scholastic Calvinism,* insisting that the atonement was the ultimate expression of God's love, not divine justice.

Bushnell's understanding of language, the organicism of his theology, and his evolutionary and developmental conception of faith* made a powerful impact on the Christian education* movement, the social gospel, and Protestant modernism. His principal works were *Christian Nurture* (1847); *God in Christ* (1849); *Nature and the Supernatural* (1858); and *The Vicarious Sacrifice* (1866).

B. M. Cross, *Horace Bushnell* (1958); W. A. Johnson, *Nature and the Supernatural in the Theology of Horace Bushnell* (1963); H. S. Smith, ed., *Horace Bushnell* (1965).

JOHN M. MULDER

Caird, John (1820–1898)

Scottish Presbyterian philosopher-theologian, educated at the University of Glasgow and Divinity Hall. After parish work, Caird taught theology at Glasgow (1862) and became university principal (1873).

Caird emphasized union with the living Christ rather than the atoning death. In his philosophical writings, in idealistic fashion, he asserted the continuity of all things in the Absolute Mind. Influenced by Hegel, he nevertheless admitted that Hegelian philosophy could not elucidate the mystery of the Trinity.

Caird published sermons and addresses as well as philosophical works: *An Introduction to the Philosophy of Religion* (1880); *Spinoza* (1888); and *The Fundamental Ideas of Christianity* (1900; with memoir by E. Caird, his brother).

DNB; H. M. B. Reid, *The Divinity Professors in the University of Glasgow* (1923); Sell, *DD* (1987); C. L. Warr, *Principal Caird* (1926).

ALAN P. F. SELL

Calling *see* Vocation

Calvin, John (1509–1564)

One of the principal leaders of the Protestant Reformation. John Calvin is chiefly remembered as a biblical scholar and a systematic theologian.

Calvin was born on July 10, 1509, in the

cathedral town of Noyon, where his father was an ecclesiastical business manager. At about age twelve Calvin was sent to Paris to prepare for theological studies at the Collège de la Marche. Progressing rapidly, he entered the Collège de Montaigu, famous for its traditional scholasticism, but after he had taken his bachelor's degree, his father redirected him toward law. He studied law both at Orléans and Bourges, finishing his degree in 1531. During this time he made his acquaintance with the new learning of the Renaissance. Pierre de l'Etoile and the great Andrea Alciati introduced him to the historical-critical method of studying law, while Melchior Wolmar introduced him to Greek as well as to the ideas of the Reformation. At this period in his life, however, Calvin was interested above all in the historical and literary pursuits of the Christian humanists* such as Jacques Lefèvre d'Etaples and Erasmus.* After his father's death (1531), Calvin was able to devote himself to literary studies at the newly founded Collège de France in Paris. There, under royal patronage, the new learning held full sway.

Calvin's mastery of this new learning, especially classical Greek and Hebrew, brought him into an elite circle of intellectuals who were committed to church reform. In November 1533 one of Calvin's friends, Nicholas Cop, rector of the University of Paris, in the course of his rectorial address espoused the reforms not only of the Christian humanists but of Protestantism as well. Calvin may have been the ghostwriter of the speech. At any rate, both he and Cop were obliged to flee. Eventually finding refuge in Basel, Cop's hometown, Calvin published the first edition of the *Institutes of the Christian Religion** (1536). Only then did it become clear that Calvin had decided for the Protestant rather than the Christian humanist approach to reform. The *Institutes* came out strongly in favor of Luther's* doctrine of justification* by faith.* With this the foundation of Calvin's theology was set.

After a considerable amount of traveling, Calvin arrived in Geneva in August 1536. There William Farel* pressed him into helping reform the church in the former prince-bishopric. Only four years before, the city council had exiled the bishop, declared for the Reformation, and called several Protestant pastors to conduct services. The council was not willing, however, to give the newly reformed church of Geneva a constitution. All decisions were to be made by the city council. Both Calvin and Farel found the situation intolerable. Much friction developed, and finally the two reformers were exiled.

This time Calvin found refuge in Strassburg. There he became the understudy of the German reformer Martin Bucer.* In 1539 he published a new edition of the *Institutes* showing a considerable development in his thought. First, it shows his deepening appreciation for the classical doctrine of the Trinity* and the Christology* of the patristic age. To these doctrines Calvin remained firmly committed throughout his life. Second, it shows his growing interest in the biblical doctrine of predestination* as it had been developed particularly by Augustine.* While Calvin saw it as a fundamental teaching of Scripture,* it was not the cornerstone of his theology. For Calvin, the point is that human destiny is in the hands of God and that salvation* therefore is a divine gift rather than a human achievement. Calvin's teaching on this subject was not a matter of theological speculation but rather a matter of biblical interpretation. The place where the apostle Paul treats the subject most thoroughly is the letter to the Romans, and Calvin wrote a very thorough commentary on Romans during this same period. He obviously intended to explore the subject as deeply as possible. The commentary is an original study of the Greek text in the manner of the new learning, the first of many commentaries treating most of the books of the OT and the NT.

Back in Geneva, the city council was beginning to recognize the need for a legitimately organized church. In 1541 Calvin was asked to return; however, the reformer would accept only if the church was granted its own constitution. This constitution included a form of prayers, a form of government, and a catechism. Although all three were accepted, the church of Geneva still had a long struggle to establish its independence.

The worship* of the Reformed church of Geneva had a strong doxological bent consistent with Calvin's doctrine of the sovereignty of God. It featured the praying of the Psalter and, quite appropriate to Calvin's doctrine of providence,* a strong ministry of intercessory prayer.* The preaching* focused on the exposition of Scripture. Calvin preached at the cathedral twice each Sunday and daily every other week at morning prayers. Others filled in the schedule at the cathedral and the parish churches. Catechetical education for children was established, and Calvin lectured regularly to theological students. He had a covenantal understanding of worship, and therefore the sacraments* of Baptism* and the Lord's Supper,* as signs and seals of the covenant,* were essential to worship. Rather than as a sacrifice, Communion was celebrated as a covenant meal.

A major problem for Calvin was to gain for the church a polity* that would make it possible for the church to be independent of the state. Unlike the Lutherans in Germany and the Anglicans in Elizabethan England, Calvin could not accept a state-controlled church. It was the Word of God* which was to have authority* in the church, and in accordance with that Word the church was to be governed. This responsibility Calvin entrusted to the "consistory," or presbytery composed of ministers and elders.* Calvin saw the church as a republic rather than a monarchy.

A reform that was only theological and liturgical and did not express itself in the ethical life of the community would have seemed quite in vain to Calvin, hence his great concern to develop a disciplined Christian life. Before the Reformation, Geneva had a reputation for loose morals and sharp business practices. The Libertines wanted to keep it that way and resented Calvin's puritanism. Although the moral code of Protestant Geneva was not much different from those of other cities of the period, under Calvin's influence it was enforced on rich and poor alike. Geneva was not a theocracy but a republic, and Calvin's "moral" influence there was due primarily to his preaching. His supporters were increasingly elected to office because the electorate sensed that the moral discipline preached by Calvin would effect a better-ordered society than the Libertines were apt to produce. Calvin's intellectual and moral leadership gave the city an international reputation which attracted great numbers of learned and industrious refugees, producing something of a population explosion.

Calvin, sad to relate, was not very skillful at dealing with his opposition. The Libertines of Geneva were a constant frustration to him until they finally discredited themselves and were voted out of office. In 1544 Sebastian Castellio attacked Calvin's interpretation of the Song of Solomon. The clash of personalities made the controversy disproportionately bitter. The most serious challenge to Calvin's leadership was that of Michael Servetus,* who had made himself odious to Catholics and Protestants alike by his abusive attacks on the doctrine of the Trinity. The Libertines tried to use the affair to discredit Calvin, encouraging Servetus to bait him, but the execution of Servetus (1553) marked the defeat of the Libertines. While Calvin made and maintained many fast friendships throughout his life, his intense and excitable nature tended to overreact when he was goaded by his opponents.

Our portrait of Calvin has changed greatly in the last few years, but the painting in of some of his features is still difficult because he rarely spoke of his personal life. We know almost nothing, for instance, of either his conversion or his ordination. The reformer's lack of interest in himself was expressed in his simple dress, his modest life-style, and his complete devotion to his work. He died on May 27, 1564, and had even taken care that his place of burial remain unknown. Far from being driven by anxiety, he was a man inspired by faith, confident that in the mysterious workings of divine providence Christ's kingdom would be established.

W. J. Bouwsma, *John Calvin: A Sixteenth-Century Portrait* (1988); E. A. Dowey, Jr., *The Knowledge of God in Calvin's Theology* (1952; repr. 1964); A. Ganoczy, *The Young Calvin* (ET 1987); J. H. Leith, *John Calvin's Doctrine of the*

Christian Life (1989); K. McDonnell, *John Calvin, the Church and the Eucharist* (1967); A. E. McGrath, *A Life of John Calvin* (1990); D. McKim, ed., *Readings in Calvin's Theology* (1984); T. H. L. Parker, *John Calvin: A Biography* (1975); C. B. Partee, *Calvin and Classical Philosophy* (1977); F. Wendel, *Calvin et l'humanisme* (1976).

HUGHES OLIPHANT OLD

Calvinism

While Calvinism bears the name of John Calvin* as the system of theology he set forth during the Reformation, he was by no means the inventor of it, for its roots go back to the Bible and to the interpretations of such early church theologians as Chrysostom and Augustine* and to medieval thinkers such as Bernard of Clairvaux. This is clear in Calvin's theological works and commentaries. Yet Calvin added much to the earlier tradition by his studies and Christian thought. So Calvinism is a summing up of the earlier tradition by an able and committed theologian of the sixteenth century.

To understand Calvin's part in this development, it is necessary to know something of his background. He came from a Roman Catholic family and planned to become a lawyer. To this end he studied first at the University of Paris, then at Orléans and Bourges. During this latter period he was influenced by the Reformation movement. The result was his setting forth Protestant views. Trained in the current methods of humanism* in reading ancient authors, he applied the same methods to his reading of OT and NT Scriptures, seeking a literal interpretation of the biblical text.

The Bible. To Calvin, Scripture was God's Word. Therefore it was to be taken literally in its presentation of God's rule over history.* Calvin was not, however, a literalist in his understanding of what today would be called natural science, as for instance in his view of the biblical account of creation.* He viewed the Genesis statements as setting forth creation but in a way that even the "rude and ignorant" could understand. At the same time, he stressed that God* was the creator of everything, though God has not revealed the methods by which creation occurred. Thus, to Calvin, the Bible as the Word of God* is the final authority* for the Christian's view of the world and life in it.

How does one come to recognize the Bible as the Word of God and understand it? Calvin's answer was by the work of the Holy Spirit,* the Third Person of the Trinity,* who opens humanity's eyes so that many are able to recognize the Bible as divinely inspired. Further, one understands the message of the Scriptures by the enlightening action of the Spirit, who enables God's people not only to understand but also to apply what the Scriptures teach. This meant to Calvin that the Bible must be interpreted historically and literally, with no place for the common practice of medieval exegesis in allegorizing biblical passages.

The Bible's prime characteristic is as the self-revelation of God. God has been revealed in creation, nature, and history as God has providentially* watched over and directed the physical and human aspects of creation. But because of human sinfulness, this is not enough. Humans need direct and specific revelation* to enable them to know and understand their relationship to God. To this end, God has given specific and direct revelation in the Bible so that humanity has in Scripture an inspired record of God's dealings with creation.

To Calvin the Bible, however, was not just a record of history and how God had dealt with creation in the past. It is a revelation of God today, as it tells much concerning God's plans and purposes throughout history. It also provides humankind with a knowledge of God's redeeming work in Christ which took place two millennia ago as well as God's providential and redeeming work today. Therefore the Bible's message is not only to be read as history but to be applied faithfully to one's life now. At the same time, Calvin stressed the mystery of God's own being and purpose, constantly quoting Deut. 29:29 that one might not reduce biblical teaching to some form of a purely human, rational system, for God can be known only as God is revealed to human creatures.

God. The God of whom Calvin wrote and spoke is the God of the Bible. God is the only God, but at the same time God is the God who is a trinity of persons: Father, Son, and Holy Spirit who are the same in substance and equal in power and glory. Here Calvin followed biblical teaching as formulated and expressed in the early church confessions. But this doctrine* was absolutely basic to his whole system of thought, and as a result he was sometimes more consistent in his theological exposition than others who, while professing a Trinitarian theology, were subordinationist in their application of the doctrine.

Equally important in Calvin's thought was the belief that God is sovereign. God is eternal, without beginning or end; and God is also infinite, an attribute on which Calvin laid great stress. This in turn means that God is self-sufficient and does not depend upon either physical forces or human cooperation to accomplish the divine purposes. God works all things after the counsel of God's own will. This brought Calvin into conflict with some other Protestant leaders and has been one of the main points of disagreement between Calvinists and other Christians since the Reformation. Because God is sovereign, God is the source of all in the universe.

On this basis, Calvin saw God as the creator and sustainer of all things. Throughout his writings, and especially in his Genesis commentary, Calvin was very insistent that nothing has come into existence by chance or accident but only in the plan and purpose of God. Further, he rejected any deistic view that God created all and then left creation to run by itself. Rather, he is equally insistent that God is the sustainer of everything, so all physical laws are expressions of God's constant care and the result of God's sovereignty. This applies not only to the physical universe. God also rules over humanity, guiding and directing history in God's foreordained* fashion. In this, Calvin laid the foundation for a Christian interpretation of science* and history.

Humanity. Calvin saw humans as the peak of creation, since they are made in God's own image, an honor conferred on no other creature. To Calvin, the image of God in humanity was not physical but spiritual, intellectual, and volitional. Moreover, God made humans capable of free choice and decision, while placing them in the position of ruling over creation as God's deputies. The deputy status comes through a covenant* relationship in which humans are commissioned to rule over the creation while also required to serve God wholly in the world. Humans receive God's blessing as long as they obey God's commands.

Desiring to be independent of God, however, humans went their own ways and broke God's command. To the question, How could they do this if God is sovereign? Calvin admitted this was a mystery. But he insisted that human responsibility and God's sovereignty are always mysterious in their relationship. Yet both are set forth in Scripture. When humans broke their covenant relationship with God, they came under divine condemnation and rejection. The result is that they are now at enmity with God, going their own ways and doing as they please. For Adam's rebellion has become characteristic of the whole human race. Humans themselves are unwilling to repent* and return to their covenant relationship with God.

Though Satan through the serpent (Gen. 3) led humans astray, God's purpose for humanity still remains. God, by God's grace,* has from all eternity chosen a great multitude of the human race to be brought back into relationship with God. Yet atonement* had to be made for humanity's rebellion, and it was for this purpose that the Son, the Second Person of the Trinity, came into the world to bear its sins.* Whether Calvin would have accepted the later doctrine of "limited atonement" may be questioned, as he seems to have believed that Christ's atonement was sufficient for all but efficient only for the elect. He did stress, however, that individuals came to accept Christ's atonement in faith* only as the result of the effectual calling of the Holy Spirit. They were then regenerated* and placed their faith in Christ, to whom they gave their obedience as Lord and King. Thus salvation* was entirely by the grace of God. Without divine grace, hell* is the only human destiny.

In stressing that the sinner was justified

by faith alone, Calvin agreed fully with Luther* and other reformers. He held firmly that it was only as one placed one's faith in Christ, trusting in Christ as the one who paid the penalty for sin and whose righteousness was imputed to the believer, that the individual would find forgiveness* and acceptance by God. Throughout Calvin's writings, one finds constant rejection of the Roman Catholic doctrine of merits through good works. In this, Calvin was very explicit.

Calvin did not, however, believe that the Christian was without moral standards and not required to perform good works. Rather, the Christian is to manifest the grace of God in all of life. As the Christian had entered into a covenant relationship with God, one was to exhibit this in all aspects of human activity. This meant not only witnessing faithfully to God's grace but manifesting the Christian faith and life in all actions and seeking to persuade others to do the same. If this were done, society as a whole would be influenced to seek to do God's will and this would have an influence on the form of government, laws, economy, and every other element of daily life.

While the individual would seek to bring about such a revolution in human society, the body that was especially appointed to this office was the church.* Composed of all who profess faith in Christ as Lord and Savior, along with their children, who were to be received into the visible church by the sign of Baptism,* the church, governed by elected elders,* was to proclaim the gospel to all people across the world. By this means it fulfills Christ's commission to the apostles before his ascension.* On this, Calvin was very insistent and did much to forward missionary work in his own day. In this way he presented a very practical agenda for Christians to follow in this life.

Calvin's influence has continued long after his death, as many accepted his teachings as being truly biblical. He gained a large following in many countries in Europe, and from there his teachings spread to America, Africa, and Asia. His theology influenced not only individuals but whole societies as well, and it continues to do so. Notable individuals in many fields of human endeavor—government, science, education, and the arts—testify to the influence of Calvin's thought, and through their efforts Calvinism has had a significant impact on world history.

J. T. McNeill, *The History and Character of Calvinism* (1954); M. Prestwich, ed., *International Calvinism, 1541–1715* (1985).

W. STANFORD REID

Calvinism in America

Originating in sixteenth-century German- and French-speaking Switzerland, Calvinism gradually spread to other areas of both eastern and western Europe where strongholds developed in the Netherlands and the British Isles. The Puritans in Holland and England, and the Scotch-Irish, were especially successful in transplanting Calvinism to America. The Puritan and Scotch-Irish forms of Calvinism were organized into Congregational,* Presbyterian,* and Baptist churches. The Dutch Reformed, German Reformed, and other immigrant groups also established American churches during the eighteenth century.

Calvinism is both a cultural system and a theology. As a theology, American Calvinism owes much to its European heritage. This heritage is rooted in the Augustinian tradition* and in the Reformation-era biblical and theological works of John Calvin,* especially his *Institutes of the Christian Religion* (1559). The Reformation-era movement was also shaped by the work of others, including Theodore Beza* of Geneva, Huldrych Zwingli* and Heinrich Bullinger* of Zurich, John Oecolampadius* of Basel, and John Knox* of Scotland. The theology of these reformers was further developed and summarized in important confessions and catechisms, particularly the Scots Confession* (1560), the HC* (1563), the Second Helvetic Confession* (1566), and the WCF* (1647).

During the post-Reformation period, a number of continental European and English theologians also produced important summaries of Calvinistic thought which reflect changing cultural, social, political, and scientific views. These presentations of

Calvinism include works by the Puritan theologians William Perkins,* William Ames,* and John Owen;* by the great Swiss scholastic Francis Turretin* (1679–85); by Dutch Reformed thinkers Abraham Kuyper* and Herman Bavinck;* and by Swiss theologians Karl Barth* (1932–67) and Emil Brunner* (1946–60). Recently, Jürgen Moltmann,* Helmut Gollwitzer,* T. F. Torrance,* and other Reformed thinkers have opened new perspectives. While many of the central concepts of Calvinism, such as the power and activity of God* as creator and sustainer of the world, as redeemer, and as Lord of history,* can be found in the works of Calvin, many post-Calvinian ideas and diverse cultural expressions have also shaped the Reformed tradition.

As a cultural system, American Calvinism emphasizes learning and stresses the importance of higher education. Approximately seventy-five American colleges were founded by Presbyterian, Congregational, and German and Dutch Reformed churches prior to the Civil War. A disproportionately high number of college and university faculty, trustees, and presidents have also been affiliated with the Reformed tradition. Reformed churches also emphasize the centrality of the OT and the NT as the authority for Christian living. The biblical witness is viewed as the basis for cultural transformation sought through social, political, and evangelical means. The Calvinistic worldview was certainly a primary influence in the life of John Witherspoon* and other patriots who participated in the American Revolution and influenced the development of democratic institutions, for example.

Traditionally, Calvinism has also stressed simplicity and hard work. While there has been much debate on the relationship between Calvinism, capitalism,* and the Protestant work ethic,* many scholars now see the contributing aspects of Reformed theology as one important factor among several that led to the development of capitalism. In its various organizational forms, Calvinism relies on a shared leadership of ministers and laity working together in partnership. Often theologically factious and divisive, the Presbyterian and Reformed denominations are also characterized by their emphasis on corporateness and catholicity. This emphasis fostered cooperative educational and mission programs, a commitment to church union, especially among Reformed churches, and development of important ecumenical organizations.

During colonial times, Calvinistic ideas flowered in the works of Puritans* who settled New England and became Congregationalists. The classic exposition of early American Puritanism is found in the lectures of Samuel Willard (1640–1707) on the Westminster Shorter Catechism. Published posthumously (1726) as *A Compleat Body of Divinity*, the lectures fill over one thousand double-columned pages. This great summa of New England theology centers around the covenant* idea (God's chosen people) which permeated all aspects of early New England life, including church,* society, politics,* and the Puritan view of history. The most important historical work written from a New England Calvinist perspective is certainly Cotton Mather's* *Magnalia Christi Americana* (1702). By recording the "wondrous works" of God in the churches of New England, Mather glorified the past and tried to halt the decline of his own day. While flawed in its presentation of history, the *Magnalia* contains aspects of Puritan thought and passages of literary excellence that make it a great work. Other important works were by Jonathan Edwards,* a seminal theologian and philosopher, including *Religious Affections* (1746), *Freedom of the Will* (1754), and *Original Sin* (1758). In these and other writings, Edwards displays philosophical and ethical insight equaled by few, if any, American theologians.

The decline of New England Puritanism was hastened by the growth of Baptist, Quaker, and other churches alongside and within the "holy commonwealth." It soon became apparent that the religious uniformity sought by the founders was not possible. At the same time, many second- and third-generation Puritans refused church membership. This erosion from within led to adoption of the Half-Way Covenant.* Religious pluralism, the Half-Way Covenant, the revivalism* of the Great Awakening,* and other troubles led to a fragmentation of the theological and social aims of the commonwealth. As a result, the "New Divinity" theologians who followed Edwards found themselves in a more theologically diverse landscape. This landscape included traditional Scotch-Irish Calvinism which rejected revivalism and pressed for a return to a pre-Awakening theology; the New Haven Theology* of N. W. Taylor* which made some concessions to revivalism but maintained Calvinistic orthodoxy; and the liberal Calvinism of William Ellery Channing (1780–1842) and others who rejected Trinitarianism, original sin,* and the atonement,* and identified with the Unitarian movement.

Amidst this growing diversity, Horace Bushnell* emerged as a mediating figure. He tried to find a middle way between Old Calvinism and Unitarianism* and between science and revivalism. In *God in Christ* (1849) and other works, Bushnell concentrated on the nature of language which he viewed as poetry and symbol rather than science. He favored the romanticism of Friedrich Schleiermacher* and was extremely critical of the theological rationalism and disciplinary system of his New England forebears. In *Christian Nurture* (1847) he presented a case for the gradual, catechetical* process through which faith* is nurtured and argued against individualism, revivalism, and the need for a conversion* experience. He also broke with more orthodox views in *The Vicarious Sacrifice* (1866) by arguing that Christ's atonement was an example of God's love rather than a reconciling act.

Bushnell, like other Presbyterian and Reformed theologians during the nineteenth century, wrestled with advances in many fields of knowledge. Scientific discoveries, including evidence of human evolution and the antiquity of the earth and solar system, were startling. New disciplines such as Freudian psychology, and new methods of biblical study using textual, literary, and historical methods, presented many challenges. Also, the growing interaction of Christianity with other world religions* posed new questions. The industrial revolution, urbanization, development of communist ideology, and the issue of slavery* also presented additional questions for theology.

Many in the Reformed community viewed these discoveries and developments with great alarm, seeing them as challenges to both traditional Calvinism and Christianity itself. In response, many embraced the conservative Princeton Theology* which defended the views of the Old Calvinism.

The Princeton Theology held sway at Princeton Theological Seminary from its founding in 1812 through the fundamentalist/modernist controversy* of the 1920s. It was probably the most dominant form of American Calvinism during this period. Archibald Alexander,* Charles Hodge,* and B. B. Warfield* were its principal proponents, though Archibald Alexander Hodge* and J. Gresham Machen* popularized many of its doctrines. Through C. Hodge's detailed *Systematic Theology* (3 vols.; 1872–73) and Warfield's numerous articles, especially on "Inspiration" (1881), the Princeton Theology became known for its high view of biblical authority and inspiration and defense of Old School Calvinism. While many considered the Princeton Theology to be "pure Calvinism," in reality its theological method was influenced by the work of Turretin, by the Scottish common sense* philosophy, and by many of the challenges cited above.

The Princeton theologians also held a static view of orthodoxy which failed to recognize the importance of historical development. In spite of shortcomings, the Princeton Theology was *the* theology of many Presbyterian and Reformed churches during the nineteenth and early part of the twentieth century.

The South was influenced by the Princeton Theology and by Turretin, whose theological textbook, *Institutio theologiae elencticae*, was used by Presbyterian seminaries in Virginia and South Carolina. Old School views were also transmitted by the two dominant theologians of the nineteenth-century South, James Henley Thornwell* and Robert Lewis Dabney.* Dabney's *Systematic and Polemic Theology* (1871) and Thornwell's *Collected Writings* (4 vols.; 1871–73) were of primary importance in shaping southern Calvinism through the 1930s. In his understanding of Old School Calvinism, however, Thornwell differed from the Princeton theologians in ecclesiology and doctrine of "the spirituality of the church." The latter doctrine holds that the church is a purely spiritual entity which should not involve itself in social or political issues. While this doctrine proved to be very influential in theological circles, in practice many southern Presbyterians took conservative positions on the controversial issues of the day, including slavery, woman suffrage, temperance, and Sabbath* observance.

In the German Reformed tradition, American scholars such as John Williamson Nevin* and Philip Schaff* broke new ground by developing the Mercersburg Theology.* In two major works, *The Anxious Bench* (1843) and *The Mystical Presence* (1846), Nevin criticized revivalism, stressed the corporateness of Christian belief, and pointed to the centrality of the sacraments.* In these and other works, the Mercersburg Theology was presented as an alternative to, and critique of, both revivalism and the Princeton Theology, which were viewed as extremes. As a theological system, the Mercersburg Theology was also important because of its attempt to reconcile German idealism with the American Reformed tradition.

More progressive in their theology were "evangelical liberals," such as William Adams Brown* and the Social Gospelers.* Brown held decidedly Christocentric views. In his textbook *Christian Theology in Outline* (1906), Brown recognized the centrality of Christ and the value of the Reformed tradition but also discarded old worldviews and "scholastic phraseology" in his attempt to present a modern Calvinism in dialogue with modern science and philosophy. Brown wanted to be both Christian and modern. Social Gospelers, led by Walter Rauschenbusch (1861–1918), and Congregational ministers Washington Gladden* and Josiah Strong (1847–1916), pressed for a number of social reforms, including labor and economic reform, in a movement that lasted from the 1890s to the 1920s. This movement was allied with the theological liberalism of William N. Clarke (1840–1912) and others who stressed education, morality, and social change.

The Niebuhr brothers, Reinhold* and H. Richard,* were important figures in the American neo-orthodox* movement of the 1930s and 1940s. In *Moral Man and Immoral Society* (1932) Reinhold Niebuhr criticized both liberal theology and the social gospel for their overly optimistic view of humanity and failure to take sin seriously. In *The Nature and Destiny of Man* (2 vols.; 1941–43) he developed a theology of sin and grace in which the struggle for social reform is paramount. H. Richard wrote a number of important works. His *The Kingdom of God in America* (1937) traced the kingdom theme in American life, and *Christ and Culture* (1951), a classic work of Christian ethics, argued for the transformation of culture.

S. E. Ahlstrom, ed., *Theology in America* (1967); G. G. Atkins and F. L. Fagley, *History of American Congregationalism* (1942); J. D. Bratt, *Dutch Calvinism in Modern America* (1984); F. J. Hood, *Reformed America: The Middle and Southern States, 1783–1837* (1980); B. Kuklick, *Churchmen and Philosophers from Jonathan Edwards to John Dewey* (1985); J. H. Leith, *An Introduction to the Reformed Tradition* (rev. ed. 1981); L. A. Loetscher, *The Broadening Church* (1954); J. T. McNeill, *The History and Character of Calvinism* (1954); A. C. Piepkorn, *Profiles in Belief*, vol. 2, pt. 3, "Reformed and Presbyterian Churches" (1978); E. T. Thompson, *Presbyterians in the South*, 3 vols. (1963–73); R. E. Thompson, *A History of the Presbyterian Churches in the United States* (1895); L. J. Trinterud, *The Forming of an American Tradition* (1949); D. F. Wells, ed., *Reformed Theology in America* (1985).

ROBERT BENEDETTO

Cambridge Platform/Synod

New England Puritans* in the mid-seventeenth century though generally holding to Reformed doctrine were not unanimous in their views on church government. In the Massachusetts Bay Colony many Congregationalist* ministers and laity strongly desired to distinguish their concept of the autonomous local church from the polity of Presbyterianism,* Separatism, and Brownism. The outbreak of the English Civil War* and the significant influence of a Presbyterian faction in the English Parliament led some Congregationalists to call for a "Presbyterian" church order (1645). Fearing a loss of distinctiveness, the General Court of Massachusetts Bay Colony called a synod composed of elders (ministers) and messengers (laity). They came from twenty-nine different churches to Cambridge, Massachusetts, and became the Cambridge Synod (1646).

The Synod's Congregationalist church government statement became known as the Cambridge Platform. This highly influential document made it clear that councils and synods have a valuable advisory role but no legal authority in local church government. On the other hand, the Platform affirmed a state-church union where civil authorities could and should discipline heresy* for the sake of unity.

The elders and messengers carefully defined and delineated basic concepts such as "the catholic church," "the visible church," and the nature of the church covenant. They set guidelines for election of church officers, ordination of ruling elders* and pastors, and the admission, discipline, and excommunication of church members. In other doctrinal matters, the Synod adopted the WCF* as its standard.

H. S. Smith et al., *American Christianity: An Historical Interpretation with Representative Documents* (1960), 1:128–40; W. Walker, *Creeds and Platforms of Congregationalism* (1893; repr. 1960).

NATHAN P. FELDMETH

Cameron, John (1579–1625)

Scottish theologian influential in the French Reformed Church. Though born and educated in Glasgow, Cameron spent most of his adult life in France, as student, teacher, and Reformed minister in Bordeaux (1608–17) and professor of divinity at Saumur (1618–20) and Montauban (1624–25). Controversy dogged him, not only in Scotland and France for his lofty views of royal power but, more important, for his espousal, though Calvinist, of the (hypothetical) universality of the atonement,* more characteristic of Arminians.* He thereby influenced Moïse Amyraut* and his school. For his learning and linguistic skills, Cameron was known as a "walking library."

G. B. Maury, "John Cameron," *Scottish Historical Review* 7 (1910): 325–45; A. H. Swinne, *John Cameron, Philosoph und Theologe* (1968).

DAVID F. WRIGHT

Cameron, Richard (c. 1648–1680)

The Lion of the Scottish National Covenant.* Charles II, restored to the throne (1660), repudiated the Presbyterian National Covenant (1638) and enforced episcopacy. The strongest opponents were called the Covenanters,* frequently attacked and tortured during hillside worship services.

Cameron was converted at a hillside conventicle. He was theologically educated in Holland and returned to preach. He believed in only one expression of faith in a nation, insisting this be the faith of the most extreme Covenanters. He was killed in a skirmish.

Cameron's followers founded the Reformed Presbyterian Church. Since their constitutional claim was not recognized, they withdrew into sectarian isolation, refusing to participate in the political process. Yet their presence helped necessitate a form of religious and civil toleration. Their dogged adherence to Presbyterianism helped determine that, from the Revolution Settlement (1688–89), the Church of Scotland would be Presbyterian.

J. Buckroyd, *Church and State in Scotland 1660–1681* (1980); G. Donaldson, *Scotland, James V to James VI* (1971); J. D. Douglas, *Light in the North: The Story of the Scottish Covenanters* (1964); A. Smellie, *Men of the Covenant* (1909).

IAN S. RENNIE

Cameronians

The Reformed Presbyterian Church (Cameronians), a church with origins in the persecution of the Covenanters* in

Scotland, who were sometimes called Cameronians after Richard Cameron,* a martyred field preacher (1680). They believed the covenants (National Covenant,* 1638; Solemn League and Covenant,* 1643) were still binding on Scotland and refused to acknowledge an uncovenanted king as head of the state or any but "King Jesus" as head of the church. They refused to enter the (Presbyterian) Church of Scotland after the Revolution (1688). Most joined the Free Church (1876), but continuing Reformed Presbyterian churches still exist in Scotland, Ireland, and the United States.

W. J. Couper, *The Reformed Presbyterian Church in Scotland: Its Congregations, Ministers and Students* (1925); M. Hutchison, *The Reformed Presbyterian Church in Scotland* (1893).

DAVID C. LACHMAN

Camisard Wars

A revolt of Protestant zealots in southern France against repression following the revocation of the Edict of Nantes* (1685). Led by millennial prophets roused to ecstasy, young Protestants assassinated a persecuting priest (July 24, 1702). Claims to direct revelation, violence, and guerrilla warfare followed in rural Dauphiné, Vivarais, and the Cévennes. Foreign Protestants sympathized. The Camisards, perhaps named after their black peasant shirts, organized and fought Louis XIV's soldiers fiercely but were effectively contained by 1704. Sporadic violence continued. French leaders and a Reformed Church synod (1715) repudiated them. They remained historically inspirational to many.

JEANNINE E. OLSON

Campbell, John McLeod (1800–1872)

Minister of the established Church of Scotland. After education at Glasgow and Edinburgh, Campbell became minister of the Rhu parish where he was intent on "awakening" his people to an "enjoyment" of God. Soon, however, he was opposed by colleagues, who with a group of disgruntled parishioners charged him with heresy.* Following appeals to the Synod of Glasgow and Ayr and the General Assembly* (1831), Campbell was deposed from the established church because his views of "universal atonement" and "assurance as being of the essence of faith" were understood as at variance with the Westminster Standards.* Refusing to establish a rival schismatic church, he spent the remainder of his ministry (until 1859) as a minister in Glasgow's inner city.

Campbell expanded the theological ideas that led to his deposition in *The Nature of the Atonement* (1856) which James Denney* regarded as the only theological classic that Scotland has produced. J. B. Torrance places it alongside Anselm's *Cur Deus Homo?* and Athanasius's *De incarnatione.* Campbell's writings also include *Christ the Bread of Life* (1851; and ed. 1869) and *Thoughts on Revelation* (1862). His work is best understood as a recovery of the Reformed conception of *sola gratia* and *sola fide*, over against all attempts to introduce into Christian faith any doctrine that would stand between persons and their free and utter dependence upon the triune God who is fully revealed in Christ. Campbell, thus, rejected federal* Calvinism, with its doctrine of "limited atonement" and quest for "assurance of election." He sought to return to Luther's* *theologia crucis* and Calvin's* view that in Christ "all parts of our salvation are complete."

Campbell's controversial conception of "vicarious penitence" is a careful restatement of earlier Reformed theology's doctrine of Christ's high priesthood. For Campbell, as for the early Fathers, Luther and Calvin, Christ is the atonement* between God* and humanity.* In contrast to recent attempts to separate representation and substitution in soteriology, Campbell holds both together in an elegant ontological framework.

Campbell's reinterpretation of the Reformed doctrine of atonement, understanding its judicial aspects in the light of the filial, did not receive wide approval in his native church. But eventually his understanding became influential in Britain and North America. Campbell's attempt to perceive atonement "in light of the incarnation" anticipated by a century advances in Trinitarian theology by Karl

Barth,* Jürgen Moltmann,* Karl Rahner, T. F. Torrance,* and others.

E. G. Bewkes, *Legacy of a Christian Mind: John M'Leod Campbell, Eminent Contributor to Theological Thought* (1937); J. B. Torrance, "The Contribution of McLeod Campbell to Scottish Theology," *SJT* 26 (1973): 303–11; G. M. Tuttle, *So Rich a Soil: John McLeod Campbell on Christian Atonement* (1986).

W. MICHAEL JINKINS

Candlish, Robert Smith (1806–1875)

Scottish preacher and churchman, New College* principal (1862), and leading figure in the Free Church of Scotland after the death of Thomas Chalmers.* Candlish was a famous preacher, ecclesiastical statesman, and biblical commentator. His theology was generally conservative and concerned to engage contemporary issues, as in his *Reason and Revelation* (1859).

R. S. Candlish, *The Fatherhood of God* (1865); *The Atonement* (1845); and *Contributions Towards the Exposition of Genesis*, 3 vols. (1842); J. L. Watson, *Life of Robert Smith Candlish* (1882); W. Wilson, *Memorials of Robert Smith Candlish* (1880).

N. R. NEEDHAM

Canon of Scripture

With reference to the Bible, "canon" means the list or collection of books that were received as divinely inspired and therefore serve as the rule or standard for belief and practice. Though recognition of the canon of the OT and the NT was of momentous consequences, history is silent on exactly how, when, and by whom such recognition was brought about. Nevertheless, it is generally agreed that the process involved the following stages of development.

Canon of the OT. Authoritative legal and prophetic literature grew up by degrees and was carefully preserved. Eventually the books of the Hebrew Bible came to be regarded as twenty-four in number, arranged in three divisions. The first, primary division is the *Torah* (Law), comprising the five "books of Moses." The second division is the *Nebiim* (Prophets), further subdivided into Former Prophets (Joshua, Judges, Samuel, and Kings) and Latter Prophets (Isaiah, Jeremiah, Ezekiel, and the Book of the Twelve). The third division is the *Kethubim* (Writings) and comprises Psalms, Proverbs, Job, Song of Solomon, Ruth, Lamentations, Ecclesiastes, Esther, Daniel, Ezra-Nehemiah (reckoned as one book), and Chronicles. These twenty-four books are identical with the thirty-nine of the Protestant OT; the difference in reckoning arises from counting the twelve ("minor") prophets separately and dividing Samuel, Kings, Chronicles, and Ezra-Nehemiah into two each.

The Septuagint, the Greek translation of the Hebrew Scriptures made in the centuries just preceding the Christian era, includes several additional books, and parts of books, not present in the Hebrew Bible. These are Tobit, Judith, Wisdom of Solomon, Ecclesiasticus (the book of Jeshua ben Sira), Baruch (including as ch. 6 the Letter of Jeremiah), 1 and 2 Maccabees, as well as six additions to Esther, and three additions to Daniel (Susanna; Prayer of Azariah and the Song of the Three Young Men; and Bel and the Dragon). These several texts were widely used in the early church and eventually were translated into Latin, becoming part of the OT as received by the Roman Catholic Church. In Protestant Bibles these books, along with 1 and 2 Esdras and the Prayer of Manasseh, were gathered together and placed between the OT and the NT in a section entitled Apocrypha (see WCF,* 1.3).

Reasons that led the Reformers to adopt the Hebrew canon of the Scriptures rather than the expanded canon of books in the Greek Septuagint and the Latin Vulgate included the following considerations: (1) Neither Jesus nor any of the writers of the NT make any direct quotation from any of these books. (2) Some of the Apocrypha contain texts that support purgatory (2 Macc. 12:43–45) and the efficacy of almsgiving in covering one's sins* (Tobit 4:7–11; 12:8–9; 14:10–11; Sirach 3:30; 35:2).

Canon of the NT. The apostolic church received from the Jews a written rule of faith, the Jewish Scriptures. Besides these writings, the oldest Christian communities accepted another authority, the words of Jesus as these were handed down, first by oral tradition and later in written Gospel. There also circulated copies of apostolic letters giving explanations of the significance of the person and work of Jesus Christ for the lives of believers. At first a local church would have copies of only a few apostolic letters and perhaps one or two Gospels. In the collections that were gradually formed, a place was found for two other kinds of books—the Acts of the Apostles and the Apocalypse of John. Thus, side by side with the old Jewish canon, and without in any way displacing it, there sprang up a new Christian canon.

The church had the task not only of collecting but also of sifting and rejecting—for many other gospels, acts, letters, and apocalypses circulated in the second, third, and succeeding centuries. Finally, after many years, during which books of local and temporary authority came and went, the limits of the NT canon were set forth for the first time by Bishop Athanasius of Alexandria (A.D. 367). But not all in the church were ready to follow him, and in the following centuries there were minor fluctuations in the canon, such as temporary acceptance by the Armenian church of Paul's Third Letter to the Corinthians and inclusion of the spurious Letter to the Laodiceans in the eighteen German Bibles printed prior to Martin Luther's* translation.

The criterion of canonicity of books of the NT appears to have been apostolic authorship or near-apostolic status, antiquity, orthodoxy, and usage throughout the churches. According to non-Reformed churches, the canon is an authoritative collection of books, whereas for Reformed churches it is a collection of authoritative books; the books had their authority before they were collected. In the most basic sense, neither individuals nor councils created the canon; instead, they came to perceive and acknowledge the self-authenticating quality of these writings, which imposed themselves as canonical upon the church. This conviction of divine authority "is from the inward work of the Holy Spirit, bearing witness by and with the Word in our hearts" (WCF, 1.5).

R. Beckwith, *The Old Testament Canon of the New Testament Church* (1985); F. F. Bruce, *The Canon of Scripture* (1988); B. M. Metzger, *The Canon of the New Testament* (1987).

BRUCE M. METZGER

Capitalism

Definitions of capitalism converge on the notion that economic well-being is best served by allowing a free flow of goods in the marketplace, unimpeded by government interference or control, so that as individuals or groups compete for markets, those who create the best balance between maximizing profits and minimizing production costs will be rewarded.

While neither the Bible nor Christian tradition endorses any one economic system, there has been a close relationship, both of support and critique, between capitalism and the Reformed tradition. The twentieth-century debate has focused on what Max Weber called "the Protestant ethic and the spirit of capitalism." Weber maintained that the Protestant emphasis, developed during the Reformation period, on fulfilling one's "calling" or vocation* under God in this life ("worldly asceticism") was a driving force away from sloth and toward hard work, frugality, and thrift. This led to worldly success and the accumulation of capital which, in turn, could be interpreted as God's blessing on human endeavor and an assurance of being one of the "elect."

Weber's critics claim that the thesis is oversimplified and neglects other factors such as the breakup of feudal holdings, introduction of a money as opposed to a barter economy, and the fact that Catholics as well as Calvinists prospered in post-medieval society. Weber's thesis better describes the later English Puritans* than the immediate followers of Calvin,* who was suspicious of profit making to the neglect of human welfare—a frequent consequence of single-minded devotion to profit making.

The resultant moral debate thus focuses on such competing claims as the following: (1) Capitalism, by proscribing state interference in the economic order, creates maximal conditions for individual initiative and freedom to be suitably rewarded and is thus consonant with Christian faith. (2) Capitalism, being based on competition rather than on cooperation, gives lavish rewards to a few but does so at the cost of consigning the majority to marginal and even subhuman existence and is thus not consonant with Christian faith.

Recent discussion over whether capitalism is bane or blessing has been sharpened by inclusion in ecumenical gatherings of representatives of churches in the third world, who have experienced capitalism through its linkage to a type of global imperialism by the affluent that has been exploitive of the indigent, increasing an already present economic imbalance so the rich grow richer while the poor grow poorer.

The belief of the Reformed tradition in the sovereignty of God* is an ongoing reminder that everything, including economic systems, stands under God's judgment and that uncritical allegiance to any human construct is an act of idolatry* and a denial of God's sovereignty.

W. F. Graham, *The Constructive Revolutionary* (1971); W. L. Owensby, *Economics for Prophets* (1988); R. H. Tawney, *Religion and the Rise of Capitalism* (1926; repr. 1962); E. Troeltsch, *The Social Teaching of the Christian Churches* (1912; ET 1931); M. Weber, *The Protestant Ethic and the Spirit of Capitalism* (1904–5; ET 1930; repr. 1958).

ROBERT MCAFEE BROWN

Capito, Wolfgang (1478–1541)

A devout scholar and reformer of Strassburg, Capito was closely associated with many early leaders of the Reformation. Educated at Ingolstadt and Freiburg im Breisgau, he was a noted Hebraist who published commentaries on Habakkuk (1526) and Hosea (1528) as well as a translation of the Psalms and a Hebrew grammar. Despite his friendship with Erasmus,* he moved gradually from scholarly labors to a more activist role as preacher and reformer. Capito, along with Matthew Zell, was a leading figure in the early Strassburg Reformation movement. Overshadowed by Martin Bucer,* he nonetheless had a shaping influence in developing a Protestant polity* for that city. With Bucer he coauthored the Tetrapolitan Confession* (1530) and drew up church orders for several other Reformed cities. He participated in the Marburg Colloquy* and was deeply concerned about issues of liturgy, preaching,* and church union. He was on friendly terms with many Anabapatists and radical reformers who frequented the Strassburg area. He preferred persuasion to coercion and was a moderating influence against the use of more drastic measures to force the conformity of dissenters. Erasmus, who could not follow Capito into the evangelical camp, referred to his former friend as a "bishop of the new gospel." Capito signed the Wittenberg Concord (1536) and spent his final years working for peace among the splintered Protestant parties. He died of the plague in Strassburg.

J. J. Kittelson, *Wolfgang Capito: From Humanist to Reformer* (1975); B. Stierle, *Capito als Humanist* (1974).

TIMOTHY GEORGE

Carey, William (1761–1834)

Pioneer English Calvinistic Baptist missionary to India. Arriving in Bengal (1793), Carey, with Joshua Marshman and William Ward, established a mission and college at Serampore, a Danish colony near Calcutta (1800). Carey is known for his Bible translations into many languages and for lexicons and grammars produced by Serampore Press. He is significant in the Bengal renaissance because he encouraged use of the vernacular, emphasized education, and opposed "certain dreadful practices" incompatible with Christianity, such as *sati.*

M. A. Laird, *Missionaries and Education in Bengal, 1793–1837* (1972); E. D. Potts, *British Baptist Missionaries in India, 1793–1837* (1967).

DUNCAN B. FORRESTER

Carstares, William (1649–1715)

Scottish churchman and statesman whose influence at the time of the Glorious Revolution (1688–90) determined the pattern of government in the Church of Scotland from then until today. The source of Carstares's influence was his close friendship with William of Orange and the trust William placed in his judgment.

Born less than two weeks after Charles I's execution, Carstares died six weeks after the battle of Sheriffmuir. He is thus an important link between seventeenth-century Covenanting wars and eighteenth-century controversies. His background was Protester, and both he and his father found refuge in the Netherlands* during the second Covenanting period. This experience confirmed his prejudice against episcopal church government and his view that Presbyterianism* commanded general support in Scotland. Carstares's friendship with William of Orange was deepened when he acted as William's confidential agent in England and Scotland and kept William's involvement secret even when tortured. Carstares convinced William that the Scottish bishops could not be persuaded to renounce the exiled Stuarts and that only Presbyterianism would secure the loyalty of the Church of Scotland. An act of the Estates of Parliament (1690) adopted the WCF,* abolished prelacy, and confirmed Presbyterian church government as "the only government of Christ's Church within this kingdom."

Carstares did much to remove misunderstandings between William and the revived General Assembly* of the church. He also persuaded the General Assembly not to oppose the parliamentary union with England (1707). He was, however, unable to prevent the passing of the Toleration Act (1689) and the Patronage Act (1712). He was principal of the University of Edinburgh (from 1703) and Moderator of the General Assembly (1705; 1708; 1711; 1715).

A. I. Dunlop, *William Carstares and the Kirk by Law Established* (1967).

HENRY R. SEFTON

Cartwright, Thomas (c. 1535–1603)

The most influential Puritan-Presbyterian theologian of the Elizabethan period. Cartwright was educated at Cambridge and throughout his theological life associated with the Reformed theology of Geneva (friend of Theodore Beza*) and Scotland. To the delight of the Puritans* he was named professor of theology at Cambridge (1570). But his outspoken opposition to the Elizabethan Settlement,* especially to the Anglican form of church government, led to his dismissal the following year. His famous and continuous adversary, John Whitgift (1530–1604), archbishop of Canterbury (from 1583), was responsible for the dismissal. The disagreement between them involved only the form of church government; Cartwright later defended the established church against separatist Puritanism. Along with an emerging tradition in Reformed theology, he advocated a church organized on presbyterian principles and established by the state, including severe penalties for offenses against the Ten Commandments (death penalty for blasphemy), but clearly separating temporal and spiritual jurisdictions. Christ alone is head of the church, of which the magistrate is only a member; the church is to exercise discipline* in the lives of its members.

Cartwright was involved in a tract conflict with the Anglicans (1572–74), primarily with Whitgift (Admonitions* controversy); Puritans hoped to move Parliament to challenge the queen on the settlement of church and church-state affairs. His fame, increased by imprisonment, continued in later Puritanism, including New England Congregationalism. John Cotton claimed agreement "in substance" with Cartwright's views of church government.

JOHN E. WILSON

Catechism

A form of instruction in the basics of the Christian faith, usually by question and answer, greatly used in Reformed and other churches. The word derives from the Greek word *katēchein*, "to instruct" (1 Cor. 14:19). In the early church a well-developed catechumenate prepared candidates for baptism (described in Hippolytus's *Apostolic Tradition* [c. 215] and reflected in a series of catechetical homilies by Cyril of Jerusalem, John Chrysostom, and others). The later prevalence of infant baptism* called for catechesis after baptism, and in the medieval era a wide variety of aids, normally focusing on the Ten Commandments, the Lord's Prayer, and the Apostles' Creed, were used.

Martin Luther's* Small Catechism (1529) fixed the name of a new genre of Christian literature. It was part of his response to the ignorance exposed during church visitations in Saxony (G. Strauss, *Luther's House of Learning* [1978]). It set a pattern that became classical, built around the traditional elements of the Decalogue, the Creed, the Lord's Prayer, and the sacraments* (with confession separating Baptism and the Lord's Supper*), with appendixes on household religion and daily Christian living. It was intended for children, but Luther also stressed the importance of verbatim repetition and memorization in instructing the young. From the Small Catechism those who were adequately taught should move to his Large Catechism, which was not in question-and-answer form.

During the Reformation numerous catechisms were compiled, not only by leading reformers (e.g., John Oecolampadius* and Heinrich Bullinger*) but also by pastors whose works were never published. These catechisms served not only as general purpose tools of Christian teaching but also specifically as preparation for confirmation,* which under the lead of Martin Bucer* took on a new lease of life as the occasion when children gave an account of their faith (*Inst.* 4.19.4, 13). Inevitably the catechisms of the Reformation and the post-Reformation reflected the distinctive emphases of contemporary controversies and so fulfilled a confessional function also. This is true even of the brief catechism of Thomas Cranmer* which was included in the *BCP** (1549). It requires recitation of the Creed, the Decalogue, and the Lord's Prayer. Only the section on the sacraments, added in 1604, used short questions and answers. It was drawn largely from one of the much-used catechisms of Alexander Nowell (d. 1602), dean of St. Paul's Cathedral, London.

Within the Reformed tradition, deserving special mention are Calvin's Geneva Catechism* for the Genevan church and the Heidelberg Catechism.* Calvin's illustrates the artificiality of the question-and-answer form; too many questions are "leading," and some become statements that the child endorses with "Correct"! The Heidelberg Catechism still enjoys wide admiration for its warm piety and doctrinal clarity.

No Reformed catechism has been more influential than the Shorter Catechism of the Westminster Assembly* (1648). Largely the work, it seems, of the English Puritan* Anthony Tuckney, it comprises 107 questions and answers that present a structured account of Christian belief (not based on the Creed) from God and creation to the final resurrection before dealing with the Decalogue, the sacraments, and the Lord's Prayer. Its distinctive emphases (e.g., the decrees of God* and the Sabbath* commandment) and weaknesses (e.g., on the church*) are not hard to seek, but its noble start ("Q. 1. What is the chief end of man? A. Man's chief end is to glorify God, and to enjoy him forever") and general dignity and economy merited the treasured place it held for centuries in church and school in Presbyterian Scotland and elsewhere.

Alongside the catechism went the practice of catechizing—the inculcation of Christian knowledge by interrogation and testing, often in families on a Sunday afternoon in response to the morning sermon. Though in recent years various attempts have been made to revive both catechisms and catechizing (e.g., the Church of England's Revised Catechism [1962]), they have rarely enjoyed much success. Yet in the "post-Christian" West, even if learning by memorization and repetition is not in vogue, appropriate catechetical instruction is urgently needed.

T. F. Torrance, *The School of Faith* (1959).

DAVID F. WRIGHT

Chalmers, Thomas (1780–1847) Scotland's greatest nineteenth-century churchman ministered at Kilmany in Fife (1803–15), at Tron Church in Glasgow (1815–19), and at St. John's in Glasgow (1819–23) before becoming professor of moral philosophy at St. Andrews University (1823–28), professor of divinity at Edinburgh (1828–43), and principal and professor of theology in the Free Church College, Edinburgh (1843–47). Converted to evangelicalism (c. 1810), Chalmers rose rapidly within the Kirk's "Popular" party. He championed its cause in the Voluntary Controversy (1829ff.) and the Ten Years Conflict (1834ff.). He led the Non-intrusionists out of the Established Church at the Disruption (1843) and became a father figure and presiding genius of the emergent Free Church of Scotland.

Parish renewal. Chalmers regarded the traditional parish—a Christian community embracing everyone (c. two thousand people) within a clearly defined area, centered on church and school, and receiving all necessary leadership from minister and kirk session—as the ideal instrument for the regeneration of a country beset by innumerable problems—economic, social, and political. In Glasgow he sought to demonstrate what it could do. Poor relief was efficiently managed by a revived diaconate; day school and Sunday school teachers provided education for hundreds of needy children; elders learned to exercise responsible pastoral oversight, and the whole congregation to consider itself a missionary agency. Chalmers and St. John's became household words throughout Scotland, and the church looked as though it would regain its place at the center of local and national life.

Poor relief. Though distressed by the sufferings of Scotland's urban proletariat, Chalmers rejected the increasingly popular solution: secular relief schemes financed by compulsory poor rates. These, he believed, would eventually result in the pauperization and demoralization of the persons they were designed to benefit. Instead, since poverty's ultimate cause is irreligion, the cure lay in combining evangelism* and Christian philanthropy (charitable doles dispensed, after rigorous inquiry, by church office-bearers). His efforts in Glasgow were successful and drew attention to the problem's magnitude. But critics abounded, and by the 1840s it was clear that the future lay with state-organized welfare rather than church-inspired charity.

Church extension. Valuing the parochial organization of the church as he did, Chalmers sought to increase its effectiveness by reducing the size of overlarge parishes and creating new ones wherever necessary. He launched a great campaign (1834) for church extension, and after four years nearly two hundred churches had been called into existence. When government withheld support for the stipends of the new ministers, he devoted himself to raising funds. Once the Disruption finally extinguished his hopes for a revivified Establishment, he presided over the even more remarkable church-building program of the young Free Church.

Establishment and ecclesiastical freedom. The centuries-old alliance between church and state had no more enthusiastic supporter than Chalmers. During the great debate of the 1830s, he argued that free trade in religion could not reclaim the non-Christian masses for Christianity. State recognition and support of one particular religious body was as desirable in nineteenth-century Scotland as in medieval or Reformation times. Alongside Establishment, however, Chalmers was equally devoted to spiritual freedom—and his experience during the Ten Years Conflict convinced him that in existing circumstances his two ideals were incompatible. Government was withholding help to which the church felt entitled; law courts and legislators were denying congregations the right to choose their own ministers. Such threats to Christ's headship and Christian liberty must be resisted, even at the cost of breaking the state connection. So Chalmers led the evangelically-minded Non-intrusionists out of a "vitiated Establishment" into the Free Church (1843).

Practical yet visionary, a spellbinding orator and a superb administrator, Chalmers combined evangelical passion with social concern, and theological orthodoxy with broad interests and catholic sympathies. He could be overbearing in personal relationships, maladroit in politics, and intensely conservative and paternalistic on social questions. But he had an unerring instinct for what was vital, and he inspired deep affection. Even his adversaries honored him. He suffered many defeats: the eclipse of his poor-relief schemes, the failure to win government backing for church extension and the tragic schism (1843). But his concept of the parish still inspires the Kirk's missionary strategy, and his twin ideals—national recognition of religion and spiritual freedom—are enshrined in the Declaratory Articles (1921; 1926), the constitutional foundation of the reunited Church of Scotland.

S. J. Brown, *Thomas Chalmers and the Godly Commonwealth in Scotland* (1982); A. C. Cheyne, ed., *The Practical and the Pious: Essays on Thomas Chalmers (1780–1847)* (1985); W. Hanna, *Memoirs of Dr. Chalmers*, 4 vols. (1849–52).

ALEC C. CHEYNE

Charismatic Movement

An ecumenical phenomenon with NT roots. The word "charismatic" refers to the grace gifts of the Spirit (1 Cor. 12–14; Rom. 12). Two aspects of this spiritual movement have concerned churches of the Reformed tradition: (1) baptism in/with the Holy Spirit; and (2) charismatic gifts for ministry. Charismatic Christians challenge the traditional ways in which the gift and the power of the Spirit have been understood and expressed.

While the writings of John Calvin* are filled with references to the dynamic work of the Holy Spirit,* the Spirit's activity in ministry was confined largely to the office of pastor (*Inst.* 4.3.6–7). The extraordinary "visible graces" of the Spirit in the ministry of Jesus and the apostles were withdrawn from the church because they were no longer needed in the full light of the gospel, and human ungratefulness quenched them.

Calvinists continued to teach that the "extraordinary" gifts of the Spirit had ceased. The Word-centered Reformed tradition was suspicious of spiritual "enthusiasm." But the dynamic work of the Spirit in Christian life was emphasized by the Puritan John Owen* and the WCF* (ch. 18). Abraham Kuyper* viewed the charismatic gifts in general as essential for the church's upbuilding and mission.

Since about 1900, experiences of Spirit empowerment (baptism in the Spirit) and gifts/miracles (charismatic gifts) have challenged American mainline churches. Early Pentecostal experience was often dismissed as mere enthusiasm. But a "second wave" of charismatic renewal (from 1960 on) sweeping the historic churches led to a flurry of official studies of the issues raised by the movement. Reformed writings provided historical background and theological understanding.

Charismatic Christians today usually try to stay in their churches because of the cautious welcome extended in the official reports and because of the work of nonofficial groups. Presbyterian and Reformed Renewal Ministries (from 1967) promotes dialogue with those interested in or troubled by charismatic renewal. Pentecostal type of experiences are interpreted in Reformed theological terms.

The main themes of official reports of General Assemblies* and General Synods have been to: (1) anchor "baptism in the Spirit" in a unified Christian initiation, while denying the Pentecostal view of a two-stage work of the Spirit; (2) affirm individual experiences of Spirit empowerment and gifts within certain pastoral limits; (3) revise the traditional view of spiritual gifts to include (with due caution) "extraordinary" charismata (tongues, healing, prophecy) as valid expressions of Christian faith; and (4) encourage sensitivity and respect on all sides with guidelines for individuals and governing bodies on how to deal with difficulties. While problems still exist, charismatic empowerment and giftedness seem now to be a permanent part of churches of the Reformed family.

Berkhof, *CFI*; J. D. G. Dunn, *Jesus and the Spirit* (1975); A. I. C. Heron, *The Holy Spirit* (1983); A. Kuyper, *The Work of the Holy Spirit* (1900); K. McDonnell, ed., *Presence, Power, Praise*, 3 vols. (1980); B. A. Pursey, *Gifts of the Holy Spirit* (1984); and *Charismatic Renewal and You* (1987); UPCUSA (1970); PCUS

(1971); RCA (1975) Reports; WCC, *The Church Is Charismatic* (1981).

BARBARA A. PURSEY

Charnock, Stephen (1628–1680)

Born in London, Charnock studied at Cambridge and Oxford. Under the Commonwealth, he preached successfully in Ireland. At the death of Oliver Cromwell*, he returned to London and studied in retirement for fifteen years. He shared a Presbyterian pulpit with Thomas Watson at Crosby Hall (from 1675). *On the Existence and Attributes of God* (1681) is one of the seventeenth century's most original theological works, thinking out the theological tradition in terms of Christian experience. James McCosh* wrote the biography for Charnock's collected works (1860).

DNB 4:134ff.

HUGHES OLIPHANT OLD

Christian Education

The institutional patterns and processes by which the church educates its members. It includes (1) handing on the Christian faith to adult converts and children of believers to support their ongoing growth in the Christian life; and (2) relating the Christian faith to the general education of the church's members. These internal and external dimensions have been important parts of the Reformed tradition.

Christian education prior to the Reformation. The first use of "Christian education" (Gr. *en Christō paideia*) is in Clement of Rome (c. A.D. 96). In Paul's writings, however, Christian parents are told to bring their children up "in the discipline and instruction of the Lord" (Eph. 6:4). As the church spread around the Mediterranean and adapted to new cultures, it sought continuity with the original teachings of Jesus and instructed children and adults in the Christian way of life.

While much Christian education took place through preaching* and, indirectly, through participation in the liturgy,* the early central focus was the catechumenate for adult converts. Lasting several years, the catechumenate involved a well-structured period of formation and instruction. Entry into the church meant a radical break with the ways of the surrounding pagan culture and an internalization of the attitudes, behaviors, and beliefs of the community of faith.

Since pagan culture was held suspect during this period, it is ironic that the church did not form its own schools. Children and youth of believing families simply attended already established schools, based on the traditions of classical humanism, to receive a general education. The only explicitly Christian "schools" to emerge were communities gathered around leading theologians to study Christian doctrine.* These were not sponsored by the church but did contribute significantly to the emergence of theology as a "sacred science" comparable to the reflection of the pagan philosophers.

With the Roman Empire's collapse and the subsequent decline of the schools it had supported, the church had to assume functions previously carried out by other agencies. The rise of the monastic schools was a particularly important trend. To study and pray Scripture, children and unlearned novices had to be taught to read. Similarly, bishops were forced to provide candidates for the priesthood with an elementary as well as a theological education. By the sixth century, the church's involvement in general education spread beyond the bishop to the rural parishes, where priests were ordered by the Second Council of Vaison to educate "worthy successors to themselves."

Christian education during the Middle Ages built on this foundation. Most formal education was for persons who were involved in an ecclesiastical function, and it occurred in monastery or cathedral schools. These schools were also important centers for theological study and writing. The prevalence of infant baptism* and the gradual separation of initiation and catechesis led to the demise of the catechumenate, leaving ordinary Christians with limited involvement in formal Christian instruction.

During the late Middle Ages, scholasticism* dominated Christian education, emphasizing logic (dialectic) in a manner mirroring the prevalent style of theological disputation. The Renaissance challenged this style of education, restoring the ideals of classical humanism.* John Calvin,* Johannes Sturm, and other Reformed educators were deeply influenced by this movement, incorporating into their educational reforms its emphasis on rhetoric, use of classical models for grammar and composition, and acceptance of historical and philological modes of investigation.

Christian education in the Reformed tradition. The Reformation was a watershed in the history of Christian education. Reformation churches took renewed interest in the education of their own members and the general populace. Calvin believed that if the Reformation was to succeed, it must find ways to support the emergence of an educated laity and a learned clergy. All persons must have direct access to the Bible and receive a basic foundation in Christian doctrine if they were to order their lives according to the purposes of God. Moreover, the general populace must be educated in the virtues of citizenship and instructed in how to find and hold their place in the social order. Accordingly, Calvin greatly emphasized both the internal and external dimensions of Christian education.

Following the lead of Martin Luther,* Calvin attempted to renew the catechumenate of the early church, focusing now on the task of teaching children the basic doctrines of the Christian faith. The family and the church were to cooperate in forming Christian piety* and understanding early in life. Calvin also encouraged ministers to teach the laity through sermons, reviving the practice of didactic preaching associated with catechesis in the early church. To carry out these tasks, ministers were to receive the best general and theological education.* In part, Calvin's desire for a learned clergy lay behind his strenuous efforts to establish a first-rate system of education in Geneva, culminating in the Academy.*

Yet his motivation went beyond this. Equally important was his belief that literacy was necessary for a healthy laity and citizenry. From the start, Calvin attempted to establish a system of education open to all, rich and poor. Here, instruction in the faith and general education were to commingle, for education in citizenship and occupation were inseparable from a theological understanding of Christian vocation.* Church and magistrate were to cooperate.

Calvin's comprehensive interest in education permanently affected the Reformed tradition. Virtually everywhere it appeared, the Reformed tradition spawned vital educational institutions. John Knox,* who studied at the Geneva Academy, gave careful attention to education in his Book of Discipline for the Scottish Reformed church. As in Geneva, church and state were to cooperate to provide universal education and institutions of higher education for the gifted. General education and education in the faith were to cooperate in such institutions. Likewise the church's internal education of its own members followed Calvin's lead, placing great emphasis on catechetical instruction and didactic preaching.

The close relationship between the Reformed tradition and Christian education is also found in Holland, England, and France. In Holland, Abraham Kuyper's* theology of "sphere sovereignty" undergirded a revitalization of education both inside and outside the church.

In America, the Puritans* continued this legacy. Ministers frequently functioned as the first teachers in a town. By the 1650s, the villages of Massachusetts were required to provide a school for the education of the community's children. Similarly, in the middle and southern colonies, Presbyterian ministers of Scottish descent were responsible for much of the formal education. Many of the first colleges in America were established to provide a learned clergy, and eventually there were colleges to train people for the teaching and other professions. Reformed churches produced a variety of educational resources, including catechisms* for children and primers that included moral and religious material.

The disestablishment of religion, however, created a new situation to which Reformed churches had to adapt. They could no longer expect the state to cooperate with the church, at least in a manner favoring a specific denomination. Three different approaches to Christian education emerged in the Reformed churches in response to this situation, each legitimately drawing on Calvin's legacy.

First, some churches, such as the Christian Reformed Church in North America, have opted for parochial schools. In the mid-1800s, this approach was feasible for many in the Presbyterian Church and was sharply debated in the General Assemblies.* Between 1846 and 1870, Presbyterians founded 264 parochial schools.

A second response has been to accept the separation of Christian education and general education and confine the church's educational efforts strictly to its own members, leaving their general education to the public schools. The cooptation of the Sunday school movement by the major denominations (late 1900s) has been a key part of this strategy. Many in the Reformed tradition have argued theologically for the universal education that the common school represents, recalling the examples of Calvin and Knox.

The third response is a mixture of the first two. In general, the separation of Christian education and general education is accepted as a necessary evil, but recognition of the difficulties involved in really separating moral and religious dimensions from public education is acknowledged. The need to teach civic virtue, for example, is seen as necessitating a religious or quasi-religious foundation. Many half measures have been tried: grounding civic duty in a "generalized" religious stance and teaching religion off school grounds or after school.

All three approaches to Christian education have been important in Reformed churches in the United States and continue to represent viable options. In an increasingly pluralistic society where Christians confront a number of conflicting beliefs and values, the need to continue the Reformed tradition's strong emphasis on Christian education is perhaps more important than ever.

F. Eby, *Early Protestant Educators* (1931); H. I. Marrou, *A History of Education in Antiquity* (1956); R. R. Osmer, *A Teachable Spirit: Recovering the Teaching Office in the Church* (1990); L. J. Sherrill, *Presbyterian Parochial Schools 1846–1860* (1932); J. Westerhoff and O. C. Edwards, eds., *A Faithful Church: Issues in the History of Catechesis* (1981).

RICHARD R. OSMER

Christology

As the study of who Jesus of Nazareth is in relation to God* and humanity,* Christology is pursued not in isolation from what Jesus achieved for humanity (the work of Christ) but in close association with it. There is a unity of the person and work of Christ, for Christ came to humanity in and through his saving work. Thus Calvin* united the person and work by presenting Christ in the threefold office of prophet, priest, and king. For conceptual purposes it is, however, convenient to look at the person and work separately. The following examines the person of Christ.

Patristic creeds. The most important doctrinal statement concerning the identity and nature of Jesus produced by the early church is the Chalcedonian Definition (A.D. 451). This christological formula was taken up by sixteenth-century Reformed theologians as a faithful reflection and statement of that to which Scripture* pointed concerning the person of Christ. The Definition first emphasizes the unity of the person of Christ by use of "one and the same" and "the same": He is "one and the same Son, the same perfect in Godhead, the same perfect in manhood, truly God and truly man, the same consisting of a rational soul and body."

Second, and of more significance, the duality of the two natures, human and divine, is underlined. "One and the same Christ, Son, Lord, Only-begotten, made known in two natures without confusion, without change, without division, without separation; the difference of the natures having been in no wise taken away by reason of the union but rather the properties of each being preserved, and both concurring into one *prosōpon* and one *hypostasis*—not parted or divided into two *prosōpa* but one and the same Son and Only-begotten, the divine Logos, the Lord Jesus Christ."

The four "withouts" serve as "No Road" notices for false paths in patristic theology (e.g., Nestorius [without division; without separation]; Arius [without change]; and Eutyches [without confusion]). Nestorianism was seen as commending a double personality in Christ as if there were two persons, not one, living inside his skin. Arianism was seen as teaching that the Logos was passible and mutable because it attributed all that was said of Jesus (e.g., his growth, temptations, and suffering) to the Logos, not the human nature. Finally, Eutyches was interpreted as teaching "two natures before the union, one nature afterward," thereby indicating that the humanity of the incarnate Logos was hardly real.

The Council of Chalcedon claimed that the incarnate Lord must be described as one person (Gr. *hypostasis* or *prosōpon*) in two natures (*physis*). Thus it was necessary to give an account of the way in which the Logos/Son could be described as the ultimate subject of two disparate natures. Thus the doctrine of *enhypostasia* (often unhappily referred to as "the doctrine of impersonal humanity") was developed in order to show that the *hypostasis* of the Logos (who is Creator) sufficed as the *hypostasis* of the humanity (the created) because the latter, never having existed on its own, had no independent *hypostasis* of its own. This means that the divinity of Christ is not really the divine nature (common to all three Persons of the Trinity) but the Person of the Logos/Son, the deity under the personal determination of the Logos. Thus it was not the divine nature which became flesh but the Logos of the Second Person of the Trinity who became flesh.

Further, in terms of the assumed human nature of the Logos, the third Council of Constantinople (681) taught (against the Monothelites) that it retains, in its unimpaired integrity, a separate will and intelligence and thus in the one Person of the Logos there are two wills, divine and human (dyothelitism), with the latter being subject to the former.

Reformed confessions. During the Protestant Reformation, the Reformed churches took up the christological teaching of the Nicene Creed, the Chalcedonian Definition, the Quicunque Vult, together with the doctrines of *enhypostasia* and dyothelitism, and applied it to their contemporary situations to present sound doctrine and set aside error and heresy.* Further, they added to their use of patristic statements of dogma many Scripture* citations to make clear they accepted the patristic dogma because it was scriptural. For example, the Belgic Confession* (1561) said the Son is one of the three Persons of the eternal Godhead (art. 8), eternally begotten of the Father (art. 9), and thus neither made nor created (thus anti-Arian in emphasis). Further, Christ's incarnation* is said to be a real and true assuming of a full human nature, body and soul, with all its infirmities, sin excepted (art. 18). Thus the error of the Anabaptists who teach that Christ did not really take flesh from Mary* must be rejected. If this is anti-docetic in emphasis, then the next article is anti-monophysite, for it clearly teaches the unity and distinction of the two natures in the one Christ in Chalcedonian style. The reality of the (now immortalized) human nature after the resurrection* is affirmed and the section ends with this declaration: "We confess that he is *very God* and *very man*: very God by his power to conquer death and very man that he might die for us according to the infirmity of his flesh."

The Second Helvetic Confession* (1566) deals with Christology (ch. 11) by affirming the Christology of the first four ecumenical councils, in particular the Chalcedonian teaching. It rejects the impious doctrine of both the ancient Arius and the modern Servetus* that Jesus was not co-equal and consubstantial in his divine nature with the Father. Further, it insists against all both ancient and modern forms of docetism that Jesus had "a soul with its reason and flesh with its senses" and suffered real pain. This human nature, while immortalized and spiritualized through resurrection and ascension,* is not localized in heaven and is not (as some Lutherans taught in connection with the real presence of Christ in the sacrament) present in this world.

The disagreement with the Lutherans about the ubiquity* of the human nature of the exalted Lord Jesus is also expressed in the Heidelberg Catechism* (1563). Here it is taught that "Christ is true man and true God. As a man he is no longer on earth, but in his divinity, majesty, grace,* and

Spirit, he is never absent from us" (HC, 47). This is possible because "divinity is incomprehensible and everywhere present" and thus "beyond the bounds of the humanity which it has assumed" (HC, 48). In other words, while the glorified human nature of Christ is localized in heaven, his infinite and eternal divine nature cannot be localized even though it is always perfectly united with his localized human nature.

This doctrine was taught by Calvin himself. For while Luther particularly insisted on the unity of the person, Calvin emphasized the integrity of the two natures, fearing it was possible to destroy both natures by insisting too much on the unity of the person. Thus Calvin opposed the Lutheran exposition of the *communicatio idiomatum* ("communication of properties") and taught that the human nature was not capable of being divinized and given the property of omnipresence. Calvin revived a form of teaching from patristic sources that, when the Logos became incarnate as Jesus, he did not relinquish the divine attribute of omnipresence but continued to fill the whole cosmos, and thus to be outside as well as inside the human nature he had assumed (the *extra calvinisticum**).

Yet it was from Lutheran sources that Reformed theologians borrowed the important concept of the two states of Christ, though they interpreted it differently. One problem with using the categories of the Chalcedonian Definition was that they are static and seem far removed from the dynamic Jesus who is encountered through the Gospels and the epistles. However, the adoption of the concept of the threefold office of prophet, priest, and king, along with that of the two states, helped give a more rounded character to Reformed Christology. On the basis of Phil. 2:5–11, Jesus as the incarnate Word (not the human nature alone but the Logos become flesh) has been presented as first in a state of humiliation (suffering, death, burial, and descent into Hades) and then in a state of exaltation (resurrection, ascension,* session, parousia). This approach provided an answer to the question, Who is the subject about whom the statements of the Chalcedonian Definition are made?

It has been noted that while classic Christology relies heavily on abstract nouns, the NT (as well as the Apostles' Creed) makes use primarily of verbs in presenting the person of Jesus. The doctrine of the two states also focuses attention on the verbal dimension—he suffered, he arose, and so forth. But Phil. 2:7, "he emptied himself," has been much discussed over the centuries, and from it what are known as kenotic theories of the incarnation have been propounded, especially by Lutherans and only rarely by Calvinists. Is the subject of the self-emptying either the preexistent Logos (as in some nineteenth-century formulations) or the Logos incarnate (Lutheran dogmaticians of the seventeenth century)? The former was a bold attempt to seek to do justice to the figure of Jesus in the Gospels who had obvious limitations in terms of his knowledge, and it may be judged to have failed because of its reducing and limiting of the Godhead in the divine nature of Jesus.

From above and from below. In modern times, there has been a determined attempt by some theologians to do justice to the true manhood of Jesus and thereby to construct a Christology from below, that is, from the account of Jesus and his ministry in the Gospels (as viewed through modern biblical criticism). In this approach, Jesus is really and truly a man (human) without reserve or ambiguity. The human experiences recorded in the texts and those which are not recorded but which all accept as belonging to humankind must be taken into account. So although Jesus, because of the quality of his life and deeds, is presented as God's Man and also God's Son, nothing must detract from the fact that he was first and foremost a man. Thus the patristic transition from God's Son to God the Son is seen as a false step. In this approach the divine disclosure took place through a man who was utterly open and transparent throughout his whole being to the living God. That man who thus lived for God is therefore God for us. His union with God is a matter of relation, function, and activity and a matter of degree not of kind. As the contemporary biblical scholar John Knox has put it: "We can have the humanity without the pre-existence and we can have the pre-existence without the humanity. There is absolutely no way of having both" (*The Humanity and Divinity of Christ* [1967], p. 106).

Classic Christology begins from the side of God—from above. Within Reformed theology the best modern presentation is undoubtedly that of Karl Barth,* whose great commitment to the Bible as the witness to God's revelation* ensures a more biblical presentation than the classical statements of the fifth and sixth centuries (see *CD* I/1; I/2; IV/1; IV/2). Barth employed the ontological framework of the classic statements but was always careful to ensure that Christology is much more than the manipulation of logical categories. The various stages in his argument are carefully checked by reference to the person and work of Christ as a whole and from the reality of Jesus Christ as fact and event. Barth's contemporary, Emil Brunner,* believed that Barth had not clarified adequately or successfully the difference between person (*hypostasis*) and personality (as used in modern psychology). Brunner addressed this in *The Mediator* (1927; ET 1934, pp. 345ff.) and argued for the inclusion of personality within nature (*physis*) and not connected with person (*hypostasis*).

Obviously, to the believer who searches for truth this whole subject has the aspects of both mystery and paradox. One is led to exclaim with Thomas, "My Lord and my God!" (John 20:28).

Heppe, *RD*; G. C. Berkouwer, *The Person of Christ* (1954); A. C. Cochrane, ed., *Reformed Confessions of the 16th Century* (1966); D. F. Wells, *The Person of Christ* (1984).

PETER TOON

Church

The following four quotations suggest some landmarks in addressing a Reformed understanding of the church. The church as a theological community is the subject of the first two. The church as a dynamic community/institution is indicated by the third. And the contemporary context as important for a Reformed understanding of the church is suggested by the last.

Q. 54. What do you believe concerning "the Holy Catholic Church"?
A. I believe that, from the beginning to the end of the world, and from among the whole human race, the Son of God, by his Spirit and his Word, gathers, protects, and preserves for himself, in the unity of the true faith, a congregation chosen for eternal life. Moreover, I believe that I am and forever will remain a living member of it (HC, in *BC* 4.054).

To be reconciled to God is to be sent into the world as his reconciling community. This community, the church universal, is entrusted with God's message of reconciliation and shares his labor of healing the enmities which separate men [*sic*] from God and from each other. Christ has called the church to this mission and given it the gift of the Holy Spirit. The church maintains continuity with the apostles and with Israel by faithful obedience to his call (Confession of 1967, in *BC* 9.31).

Ecclesia reformata semper reformanda. "The church reformed and always being reformed."

Clearly, the meaning of one's life for most Americans is to become one's own person, almost to give birth to oneself (Bellah, p. 82).

The church as a theological community. A Reformed understanding of the church begins not with the church but with God's* gracious call to be the church and, as the people of God, to be engaged in God's mission in the world. This polarity of being the church and being in mission has been nuanced differently in different historical periods. The missional element rises to more prominence, for example, in the nineteenth and twentieth centuries, as suggested by the quotation above from the Confession of 1967 (C-67). The Heidelberg Catechism, on the other hand, suggests the church as a people called into a community where there is mutual nourishment and consolation. Both statements reflect not only enduring facets of the doctrine of the church but different social and cultural environments. Heidelberg arises from a religious culture where the issue was joined between and among religious communities. C-67 reflects a church in a society where religion, including the Christian faith, has become an option, not an assumption.

The central point of agreement between Heidelberg and C-67 is a theological point, not perhaps unique to the Reformed heritage but nevertheless central to it: The church must be understood theologically in the context of the doctrine of election. The core identity of the church is its confession that it is a people chosen through Jesus Christ and by the work of the Holy Spirit.* It cannot, therefore, be self-defining. Its identity is given by the being and activity of God. The church is a theocentric community.

The church visible and invisible. "We must leave to God alone the knowledge of his church, whose foundation is his secret election," wrote Calvin* (*Inst.* 4.1.2). Calvin, the engendering agent of the Reformed heritage, grounds the church in God's action but provides for a distinction between the invisible and the visible church. The former is the true and full church. But it is known only to God. Hence, one must be cautious in making judgments about others and humble about one's own condition. The invisible church is the whole number whom God has chosen, living and dead, the communion of saints,* perhaps even those who appear to our eyes as reprobate, and excluding some who appear to be genuinely righteous and godly. But to say the church is invisible is to rest its identity solely in God.

The visibility of the church is, however, equally as important as the church invisible. Indeed, to separate the two would be as great an error as to identify them as one. For the visible church, with all its deficiencies and sins,* is grounded upon God's gracious provision for our lives, individually and corporately. It is the visible church which Calvin strikingly calls "our mother." "For there is no other way to enter into life unless this mother conceive us in her womb, give us birth, nourish us at her breast, and lastly, unless she keep us under her care and guidance until, putting off mortal flesh, we become like the angels [Matt. 22:30]. Our weakness does not allow us to be dismissed from her school until we have been pupils all our lives" (*Inst.* 4.1.4).

The visible church is absolutely essential. It is not an option. It is God's provision for our fallen world, God's accommodation* to our fallen state. God's election creates a people who live in this world, not in some other. This is the good news associated with the church as we know it. It is not only a house of hypocrites. It is a community/institution which God provides as an agency for God's saving, justifying, and sustaining activity. It is, to use Karl Barth's* striking phrase, "the earthy-historical form of existence of Jesus Christ Himself" (*CD* IV/1, 661). It is, to use the biblical metaphor, the body of Christ. Clearly, the dangers in such a proposal are immense—pride, self-congratulation, and idolatry.* But since Jesus Christ is the center of the church, the head of the body, the visible church is defined by one who emptied himself, taking the form of a servant (Phil. 2:7). The true church is instrumental to God's mission of serving.

In the Reformed heritage the church is both visible and invisible, sometimes more and sometimes less visible! Yet its authenticity rests not upon itself but upon its center—Jesus Christ, who calls this people into being and gives them life through the power of the Holy Spirit. Through the Spirit the people know their election in Jesus Christ and render their thankful praise and service. Such knowledge is cause for rejoicing but not boasting. It is grounds for serving, not being served.

The one church. Theologically, the church in the Reformed tradition claims that its commitment is to the ecumenical church. What it holds in common with other traditions is more important than what separates it. A Reformed understanding of the church includes, therefore, the four classical, theological characteristics associated with the ecumenical church. The church which is Reformed is one, holy, catholic, and apostolic.

To say the church is one is to assert that all churches find their unity not in their common practices but in their common source: Jesus Christ. The oneness of practices and understanding is not unimportant. Far from it. But these matters are subordinate to the fact that in Christ all are one. To be "in" Christ is to be a member of the church. Such deficiencies of unity and scandals of separation as there are in the visible church are negative reminders of the oneness given in Christ. Oneness is an eschatological dimension of the church, avidly to be sought now and to be received in the future.

Similarly, the church's holiness is not its perfection or purity. Holiness is the holiness of Jesus Christ who bestows upon the church the righteousness it cannot attain for itself. Therefore to be holy is to depend on Christ who "is daily at work in smoothing out wrinkles and cleansing spots. . . . The church is holy, then, in the sense that it is daily advancing and is not yet perfect" (*Inst.* 4.1.17). The Holy Spirit leads the church into righteousness. But this leading of the church into righteousness is not only the sanctification* of the believers. It is the believers' engagement, individually, corporately, and with others in reaching out to and transforming the "unholy," in seeking to build community among all, the so-called sheep and goats, and in doing justice* in the world. It is the engagement through Christ and in Christ with the struggles for a world where the hungry are to be fed, the homeless to be sheltered, and the lost to be found. It is, as C-67 puts it, allowing the life, death, resurrection,* and promised coming of Jesus Christ to "set the pattern for the church's mission" (*BC* 9.32).

The church is catholic. This affirmation locates the church simultaneously in relationship to Jesus Christ and to Jesus Christ's being confessed. Ignatius of Antioch wrote, "Wherever Jesus Christ is, there is the catholic church" (*Smyrneans* 8.2). So understood, catholicity or universality is, like holiness and oneness, grounded in the universal Lordship of Jesus Christ. The given universality in Jesus Christ leads the church to be inclusive in its life and leave no realm of life exempt from the Lordship of Christ. The church as catholic understands Christ's Lordship as embracing all geographic arenas and all spheres of life within geographic units. Jürgen Moltmann* writes: "The goal of the church's mission remains universal. In the new people of God the divisions that destroy mankind [*sic*] will be deprived of their force here and now. The barriers which people set up against each other . . . will be broken down through mission and fellowship" (Moltmann, p. 351).

The church is apostolic. By apostolic is meant both the legitimate source of the church's message and its mission. By source is meant the apostolic witness to Jesus Christ as received in the Scriptures.* These testimonies are the touchstone for current apostolic faithfulness. Where the church does find its legitimacy is in its consistency with the message of those who saw the Lord "face to face." The church is apostolic as it is instructed and disciplined by the apostles and as it carries into the whole inhabited earth the good news that all, including the church, need to hear. It is apostolic as it fulfills its purpose, put simply by H. Richard Niebuhr, as the increase of the love of God and the neighbor among humans (Niebuhr, p. 31).

In the Reformed tradition, thinking about the nature of the church holds firmly to these marks of self-understanding: one, holy, catholic, and apostolic. The church which is centered in Jesus Christ is instructed and commissioned by the apostolic witness; it proclaims by word and deed the universal rule of God in Jesus Christ; it trusts in God's Spirit to lead it into and to contribute to the holiness God intends for all the world; and it clings to the unity it has in Christ and which it seeks institutionally. For Reformed Christians, the church is, therefore, inevitably ecumenical, engaged with the world; and informed and held under scrutiny by the words and deeds of the earliest witnesses.

The church as a dynamic community/institution. Inasmuch as the church is a human instrument, indeed, an "earthen vessel," there is need to attend to such matters as ministry,* sacraments,* and church order. These are by no means issues of indifference to the Reformed way of thinking. They are, in some cases, distinctives. They are means of grace* God provides and uses to provide for the church and the world. They are necessary furnishings for the visible church.

Calvin wrote: "From this the face of the church comes forth and becomes visible to our eyes. Whenever we see the Word of God purely preached and heard, and the sacraments administered according to Christ's institution, there, it is not to be doubted, a church of God exists" (*Inst.* 4.1.9). Such a statement does not resolve all confessions or disagreements. Persistent questions remain. The Reformed acceptance of two sacraments—Baptism* and the Lord's Supper*—set it apart from the Roman Catholic Church.* Disagreement about the meaning of these two sacraments divided and still divides today Reformed Protestants from Lutheran and Anabaptist Protestants. But these visible marks of the true church are central to the Reformed understanding of the church. Note that the "preaching"* mark of the church includes both *proclaiming* and *hearing*. This interactive setting emphasizes the responsibility of the whole people of God to discern the Word that God speaks by the power of the Spirit. Word, Spirit, and people are inextricably tied together. All in the church are active participants in discernment.

The Reformed tradition today embraces a high view of the church as a people whom God calls. It endorses the perspective that two marks of the church are as stated above. But there is as well a third mark associated with this tradition—discipline.

The Scots Confession,* following a description of the first two marks of the church as true preaching and the right administration of the sacraments, affirms another mark: "lastly, ecclesiastical discipline uprightly ministered, as God's Word prescribes, whereby vice is repressed and virtue nourished" (*BC* 3.18). Church discipline* is instrumental to faithful discipleship.

Since it is a Reformed insistence that the church is to be ordered by the Word and Spirit, the issue of how that ordering is to be done is not a trivial matter. While there is no one polity* or system of discipline mandated for every Reformed community, there are shared points of agreement among them.

One agreement is the importance of the elder* as an agent of the church's disciplines. This lay officer shares with the minister of Word and Sacrament in the positive task of providing for the spiritual well-being of the church. Further, there is agreement that discipline is the constructive task of providing for the structures, processes, and programs that build up the church and enable it to carry forward its mission. Such discipline is exercised through a series of ascending governing bodies, in which clergy and laity share responsibility in a representative system.

Some features of discipline, of course, must be determined in the light of changing conditions. The flexibility of church discipline illustrates the motto that is identified widely with a Reformed understanding of the church: *Ecclesia reformata semper reformanda* ("The church reformed and always being reformed").

Within this Reformed understanding of the church there is the affirmation of the church as a dynamic community, dependent upon a living Lord as it seeks to be in mission in a changing world. One should note that the subject of the reform of the church is not the church. The church is the object of reform—it is "always being reformed." The agent of legitimate reform is the Holy Spirit. It is the dynamic element of the Spirit's work that emboldens the church to be open to and seek new forms of discipline, including new confessions of faith. Calvin wrote: "Our constant endeavor, day and night, is not just to transmit the tradition faithfully, but also to put it in the form we think will prove best" (*Defense Against Pighius*). So Reformed churches understand themselves as part of an open tradition. In such a tradition, one understands, for example, confessions* of faith as necessary disciplines for the church's life and mission. But one also knows that such confessional standards and other forms of discipline arise under specific conditions and address needs of a particular time and place. Subordinate to Scripture, such disciplines order and inform the life and convictions of the church.

The church in the Reformed tradition

understands itself in a dynamic tension with the culture and the state. As the Lord of the church is the Lord of the world, so the church is called to discern and respond to God's creating, redeeming, and ordering work in the world. The church seeks the public good. With reference to civil government,* for example, there is a high view of the calling of the state. It is to provide for justice, order, freedom,* and peace,* to enact and enforce policies that liberate those who are oppressed or victimized. But the church has the positive task of addressing the state and society as to what the church believes makes for peace, justice, freedom, and order.

In the Reformed tradition, the church is the communion of saints. It is the communion of Christians of all times and all places. But this phrase is something more. It points to the church as a community marked by mutual care and bearing of burdens. It is the community where sins are forgiven, encouragement is shared, and faith is deepened and corrected. It is the people who know and live as members one of another because they are members of Christ's body. It is the community of the elect who exercise toward each other and toward all neighbors the love and justice of Jesus Christ. It is the community of the Holy Spirit.

The challenge of individualism. Perhaps one of the greatest challenges to the corporate view of the church in the United States, and possibly in the world, is indicated by the concluding quotation at the beginning of this article. "To become one's own person" and "to give birth to oneself" reflect a view of the self and community where the community drops away or recedes so far into the background that only the separate and self-reliant individual comes into focus. This self is the individual who has no necessary relationships of mutuality, whose individual accomplishments overshadow the sense of gifts received, where one "makes it" alone or not at all, where consuming goods takes precedence over public responsibility, where the church as our mother is replaced by self-birthing.

To this radical individualism as a cultural value the Reformed understanding of the church addresses a good word. It is the word that true life is life in community. It is the good word that life in community rests firmly on a foundation that endures, the gracious calling into the community of all of God's creation, through Jesus Christ and by the power of the Holy Spirit. That is a hard word to hear for the radical individualist in and outside the church. But beyond that, it is a graceful Word, full of truth. For the nature of the church is finally not a doctrine* but a life lived in, from, and by the Word of God.* It is the life of a people who are in relationship with each other because they share a relationship with Jesus Christ which defines who they are—children of God and sisters and brothers in Christ.

Robert Bellah et al., *Habits of the Heart* (1985); T. George, ed., *John Calvin and the Church* (1990); H. Küng, *The Church* (1967); J. T. McNeill, *The History and Character of Calvinism* (1954); J. Moltmann, *The Church in the Power of the Spirit* (1977); H. R. Niebuhr et al., *The Purpose of the Church and Its Ministry* (1956); L. Vischer, ed., *Reformed Witness Today* (1982).

JACK L. STOTTS

Church of Scotland Act

The United Kingdom Parliament's settlement of the present relationship between the national Church of Scotland and the state (1921). It decreed the lawfulness of the "Articles Declaratory of the Constitution of the Church of Scotland in Matters Spiritual" (1926). The whole settlement (with an Act regulating finance and property [1925]) was to facilitate the union of the Church of Scotland and United Free Church (1929) by unambiguously securing the national church's independence from state control and its full internal autonomy.

J. T. Cox, ed., *Practice and Procedure in the Church of Scotland*, 6th ed., ed. D. F. M. MacDonald (1976); F. Lyall, *Of Presbyters and Kings* (1980).

DAVID F. WRIGHT

Clarendon Code

A series of acts of the English Parliament (1661–66) during the Restoration following Oliver Cromwell's* Protectorate. The Clarendon Code was named after the lord chancellor, first Earl of Clarendon, who was the agent of royal ecclesiastical policy during the Restoration. It included the Corporation Act (1661), the Act of Uniformity (1662), the Conventicle Act (1664), and the Five Mile Act (1665). These sought to bring about loyalty to the king, conformity to Anglicanism, and suppression of Presbyterian* Puritanism.*

H. Gee and W. J. Hardy, *Documents Illustrative of English Church History* (1921); I. M. Green, *The Re-establishment of the Church of England 1660–1663* (1978).

JOHN H. PRIMUS

Clark, Gordon H. (1902–1985)

For over fifty years, Clark did not cease from teaching or writing, justly earning his reputation as a leading Christian philosopher. His teaching at the University of Pennsylvania, at Wheaton College, at Butler University, and in retirement at Covenant College and Sangre de Cristo Seminary exemplified the Socratic method. His writings were in a similar vein. Through his numerous assessments of the thinking of other philosophers their systems of truth, methods of ethics, and scientific theorizing were seen as containing basic contradictions and, even worse, as manifesting an unwillingness to acknowledge their philosophical starting points.

Clark's philosophical aim, in contrast to the approaches he thought deliberately obscured epistemological or metaphysical assumptions, was to show clearly the platform on which philosophical and theological structures are to be erected. His task, like that of Ludwig Wittgenstein, was to "unpack" theological and philosophical statements. But unlike the thinking of other modern ordinary language philosophers, his analysis led to the necessity of assuming the authority and sufficiency of Christianity's biblical revelation.* Its statements were to be taken as a comprehensive a priori from which a consistent and substantial view of the world and life in it could be deduced.

In addition to establishing this apologetical starting point, Clark took very seriously, in good Reformed fashion, the further task of explicating the unity and practicability of the Bible's contents. The books that he wrote in his later years showed the same rigorous skills characteristic of his philosophical output, but now the titles were more theological: *The Trinity* (1985); *The Atonement* (1987); *Biblical Predestination* (1968); *What Do Presbyterians Believe?* (1956); and *Karl Barth's Theological Method* (1963). One work of which he was particularly fond was his *The Johannine Logos* (1972). In it he showed the foundational character of epistemology and expressed his conviction that true knowledge of God* is possible. Interspersed among Clark's theological works were his commentaries covering most of the NT epistles. These are the capstone of Clark's calling and underline his captivity to Christ and the "unsurpassable" Scriptures. The Sangre de Cristo Seminary in Westcliffe, Colorado, and the Trinity Foundation in Jefferson, Maryland, are dedicated to teaching and publishing Clark's views. His papers are in the archives of the Presbyterian Church in America at Covenant Seminary, St. Louis.

THOMAS M. GREGORY

Cocceius, Johannes (1603–1669)

A foremost seventeenth-century biblical interpreter, Johann Koch (Lat. Cocceius) is known for federal* or covenant* theology. German by birth, he taught at Bremen, Franeker, and Leiden, where he was professor of theology (1650–69).

Cocceius's writings include commentaries; works on biblical theology, including *Doctrine of the Covenant and Testament of God (Summa doctrinae de foedere et testamento Dei* [1648]); and volumes on philology, dogmatics, and ethics. He led in revitalizing theology in the Reformed churches.

Cocceius sought to formulate a biblical dogmatics closer to faith than to theological speculation. He employed "covenant," rather than the "eternal decrees,"* to speak of the relation of God* to humanity,* interpreting God's dealings with creation* dynamically. Cocceius defined the covenant as "nothing other than a divine declaration of the method of perceiving the love of God and of obtaining union and communion with Him" (*Doctrine of the Covenant*, 1.5). Though initiated by God, as a mutual covenant, the covenant demanded a human response. As with earlier developments, Cocceius distinguished a covenant of works and a covenant of grace.* When the former was violated by disobedience an alternative way of salvation* was established in the covenant of grace which Cocceius divided into different periods. The climax of the series of covenants in a future consummation gave his system a strong eschatological character. Cocceius influenced the later significant theologians Franz Burmann (1628–79) and Hermann Witsius (1636–1708).

J. H. Cocceius (son), ed., *Works*, 8 vols. (1673–75); Barth, *CD* IV/1, 54ff.; G. Schrenk, *Gottesreich und Bund im älteren Protestantismus* (1923; repr. 1967).

WILLIAM KLEMPA

Coffin, Henry Sloane (1877–1954)

Liberal Presbyterian minister and educator. Coffin was raised in New York City and educated at Yale, New College* (Edinburgh), Marburg, and Union Seminary (N.Y.). Ordained in the Presbyterian Church in the U.S.A. (1900), he served in the Bronx (1900–1905) and at Madison Avenue Presbyterian Church (1905–26). He became a renowned preacher and college speaker, taught part-time at Union, and published numerous books.

A prominent liberal or modernist and advocate of the social gospel,* Coffin led the liberal forces during the fundamentalist/modernist controversy* in the Presbyterian Church (1920s). A key proponent of the Auburn Affirmation,* he believed the church had to accommodate its doctrine to the prevailing ideas of the age or perish for lack of relevance. He therefore fought doggedly against conservative efforts to maintain traditional theological guidelines in the church. He helped convince the church to broaden its doctrinal boundaries in order to preserve its unified mission to the world.

Coffin was president of Union Seminary (1926–45) and attracted Reinhold Niebuhr* and Paul Tillich to Union's faculty. A devout advocate of Christian unity, he worked unsuccessfully to unite northern and southern Presbyterian churches while he was Moderator of the General Assembly* (1943–44). Though Coffin's modernism was chastened with the advent of neo-orthodoxy* (1930s–40s), he never explicitly abandoned his liberal convictions.

B. J. Longfield, *The Presbyterian Controversy: Fundamentalists, Modernists, and Moderates* (1991); M. P. Noyes, *Henry Sloane Coffin* (1964).

BRADLEY J. LONGFIELD

Common Order, Book of

The order of worship* adopted during the Reformation in Scotland, authorized by the General Assembly* (1562). Its first part is John Knox's* adaptation (1556) of Calvin's* "Forme des Prières," used by the English-speaking congregation of Marian exiles* in Geneva. To this was added a metrical version of the psalms and Calvin's Catechism. Knox's Genevan order of worship represented the rejection by the more Reformed wing of British Protestantism of the second Edwardian *BCP* (1552), seen as still containing unacceptable nonbiblical and wrong elements of Roman Catholic ritual. In distinction from the Edwardian Prayer Book, *Book of Common Order* prayers were not unalterable prescribed words but were meant as a guide or directory. Because of the alliance with English Presbyterians and participation in the Westminster Assembly,* the Church of Scotland officially replaced the *Book of Common Order* with the Westminster Directory for Public Worship (1645). The name *Book of Common Order* (or simply *Book of Order*) has more recently been revived as the title of books of discipline and worship in Scotland and churches tracing their descent from Scottish Presbyterianism.

D. Laing, ed., *The Works of John Knox* (1964; repr. 1966), vols. 4, 6; W. D. Maxwell, *The Liturgical Portions of the Genevan Service Book . . . 1556–1569* (1931; repr. 1965).

JOHN E. WILSON

Common Prayer, Book of

The first *BCP* appeared in 1549, during Edward VI's reign. Largely the work of Thomas Cranmer,* it combined a translation of the Latin Sarum Rite and continental Reformation liturgies, especially of Lutheran origin. In 1552 the Second Prayer Book of Edward VI appeared. In this revision, Reformed elements, especially the views of Huldrych Zwingli,* were much more dominant. Slightly revised, this version was adopted (1662) as the standard version for the Church of England.

After the Revolution, the Episcopal Church in the United States adopted a version influenced by the usage of the Scottish Episcopal Church (1790). Both in Great Britain and in the United States there have been several revisions, most recently the American version (1979).

It would be impossible, however, to estimate the *BCP*'s influence on the life of English-speaking Reformed and Presbyterian churches. Many of its phrases and some of its prayers have become part of the worship traditions of these churches. Much of this can be ascribed to Cranmer's literary genius in producing a book for genuine *common prayer*. Despite its many revisions, the majority of his work has remained untouched except for eliminating a few obscure words and some horizontal sexist language.

HOWARD G. HAGEMAN

Common Sense Philosophy

Also called common sense realism, it was an intellectual product of the Scottish Enlightenment associated with Thomas Reid* and Dugald Stewart and also with George Campbell and James Beattie. It had major influence in the United States, both in the academic culture of the late eighteenth and nineteenth centuries and in several theological traditions.

Reid published *An Inquiry Into the Human Mind on the Principles of Common Sense* (1764) and expanded its ideas into later volumes. Influenced by Francis Bacon and John Locke, Reid wished to combat the influence of David Hume and the dangerously speculative philosophical tendencies he believed Hume had influenced. Reid's epistemology was grounded in the conviction that perception is always of existing objects, that knowledge is not restricted to perceptions in the mind alone. More important for its religious use, Reid's philosophy adhered to a rigorous dualism of material and spiritual being.

Common sense philosophy emerged in the American colonies when John Witherspoon,* a product of the evangelical movement in Scotland, became president of Princeton College (College of New Jersey) in 1768. Witherspoon discovered the ideas of George Berkeley in fashion at the college and worked to discredit them through a philosophy of realism. He laid the foundations for a long tradition of academic philosophy in the United States; by the early nineteenth century, works in the common sense genre were in wide use in American colleges. Stewart's *Elements of the Philosophy of the Human Mind* (3 vols.; 1792–1827) was a popular text.

Within the Reformed tradition, common sense realism was particularly important at Princeton Seminary (1812), the major citadel of "orthodox" Presbyterianism* in the United States. The Scottish influence was evident in Charles Hodge,* Samuel Miller,* and Archibald Alexander.* The Princeton Theology* opposed metaphysical influences associated with certain varieties of German philosophy and American transcendentalism and sought to temper the excesses of revivalism* by establishing faith* on a strong intellectual base. Building on the empirical data of consciousness, and deriving moral and spiritual laws from this source, the inductive method of the Scots, in the tradition of Bacon, helped accommodate Reformed thinking to a new spirit of science* and a new challenge from scientific methodology.

Common sense philosophy was remarkably adaptable. It fortified conservative theology, as at Princeton, but was widely implemented in more liberal movements. It influenced the New Haven Theology* of N. W. Taylor* and the Unitarianism* of William Ellery Channing. Channing was introduced to Scottish philosophy at Harvard and used Reid's dualism to defend a rational belief in the supernatural against rival philosophies of materialism. Common sense philosophy was a kind of Protestant scholasticism that gave something of a common base to Reformed and non-Reformed religious intellectual traditions.

T. D. Bozeman, *Protestants in an Age of Science: The Baconian Ideal and Antebellum American Religious Thought* (1977); D. Meyer, *The Instructed Conscience* (1973); Rogers and McKim, *AIB*; D. Sloan, *The Scottish Enlightenment and the American College Ideal* (1971).

J. DAVID HOEVELER, JR.

Common Sense Realism *see* **Common Sense Philosophy**

Common Worship, Book of

The first officially prepared set of prayers and services in American Presbyterianism (1906). The *BCW* was extensively revised (1932; 1946). The PC(USA) publishes it as well as *The Worshipbook* (1970) and *The Service for the Lord's Day* (1984). When the first General Assembly* revised the Westminster Directory for Worship (1788), antiliturgical elements successfully opposed adding pattern prayers. For over a century the only official worship guidance was this relatively "nondirective" Directory. Experimentation in worship, by pastors "formal" and "evangelistic," was frequent, and controversies over what practices were and were not "Presbyterian" often ensued. Among influences that finally moved the church to provide more specific worship materials were its rediscovery of a pre-Puritan Reformed liturgical heritage, "churchly" developments in Scotland, surveys regarding worship practices, responsive services in Sunday schools, and the appearance and use of privately prepared worship manuals. Two key advocates of improved worship became editors of the 1906 book: pastor and author Henry van Dyke* and the denomination's hymnal compiler, Louis Benson.*

Though influential, the book did not displace a long-cherished pattern of local freedom in worship. Its title page said, "For Voluntary Use." Van Dyke composed fine materials, and all three editions drew from a variety of sources—ancient Catholic, more recent ecumenical, but primarily Reformed and Anglican liturgies.

J. Melton, *AP* 66 (1988): 299–303; *Presbyterian Worship in America* (1967); and *Reformed Liturgy and Music* 21 (1987): 80–88.

JULIUS MELTON

Communion of Saints

The Apostles' Creed's *sanctorum communio* can have seven grammatical translations. Three major theological interpretations have emerged. The sacramental, prominent in the Middle Ages, linked the believer to salvation through "participation in holy things"—the sacraments. Second, the phrase can mean the church here and now, the "union of saints" in fellowship and mutual love. A further Reformed emphasis, however, is the whole company of God's people—past, present, and future. This is a comprehensive picture of "church," grounded in God's election (*Inst.* 4.1.3).

DONALD K. MCKIM

Confession of 1967

Part of the *Book of Confessions* in the *Constitution* of the PC(USA), representing the first major revision of formally approved doctrine in American Presbyterianism.* The Confession of 1967 (C-67) is founded on the biblical doctrine of reconciliation (2 Cor. 5:18ff.), a fundamental motif comparable to, and almost identical with, the doctrine of justification* at the time of the Reformation. Classical Trinitarian and christological* doctrines are "recognized and reaffirmed" but not restated—as they appear in other parts of the *BC* as described in the Preface of C-67.

Part I, "God's Work of Reconciliation," begins with the ministry as well as the death and resurrection* of Jesus Christ and affirms the universality of Christ as savior and judge. This point of departure leads to a doctrine of universal sin, from which Christ is the sole redeemer, and thence to creation* as a work of the same universal and sovereign love of God* known in Christ. Next, "The Communion of the Holy Spirit" describes the "new life" of the Christian, which results when Christ's cross becomes "personal crisis and present hope." It is always a life in community (the church*), still in conflict with sin, but finding its direction and pattern in the life of Jesus, and trusting that "God's purpose rather than man's schemes will finally prevail." Also under the teaching on the Spirit is a section on the Bible, which is "received and obeyed" as the Spirit's "authoritative witness" to "the one sufficient revelation of God" in "Jesus Christ, the Word of God incarnate." This founding of authority* in the Word revealed in Christ, rather than on the inspiration of a sacred text, was an intentional development beyond the WCF* (1647). C-67 then presents the NT as the confessional access to the OT and requires "literary and historical understanding" of the "views of life, history, and the cosmos," found in various documents that make up Scripture.* The persistence of the Word through "diverse cultural situations" gives confidence that God "will continue to speak through the Scriptures in a changing world and in every form of human culture."

Part II, "The Ministry of Reconciliation," deals first with the "direction" of the church's mission and the "forms and order" which take shape from the message preached and the "pattern" of the life, death, resurrection, and promised coming of Jesus Christ, carried forward in different times and places. C-67 is compressed, but it is quite elaborate about characteristics and norms of the church as an institution.

"Revelation and Religion" deals with the mission encounter with world religions,* confessing that the gospel judges also the "Christian religion" but is to be carried to the whole human race. The mission of "Reconciliation in Society" offers four paradigms that have to do with racial injustice, war,* poverty, and sexual anarchy, in which the church "seeks to discern the will of God and learn how to obey." Here church responsibility toward social evil in addition to that of private Christians represents a development beyond other documents in the *BC*. This section, together with that of Scripture, was the focus of thorough study and considerable controversy in the adoption process. "The Equipment of the Church" for its mission is presented under the topics "Preaching and Teaching," "Praise and Prayer," "Baptism," and the "Lord's Supper."

Part III, "The Fulfillment of Reconciliation," is a brief eschatology* of the kingdom,* which images Christian hope* as "the triumph of God over all that resists his will and disrupts his creation." The concluding words are the ascription of praise from Eph. 3:20.

E. A. Dowey, Jr., *A Commentary on the Confession of 1967 and an Introduction to "The Book of Confessions"* (1968); and "Reconciliation and Liberation—The Confession of 1967," issue of *JPH* 61, no. 1 (1983).

EDWARD A. DOWEY, JR.

Confessions of Faith *see* Creeds and Confessions

Confirmation/Admission to the Lord's Supper

John Calvin* regarded confirmation as one of the five "bastard Sacraments" of the Roman Church. It has no institution in the Word of God,* and it is "a noted insult to baptism." Martin Luther* also regarded confirmation as "a human invention" and considered it "preposterous to think confirmation could add something to baptism that baptism lacked." Calvin, nevertheless, believed it was an ancient custom that those baptized as infants should, in adolescence, be examined in the catechism* and blessed. "This laying on of hands, which is done simply by way of benediction, I commend, and would like to see restored to its pure use in the present day" (see *Inst.* 4.19.4–13). He was decisively rejecting any view that the laying on of hands had a sacramental quality or conferred a special grace.*

In the Western church, confirmation, as distinct from Baptism,* arose when one of the ceremonies by which Baptism had been elaborated came to be reserved to the bishop and administered at a later date. Since anointing or the laying on of hands (and there is always dubiety as to what the "matter" of confirmation is) was intended to symbolize and underline the work of the Holy Spirit* in Baptism, its separation from Baptism could not detract from the fullness of that rite, and there have been few, until recent times, who would have argued that it did.

Once the rite of confirmation had been separated from Baptism, the problem was to find a meaning for it. The medieval view that confirmation confers an increase of grace can be traced back to the fifth century and was given definition by Thomas Aquinas in the context of his view of sacraments* as conferring special graces for the different stages and states of life.

This was rejected by all the Reformers, but the proposal of Erasmus,* Bucer,* and Calvin to link the service in some way with catechizing and profession of faith* came to be accepted. In the Church of Scotland, young people were catechized by the kirk session* and admitted to Communion, and this was seen as a disciplinary rather than a ritual matter. In the Church of England, confirmation was reserved to the bishop and the medieval view prevailed, until, beginning in the late nineteenth century, a radically new view was propounded that separated the gift of the Holy Spirit from Baptism and attached it solely to confirmation: "In baptism, he is the agent, in confirmation the gift." This view, associated with the names of F. W. Puller, A. J. Mason, L. S. Thornton, and Gregory Dix, has had support among Anglo-Catholics but not in official statements. The view was ably countered by G. W. H. Lampe (*Seal of the Spirit* [1951]).

In other Reformed churches, notably the Church of Scotland, admission to the Lord's Table began to take place at public worship,* and in the orders of service that were provided the word "confirmation" began to be used. The most widely influential of these was in the *Book of Common Order* (1940). The Scoto-Catholics who produced that book were vague enough about the meaning of "confirmation" but tended toward the medieval view rather than the view of Mason and Dix—as did the Church of Scotland's Panel on Doctrine in a 1967 report. The result is a vague idea of confirmation as conferring something by the hands of the minister. Such a mechanical, clerically operated view of grace is strangely out of place in a Reformed church. The recovery of a Reformed understanding of God's prevenient grace might yield a more robust theology of Baptism and remove the need for a medieval theology of confirmation.

The place of confirmation has become even more problematic with the increasing tendency of Reformed churches to welcome children to the Lord's Table at an age much younger than admission (or confirmation) has traditionally been granted.

J. D. C. Fisher, *Confirmation Then and Now* (1978).

JAMES A. WHYTE

Congregationalism, American

Congregationalism is that form of church polity* which affirms Christ as the sole head of the local church.* There is no ecclesiastical authority, such as the presbytery or bishop, over the local congregation. However, the majority of early Congregationalists in England and America, as seen in the writings of William Bradshaw and John Robinson,* were not Separatists but stressed the mutual recognition of churches; and in the nineteenth and twentieth centuries, Congregationalists have been persistent advocates of cooperation and ecumenism.*

Though the first Congregationalists were theological heirs of John Calvin,* Theodore Beza,* and Heinrich Bullinger,* their emphasis on the autonomy of the congregation distinguished them from Reformed groups in Europe and England which were presbyterian in governance. Henry Jacob (1563–1624) is usually considered the founder of Congregationalism, but congregationalist tendencies are seen as early as 1562 in Jean Morély, a French émigré in Geneva.

Congregationalism spread to America through the founders of Plymouth Plantation (1620) and Massachusetts Bay Company (1630). It became the dominant religious force in New England and the established religion of Massachusetts, New Hampshire, and Connecticut.

Colleges such as Harvard and Yale were established to train ministers, and orthodox Reformed thought was perpetuated through the theological manuals of William Ames* and Johannes Wollebius,* which were widely used into the late 1700s. Traditional themes of Reformed theology were the foci of both conservative theologians, such as Jonathan Edwards* (1700s), and liberal thinkers, like Horace Bushnell* (1800s).

However, theological differences over revivalism* in the first and second "Awakenings," a concern over maintaining its establishment privileges, and eagerness to respond to missionary demands of the expanding western frontier—as well as its emphasis on local autonomy—prevented Congregationalism from developing any theological unity. No statement of faith was issued from 1648 to 1865, and modern Congregationalists insist that such statements are a "witness to faith," not a "test of faith."

Following the demise of the "New England Way," Congregationalism has seen theology as personal, but on many occasions this private faith could be marshaled to support social reform. From the antislavery drive (mid–1800s) and the social gospel movement* of the late nineteenth and early twentieth centuries, to contemporary civil rights protests, Congregationalists have been leaders in social concerns.

In the twentieth century, congregationalism continues in the United Church of Christ, formed by the 1957 merger of the Congregational Christian Churches and the Evangelical and Reformed Church. Because of disputes over polity and doctrine, several hundred congregational churches did not join the United Church of Christ. Some formed the Conservative Congregational Christian Conference, and others the National Association of Congregational Christian Churches.

The theology of American Congregationalism since the Civil War is Reformed in tradition, but not by intention. Diversity is the only constant. But if Congregationalism has not perpetuated an undivided theological tradition, it can be said its concern about local autonomy is a characteristic of all American churches.

L. Gunneman, *The Shaping of the United Church of Christ* (1977); D. Horton, *Congregationalism* (1952); P. Miller, *Errand Into the Wilderness* (1956); R. S. Paul, *Freedom with Order* (1987).

DAVID FOXGROVER

Congregationalism, British

The harbingers of congregationalism (a polity practiced by Baptists and others as well as by Congregationalists themselves) were such Separatists as Richard Fitz and Robert Browne* (c. 1550–c. 1633) and martyrs Henry Barrow (c. 1550–93), John Greenwood (d. 1593), and John Penry (1563–93). These persons, when national unity was deemed to necessitate religious uniformity, opposed church establishments in favor of the conviction that the church comprises gathered, regenerate saints. During the reign of James I (1603–25) many Separatists fled to Holland for safety. In 1620 some of the exiles went, with others from England, as pilgrims to the New World.

Meanwhile, despite difficulties, Separatist groups were multiplying in England. Prominent was the church gathered under Henry Jacob at Southwark (1616), and by 1631 there were eleven such churches in London. The commitment of Charles I (1625–49) to the notion of the divine right of kings, with his wife's Roman Catholicism and the vindictive activities of Archbishop Laud, led to the Civil War* (1642–51). The king was beheaded, and the Commonwealth and Oliver Cromwell's* Protectorate (1653) followed. The Savoy Declaration of Faith and Order* (1658) was published, and John Owen* (1616–83) became prominent.

With the Restoration of the monarchy (1660), a harsh drive for episcopalian uniformity was expressed in the Clarendon Code*—a series of punitive acts, including the Act of Uniformity* (1662), the Conventicle Act (1664), and the Five Mile Act (1665). The first brought the period of the Great Ejectment to a head, with some two thousand clergymen leaving their livings rather than give their "unfeigned assent and consent" to the Church of England's *Book of Common Prayer** (1660–62). The second was directed against gathered churches, and the third was designed to keep ejected ministers away from their former flocks. Eventually the Toleration Act (1689) gave freedom of worship to orthodox Dissenters (though not to Roman Catholics). Now legalized, Dissenters were kept socially subservient for the next two centuries. Nevertheless they erected meetinghouses, opened Dissenting Academies,* and entered into a period of dull consolidation, alleviated by the hymns of Isaac Watts* and Philip Doddridge.*

Though some Congregationalists were suspicious of evangelical "enthusiasm," the revival of the second half of the eighteenth century (Le Réveil*)—especially its Calvinistic wing through the Countess of Huntingdon* (1707–91) and George Whitefield* (1714–70)—provided impetus to mission at home and abroad. The London Missionary Society* (founded 1795; LMS) was largely supported by Congregationalists who began to establish home mission societies and county unions of churches. The Congregational Union of England and Wales was formed (1831), and Britons were prominent in the International Congregational Council from its inception (1891).

Through the nineteenth century, English Congregationalists became increasingly influenced by biblical higher criticism and evolutionary thought. R. J. Campbell (1867–1956) was among the more extreme exponents of the "New Theology," until he recanted and ended in Anglican orders. He was resolutely opposed by the erstwhile liberal theologian P. T. Forsyth.*

Following World War II, the so-called "Genevan" group, including Nathaniel Micklem and John Whale, urged recovery of Reformed theology. Afterward, younger leaders, including W. John F. Huxtable, successfully promoted a national covenant—hence the Congregational Church in England and Wales (1966; CCEW), whose Declaration of Faith (1967) is one of the most impressive twentieth-century confessional documents.

The Fellowship of Evangelical Congregational Churches (1966) comprises those who declined to enter the national covenant; and the Congregational Federation (1972) was constituted by others who on ecclesiological grounds did not enter the United Reformed Church—the union (1972) of the majority of the churches of the CCEW with the Presbyterian Church of England, which union was joined by the majority of the British Churches of Christ (1981).

The roots of Congregationalism in Wales are Puritan.* In November 1639 a church "according to the New England pattern" was formed at Llanvaches, with Henry Jessey of "old" England participating. The congregation was dispersed during the Civil War, Wales being strongly Royalist, and its ideals spread. The Welsh story roughly parallels the English during the Commonwealth and pre- and post-Toleration periods. From 1815 to 1850 Welsh Independents were especially influential in nurturing the minds and morals of the nation—especially through the adult Sunday schools. Thereafter the elevation of the "prince of the pulpit" above pastoral concerns, and liberal theology, took their toll. The Union of Welsh Independents was formed (1876). It yielded many supporters to the Welsh Language Society, and two of the first three presidents of the Welsh Nationalist Party were Independents. English county unions were formed in South Wales (from 1867), and the North Wales English Union was established (1876). The majority of English-speaking Welsh Congregationalists entered the United Reformed Church (1972).

Irish Congregationalism derives from Cromwellian chaplains and soldiers, though fresh impetus came from the evangelistic work of the Scottish Haldane movement (see below). The Congregational Union of Ireland was formed (1829). Recently it has become almost entirely conservative in theology and has withdrawn from the Council for World Mission (successor to the LMS) and the WCC.*

Though Congregationalism was quite strong in some parts of Scotland during the Cromwellian period and the influence of Glasite voluntarism and small groups of Old Scots Independents and Bereans may not be discounted, the vital roots of Scottish Congregationalism are in the revival associated with Robert Haldane (1764–1842) and James Haldane (1768–1851), defectors from the Church of Scotland who became Baptists (1808). Unlike early Separatists and Independents, the Scots were motivated not ecclesiologically but evangelically. They "came by" their congregational polity, shaped for them by Greville Ewing (1767–1841). The Scottish Congregational Union (1812) was united with the Evangelical Union (1843) in 1896.

H. A. Escott, *History of Scottish Congregationalism* (1960); J. M. Henry, "An Assessment of the Social, Religious and Political Aspects of Congregationalism in Ireland in the Nineteenth Century" (diss., Queen's University of Belfast, 1965); R. T. Jones, *Congregationalism in England, 1662–1962* (1962); and *Hanes Annibynwyr Cymru* (1966); A. P. F. Sell, *Saints: Visible, Orderly and Catholic. The Congregational Idea of the Church* (1986).

ALAN P. F. SELL

Conscience

Paul's allusions to conscience (Rom. 2:15; 1 Cor. 4:4) assured this topic a place in Reformed theology, where the condemning conscience ("the worm of conscience") has been more prominent than the guiding conscience.

John Calvin* defined conscience as a "sense of the divine judgment" and a "medium between God and man" which "does not allow a person to suppress what he knows" (*Inst.* 3.19.15). However, the Reformers also stressed that "peace of conscience," or "good conscience," is possible through—but only through—faith* in God's free redemption in Christ.

Romans 2:15 and 1 Cor. 4:4 display a tension always present in Reformed treatments. "Written on their hearts" (Rom. 2:15) could mean that conscience is a faculty of the soul that pronounces God's verdict on the morality of an act or decision. But when Paul says (1 Cor. 4:4) he is not acquitted even though his conscience is clear, he suggests that conscience is relative to God's judgment. For Calvin, conscience mediates and can even anticipate God's judgment but cannot be separated from God's judgment.

After Calvin, conscience continued to be important in Reformed thought, especially in William Ames's* "cases of conscience" and with others who dealt with "assurance of salvation"* as well as with conscience providing guidance in making moral decisions. The emphasis on the practical syllogism and conscience as an act of practical reason are reminiscent of medieval discussions. Some might argue that these theologians returned to conscience as linked to the will or reason rather than seeing it as a description of the whole person before God.* However, the works of Francis Turretin* show that this latter idea was still present among Reformed thinkers.

Later Reformed theologians, such as Friedrich Schleiermacher,* continue to treat the concept. For Schleiermacher, conscience "expresses the fact that all . . . activity arising from our God-consciousness . . . confront[s] us as moral demands" (*CF*). Conscience is important because it is directly related to the central concept of the feeling of dependence.

Among twentieth-century Reformed theologians, conscience has not been a significant topic. This is clearly due to Freud's criticisms. For him, the guilty conscience was the result of parental and societal injunctions and the price paid for civilization. However, Reinhold Niebuhr* defined conscience as the "sense of being . . . judged" by God, and he frequently criticized the "easy conscience" of contemporary persons.

Paul Lehmann* attempted to reclaim conscience as an important ethical concept by redefining conscience in dependence on Reformation insights, while taking account of the criticisms presented by modern psychology. For him, conscience "forges the link between what God is doing in the world and man's free obedience to that activity" (*Ethics in a Christian Context,* p. 350).

Studies of the sociological and psychological stages of moral development by psychologists critical of Freud may foster a renewed interest in conscience among Reformed theologians.

W. Ames, *De conscientia* (1622; 1630; ET *Conscience with the Power and Cases Thereof* [1639]); P. L. Lehmann, *Ethics in a Christian Context* (1963); Reinhold Niebuhr, *The Nature and Destiny of Man*, 2 vols. (1941–43).

DAVID FOXGROVER

Consensus of Geneva

John Calvin* composed this treatise to defend his predestination* teachings, and it was subscribed to by the Genevan pastors (1552). The work responded to anti-predestinarian critiques by Roman Catholic Albertus Pighius (1542) and the temporary Protestant, onetime colleague of Calvin who became his fierce enemy, Jerome Bolsec,* as well as by one George of Sicily. Pighius and George advocated a semi-Pelagian view of the freedom of the human will, and Bolsec held that Calvin's view of divine sovereignty and human inability made God the author of sin* and encouraged immorality.

Reminiscent of Romans 9–11, Calvin replied that there is no moral standard of judgment outside and above the character and will of God* by which humans can negatively assess God's choices. God's sovereign election of sinners is the most solid foundation for believers' assurance, and divine "passing by" the lost is in accord with God's righteousness, which requires God to punish sin,* not obligating God to save anyone.

Though Calvin hoped for support from pastors and civil authorities of other Swiss cities, the strident and sometimes bitter polemical tone of the Consensus prevented its acceptance beyond Geneva. Other Protestants, such as Heinrich Bullinger* and Philipp Melanchthon, desired a more moderate and irenic predestination statement.

CO 8:249–366; H. A. Niemeyer, *Collectio Confessionum* (1840), 218–310; J. K. S. Reid, ed., *Concerning the Eternal Predestination of God* (1961); Schaff, *Creeds*, vol. 1.

DOUGLAS F. KELLY

Consensus Tigurinus

("Agreement of Zurich.") A statement of faith composed principally by John Calvin* and Heinrich Bullinger* to provide concord on eucharistic theology and practice between the French-speaking and German-speaking Swiss Reformed churches. The need arose from intense disputes over the Eucharist between Zwinglians and Lutherans. In international politics, the militant Roman Catholic maneuvers against the Reformers demanded a united Swiss Protestant response. Calvin and William Farel* traveled to Zurich (May 1549) to sign the accord with Bullinger and other city ministers. The document reflected several years of extensive negotiations between Calvin and Bullinger.

The Consensus (1551) had twenty-six articles. It was eventually adopted by the other Swiss Reformed churches, providing an important step toward the Second Helvetic Confession* (1566). It states that Christ truly "exhibits" himself to believers in the Lord's Supper* which is a mark or badge of the Christian life. However, apart from faith,* the sacraments* are nothing but "empty masks." Sacramental efficacy is thus related to the doctrine of predestination*: "God does not exert his power indiscriminately in all who receive the sacraments, but only in the elect." A materialist view of the Eucharist is rejected by emphasizing spiritual communion with Christ and the lifting of the believer's heart to heaven (*sursum corda*) by the power of the Holy Spirit.

The Consensus brought Swiss Reformed churches closer, but it occasioned still another eucharistic controversy as Calvin was forced to defend it against renewed assaults from the Lutherans. The meaning of the Consensus has been debated by subsequent Reformed theologians such as Charles Hodge* and John Williamson Nevin.*

U. Gäbler, "Das Zustandekommen des Consensus Tigurinus im Jahre 1549," *Theologische Literaturzeitung* 104, no. 5 (1979): 321-32; T. George, "John Calvin and the Agreement of Zurich" in *John Calvin and the Church*, ed. T. George (1990); P. Rorem, *Calvin and Bullinger on the Lord's Supper* (1989); O. Strasser, "Der Consensus Tigurinus," *Zwingliana* 9, no. 1 (1949): 1–16.

TIMOTHY GEORGE

Conversion

The experience of God's forgiveness* and love and the reorientation of an individual's life away from sin* to grace* and faith.* Though the Hebrew and Greek Scripture texts rarely use the word for "conversion," the Bible is filled with references embodying the root meaning—to turn or to turn around. All understandings of conversion involve three dimensions: the act of repentance, the experience of grace, and a new life of discipleship.

The history of Reformed theology has been marked by sharp and bitter debates about the nature of conversion. While John Calvin* conceded that knowledge of God* and knowledge of self were so intertwined that they could not be separated, scholastic Calvinism increasingly insisted on a more rigid view of God's sovereignty and humanity's inability to do anything to achieve salvation.* This debate over human will and free will* lay at the heart of the Arminian* controversy and continued to shape Reformed attitudes toward evangelicalism and revivalism* in the eighteenth, nineteenth, and twentieth centuries.

The conversion debate decisively molded New England Puritanism* and its doctrine of the church.* At first, membership was restricted only to persons who could recount conversion experiences; later, the Half-Way Covenant* was introduced to extend baptism* to children of unregenerate parents. Central was the dispute over whether the church should include only persons who have been converted or whether its fellowship should extend to persons who have not yet had a definable and describable grace experience.

At the heart of the broad movement of Protestant evangelicalism, conversion was understood as a particular event in one's life. Though many, such as Charles G. Finney* and Alexander Campbell, rebelled against scholastic Calvinism's determinism and predestination emphasis, others, such as Horace Bushnell,* questioned the legitimacy of defining grace in terms of solitary events. He insisted that children should grow up never knowing themselves to be anything other than Christians.

Whether it is predestined by God or is an act of individual submission, whether it is one event or a series of experiences over a lifetime, whether it should be the primary requirement for church membership instead of a confession of faith, conversion remains a mystery of God's grace. In John 3, Jesus does admonish Nicodemus to be "born anew" or "born again." But when Nicodemus asks how this is possible, Jesus replies, "The wind blows where it chooses, and you hear the sound of it, but you do not know where it comes from or where it goes. So it is with everyone who is born of the Spirit" (John 3:8).

Conversion becomes the sign of a turning away from sin and doubt to a new life of joy and faith through the work of the Holy Spirit.* The Reformed tradition also stresses that this inner regeneration is accompanied by a life of discipleship and service. The link between conversion and witness is one of the distinctive marks of Reformed piety.*

W. E. Conn, ed., *Conversion: Perspectives on Personal and Social Transformation* (1978); B. R. Gaventa, *From Darkness to Light: Aspects of Conversion in the New Testament* (1986); W. James, *The Varieties of Religious Experience* (1902); A. D. Nock, *Conversion* (1933).

JOHN M. MULDER

Cosmology

The study of the arrangement and dynamics of the sun, the moon, planets, comets, and stars. At the time of the Reformation, European schools had been teaching Aristotle's cosmology for three centuries. The earth was at rest, the cosmos was finite, and speculation about what lay beyond its outermost sphere was problematic.

John Calvin* wondered why the earth should be attracted to a bare point at the center of the cosmos and remain perfectly motionless in the midst of the huge revolving spheres around it. These must be signs of the particular providence* of God, he argued. Though he left nothing in writing about the heliocentric theory of Copernicus (1543), Calvin ridiculed the very suggestion that the earth might be moving as a subversive ploy of skeptics like Sebastian Castellio to cast doubt on the truth of biblical faith.

Copernicus restructured Western cosmology by setting the earth in motion, placing the sun at the center, and greatly increasing the distance to the stars, now "fixed" at the circumference of the cosmos. The English Protestant Thomas

Digges (1576) first suggested that an infinite expanse of stars was suited to the infinite power and majesty of their creator. Calvin's commitment to Aristotelian cosmology was easily forgotten!

The dynamics of the moving planets were worked out by Isaac Newton (1687). Though mathematical and predictable, they still required God for their origin and maintenance. Within a century, however, God was no longer needed for either reason. The French agnostic, Pierre Simon Laplace, was largely responsible for convincing the scientific world that a completely mechanical cosmology was feasible.

In the early eighteenth century, Reformed theologians such as Isaac Watts* and Jonathan Edwards* had already accepted the Epicurean notion that the formation of all aspects of the world—inanimate ones, at least—was explicable in purely mechanical terms. A Scots astronomer, James Ferguson, even anticipated Laplace's theory that the formation of the solar system could be explained by the clustering of atoms in accordance with Newton's law of gravitation. Such was the skill of the Creator in giving motions and powers to the atoms in the beginning!

Though belief in creation was not ruled out, particular providence had disappeared from scientific cosmology by the end of the eighteenth century. Thomas Chalmers,* leader of the Free Church of Scotland, was one who questioned the completeness of Laplace's account of things and because of this favored Catastrophist understandings of natural history. Singularities and instabilities have regained prominence in twentieth-century cosmology, but the debacle of nineteenth-century Catastrophism has made most Reformed theologians shy away from the issue.

C. B. Kaiser, "Calvin's Understanding of Aristotelian Natural Philosophy," in *Calviniana*, ed. R. V. Schnucker (1988), 77–92.

CHRISTOPHER B. KAISER

Cotton, John (1585–1652)

The preeminent preacher, theologian, and civic leader in Boston from the time of his arrival there (July 1633). Cotton was born in Derby, England, educated at Trinity College, Oxford, and became Emmanuel College's most outstanding scholar and preacher. His spiritual conversion* began from a sermon by Richard Sibbes, and after three years of agonized soul-searching, Cotton became a convinced Calvinist* and Puritan. He became a vicar in Lincolnshire (1612) but was removed as a nonconformist* (1632), escaping by emigrating to Massachusetts. He soon became Teacher of Boston's First Church (1633).

Cotton supported the Calvinist doctrines of God's eternal unconditional election, limited atonement,* irresistible grace,* and the impossibility of the believer's fall from grace. He believed a conversion experience was necessary evidence of the working of divine grace in the believer and led the effort to make a person's ability to recount this experience a requirement for church membership. His emphasis on the inner experience of the Spirit's work led him to support Anne Hutchinson in the antinomian controversy until her banishment (1637). He was a vigorous proponent of Congregational Church polity and theology in his *The Way of the Churches of Christ in New England* (1645) and *The Way of Congregational Churches Cleared* (1648). His *Spiritual Milk for Babes* (1646) was a children's catechism.

C. Mather, *Magnalia Christi Americana* (1702); A. Young, *Chronicles of the First Planters of the Colony of Massachusetts Bay from 1623 to 1636* (1846).

JAMES L. BREED

Covenant

In Reformed theology, "covenant" usually refers to God's* gracious promise to Abraham and his spiritual descendants that God will be a God and father to them and that they, enabled by God's grace,* will live before God in faith* and loving obedience. It has a richer theological meaning and more frequent usage in the Reformed tradition than in any other.

Though both the expression and that which it denotes lie at the heart of both Testaments, there was no development of the doctrine until the sixteenth century, and that development was confined to Reformed theology. Zwingli* and Bullinger* were the first to emphasize scriptural teachings on the covenant, reacting to Anabaptism in and around Zurich. Thereafter Reformed theologians, including Calvin,* made increasingly frequent mention of God's covenant with humanity.*

In the seventeenth century, a "covenant theology" was developed which received heavy emphasis and sometimes played a dominant role in the system of doctrine* expounded. Thus Johannes Cocceius* wrote *Doctrine of the Covenant and Testament of God* (1648), Hermann Witsius entitled his three volumes on God's relationship to the human race *The Oeconomy of the Covenants* (1685), and the Westminster Standards gave the theology of the covenant prominence in 1646–48 (WCF,* chs. 7, 29, 30, 32.3; WLC, qq. 20; 30–36; 57; 79; 80; 97; 162; 165; 166; 174; 176; WSC, qq. 12; 16; 20; 92; 94). Inasmuch as Puritanism* embraced this covenant, or federal, theology,* it was woven into the fabric of New England's early church life and played an important role in Presbyterian* and Dutch Reformed churches.

Though the etymology is unclear, "covenant" probably comes from the Assyro-Babylonian and Hebrew word meaning "to bind" or "to fetter"; hence, the two covenant parties are bound together by oath. Originally the word was applied to two contracting human partners. When "covenant" came to be used in a religious meaning among the Hebrews, the meaning shifted to a divine bestowal of grace by which God took chosen people into fellowship, telling them that God would be their God and they should live as God's people. In some Reformed theology the covenant was seen as a relationship that God bestowed on humankind as a reflection of a covenantal relationship thought to subsist among the three Persons of the Trinity.*

As this emphasis on God's interaction with humanity in history developed in Reformed circles, attention was shifted away from the theology of the divine decree* and predestination* which was prominent from the time of Calvin's controversy with Jerome Bolsec* to the Synod of Dort* in the next century. A connecting link between the divine decree and God's covenant with humanity was the covenant of redemption which many Reformed theologians defined as the eternal pact between the Father and the Son whereby the Father commissioned the Son to be the Savior and gave him a people. The Son agreed to fulfill all righteousness and give his life for the salvation* of humankind. Thus, before the foundation of the world a covenantal relationship existed in the Godhead as the archetype of that which was to appear later in history. Scriptural support stemmed from John 3:16; 5:20, 22, 36; 10:17, 18; 17:2, 4, 6, 9, 24; Ps. 2:7, 8; Heb. 1:8–13.

Covenant of works. In elaborating the theology of the covenants, some Reformed theologians taught a covenant of works as God's first covenant in history. This consisted of the promise of eternal life and confirmation in righteousness for Adam if he would be obedient throughout a probationary period and death if he were disobedient. As the father of all humankind, Adam was a public person and not acting only for himself. His fall, therefore, affected all who were to come after him, so we are all conceived and born in sin. The problem in the covenant of works is the promise to life, an idea not found in Scripture, though Rom. 10:5 and Gal. 3:12 have been cited as support. Moreover, some feel the covenant of works to be a legitimate inference from that which has been revealed.

Covenant of grace. This covenant, beginning with the call of Abraham (Gen. 12; 13; 15; 17:1–7), lies at the heart of Scripture.* Frequently mentioned in the Psalms (Ps. 89; 105) and the prophets (Jer. 31:31–34), it was given a new form and richer meaning by Jesus Christ (Matt. 26:28; Mark 14:24; Luke 22:20; 1 Cor. 11:25). Appearing often in the epistles (2 Cor. 3:6; Heb. 8–10; 12:24; 13:20), the teaching of the covenant that God established with the people of God and sealed with the blood of Jesus Christ is a major NT theme, just as its fundamental idea was at the center of Israel's religious life. It runs throughout the two Testaments as a golden chain holding them together, with Jesus Christ the connecting link. Thus Paul saw both OT Israel and believers in his day as bound together in Christ. That was God's intention with the call of Abraham; the covenant made with him was eventually to include Gentile nations. In Abraham all families of the earth would be blessed. This promise Paul recalled in Gal. 3:7–9, 14, 27–29.

The continuity of the two covenants, Old and New, is portrayed by Paul through the figure of an olive tree. Some natural (Jewish) branches were broken off; Gentile branches were grafted in. The tree itself, spanning both dispensations, is the continuing community of those who know and serve God (Rom. 11:17–24). Jesus' parable of the wicked husbandmen (Matt. 21:33–46) teaches the same truth, climaxing with Jesus' words to Jewish leaders: "The kingdom of God will be taken away from you and given to a nation producing the fruits of it" (v. 43). That nation, or people (alternative translation), can be none other than the Christian church* which is now God's covenant community. The new covenant, that is, the new form of the old covenant with Abraham, has been established with it.

In Jer. 31:31–34 God promises a new covenant with God's ancient people. In Hebrews 8, that passage is quoted to teach that the covenant promised to Israel has been given to the church. The author clearly understood the Christian church to be the covenant people of God. Jesus had instituted the Lord's Supper* before his crucifixion by saying, "This is my blood of the new covenant which is shed for many for the remission of sins" (Matt. 26:28). Thus the author wrote that "for this cause he is the mediator of a new covenant" (Heb. 9:15; cf. 7:22). So, Paul reminded the Corinthians that Christ had made them "ministers of a new covenant" (2 Cor. 3:6). New Testament writers were aware that the new form of the old covenant had been promised to Israel and claimed that this promise had been fulfilled in the church.

This is the uniform NT teaching. Since Christ has come and established the new form of the covenant, distinctions formerly prevailing in Israel are no longer binding. The old dietary laws became obsolete (Acts 10:28, 34–35). One is not a Jew who is one outwardly; the real Jew is the person whose heart is right with God (Rom. 2:28–29). The "dividing wall of hostility" that once separated Jews and Gentiles is said to have been removed. Gentiles are no longer "alienated from the commonwealth of Israel, and strangers to the covenants of promise, . . . no longer strangers and sojourners, but . . . fellow citizens with the saints and members of the household of God, built upon the foundation of the apostles and prophets, Christ Jesus himself being the cornerstone, in whom the whole structure is joined together and grows into a holy temple in the Lord" (Eph. 2:11–21). The temple is the church which traces its descent from Abraham, the father of all the faithful. Believers in the Lord Jesus Christ are the Israel of this age.

Sinaitic covenant. Within Israel's history before the coming of Christ, God implemented and strengthened the earlier covenant. At Sinai (Ex. 19–24) the covenant assumed a national form with many commandments and prohibitions and with special stress on the law* of God. This was not to lessen the gracious character of the earlier covenant (Gal. 3:17–18) but to train Israel until God would appear in its midst. The Davidic covenant (2 Sam. 7; 1 Chron. 17; Ps. 80) also is no break in the Abrahamic covenant but a high moment in the latter's realization, to come to fruition in David's greater son, the Lord Jesus.

Mediator of the new covenant. When Christ fulfilled the OT promises by his perfectly obedient life, sacrificial death, and resurrection,* he became the mediator of the new covenant, that is, the new and better form of the covenant of grace. Jesus is mediator by virtue of his saving work (Heb. 8:6; 9:15; 12:24) and not only because he is the arbitrator between God and humankind. Because in Jesus salvation is sure, Jesus is called the "surety" or "guarantee" of a better covenant than that which came from Moses (Heb. 7:22). There is a direct relationship between Hebrews 7 and 8 and the institution of the Lord's Supper (Matt. 26:28; Luke 22:20) and the sealing of the Sinaitic form of the covenant (Ex. 24). Moses sacrificed an animal and sprinkled its blood on the altar and the people. Christ must have had that in mind when he said his blood was poured out for his people for the forgiveness of their sins.

This teaching of the unity of the covenant of grace is fundamental to the Reformed understanding of the church. The Christian church is the new covenant form of the people of God, the Israel of this age. It lives as the body of Christ, in communion with its head. It is as much a holy people, separated unto God, as was Israel of old. It is *in* the world but not *of* it. Its present existence is a pilgrimage, its destination eternal life with God.

Practical application. The application of the doctrine of the covenant for life is that Christians, who are members of Christ (1 Cor. 12:12–27; John 15:1–8; Eph. 4:4–16), are not their own but belong to Christ (1 Cor. 6:19–20). They live in union with Christ* and glorify him through the power of his Spirit (Rom. 6; Matt. 5–7; Col. 3:1–17; Rom. 8). The fruit of the Spirit is evident in their lives (Gal. 5:22–25), and they are lights to shine in a dark world so others may see their good works and glorify God (Matt. 5:14–16). In the Reformed tradition, this practical aspect of living for the Lord is known as "calling" or "vocation,"* an idea inherited from Luther* and developed in Calvinism.* As children of the covenant and members of Christ, Christians are to dedicate their lives to Christ as "a chosen race, a royal priesthood, a holy nation, God's own people" (1 Peter 2:9–10).

L. Berkhof, *Reformed Dogmatics* (1941); E. M. Emerson, "Calvin and Covenant Theology," *CH* 25 (1956): 136–44; Heppe, *RD*; E. Kutsch, *Neues Testament—Neuer Bund?* (1978); C. S. McCoy, "Johannes Cocceius: Federal Theologian," *SJT* 16 (1963): 352–70; M. E. Osterhaven, "Calvin on the Covenant," in *Readings in Calvin's Theology*, ed. D. K. McKim (1984); G. Schrenk, *Gottesreich und Bund im älteren Protestantismus* (1923; repr. 1967); H. H. Wolf, *Die Einheit des Bundes* (1958).

M. EUGENE OSTERHAVEN

Covenant, National

The symbol of the movement in seventeenth-century Scottish Presbyterianism known as the Second Reformation. During the reign of King James (VI of Scotland; I of England), modifications were introduced in the Presbyterianism of the Church of Scotland, typified by a moderate episcopacy. Then James's son, Charles I, dedicated to the divine right of kings, deeply committed to the type of Anglicanism being developed by his archbishop of Canterbury, William Laud, and particularly insensitive to the attitudes of his Scottish subjects, unilaterally forced a Book of Canons on the Kirk (1636) and a comprehensively liturgical Prayer Book worship (1637).

These policies aroused the fear and the ire of most Scottish Presbyterians. The Erastian* assumption of royal prerogative over the church denied the Reformed claim of the church's spiritual independence—that while state and church were to be mutually supportive, the former was not to interfere with the "spiritual" or "internal" operations of the latter. Church authority transferred to the bishops denied the Reformed conviction of the parity of the clergy and presence of lay eldership. Additionally, there was the fear that Charles, with his actively Roman Catholic wife, might be leading the Kirk back to the papacy.

Scottish leaders harnessed and directed this dynamic national movement. They prepared a legal bond of association—the National Covenant (1638)—which was a confession of faith and a call to action. It affirmed the Reformed faith in doctrine,* worship,* and discipline* as established by law in the first phase of the Reformation, disregarded the changes recently implemented until discussed in Parliament and General Assembly,* and in common with many movements of national Christianity envisioned the nation as the New Israel and the supreme hope of Christendom. All Scots were to sign the Covenant. It was not simply a personal or a congregational act but a supreme example of a people recognizing and committing themselves to the Lordship of Christ and becoming the godly nation par excellence. This has always been regarded as one of the high-water marks of Scottish Presbyterianism.

When the royal army was defeated by the Covenanting forces, Charles finally succumbed and accepted the Covenant. It continued in force after his execution during the Cromwellian* Interregnum. When Charles II rejected the Covenant at his restoration (1660), the more extreme supporters of the Covenant, the Covenanters,* mounted their opposition, particularly in southwestern Scotland. Although the Revolution Settlement (1688–89) did not acknowledge the Covenant as such, Presbyterianism has ever since been the unquestioned established faith of Scotland.

G. Donaldson, *Scotland, James V to James VI* (1971); J. D. Douglas, *Light in the North: The Story of the Scottish Covenanters* (1964); J. Lane, *The Reign of King Covenant* (1956); W. Mackey, *The Church of the Covenant 1637–1651* (1979); A. Smellie, *Men of the Covenant* (1909).

IAN S. RENNIE

Covenant Theology *see* Federal Theology

Covenanters

Public covenants were important in the history of Reformed churches in Scotland. The persons who subscribed those covenants were called Covenanters. The term is used in both a broader and a narrower sense.

Broadly, the Covenanters were those who revolted against Stuart absolutism in the seventeenth century. They drew up and signed the National Covenant* (1638) and the Solemn League and Covenant* (1643; including England and Ireland). These covenants included an oath-bound pledge to be faithful to the tenets of the Reformation; to oppose those who held contrary views; to be loyal to the king when he shared their goals; and to give mutual support to those subscribing the covenant.

The covenants initially attracted widespread Scottish support. Most national leaders and the common people signed them. Approval of the Solemn League led to Scottish Covenanters' participation in the Westminster Assembly.* Charles II signed the covenants as a condition of his coronation (1651). At the Restoration (1660), Charles repudiated the covenants and fiercely persecuted those who continued to be faithful to them. The persecuted minority came to be known as the Covenanters in the narrower sense.

After the Revolution Settlement (1688–89), these strict Covenanters continued their ecclesiastical existence as the Reformed Presbyterian Church. Daughter denominations exist today in Scotland, Ireland, North America, and Australia.

J. D. Douglas, *Light in the North: The Story of the Scottish Covenanters* (1964); E. Whitley, *The Two Kingdoms* (1977).

WAYNE R. SPEAR

Cranmer, Thomas (1489–1556)

Born in Nottinghamshire, Cranmer studied at Cambridge and became a fellow of Jesus College. He was ordained (1523) and attracted the attention of Henry VIII, who sent him on an embassage to Europe (1529). In 1532 Henry appointed him, much against his will, archbishop of Canterbury. Cranmer cautiously promoted reform of the Church of England. After William Tyndale's martyrdom in Belgium (1536), Cranmer, with Thomas Cromwell, helped procure authorization for the use of the English Bible. With the accession of Edward VI (1547), Cranmer's reforming policies rapidly advanced.

Cranmer had great erudition and collected a famous personal library. He was without peer as a liturgical scholar. Cranmer was architect of the English *Book of Common Prayer** (1549; rev. 1552), providing for worship in the common language and laying the basis of Reformed worship in the Church of England for centuries.

Cranmer was also responsible for, and in part the author of, the Forty-two Articles of Religion which, under Elizabeth I,* became the Thirty-nine Articles.* These stated the doctrinal position of the Church of England, mainly in contrast to the Church of Rome, particularly with reference to the authority of Scripture, justification of the sinner, and the nature of the sacraments.

Peter Martyr Vermigli* and Martin Bucer* accepted Cranmer's invitation to England to assist in church reform and served as professors at Oxford and Cambridge respectively. Cranmer was an advocate of Reformed ecumenicity and had plans, with Calvin's* enthusiastic approval, to assemble an international conference of Reformed theologians, which, because of Edward VI's early death and the accession of Mary Tudor, were not realized. Under Mary, who reinstituted the papal power and religion in England, Cranmer was arrested and imprisoned, and was burned at the stake in Oxford (March 21, 1556).

PHILIP E. HUGHES

Creation

Understandings of creation within the Reformed tradition include classical emphases found in other Christian traditions, revisions due to modern developments also affecting other traditions, plus its own characteristics. Emphases shared with other traditions include belief in creation as a free act of God* performed through the eternal Word, creation of the world along with time out of nothing, a very good creation, and God's continuing sustenance and governance of the created order. Through these emphases is the pervasive belief that the creation is neither absolute nor divine but is forever contingent upon the eternal and self-existent creator.

Along with other Christian traditions, the Reformed understanding of creation has been altered by consequential modern developments, including the rise of historical-critical biblical studies, the Copernican revolution, Darwin's evolutionary theories, Einstein's theories of relativity, the emergence of process thought, and more recently the big bang cosmogony. These fostered a diminution of Christian cosmogonic and cosmological commentary, the differentiation of divinely revealed truth and obsolete worldviews through which it was conveyed, plus a movement away from literalistic interpretation of biblical accounts of creation to more textually informed interpretations.

The confessional sources of the Reformed doctrine of creation include Calvin's Geneva Catechism* (1541), the Scots Confession* (1560), the Belgic Confession* (1561), the Heidelberg Catechism* (1563), the Westminster Confession of Faith* (1647), and more recently the Presbyterian Confession of 1967.* Major theological contributions to the Reformed understanding include those of John Calvin,* Jonathan Edwards,* Herman Bavinck,* Karl Barth,* Emil Brunner,* and T. F. Torrance.* While these confessions and theologians certainly do not constitute a uniform Reformed witness, there are prevailing Reformed perspectives on creation.

Beginning with Calvin and the HC and culminating in Barth, God the Creator is believed to be our Father because of Christ the Son who is also the Creator. Closely allied with this is the belief in creation found in Calvin and the WCF as the work of the triune God. Another persistent emphasis is on the close connection between creation and providence,* made so clear in the HC and in the Second Helvetic Confession where a chapter on providence precedes one on creation. The Reformed emphasis on God's ongoing involvement in creation is a kind of *creatio continua* held alongside a *creatio ex nihilo*. Allied with this emphasis is the epistemological role given to the created order in general revelation.* Here we have Calvin's glorious or beautiful theater which as a mirror reflects God's power, wisdom, and goodness. But human wickedness, consequent ignorance, and error suppressed God's truth and negated this revelation. The Reformed view is also very theocentric in that creation's ultimate purpose is the glorification of God through humankind serving God, to which end other creatures were made for the sake of humankind. This emphasis plus a belief in an active Creator who continues to be faithfully involved with the creation has fostered sustained inquiry into its workings.

Barth, *CD* III/1–4; Berkhof, *CFI*; T. F. Torrance, *The Ground and Grammar of Theology* (1980).

ROBERT J. PALMA

Creeds and Confessions

The people of God have always paused at critical historical moments to summarize and declare who they are and what they most deeply believe. These high moments are remembered and passed on to succeeding generations to preserve the identity and vitality of the community.

Precursors of Creeds in Scripture.

Old Testament. Deuteronomy 6:4–9 records one such moment. God had rescued the covenant* people from slavery. They had disobeyed and wandered forty years in the wilderness. Now they were finally about to enter the Promised Land. The law* had been given on Sinai. The issue was how to keep the law and prosper as a nation in the new land. All that they had experienced and been taught was summed up in one stirring sentence: "Israel, remember this! The LORD—and the LORD alone—is our God" (TEV). Then came the exhortation to put that declaration into practice: "Love the LORD your God with all your heart, with all your soul, and with all your strength" (TEV). That was followed by the necessary injunction to teach this to their children by building it into the fabric of their daily lives.

The ritual offering of the firstfruit of the harvest was a time for remembering God's greatness and goodness. The story of God's deliverance was recited at the time of presenting an offering to the priest. Deuteronomy 26:5–9 records an early faith affirmation in narrative form beginning with the words "My ancestor was a wandering Aramean" (TEV).

New Testament. Those close to Jesus, at certain crisis moments, came to stark clarity in response to his questions. Jesus asked Peter, "Who do you say I am?" Peter replied, "You are the Messiah, the Son of the living God" (Matt. 16:15–16, TEV). After Lazarus's death, Martha ran to meet Jesus, sorrowing that he had not been present to prevent the tragedy. Jesus declared to Martha, "I am the resurrection and the life," and then asked her, "Do you believe this?" Martha confessed, "Yes, Lord! . . . I do believe that you are the Messiah, the Son of God, who was to come into the world" (John 11:25–27, TEV).

Paul in 1 Corinthians and Romans makes brief summary statements of the significance of Christ's life, death, and resurrection for our sake (1 Cor. 15:3–4; Rom. 1:3–4). He urges the verbal confession of these succinct statements of essential Christian truth (Rom. 10:9; 1 Cor. 12:3). Philippians 2:11 retains what is possibly the oldest crystallized confession of the early Christian community in the phrase "Jesus Christ is Lord."

No formal creeds, confessions, or catechisms are found in Scripture. Present, however, is a common body of belief, accepted by all, as the faith affirmation of the Christian community (Kelly, pp. 23–24). This pattern of commonly accepted affirmation set the stage for the development of formalized and repeated creeds in the first centuries of the church's life. A creed, confession, catechism, statement, or declaration is, therefore, a formal statement of a group's set of beliefs (Plantinga, p. 5).

Ancient Creeds of the Early Church.

The early church built on the biblical examples of terse affirmations of faith and developed "creeds." The Latin word *credo* means "I believe" and points to the personal character of the earliest creeds.

Individual confession at baptism. When early converts asked how they could become part of the Christian community the answer was: By being baptized. This baptism* took place according to Christ's command: "in the name of the Father, the Son, and the Holy Spirit" (Matt. 28:19, TEV). Candidates for baptism became catechumens, learners, instructed in the meaning of this belief in one God in three persons. After a training period, the initiates recited a creed summarizing the truth they were going to profess.

Reciting a creed in this context was equivalent to taking a sacred oath, the original meaning of the word "sacrament."* Another common name for the creed was "symbol." It was a sign pointing Christians back to their baptism and their solemn oath of trust in the triune God.

By the second half of the second century, Christians generally knew a summary of Christian doctrine called "the rule of faith." Because of fear of persecution, this was not written down. It was, however, memorized and recited, often in connection with the sacraments of Baptism and the Lord's Supper.*

First to take definitive form in a local

area was the Old Roman Symbol. Toward the end of the second century, this expansion on the Trinitarian baptismal formula became known and used. The Apostles' Creed is a descendant of this Roman creed. The present form of the Apostles' Creed is an expanded version that developed in the south of France between the fifth and the eighth century. By the ninth century, the Creed, in its present form, was sanctioned for use in Christian instruction by the Holy Roman Emperor, Charlemagne, and incorporated into the Roman liturgy by the papacy.

Community identity through church councils. The Nicene Creed, from the fourth century A.D., has a different beginning and serves some additional functions. It begins, "We believe . . . " and primarily proposes to solidify the identity of the Christian community. When differing interpretations of Scripture threatened the unity of the church it became necessary to identify orthodoxy (correct opinion) and differentiate it from heresy* (choosing another way). After two church councils convened by emperors (Nicaea, A.D. 325; Constantinople, A.D. 381), the Nicene Creed developed to affirm the full deity and humanity of Jesus Christ* and the reality of the Holy Spirit.*

Creeds are a way of passing on the Christian tradition. There is risk involved. The Latin word *tradere* can mean "to hand on" and also "to betray." The responsibility to pass on the truth of the Christian tradition necessitates objectifying the experience of a people so that subsequent generations can analyze and, it is hoped, appropriate it as their own (Routley, pp. 1, 4). Creeds intend to describe the faith of the whole, undivided Christian church. They are symbols of unity and givers of identity. They become vehicles of praise to God; are used in the worship of God, especially in connection with the sacraments; and serve as standards for preaching and instruction. Creeds are also guides in the interpretation of Scripture, indicating how the church has read its Holy Books in the past. They clarify the identity of the community by demarcating orthodoxy and rejecting heresy. They become a testimony, a witness, sometimes even a battle cry, as the church encounters the world (Leith, "History," pp. 35–39).

Reformation Confessions.

The intent to be catholic. Confessions presuppose creeds. Often they explicitly affirm their adherence to the ancient creeds. Whereas creeds are brief summary statements of the belief of the whole church, confessions are more elaborated statements intended as the application of Christian faith to one group or region. During the Protestant Reformation of the sixteenth century, the renewal of the church took shape along national lines. Nations often used confessional documents to clarify their Christian and national identity.

National confessional distinctives. These confessions not only affirmed generic, catholic Christianity but also objectified the differences between a particular national church and others. All Protestants distinguished themselves from the Roman Catholics. Justification* by grace* through faith* became a Protestant distinctive, a virtual thirteenth article of the creed (Routley, p. 11). Internal Protestant differences quickly arose. German Lutherans made clear their distinctions from the Swiss Reformed. The Swiss Reformed distanced themselves from both the German Lutherans and the Anabaptists in their midst. The Anglicans declared what they perceived to be a more excellent middle way between Protestantism and Catholicism.

Most of the Reformers did not intend or desire to be sectarian in any way. They wished only to articulate the undivided catholic faith in their confessions. They hoped all Christians would come to agree with the rightness of their formulations. But because these confessions were developed in differing historical and theological contexts, they inevitably took on distinctive colorations and tones and textures. There came to be theological traditions within Protestantism—for example, Lutheran, Anglican, Anabaptist, and Reformed. Within each tradition, national and regional groups produced their own distinctive confessional statements.

The sixteenth century also saw the production of catechisms.* These were teaching tools, often in question-and-answer form intended to guide preaching and instruct the young. Luther's Small Catechism was widely used. Calvin's Geneva Catechism* (1541) provided the basis for a dialogue on Christian faith between a minister and a child. The Heidelberg Catechism* (1563) became the chief theological standard for the Reformed communities in Germany, Hungary, Belgium, and the Netherlands. In 1609 Dutch explorers brought it as the first Reformed statement of faith in the New World. It was approved for use in Presbyterian congregations in the United States (1870). The Westminster Larger Catechism (for preachers) and the Westminster Shorter Catechism (for children) proved influential in the Anglo-Saxon world from the seventeenth to the mid-twentieth century.

Reformed confessions. Of all the Protestant theological traditions, the Reformed has been the most prolific in producing confessional documents. Anglicans find their theology primarily in the liturgy. The Lutherans will interpret the Augsburg Confession (1530) but refuse to change or supplement it. The Anabaptists have statements such as the Schleitheim Confession (1527) and the Dordrecht Confession (1632). But they find their distinctiveness more in their way of life than in their confessional documents.

Sixteenth-century Reformed groups and their descendants have taken seriously their motto *Ecclesia reformata semper reformanda*. They have attempted both to be Reformed, rooted in a tradition, and always open to being further reformed according to the Word of God and the call of the Spirit. Reformed communities produced at least fifty confessional documents of some substance in their first fifty years of existence. Harmonies of Reformed confessions have sometimes been produced to show general doctrinal agreement among them. The Second Helvetic Confession* was used as an outline for the Harmony of Reformed Confessions (1581; ET 1842; see Leith, *Creeds*, pp. 128–29; Dowey, pp. 243ff., for a harmony of the *BC*). The WARC* issued a collection of thirty-three Reformed statements of faith produced in many countries in this century (see Vischer).

Contemporary Reformed Confessions.

New forms to meet new needs. In the twentieth century, another theological genre came into use. The Theological Declaration of Barmen* (1934) was an "explanation," or "clarification," of the meaning of previous creeds and confessions. It applied Reformed principles to the menacing intrusion of German national socialism into the churches' life. Using only biblical and theological language, it made clear that the affirmation "Jesus Christ is Lord" meant that Adolf Hitler is not Lord.

The Confession of 1967* in the United States followed the style and substance of the Barmen Declaration. Though much longer, it was structured around one doctrine, reconciliation. It was not to be a summary statement of Christian doctrine but applied the doctrine of reconciliation to the pressing social problems of the time, including racism,* war,* poverty, and anarchy in sexual relations.

A Brief Statement of Faith. In the late twentieth century, the Presbyterian Church (U.S.A.) developed "A Brief Statement of Faith."* A Special Committee was called into being by the reunion of northern and southern branches of American Presbyterianism (1983). After a year of wrestling with its task, the committee concurred that a primary need was for a renewed sense of identity in the reunited church. The form chosen was a brief, liturgically usable document. The models were not Barmen or the Confession of 1967 but the Apostles' Creed and the Nicene Creed. The Statement was simply to summarize the Christian faith in its Protestant and Reformed expression in contemporary terms.

Although there was no intention of breaking new ground, the writers were compelled to extend the Reformed tradition into new areas. They introduced into Reformed confessional literature a narrative of Jesus' life and ministry; a clear assertion of the equality of women and men in the image of God and their fitness to be called to all the ministries of the church; a warning of the sins that threaten death to the planet entrusted to human care; and a modeling of both masculine and feminine imagery in speaking about God.

How We Confess the Faith Today. Contemporary Reformed Christians take their confessional documents very seriously but not with slavish literalism. Office-bearers are asked to "receive" and "adopt," to be "instructed" and "led." In most Reformed churches they are not required to subscribe to every word of every confession. Rather, they are asked whether they stand "in this succession, recognizing the road marked out by these confessions as that of a church obedient to its calling" (Smart, p. 6). Charles Hodge* declared that subscription to the Westminster Standards asked one to affirm that she or he was Christian, Protestant, and Reformed (quoted in Leith, "History," p. 44). Contemporary creedal affirmation is a way of saying there is latitude within limits. Confessions are subordinate standards to the revelation of God in Jesus Christ recorded in Scripture. But they are standards. They represent the careful reading of Scripture by our parents in the faith. They cannot be treated casually. Governing bodies have the right to use them as a measure of whether or not someone is willing to function with integrity as a member of the community. Yet there must be responsible latitude for creative expression of theological thought alongside the essential affirmations. It is not every historically conditioned detail or the nuance of a word prescribed by a particular theological school which is definitive in the confessions. Rather, it is the common themes, the continuing principles, the central affirmations of the Reformed confessions which form the essential tenets or set the parameters that point us to the center of the Reformed tradition we share (Rogers, pp. 24–26).

E. A. Dowey, Jr., *A Commentary on the Confession of 1967 and an Introduction to "The Book of Confessions"* (1968); J. N. D. Kelly, *Early Christian Creeds*, 3rd ed. (1981); J. H. Leith, "A Brief History of the Creedal Task: The Role of Creeds in Reformed Churches," in *To Confess the Faith Today*, ed. J. L. Stotts and J. D. Douglass (1990); and, ed., *Creeds of the Churches*, 3rd ed. (1982); C. Plantinga, *A Place to Stand* (1979); J. B. Rogers, *Presbyterian Creeds: A Guide to The Book of Confessions* (1985); E. Routley, *Creeds and Confessions* (1962); J. D. Smart, "The Confession of 1967: Implications for the Church's Mission," *Monday Morning* 33 (May 6, 1968): 15–30; T. F. Torrance, *The School of Faith* (1959); L. Vischer, ed., *Reformed Witness Today* (1982).

JACK B. ROGERS

Cromwell, Oliver (1599–1658)

Lord Protector of England (1653–58). Cromwell was a Parliament member before becoming, in the war with the king, a great cavalry leader of the New Model Army. He rejected the English Episcopal national church and sought to replace it, when Protector, with a national system of supervision of parishes, where ministers could be Congregationalist* or Presbyterian* but not Episcopalian. He was advised by the leading Puritan* (Independent*) divines of the time, and he helped ensure that England would be ruled by Parliament, not by absolute kings.

R. S. Paul, *The Lord Protector* (1955).

PETER TOON

Crypto-Calvinism

A sixteenth-century term using crypto (Gr. *kryptos*, hidden, secret, concealed) as a prefix to describe Lutherans in Germany and Scandinavia who privately held or sympathized with Calvinist tenets and, less commonly, in France to those professing Roman Catholics accused of secretly being Calvinists. In Germany particularly, charges of crypto-Calvinism had serious repercussions for the future of Lutherans and Calvinists. After Luther's death (1546), as Lutheranism struggled to define itself, Lutheran rigorists (Gnesio-Lutherans) often accused Philipp Melanchthon and his followers (Philippists or Melanchthonians) of covertly holding Calvinist views or tolerating those who did.

The controversy that erupted divided Lutheranism theologically and politically. Theologically, it centered on the

Lord's Supper* concerning which Melanchthon and many Lutherans held views similar to those of Calvin.* Thus, Melanchthon changed his Augsburg Confession to omit from its article on the Supper the phrase "truly present" and its condemnation of differing views (1542). Hard-line Lutheran theologians suspected that Melanchthon had decided to embrace Calvin's rejection of the doctrine of ubiquity* (omnipresence) in which the resurrected Christ was believed to be corporeally present in the eucharistic elements, and instead accepted a real spiritual presence made possible through the intermediary of the Holy Spirit.*

In political terms, the controversy made cooperation among various Lutheran German states more difficult in the last half of the sixteenth century. This was especially true when Electoral Saxony was governed successively by two Philippist Lutherans (Augustus, 1553–86; Christian I, 1586–91) who knowingly harbored Calvinist sympathizers before strict Lutheran orthodoxy was reestablished by succeeding rulers. This, in turn, made it harder for German Protestants to maintain a common front against Rome and its allies. However, the theological consensus achieved by the Formula of Concord (1577) enabled a reunion of the various Lutheran factions, and after 1600, crypto-Calvinism was no longer a vital theological concern of Lutheranism.

T. Klein, *Der Kampf um die zweite Reformation in Kursachsen, 1586–1591* (1962); R. D. Linder, "The French Calvinist Response to the Formula of Concord," *Journal of Ecumenical Studies* 19 (Winter 1982): 18–37; J. Moltmann, *Christoph Pezel (1539–1604) und der Calvinismus in Bremen* (1958); R. D. Preus, *The Theology of Post-Reformation Lutheranism*, vol. 1 (1970); D. Visser, ed., *Controversy and Conciliation: The Reformation and the Palatinate, 1559–1583* (1986).

ROBERT D. LINDER

Cunningham, William (1805–1861)

Nineteenth-century Scotland's most distinguished Reformed theologian. Cunningham played a leading role in the Disruption (1843) and founding of the Free Church of Scotland. He was principal of New College* (from 1845). His writings display a brilliant mastery of Reformed scholastic theology, whose central features he expounded and championed. Though Scotland and the Free Church took a different doctrinal course after Cunningham's death, his writings continue to be reprinted.

W. Cunningham, *Discussions on Church Principles* (1863); *Historical Theology*, 2 vols. (1862); *Lectures on Subjects Connected with Natural Theology* (1878); and *The Reformers and the Theology of the Reformation* (1862); J. Mackenzie and R. Rainy, *Life of William Cunningham* (1871).

N. R. NEEDHAM

Dabney, Robert Lewis (1820–1898)

Old School Presbyterian theologian, professor, and statesman of the (Southern) Presbyterian Church. Dabney was born in Virginia and educated at Hampden-Sydney College, the University of Virginia, and Union Theological Seminary (Va.). After a pastorate at Tinkling Spring Church (Va.), he became professor of church history (1853) and then theology (1859–83) at Union.

Dabney served as chief of staff to Confederate General Thomas J. "Stonewall" Jackson during the War Between the States and wrote a biography of Jackson (1866). He was Moderator of the Southern Presbyterian Church (1870). He moved to Texas as professor of philosophy at the University of Texas (1883–94) and taught theology at Austin Seminary (1884–95), which he helped establish. He became blind (1890) but continued lecturing and writing.

Firmly rooted in the conservative Calvinist tradition, Dabney was heavily influenced by the seventeenth-century Reformed orthodoxy* of Francis Turretin* and John Dick.* Avoiding speculation, he followed the generally moderate Calvinism* of the Westminster Standards, seen in his *Lectures in Systematic Theology* (1871). A keen social critic of industrial materialism and opponent of American theological liberalism, Dabney remained an ardent defender of the Old South.

R. L. Dabney, *Discussions*, 4 vols. (1890–97); *A Defence of Virginia* (1867; repr. 1969); and *The Sensualistic Philosophy of the Nineteenth Century* (1875; new and enl. ed. 1887); T. C. Johnson, *Life and Letters of R. L. Dabney* (1903); D. F. Kelly, "Robert L. Dabney," in *Southern Reformed Theology*, ed. D. F. Wells (1989).

DOUGLAS F. KELLY

Daillé, Jean (1594–1670)

French Protestant pastor, theologian, and man of letters. Born to Protestant parents (at Châtellerault in Poitou), he studied theology under John Cameron* at Saumur while a tutor in Philippe Duplessis-Mornay's household. He represented the ideas of both throughout his life (he edited Duplessis-Mornay's *Memoirs*). A great pastor (Paris [Charenton] Reformed Church [1626–70]) and churchman (moderator of the final Huguenot* national synod), he was arguably the greatest Huguenot scholar after John Calvin. His *Traité de l'employ des saints pères* (1632), for example, demanded criticohistorical use of the sources. But he has been largely neglected by scholarship.

BRETT ARMSTRONG

d'Albret, Jeanne (1528–1572)

Queen of Navarre (from 1555), Jeanne d'Albret was an outspoken leader of the French Reformed church (from 1560). She was daughter of Marguerite of Angoulême,* niece of Francis I, and mother of Henry of Navarre (i.e., Henry IV, promulgator of the Edict of Nantes* [1598]). Intellectually keen, stubborn, argumentative, often offensive and easily offended, she skillfully took advantage of shifting French political and military fortunes to develop a Calvinist religious establishment in Béarn, including church reorganization modeled on Geneva, and support for the ministry, poor relief, and education.

N. L. Roelker, *Queen of Navarre* (1968).

ROBERT M. HEALEY

Dale, Robert William (1829–1895)

English Congregational minister and theologian. Dale was educated at Spring Hill College, Birmingham. He joined John Angell James at Carr's Lane Chapel, Birmingham (1853; in charge, 1859–1895), and was active in many areas of civic life and theological education. He was also a prolific writer. His theological reputation rests on *The Atonement* (1875), in which he attempted an ethical rather than a forensic defense of penal substitution. Alive to modern thought, yet rooted in the faith of the ages, Dale caused some distress when he embraced annihilationism.

A staunch churchman, Dale was chairman of the Congregational Union of England and Wales (1869; he left the Union over the Irish question [1888]) and first president of the International Congregational Council (1891). *A Manual of Congregational Principles* (1884) was followed by his *History of English Congregationalism* (1907), which was finished by his son.

DNB; A. W. W. Dale, *The Life of R. W. Dale of Birmingham* (1898); L. H. Hough, *Dr. Dale After Twenty-five Years* (1922); M. D. Johnson, *The Dissolution of Dissent, 1850–1918* (1987).

ALAN P. F. SELL

Daneau (Danaeus), Lambert (1530–1595)

French Reformed theologian. After studying law, Daneau went to Geneva (1560) and followed Calvin's* lectures. He became pastor at Gien, returned to Geneva (1572), and taught at the Academy* with Theodore Beza.* Teaching at Leiden (1581–82), Daneau advocated independence of the church from the state. He then took pastoral and teaching positions at Ghent, Orthez, Lescar, and Castres. His many works include an introduction to dogmatics, *Christiana Isagoge* (1583–88); *Ethice Christiana* (1577), which first treated ethics* apart from Reformed dogmatics; a Christian physics; and a Christian politics. Daneau contributed to the early development of Reformed scholasticism.*

O. Fatio, "Lambert Daneau," in *Shapers of Religious Traditions*, ed. J. Raitt (1981), ch. 7.

DONALD SINNEMA

Deacons

The diaconate in the Calvinist tradition is one of four church offices (pastor, teacher, elder, deacon). Its responsibility is institutional leadership in caring for the poor and those who physically suffer. Calvin identified two diaconal functions: administration of benevolence and personal care for the needy, tasks he believed were scripturally assigned to men and women (Acts 6:1–6; 1 Tim. 3:8–13; 5:9–10; Rom. 12:8; 16:1–2). Following sixteenth-century cultural biases, women were subordinated to men. Deacons, who should be ordained by the laying on of hands, are ministers of the church, not deputies of the pastor. Deacons do not preach or administer the sacraments independently but may appropriately collect the offering (alms) and offer the cup in the Lord's Supper, as expressions of the spiritual character of their charitable ministry. Calvin insisted that the office of deacons is permanently necessary for right church order.

The distinctiveness of the Calvinist diaconate is seen by comparison and contrast with: (1) the vocation of all Christians and (2) other diaconates.

1. Calvinists, like other Christians, teach that every believer is called to *diakonia*, love of neighbors. The diaconate is the institutional expression of *diakonia*, leading and giving structure but not replacing individual service to neighbors. (2) In medieval Catholicism, the diaconate was a sacramental ministry; money matters were considered inappropriate for a church ministry. Protestants insisted that charity is a religious ministry but disagreed about who is responsible for it. This is particularly evident in the differences between the two branches of the Reformed tradition itself. For Zwinglians, church order was based on the OT as well as the NT. As in Israel, church and state were not clearly distinguished, so Christian rulers were responsible for all practical ministries, including poor relief. In many Zwinglian churches, organized *diakonia* eventually lost its ecclesiastical roots and became simply a part of secular government. For Calvinists, church order was based on the NT, where ecclesiastical offices are distinguished from civil ones; thus the diaconate should be distinct in theory, though not necessarily in practice, from state welfare. Deacons are essentially ministers of the church. In a Christian state, civil welfare and ecclesiastical diaconate may coincide or cooperate, but the Calvinist diaconate is not dependent upon the state for its existence.

Calvinist practice and theory of the diaconate varied in different places and times. Often the responsibilities of elders* and deacons were not clearly distinguished. A few churches experimented with women deacons, but most diaconates were exclusively male (as was Geneva's, to Calvin's regret). Formal diaconates continued in many places, but sometimes later churches were established without diaconates, though *diakonia* might be done by voluntary associations loosely related to churches. Today's most significant factors are the concern for justice as well as charity, ordination of women as full deacons, and participation in the ecumenical renewal of the diaconate.

R. M. Kingdon, "Social Welfare in Calvin's Geneva," *ARH* 62 (1971): 50–69; E. A. McKee, *John Calvin on the Diaconate and Liturgical Almsgiving* (1984); and *Diakonia in the Classical Reformed Tradition and Today* (1989); J. E. Olson, *Calvin and Social Welfare* (1989).

ELSIE ANNE MCKEE

Death

Scripture* reveals the "*living* God" who creates life and then re-creates it in Jesus Christ. Death appears in Genesis 3 as an unnatural interloper. Death is both universal and final. It comes to humans and beasts, rich and poor, wise and foolish (Ps. 49; Eccl. 3:19–20). In the OT, believers sought God for prolongation of life, for Sheol separated them from God's presence (Ps. 6:5). The NT teaches continuation of life beyond the grave and resurrection* of the body. Paul says death is the "wages" of sin (Rom. 6:23), experienced in solidarity with Adam (Rom. 5:12–21). But in Christ we are resurrected to eternal life (1 Cor. 15). Death is the last enemy to be destroyed (1 Cor. 15:26). Then all creation* will share our perfection (Rom. 8:18–19).

Augustine's* doctrine of original sin* tightly knitted sin and death. The Vulgate text of Rom. 5:12 says, "In Adam all sinned." First Corinthians 15:22 says, "In Adam all die." Thus death, the punishment for Adam's sin, is inherited by all of Adam's children. This view persisted through the medieval period, the Reformation, and to our own times.

The classic Reformed doctrine, taught by John Calvin,* the WCF,* Charles Hodge,* and A. A. Hodge,* is that death came into the world through human sin: the spiritual death of sin led to physical death. In death, mortal body and immortal soul are severed. In the general resurrection, body and soul will unite again—unto eternal life or eternal death.

Karl Barth,* Emil Brunner,* Gerrit Berkouwer,* Hendrikus Berkhof,* and others have revised classic ideas of the relation of sin to death. New translations of Rom. 5:12 removed the genetic inevitability; death extends to all because all have sinned (RSV). From a modern scientific perspective, suffering, death, and struggle were in the world long before humanity appeared. All creatures are finite; death is biologically *natural* and necessary. It seems that God's good creation is provisional—perfection lies ahead, not in the past. Unlike the beasts, we know we will die—and death always seems *unnatural.* We live and die before God. Jesus in his death and resurrection delivers us out of the nexus of sin, guilt, and death. For Christians, death remains a sign of judgment, but it has lost its sting. Through faith* in Christ, death becomes a "gracious ending" free of sin's curse.

Death also refers to the process of sanctification* in both the NT (Rom. 6–8) and the Reformed tradition. For Calvin, death teaches Christians not to cling to this life but to live in communion with Christ. Through Christ's death we enjoy both liberation from the power of death and mortification of our old nature through self-denial (*Inst.* 2.16.7). By faith we overcome the horror of death and face with courage the afflictions that are the harbingers of death.

Barth, *CD* III/2, sec. 47.5; Berkhof, *CFI*; R. S. Wallace, *Calvin's Doctrine of the Christian Life* (1959); Weber, *FD*.

BARBARA A. PURSEY

Declaratory Acts

Measures by two Scottish Presbyterian churches—the United Presbyterian Church (1879) and the Free Church (1892)—to express how office-bearers are free to understand their confession* of faith. They intended to secure liberty for more liberal-minded Calvinists to remain in the church without fear of discipline for departing from the Westminster Confession.* Both acts emphasized God's love, human responsibility, and the duty of evangelism;* the United Presbyterian act specified the six days of Genesis 1 as a subject on which interpreters could differ. The Free Church act aroused controversy and led to a small secession which called itself the Free Presbyterian Church, pledged to a full-blooded Westminster Calvinism.* The established Church of Scotland decided that such a declaratory act would be *ultra vires*, but its Act on the Formula (1910) had a similar effect, and the United Free Church of Scotland (from 1929) gave clear recognition to liberty of opinion on nonfundamentals.

J. T. Cox, ed., *Practice and Procedure in the Church of Scotland,* 6th ed., ed. D. F. M. MacDonald (1976); A. Stewart and J. K. Cameron, *The Free Church of Scotland 1843–1910* (1910); A. Thomson, *Life of Principal Harper* (1881).

N. R. NEEDHAM

Decree(s) of God

Reformed scholastic* doctrine rooting in God's* sovereignty (power) as theological starting point. The focus is on God's determining in God's eternal decree (plan) whatever occurs in heaven and earth. In the background is Aristotle's fourfold causality: the decree as efficient cause; Christ as material; faith* (Spirit) as instrumental; and the glory of God as final cause (*Inst.* 3.14.17, 21; *Commentary* on Eph. 1:4; continued in Theodore Beza* and the Canons of Dort*).

Nature of the decree. The decree is finally one, and equated with God's "purpose" in the destinies of people. Some are chosen "before the foundation of the world . . . for the praise of his glory" (Eph. 1:4, 11f.), while others are condemned. Moreover, by God's "most wise and holy counsel," God did "freely and unchangeably ordain whatsoever comes to pass" (WCF, 3.1). The Reformed scholastics focused on God in God's self and not in covenantal relations. God foresees all things *because* God decrees them eternally. Against semi-Pelagians and Arminians,* the decretal theologians taught that God's predeterminations do not *depend* on God's foreknowledge* of free agents. These thinkers also distinguished God's immanent works (*opera ad intra*) from God's extrinsic (*ad extra*) and limited the decree to the latter—including all reactions of free creatures. God effects some of these directly but renders others certain by God's "permissive decree." The blame for sin* rests on "secondary causes" or "instruments" (again, à la Aristotle).

The scholastics said this decree roots in God's essential attributes—including a balance of love/hate or mercy/justice. They inadequately appreciated that these qualities imply a relation to creatures in history.* They distinguished sharply God's decree to act (eternal "cause") and humanity's activity ("secondary cause"), and thus the decree itself and its execution. Beza particularly made this distinction, though it is already present in medieval nominalism.

Characteristics of the decree. This decree is founded in God's wisdom ("counsel") and presumes a consultation in the Trinity,* a rational actualization in history, and immutability throughout the ages. Its "parts" are related logically but not chronologically. Nevertheless, the proponents have frequently used chronological language. The decisive action occurs in a "prior" eternity, and history "effects" what God has (already) "caused." Faith is the product of the decree—and Christ is the "executor" or ground for assurance of salvation* (the "mirror of election"). Christ is in the decree, instead of the decree in him (as "author"). Finally, the decree is the starting point for all theological reflection. The idea of reprobation "naturally follows from the logic of the situation," since "the decree of election inevitably implies the decree of reprobation" (L. Berkhof, p. 116). The fall (*lapsus*) is therefore necessary for God to realize both mercy and justice in history.

Neo-Reformed scholars, such as Karl Barth,* Emil Brunner,* Gerrit Berkouwer,* Otto Weber,* Hendrikus Berkhof,* James Daane, Neal Punt, and Harry Boer, have rejected this view of reprobation. They contend—in line with Jerome Bolsec* (early 1550s)—that the Bible does not teach eternal reprobation and subjection of Christ to the decree. But traditional Reformed theology has gone in two directions here. "Supralapsarianism"* began with Beza* and included Franciscus Gomarus,* Peter Martyr Vermigli,* Girolamo Zanchi,* William Perkins,* and recently Herman Hoeksema. "Infralapsarianism"* arose as a reaction, though still presuming the necessity of the *lapsus.* It included Pierre Viret,* Petrus van Mastricht,* Francis Turretin,* and more recently Herman Bavinck,* and Louis Berkhof.* The Reformed creeds* are infralapsarian. The difference between these two views relates to this question: Did God regard the objects of election and reprobation as not-yet-created or as already-created-and-fallen? Supralapsarians say the former and put the *lapsus* "before" creation* in God's mind, while infralapsarians say the latter and set the fall logically "after" creation. But both have stressed the sequence from eternity to time and contended that God's decisive action occurred in the former (thus a certain metaphysics is implied).

Objections to decretal theology. 1. Is decretalism consistent with human moral freedom? Reformed thought has distinguished between necessity and compulsion: Free agents act necessarily, according to their disposition and God's decree, without being externally coerced. Freedom* is incompatible with compulsion but entails the necessity to act in terms of who we are (Jonathan Edwards*). The question is finally this: Is a previous certainty consistent with free agency? Reformed decretalism has underscored the distinction between determination and determinism.

2. Does decretalism eliminate incentives for human effort? If all things are necessary, does human responsibility make sense? Reformed theologians have said God's initiative requires human response and the "final cause" is only attained through the "means" of obedience and disobedience. It is also an empirical fact that Reformed piety has usually been dynamic. The glory of God is the highest motivation.

3. But is God the "author of sin"? Decretalism has maintained that God creates free agents, who are themselves culpable. Again, it has used the distinction of "efficient" and "permissive." The neo-Reformed have argued that mechanical "causality" is inappropriate to the personal relations of God and human beings, and sin is a "riddle" which cannot be rationalized (Barth, Berkouwer). Some scholastics have responded that God has "deemed it wise, for the purpose of His self-revelation, to permit moral evil, however abhorrent it may be to His nature" (L. Berkhof, p. 108). Others have said that sin is necessary for God to realize God's glory by revealing both mercy and wrath (Beza).

The neo-Reformed have rejoined that we cannot speak of God's decree apart from God's revelation in the historical Christ. There is no *decretum absolutum*. Faith enables us to see that God has eternally willed to give people the dignity of being God's "covenant partners." There is no eternal decree of reprobation (for Barth, this implies an incipient universalism*). Election in Christ "before the foundation of the world" suggests that nothing in this world can shake the salvation we have in him (Rom. 8:18ff.; esp. vs. 38–39; again this presumes a different metaphysics of "causality" and the relation of eternity and history). With Calvin in the *Institutes*, the neo-Reformed have refused to focus on God in God's self and have limited their discussions to God in creation, redemption, and history.* Instead of a triumph of power, they want a "triumph of grace" (Berkouwer's description of Barth).

In past years, some theologians have interpreted Calvin (too much) in a quasi-Barthian way (Berkouwer, Weber, Daane). But others have argued (too much) that the early Reformed were not guilty of abstract decretalism (Muller). One thing is clear: One's view of the decree lies at the heart of what it means to be "Reformed."

Calvin, *Inst.* 1.17.3, 13–14; 2.12.1; 2.17.1; 3.21–23. For Reformed scholasticism: T. Beza, *The Sum of All Christianity* (1555); J. Wolleb and F. Turretin selections, in *Reformed Dogmatics*, ed. and trans. J. W. Beardslee III (1965); C. Hodge, *Systematic Theology*, vol. 1 (1871); L. Berkhof, *Systematic Theology* (4th rev. and enl. ed. 1949); H. Hoeksema, *Reformed Dogmatics* (1966).

For older Reformed theologians: Heppe, *RD*. For a more covenantal approach: J. Edwards, *Freedom of the Will* (1754). For the neo-Reformed: Barth, *CD* II/2; E. Brunner, *The Christian Doctrine of God* (1946; ET 1950); G. C. Berkouwer, *Divine Election* (1960); and *Sin* (1971); Berkhof, *CFI*; Weber, *FD*; J. Daane, *The Freedom of God* (1973); N. Punt, *Unconditional Good News* (1980); H. R. Boer, *The Doctrine of Reprobation in the Christian Reformed Church* (1983). Also, R. A. Muller, *Christ and the Decree* (1986); P. C. Holtrop, *The Bolsec Controversy* (1991).

PHILIP C. HOLTROP

Denney, James (1856–1917)

Influential Scottish Reformed leader born in Paisley and a graduate of the University of Glasgow (1879). A member of the small Reformed Presbyterian Church, Denney studied theology at the Free Church College in Glasgow. Following three years in inner-city mission work, he served the East Free Church in Broughty Ferry, near Dundee.

The Free Church of Scotland elected Denney professor of systematic and pastoral theology at its Glasgow College (1897), where he moved to the chair of New Testament (1900) and was named principal (1915). He had qualities of a master teacher—profound spiritual insight, broad background of culture, deep and penetrating scholarship at once as exact and critical as far-seeing and constructive, and a unique gift of clear and trenchant speech. His writings influenced many churches. He continued to preach regularly and was active in the leadership of the General Assembly of the then United Free Church and in struggles over pressing social issues in Scotland and beyond.

Denney's theology pivoted on the cross which influenced and integrated all his thought. From that primary focus he reflected widely and anticipated many of the emphases of the coming neo-orthodoxy.* He was a man ahead of his time, whom P. T. Forsyth* called "the theological prophet." He expressed his envy of the Roman Catholic priest who could hold before the eyes of a dying person the form of a crucifix and say, "God loves like that!"

J. Denney, *Studies in Theology* (1894); *The Death of Christ* (1902); *Jesus and the Gospel* (1908); *The Way Everlasting* (1911); *The Christian Doctrine of Reconciliation* (1917); and commentaries on Romans, 2 Corinthians, 1 and 2 Thessalonians.

J. RANDOLPH TAYLOR

Descent Into Hell

Christ's descent to hell after his crucifixion (Matt. 12:40; Eph. 4:9; 1 Peter 3:19) appeared in the Creed by the fourth century. Understood as the release of the OT faithful, it became a graphic element in medieval belief. The Protestant Reformers generally rejected this "limbo of the fathers," believing that pre-Christian saints went immediately to God's presence, but otherwise disagreed on the meaning of the descent. Lutheran theology (though not Luther*) affirmed a descent to triumph over the power of hell. Reformed theology offered several alternatives to a spatial descent. Huldrych Zwingli* and Heinrich Bullinger* thought Christ's descent meant that his saving work extended spiritually to the pre-Christian righteous. The modern theologian Emil Brunner* found hope for those who never heard of Christ in this interpretation. Martin Bucer* and Theodore Beza,* echoed by Charles Hodge* in the nineteenth century, considered the descent synonymous with Christ's death and burial. John Calvin,* however, interpreted it psychologically: Christ, on the cross, suffered in soul the wrath of God, or "hell." Many Puritans* accepted this view; Karl Barth* developed a modern form of it. Seventeenth-century philological scholarship concluded that the hades-sheol of the descent was the state and power of death, under which Christ's human soul remained until his resurrection. Reformed scholasticism* distinguished a strict meaning (the grave and persisting under the power of death) from a metaphorical one (suffering God's wrath) and held, against Lutheran orthodoxy, that the descent belonged to Christ's humiliation rather than to his exaltation.

D. D. Wallace, Jr., "Puritan and Anglican: The Interpretation of Christ's Descent Into Hell," *ARG* 69 (1978): 248–87.

DEWEY D. WALLACE, JR.

Dialectical Theology

Theological perspectives developed about 1920 in German-speaking territories under the leadership of Karl Barth,* Emil Brunner,* Rudolf Bultmann, Friedrich Gogarten, Eduard Thurneysen, and to a lesser extent Paul Tillich. Those outside the movement called it "dialectical theology," a term only partially characterizing its concerns. The leaders, however, understood their concern as a "theology of the Word of God," since Barth and Thurneysen saw the impulse for it not in a problem of thought but in the problem of preaching.* Because of the movement's relation to the crisis mentality existing in the spiritual and cultural milieu after the end of World War I, it was also called "theology of crisis" (Tillich). It communicated through the periodical *Zwischen den Zeiten* (1922–33), and its chief document was Barth's *Der Römerbrief* (2nd ed. 1922). Rather than a unified school of thought with its own program, from the beginning it existed only as a loose working fellowship.

This fellowship was initially united by its fundamental critique of the previous era of theology and church, summarily named "neo-Protestantism." The critique applied both to the "positive," that is, the more conservative or orthodox form of neo-Protestantism as well as to its liberal form, out of whose school the leaders of the new movement had come. Its protest was directed point-blank "against the forfeiture of theology at the hands of the theologians" (Moltmann, *Anf.*, 1:ix). Bultmann formulated it in a way that also faithfully represents the conviction of Barth and Gogarten: "The object of theology is God,* and the charge against liberal theology is this: that it did not deal with God, but rather with humans" (*GV*, p. 2). The goal of the critique was not that there be more speaking about God but that speaking about God had to mean something different from "talking about humanity* in a somewhat elevated tone" (Barth, *WG*, p. 164). According to the critique, neo-Protestant theology's shortcoming was that in its speaking about God it was actually only speaking about "something" in *humanity* and its *world* and therefore not speaking of God. So a "No" was said to a dissolving of God into human religion, morals, and culture. This threatened dissolution was understood as an unavoidable consequence of the titanic attempt of humanity to take God into its possession and disposition.

What united the circle of dialectical theology on the constructive side was its determination to break away from neo-Protestantism in order to forge a new basis for evangelical theology. However, this circle believed it first had to accomplish some essential preparatory tasks. They saw themselves in a time "between the times" (Gogarten; see Moltmann, *Anf.*, 2:95). As the theme of theology, discourse of humanity about itself did not qualify, nor did discourse about God as a factor in human life. It had to be strictly the word of God directed to humanity, identical with the "Word in the words" of the Bible (Barth, *R*, p. xiii). It is therefore really impossible for us to speak of God. For us remains only the recognition that God is the "wholly other," that "God is God" (Barth, *WG*, p. 85; *R*, p. 326). God is not a God of mere otherworldliness, for the otherworldly is a part of the given reality of the world as its converse. Also, God is not God simply by virtue of being different from humans, who could then be simply left to their own devices. God is neither this-worldly nor otherworldly; God is "the one who, doing without all the qualities of an object, is the source of the *krisis* of all objectivity," of all actualities, of all holding tight to what exists as though one could possess it (Barth, *R*, p. 57). As the wholly other, God is not distant from humanity but rather "reveals" God's own self in humanity. God does this, not in order thereby to inaugurate a new kind of "possessing," but rather in this way to carry out toward humanity the *krisis* of all "possessing"! Therefore God reveals God's self "as the unknown God" (Barth, *R*, p. 88), as the crucified, as the judge, in "radical denial and dissolution of humanity" (Bultmann, *GV*, p. 2). Yet in this way God actually does make God's self known. The crucified is also the risen one. Judgment is also grace.* The "No" is also the "Yes" for humanity and the *krisis* is also the "source" of the unity of God and humanity. To be sure, this "Yes" is only given in the "event" of the Word of God,* which cannot be viewed, cannot be deduced, and in this sense comes "vertically from above." This "Yes" is given to humans strictly in faith and hope, only in "the justification* of the sinner," never as a kind of visible possession. On the side of what can be viewed, no reality can be ascertained, but rather there is only "vacant space" (Barth, *R*, p. 17), only allusion and parable. In these principles, dialectical theology believed it was renewing Reformed theology. The expression "dialectical theology," is appropriate insofar as here the structure of the relation of God to the reality of humanity is thought of dialectically. That is, it is thought of as a paradoxical conjuncture of transcendence and immanence, of revelation and veiling, of judgment and grace, of the invisible "Yes" and the visible "No." The dialectic is not to be understood as though what is posited and what is negated could be gathered together intellectually in a higher unity (Hegel). It is understood, rather, that the conjuncture of both, existing only through God in the event of a word, always remains a paradox for our thinking (Kierkegaard). Because of this, dialectical theology holds that theological thinking itself has to be dialectical and constantly has to "correlate every position and negation one against the other, to clarify 'Yes' by 'No' and 'No' by 'Yes,' without persisting longer than a moment in a rigid 'Yes' *or* 'No' " (Barth, *WG*, p. 172).

The breakup of the circle of dialectical theology (1933) over opposing stances to the new political conditions in Germany clarified long-standing differences among its leaders, or even a "productive misunderstanding" (Barth, *ZZ*, 1933, p. 54) existing from the beginning over what they wanted to do. Though they were united against neo-Protestantism, there was a deep difference: either to maintain methodologically over against the subjectivism of neo-Protestantism the *category* of "Word," or "Reality" (Gogarten), or "Event" (Bultmann), or "I-Thou relationship" (Brunner), or—in concern about the threat from this direction of a new anthropological fettering of theology—to base everything referring to the "Word," "Reality," "Event," and "I-Thou relationship" on the revelation of *God* (Barth, Thurneysen). While united against neo-Protestantism in recognizing that God is not at our disposal, there were also deep differences: either to postulate from this recognition a secular world as a law unto itself (Gogarten); or, in conjunction with renunciation of direct speech about God, to talk of human existence which is capable of receiving this speech (Bultmann); or to understand the reality of God as a critical counter-reality to the present worldly reality, with divine reality acting in contradiction to the present reality to bring it into correspondence with itself (Barth). In Barth's unique conception, it is apparent that influences of Calvin's* theocentric thought were at work as well as the eschatology* of Johann Christoph Blumhardt and Christoph Blumhardt.* However this may be, dialectical theology showed itself to be a theology "between the times," whose unforgettable impetus for taking seriously the Godness of God had to lead, and did lead, beyond the immediate impetus to further clarification and development.

G. Merz, ed., *Zwischen den Zeiten* (periodical; Munich, 1923–1933; *ZZ*); K. Barth, *Der Römerbrief* (1919; 1922[2]; 1923[3]; ET 1932; *R*); and *Das Wort Gottes und die Theologie* (1924; ET 1928; *WG*); R. Bultmann, *Glauben und Verstehen*, vol. 1 (1933; ET 1969; *GV*); J. Moltmann, ed., *Anfänge der dialektischen Theologie*, vols. 1–2 (1962–63; *Anf.*); ET, see *The Beginnings of Dialectic Theology*, vol. 1, ed. J. M. Robinson, 1968); T. Siegfried, *Das Wort und die Existenz: Auseinandersetzung mit der dialektischen Theologie*, 3 vols. (1930–33); C. Van Til, *The New Modernism* (1946); H. Urs von Balthasar, *Karl Barth* (1951; repr. 1961); C. Gestrich, *Neuzeitliches Denken und die Spaltung der dialektischen Theologie* (1977); W. H. Ruschke, *Entstehung und Ausführung der diastasen Theologie in Barths zweiten "Römerbrief"* (1987); M. Beintker, *Die Dialektik in der "Dialektischen Theologie" Karl Barths: Studien zur Entwicklung der Bartschen Theologie und zur Vorgeschichte der "Kirchlichen Dogmatik"* (1987); W. Pannenberg, "Dial. Theol," *RGG*[3] 2:168–74. Cf. W. Haerle, "Dial. Theol," in *TRE* 9:683–96.

EBERHARD BUSCH

Dick, John (1764–1833)

Scottish Secession Church theologian. After fourteen years in Slateford (near Edinburgh), where he published his influential *An Essay on the Inspiration of the Holy Scriptures* (1800; 3rd ed. 1813), Dick was called to Glasgow. His *Lectures on the Acts* (1808) and *Sermons* (1816) were published, and he was awarded a D.D. by the College of New Jersey (now Princeton University; 1815). Dick was appointed professor of theology (1820) to the newly united Secession Church, continuing in both charges until his death. His *Lectures on Theology* was published posthumously (4 vols.; 1834). Though reprinted and influential in Scotland and England, these lectures were more frequently published in the United States, where they became the standard system of theology in the Secession churches, or Seceders* (subsequently United Presbyterian Church of North America).

DAVID C. LACHMAN

Discipline, Books of

The Scottish Reformation produced two sixteenth-century works to reorganize Protestant churches and shape the relationship between church and state in accordance with Reformed principles: the First Book of Discipline (1560) and the Second Book of Discipline (1578). Both are Protestant in rejecting papal government but also Reformed in representing attempts by Reformed leaders to establish a church government modeled after Genevan polity* under Calvin* and Beza.* This meant rejection of the Reformed polity of England's episcopal and hierarchical system, and in place of a state-appointed hierarchy came church leaders and assemblies selected by churches themselves and by representative ecclesiastical church assemblies whose membership came from the church's leadership. Though not hierarchical, neither was this system democratic. Both books of discipline were composite works, but two prominent names associated with them are John Knox* (First Book) and Andrew Melville* (Second Book).

The First Book of Discipline called for government by clerical and lay leaders: superintendents,* ministers, doctors (teachers), elders,* and deacons;* it was in many ways modeled after what Knox saw functioning in Geneva and himself had attempted to develop (1554–55) at Frankfurt-am-Main. There, as later in Scotland, Knox was opposed by Reformed Protestants who disliked heavy reliance on lay leaders and rejected equality among pastors. At Frankfurt this latter group was led by Richard Cox. Though an admirer of Calvin's theology, Cox insisted on clerical domination of church government and demanded that the exile church in Frankfurt have "the face of an English church." When the exile ended, Cox and his followers supported England's episcopacy, while Knox's followers for the most part became puritan critics of England's episcopacy and Knox himself helped a new polity in Scotland.

The First Book was threatened by lack of full harmony in church-state relations. In addition, many Scottish Protestants supported an episcopal hierarchy patterned after the English example rather than Scottish use of a reformed episcopacy in conjunction with church councils. Given the fluid political and economic situation (1560s), as well as lack of agreement on "true" polity among Reformed Protestants, the First Book did not survive the convention of Leith (1572). Reemphasis on the role of bishops at Leith proved unacceptable, as did the new policy of allowing the regent to appoint bishops; and dissatisfaction led to a new committee's production, the Second Book of Discipline.

Melville led the group which advocated thorough presbyterianism* by means of the Second Book. This work, adopted by the Scottish church (1578), was part of the broader presbyterian movement which was led in England by Walter Travers* and Thomas Cartwright,* was established in France and the Netherlands, and was aggressively promoted by Beza. The Second Book placed ecclesiastical supervision fully in the hands of groups of elected church leaders: presbytery, synod, general assembly.* Excluded from supervision were secular governors and appointed bishops. The Second Book, however, did not provide all the elements of presbyterianism; and presbyteries were largely assumed to take over the functions previously performed by bishops, such as ordination,* supervision, and discipline.* All jurisdiction was not fully spelled out.

The Books of Discipline were part of Reformed attempts to find a biblical, yet workable, polity. Practical politics and economic necessities interfered with Knox's and Melville's ideals, as did traditional ways of conducting ecclesiastical life in Scotland. Also, Reformed theology failed to produce a uniform polity, for Calvin's refusal to demand a single ecclesiastical system gave hope to episcopal, presbyterian, and congregationalist* followers alike.

I. B. Cowan, *The Scottish Reformation* (1982); G. Donaldson, *The Scottish Reformation* (1960).

RONALD J. VANDERMOLEN

Discipline, Church

Church discipline has always been a major concern within the new Reformed churches. Three basic issues were involved. First, would the new Reformed churches discipline their members with excommunication as in the past? Second, would discipline fall under the jurisdiction of the civil magistrate or an ecclesiastical court? Third, how would the church relate to the civil community? The proposed solutions to the problem resulted in three basic types of church discipline and polity* within the Reformed tradition.

Reformed Protestantism began in Zurich (1520s) under the leadership of Huldrych Zwingli.* Zwingli and Heinrich Bullinger,* his successor, developed a theory of discipline that was the basis for the system in Zurich. They saw Zurich as a single, unified Christian community, where the civil magistrate held supremacy over all external matters. Clergy had no coercive power. There was no separate church discipline, not even excommunication. The church and the Christian were equivalent to the civil community and the citizen. Civil magistrates thus ruled over both the church and the civil community.

John Oecolampadius* offered the Basel magistrates a second solution (1530). He unsuccessfully proposed, first, that excommunication was an absolute necessity for a fully reformed church; and, second, that excommunication and other forms of church discipline must be imposed by an ecclesiastical court of elders or presbyters, chosen from the clergy and the laity.

Martin Bucer,* who originally agreed with Zwingli on discipline, came to Oecolampadius's viewpoint (early 1530s). Partially because of Bucer, and perhaps because of Oecolampadius's writings, John Calvin* came to advocate the newer ideas on church discipline.

Calvin attempted to implement his more developed Oecolampadian version of discipline in the Ecclesiastical Ordinances* (1541). The Geneva Consistory* was composed of all pastors and twelve lay elders. It was to be in charge of church discipline, consisting of admonishing offenders and, if necessary, excommunicating them. For Calvin, the goals of church discipline were those of protecting the purity of the church, shielding the good Christian from the influence of the wicked, and the repentance of sinners.

When Calvin tried to impose this discipline on Geneva all Protestant cities in Switzerland, and also South German cities, had a system similar to Zurich's, with the civil government in control of Christian discipline, supreme in its control over the entire community. But Calvin's concept distinguished between civil and ecclesiastical jurisdictions. Though not denying the proper authority of the magistrate, he proposed a separate church discipline under Consistory control. It took Calvin nearly fifteen years to establish the independence of the Consistory in Geneva and make the system work.

In the second half of the sixteenth century, the Calvinist and Zwinglian approaches came into conflict in the Swiss cities, Germany, England, and the United Provinces. One key battle was at Heidelberg, where Thomas Erastus, a disciple of Zwingli and Bullinger, defended Heidelberg's current Zurich style against Calvinists who wanted to establish a Genevan system. The Calvinists won. The Zwinglian approach to the Christian community and discipline was thereafter often called Erastianism.*

In French and Scottish Reformed churches the Calvinist discipline system developed into Presbyterianism.* In France, a Presbyterianism loosely modeled on the Genevan system emerged under the guidance of Theodore Beza.* Andrew Melville* was responsible for the fully developed Presbyterian church discipline and government in Scotland.

In 1562 Jean Morély suggested a third approach to discipline for the French Reformed church, Congregationalism,* where discipline would be imposed by the local congregation. Beza's party defeated the proposal.

In England, under Elizabeth I, the established Erastian system met opposition from "Congregationalists" such as Robert Browne* and "Presbyterian" advocates such as Thomas Cartwright* and Walter Travers.* At the Westminster Assembly* (1640s), the Presbyterians appeared to be triumphant, but the

Congregationalists won in the end. The religious settlement under Oliver Cromwell* (1652) established Congregationalism in England. These events also had an impact on the American colonies, especially those in New England, where Congregationalism prevailed.

During the seventeenth and eighteenth centuries, the three Reformed approaches to discipline continued to compete for acceptance. However, the Zwinglian approach, Erastianism, was doomed to failure because it could function only in a unified Christian community. It could not adjust to a modern pluralistic community, where the civil government did not impose religious uniformity. Presbyterianism, though it was similarly wedded to the idea of a Christian commonwealth, could operate independently of government. There had been an implicit separation between the ecclesiastical jurisdiction and the civil jurisdiction since Calvin's time. Therefore, when forced, Presbyterian discipline could exist and even flourish in a pluralistic society. Congregationalism was less wedded to the concept of a unified Christian society. By definition, each congregation was self-governing and self-disciplining. It was therefore easily adaptable to a pluralistic milieu.

J. W. Baker, "Calvin's Discipline and the Early Reformed Tradition," in *Calviniana: Ideas and Influence of Jean Calvin* (1988), 107–19; R. M. Kingdon, *Geneva and the Consolidation of the French Protestant Movement* (1967); J. T. McNeill, *The History and Character of Calvinism* (1954); A. Simpson, *Puritanism in Old and New England* (1955).

J. WAYNE BAKER

Dispensationalism

Also called dispensational premillennialism, it is a scheme of history* based on a complex literal interpretation of the prophetic books of the Bible. Developed primarily by the Englishman and Plymouth Brethren John Nelson Darby (1800–1882) in the mid-nineteenth century, dispensationalism was popularized in the United States by annual Bible and prophetic conferences initiated in 1875, publication of *The Scofield Reference Bible* (1909), and at schools such as the Moody Bible Institute.

Though there are various dispensational schemes, most divide world history into seven eras or dispensations, including the historical "parenthesis" of the current church age. In this plan, the present age will steadily deteriorate until the secret rapture of the church, the return of Christ, and the establishment of God's kingdom.* Included too is a strict division between Israel and the church.

Early dispensationalist leaders were largely drawn from Presbyterian and Baptist communions, and most of the early dispensationalists were broadly Reformed. However, the General Assembly* of the PCUS (1944) condemned dispensationalism as "out of accord" with the church's confession.

Dispensationalism continued to attract interest and adherents in the late twentieth century, especially in fundamentalist circles, as evidenced by the immense popularity of Hal Lindsey and C. C. Carlson's dispensationalist book, *The Late Great Planet Earth* (1970), which has sold millions of copies.

E. R. Sandeen, *The Roots of Fundamentalism* (1970); T. P. Weber, *Living in the Shadow of the Second Coming* (1983).

BRADLEY J. LONGFIELD

Disruption, Scots

"From the time when it was re-enacted in 1712 until it was repealed in 1874, the Law of Patronage hung like a great black cloud over the Kirk, and to its baneful influence can be traced . . . most of the ills that afflicted her during that century and a half" (Herron, p. 89). It was primarily the issue of lay lairds "intruding" (forcing) upon churches pastors they did not choose that caused all the secessions from the Church of Scotland. Patronage was the issue when Ebenezer Erskine* led the Seceders into the Associate Synod (1733) and when Thomas Gillespie was expelled by General Assembly and helped found the Presbytery of Relief (1761). The Disruption that created the Free Church of Scotland began with the 1835 Veto Act, whereby General Assembly ruled that a minister would not be intruded upon a congregation if half the male heads of families rejected the patron's choice. When an intruded minister was rejected by the Kirk of Auchterarder, the patron sued and the church was taken before the Court of Session (the highest civil court of the land), where it was overruled. The General Assembly appealed to the House of Lords and lost. With the church overruled by secular courts and pressure for democracy growing, it is not surprising that many simply decided on independency from governmental restrictions as well as from patrons. So in 1843, led by Thomas Chalmers,* nearly one-third of the ministers and half the membership left the established church and founded the Free Church of Scotland. In 1900 the Free Church united with the United Presbyterian Church (formed from a union of the earlier sessions) to form the United Free Church, which reunited with the Established Church of Scotland (1929). Two small churches refused to be part of these mergers, the Free Church and the United Free Church, and the former church is often tagged the "Wee Frees" today.

S. J. Brown, *Thomas Chalmers and the Godly Commonwealth in Scotland* (1982); A. Herron, *Kirk by Divine Right* (1985).

W. FRED GRAHAM

Dissenters *see* Nonconformity

Dissenting Academies

Excluded from the ancient English universities by the Clarendon Code,* Dissenters established academies of general and theological education. Among the earliest was Richard Frankland's at Rathmell (1670). Post-Toleration academies were supported by such bodies as the Presbyterian Fund (1689), the Congregational Fund Board (1695), and the King's Head Society (1730). Newer, independent academies followed. By mid-nineteenth century many had closed, a few became public (=private) schools, and some fed into nonconformist* theological colleges. Courses varied, some pioneering in science and mathematics. Alumni have included Daniel Defoe, Isaac Watts,* Philip Doddridge,* Joseph Priestley, and Thomas Godwin.

H. McLachlan, *English Education Under the Test Acts* (1931); I. Parker, *Dissenting Academies in England* (1914); J. W. A. Smith, *The Birth of Modern Education* (1954).

ALAN P. F. SELL

Doctrine

The term derives from the Latin word *docere* ("to teach"). In contemporary usage it may mean the general teaching of the church* (e.g., Christian doctrine), teachings of a church or tradition (e.g., Presbyterian; Reformed doctrine), or a specific tenet of faith* (e.g., the doctrine of predestination*). Doctrine may be seen as constitutive, authoritative, normative, and/or descriptive. A given doctrine, or doctrinal system, may be judged true or false, sufficient or deficient, essential or nonessential.

The Reformed tradition, from its beginning, acknowledged that the formulation of doctrine is an appropriate and necessary task of the church. In accord with the *sola Scriptura* of the Reformation, the Reformers taught that doctrine must derive from and communicate the truth of the Bible. Thus the formulation of doctrine is not an endeavor that builds on a prior interpretation of Scripture* but is offered as the initial interpretation itself. It is a primary rather than a secondary hermeneutical endeavor. Calvin's *Institutes of the Christian Religion,** for example, was written as a summary of the Christian religion for use by theological students in their biblical studies. Thus there is no prior norm for doctrine imposed on Scripture; the Word of God* provides both the content and the norm for the teachings formulated from it.

Doctrine is thus viewed by the Reformed reformers as an organized statement of the teaching of Scripture for the use of the church. Every aspect of the church's life must be grounded in the Word of God: doctrine is the link between the Bible and the preaching,* teaching, worship,* order, and service of the Christian community. Formation of doctrine is not an end in itself but is undertaken for the sake of the church and the believer. When it is understood in this way, defining the duties of the deacon,* for example, is as much a doctrinal matter as a confessional statement concerning election.

In the sixteenth and seventeenth centuries, doctrine in the Reformed tradition was articulated through confessions.* Since then, with a few exceptions (such as the United Church of Christ in the United States), Reformed churches have continued to be confessional churches, with a flowering of new confessions in the twentieth century. Confessions are not intended to be innovations but faithful expositions of biblical and apostolic faith. Consequently, most Reformed churches are also creedal, subscribing to the Apostles' Creed and the Nicene Creed and, less commonly, the Athanasian. Apostolicity in the Reformed tradition is not invested in the office of bishop but in the confessions of the church. Twentieth-century confessions seek to formulate biblical teachings in terms relevant to the issues of our time and also to present a range of ethical concerns confessionally.

Reformed theology and polity* have placed responsibility for sound doctrine in certain offices of the church: doctor, minister of the Word, and governing elder.* Most Reformed bodies no longer recognize a distinct teaching office, subsuming the responsibilities of the doctor under the minister of the Word. The minister of the Word has been specifically charged to preach and teach the doctrines of the Bible, in some cases through the requirement that theological points of a confessional statement be systematically presented. A responsibility of those ordained to the office of governing elder is to assure the faithful performance of this task.

Since the Reformation, doctrine has been understood in a variety of ways. Already in the sixteenth century, Reformed scholasticism* began to distill sharply defined doctrinal propositions from Scripture and organize them in logical systems which today seem often to distort rather than faithfully represent biblical teaching. The development of biblical scholarship as a discipline placed responsibility for determining the teaching of Scripture in the hands of those pursuing scientific knowledge. Early in the nineteenth century, the understanding of doctrine was recast by Friedrich Schleiermacher,* who taught that the doctrines of the Christian faith are descriptive rather than constitutive. Karth Barth,* in opposition, held that the community of faith is created only by the Word given testimony in Scripture, and apart from the teachings of the Bible neither faith nor church can exist. Jürgen Moltmann's* emphasis on the doctrine of hope has resulted in a focus on sound practice (*orthopraxis*) alongside sound teaching (*orthodoxy*). Liberation, feminist, and minjung theologies claim that doctrine may be articulated only by persons who experience a certain kind of oppression.

H. Berkhof, *Introduction to the Study of Dogmatics* (1985); Heppe, *RD*; Weber, *FD*.

PAUL R. FRIES

Dodd, Charles Harold (1884–1973)

One of the twentieth century's most significant NT scholars. Dodd was born in Wales, studied classics at Oxford, and was ordained in the Congregational church (1912). After three years of parish ministry he became professor at Oxford, Manchester, and Cambridge universities. His Cambridge appointment (1935) as Norris-Hulse Professor of Divinity made him the first non-Anglican to hold a chair of divinity at Cambridge or Oxford since the seventeenth-century Restoration. Dodd became famous for his emphasis on "realized eschatology" and the kerygma. He wrote twenty books, including two magisterial volumes on the Fourth Gospel. A leading ecumenical churchman, he was general director of the New English Bible translation.

DONALD A. HAGNER

Doddridge, Philip (1702–1751)

English nonconformist leader. He was pastor of an Independent/Congregational* chapel in Northampton (1729–51) and participated actively in an academy for ministerial students. Doddridge embodied many of the influences affecting evangelical nonconformity.* He maintained an orthodox yet moderate Puritan* theology (akin to that of Richard Baxter*). In the Puritan tradition he valued the life of the mind and was famous for attempting to teach his students to think. Interacting with the thought of an early Enlightenment figure such as Jean LeClerc, Doddridge helped develop the plenary theory of biblical inspiration which would commend itself to most English-speaking evangelicals for a century or more.

Doddridge was one of the first nonconformists to welcome the Evangelical Awakening. He valued the spiritual and theological work of Jonathan Edwards,* broke out of the rigid separatism of late Puritanism into the interdenominational fellowship that the Awakening made possible, and encouraged others to share in the new life. He produced a classic of evangelical spirituality, *The Rise and Progress of Religion in the Human Soul* (1745), and, after Isaac Watts,* was the second greatest hymn writer of eighteenth-century English nonconformity. "O God of Bethel, by Whose Hand" is expressive of pure worship;* "Hark, the Glad Sound! the Savior Comes," an exhortation to worship; and "O Happy Day, That Fixed My Choice" is a Reformed testimony to the reality of conversion.*

The Works of the Rev. P. Doddridge, 10 vols. (1839); G. F. Nuttall, ed., *Philip Doddridge, 1702–51* (1951).

IAN S. RENNIE

Dooyeweerd, Herman (1894–1977)

Professor of legal philosophy, law, and medieval Dutch law at the Free University of Amsterdam* (1929–1965). Cofounder (1935), with his brother-in-law Dirk Hendrik Theodoor Vollenhoven, of an international Christian philosophical movement of reformational character oriented to Dooyeweerd's three-volume magnum opus published as *De Wijsbegeerte der Wetsidee* (Philosophy of the Law-Idea; 1935–36) and as *A New Critique of Theoretical Thought* (1953–58; repr. 1983). He edited the movement's journal *Philosophia Reformata* (1936–76) and was a member of the Royal Dutch Academy of Science (secretary-treasurer, 1954–64). In *The Legacy of Herman Dooyeweerd*, North American students introduce his thought (C. T. McIntire, ed., 1985).

Dooyeweerd carried on critical dialogue with contemporaries about the autonomy of theoretical thought. Thus he was an early critic of today's foundationalism. He rejected the absolutization of reason and developed a transcendental critique of thought exposing the Enlightenment's pretended lack of prejudice. His epistemological and metaphilosophical ideas received a context in a fully developed cosmology and penetrating analysis of the history of philosophy. Reality is creation,* called into being by God,* subjected to a temporal order which guarantees its coherence. Philosophy is historically developed in terms of four religious motives: form and matter in Greek philosophy, nature and grace* in medieval synthesis philosophy, freedom* and nature in modern humanist philosophy, and creation-fall-redemption in biblical philosophy.

HENDRIK HART

Dort, Synod of

This assembly, the most significant national synod of the Reformed Church of the Netherlands,* settled the predestination* controversy between Arminians and Calvinists by condemning Arminianism.*

After Jacobus Arminius's death, the Arminians (or Remonstrants*) drew up a Remonstrance (1610) which presented their views in five articles. These became the basis of the increasingly bitter controversy that climaxed at the Synod of Dort. Convened at Dordrecht by the States General of the Netherlands, the synod lasted 180 sessions (November 13, 1618, to May 29, 1619). Its Dutch delegates included fifty-eight ministers and elders sent by provincial synods and five theologians (including Arminius's adversary Franciscus Gomarus*) from different Dutch academies. The States General sent eighteen civil delegates to protect government interests. Also represented were twenty-six Reformed theologians from eight foreign lands (Great Britain, the Palatinate, Hesse, Switzerland, Nassau-Wetteravia, Geneva, Bremen, and

Emden), giving the synod an international character. Leeuwarden pastor Johannes Bogerman was chosen president.

The synod summoned thirteen Remonstrant leaders, not to be delegates, but to examine and pass judgment on their views. Prior to their arrival, the synod dealt with issues of Bible translation, catechism* preaching,* catechetical instruction, baptism* of slaves, the status of theology students, and censorship.

The arrival of the Remonstrants on December 6, headed by Leiden theologian Simon Episcopius, initiated five weeks of procedural wrangling. The Remonstrants protested the synod's authority to act as judge and called for a conference between equals. Though both sides made procedural concessions, Remonstrant failure to cooperate fully led ultimately to their expulsion from the synod. After a government decision that the Remonstrants be judged from their writings, Bogerman expelled them with an angry speech (January 14).

For the next three months the synod studied the issues before making its judgment. The debate was sometimes heated, especially between the supralapsarian* Gomarus and the English and Bremen delegates. On the basis of reports from all nineteen delegations a committee of nine drafted the Canons of Dort, which condemned Remonstrant views and affirmed: God elects and reprobates, not on the basis of foreseen belief and unbelief, but by his sovereign will, though the reprobate perish by their own fault; Christ's death was sufficient for all but effective only for the elect; by the fall, humanity was totally corrupted, though it remained human; God's grace works effectively to convert the unbeliever, though not by coercion; and God preserves believers so they cannot totally fall from grace. These have been popularly described by the acronym TULIP: Total depravity, Unconditional election, Limited atonement, Irresistible grace, and Perseverance of the saints.* The Canons, signed by all delegates, accommodated significant theological diversity among them and represented the triumph of a moderate Calvinism.*

Then, after approval of the Belgic Confession* and the HC,* the foreign delegations returned home. The remaining sessions, beginning on May 13, dealt with such church matters as revision of the church order, liturgical forms, and Sunday observance.

The Synod of Dort's decisions on doctrine and church order defined the Dutch Reformed church for two centuries and continue to shape Reformed churches of Dutch heritage.

Acta Synodi . . . Dordrechti (1620); G. Brandt, *History of the Reformation . . . in . . . the Low Countries* (1733; repr. 1979, 4 vols. in 2), vol. 3; Schaff, *Creeds*, vols. 1 and 3.

DONALD SINNEMA

Downame, George (1565?–1634)

Important Puritan theologian who was professor of logic and Fellow of Christ's College, Cambridge (1585–96). Downame wrote theological treatises, including *The Christians Sanctuarie* (1604); *Lectures on the XV Psalme* (1604); *Papa Antichristus* (1620); and *The Covenant of Grace, or an exposition upon Luke I* (1631). His commentary on the logic of Peter Ramus* (*Commentarius in Rami dialecticam* [1605]) was nearly five hundred pages long, his theological works displaying his debt to the Ramist method. Downame and his brother John, another significant Puritan theologian, imbibed their Ramism from William Perkins* and stand in the line of Christ's College Puritan Ramists from Perkins to John Milton* who used Downame's work on logic as a source for his own *Art of Logic* (1672). It was said of Downame that "no man was then and there better skill'd in *Aristotle*, or a greater Follower of *Ramus*" (Thomas Fuller, *The History of the Worthies of England* [1662]). Downame became bishop of Derry, Ireland (1616), and got into trouble with Archbishop Laud for publishing an attack on Arminianism* (1631).

W. S. Howell, *Logic and Rhetoric in England 1500–1700* (1956); D. K. McKim, *Ramism in William Perkins' Theology* (1987).

DONALD K. MCKIM

Drummond, Henry (1851–1897)

Evangelist, theologian, and scientist, and professor of natural science in the Free Church of Scotland College, Glasgow. Drummond became a prominent preacher, working with the campaigns of Dwight L. Moody and Ira D. Sankey (1870s). His popular success in using science to illumine theology was probably due more to his felicitous literary style than to scientific or theological profundity. Theologians criticized him for uncritically accepting the evolutionary theories of Charles Darwin and Herbert Spencer.

H. Drummond, *The Ascent of Man* (1894); *Natural Law in the Spiritual World* (1883); and *The Ideal Life* (1897); G. A. Smith, *The Life of Henry Drummond* (1899).

N. R. NEEDHAM

Duff, Alexander (1806–1878)

At St. Andrews University, Duff was influenced by Thomas Chalmers* and went to Bengal (1829) as the first official missionary of the Church of Scotland. In Calcutta he found a tremendous thirst for Western education among intelligent young Bengalees caught between tradition and Western modernity. Duff saw this as his evangelistic opportunity. He established a college to teach Western learning and Christian truth through English. He lectured on the evidences of Christianity to packed and excited audiences. He baptized many exceedingly able young Bengalees, most of whom were ordained after undertaking the equivalent of the full Scottish divinity course.

Duff became the leading strategist, apologist, and theorist for missionary education. He saw Western education on a Christian basis as laying a mine that would eventually destroy the whole edifice of Hinduism, a kind of preparation for the gospel. He also sought to raise up by English education a whole generation of "Indian Luthers, Calvins and Knoxes" who would, using Indian languages, be agents of an Indian reformation that would ultimately lead India to freedom. For Duff, as for most Scots of his day, evangelism* and enlightenment were so closely allied as to be virtually indistinguishable; and he saw education as the spearhead of mission.

After returning from India (1867), Duff occupied the new chair of evangelistic theology in New College,* Edinburgh.

M. A. Laird, *Missionaries and Education in Bengal, 1793–1837* (1972); G. Smith, *The Life of Alexander Duff*, 2 vols. (1879).

DUNCAN B. FORRESTER

Dutch Reformation

The Dutch Reformation began with the Brethren of the Common Life in the fourteenth century, continued with Erasmus* and the humanists,* became less gentile with the importation of German goods and Lutheran ideas, was radicalized among the lower classes with Anabaptist commitments, and found fruition in Calvinism.*

Reform conflicted with the conservative Catholicism of Philip II. The first blood that was shed was Lutheran, then Anabaptist. The armed conflict by which reform was secured was far from purely religious, nor were the sides divided on present religious, geographic, or political lines. A revulsion at the Inquisition and the cruelty of Fernando Álvarez de Toledo, Duke of Alva; the detestation of Spanish troops; the desire of the nobility and urban oligarchies to retain privilege against Spanish absolutism; economic outrage over a 10 percent sales tax; the democratization of the lower classes; a rising national religious commitment on the part of some; consciousness and forceful personalities—all contributed to the armed conflict, but ultimately the geography of the Netherlands determined the possibility for the ultimate success of Calvinism in the north and east and maintenance of Catholicism in the south and west.

During the 1540s, Calvinism's existence outside the borders of the Hapsburg Netherlands was primarily at Emden and London. The first formal confession (Belgic Confession,* 1561) was by Guido de Brès, who ministered in Tournai, Mons, and Lille. After Spain's peace with France (1559), Philip could turn his attention to exterminating heresy. In 1566 some four hundred nobles from all parts of the Netherlands presented a petition to the governess, Margaret of Parma, to abolish the Inquisition. It was met with a derisive remark about the impudence of these "beggars," from which term the subsequent resistance movement took its name.

This expression of Netherlandish nationalism gained momentary freedom for "hedge-preachers," and animosity for the old regime soon broke out in the destruction of images and the looting of church properties. This destruction robbed the movement of national cohesiveness as the vast majority of the people were loyal to the old religion, if not to Spain. An "Accord" granted freedom to preach and proscribed interference with the old religion. Peace was possible, but Philip meant to extirpate heresy through Alva and his nine thousand Spanish troops.

In Alva's six-year rule (1567–73), a thousand rebels were executed, the country subdued, an invasion by William of Orange from Germany repelled, the Inquisition exercised, and a 10 percent tax imposed. The severity of Alva's reign gave new life to the nationalist cause, but opposition had been crushed, with the exception of the Sea Beggars—privateers who preyed on Spanish shipping.

Ordered out of English ports in April 1572, the Sea Beggars captured Brielle and then Flushing. Soon almost all the provinces of Holland and Zeeland (Amsterdam excepted) had fallen to them, aided by Calvinists and Orangeists. Alva soon reasserted his control, but north of the great rivers logistical difficulties increased. Ultimately, Alva failed—at Alkmaar—and asked to be recalled.

In November 1576, Spanish troops ran wild in Antwerp, killing seven thousand in eleven days of pillage and massacre. Again, excess turned the tide, and a revulsion toward all things Spanish united all the provinces in their desire for the expulsion of Spanish troops, the first demand of the Pacification of Ghent,* which included suspension of Philip's edicts against heresy and freedom for Calvinists in Holland and Zeeland, and no anti-Catholic action.

Calvinists exercised freedom in Brabant and Flanders as well, where the movement had first gained strength. But religious excess combined with social unrest resulted in iconoclasm and uprisings, with the resultant League of Arras to protect the Catholic faith and the Union of Utrecht to protect the Calvinists. While Orange had always worked for a united Netherlands with religious toleration, religious zeal and persecution on both sides caused increasing division.

Spain now sent Parma to subdue the country. Calvinists from the southern provinces flocked north by the thousands, while Catholics in the north headed south. Parma was able to assert Spanish authority in the provinces south of the delta of the Rhine, while the seven northern provinces of Holland, Zeeland, Utrecht, Gelderland, Friesland, Overijssel, and Groningen declared their independence from Spain (1581).

Ultimately, it was the great rivers that set the boundaries, while Catholics and Calvinists operated within their provinces to maintain control and exclude dissent. The toleration of William of Orange found expression, not in a united Netherlands where both Catholics and Calvinists could worship,* but in a northern Netherlands where Anabaptists were first given national rights of worship (1577).

In polity,* the Dutch Reformed Church sought to follow Calvin. Early synods in Wesel (1568) and Emden (1571) were held out of the country. By 1574, the Calvinists had sufficient strength to hold a national synod at Dordrecht (however, Pieter Geyl estimates that even in 1587 only 10 percent of the Province of Holland was Calvinist!). Local privilege of nobility and oligarchy everywhere set limits on the church, and the Arminian* controversy was as much about polity as theology. Even after the great Synod of Dort* (1618–19), polities in the provinces varied, as did the nuances of theology.

For a more complete telling of the tale, John Lothrop Motley communicates the religious fervor of the Calvinist cause, while Geyl dispassionately conveys the multifaceted nature of the conflict without a good/bad portrayal.

C. Bangs, *Arminius* (rev. ed. 1985); P.

Geyl, *The Revolt in the Netherlands, 1555–1609* (1962); J. L. Motley, *The Rise of the Dutch Republic* (1856).

DONALD J. BRUGGINK

Dwight, Timothy (1752–1817)

Congregational educator and theologian. Born in Northampton, Massachusetts, Dwight attended Yale College and served as chaplain in the American Revolution. He ran a school in Northampton and served in the state legislature (1779–83). After 1783 he pastored a Congregational church in Greenfield, Connecticut, taught school, published poetry, and was a recognized educator and leader of Connecticut Congregationalism.*

Dwight became president of Yale and professor of divinity (1795). He reformed administration and curriculum, and tripled the enrollment. Despite the lack of piety and the prevalence of Deism and unbelief, a revival occurred under his preaching, and by 1802 a third of the students were converted. This fueled the Second Great Awakening.* Dwight's chapel sermons, constituting a system of theology, were posthumously published as *Theology, Explained and Defended* (5 vols.; 1818–19).

In the interests of revivalism* and reform, Dwight, a moderate Calvinist, modified the theology of his grandfather, Jonathan Edwards,* by rejecting doctrines of the imputation of Adam's sin,* natural inability, and limited atonement.* A conservative and federalist, he defended the standing order and established (Congregational) church against infidelity and democratic sentiments. He wrote the hymn "I Love Thy Kingdom, Lord" (1800).

S. E. Berk, *Calvinism Versus Democracy: Timothy Dwight and the Origins of American Evangelical Orthodoxy* (1974); C. E. Cunningham, *Timothy Dwight 1752–1817* (1942); J. R. Fitzmier, "The Godly Federalism of Timothy Dwight" (diss., Princeton University, 1986); K. Silverman, *Timothy Dwight* (1969); A. Wenzke, "Timothy Dwight: The Enlightened Puritan" (diss., Pennsylvania State University, 1983).

ALBERT H. FREUNDT, JR.

Ecclesiastical Ordinances

The document drawn up at the insistence of John Calvin* as a constitution for the Reformed church of Geneva upon his definitive return (1541). The Genevan Small Council, realizing that the 1538 policy of banishing Calvin had been a political and ecclesiastical disaster, invited him to return as chief minister of the church (September 21, 1540). Calvin agreed, but on his own terms. He wanted to establish a church* governed by the Bible and the system of discipline* that he had tried to enforce during his previous tenure in the city. Therefore, on the day of his arrival (September 13, 1541) he appeared before the Small Council to demand that the magistrates name a committee, including himself, to prepare a written constitution for the Genevan church. The resulting Ecclesiastical Ordinances were subsequently modified by the Small Council and the Council of Two Hundred before being approved by the General Assembly of Geneva (November 20, 1541).

The stated work of the church was to preach the gospel and administer the sacraments,* to teach believers the Scriptures,* and to care for the needy. To implement this, the Ordinances settled the practical details of church life and focused on the functions of four ministerial offices, two ecclesiastical and two lay: pastors, teachers, elders,* and deacons.* Each had its own service sphere under ultimate oversight of the civil authorities. Pastors, elected by the Venerable Company of Pastors* (all the resident pastors) and confirmed by the Small Council, were to preach the Word of God,* administer the sacraments, and assist in exercising discipline. Doctors (teachers), chosen in the same manner as the pastors, were to catechize the young, instruct adult believers in true doctrine,* and provide general education for the community. Twelve elders, chosen from the Councils, nominated by the Small Council and elected by the Council of Two Hundred, were all laymen who were to help the pastors maintain discipline and spiritual oversight. Deacons, laymen elected in the same manner as elders, were responsible for the care of the sick, the poor, and the needy.

The machinery of discipline was in the hands of the Consistory,* an ecclesiastical court composed of the Company of Pastors and the elders. Calvin saw this as an essentially remedial body, one phase of the care of souls. It not only admonished the wayward but also determined whether the Lord's Supper* should be withheld from anyone or whether excommunication should be exacted. The most original feature of Calvin's Consistory was its power of excommunication—claimed somewhat ambiguously in the 1541 Ordinances but definitely confirmed by 1555 and written into the 1561 document's revision. Elsewhere in Protestant Europe, excommunication remained the prerogative of the civil government.* The Ordinances also affirmed the principle of a representative church polity* in which clergy and laity shared authority.

J. W. Baker, "Christian Discipline and the Early Reformed Tradition," in *Calviniana*, ed. R. V. Schnucker (1988), 107–19; J. F. Bergler, ed., *Registres de la compaignie des pasteurs de Genève, 1546–1553* (1964); R. M. Kingdon, "Calvin's Ideas About the Diaconate," in *Piety, Politics, and Ethics*, ed. C. Lindberg (1984); E. A. McKee, *Elders and the Plural Ministry* (1988); E. W. Monter, *Calvin's Geneva* (1967); J. E. Olson, *Calvin and Social Welfare* (1989).

ROBERT D. LINDER

Economics

The study of patterns of production, exchange, and consumption of "goods" to fulfill human needs and desires. In European civilization, no religious people paid more systematic attention to economics than the Calvinists.

Unlike their medieval predecessors, Calvinists neither downgraded nor episodically concerned themselves with poverty, wealth, and questions of economic justice. Instead, they sought to bring the economic realm—like every other human realm—into conformity with the realm of God.*

Indeed, says R. H. Tawney, Calvinism* "is perhaps the first systematic body of religious teaching which can be said to recognize and applaud the economic virtues. Its enemy is not the accumulation of riches but their misuse for purposes of self-indulgence or ostentation. Its ideal is a society which seeks wealth with the sober gravity of men who are conscious at once of disciplining their own characters by patient labor, and of devoting themselves to a service acceptable to God" (Tawney, p. 105).

Calvin's* Geneva was the laboratory of this development. Its church and government leaders devised and enforced an economic discipline that touched all facets of that city's material life. Laws requiring church attendance and education of children combined with laws for public sanitation, family health practice, and the founding of new industry. Under Calvin and the Councils, Genevans acquired latrines and balcony railing in their houses, better home-heating systems, licensed dentists, new hospitals, and their first textile factory (McNeill). Most of all, they acquired theology, law, and active church-state controls of the ancient human vice of greed as practiced in the new commercial culture of capitalism.* "The hungry are defrauded of their rights," said Calvin, "if their hunger is not relieved." Therefore, charging the poor high prices for bread when bread is scarce may be market ethics, but not Christian ethics.

Calvinism's influence in shaping capitalism has elicited much scholarly debate. Like the parallel dispute regarding its contribution to the emergence of democracy, its contribution to capitalistic theory and practice over the centuries is undoubtedly partial, complex, a mixture of "affinity" and antagonism. Calvinists have to begin their thinking about economic life with a certain cluster of unambiguous general principles. For example, there can be no "autonomous sphere" of economics in a world governed wholly by a sovereign God;* rules of justice* and fairness apply to market exchanges just as much as to any other human relationships; God loves poor people as much as rich people but requires of the rich particular concern for the needs of the poor; greed remains a besetting human sin and the rich are especially vulnerable to it. These principles root in a biblical tradition more ancient than Calvinism—the

Bible,* where Calvinists mean to start their cultivation of an economic ethic.

Max Weber believed that the only powerful surviving modern fruit of this rootage is the "Protestant ethic"* and its associated personal character—the frugal, hardworking, wealth accumulator who became Karl Marx's stereotype of the capitalist. Tawney, in accusing Weber of oversimplifying this history, underscored the truth in it when he observed that Calvinists, from the Puritans* to modern Presbyterian business persons, have progressively suffered from the atrophy of one-half of their ethical roots: they acquired freedom of economic striving and lost collective discipline of that striving. Calvinism's "theory had been discipline; its practical result was liberty," in both Puritan England* and Protestant America.

The ironic result of this four-century erosion of the sense of social justice, social control, and social responsibility of all economic enterprise has been the clamor, in an America of the 1990s, for a new "business ethic." Modern adherents of the Reformed tradition have much thinking to do if they are to combine the old, basic Calvinist principles with the new world of global economics and multinational corporations. They will probably have to begin their recovery of tradition and their new thinking about it in the company of fellow church members rather than exclusively in the company of associates in business. In the former company, they are more likely to become sensitive to the basic ethical-theological wisdom of Tawney, a practicing economic historian and practicing Christian, when he wrote:

> If . . . economic ambitions are good servants, they are bad masters. Harnessed to a social purpose, they will turn the mill and grind the corn. But the question, to what end the wheels revolve, still remains; and on that question the naive and uncritical worship of economic power . . . throws no light. . . . For the condition of effective action in a complex civilization is cooperation. And the condition of cooperation is agreement, both as to the ends to which effort should be applied, and the criteria by which success is to be judged. (Tawney, p. 282)

W. J. Bouwsma, *John Calvin: A Sixteenth-Century Portrait* (1988); J. T. McNeill, *The History and Character of Calvinism* (1954); R. H. Tawney, *Religion and the Rise of Capitalism* (1926; repr. 1962); M. Weber, *The Protestant Ethic and the Spirit of Capitalism* (1904–5; ET 1930; repr. 1958).

DONALD W. SHRIVER, JR.

Ecumenism

The movement through which divided churches seek to manifest afresh the unity given and willed by Jesus Christ. The term "ecumenism" is from the Greek word *oikoumenē*, meaning the "inhabited earth." The noun "ecumenism" is a construct of relatively recent date, coming into general use through the Second Vatican Council.

Reformed churches are divided in their attitude toward the ecumenical movement. While the majority participate with great openness and can be considered to be a driving ecumenical force, others are skeptical or even hostile toward it. Basic for the Reformed understanding of ecumenism is that the Reformers did not intend to found a new church but sought reform of the whole church. Reformed churches open to the ecumenical movement see it as an opportunity to resume the dialogue with other churches that was prematurely disrupted in the sixteenth century. In a certain sense, the ecumenical movement is the fulfillment of the deepest intentions of the Reformation.

John Calvin* considered unity to be part of the nature of the church.* His fourth book of the *Institutes* is a vivid expression of this conviction: "On the True Church with whom We are to Cultivate Unity because She is the Mother of all Faithful" (*Inst.* 4.1). He made repeated efforts to avoid the final rupture with the Church of Rome. In particular, he worked indefatigably for the unity of the various Reformation churches. In this respect, his assumption was that as long as agreement on the essentials of faith was assured, diversity among the local churches was admissible. The Consensus Tigurinus* (1549) made it possible to maintain fellowship with the Reformation of Zurich, but for centuries it created an obstacle to the rapprochement with the Lutheran tradition.

When separate Reformed churches had been established, the question of the status of other churches arose. In what did the Reformed church claim to be or to represent the church of Jesus Christ? French theologians (primarily) developed the concept of the church of Jesus Christ being alive in all churches, in some purer and in others in less pure form. "Identifying a particular church with the *una sancta* is as inappropriate as calling the sea of Bretagne the whole ocean" (Philippe Duplessis-Mornay [1549–1623]). The one church consists of several Christian communions that are one in the essentials of the faith and recognize one another on this basis (Pierre Jurieu [1637–1713]). Reformed theologians persisted in hoping that one day the divided churches would gather in a universal council and confess together the fundamental truths of the gospel.

In the course of the centuries, Reformed churches were at the origin of many initiatives toward unity—both internal and intraconfessional. The hardening of the Reformed tradition into Reformed orthodoxy in the seventeenth and eighteenth centuries and resulting splits provoked countermovements. Both in Pietism and the revival movement the quest for unity was alive. At the beginning of the nineteenth century, the Disciples of Christ movement split from the Presbyterian Church because it wanted to provide a platform for intraconfessional unity. Reformed Christians actively participated in the foundation of the Evangelical Alliance (1846).

Reformed theologians played an outstanding role in the beginnings and shaping of the modern ecumenical movement (e.g., F. F. Ellinwood, William Paton, Wilfred Monod, Adolf Keller). The first two General Secretaries of the WCC* were from Reformed churches (W. A. Visser 't Hooft,* Eugene Carson Blake*). The thought of some Reformed theologians had a decisive influence on the nascent ecumenical movement (Karl Barth,* Josef Hromádka,* John Mackay,* Lesslie Newbigin,* Hendrikus Berkhof,* etc.).

An important step was taken after World War II with the decision of the WARC* to consider itself an instrument in the service of the ecumenical movement. The General Council at Princeton (1954) developed the idea that "Jesus Christ himself breaks down all barriers of separation and, in obedience to him, the various forms of faith and life become means of serving the unity of the Spirit in the bond of peace." The Council declared that the Reformed churches recognized the ministry,* the sacraments,* and members of all churches that, according to the Bible, confess Jesus Christ as Lord and Savior and that they were prepared to invite all members of such churches to participate in the celebration of the Lord's Supper.* Not all Reformed churches shared this emphasis on openness. In 1946 the Reformed Ecumenical Synod (since 1988 Reformed Ecumenical Council) was founded, an association of churches with a clear allegiance to the classic Reformed confessions. A militant opponent of the ecumenical movement is the Presbyterian pastor Carl McIntire, founder of the International Council of Christian Churches.

Reformed commitment to the ecumenical movement also found expression in bilateral dialogues. On the basis of extended theological conversations, European Reformed churches declared "church fellowship" with the Lutheran churches (Leuenberg Agreement; 1973). At the international level, dialogues were conducted with the Disciples of Christ (concluded 1988), the Anglican Communion (1984), Baptist World Alliance (1982), Lutheran World Federation (1989), World Methodist Council (1988), and Mennonite World Conference (1984). While these conversations aimed at full communion, dialogues with the Roman Catholic Church (1990) and the Orthodox Church (started in 1988) served the purpose of better mutual understanding. Analogous conversations took place with all partners at the national level. In the course of the twentieth century, several Reformed churches decided to enter into united churches (Canada, India, Australia, etc.).

Internal division remains, however, a characteristic of the Reformed family. While in some countries reunion of divided Reformed churches was successfully achieved (United States, Holland), the movement of dividing continues in other countries (e.g., Korea*). The WARC has in recent years recognized the problem which was one of the major themes at the 22nd General Council in Seoul, Korea (1989). At the same time, the Alliance emphatically confirmed its commitment to the ecumenical movement.

LUKAS VISCHER

Edwards, Jonathan (1703–1758)

Prominent eighteenth-century New England pastor, revivalist, and theologian. Edwards served as minister of the church of Northampton, Massachusetts (1729–50), missionary to Indians in Stockbridge (1751–57), and president of the College of New Jersey (January–March 1758).

Edwards was born in East Windsor, Connecticut, into a culturally enlightened and theologically conservative family. An only son, he was prepared from an early age for the ministry and a life of thought. His childhood education and his undergraduate (1716–20) and graduate studies (1721–22) at Yale College immersed him not only in the most current thought emerging from Europe, such as British empiricism and continental rationalism, but also in the debate between the orthodox Calvinism* of his Puritan* forebears and Anglican Arminianism.*

In Anglo-American society during the late seventeenth and early eighteenth centuries, an important aspect of theological controversy was the impact of the teachings of Jacobus Arminius, a sixteenth-century Dutch theologian. Arminius opposed Calvinist doctrines of irresistible grace,* predestination,* and election. Eventually, the English school of thought that carried his name advocated the undetermined freedom of the will,* the graciousness of works, natural virtue, and moderation in church admission policies. By 1700, virtually all clergy of the Church of England subscribed to this way of thinking. To those descendants of the New England Puritans intent on preserving the doctrines of God's absolute sovereignty and humankind's absolute dependence on God for grace, Arminianism* was a reprehensible theology. They argued that if works alone were meritorious of grace, and if mere striving was sufficient to earn salvation,* then God's sovereignty was compromised and Christ's atonement* unnecessary. Into this ideological civil war Edwards was recruited.

The necessity of challenging the Arminian heresy became immediately apparent to Edwards when the rector and tutors of Yale, in what became known as "The Great Apostasy," converted to Anglicanism (1722). Returning to Connecticut after serving a Presbyterian church in New York City (autumn 1722–spring 1723) and in Bolton, Connecticut (October 1723—May 1724), he assumed the position of senior tutor at Yale until 1726. Here he began his life's work of combating the spread of Arminian thought.

In August 1726 Edwards was called by the church of Northampton, Massachusetts, as an assistant to the aged and sickly Solomon Stoddard. Stoddard, Edwards's grandfather, was a renowned minister and distinguished revivalist. But he was also controversial for his denunciation of congregational* polity.* He denied the legitimacy of church covenanting and espoused instead an ecclesiastical hierarchy. In place of tests for admission, Stoddard substituted an "open" policy allowing anyone of good behavior and reputation into the sacraments,* which, he maintained, were "converting ordinances." To Edwards, this resembled the Arminian tenets he opposed. However, the post was too prestigious for the ambitious Edwards to refuse, and, despite misgivings about Stoddard's principles, he was ordained (February 1727).

Solomon Stoddard died in February 1729, leaving Edwards fully in charge of western New England's most important pulpit and free to pursue his anti-Arminian agenda. In 1731 Edwards preached "God Glorified in Man's Dependence" at Boston. This sermon clearly demonstrated his loyalty to orthodoxy and his radical view of the nature of grace. In his preaching at Northampton, Edwards aimed at being the instrument of a revival to make his congregation realize the futility of trusting in their own righteousness and their need for the "divine light," or saving grace, to change their nature completely. As he described in *A Faithful Narrative of the Surprising Work of God* (1737), his people—especially the young people—began to show signs of a change of heart in 1732–33. During 1734–35, a full-scale awakening occurred in the town. Edwards's summary of the revival, published in London, gained him international recognition.

The widespread revivals of the early 1740s, known as the Great Awakening,* were a seminal period for Edwards. He was both exulted and disheartened by what he saw and heard. The frequency and intensity of reported conversions made Edwards look optimistically to the coming of the millennium, the thousand-year reign of peace on earth that would follow the defeat of Satan. However, he was disturbed by some of the consequences of the revivals, including anticlericalism, lay exhortation, separatism, and irrational behavior that did not, in his view, accord with true conversion.* Critics assailed the convictions of many supposed converts as illusory and even the work of the devil. Edwards became a cautious defender of the revivals. In *The Distinguishing Marks of a Work of the Spirit of God* (1741), *Some Thoughts Concerning the Present Revival* (1742), and *A Treatise Concerning Religious Affections* (1746), he sought to isolate ways of discerning true workings of grace from self—or even devil-inspired delusions. In *Religious Affections*, his most searching psychological treatment of conversion, he demonstrated through twelve "signs" that though true religion consists in "holy affections," those affections do not violate the reasonableness of God and Christianity. For Edwards, a balance of emotion and reason,* manifested in a corresponding balance of sincere profession and godly actions, was an essential indication of election.

With the decline of the awakenings abroad and in Northampton, Edwards and his congregation experienced a slow process of alienation. In 1744 his heavy-handed manner of disciplining young men of the town for distributing a book on midwifery drew the ire of many in his church. Salary disputes, punctuated by resentment over the purportedly high life-style of the Edwards family increased friction. Edwards's efforts to exercise ministerial authority in a paternity case only exacerbated matters (1748). Most important, his view of visible sainthood gradually overcame his former tolerance of the "lax mode of admission" practiced in the Northampton church.

In the aftermath of the awakenings, Edwards's study of Scripture and the ecclesiastical problems posed by the Great Awakening left no doubt in his mind about the need for stricter terms for church admission. He could no longer abide by Stoddardean practices or see warrant for keeping known hypocrites in communion. For Edwards, the ordinances were not means of conversion but seals of a preexisting faith. By 1748 he publicly insisted that applicants would have to make a sincere profession "of the things of which religion consists." His concern was with keeping the church pure so as to preserve it. These principles were published in *An Humble Inquiry . . . Concerning the Qualifications Requisite to a Complete Standing and Full Communion in the Visible Christian Church* (1749). But the majority of the Northampton congregation were for preserving its old polity. A bitter struggle ensued that ended with Edwards's dismissal on June 22, 1750.

Edwards went to Stockbridge, Massachusetts, to become pastor to the Mahican Indians and to a small English congregation. Since the beginning of the revivals he had an interest in evangelizing the native Americans as part of the work of ushering in the millennium. His 1747 work, *An Humble Attempt to Promote Explicit Agreement and Visible Union of God's People in Extraordinary Prayer*, part of a larger movement toward Anglo-American "concerts of prayer," dealt with the importance of evangelizing. In addition, he had published *The Life of David Brainerd** (1749), who until his death (1747) had been a tireless missionary. Edwards proved to be an able administrator of the mission and a stringent advocate of the exploited Mahicans. He even remained at the exposed western outpost when the French and Indian War began (1756).

At Stockbridge, Edwards wrote many of his major works that addressed the Arminian controversy. Foremost were *A Careful and Strict Enquiry Into Modern Prevailing Notions of . . . Freedom of the Will* (1754), in which he showed that the will was determined by the inclination of either sin* or grace in the soul, and *The Great Christian Doctrine of Original Sin Defended* (1758), in which he asserted that all humankind had a natural propensity to sin due to its "constitutional unity" in Adam.

Edwards served at Stockbridge until January 1758. He then went to Princeton, New Jersey, to become the new president of the College of New Jersey. He died on March 22 after having received a month earlier an inoculation for smallpox that proved to be infected.

Following Edwards's death, his reputation grew. Posthumously published works included *The Nature of True Virtue* and *The End for Which God Created the World* (1765), two major statements on ethics; *A History of the Work of Redemption* (1774), which laid out Edwards's vision of the faithfulness of God to God's promises throughout history; *Miscellaneous Observations on Important Theological Subjects* (1793) and *Remarks on Important Theological Controversies* (1796), which contained excerpts from his exegetical writings and private notebooks.

Edwards's influence on American thought and life has been profound. His writings laid the groundwork of the New England Theology;* determined the parameters for debate on religious psychology, human liberty, and social ethics; helped shape frontier piety as America expanded westward; informed the natural theology of the Transcendentalists; and were factors in abolitionism, missionism, and the moral reform movements of the nineteenth century. Even today, the breadth and the depth of Edwards's thought make him one of the most intriguing and studied figures of early American history.

C. Cherry, *The Theology of Jonathan Edwards: A Reappraisal* (1966; repr. 1990); N. Fiering, *Jonathan Edwards's Moral Thought and Its British Context* (1981); R. Jenson, *America's Theologian: A Recommendation of Jonathan Edwards* (1988); M. X. Lesser, *Jonathan Edwards: A Reference Guide* (1981); P. Miller, *Jonathan Edwards* (1949); I. H. Murray, *Jonathan Edwards: A New Biography* (1987); J. E. Smith, ed., *The Works of Jonathan Edwards* (1957–); O. E. Winslow, *Jonathan Edwards* (1940).

KENNETH P. MINKEMA

Effectual Calling *see* Predestination

Elders

The Calvinist office of elders is one of four church ministries. With pastors and teachers, elders are presbyters; the fourth office is the diaconate. Presbyterial functions include preaching, teaching, administering the sacraments, and governing; pastors, who have all functions, share government with the lay elders, and together pastors and elders form a governing council called the consistory (session). Church government is usually identified with "discipline," but this concept must be rightly understood. Discipline* is not primarily punishment but guidance, counseling, rebuke, reconciliation, and only finally "excommunication" if other measures have not brought repentance* and renewal. Traditionally, discipline has been based on Matt. 18:15–18, and usually the "church" (v. 17) which disciplines the unrepentant sinner has been understood as a body representing, acting for, the whole. John Calvin* believed that in Matthew, Jesus was speaking of a Christian version of the Sanhedrin; he considered Rom. 12:8; 1 Cor. 12:28; and 1 Tim. 5:17 Pauline references to lay Christians elected to share church government with pastors. Modern study of Calvin's Geneva Consistory* reveals that its work went far beyond "discipline" as rebuke, to include religious education, corporate counseling, and efforts to build and rebuild Christian community.

The office of elders was the most controversial of Calvin's four; its distinctive Calvinist Reformed character is best seen by comparison with other Christian agencies of discipline. Until the Protestant Reformation, Matt. 18:17 was normally read as assigning discipline to the clergy, but control of excommunication became a source of contention in Christendom, as princes vied with bishops for the power to exclude citizen-Christians from common life. Protestants expanded the interpretation of Matt. 18:17 to include laity, but after some hesitation most groups concluded that discipline should be handled for the community by senior members (men). Differences arose primarily over which laity should represent the church. Zwinglian Reformed (like Lutherans) assigned discipline to Christian rulers. Zwinglians based church order on the OT as well as on the NT; 2 Chronicles 19 was a favorite text supporting magisterial control of ecclesiastical discipline. Calvinist Reformed insisted on the NT model for right church order, distinguished church and state, and advocated and struggled for autonomy in ecclesiastical government. The same person might be Christian magistrate and elder, but the offices are different and distinct.

The elders' office has a varied history, partly because of its nontraditional character as a "lay ecclesiastical" office. In some places, the responsibilities of elders and deacons* were not clearly distinguished. Where congregationalist polity* developed, elders were discontinued. Today, in many churches women as well as men serve as elders. However, though communal oversight of personal life has come to seem an invasion of privacy, and practice of discipline has changed, the Reformed office of elders continues to represent the importance of corporate responsibility for the quality of Christian life.

P. De Klerk, ed., *Renaissance, Reformation, Resurgence* (1976), 63–84 (E. W. Monter), 95–106 (R. M. Kingdon); R. M. Kingdon, "Calvin and the Establishment of Consistory Discipline in Geneva," *Nederlandsch Archief voor Kerkgeschiedenis* (1990); E. A. McKee, *Elders and the Plural Ministry* (1988).

ELSIE ANNE MCKEE

Election *see* Predestination

Elizabethan Settlement

The reestablishment of the Protestant and Reformed faith in England under Elizabeth I (1558–1603). She succeeded Mary Tudor (1553–58), who had brought back Roman Catholicism and the papal supremacy. The Act of Uniformity* (1559) regularized the Church of England's course along the lines established during Edward VI's reign (1547–53). The use of Thomas Cranmer's* second *Book of Common Prayer** (1552) was restored, the Articles of Religion (reduced from forty-two to thirty-nine) were reenacted, and archbishops and bishops were appointed who promoted the cause of the Reformation.

PHILIP E. HUGHES

Ellul, Jacques (1912–)

Professor Emeritus of the History and Sociology of Institutions at the University of Bordeaux, France, Ellul holds degrees in history, sociology, and law and an honorary doctorate from the University of Amsterdam. During World War II he was a leader in the French Resistance. A member of the Reformed Church of France, he also served on the Committee on Work of the WCC.*

Author of more than thirty books, Ellul is best known for his sociological trilogy (*The Technological Society* [1967], *Propaganda* [1973], and *The Political Illusion* [1972]) depicting the domination of Western society by "technique," a force neither neutral nor within human control. Ellul refers to the whole of his work, however, as "a composition in counterpoint" in which sociological investigation is confronted with biblical and theological interpretation. In theological works, *The Meaning of the City* (1970), *The New Demons* (1975), and *The Politics of God and the Politics of Man* (1972), he presents the city and its politics as humanity's rebellious attempts to secure life and society apart from God.

While Ellul may be placed in the Reformed tradition, he has increasingly distanced himself from Calvin* and moved by his own account toward Barth* and Kierkegaard. "I am not a Calvinist," he claims in his *In Season, Out of Season* (1982), adding, "I have developed in the direction of openness." One sign of this openness is his belief in universal salvation. Like his mentors, however, he has remained critical of rationalist philosophy and natural theology, both of which he views as attempts to constrain God's sovereign freedom.

J. Ellul, *To Will and To Do* (1969); *The Ethics of Freedom* (1976); and *Hope in Time of Abandonment* (1978); C. Christians and J. M. Van Hook, eds., *Jacques Ellul: Interpretive Essays* (1981); D. Fasching, *The Thought of Jacques Ellul: A Systematic Exposition* (1982); J. Holloway, ed., *Introducing Jacques Ellul.*

JAY M. VAN HOOK

English Civil War

The crisis that precipitated the Civil War in England emerged from Charles I's imposition of a liturgy on Scotland that replaced the Service Book which derived from John Knox* without channeling his action through the Kirk Assembly (1637). This provoked resistance for which Charles's military forces were inadequate. The Scots occupied northern England and required payment before they would leave. To obtain funds, the king called a Parliament for November 13, 1640.

Religion stood out among the issues. There was opposition to the preference of Arminians for church offices over those who represented orthodox Reformed theology. New liturgical forms were perceived as "popery." Statutory reformation of church government was desired.

During the first year of the Long Parliament, Charles obtained settlement in Scotland by conceding to the demands of the Scots. But he had to accept the execution of his chief adviser for suggesting use of Irish troops to put down opposition. In December 1641 the bishops were imprisoned in the Tower. A rebellion in Ireland hurt the king's position, for English Protestants saw this as part of a worldwide popish conspiracy.

In January 1642, after attempting to arrest parliamentary leaders, the king left London. After negotiations and much propaganda, Charles raised his standard at Nottingham on August 12, 1642. The king had support in the north and west. Parliament put its forces under the Earl of Essex and controlled the navy under the Earl of Warwick. The first battle took place at Edgehill on October 23, 1642. Charles established a capital at Oxford. Royal success (1643) caused Parliament to join in a Solemn League and Covenant* with the Scots which changed the committee for church reform, known as the Westminster Assembly,* from modifying standards of the English church to producing forms that would also be satisfactory to Scotland.

The tide turned at Marston Moor (July 2, 1644) when Scots Thomas Fairfax's infantry and Oliver Cromwell's* cavalry defeated Royalist forces under Prince Rupert. When the Earl of Essex became trapped in Cornwall, this new leadership took over. The defeat of the royal forces at Naseby (June 1645), the surrender of Bristol, and the defeat of Montrose at Philiphaugh in September, left the Royalist cause too weak to continue much longer. As Charles's hopes faded, he surrendered to the Scots (April 1646), bringing bloody conflict to an end.

After months of negotiations, the king was turned over to parliamentary forces (February 1647). Both the Scots and Parliament maintained that they were fighting for the proper relationship of king and parliament and not for the destruction of monarchy.

A rising of Royalist forces (early 1648) with Scots support was put down by the army with hard-won victories. Charles was now seen as a war criminal. After a trial was authorized by the Rump Parliament which had been purged of members not desired by the army, King Charles was convicted and beheaded (January 30, 1649). This ended "personal rule" and the possibility of a comprehensive national church.

JAMES C. SPALDING

English Reformation

Initially the Reformation in England had more to do with concern for reform of canon law than with theology or worship. This was due partly to Henry VIII's need for annulment of his marriage with Catherine of Aragon. But many inside and outside Parliament had grievances against aspects of canon law that contradicted common law tradition. The break with Rome dates from the forced Submission of the Clergy (May 15, 1532). When ratified by Parliament and affirmed by the Crown, this submission subordinated canon law to the laws of the realm. As a result of the submission, the most powerful defender of the old order in the church, Sir Thomas More, resigned as chancellor of England. However, people of diverse theological tendencies and for various reasons supported this separation from Rome.

The church under Henry's vicegerent Thomas Cromwell moved in a Lutheran direction theologically and politically. Following Cromwell's arrest and execution (1540), there was Catholic reaction until Henry's death (1547).

Reformed influences from Switzerland and the Rhineland surfaced during the reign of Edward VI when Martin Bucer* (Calvin's mentor) came to Cambridge University; Peter Martyr Vermigli* came to Oxford; Zurich-trained John Hooper became bishop; Dutch and French refugees established the Church of the Strangers along Reformed lines in London; and the Church of England leadership sought the counsel of Calvin from Geneva and Bullinger* from Zurich. Documents that showed Reformed influence and were of lasting importance and became statutory law were the Forty-two Articles, the accompanying Catechism, and the Second Prayer Book of Edward VI.

In keeping with the revision sought for in 1532, a *Reformation of the Ecclesiastical Laws* was completed (1552) to make canon law consistent with common law and the statutes of the realm. The typically Reformed church consistory of elders meeting regularly with the pastor of a congregation to supervise discipline* was proposed. Unlike the Articles and the Prayer Book, the revised canon law had not cleared passage in Parliament before Edward VI's death (1553).

Mary I's attempt after 1553 to restore Roman Catholicism to England resulted in martyrs' deaths for about 288 Protestant leaders in the Church of England. Many took refuge on the Continent in important Protestant cities, including Reformed centers such as Geneva, Basel, and Zurich. Still others, like Elizabeth's Archbishop of Canterbury Matthew Parker, who considered Bucer his mentor, survived in England while keeping a low profile.

Just as Mary's legitimacy had depended on her being Roman Catholic, so Elizabeth I's legitimacy depended on her being Protestant when she came to the throne (1558). Though Elizabeth wanted a Church of England as comprehensive as her father's, she had to rely on Protestant leadership, including returnees from the Continent, to staff her bishoprics and deaneries. The Puritan* controversies during her reign were carried on within the parameters of Reformed theology. Even Peter Baro, the Cambridge professor whose teaching generated English Arminianism,* had studied and been ordained in Calvin's Geneva.

JAMES C. SPALDING

Erasmus, Desiderius (1466–1536)

Born in Rotterdam and educated in Deventer and Paris, Erasmus lived in England, Louvain, Basel, and Freiburg in Breisgau. He was drawn to the *devotio moderna* and favored educational and disciplinary reforms of church and clergy. He had voluminous correspondence with prelates, rulers, and reformers but did not support any of the protestant Reformation movements. To the end he argued for maintaining ecclesiastical unity, for which he was willing to concede Communion in both kinds and marriage of priests. He was most upset about the effect of theological polarization on the freedom of learning.

Erasmus provided a new Latin translation of the NT. His preface, in which he exhorted an educated laity to study the Scriptures which he believed should be made available in vernacular languages, was most influential. He wrote against

Luther's views on the enslaved will and provided new editions of the collected works of such fathers as Jerome and Augustine.* His works were placed on the Index of Forbidden Books by the Council of Trent (1559). Erasmian is a much-abused term used to describe the moderate as well as the doctrinally uncommitted city magistrates, literati, and theologians in both camps (e.g., Julius Pflug and Philipp Melanchthon) who participated in unification colloquia.

Opera Omnia Desiderii Erasmi Roterodami, ed. J. Waszink et al. (1969ff.); and *Collected Works*, ed. C. R. Thompson et al. (1974ff.); C. Augustijn, *Erasmus von Rotterdam* (1986); J. Huizinga, *Erasmus of Rotterdam* (1952).

DERK VISSER

Erastianism

The doctrine that the civil state has final earthly authority over expression and practice of religious beliefs and over ecclesiastical organization. It found its most characteristic form in the middle of the seventeenth century during and after the Westminster Assembly* (1643–49) debates concerning the shape and organization of English religious life. Thomas Hobbes and John Selden, the influential jurist and scholar of the period, were notable proponents. The doctrine is named from Thomas Erastus (1524–83), a Swiss theologian and physician, though he advocated a much less one-sided version of church-state relations.

DAVID LITTLE

Erskine, Ebenezer (1680–1754)

Leader of a "secession" from the Church of Scotland (1733–40) which became a vigorous church movement. After ordination (1703), Erskine awoke to a lively faith in Christ and became a strong preacher and diligent pastor. His views of the Lordship of Christ, the "open offer of the gospel," and the role of laity in calling ministers led him to prominence and dissent against the state church, which deposed him. While orthodox in theology, Erskine adapted Scottish Presbyterianism to emerging trends in Reformed Pietism, church liberty from state control, and voluntary forms of church life.

MERWYN S. JOHNSON

Erskine, Ralph (1685–1752)

Minister in Dunfermline, Scotland. Younger brother of Ebenezer Erskine,* he participated in the Marrow controversy* and opposed the forced settlement of churches against the will of the people. He joined the Secession in 1737 and opposed the Cambuslang Revival, writing *Faith No Fancy* (1745) against it.

Erskine's sermons, full of God's love for sinners and offers of Christ in the gospel, were highly regarded. He had a considerable reputation as a poet. His *Practical Works* (1764–65) was reprinted several times, and his writings were long influential throughout the English-speaking world and, as translated into Dutch, in the Netherlands* as well.

D. Fraser, *The Life and Diary of . . . Ralph Erskine* (1834); A. R. MacEwen, *The Erskines* (1900).

DAVID C. LACHMAN

Eschatology

The doctrine of "the last things" (called "eschatology" only since the nineteenth century), often appearing last in expositions of Reformed faith. It has traditionally dealt with the end of the world: the return of Christ—before, after, or without a millennium (pre-, post-, or a-millennialism*), the last judgment; and the end of a person's life: death* and the hereafter, heaven* and hell.* In contrast to these terminal and individual emphases, one finds, partly in Calvin* and most fully in contemporary Reformed theology, the recovery of a more dynamic and cosmic eschatology.

Pre-Reformation. Original anticipations of the ascended* Christ's immediate return soon yielded to the task of being his church* in the interim before history's* certain, but possibly distant, culmination. Some retained apocalyptic visions, often based on the "thousand years" of Revelation 20, of an earthly triumph for God's saints over the pagan powers. Others denounced this millennialism (or chiliasm) as too literal, materialist, and chronological, and a more figurative, spiritual, dehistoricized eschatology dominated the Middle Ages. For Augustine,* the millennium represented the whole Christian era, whose eventual ending, with the judgment of Antichrist, would halt history rather than renew it, as time gave way to eternity. Meanwhile the City of God could be distinguished from the city of the devil not by visible, worldly marks but by spiritual and inward ones: love of God, not of self.

Reformation. Events around them convinced the Reformers that God was actively redeeming history. Luther* expected Christ's cataclysmic return, to resolve the conflict between God and the devil. Yet his "two kingdoms" preserves the unhistorical inwardness of Augustine's "two cities." To live by faith in the kingdom of Christ means inner warfare between gospel and law.* Hope provides more consolation until the world is overcome than anticipation that the world shall itself be sanctified.

Calvin envisaged more clearly creation's* restoration. Predestination* does not rob history of meaning in subjection to God's eternal will but promises that history has a destiny and goal. Dismissing a millennium as too brief an earthly rule, Calvin still affirmed that Christ would come again, and the renovation of the world had "in a manner" already begun, in Christ's glorified humanity. As Christ Ascended awaits his final reign, the church, in union with him, waits too. That means humiliation for now; but we treat our sufferings with contempt and meditate on the future life, when we shall share Christ's glory (*Inst.* 3.9, 25). Meanwhile the church advances and actively engages with the world, promoting a godly commonwealth as visible firstfruits of Christ's dominion.

Yet Calvin's (and the Reformed confessions') eschatology is often individualistic, propounding the biblically questionable view that at death the immortal soul is separated from the body. Still, this immortality is not a Platonic divine essence but God's gift to humanity,* grounded in creation and redemption. In his early *Psychopannychia* (1534), Calvin affirms that the departed soul is not asleep but awake to enjoy God's presence and anticipate everlasting joy (or, in the case of the impious, fearfully to await damnation). Like the later confessions, he teaches that the souls of the elect will be reunited at the end with their now transfigured bodies.

Post-Reformation. As Calvinists struggled against oppression, futuristic hopes sometimes arose. Jonathan Edwards* foresaw a millennium beginning in New England, while some seventeenth-century English Puritans* grounded their revolutionary politics in the impending reign of Christ and defeat of the papal Antichrist. The contemporaneous Westminster Assembly,* though, was more Augustinian than millenarian (cf. WLC, q. 191).

The WCC,* embodying a covenant* framework shaped by Johannes Cocceius,* exemplifies Reformed orthodoxy's* efforts to develop Calvin's historical instincts. Yet covenant theology often lapsed into dispensationalism* (which periodized history and found eschatological significance only in the final epoch), or else reduced the interval from resurrection* to last judgment to a static, necessary outworking of Christ's completed work. This left Calvinism* ill-placed to resist the post-Enlightenment reduction of eschatology to secular progress or to liberalism's moralized, this-worldly kingdom of God.*

Contemporary. Reformed theologians led twentieth-century interpretation in quite new directions, embracing eschatology as the key to biblical reality. Karl Barth's* *Commentary on Romans* (1919; 1922²; 1923³; ET 1932) emphasized the alienness of the kingdom. Eschatology articulates God's eternal Otherness, which intersects time and subverts human hopes. Later, in his *Church Dogmatics* Barth set the judgment of last things firmly within the graciousness of Christ, the Last One; yet he never conceded that the future could add anything new, beyond fuller disclosure of the revelation* already completed. Jürgen Moltmann* has since given priority to hope* and promise over fulfillment; conceived of the future, in its tension with the present, as a "new paradigm of transcendence"; and, with others, has extended Barth's re-thought doctrine of God,* not as static "being," but as a process of "becoming" through the still unfinished "history" of the Trinity.

Like Barth, Moltmann draws radical political conclusions from eschatology. Because the ultimate future rests with God, not with human planning or ideals, we are freed and summoned to struggle for penultimate, human justice* corresponding to the coming triumph of God's righteousness. Contemporary eschatology relativizes individual concerns and questions of chronology. Yet inheritors of Reformed millenarianism still predict imminent Armageddon, interpreting the nuclear threat, for example, as fulfilling biblical prophecies. Between such literalism and the disavowal of a realistic second coming altogether, Reformed eschatology still struggles to take history and the future seriously yet affirm not their annihilation but their consummation.

Barth, *CD* III/2, 437–511, IV/3, 274–367; and *The Christian Life* (1981); G. C. Berkouwer, *The Return of Christ* (1972); A. Hoekema, *The Bible and the Future* (1979); D. E. Holwerda, "Eschatology and History," in *Readings in Calvin's Theology*, ed. D. K. McKim (1984); J. Martin, *The Last Judgment in Protestant Theology* (1963); J. Moltmann, *Theology of Hope* (1967); H. Quistorp, *Calvin's Doctrine of the Last Things* (1955); P. Toon, ed., *Puritans, the Millennium and the Future of Israel* (1970); T. F. Torrance, *Kingdom and Church* (1956).

ALAN E. LEWIS

Eternal Punishment *see* Hell

Ethics, Social

To speak of social ethics and in the Reformed tradition involves making arbitrary distinctions. In a basic sense, all ethics is social because it involves the interaction of human beings, even when it concerns their motivations and character. All social ethics is personal, for the same reason.

The Reformed tradition cannot be exclusively defined. Reformed theologians have always made ecumenical claims for their insights and developed their ethics in interaction with the perspectives and experience of other branches of the Christian church. At best, one can speak of a Reformed emphasis within the common enterprise of Christian ethics based in Holy Scripture and informed by the whole tradition of the church catholic and ecumenical.

Nevertheless, social ethics is understood as dealing with the corporate or collective life of society in areas such as the church and in structures of government and economic life. The Reformed tradition is that movement of theology and church life which, with roots in Scripture and the church catholic during the first fifteen centuries, sought and still seeks the reformation of that church from the sixteenth century to the present. Its formative theologians were John Hus, Martin Luther,* and John Calvin,* with their sixteenth-century colleagues and the church confessions. It is a living tradition, constantly criticized and reformed to the present.

Christian life in the church. All ethics in the Reformation tradition is rooted in the message of the apostle Paul, reasserted by Luther, that the Christian lives by free and grateful response to God's grace in Jesus Christ justifying and transforming a sinful world. This is a radical protest against all forms of human self-justification and sanctification, even those which bear the name "Christian." Humans are not saved by works—of personal virtue, social justice, or sacramental order—important as these are as faithful, fallible witnesses to God. Calvin applied this insight directly to the church. *Ecclesia semper reformanda*—the church always being reformed by the living word of God—meant first that no human authority or structure is finally authoritative. The church is one, catholic and universal, the given reality of the body of Christ being built up in love. But it has no head except Christ. Its forms must continually be sought by faithful, fallible human work.

This principle caused much tension and struggle. Yearning for a final human authority to define the Word of God and the order of the church has not ceased. A "verbally inspired" Bible, a particular confession, a new episcopal order, and the people in their various self-expressions have been suggested. Reformed and Lutheran churches have divided over these issues. An open, free, and reformable ecclesiology, however, reaffirmed in the twentieth century by such theologians as Karl Barth,* Reinhold Niebuhr,* Dietrich Bonhoeffer, and Jürgen Moltmann,* and modern church confessions, continues as the Reformation tradition's basic witness.

Second, the triune God alone is the source of truth and Lord of the conscience. The doctrine of the church is confessional, the living response to the Word of God revealed in Scripture which a historical time and place requires. There is authoritative doctrine that includes authoritative ethics, but it must continually be expressed anew as redeemed but sinful human beings, inspired by the Holy Spirit, discern in each time and place the Word of God that judges and saves the world.

Third, the task of ordering the church is political and constitutional. Power and authority must be so balanced as to allow the Word of God to prevail over human emotions and interests. Calvin, adapting NT prototypes, developed the structure of ministers, elders,* and deacons* still used today. Teachers and current church leaders in presbytery were given a special role in the selection of new officers but always in the presence, and with the confirmation, of the people. Authority lies not with the ministers, the elders, or even the people, but with the process, informed by the Holy Spirit,* whereby the church seeks guidance in the selection of its leaders, in the form of its confession, and in its witness to the world on public policy.

Christian responsibility in politics. The sixteenth-century Reformers were not democrats, nor were individual rights a center of their concern. For both Luther and Calvin the freedom* of a Christian is given by grace* through faith* in the community of believers. It is not therefore a freedom to pursue self-interest, or even to assert just claims, by political action. Governments* are ordained by God to establish just order and restrain the anarchic drives of human sin.* Still no general right of resistance* to unjust and tyrannous authority is permitted. God will judge and destroy tyrants in God's way. Christians must speak prophetic words to governors about the governors' misuse of authority, but Christians must crown their witness by suffering under, rather than seeking to overthrow, those governors.

Nevertheless, political ethic in Reformed tradition has developed in ways undergirding modern democracy and superseding the teachings of the Reformers. The reason lay most deeply in the life of the church itself and the model it offered for a changing world. The model was neither democratic nor hierarchical, but constitutional. In analogy to the covenant* of God with the company of believers, the Puritans* in seventeenth-century Massachusetts attempted to establish constitutional structures for government. Suspicious of all unchecked human authority and power, they sought to balance that power by denying the clergy political office and providing for popular participation in the choice of political leaders and legislation. Aware that structures of government, like those of the church, must always be reformed, they provided processes for amendment and change. By analogy with the calling of the Christian to be a servant of others in love, they based participation in the political process on a calling to responsible citizenship. Similar developments took place in Scotland, England, and Holland. Furthermore, this calling led, beginning in a limited way with Calvin and Knox,* not to the right but the duty of active citizens to resist unjust tyrannous authority for the sake of the God-ordained function of government itself.

This theology made its contribution both to revolution and to democratic political constitutions in Europe, America, and Africa from the sixteenth century to the twentieth. In modern times, however, it has undergone a decisive transformation. Though government continues to be described by some as deduced from (and limited by) the sovereignty of God (Abraham Kuyper) or an order of creation (Emil Brunner), the trend has been to understand it in the context of the Lordship of the risen Christ in human affairs and the promise of his coming again. For Bonhoeffer, government is a mandate, an area of human life to be organized responsibly, in penultimate witness to the reality of Christ taking form in the world. For Barth, political relations should be secular parables of the kingdom of God* in the world in the way they organize justice* and preserve freedom in the civil community. Reinhold Niebuhr understood government's task to be the coercion of competing vitalities and powers in society into a relative justice, subject to the continual judgment and inspiration of the higher mutualities of love revealed in Jesus Christ. Politics in these and other modern expressions of the Reformed tradition is a relative, sinful yet promising area for the achievement of those forms of provisional, reformable justice which bear external witness to the realization of human community and love in Jesus Christ.

Economics and the gospel. In *The Protestant Ethic and the Spirit of Capitalism* (ET 1930), Max Weber argued that Calvinist-Puritan theology created the ethos of inner-worldly asceticism in which modern capitalism developed. Calvinism,* he claimed, stressed the importance of successful work, organizing this world to the glory of God, as evidence of saving grace at work among God's chosen people. The energy and the discipline this released has propelled the commercial and industrial development of the modern world and was an implicit sanctification of the capitalist system. R. H. Tawney, in *Religion and the Rise of Capitalism* (1926), presented a more subtle version of the thesis. He showed that Calvin and later Calvinists, though positive toward the developing economy of their time, attempted to exercise moral and ecclesiastical control over it. Laws governing rates of interest and conditions of loans, just wages and prices, the conditions of labor and limitation of profits, were all part of the Puritan ethic, and the sin of avarice was under constant surveillance.

Only when the church lost its disciplinary power to enforce an economic ethic, when social control gave way to individual admonition, did the Protestant work ethic turn into the sanctification of economic success. Individualism and private spirituality took over in the sphere of economics* from the Reformed ethic.

The twentieth century has witnessed a recovery from this failure, in the form of an ecumenical economic ethic to which the Reformed tradition has made a substantive contribution. Swiss reformers Hermann Kutter and Leonhard Ragaz joined with Americans Washington Gladden and Walter Rauschenbusch, the German Christoph Blumhardt, and British Anglicans Charles Gore and William Temple among others to define the social gospel.* Reinhold Niebuhr and John Bennett in the United States gave the movement greater realism and depth, analyzing economic power as a social expression of human sin and proposing strategies of prophetic witness and action to confront this power with the command and promise of God. American church studies and denominational statements on social questions continue to follow their guidance. Reformed economic ethics today must avoid idealism on the one side that judges all existing economies against an absolute standard of loving sinless human community, and blessing successful economic power on the other side, however unjust and inhuman its consequences for the disadvantaged of the world. Its principles here also are, no unquestioned human authority, whether revolutionary or conservative, but the church's continual participation in the search for more just and responsible ways of producing and distributing the goods and services of an economy, with special concern for the poor, while cultivating our common environment in the power and promise of God "in the economy of the fullness of times to gather up all things in Christ" (Eph. 1:10).

CHARLES C. WEST

Ethics, Theological

Theological ethics in the Reformed tradition has stressed the active power and presence of God* and the need for conscious response in piety* to God's rule. As a result, this tradition has emphasized the need to comprehend and order all life in faithfulness to the One made known in Jesus Christ and in ancient Israel. These themes are not exclusive to the Reformed tradition; they are grounded in Scripture* and expressed in the wider Christian community. Still, they came to forceful expression in the movement that emerged from Geneva and were further developed in Puritanism.*

Calvin* emphasized the radical priority of God's power and presence to human response. God is the creator from whom comes every good gift, the governor who rules the whole of nature and history,* and the redeemer whose present purposes shall finally be vindicated. Piety is the conscious human response to God's power and presence, an attitude of heart and mind that inclines the believer to faithfulness and the subordination of self-concern in the service of God's reign. The Christian life is envisioned as a "sentry post" at which the Lord has posted us, which we must hold until God recalls us (*Inst.* 3.10.6). In the language of the sociologist Max Weber, Calvin's thought supports an attitude of "inner-worldly asceticism"; called to God's service in this world, Christians are under divine orders to use the goods of the world to God's glory.

The priority of God and the need for piety also are reflected in Calvin's distinctive understanding of the law.* For Calvin, the divine law disclosed in Scripture includes the moral precepts of natural law and equity which are universally distributed. Found in the Decalogue, these are intensified and extended in Jesus Christ. God's law shows sinners how short they fall of God's purposes, and it restrains sin* and evil. Its principal use, however, is to provide guidance for renewed hearts and minds who seek to follow God's will. In this sense, the law limits and directs faithful living in political and economic institutions as well as in family and church.*

The movement that emerged with Calvin soon faced significantly changed social conditions. In the midst of bitter religious conflicts, different national governments supported different branches of Christianity. Calvinist churches sought recognition and toleration* in hostile lands. The result was a modification of theocratic impulses and development of the church as a voluntary community, often in tension with its dominant society.

Covenant* theology flourished under these conditions, especially among Puritans in England and America who endorsed the theology of the Calvinist Reformation—the priesthood of all believers,* justification* by faith,* the sanctification* of believers, and the authority of Scripture*—while emphasizing the sovereignty of God who calls humans to service in the world. The Puritan movement was fueled by piety, an affective orientation of the heart, that led to introspection and the need for a narratable conversion* experience as well as to practice. Indeed, if it is defined as those influenced by the theology,* piety, and traditions that emerged from Geneva, Puritanism encompasses a broad range of figures and communities, from the Presbyterians* and Thomas Cartwright* to Roger Williams and the Rhode Island experiment.

As apparent from the writings of William Perkins,* William Ames,* William Preston, Richard Baxter,* and others, Puritans used the language of the covenant to refer to the proper ordering of the entire nexus of human relations under God. Covenants bound parties together by mutual agreements made with respect to the natural order and special circumstances. Marriage* and friendship, as well as business and political relations, were defined and understood as partnerships with reciprocal interactions, responsibilities, and obligations. For example, covenant theology emphasized mutual companionship as the chief end of marriage. Eventually, it also led to a nonhierarchical view of church polity,* separate and distinct from civil government* and the economic sphere. Nevertheless, Puritan ecclesiastical life came to be imbued with democratic tendencies that had broad political and economic consequences. Indeed, following the Puritan revolution, covenant thinking led toward republican government, as Puritans and their sometimes secular descendants argued first for toleration and then, in America, for a separation of church and state which culminated in the notion of a limited state and separation of government powers. In the economic sphere, the covenant theology which linked the call of the sovereign God to service in the world became associated with a market free of excessive control by family or by state. Throughout the Puritan movement, covenantal thinking was accompanied by a casuistry that talked of particular vocations* and cases of conscience* with critical scrutiny, exemplified in Perkins's *Whole Treatise of Cases of Conscience* (1606) and Baxter's *Christian Directory* (1673).

During the Great Awakening* in America, Jonathan Edwards* developed an understanding of the moral life based in true charity or love of God as a new affective principle and sense of the divine excellence that results from regenerating grace* and reorients the person. Transformed by grace, the moral agent is inclined toward virtuous participation in the universal system of being under God rather than toward some limited participation in a restricted or limited circle, for example, one's family or nation. The sinfully contracted moral sensibilities, judgments, and discernments of the person are thereby enlarged and corrected so that life may be ordered in a fashion that is more truly responsive to God's sovereign reign.

Many of the intellectual challenges facing Reformed theology and ethics at the beginning of the nineteenth century were set by the impact of modern science* and a growing confidence in the powers of human reason.* In opposition to what they regarded as the credulity of traditional religion, proponents of the Enlightenment and their heirs claimed that human reason, by itself, could furnish a universal ethic, unencumbered by superstition. Friedrich Schleiermacher* responded by claiming that human affections are central for ethics, and Christian ethics is based, not in universal reason, but in the historically particular qualifications of human inclination wrought by the specific form of piety expressed in the Christian community and its tradition. Thus for Schleiermacher, Christian ethics is grounded in the Christ-shaped or Christ-determined feeling of absolute dependence on God. This becomes the foundation for a particular way of life; and Christian ethics is the reflective work of describing what a person whose emotions are formed in this way will be inclined to do.

From about the mid-nineteenth century through the early twentieth century challenges provoked by the growing differentiation of Western societies and the growth of industrialization came to the fore. In the United States, proponents of the social gospel* movement included representatives of many Protestant churches who focused attention on faithful service in the midst of interdependent social relations. For example, Richard T. Ely, an economist with theological concerns who was raised a Presbyterian and later became an Episcopalian, developed an idea of "social solidarity" or the notion that we are not isolated individuals but participants in a vast matrix of interests, possibilities, and responsibilities. This idea, he said, was beginning to be glimpsed by social philosophy and the sciences, though its longer heritage includes biblical understandings of human community before God and the organic unity of the church.* Combining social solidarity with a prescription to love God and neighbor, Ely promoted a social ethic concerned with works of justice* and reform in law and government, business and labor, education, and housing. These and similar concerns found institutional embodiments in both denominational and ecumenical bureaucracies which continue to be important today.

The twentieth century witnessed not only the ongoing impact of urbanization and industrialization but also the advent of totalitarianism, severe world economic crises, and two world wars. In response to these and other challenges, Karl Barth* sought to protect the sovereignty of God by founding Christian ethics on the Word* and command of God alone. In the Theological Declaration of Barmen* (1934), he contrasted idolatrous reliance on cultural norms with genuine Christian faithfulness. The Declaration, adopted by the Confessing Church in Germany, acknowledged the "divine appointment" of the state to work "for justice and peace," yet insisted the state should not "become the single and totalitarian order of human life, thus fulfilling the Church's vocation as well" (*BC* 8.22, 23).

Against the separation of law and gospel espoused by some European theologians, Barth insisted that "law is a form of the Gospel." He also stressed the particularity of the divine command. "Nothing either outward or inward," including principles or rules, can anticipate the command and so reduce God's sovereign freedom to command. Nevertheless, Barth maintained these commands are given within certain "spheres" of human interaction and that genuine faithfulness is more likely to receive these commands if it attends to "prominent lines" or directions in Scripture. In sum, Barth insisted on God's sovereignty over all of life, or over the multiple spheres of human conduct in which the command is given, and the urgency of genuine faithfulness.

In America, H. Richard Niebuhr* argued that Christian ethics is based in faith as trust in and loyalty to the universal God who creates, governs, and redeems all things. Like Edwards, he argued that such a faith renders one responsive to the entire community of being. It is radically monotheistic in that it expands the community of moral responsibility beyond all partial contexts and so both affirms and relativizes our allegiances to lesser objects and communities. Informed by radical faith, cultural pursuits in religion, politics, and science are practiced with a kind of universal intent that opposes the constricted and hegemonic tendencies that arise when they are practiced in the service of idolatrous devotions to less than radical objects, for example, church, nation, or race. The moral life becomes the effort of persons and communities to order their lives appropriately in response to God in the midst of mundane relations and interdependencies.

Important challenges continue to face the Reformed community at the close of the twentieth century. In South Africa,* where Calvinist doctrine has often been used in the service of racial oppression, a number of Reformed ministers and theologians currently are engaged in the work of reclaiming a tradition of conscience, justice, and compassion. In Ireland* an unrelenting spiral of violent conflict continues among Roman Catholic,* Reformed, and other Protestant factions. The churches of central Europe, recently released from decades of official suppression, must once again ponder their appropriate roles in public life. The Reformed communities in the United States, along with other progressive churches and synagogues, need to devise distinctive and engaging interpretations of their increasingly secular and pluralistic society within a matrix of global interdependence. In these and many other contexts, Reformed churches and their theologians will remain true to a rich and distinctive heritage to the extent that they are able to connect a vigorous piety with the vision of a sovereign God who calls persons to faithful service in every area of life.

J. Edwards, *Ethical Writings*, ed. P. Ramsey, *The Works of Jonathan Edwards*, vol. 8 (1989); D. Little, *Religion, Order, and Law: A Study in Pre-Revolutionary England* (1969); R. W. Lovin, *Christian Faith and Public Choices: The Social Ethics of Barth, Brunner, and Bonhoeffer* (1984); P. Miller, *The New England Mind: The Seventeenth Century*, 2 vols. (1939; repr. 1961); D. F. Ottati, *Meaning and Method in H. Richard Niebuhr's Theology* (1982); F. Schleiermacher, *An Introduction to Christian Ethics*, trans. J. C. Shelley (1989); E. Troeltsch, *The Social Teaching of the Christian Churches* (1912; ET 1931).

CHARLES M. SWEZEY

Eucharist *see* **Lord's Supper**

Evangelism

Evangelism as a message is the authoritative summons of God to repentance* and faith* in the crucified and risen Christ, the inaugurator and consummator of the eschatological kingdom of God.* Evangelism as a method is so to present Christ that, by the power of the Holy Spirit,* people may come to God through him, grow in Christ, and serve him as Lord in the fellowship of his church and in the extension of his reign in the world. Various components of these definitions are stressed in the Reformed community; others are held in common with other theological traditions.

The God-centered message. Calvin* with Luther* rediscovered the message of evangelism—grace* alone, faith* alone, Christ alone. Not our work, but God's electing love redeems: "Salvation is of the Lord." Calvin also emphasized our obligation to demonstrate the Lordship of Christ in all life—society, politics, family, and church.* The Puritans* underlined this in their vision for the "wilderness" of America where the garden of God would be planted.

An invitation to a new birth. In the face of spiritual decline in the colonies, the Great Awakening* (which peaked in the 1740s) called for the revival of holiness and the new birth, for a living, personal faith in Christ. Jonathan Edwards* married the Puritan message on God's eschatological* consummation to evangelism as a method, an invitation to accept Christ and become part of his new earthly community. Our mission was to call people to fulfill God's predestined* design—a creation fully subject to its creator's eternal purposes.

Foreign missions and new struggles. Following European Pietism and British Calvinists like William Carey,* the nineteenth century brought a new emphasis on the kingdom of God's global extension. Puritanism's "grand scheme" was to be exported to the ends of the earth. This emphasis brought two movements that began to erode Calvinism's earlier emphases. Charles G. Finney's* revivalism,* shaped by Arminian* theology, began to overpower Puritanism's holistic ministry and reduce evangelism to special meetings and new techniques. Calvin's emphasis on conversion* as a "continuous process" of the whole person was reduced to a simple, one-step decision which the "old side" Calvinist viewed with growing skepticism.

Theological liberalism also began to question earlier commitments of the lostness of humanity and the uniqueness of Christ. In the United States it overwhelmed Calvinism's interest in society and became identified with the social gospel* movement. Evangelism was transformed into an emphasis on social reform and change.

Contemporary emphases and reinforcements. At least four themes have become focuses of the message and methodology of Reformed evangelism in the twentieth century: (1) renewed interest in the kingdom of God* as the comprehensive evangelistic message of Jesus; (2) renewed connection between evangelism and incorporation into the life of the institutional church, an emphasis of the Church Growth school; (3) growing recognition by a now-global church of evangelism's ethnocultural dimensions and a new sensitivity to the cultural lines along which the Holy Spirit worked in evangelism; and (4) expanding concern for relating evangelism to justice* and the special needs of the poor and oppressed.

Agenda issues for the future. Theological pluralism and the global shape of the Reformed community raise these issues:

1. Who are the objects of evangelism? The traditional category of the lost; the poor and oppressed; or both?

2. What is the connection between verbal proclamation and social responsibility? Word or deed; orthopraxy or orthodoxy; or both?

3. Where is the boundary between the church and the world? Which is the main arena of God's activity; what is the role of the church in the world?

4. How do we see the place of Jesus in terms of other religions? Historic Reformed theology has stressed his uniqueness. Modern trends press for a universal extension of God's salvation that incorporates, not excludes, the world's faiths.

W. J. Abraham, *The Logic of Evangelism* (1989); D. Bosch, "Evangelism," *Mission Focus* 9, no. 4 (1981): 65–74; C. L. Chaney, *The Birth of Missions in America* (1976).

HARVIE M. CONN

Ex opere operato

The phrase meaning "from the work worked" is from the Council of Trent (1545–63; decree on sacraments, seventh session), where if any say that "grace* is not conferred by the performance of the rite itself," they should be anathema. This seeks to affirm that the objective efficacy of the Christian sacraments* is not dependent on the subjective worthiness of the recipient. In a way, this extends Augustine's* argument (against the Donatists) that the unworthiness of the minister does not affect sacramental validity. It contrasts to those who affirm that the efficacy of the sacraments derives "from the work of the worker" (*ex opere operantis*). By implication, the notion of *ex opere operato* is sometimes understood to suggest that the power and the efficacy of the sacraments are intrinsic, that the sacraments "contain" grace and work almost automatically (or "magically"), apart from God's Spirit or human faith.

For John Calvin,* as for Augustine, God is the true minister of the sacraments; and Calvin (critiquing Trent) questions the *ex opere operato*. While the sacraments are among the "means" by which God promises to give grace, God is not "tied" to the sacraments. While through God's gracious ministry the sacraments give what they signify, they do not (in and of themselves) have any power. Not magical, the sacraments work, as instruments of God's grace, only where they are received in faith.*

J. Calvin, *Tracts and Treatises Relating to the Reformation*, trans. H. Beveridge, vol. 3 (repr. 1959); K. Rahner, *The Church and the Sacraments* (1963); Schaff, *Creeds*, 2:118–22; 3:285–89.

JOHN E. BURKHART

Experience

Etymological roots of "experience" suggest testing or experimenting to ascertain the truth. Current English usage defines experience as the state of being consciously affected by something or the conscious content of the life of an individual, group, or community. Theologically, the term is used in all three senses.

The Reformed tradition has expressed ambivalence about the role of experience in theology*—an ambivalence traceable to John Calvin.* He speaks of experience as common human experience and specifically Christian experience. Either may be probative. The ambivalence arises in trying to discern whether in a specific context Calvin values experience as such and finds it trustworthy or sees it vitiated by sin and needing judgment and grace.

In the *Institutes*, Calvin speaks positively about common human, and specifically Christian, experience. Common human experience can tell us that the seed of religion has been planted in every human being (1.4.1), that God is Father (1.5.3), that the world is governed by providence (1.16.3), and that our will is not completely free (2.2.3). Christian experience convinces us of the authenticity of Scripture (1.7.5), the need for the Sabbath (2.8.32), that though faith is always mixed with unbelief it cannot be conquered by it (3.2.4, 37), and that God is faithful even in the midst of adversity (3.8.3). However, Calvin also speaks negatively of both kinds of experience. Common human experience tells us that our understanding always reaches for the truth but, left to its own devices, cannot attain it (2.2.12). The daily experiences of Christians do not always assure them of their election; rather, Christians must turn from themselves to the Word of God,* specifically to Christ (3.24.4, 5).

Friedrich Schleiermacher* was interested in common human religious experience but saw the thematization of Christian experience as the actual task of dogmatics (*CF*, sec. 15). Scripture records the original, and therefore normative, expression of encounter with Christ. In this sense, it is the first in a series of presentations of Christian experience but retains its uniqueness because all subsequent presentations can only be developments of the apostolic preaching (*CF*, sec. 129). Scripture* and experience, therefore, are not antithetical as independent sources of the knowledge of God.*

Karl Barth* picks up more of Calvin's negative statements about experience. Theology does not reflect on the experience of believing Christians but on the Word of God (*CD* I/1, 198–227). While people may have an experience of God's Word (i.e., for their existence to be determined by it), it is impossible for that experience to come from themselves. Nothing in human beings as such connects with the Word of God. God's image in humanity* has been annihilated and must be created anew by God in Christ (*CD* I/1, 238–40). Therefore, to speak about human experience in dogmatics is to miss the real object of theology: God's self-revelation in Jesus Christ.

Neither Schleiermacher nor Barth precisely reproduced Calvin's own ambivalence about experience. Schleiermacher perhaps did not fear the self-deception that, because of sin, is still a part even of Christian experience. Barth, though, did not do justice to Calvin's recognition that there is a knowledge of God in common human experience: "Scripture, gathering up the otherwise confused knowledge of God in our minds, having dispersed our dullness, clearly shows us the true God" (*Inst.* 1.6.1).

DAWN DE VRIES

Extra Calvinisticum

The so-called *extra calvinisticum* is the doctrine that after the incarnation the Eternal Word by whom all things were made continues to be present and active also beyond the flesh (*etiam extra carnem*) united to himself. This teaching was widely held in the Catholic tradition, but in debates among Lutherans it came to be referred to as that "Calvinistic extra" (*extra calvinisticum*). The term appears to have been used first in controversies (1620s) between the rival Lutheran schools at Tübingen and Giessen. Both sides agreed that in the incarnation the divine nature's power to be everywhere was communicated to the human nature. The Tübingen school maintained that during the period of his earthly ministry Christ simply hid his power of bodily ubiquity.* The Giessen school maintained that during that period Christ actually emptied himself of that power. To teach the latter position, objected T. Thumm of Tübingen (1623), would be to reintroduce *illud extra calvinisticum.* Two years earlier, Balthasar Mentzer had employed the synonymous *extra calvinianum.* The term, in whatever form, reflects the assumption among many Lutherans, and by the 1620s Lutheran and Reformed representatives. By 1564, in polemical debate "Calvinist" had become the equivalent of "Zwinglian" to refer to opponents classified as the "sacramentarians," namely, those who taught that Christ was only "sacramentally," not really, present in the Eucharist. This classification was inaccurate, since Calvin* himself objected to the sacramentarian position thus understood. He taught (*CO* 9, cols. 194–95, 507) that the whole Christ, but not everything that is Christ's (*Christus totus sed non totum*), is really (*realiter*) present in the Lord's Supper* by the power of the Holy Spirit.*

These eucharistic debates undoubtedly saw overzealous denials, almost Eutychian in tendency, of the teaching that even after the incarnation the Eternal Word was present and active also beyond the flesh. The debates, however, undoubtedly also saw the use, almost Nestorian in tendency, of exaggerated arguments that too often emphasized the "beyond the flesh" at the expense of the confession of the unity of the Person which, after all, the doctrine was meant to serve. Nonetheless, the occasional abuse of this doctrine does not alter the fact that the so-called *extra calvinisticum* was taught in some form by almost all the most prominent theologians of the Catholic tradition. Even a partial list includes Athanasius (*On the Incarnation* 17); Augustine* (*Letters* 137.2, *To Volusian*); Cyril of Alexandria (*Ep.* 17); Peter Lombard (*Sentences* III, d. 22, 3); and Thomas Aquinas (*Summa Theologica* 3.10.1, ad 2). In fact, so widespread is the doctrine that it could just as well be called the *etiam extra catholicum.*

The term's origin, accuracy, and prominence in the tradition is how this commonly held doctrine can function differently in diverse historical settings. At least in Calvin's theology (e.g., *Inst.* 2.13.4; 4.17.30) and in the HC* (q. 48), the doctrine does not function to encourage speculation about some other Word than the one united to the flesh to constitute the one Person. In Calvin's thought, it functions to support a fully Trinitarian doctrine of the knowledge of God* and of self. It strengthens the confession of the identity of the redeeming Word and the Word by whom and with whose Spirit all things are created. Werner Krusche rightly argues that Calvin's doctrine of the Holy Spirit reinforces these Trinitarian functions of the *extra calvinisticum.* This is the same function the doctrine also appears to serve in most of the theologians of Reformed orthodoxy.*

Barth, *CD* I/2, 159–71; IV/1, 180–81; A. Heron, "Extra Calvinisticum," *Evangelisches Kirchenlexikon: Internationale theologische Enzyklopädie* 1 (1986): 1247–48; W. Kreck, "Extra Calvinisticum," *Evangelisches Kirchenlexikon: Kirchlich-theologisches Handwörterbuch* 1 (1956): 1245–46; W. Krusche, *Das Wirken des heiligen Geistes nach Calvin* (1957); W. Niesel, *The Theology of Calvin* (1956); F. Wendel, *Calvin* (1950); E. D.

Willis, *Calvin's Catholic Christology: The Function of the So-called Extra Calvinisticum in Calvin's Theology* (1966).

DAVID WILLIS-WATKINS

Fairbairn, Andrew Martin (1838–1912)

British Congregational theologian who taught at Mansfield College, Oxford (1889). Fairbairn opposed skepticism, maintaining that "the highest truth of reason is one with the highest object of faith," and cast evolution in theistic terms. Social ethics,* the Protestant understanding of catholicity and abhorrence of sacerdotalism, and world religions were all interests. Biblical criticism held no fears, and the widely prevalent philosophical determinism was despised as simply "Calvinism* with God dropped out."

By exalting the Fatherhood of God and the human consciousness of Christ, Fairbairn exemplified strengths and weaknesses of the then current liberal theology. He wrote *The City of God* (1892); *Christ in Modern Theology* (1893); *Catholicism, Roman and Anglican* (1899); and *The Philosophy of the Christian Religion* (1902).

DNB; R. S. Franks, "The Theology of Andrew Martin Fairbairn," *Congregational Historical Society Transactions* 13 (1937–39): 140–50; W. B. Selbie, *The Life of Andrew Martin Fairbairn* (1914); A. P. F. Sell, "An Arminian, a Calvinist and a Liberal," in *Dissenting Thought and the Life of the Churches* (1990).

ALAN P. F. SELL

Faith

Christian faith is trust in God* whose steadfast love and free grace* are decisively revealed in Jesus Christ. Because faith is a personal response of confidence in and fidelity to the living, gracious God, it is altogether different from blind submission to church teachings or mechanical adherence to a set of religious beliefs and practices. While some sort of faith—in oneself, family or friends, some ideal or cause, or simply in the worthwhileness of life—is often claimed as a necessary element in all human experience and development, faith in the NT sense refers more specifically to a free and wholehearted trust in God whose goodness, mercy, and faithfulness are disclosed in Christ.

Emphases of a Reformed understanding of faith. Reformed theology is not primarily concerned to secure its distinctiveness among the various Christian traditions of faith. Its aim is ecumenical as well as evangelical, that is, to recover the truth of the gospel message as attested in Scripture* for the continual reform and renewal of the church catholic. With this proviso, several prominent emphases of the understanding of faith in Reformed theology may be identified.

1. The object of faith is *God alone* whose grace is known to us supremely in Jesus Christ through the witness of Scripture illuminated by the Holy Spirit.* According to Calvin's* celebrated definition, faith is "a firm and certain knowledge of God's benevolence toward us, founded upon the truth of the freely given promise in Christ, both revealed to our minds and sealed upon our hearts through the Holy Spirit" (*Inst.* 3.2.7). Only the living and sovereignly gracious God is to be the object of our faith. To elevate anything else to this position—whether nation, culture, reason, religious experience, church doctrines, or the text of Scripture itself—is idolatry.*

2. The subject of faith is the *whole* person—mind, affections, and will—in response to God's goodness, faithfulness, and forgiveness* of sins* in Christ. Faith is a response of the "heart" and not the mind alone (cf. Calvin's emblem of the Christian life as a flaming heart offered to God). To be sure, there is a cognitive dimension of faith; it is "knowledge" of the truth and not a blind leap in the dark or mindless assent to whatever the church teaches (in this sense the notion of "implicit faith" was rejected by the Reformers). That faith seeks understanding and is no enemy of reason* is a familiar motif of Reformed theology. Yet this emphasis goes hand in hand with the insistence that true knowledge of God is inseparable from the spirit of "piety,"* that is, a reverence for and love of God, a readiness to be taught and guided by God's Word and Spirit, a valuing of prayer* as "the chief exercise of faith" (*Inst.* 3.20), and a hum-

ble recognition that "we are not our own; we are God's" (*Inst.* 3.7.1).

3. Faith is both a *gift of God* and a *free human response*. For Reformed theology, faith is a gift of God (Eph. 2:8–9) rather than a human achievement. We receive the grace of God with empty hands and have no grounds for boasting. Yet as the gift of the Holy Spirit who works liberatively rather than coercively, faith is also an act of human freedom.* Genuine human freedom and humility before God stand in direct rather than inverse proportion. We are never more truly free than when we live by the grace of God alone. As a gift of God, faith brings liberation from all idols of self and world, empowering us for new life and service.

4. Faith comes from *hearing the gospel* of Christ (Rom. 10:17). While faith may arise in unpredictable ways and widely diverse circumstances, it is ordinarily fostered and strengthened in the life of Christian community where the Word of God* is rightly preached and heard, the sacraments* properly administered, and Christian discipleship responsibly cultivated. Reformed theology sees the awakening and nourishing of faith as a profoundly communal rather than individualistic process. This is summed up by Calvin's description of the church as the "mother" of our faith (*Inst.* 4.1.1). Faith in God is intertwined with life in community and fidelity in personal relationships.

5. We are saved by grace through faith alone, but such faith is always coupled with *works of love* and service to the glory of God. While the Reformers objected to the view that faith is mere assent to the church's teachings and must therefore be perfected by our acts of love, they nevertheless insisted that true faith expresses itself naturally and unpretentiously in love and service of God and the neighbor, just as a healthy tree bears good fruit. Motivated by thankfulness (cf. HC, pt. III), authentic faith does not fail to produce works of love (Gal. 5:6). Hence for Reformed theology there is no contradiction between the Pauline doctrine of justification* by faith (Rom. 3:27) and James's warning that faith without works is dead (James 2:26). Justification is the basis of sanctification,* and sanctification the goal of justification (hence the characteristically Reformed "third use of the law"*).

6. Faith and *hope* are inseparable. While God has acted decisively for the world in Christ, the work of redemption is not yet complete. At present, believers see in a mirror dimly (1 Cor. 13:12) and do not yet experience the promised triumph of God's grace throughout the whole creation (Rom. 8). Sin and suffering are still evident in the world and in the lives of believers. Thus together with the groaning creation believers pray for God's kingdom,* struggle against injustice, and work for the transformation of all things. Faith and hope are mutually supportive, for faith without hope becomes arrogant and triumphalistic, and hope without faith falls victim to religious escapism or secular utopianism.

7. Within the Reformed tradition, faith in God's grace is not only personally renewing but *world-transforming*. While faith is no mere projection of the ideas, wishes, and interests of believers, it nevertheless seeks transformation of all things to the glory of God and thus acts as a *catalyst of human creativity, imagination, and permanent reformation* in all spheres of culture. The steadfast and holy love of God manifest in Christ continually illumines, judges, revolutionizes, and transforms our understandings of God, the world, and ourselves. This world-transforming view of faith informs the characteristic participation of Reformed Christians in many social, political, and cultural reform movements.

8. Recognition that our Christian faith, love, and hope are also *always in need of reform* is a hallmark of Reformed theology. As evident in the *BC*, Reformed churches have produced many confessions* of faith in different times and places. They have underscored the freedom and responsibility of a believing community to bear witness to its faith in timely words and pertinent deeds to meet the challenges and needs of new situations. Faith is no mere inner disposition that remains indifferent to the crises and possibilities of the public domain. By courageous witness and concrete forms of costly discipleship, faith seeks to shape

life and culture in the direction of the coming reign of God.

History of Reformed theologies of faith. The history of Reformed theological reflection on faith shows continuity and diversity. For the sake of simplicity, five major periods can be distinguished:

1. The period of the sixteenth-century Reformation when in the wake of Luther's reform movement Calvin, Bullinger,* Beza,* Zwingli,* Knox,* and others recovered the biblical understanding of faith as reliance on the gracious promise of God contained in the biblical witness and centered in the reconciling work of Christ.

2. The period of seventeenth-century Reformed orthodoxy, represented in Europe by Francis Turretin,* Amandus Polanus,* and Johannes Cocceius* and defended in nineteenth-century North America by the old Princeton* school of Charles Hodge* and B. B. Warfield,* which tended to stress the cognitive side of faith and the propositional nature of revelation.*

3. The period of eighteenth-century Reformed evangelicalism and nineteenth-century Reformed liberalism, which attempted in very different ways to recover the affective and ethical components of faith (cf. Jonathan Edwards's* sensitivity to the importance of the affections in the life of faith; and Friedrich Schleiermacher's* association of faith with the "feeling of absolute dependence").

4. The period of neo-Reformed theology, led by Barth* and Brunner,* which in opposition to all historicist, psychological, and cultural domestications of faith reasserted the freedom of God's grace and the orientation of faith on the revelation in Christ.

5. The contemporary period of Reformed theology whose emphases include H. Richard Niebuhr's* radically theocentric description of faith; Jürgen Moltmann's* recovery of the critical and transformative significance of hope in God's promise for every aspect of Christian faith and discipleship; and the interpretation of Reformed faith as liberative, contextual, and oriented to "political" praxis (cf. Paul L. Lehmann,* A. A. Boesak,* Letty Russell).

Barth, *CD* IV/1, 608–42, 740–49; A. A. Boesak, *Black and Reformed* (1984); Heppe, *RD*; J. Moltmann, *Theology of Hope* (1967); H. R. Niebuhr, *Faith on Earth* (1989); N. Wolterstorff, *Until Justice and Peace Embrace* (1983).

DANIEL L. MIGLIORE

Farel, William (1489–1565)

Red-haired Farel, best remembered as the reformer of Neuchâtel, was born near Gap, Dauphiné. While at the University of Paris (1509), he was powerfully influenced by Jacques Lefèvre d'Etaples (Jacobus Faber)—some of whose theological views anticipated those of Martin Luther.* For a while Farel was associated with the reforming group at Meaux under the protection of Marguerite of Angoulême,* sister of Francis I.

When the pace of reformation in France was too slow for Farel, he returned to Switzerland. After expulsion from Basel, he evangelized the French-speaking territories of the canton of Bern. Farel introduced the Waldenses* to the wider reformation and was instrumental in bringing Protestantism to Geneva (1532).

When Calvin was passing through Geneva on his way to a life of quiet study (1536), Farel confronted the shy, young scholar with the demand that he remain. Both were banished (1538), but Calvin was invited to return (1541). Farel continued in Neuchâtel, where he had initiated the reformation (1530).

For some years Farel was the most eminent French-speaking, Protestant theologian. However, he recognized that Calvin, twenty years younger, was his theological superior and happily recommended Calvin's works.

Farel was more active than contemplative, and his reckless energy and courage nearly always outraced his discretion. His abilities were more fitted for storming a bastion than holding a fortress, but he was too noble to resent others building on foundations he laid.

In the Neuchâtel church a brass plaque on a pillar reads: "On the 23rd October 1530, idolatry was overthrown and removed from this church by the citizens." In the yard outside is a statue of Farel with the Bible held aloft.

CHARLES PARTEE

Federal Theology

Federal theology, or covenant theology (Lat. *foedus*, "covenant"), is a theological approach depicting the divine-human relationship as covenantal. It became an important school of Reformed theology in the seventeenth century and influenced Reformed thought and practice in many areas.

God's covenant* with Israel is a central theme of the Bible, and occasionally it appeared as a theme in patristic exegesis. Some late-medieval theologians, especially Nominalists, thought in covenantal terms, arguing that God's absolute power was constrained by God's ordaining to act in certain stipulated ways with respect to creation. In the early Reformation, Martin Luther* and Huldrych Zwingli,* claiming to return to a more biblical outlook, gave renewed importance to the covenant.

Heinrich Bullinger,* the leading theologian of Zurich after Zwingli's death, devoted a whole treatise to the subject, making it central in his thought. Bullinger followed Zwingli in seeing in the Bible and the church's history one long story of God's covenant relationship with humankind: God promised grace* to Adam and the patriarchs, revealed "types" of it in the law of Moses, and fully manifested it in Christ. The histories of Israel and the church* belonged to this covenant scheme and consisted of periods of decline and revival as God's people were more or less obedient to the divine will. The Reformation, like the time of King Josiah in ancient Israel, was seen as a period of the overthrow of idolatry. To Bullinger, God had made but one covenant with humankind, that of grace, known by anticipation before Christ and remembrance thereafter. Each period had its own sacraments,* circumcision being a sacrament of anticipation which had been replaced by Baptism.* The covenant was mutual and conditional: God willed to redeem those who fulfilled its terms of faith* and repentance,* though Bullinger also thought God's grace made such fulfillment possible. His theology was thus built upon the history of salvation,* and the covenant was the chief principle for interpreting the Bible and understanding God's rule in history.* The covenant also had social implications for Bullinger: in a truly Christian society, covenant obligations of justice* and pure worship* would be met.

Calvin* gave the covenant less attention than did Bullinger and emphasized its testamentary quality as God's promise of grace more than its conditionality. For Calvin too there was but one covenant—grace—administered differently in OT and NT times. For Calvin, as well as for Zwingli, Bullinger, and later Reformed theologians, the covenant was entirely compatible with predestination* (many of the strictest double predestinarians were also federal theologians). Though federal theology spoke of God's will as conditional, the covenant was always regarded as the means, in historical time and through human volition and secondary causality, by which God effected his unconditional will. But it did supplement the predestinarianism of Reformed theology with a biblical language stressing history and human responsibility.

A new idea entered covenant thinking at the end of the sixteenth century with the appearance of a covenant of works separate from and antecedent to the covenant of grace. This view first appeared with the Heidelberg theologians Zacharius Ursinus,* Caspar Olevianus,* and Franciscus Junius, then with those who came under their influence, including the English Puritans Thomas Cartwright* and Dudley Fenner. Later Reformed scholastic theologians further developed it. According to this view, God made a covenant of works with Adam, the "federal head" of all humanity, enjoining obedience to a perpetually binding moral law identified variously with the Ten Commandments (known to Adam before being given to Moses) and the law of nature. After Adam and his posterity with him fell, salvation was no longer available through the first covenant, so God established the covenant of grace, in which Christ fulfills the law and atones for its breach, becoming the "federal head" of believers. This covenant of grace was given as promise in the OT and fulfillment in the NT. Both covenants are "one-sided" insofar as God ordained them but "two-sided" insofar as by them humankind became God's covenant partner. All are under the covenant of works as obligation; but elect believers are also under the covenant of grace and thereby confront obligations of the covenant of works not only as condemnation but also as a pattern for a devout life possible for them through sanctifying grace. Thus the covenant of works became a means for regarding certain moral obligations as universally binding. Since these obligations included those of the Decalogue, Reformed Sabbatarianism,* especially evident among the Puritans, can be seen as related to federal theology.

By mid-seventeenth century, the double covenant was a commonplace of Reformed theology. It appeared in the WCF* (1646) and became the central organizing principle in the writings of Hermann Witsius and Johannes Cocceius* in the Netherlands. Cocceius developed yet a third covenant, that of redemption, whereby Christ made a pact with the Father to atone for the sins of the elect. This pushed the covenant pattern back into the inner life of the Trinity.*

The Puritans, who produced numerous sermons and treatises on the covenant, removed it from abstract theology and related it to personal piety.* It enabled them to stress the obligations of conversion* and holiness as well as the assurance found in consideration that God dealt predictably with humankind. Federal theology had significant social ramifications: the disciplined society that Reformed thinkers envisaged was rooted not only in the moral demands made upon believers but also in universal moral obligations of humankind. Moreover, covenanting was applicable to congregational and political life, as evidenced in English Congregationalist* polity* and Scottish Presbyterian political protest. The contractual model it entailed influenced political philosophy, as in John Locke, and led to notions of responsible, democratic government.

J. W. Baker, *Heinrich Bullinger and the Covenant* (1980); M. McGiffert, "Grace and Works: The Rise and Division of Covenant Divinity in Elizabethan Puritanism," *Harvard Theological Review* 75, no. 4 (1982): 463–502; and "From Moses to Adam: The Making of the Covenant of Works," *SCJ* 19, no. 2 (1988): 131–55; J. Von Rohr, *The Covenant of Grace in Puritan Thought* (1986); D. A. Weir, *The Origins of the Federal Theology in Sixteenth-Century Reformation Thought* (1990).

DEWEY D. WALLACE, JR.

Feminist Theologies

Feminist theologies reflect on God* as God is known in and through the experience of those who advocate the full humanity* of women together with men. Fully consistent with the Reformed tradition of searching out reconciliation in the midst of "a ferment" of the world, feminist theologians are exposing the cause of painful divisions and calling for repentance* and new life in the church* (*BC* 9.54).

There is no one description of feminist or one type of feminist theology. But there is a consensus that feminist theologies seek to act and reflect upon the search for liberation from all forms of dehumanization, joining God* in advocating full human dignity for each and every person. Such advocacy includes all women and men, not just white educated inhabitants of North Atlantic nations. Although I write theology as a white, middle-class woman from the northeastern part of the United States, raised in the Reformed tradition, as a feminist I am committed to working for the equality of all women and men of every race, class, and nationality.

Many feminist theologies use a style similar to other liberation theologies* such as Latin American, black, and Asian liberation theologies. The reflection begins with the *commitment* to act on behalf of the oppressed in the light of God's liberating action in the exodus and the resurrection. It is based in a concrete situation or *context*, asking about the problems, questions, and insights that arise in that context. Because of their incarnational nature these theologies are rooted in a variety of contexts and traditions on all continents, and therefore there is no *one* feminist theology but rather a host of feminist theologies.

The style is often *communal* as well. Everyone involved in a particular community of faith and struggle is invited to take part in the action and reflection. Pastors, lay people, activists, teachers, and students are asked to reflect together on the work of the church in the world. Groups of women often gather in Bible studies and develop their own theological perspectives using this communal process.

The process is also *critical*, since it seeks to test the authority and the tradition of the church and reinterpret biblical tradition in the light of the experience of women and all people struggling to be free. Here an aspect of Reformed tradition appears in the stress on an educated congregation where all are able to read the Bible and to guard the Word through a process of active discernment. This style of committed, contextual, communal, and critical theological reflection is very much suited to a continuation of the Reformation in our own time.

Unlike the Reformed tradition that begins with God's revelation,* the method of feminist theologians is to begin with the experience* of those struggling against oppression and ask how God is involved in that struggle. After analyzing this experience to understand the social, economic, historical, and ecclesial causes of the oppression, they begin to look at the biblical and church traditions from this perspective of marginal and voiceless persons in society. In the light of this, they ask in what ways the tradition needs reinterpretation and reshaping and what God is calling us to do in response to this understanding of faith. The understanding here is not that God is slighted in the name of women's experience but that God is often known among those "of low estate" and the gospel message is often discerned through a theological process of action and reflection.

Like Reformed theologies, feminist theologies take seriously the present reality of sin and need for a strong eschatology* which affirms the reality of God's love that is stronger than sin,* death,* and domination. Women can appeal to the authority of their experience, but this experience is primarily of the old creation and the structures of patriarchy in church and society. They do not yet know what real live children of God will look like (Rom. 8:19).

Nevertheless, many feminist theologies struggle to express a vision of God's intention for a mended creation, and this hope helps women "keep on keeping on." In an important sense, Christian feminists only have this future, for the patriarchal structures that have shaped Scripture,* tradition,* church, and theology* are such that the process of reconstruction of women's place in man's world requires a utopian faith which understands God's future as an impulse for change in the present.

C. P. Christ and J. Plaskow, eds., *Womanspirit Rising* (1979); S. McFague, *Models of God* (1987); R. R. Ruether, *Sexism and God-Talk* (1983); L. M. Russell, *Household of Freedom: Authority in Feminist Theology* (1987); and ed., *Inheriting Our Mothers' Gardens* (1988); E. Schüssler Fiorenza, *Bread Not Stone* (1984); P. Trible, *God and the Rhetoric of Sexuality* (1978); J. L. Weidman, ed., *Christian Feminism* (1984).

LETTY M. RUSSELL

Field, John (1545–1588)

Leader and propagandist of the nonconformist cause in Elizabethan England. Field was ordained a priest at the age of twenty-one after studying at Christ College, Oxford. He was summoned by the Ecclesiastical Commission and asked to sign a threefold statement accepting the Thirty-nine Articles, the *BCP*, and the surplice (1571). For noncompliance, he was barred from preaching. Field and Thomas Wilcox wrote the controversial Admonition to Parliament* (1572), his vituperative part entitled "View of popish abuses yet remaining in the English Church." Each writer was sentenced to a year's imprisonment.

Field later solidified his place in the international Calvinist movement. Not a Separatist, he wanted imposition on the commonwealth by law and discipline of a devotion to the Calvinist ideal of a Christian society in which the godly magistrate underwrote the reform of the church.

DNB 22 (Suppl. 1917); Collinson, *EPM*.

DAN G. DANNER

Finitum non capax infiniti

Some (H. Baucke, W. Elert, F. Loofs) have argued that the differences between Lutheran and Reformed Christologies* reflect a more fundamental philosophical difference over whether the finite is capable of receiving the infinite. The Reformed, they say, reject the doctrine of Christ's bodily ubiquity* because they apply to the incarnation* the philosphical principle that the finite is incapable of receiving the infinite (*finitum non capax infiniti*). This principle supposedly influences the whole of Reformed theology for which, finally, there remains an unbridgeable distance between God* and creation.*

There is, understandably, a paucity of documentation in Reformed materials to confirm the presence of this philosophical principle. Maintaining that the distinction (not the distance) between God and the creature is common to all Christian theology and Reformed theology is not an exception (cf. the section on the attributes of God in Heppe, *RD*, pp. 57–104). Central to Reformed theology is the conviction that the triune God is known (*Inst.* 1.5.9; 3.1.1) precisely because God does not stay to God's self but accommodates* Godself to create and redeem. God does more than draw near the creature. In the incarnation, God is united to the flesh; and by the bond of the Holy Spirit,* believers are united to Christ (*Inst.* 3.11.10). This presence of God is the infinite creating in the finite conditions for reception and transformation. In terms of the philosphical formula, this means that by grace* the finite is indeed made capable of the infinite; but, more pointedly, it means that out of God's covenanting fidelity, the finite is taken up and transformed in God's freedom to be human—*Deus capax humanitatis.*

Barth, *CD* I/2, 484–91; H. Bauke, "Christologie II: Dogmengeschichte," *RGG*[2], vol. 1, col. 1628; G. C. Berkouwer, *The Person of Christ* (1954); W. Elert, "Über die Herkunft des Satzes 'Finitum infiniti non capax,'" *Zeitschrift für systematische Theologie* 16 (1939): 500–504; F. Loofs, "Christologie," *Realenzyklopädie für protestantische Theologie und Kirche*, 3rd ed. (1896–1913), 4:54; A. Schweizer, *Die Glaubenslehre der evangelisch-reformirten Kirche*, vol. 2 (1847), 296, 303; E. D. Willis, *Calvin's Catholic Christology: The Function of the So-called Extra Calvinisticum in Calvin's Theology* (1966).

DAVID WILLIS-WATKINS

Finney, Charles Grandison (1792–1875)

Reformed revivalist, Finney grew up in New York and became a lawyer (1818). Impressed by the Mosaic law, he studied Scripture, was converted, and determined to draw others to the faith. After study with George W. Gale, Finney was ordained by the Presbytery of St. Lawrence (1824). He led revival efforts in U.S. cities, stressing the depth of human guilt, the fear of God, and God's power in Christ to turn people from sin. Thousands responded with fainting, "melting," and other physical manifestations of the power of the Spirit. Converts sought to live purer lives, with whole communities experiencing change after his revivals in Utica, Rochester, and elsewhere.

Finney became pastor of the Second Free Presbyterian Church in New York City (1832) but relocated to form the Broadway Tabernacle when Presbyterian strictures and carping against him persisted. His *Lectures on Revivals* (1835) outlined his use of the "anxious bench," the "protracted meeting," and other revival methods, as well as his evangelical Calvinism* and anti-slavery* views.

Finney became president of Oberlin College, Ohio (1835), which was formed as ex–Lane Seminary students sought radical theological education. He led revivals in America and Great Britain, continuing to pastor a church, while also writing and teaching at Oberlin. His theology emphasized human ability as well as God's sovereignty. He urged Christians to "cast out sin" and replace sin with holiness. "Oberlin perfectionism" became a heresy among traditional Calvinists, though it tremendously influenced popular American Reformed Christianity and the rest of Protestantism.

LOUIS B. WEEKS

Fisher, George Park (1827–1909)

Yale historian and theologian who helped adapt New England Congregationalism* to nineteenth-century romanticism, scholarship, and science. Fisher studied divinity at Auburn, Andover, and Yale and then spent two years in Germany acquainting himself with its theological innovations and historical research methods. After returning to America (1854), he became professor of divinity, pastor of Yale's college church, and professor of church history (1861–1901). He was third president of the American Society of Church History (1896–97).

Fisher's wide-ranging historical works touched all periods of Christianity, and he also wrote about secular history. Here he strove for an objectivity excluding personal prejudices; but unlike many scientific historians, he simultaneously emphasized that the essence of history* was a moral drama in which individuals constituted the major actors. Moreover, Fisher transmuted older providential* readings of the past into a semisecular vision of human progress under Christian aegis. He also wrote apologetic works to refute radical German theories of the Bible and restated many of the traditional arguments for the veracity of Christian revelation.* However, his apologetic work also showed the distinct influence of liberalizing currents, for he eschewed notions of biblical inerrancy, emphasized internal evidences for Christianity far more than the older apologetic was wont to do, and recast the traditional argument from design to make room for evolutionary theory.

R. H. Bainton, *Yale and the Ministry* (1957); L. L. Stevenson, *Scholarly Means to Evangelical Ends* (1986).

JAMES H. MOORHEAD

Flavel, John (1627–1691)

The "seaman's preacher." Flavel studied at Oxford and was presbyterially ordained at Salisbury (1650). He was elected pastor of the port city of Dartmouth according to the order of the Church of England during the Commonwealth (1656). With the restoration of episcopacy (1662), he was ejected and yet continued to serve his seafaring congregation, preaching from a rock in the harbor. His important literary legacy includes theological treatises, manuals of devotion, sermons, and a commentary on the WLC (1693) with an introduction by Increase Mather (repr. 1982).

HUGHES OLIPHANT OLD

Flint, Robert (1838–1910)

Scottish Presbyterian philosopher-theologian who taught at St. Andrews (1864) and Edinburgh (1876–1903). Though keenly interested in evolutionary thought, methodologically Flint was more in the line of Joseph Butler and cautious vis-à-vis emergent philosophical idealism.

He wrote *Vico* (1884) and *Socialism* (1894), but his most notable work was in natural theology and apologetics: *Theism* (1877), *Anti-Theistic Theories* (1879), and *Agnosticism* (1903); and in the history of ideas: *The Philosophy of History in France and Germany* (1874) and *History of the Philosophy of History* (1893).

DNB; D. Macmillan, *The Life of Robert Flint* (1914); A. P. F. Sell, *DD*.

ALAN P. F. SELL

Foreknowledge

God's knowledge of all future possibilities, contingencies, and actualities. John Calvin* defined it from God's point of view (similar to Duns Scotus): "All things always were, and perpetually remain, under his eyes, so that to his knowledge there is nothing future or past, but all things are present" (*Inst.* 3.21.5).

In classical Reformed thought (scholasticism*), this is the logical correlate of omniscience and a conclusion from biblical texts stressing the "perfection" of God's knowledge (concerning the outcome of human actions, the world, etc.). God's "almightiness" is emphasized against immanentistic or pantheistic thought.

Some important distinctions are the following:

1. Reformed scholasticism has said that while God's "necessary" foreknowledge (by virtue of being God) logically precedes God's decree,* God's "free" foreknowledge (of things happening) logically follows. This implies a sharp distinction of eternity and history,* decree and execution, where the former terms precede logically (if not chronologically) the latter. It presumes a "sequential" metaphysics of eternity and time.

2. Foreknowledge means more than intellectual precognition (prescience) and implies God's will concerning the destinies of people (predestination*). That raises the question of freedom. Reformed thought responds that the human will is not indeterminate (to be turned in any direction) but roots in human nature—being connected with humanity's deepest instincts and personality ("heart").

3. Freedom* is reasonable self-determination, not indifferent choice (arbitrariness). A free person is reliable—acting necessarily in accord with who one is but not by external compulsion. Thus traditional Reformed thought has tried to combine foreknowledge with a viable concept of freedom.

L. Berkhof, *Systematic Theology* (4th rev. and enl. ed. 1949); C. Hodge, *Systematic Theology*, vol. 1 (1871).

PHILIP C. HOLTROP

Foreordination

Part of the cluster of doctrines to explain and defend the absolute sovereignty of God* in creation* and providence,* grace* and redemption, and faith* and election. As such, it must be correlated with divine foreknowledge* and human free will,* cause and effect, necessity and permission, and so forth.

"Foreordination" is used in Rom. 8:29–30; 1 Cor. 2:7; Eph. 1:5, 11; and Acts 4:28. The Greek root word *horizō* means to determine, to ordain, or to appoint. With the prefix and when applied to divine determination, *proorizō* is translated "to predestine" or "to foreordain."

The doctrine of foreordination is understood as a theologically legitimate extension of belief in "God Almighty" by whose will all things are not only created but governed.

In Scripture, foreordination and foreknowledge (e.g., Rom. 8:29) emphasize the marvelous grace of the loving God toward the faithful rather than God's determining power over the world. Sometimes God's foreknowledge has been asserted without foreordination. That is, God's omniscience* is taken to include everything that happens, but events that occur within God's omnipotence* are not considered directly determined by God's will.

While Calvin* affirmed human free will, sin,* and evil, his chief insistence was on God's continual governance of all things. God's providence is "the determinative principle of all things in such a way that sometimes it works through an intermediary, sometimes without an intermediary, sometimes contrary to every intermediary" (*Inst.* 1.17.1). This view is not an abstract speculation but a doxological confession.

In recent times human freedom, choice, and responsibility have been affirmed in such ways that God's foreordination, and doctrines closely associated with it, while seldom directly denied, are rather deemphasized in Reformed theology.

CHARLES PARTEE

Forgiveness

The doctrine of forgiveness (or justification*) affirms that in Christ sinful people are accounted righteous before God, spared divine condemnation, and made fellow heirs with Christ of eternal life in his heavenly kingdom.

Reformed theology presupposes the ubiquity of sin* in human life, good works included, making need for divine forgiveness universal. It shares the general Protestant affirmation that such forgiveness is wholly the gift of divine grace,* given apart from any consideration of merit or worthiness in the recipient. God effects this forgiveness by crediting sinners with the righteousness of Christ as a gift. This "alien" or "imputed" righteousness therefore lacks any foundation in the sinner's good works, being entirely the product of Christ's obedience. Believers appropriate forgiveness by faith* alone, apart from any necessity of ceremonial or priestly absolution.

While God's gift of forgiveness is not based in works, Reformed theology characteristically insists that it is not separable from works either. Forgiveness is one aspect of the total work of divine grace in the sinner's life. Other manifestations include faith, repentance,* holiness of life, and obedience to God's commands.

G. C. Berkouwer, *Faith and Justification*, trans. L. B. Smedes (1954); H. Bushnell, *Forgiveness and Law* (1840); P. L. Lehmann, *Forgiveness* (1940); H. R. Mackintosh, *The Christian Experience of Forgiveness* (1927); W. Niesel, *The Theology of Calvin* (1956).

P. MARK ACHTEMEIER

Forsyth, Peter Taylor (1848–1921)

British theologian. Forsyth was born in Aberdeen, where he took a "first" in classics at the university, followed by theological study at Göttingen and at Hackney College (now New College), London. After twenty-five years in five pastorates, Forsyth served for twenty years as principal of New College, London. His mind worked with lightning speed; though weighted with many pastoral, academic, administrative, and civic duties, and laboring under the drag of continually poor health, he produced a steady stream of theological writings—nearly thirty books, almost fifty pamphlets, and about 280 periodical articles. His best-known works are *Positive Preaching and the Modern Mind* (1907); *The Person and Place of Jesus Christ* (perhaps his best, 1909); *The Work of Christ* (1910); *The Principle of Authority* (1913); *The Justification of God* (1916); and *The Church and the Sacraments* (1917).

Forsyth began his ministry as a flaming liberal, keeping his hearers "shocked" by the latest German biblical criticism. He is reticent about details of his theological "conversion"; but through his pastoral relation "of life, duty and responsibility to others" in his word to them "in doubt, death, grief and repentance," along with a new revelation of God's "holiness and grace" through the Bible which brought home to him his "sin in a way which submerged all the school questions in weight, urgency and poignancy," he was "turned from a Christian to a believer, from a lover of love to an object of grace." Henceforth, all his effort was given to a proclamation of the gospel of God's grace* made known in the Bible, especially in Paul.

He remained liberal to the end in his methodology, welcoming all the gains that the critical study of the Bible made possible and freely utilizing his conception of grace to criticize the theological tradition of the church* where he felt it to be time-bound and sterile; yet his religious and theological outlook was "evangelical" in the best sense of the word. Both the Bible and the church were to be measured by that which preceded them and brought them into being—the gospel of God's grace in a cosmic redemptive deed in God's Son. Forsyth was a forerunner of the neo-orthodoxy* of Karl Barth* and Reinhold Niebuhr,* with a remarkable prescience which saw, long before World War I, the coming bankruptcy of the optimistic faith in progress which these others sought to interpret and correct after the collapse had come. The cosmic tragedy and victory of the cross became the touchstone for him in interpreting authority,* anthropology, Christology,* soteriology, ecclesiology, eschatology,* and ethics.*

W. R. Bradley, *P. T. Forsyth: The Man and His Work* (1952); R. M. Brown, *P. T. Forsyth: Prophet for Today* (1952); D. G. Miller et al., *P. T. Forsyth* (1981); J. H. Rodgers, *The Theology of P. T. Forsyth* (1965).

DONALD G. MILLER

Foxe, John (1517–1587)

Author of *Foxe's Book of Martyrs*, or, as Foxe titled it, *Acts and Monuments of Matters Happening in the Church*. The brief first Latin versions were published at Strassburg and Basel during the Marian exile.* The first English edition (1563) was published, with nearly eighteen hundred pages. Success was so great that Foxe issued a second edition (1570), twice as long as the first. Before his death, two other editions were published containing only small additions to the 1570 edition. The book was ordered placed for public use on the property of major churches (1571). It is most famous for its account of the persecution (burnings) of Protestants during Catholic Mary Tudor's reign (1553–58), but its scope covers the whole of church history.

Foxe was educated at Oxford during the latter part of Henry VIII's reign and associated especially with the group around the reformer Hugh Latimer. He first came to prominence in England with his *Book of Martyrs.* During the Marian exile he was not identified with either the Anglican or Puritan parties, but his sympathies lay more with John Knox.* A strong royalist and venerator of English tradition, Foxe generally accepted the Elizabethan Settlement* but agreed with the Puritans* on vestments and ceremonies, refusing to wear the prescribed Anglican vestments. His histories have been criticized for their inaccuracies and for sometimes being fanciful.

JOHN E. WILSON

Free Church *see* Nonconformity

Free University of Amsterdam

An ecumenical Christian university in Amsterdam, founded by Abraham Kuyper* (1880), called "free" to express political and theological independence. The Reformed origin remains visible in the continuation of the founders' critique of the Enlightenment, scientism, and rationalism. It is increasingly characterized by other Christian intentions, especially social service, particularly in underdeveloped countries. The twelve thousand students attend fifteen faculties and several institutes, offering some forty areas of study. The two hundred and fifty professors are expected to support the aims. The school is characterized by reflection on basics, social responsibility, scholarly excellence, and critical loyalty to its reformational character.

HENDRIK HART

Free Will

Historical discussion has made "free will" a systematically ambiguous phrase. It is used to mean:

1. Free agency, that is, ability to make and execute one's own decisions, thus incurring accountability for what one does. All Western philosophies and theologies assert free will in this sense, except behaviorism that sees mental and volitional acts as by-products of physical processes. The assertion means we are not robots, nor are we programmed by some other mind, as computers or persons under hypnotism are, nor are our actions mere conditioned reflexes like those of Pavlov's dogs. But we are moral agents expressing our authentic selves in our conduct. The will is here conceived psychologically and dispositionally, as the directedness of human nature whereby preferences, resolutions, and impulses come to be acted out. Free agency is entailed by the scriptural insistence that humans are answerable to God,* the judge of all.

2. Ability to trust, obey, and worship God, that is, power to respond to God heartily and happily in service that shows a loving desire for God's company and a purpose of exalting and honoring God. Reformed theology,* following Augustine,* Luther,* Calvin,* and Edwards,* unanimously denies the existence of free will in this sense in any except the regenerate, in whom this capacity is partly restored now and will be perfected and confirmed in heaven. Augustine first schemed out the fourfold state of humans as freedom* in Eden to sin* (Lat. *posse peccare*), no freedom in our fallenness not to sin (*non posse non peccare*), partial freedom in the present life of grace* not to sin (*posse non peccare*), and full bestowal in the future life of glory of inability to sin (*non posse peccare*)—which for Augustine meant perfect freedom from all that is truly evil for all that is truly good. In English-speaking Reformed theology of the past four centuries' idiom, the denial of free will to the unregenerate is correlative to the assertion of total inability to merit, due to total depravity (total not in degree, as if all are as bad as they could be; but in extent, meaning that all human activity is morally and spiritu-

ally flawed at some point, so none are as good as they should be). This in turn is correlative to assertions that sin has dominion over fallen humanity,* that original sin* is the universal human condition, and that monergistic regeneration* through sovereign grace is the necessary and sole source of such faith,* repentance,* and godliness as emerge under the Word.

Against this, Pelagianism ancient and modern holds that free will in the defined sense remains intact in all humanity despite the fall, and semi-Pelagianism sees it as diminished but not destroyed. Semi-Pelagianism, viewing humanity as essentially good though weak through sin rather than essentially bad but restrained by common grace, appears substantively, if not under that name, in Arminian* and liberal Protestantism; in Eastern Orthodoxy, which follows the free will teaching of the Greek Fathers; and in pre- and post-Tridentine Roman Catholicism,* which sees human merit as decisive for salvation.*

The conception of free will throughout this debate is narrower than in the "free agency" (no. 1 above) view. Free will here means, quite precisely, being able to do what appears good, wise, right, and pleasing to God, out of a heart that rejoices in it just because it has these qualities.

3. Metaphysical (ontological) indeterminism, that is, the state of not being fully controlled by one's insights (i.e., one's understanding of what is best to do), nor by one's character, nor (some would add) by God. Free will here signifies power to act irrationally and at random, which is certainly a fact of life: it is sometimes dignified with the name of liberty of indifference or the power of contrary choice.

Does this fact, which makes everyone's future acts unpredictable to a degree so far as humans are concerned, imply that God's predetermining foreknowledge* of each person's future behavior is in any respect incomplete, so what is done is not always God's will? A spectrum of semi-Pelagian positions, from classical Arminianism with its concept of God's self-limitation to process theology with its doctrine of the finitude and relative impotence of God, say yes; Reformed theology, with the Bible, asserts that no future event is unknown or indeterminate to God and that contrary views err by conceiving God in humanity's image. There seems to be no need to buttress this scriptural position by claiming that the will (i.e., the agent) is always moved by the strongest motivational drive operative at that moment, as Edwards* did. This claim seems to deny the reality of random action, which is implausible.

Augustine, *Enchiridion*; and *On Grace and Free Will*; D. and R. Basinger, eds., *Predestination and Free Will: Four Views of Divine Sovereignty and Human Freedom* (1986); Calvin, *Inst.* 2.1–4; J. Edwards, *Freedom of the Will*, in *Works*, vol. 1 (1957); M. Luther, *The Bondage of the Will*, trans. J. I. Packer and O. R. Johnston (1967).

JAMES I. PACKER

Freedom

In the history of Christian doctrine and the Reformed tradition, freedom has three basic foci: the freedom of God in the work of creation* and redemption; the basic freedom of willing* and choosing with which human beings are endowed by nature, underlying all teaching concerning their responsibility before God* and to their fellow human beings; and the Christian freedom that rests on the redemptive grace* of God and follows as a corollary on the doctrine of justification.*

Freedom of God. Freedom, like the various other attributes of God, stands both as a distinct attribute and as a major qualification and explanation of the other attributes. God is free in being and in action, in self and in relation to God's creatures; God's sovereignty is a sovereign freedom; and God's power is a free exercise, devoid of all constraint. The Reformed approach to divine freedom is nowhere more apparent than in the doctrine of the eternal decrees*: God freely wills the existence and preservation of the created order and freely determines the eternal destiny of all creatures, solely on the ground of God's goodness and solely for the sake of God's ultimate glory. In creation and providence* God encounters no barriers to the exercise of God's will, and in the work of redemption God acts utterly graciously, apart from any merit belonging to the creature.

In the twentieth century, Karl Barth* has offered the most eloquent exposition of the freedom of God in his understanding of the incarnation* as "God's freedom for man" and in his discussion of the divine perfections or attributes under the rubric of "the Being of God as the One who loves in freedom." The merit of Barth's discussion lies in his clear identification of the divine freedom as a positive freedom for relationship rather than as a negative freedom from restriction.

Freedom of human beings. Human freedom, unlike the freedom of God, is a relative freedom, bounded not only by our nature as given in the act of creation but also by the acts of other creatures, by the natural order around us, and by our sinfulness. Nonetheless, the Christian tradition has almost invariably assumed the fundamental freedom of the human will from external constraint and has tended to understand the boundaries of freedom in terms of the larger category of human nature or the more limited category of choice. Reformed theology has followed an Augustinian* paradigm in its understanding of human freedom, noting distinctions between the capability of unfallen human beings and human beings after the fall, under grace, and in final fellowship with God. In their original condition, humans were capable of not sinning, because the freedom of choice (*liberum arbitrium*) remained whole. After the fall, though the will itself remained free, its capacity for choice was limited by the sinfulness of human nature. The issue is not the loss of freedom in the will itself which, according to the older Reformed theology, remains uncoerced and under no externally imposed necessity, but the restriction of free choice by the pervasive sinfulness of fallen humanity. Human beings retain the capacity for choice, but all choosing occurs in the context of sin*—so the defect belonging to human nature after the fall renders even the choice of good things sinful. The entrance of grace and salvation* into human life restores the ability to do the good, but imperfectly, in and through the power of God's grace. Only in the next life, in union with Christ,* is there a total restoration of goodness and, indeed, the ultimate removal of the ability to sin.

Christian freedom. Christian freedom in Reformed theology relates, on the one hand, to the Augustinian categories of human choice and, on the other, to the somewhat paradoxical relationship of Christians to the law* in the light of their justification by grace through faith* alone. The new relationship to Christ brought about by faith results in a free obedience unfettered by fears of the law. Luther* summed up this freedom in two maxims: "A Christian is a perfectly free lord of all, subject to none" and "A Christian is a perfectly dutiful servant of all, subject to all." The paradox of this freedom arises from the fact that justification by faith opens the Christian life to a new obedience in which law no longer has the power to condemn.

Calvin,* with considerably less paradox than Luther, brought this understanding of Christian freedom into the Reformed tradition: Christians, justified by faith, though still imperfect, are freed from slavery to sin for a new obedience. For Calvin, this free obedience is understood in terms of the third use of the law, the so-called "normative use" where the law functions as a model for life rather than as a condemnation. This obedient life, rightly directed by God's grace, brings with it a freedom from the constraints of the law and, specifically, from "indifferent" regulations (*Inst.* 3.19.7; Gr. *adiaphora*) such as fasts, vestments, and outward ceremonies. In sum, Calvin understands Christian freedom as the peace of conscience* that opens Christians to the use of God's gifts according to their true purposes. This understanding of Christian freedom also appears in the Heidelberg Catechism,* where the Decalogue is treated, with the Lord's Prayer, under the rubric of "Thankfulness" and law is understood as a goal to be sought in faith rather than as a condemnation and burden.

In the twentieth century, the theme of Christian freedom has become the central focus of the ethics* of Jacques Ellul.* Christ, according to Ellul, offers us both the revelation of the freedom of God and the identification of true human freedom in the face of the choices pressed upon humanity by the sinful world—in God's choices to be incarnate, to fulfill the law, to live out the will of God, and to die. This freedom, as evidenced by Christ's temptations, is served not by the exercise of power but by seeking first and foremost the kingdom of God.* In Christ and through the Word of God* this freedom becomes possible for Christians in service to God, in the confession of faith, and in right observance of the Sabbath,* all of which point toward freedom in Christ from self, from our past, and from the world.

Augustine, *On Free Will*, in *Augustine: Earlier Writings*, LCC, vol. 6; Barth, *CD* I/2; II/1; Calvin, *Inst.* 3.19; J. Daane, *The Freedom of God* (1973); J. Ellul, *The Ethics of Freedom*, trans. G. W. Bromiley (1976); M. Luther, *The Freedom of a Christian* (1520), in *Luther's Works*, vol. 31, ed. H. J. Grimm (1957).

RICHARD A. MULLER

Frelinghuysen, Theodore Jacobus (1691–1748?)

Ordained to the Dutch Reformed ministry (1719), Frelinghuysen settled in the New Jersey Raritan Valley. There he fervently preached on the inner struggles of the Christian life and asserted the necessity of conversion* and high moral standards for church* membership. Resisting his own congregation's staunch opposition, Frelinghuysen effectively spread his evangelistic message to other Dutch Reformed communities. He influenced many Presbyterian pastors, including Gilbert Tennent* and Jonathan Dickinson, whose revivalistic zeal played a significant role in the Great Awakening* (1740s) and the expansion of American Presbyterianism.*

R. DOUGLAS BRACKENRIDGE

French Confession

Also called Gallican Confession and Confession of La Rochelle. Official confession of the French Reformed Church, adopted at the first National Synod (Paris, 1559), then more or less definitively ratified at the seventh National Synod (La Rochelle, 1571), though continuously revised by later national synods. (The controversial statement identifying the pope as the Antichrist adopted at the Synod of Gap [1603] shows the turn these revisions might take.) The confession was basically replaced by the Canons of the Synod of Dort* when the National Synods of Alais (1620) and Charenton (1623) accepted them and required subscription by all church officials.

Impetus for a confession came from a conflict over predestination* in the Poitiers church (c. 1556). An appeal to the church of Paris led, after considerable discussion with the Parisian minister Antoine de la Roche Chandieu, to the decision to create a national organization and confession. John Calvin* was consulted and, though not in accord with such formal structures, provided the resultant synod of Paris with a brief, thirty-five article confession. Under Chandieu's direction it was adopted by the synod, with revisions (principally the addition of five articles). Because both the thirty-five article confession and the forty article confession were subsequently published, the latter was reaffirmed at La Rochelle (1571) without change.

The structure and the content of the confession are very similar to Calvin's Confession (1537) and the Geneva Catechism,* except for the first five articles (added by the synod) which present a scholastic* definition of God* (arts. 1–2), and a section on Scripture* (arts. 3–5). In addition, the confession attests the creating and preserving activity of the triune God (arts. 6–8); the disabling corruption of an originally pure human race (arts. 9–11); God's decision to call some to himself (art. 12); the incarnate Christ's redeeming work, which restores righteousness and eternal life to fallen humanity (arts. 13–14); justification* through faith* alone in God's free promises, which faith is engendered by the secret, regenerating* work of the Spirit (arts. 18–22); Christ as the end of the law and only mediator (arts. 23–24); that the true church exists only where right preaching* and proper administration of the sacraments* is found (arts. 25–28); that it will be governed by pastors, elders,* and deacons* who have a true calling; that all pastors have equal authority and that all is done under Christ's authority and in subjection to one another (arts. 29–33); that the sacraments are two, are aids to faith and external signs of an inward grace which, through faith, unites us to Christ (arts. 34–38); and that God, having set up kingdoms and governments, would have us obey them, even if administered by unbelievers (arts. 39–40).

The confession was adhered to through seventeenth-century doctrinal disputes and "the church of the desert" of the eighteenth century, until a major revision (1872), which divided the French Church into liberal and conservative factions.

H. Jahr, *Studien zur Überlieferungsgeschichte der Confession de foi von 1559* (1964); J. Pannier, *Les origines de la confession de la foi* (1936).

BRIAN G. ARMSTRONG

French Reformation

Unlike the other Protestant reformations, the French was not the product of one person or cause. It sprang from many reform impulses, had a varied cast of characters with varied agendas, and was shaped by a hostile environment. It was characterized by ambiguity, and there were few, if any, decisive events such as Martin Luther's* "posting" of the ninety-five theses. The "Father" of French reform, Jacques Lefèvre d'Etaples (d. 1536) remained within the Roman Church but did sow the seeds of reform from his post at the great Saint-Germain-des-Prés Church near Paris. Trained in Italy, he was influenced by Neoplatonic spiritualism and, especially, by the philological program of Renaissance humanism.* He seems also to have embraced a strong Gallicanism (French control of French Church affairs) and a strong sense of the need for church reform.

Lefèvre's commentaries on the Psalms (1509) and on Paul's epistles (1512) contained, *inter alia*, a doctrine of justification* by faith* alone. They influenced Luther and most of the leading French reformers, including William Farel* and John Calvin,* who shared his spiritualism, Christian humanism, and Gallicanism. Crucial to this program was the humanist, historico-literal interpretation of the biblical text which appealed to the learned "circles" (or, loosely, academies) of the court of Francis I and especially his sister Marguerite of Angoulême.*

Reform ideas were in place by the time Luther's Latin treatises began to circulate in France (c. 1518). By 1523 the Sorbonne had condemned Lefèvre, Luther, and many others, but its negative defense of orthodoxy could not overcome the powerful impulse for reform which broke out everywhere, principally among the learned, the nobility, and artisans. Several nascent churches were established by 1534, the year in which reform placards were posted throughout Paris. This event brought on violent, continuous persecution, but the fires of persecution were countered by the fiery evangelism of reformers like Farel. With the publication of his *Institutes* (1536), Calvin became the leading defender and spokesman of the movement. Established in Geneva, he sent a steady stream of pastors into France.

The Paris church had been established by 1555. Under the nobleman and pastor Antoine de la Roche Chandieu, a confidant of Calvin, it became the leading voice of the French Reformed Church. By 1559 a representative form of government permitted the meeting of the first National Synod at Paris; it adopted a book of discipline and the French Confession.*

Among the noble families that joined the movement were the powerful Montmorencys and the Bourbons (the collateral royal line). Gaspard de Coligny of the former and Henry, king of Navarre, of the latter were principal leaders. This political threat led to the devastating religious wars of the latter third of the century and resulted in the assumption of the throne by Henry (as Henri IV; 1593) and establishment of the French Reformed Church as an official body via the Edict of Nantes* (1598).

M. Greengrass, *The French Reformation* (1987); E. G. Léonard, *Histoire général du protestantisme*, 3 vols. (1961–64; ET *History of Protestantism*, vol. 1, 1968); J.

T. McNeill, *The History and Character of Calvinism* (1954).

BRIAN G. ARMSTRONG

Fuller, Andrew (1754–1815)

Baptist theologian and advocate of foreign missions. Fuller was minister of Soham Baptist church, Cambridgeshire (1775), and Kettering Baptist church, Northamptonshire (1782). He was self-taught and studied Scripture and such authors as Jonathan Edwards.* Thereby he evolved an evangelical Calvinism,* leading him to oppose both hyper-Calvinism* and all forms of rationalist divinity. He was a founder and first secretary of the Baptist Missionary Society. It was said the burden of missions lay on his heart more powerfully than on any other person in England.

Fuller's commendation of evangelical Calvinism was *The Gospel Worthy of All Acceptation; or, The Obligation of Men Fully to Credit and Cordially Approve Whatever God Has Made Known* (1785). It profoundly affected William Carey, the first missionary of the Baptist Missionary Society. His works were published in several editions in the mid-nineteenth century. Yale and Princeton awarded him the degree of D.D., recognizing him as the greatest original theologian among English Calvinist Baptists of his day.

PETER TOON

Fundamentalist/Modernist Controversy

A conflict (1920s) when militant conservative Christians sought to curtail the advance of U.S. Protestant liberal theology and oppose trends in American culture at large, focusing especially on the teaching of biological evolution.

After the American Civil War, intellectual and cultural developments broke down the broad evangelical consensus of mid-nineteenth-century American Protestantism. Advances in science,* history, biblical studies, and the social sciences challenged traditional Christian theology. Concurrently, rapid urbanization and industrialization and vast immigration added to the cultural disruption.

Many Christians sought to save Christianity's cultural influence by accommodating the traditional faith to the new knowledge. These liberals or modernists emphasized the role of ethics* and experience* in religion and God's immanence in the progress of history* to the detriment of traditional views of doctrine,* the authority of Scripture,* and the transcendence of God.*

Concurrently, conservative Christians adopted innovations of their own such as dispensational* premillennialism, which found support for its high view of Scripture in the doctrine of scriptural inerrancy developed by theologians at Princeton Seminary, and Keswick holiness theology.

After the cultural crisis following World War I, these long-developing differences exploded in the fundamentalist/modernist conflict. With increased modernist aggressiveness in the 1920s, militant conservatives (fundamentalists) united to mount a conservative counteroffensive. Fundamentalists sought to rescue their denominations from the growth of modernism at home and on mission fields by requiring subscription to traditional doctrines such as the inerrancy of Scripture and the virgin birth and bodily resurrection of Jesus Christ.

Modernist/fundamentalist battles were especially fierce among the northern Baptists, the northern Presbyterians, and the Disciples of Christ who had strong contingents of liberals and conservatives. In the northern Methodist and Episcopal churches, where liberals and moderates dominated, and in most southern churches, where conservatism held sway, fighting was much less intense. By 1926 the liberal appeal for tolerance in the churches prevailed and, to the chagrin of the fundamentalists, modernists were not excised from the churches.

In the broader culture, fundamentalists, convinced that a Darwinist "Might makes right" philosophy had dragged the world into war and threatened America's moral basis, worked to arrest the teaching of biological evolution in public schools. A range of interdenominational organizations, such as the World's Christian Fundamentals Association, and numerous individuals, most notably William Jennings Bryan,* led this crusade which culminated in the Scopes* "monkey trial" (1925) in Dayton, Tennessee. Though

John Scopes was convicted of teaching biological evolution, the national press ridiculed Bryan, counsel for the prosecution, and portrayed fundamentalism as a function of rural ignorance to be overcome eventually by the advance of an urban, cosmopolitan culture. This, combined with Bryan's death shortly after the trial, led to the eventual decline of the anti-evolution movement for the near future.

Though both fundamentalism and modernism underwent important changes after 1930, divisions between conservative and liberal Christians would henceforth far outweigh traditional denominational distinctions among mainstream Protestants.

W. Hutchinson, *The Modernist Impulse in American Protestantism* (1976); G. M. Marsden, *Fundamentalism and American Culture* (1980); F. M. Szasz, *The Divided Mind of Protestant America, 1880–1930* (1982).

BRADLEY J. LONGFIELD

Gaussen, [François-Samuel-Robert] Louis (1790–1863)

Genevan Reformed pastor and professor of theology. After studying theology, Gaussen was ordained in the Church of Geneva (1814). Convinced by Robert Haldane to follow orthodox Calvinism, Gaussen co-edited, with J. I. S. Cellérier, a new edition of the 1566 Second Helvetic Confession. He founded the Evangelical Society of Geneva and taught in the School of Theology (1831). He is known for his defense of biblical inerrancy (*Theopneustia* [1841]) and his interest in the Sunday school movement (*Prophet Daniel . . . for a Sunday-school* [1840]).

O. Fatio, ed., *Genève protestante* (1983), 67–89; L. E. Froom, *The Prophetic Faith of Our Fathers*, 4 vols. (1946–54); H. v. d. Goltz, *Genève religieuse* (1862).

JOHN B. RONEY

General Assembly

The General Assembly (sometimes National Synod or Synod) is the highest governing body of Reformed denominations in a system of church government that traditionally consists of four levels of representative church courts—sessions (consistories), presbyteries (colloquies or classes), synods (provincial synods), and general assemblies (national synods). The system of ascending church governing bodies, characteristic of Reformed polity,* combines the principles of local freedom and central unity. The French Reformed Church organized the first National Synod (1559) and adopted a book of discipline* that laid the foundation for a more fully developed Presbyterianism than established by John Calvin* in Geneva. The Scottish Kirk formed a General Assembly (1560), and other continental Reformed churches subsequently created similar provincial or national governing bodies. In 1789, the Presbyterian Church in the U.S.A., consisting of four synods and sixteen presbyteries, convened its first General Assembly in Philadelphia, with John Witherspoon* as Moderator.

General Assemblies usually meet annually, with representatives being clerical and lay commissioners from each presbytery, the total number of which is proportional to the membership of the governing body. Although commissioners represent specific presbyteries, they are not instructed how to vote. A moderator who presides over the Assembly is elected for a one-year term. The chief executive officer of the General Assembly, the Stated Clerk, is elected for a designated term and eligible for reappointment. As the highest representative body in the Reformed system of government, the Assembly has authority to set denominational policies and supervise operations of various church boards and agencies. It also oversees and reviews decisions of lower governing bodies, which in turn overture or appeal to the General Assembly. The Assembly, however, has limited, defined, and delegated powers subject to the authority of the Constitution of the church. Changes in the Constitution and amendments to confessional standards can be implemented only after an affirmative vote (usually two-thirds) by presbyteries.

Among Reformed denominations, the precise authority of General Assemblies varied, often according to the historical circumstances under which they were constituted. In Scotland, where the Parliament officially adopted Presbyterianism and created the Assembly before lower governing bodies were established, the General Assembly has functioned with considerable autonomy. The moderatorial nominee is selected by a committee in advance of the annual meeting and after his or her year of service becomes a continuing member of the Assembly. Meetings are always held in Edinburgh and attended by representatives of the British monarchy. In the United States, where the lower governing bodies (presbyteries and synods) created the General Assembly, moderatorial candidates are nominated by presbyteries and the moderator is elected by the Assembly. Moderators do not become permanent commissioners, and annual meetings vary in location to acknowledge different regions of the national church. The American Reformed tradition has also emphasized the concept that undelegated powers remain in the presbyteries and not in the General Assemblies.

R. DOUGLAS BRACKENRIDGE

Geneva, Free Evangelical Church of

Founded (1849) as the last of a series of events in Geneva that began with the 1813 revival. Initially, conflict arose between revival advocates and leadership of the Church of Geneva, which, strongly under the influence of the French Enlightenment, prohibited the teaching of certain traditional articles of faith. The contradiction between an interpretation of Christianity according to Enlightenment principles, on one hand, and evangelicalism, on the other, remained the core problem. A separate theological school was founded (1832). The Free Evangelical Church's creed is inclusive as being simply biblical (primitivism); its polity* is Reformed.

M. Lador, *L'Eglise évangélique libre de Genève 1849–1949* (1949).

JOHN E. WILSON

Geneva Academy

In 1559, in order to train leaders of the Reformed movement the government of Geneva, at the urging of John Calvin,* established a college for instruction at the secondary level and an academy for higher education. The Academy took over for French Switzerland many of the functions that had been filled by another academy in Lausanne, which had recently been purged of much of its faculty and students by the government of Bern. Theodore Beza* came from Lausanne to become the first rector. Initially its faculty consisted of five lecturers—two in theology (Calvin and Beza) and three more, in Hebrew, Greek, and the arts. Its first curriculum was of a humanist* character, giving more training in languages than did universities of the period. Its primary purpose was to train candidates for the Christian ministry. The Geneva Academy soon attracted significant numbers of students from all over western and central Europe, many of whom entered the ministry in their home countries, often in positions of leadership. It was thus of crucial importance in spreading the Reformed version of Protestant Christianity throughout Europe. In later decades occasional instruction in law was added to its curriculum. In later centuries instruction in medicine was also added. The Academy served as the nucleus out of which the present University of Geneva grew.

C. Borgeaud, *Histoire de l'Université de Genève,* vol. 1: *L'Académie de Calvin, 1559–1798* (1900).

ROBERT M. KINGDON

Geneva Bible

English Bible translation by Marian exiles* in Geneva (1555–60) under the tutelage of John Calvin.* William Whittingham, a chief compiler, had published his NT (1557), and the complete Bible with fuller annotations, including a preface to each book, was an extension of Whittingham's work. He was the driving force behind the complete Bible but was assisted by Genevan exiles, notably Anthony Gilby. It was printed initially in Geneva on May 10, 1560.

The translation was never sanctioned by the English government but became immensely popular with English nonconformists. It went through numerous reprintings in England, after Edmund Grindal's appointment as archbishop of Canterbury (1575), and no English Bible could match its success. It began a new era of English translations, with many innovative features. Along with John Foxe's* *Acts and Monuments of Matters Happening in the Church* it became one of the most popular books in Tudor-Stuart England. The theological sentiments of its annotations appealed to many; from these, much of the distinctively English Protestant ethos that flourished in the Elizabethan puritan* movement received corroboration.

Though Calvin assisted in determining the exiles' view of church order, his theological influence on the Geneva Bible compilers was minimal. The Protestantism of the Genevan exiles was clearly in line with many Lutheran and Reformed positions but was crystallized before they came under Calvin's personal influence. In the Geneva Bible, the principle of *sola Scriptura* was given special meaning, since the English reformers were convinced the Bible contained a primitive, apostolic pattern that was mandated for England's national destiny.

L. E. Berry, ed., *The Geneva Bible: A Facsimile of the 1560 Edition* (1969); D. G. Danner, "The Contribution of the Geneva Bible of 1560 to the English Protestant Tradition," *SCJ* 12, no. 3 (1981); C. Martin, *Les protestants anglais réfugiés à Genève au temps de Calvin 1555–1560* (1915).

DAN G. DANNER

Geneva Catechism

During his first Genevan period (1536), John Calvin* prepared a short catechism to provide Christian instruction for the young and to secure greater unity in the Reformed faith. After his reluctant but dutiful return from a happy exile in Strassburg, he rewrote and expanded it.

In his introduction, Calvin mentions the universal concern that children be taught the basic doctrines* of the Christian faith, done in former and better times by catechisms.* Doubtless, he says, a single catechism for all the churches is desirable, but for many reasons each church is likely to use its own. This variety is acceptable to the extent "that we are all directed to the one Christ, by whose truth, if we be united in it, we may grow together into one body and one spirit, and with one mouth also proclaim whatever belongs to the sum of the faith" (Reid, p. 89).

The Geneva Catechism is divided into four (sometimes five) parts: the first, concerning faith,* explains the Apostles' Creed; the second, concerning the law,* deals with the Ten Commandments; the third, concerning prayer,* expounds the Lord's Prayer. If the Word of God* is considered the fourth division, then the fifth concerns the sacraments.* Otherwise the sacraments are the fourth subject, with Calvin's exposition of the Word of God forming an introduction to them.

J. K. S. Reid, trans., *Calvin: Theological Treatises* (1954), 83–139.

CHARLES PARTEE

Geneva Company of Pastors

The Protestant Reformation in Geneva replaced a church governed by a single person, the bishop, with one governed by a group, the Company of Pastors. This group was informally created by William Farel* and others as the Reformation began in the 1530s. It was described in writing in the Ecclesiastical Ordinances* drafted by Calvin (1541; 1561) and assumed more formal shape as it functioned. In its mature form the Company met every week. The announced purpose of these meetings was simply to discuss Scripture* and reach consensus on its interpretation. The meetings were also used to engage in mutual criticism, prepare positions for negotiation with the city government, and examine candidates for the ministry and assign them to parishes in Geneva or, increasingly, elsewhere—particularly France. The Company had two officers. One was a secretary, who kept written registers of its deliberations. The other was a moderator, who presided over its meetings and negotiated on its behalf with outsiders. Calvin was moderator until his death in 1564; Theodore Beza* held the position until 1580; since then, it has been held for shorter terms of varying length. The Company of Pastors represents in concrete form the commitment of the Reformed movement to collective rather than individual leadership within the church.

R. M. Kingdon, "Calvin and 'Presbytery': The Geneva Company of Pastors," *Pacific Theological Review*, 1985, 43–55.

ROBERT M. KINGDON

Geneva Consistory

The Geneva Consistory was established by John Calvin* to control as closely as possible Christian behavior as distinct from Christian belief. It was a model for similar disciplinary institutions in most early Reformed communities. Calvin insisted on the Consistory's creation before he agreed to return to Geneva (1541), personally drafted the legislation that created it, participated actively in its deliberations, and fought for its sole right to excommunicate people who would not accept its discipline. In legal form the Consistory was a standing committee of the local government. It was made up of lay elders,* elected annually; all the ordained pastors, ex officio; and one of the four municipal syndics (or ruling magistrates) who served as its presiding officer. It met once a week to examine community members referred to it on suspicion of misbehavior, including "superstitious" religious practices, marital and sexual problems, disorderly conduct, and disrespect for church and state authorities. It could provide counseling, excommunicate, or refer to city courts. At its height, shortly after Calvin's death, it summoned a significant percentage of the entire Genevan population. It had a great impact on the behavior of the people of Geneva.

W. Köhler, *Züricher Ehegericht und Genfer Konsistorium*, vol. 2 (1942), 505–652; E. W. Monter, "The Consistory of Geneva, 1559–1569," *Bibliothèque d'humanisme et renaissance* 38 (1976): 467–84.

ROBERT M. KINGDON

Geneva Gown

Traditionally the vestment of most Reformed and Presbyterian ministers. The Geneva Gown is an adaptation of the outdoor dress of the clergy of the Middle Ages and was originally a black gown worn over a cassock as clerical street dress. John Calvin* objected to medieval church vestments and brought clerical street dress into the church as the vestment for the Sunday service. Though still often worn with a cassock, the outer gown is frequently worn alone today. It may be worn with two linen strips called bands, the medieval mark of an educated person.

HOWARD G. HAGEMAN

Genevan Reformation

Before the Reformation, Geneva was the capital of an ecclesiastical state, ruled by a prince-bishop allied closely with the neighboring duchy of Savoy. The purely internal government of the city was handled by elected representatives of the local population. In the 1520s those representatives, encouraged by the neighboring city-state of Bern, began taking over one after another of the broader governmental powers of the bishop, until he, most of the local clergy, and agents of Savoy left the city. At the same time, preachers sponsored by Bern, led by William Farel,* were urging Genevans to embrace Protestantism. These dual political and religious revolutions climaxed (1536) when a general assembly of the citizenry voted that the city would henceforth live according to the gospel and the Word of God, renouncing the Mass and all other papist abuses. A few months later John Calvin* was hired as a public lecturer.

In 1538 both Farel and Calvin were expelled from Geneva for refusal to follow governmental orders; in 1541 Calvin alone was invited back and given power to shape a truly Reformed church for the city-state. He drafted a set of ecclesiastical ordinances* creating a church* built around four ministries: (1) pastors to proclaim the Word of God* and administer the sacraments* in the parish churches of the city and in a few neighboring villages remaining under city control; (2) doctors to teach the Word of God, at first in informal lectures, later in the formal curriculum of an Academy* (1559); (3) elders* to maintain Christian discipline as members, with the pastors, of a semijudicial body, the Consistory;* and (4) deacons* to collect alms and distribute them to the poor, in the beginning primarily through an all-purpose charitable institution called the General Hospital. Almost all the pastors and doctors were highly educated immigrants from France, who became salaried employees of the state. Almost all the elders and deacons were prominent local business and professional men, elected once a year, many of whom received nominal payments for their work.

At first the new church encountered stiff local opposition to some reforms, particularly those involving the Consistory's use of excommunication as a tool for maintaining discipline. After bitter controversy, the faction of prominent local citizens and a rapidly increasing number of religious refugees supporting Calvin won complete control of the city (1555). Thereafter Calvin's power within Geneva was absolute. The reputation of the Reformed church he created there spread rapidly, at first into neighboring France, but soon into Scotland and England, the Netherlands, parts of western Germany, and sections of Poland, Czechoslovakia, and Hungary. Geneva's church became and to a certain degree remains a mother and model to the entire Reformed movement.

E. W. Monter, *Calvin's Geneva* (1967); H. Naef, *Les origines de la réforme à Genève*, 2 vols. (1936–68).

ROBERT M. KINGDON

Ghent, Pacification of

An alliance (November 8, 1576) among the northern and southern provinces of the Netherlands, not including Luxembourg, provoked by the Spanish fury at Antwerp, calling for expulsion of Spanish troops and suspension of Philip II's antiheresy edicts. It acknowledged Reformed Christianity in Zeeland and Holland, forbidding anti-Catholic activity elsewhere. Viewed by some as an opportunity to unite the Low Countries above denominational lines, inspired by William of Orange, it failed to resolve constitutional and religious issues and keep peace.

E. H. Kossman and A. F. Mellink, eds., *Texts Concerning the Revolt of the Netherlands* (1975), 24–32, 126–32.

JEANNINE E. OLSON

Gill, John (1697–1771)

A strong proponent of Calvinism as the Baptist pastor at Horsley-Down, Southwark, for fifty-two years. Though he received the D.D. from the University of Aberdeen (1748), Gill was largely self-educated and known for his rabbinical learning. His greatest fame was his effect on Particular Baptist theology. He attacked Deist Anthony Collins for interpreting the OT allegorically, Methodist John Wesley for not understanding the covenant* of grace,* and anti-Calvinist Daniel Whitby for denying Dortian Calvinism's five points. Gill expounded his views in many publications (1728–70) and in his midweek lectures at Great Eastcheap (1729–56).

RONALD J. VANDERMOLEN

Gillespie, George (1613–1648)

Scottish theologian. After study at St. Andrews, while serving as domestic chaplain, Gillespie published *A Dispute Against the English-Popish Ceremonies* (1637), thereby gaining a considerable reputation. Subsequently he was called to an important Edinburgh church and was sent as one of the Scottish commissioners to the Westminster Assembly.* There he took a significant part, particularly in debate. His magnum opus, *Aaron's Rod Blossoming* (1646; repr. 1985), has been characterized as the *chef d'oeuvre* of Scottish ecclesiastical theology. Exploring the relationship of civil and ecclesiastical power, Gillespie both expounded the classic Reformed view and opposed Erastianism.*

DAVID C. LACHMAN

Gladden, Washington (1836–1918)

A most influential clergyman, Gladden lectured, published, and edited from the late 1860s and while pastor of the First Congregational Church of Columbus, Ohio (1882–1914). He expressed an outspoken, biblically rooted commitment to the justice of God, the moral and social nature of Christian commitment, and the social and economic implications of the

Christian message for workers and the underprivileged. This is seen in nearly forty books, his work for interdenominational understanding, and his term on the Columbus City Council (1900–1902). His theology and life are summed up in his much-loved hymn, "O Master, Let Me Walk with Thee."

J. H. Dorn, *Washington Gladden: Prophet of the Social Gospel* (1966); R. D. Knudten, *The Systematic Thought of Washington Gladden* (1968).

PHILIP W. BUTIN

Glasgow Missionary Society

Formed in February 1796, the Society was an interdenominational Presbyterian body. Initial attempts to work in West Africa failed disastrously, but in 1821 it began a successful venture in South Africa among the Kaffir people. Mission stations were established in Chumie (1821), Lovedale (1824), Balfour (1828), Burnshill and Pirie (1830), and Iggibiha (1836). The Society was fragmented by the Scottish controversy (1837) over whether churches should be "voluntary" or established. The pro-establishment Church of Scotland faction retained the Society's name and transferred its missions to the Free Church (1844) after the Disruption* (1843). The anti-establishment faction, Glasgow African Missionary Society, transferred its missions to the United Presbyterian Church, a voluntary denomination (1847).

J. L. Aikman, *Cyclopaedia of Christian Missions* (1860); E. G. K. Hewat, *Vision and Achievement 1756–1956* (1956).

N. R. NEEDHAM

God

The doctrine of God is the beginning of the early creeds,* the foundation for all that follows. In the Reformed confessions, it is first in some, and follows immediately upon the issue of the source of our knowledge* of God* in some or our desperate need for God in others. Since it is so basic, one could incorporate much of Christian doctrine* into this single issue. However, the doctrine of God has traditionally been subdivided into several others, including the Trinitarian nature of God, the incarnation* of the Second Person of the Trinity,* and the works of God in creation,* providence,* and redemption.

In the following sections, the specific issues of the understanding of God's oneness and attributes in the Reformed tradition will be discussed.

Background. Perhaps in this doctrine more than in almost any other, the Protestant tradition in general and the Reformed tradition in particular were dependent on the Hebrew tradition. The monotheistic belief was undeniable for Christians and had been maintained continuously. God is one; there is no other. Further, this God is the creator of all that is, not subject to preexistent matter or conditions. God is the ruler of all—the Almighty. Nothing is outside God's governance. This is the first and essential confession of faith.

The late-medieval period, immediately preceding the Reformation, had seen great interest in the nature of God. Was God to be thought of primarily as will, whose actions determined what was right and wrong rather than being subject to criteria external to the will of God? Was God to be thought of as supremely good and wise, whose goodness and wisdom were reflected, however dimly, in human understandings of goodness and wisdom? The Reformation discussions are best seen as continuations of this earlier debate. However, they were not a mere continuation. Particularly in Martin Luther,* the issue of God's power was placed in the context of God's gracious love. The development of the Reformed tradition must be seen in this setting.

Huldrych Zwingli. The earliest representative of the Reformed tradition is Zwingli,* who was far less dependent on Luther's work than later Calvin* would be. Zwingli's reform began in Zurich (early 1519). Radical reform was in the air but was not yet very clearly defined. The Diet of Worms had not yet taken place; Luther's great treatises had not yet been written. Zwingli's work had different roots and outcomes from Luther's. G. W. Locher has written: "[B]oth reformers were awakened to their task through fear of the judgment. With Luther, this meant fear of being punished in hell for his sins;

whereas with Zwingli, it was fear that the curse of God must fall upon Christendom, divided and betraying its Lord in bloody wars."

Zwingli is very important for the development of the Reformed understanding of God. For him, the holiness and majesty of God were paramount and were seen also in the Lordship of Christ. His basic concern was not salvation per se but the question of a holy God who chose a people and expected them to live under God's rule. Sin* was real, and forgiveness* was the gracious message of the gospel. Yet this grace* should not be so interpreted that it lessened the need for holiness in God's people.

Zwingli shows clearly the tension always present in the Reformed understanding of God: between God's holiness and majesty, on the one hand, and God's grace and love on the other. These cannot be arranged in a chronological order, that first we must know the holiness which puts us under judgment in order then to experience the grace that overcomes judgment. For the Reformed tradition, God's holiness and grace cannot in any way be played off against each other. Grace is to lead us to true holiness. Holiness has as its content not only piety but lives dedicated to living as God intends us to live, both as individuals and as a community.

Further, the incarnation* tells us of God's nearness to us. But the astonishing majesty of God cannot be overlooked or made irrelevant by the incarnation. Not even in the Second Person can the divine majesty be overshadowed by humanity. God is One, Holy, Creator, Redeemer. Creatures are to worship, obey, and honor this One. Human rulers pale in comparison. Idolatry* is the chief sin, for it denies this ultimate claim and results in disobedience. God is sovereign; there is nothing out of God's control and providence. From this the doctrines of divine election and predestination* readily flow and are understood by Zwingli as directly derived from God's sovereignty over all creation.

Following Zwingli's death (1529), Heinrich Bullinger* became leader of the Zurich church. His last confession of faith, put into the form of the Second Helvetic Confession* (1566), stresses these elements: "We believe and teach that God is one in essence or nature, subsisting in himself, all sufficient in himself, invisible, incorporeal, immense, eternal, Creator of all things both visible and invisible, the greatest good, living, quickening and preserving all things, omnipotent and supremely wise, kind and merciful, just and true" (3.1).

John Calvin. Calvin is a second-generation reformer, building on the work of Zwingli, Luther, Bullinger, and many others. On the doctrine of God, he was strongly influenced by Luther, holding firmly to the primacy of grace, the astonishing act of the sovereign God who deigns to come among us with forgiveness and love. Yet this still must be placed within the framework that Zwingli provided: God's grace is for holiness; God's concern is for the creation of a holy and just people, visible as such in the world; God's love and condescension cannot be seen as lessening the awesome majesty of this One who by election and grace will create such a people. In Calvin, because of Luther's influence, there is a clear alteration, a softening of what can appear as harshness in Zwingli. However, it is not a compromise between the two positions; it is, rather, a new and creative structure that takes into account the emphases of both. In some of his writings, Zwingli has a more philosophical and speculative interest which also increases the starkness of his doctrine of God, particularly in the emphasis on God's sovereignty that governs all things. Calvin is less speculative, and more concerned to interpret God's sovereignty in ways that leave room for secondary causes, including human wills.

By the end of the sixteenth century, when the Reformed tradition was increasingly delineated from both the Roman Catholic* and the Lutheran traditions, the distinctive emphases would be in place: God's sovereignty, which governs all things; God's grace, which allows the faithful to trust that God's sovereign will works for our good; and sanctification* as the goal of God's redemptive work in us, since we are to mirror God's holiness, both as individuals and as the community.

Calvinist scholasticism. The seventeenth century saw the development of detailed theological systems within confessional Protestantism, incorporating the use of Aristotelian logic and deducing the systems from scriptural statements. Within Calvinism,* the results of this orthodoxy are recognized in various theologians and some confessional statements. For English-speaking Reformed churches, the classical formulation of this period is to be found in the WCF.* In it one finds the doctrine of God as the second chapter, immediately following the opening section on Scripture* as the source of all human knowledge of God and of God's will and intention.

In the doctrine of God, the attributes of sovereignty and righteousness of God are very strong, and the chapter leads immediately into the doctrine of election (WCF, ch. 3). The structure is more that of Zwingli than Calvin, and the softening aspects of sheer astonishment at the grace and love of such a God toward us are therefore far less than in Calvin. Yet the confession clearly maintains the reality of created wills and secondary causes, thus limiting the direct determination of all things by God, as was more Zwingli's tendency. One needs to see the controversy around Arminius at least partly as a reaction to this stress on the sovereignty of God that appeared to lessen the gracious love, especially as manifested in the increasing prominence of the doctrine of predestination as directly derived from God's sovereign omnipotence.

Eighteenth century. The tension between the scholastic stress on the sovereignty of God and emphasis on the experience of God's graciousness—held together by Calvin—could not bear the strain under the pressure of the evangelical revivals* of the eighteenth century. Particularly in the British colonies in America, and later in the young nation, the stress on the experience of God's gracious, forgiving love would become dominant and the orthodox stress on God's sovereign election would be challenged by an increasing Arminianism* that fit the experience of surrendering to God's grace in the revivals. Jonathan Edwards* was the major theologian who held together traditional emphasis on God's sovereignty seen in election and revivalist experience of conversions.* Others could not do so, and the splits in churches such as the Presbyterian—between New Lights and Old Lights; New Side and Old Side—institutionalized this division for decades.

These divisions—between the older scholastic forms of Calvinism and new, pietistic or evangelical forms—continued well into the nineteenth and twentieth centuries. The ongoing power of scholastic Calvinism is seen in the writings of Charles Hodge* and the Princeton Theology.* Especially in the United States and in churches founded through its missions, those who emphasized the conversion experience by God's grace vied with those who continued the orthodox emphasis on God's sovereignty. Both would maintain the traditional stress on God's holiness and the counterpart of human sanctification.

Nineteenth and twentieth centuries. There have been two very important systematic formulations of the Reformed tradition in the nineteenth and twentieth centuries. Both seek to retain the tension, present in Calvin, between God's character as absolute sovereign and God's gracious love, within the context of God's holiness. The first is that of Friedrich Schleiermacher;* the second, that of Karl Barth.* Both rejected the orthodox tendency to emphasize sovereignty or holiness at the expense of graciousness.

The structure of Schleiermacher's theology assumes the absolute dependence of the whole creation on the One who created it. Faith* is the human creature's response to this One who is the Sovereign of all. This clearly parallels the traditional beginning point in Reformed dogmatics. In structuring his system in *The Christian Faith* (1821–22), however, Schleiermacher divides the experience of faith between consciousness of sin and consciousness of grace. The attributes of God paralleling the first are God's holiness and justice; those paralleling the second are God's love and wisdom. Both consciousness of sin and consciousness of grace continue in the person of faith, though the sense of guilt is always overcome by the sense of grace. The balance has returned, though in a form quite different from in Calvin. These attributes of God—holiness and love—are equally stressed in the human experience of regeneration* and sanctification*—where we see the Reformed emphases. In a unique and powerful way, Schleiermacher blends concern for the sovereignty of God and human appropriation of God's graciousness. Not accidentally, Schleiermacher places the doctrine of election within the experience of God's graciousness, as in Calvin, in contrast to being an aspect of God's sovereignty, as in Zwingli and Calvinist orthodoxy.*

Barth long argued with Schleiermacher on both the method and the content of theology. But there are parallels in Barth's concern to preserve in balance the sovereign character of God, as the first and unalterable statement of theology, and the graciousness of God which raises up to unimagined heights the human creature who has no claim upon such a creator. Barth also emphasizes sanctification as the goal of God's grace and states the Reformed tradition in a way that bypasses the harshness of orthodoxy on the doctrine of God. Though he stresses as unambiguously as possible human dependence on God's revelation,* and the sovereignty this dependence involves, the content of that revelation is gracious. Always the initiative is with God. Always the "yes" of God's graciousness involves a "no" against human waywardness. Judgment is inevitable. Redemption is only because of God's initiative, not human choice. God's election is the election of Jesus Christ, in whom is found the new creation. Barth's understanding of God, combining graciousness and sovereignty, has led to his being accused of holding to universal salvation—a rare charge indeed against a Reformed theologian, and one he denied affirming explicitly.

Conclusions. Within the Reformed tradition, the doctrine of God tries to hold in balance the sovereignty of God, the holiness of God, and the gracious love of God. Where the balance is lost, historically it has usually been the graciousness that has received less emphasis. It would be difficult to recognize as authentically Reformed any doctrine of God that compromised the sovereign omnipotence of God, or lessened the emphasis of God's holiness, with the corresponding requirement of human sanctification. In the creative and comprehensive systems that have emerged in the Reformed tradition—notably in Calvin, Schleiermacher, and Barth—all three of these characteristics have been central to the systems, and God's love and grace have not been minimized. In lesser hands, the limitation of God's love often appears to be the simplest solution to combining sovereignty, holiness, and love. The strength of the tradition is that it clearly prevents a view of God as one who readily fulfills human wishes or one who fails to take sin with utmost seriousness and makes no demands. In much of contemporary church life, that in itself is a great contribution.

J. O. Duke and R. F. Streetman, eds., *Barth and Schleiermacher: Beyond the Impasse?* (1988); G. W. Locher, *Zwingli's Thought* (1981); W. P. Stephens, *The Theology of Huldrych Zwingli* (1986).

CATHERINE GUNSALUS GONZALEZ

Gollwitzer, Helmut (1908–)

Son of a Lutheran pastor, Gollwitzer studied at Munich, Erlangen, Jena, and Bonn; did pastoral work in Berlin; opposed national socialism; was prisoner of war in Russia; then became professor of systematic theology at Berlin Free University. Influenced by Karl Barth,* prevented only politically from succeeding him, Gollwitzer applied Barth's thinking to contemporary developments, presenting the Marxist challenge in *The Christian Faith and the Marxist Criticism of Religion* (1962), confronting Herbert Braun, Rudolf Bultmann, and James M. Robinson in *The Existence of God as Confessed by Faith* (1963), espousing vicarious reconciliation against Dorothee Sölle in *Von der Stellvertretung Gottes* (1967), and discussing interfaith dialogue and social issues in *An Introduction to Protestant Theology* (1978).

GEOFFREY W. BROMILEY

Gomarus, Franciscus (1563–1641)

Reformed minister and theologian. Born François Gomaer in the Walloon-Flemish borderland in Bruges, Gomarus and his parents became religious refugees after embracing the Reformed faith (late 1570s). A precocious child, he was educated at Strassburg (with humanist* Johannes Sturm), Neustadt (where he studied theology with Girolamo Zanchi,* Daniel Tossanus, and Zacharias Ursinus*), Oxford (with John Rainolds), Cambridge (with supralapsarian* William Whitaker; degrees in 1583 and 1584), and Heidelberg (doctorate; 1594). He was pastor of the refugee Walloon Reformed Church in Frankfurt (1587–93). He became professor of theology at Leiden (1594) but resigned because of the Arminian* controversy (1611). After ministering at Middelburg in the Netherlands, Gomarus taught theology at the Protestant seminary in Saumur, France (1614–18), and at Groningen (1618–41).

Gomarus's Reformed scholasticism* was in the mold of Theodore Beza* and Petrus Plancius. Thus, in his theology, supralapsarian predestination* became Calvinism's* central doctrine. Described by contemporaries as brilliant, disputatious and irascible, he led the attack on Jacobus Arminius at Leiden (1604–9) and was instrumental in securing condemnation of Arminianism and the adoption of scholastic Calvinism as orthodoxy by the Synod of Dort* (1618–19). The high-water mark of Calvinist creed making and unconditional predestination, Dort ironically did not adopt Gomarus's supralapsarian views.

The theological controversy between Gomarus and his followers (Gomarists) and Arminius and his followers (Remonstrants*) also generated civil strife, badly dividing the Protestant Netherlands. This conflict led to the establishment (1618) of a temporary dictatorship by the stadtholder Maurice of Nassau (1588–1625) and the subsequent execution, imprisonment, or exile of many Remonstrant leaders.

F. Gomarus, *Opera theologica omnia*, 3 vols. (1644); C. Bangs, *Arminius* (rev. ed. 1985); P. Y. DeJong, *Crisis in the Reformed Churches* (1968); G. P. Van Itterzon, *Franciscus Gomarus* (1930).

ROBERT D. LINDER

Goodwin, Thomas (1600–1680)

Puritan* divine of the Congregational* Way. Goodwin led the Congregationalists within the Westminster Assembly* and later became president of Magdalene College, Oxford, and a confidant of Oliver Cromwell.* He took a leading part in the Savoy Assembly* of Congregational ministers (1658) and became a nonconformist* at the Restoration (1660). He wrote much, and several of his works deserve the title of classics, for example, *The Heart of Christ in Heaven* (1642).

PETER TOON

Government, Church *see* **Polity**

Government, Civil

John Calvin's* understandings of church* and state took practical shape through his leadership of the Genevan church in relation to the city's governing body, the Council. The church and the Council were separate bodies and their duties did not ordinarily overlap. Together, Calvin held, church and state are responsible for fashioning a society where justice* is done, where works of compassion are carried out, where the poor are maintained, and where civil stability allows citizens to live in peace. The Company of Pastors* existed separately and it generally saw to the ordering of the church's life in the ordination* and calling of pastors, catechetical* instruction, and the like. The city's Small Council, which oversaw daily civic life, had no pastors as members, though it was occasionally visited by a pastor delegated to bring some matter to its attention. This separation of spheres of oversight between the Company of Pastors and the Small Council clearly illustrates the separation Calvin enjoined in the *Institutes*.

Cooperation took place through the Consistory.* All Genevan pastors belonged to it as well as (theoretically) did those in the countryside under the city's control, though country ministers did not often attend meetings. A number of lay elders* commissioned by the Council were members. The Consistory was moderated by one of the Council's four syndics (governing magistrates) elected yearly by the citizenry. Here issues of church and state sometimes became confused, such as when adulterers were admonished or excommunicated by the Consistory and then sent to the Council for sentencing—perhaps on bread and water for a few days in addition to an obligatory appearance before the worshiping congregation.

This "mixing of magistracy," which Calvin deplored but tended in practical moral matters to insist on, gave Reformed churches a reputation as "meddlers in magistracy." This was the charge for which Calvin was discharged from his Genevan pastorate and exiled (1538). All the Protestant Reformers believed that "a government will use every effort that the pure Word of God be faithfully proclaimed" (First Helvetic Confession,* 1536), that the church and its ministers should be maintained, and that both church and state cooperate in diaconal and educational matters.

The charge that Calvin was a "theocrat" or "clerocrat"—both terms used to describe a clergy-dominated political order—are not well founded. More accurately, in Geneva Calvin was able to imbue civic leaders with moral energy to perform their political work as "vicars and lieutenants of God" (Geneva Confession of Faith, 1537).

When Reformed churches were established in less friendly lands, insistence on obedience to the magistrate was maintained in confessions of faith,* except where obedience meant disobedience to God.* The French Confession* (1559), written when many had suffered at the hands of the government, still contended that magistrates should "suppress crimes against the first as well as the second table of the Commandments of God." So, though a minority faith, the Reformed insisted (still living in the "shadow of Constantine"!) that government maintain the church and use the temporal sword to punish offenders against religion. Calvin's own insistence on obedience to rulers as God's servants was so complete that his counsel in the last chapter of the *Institutes* (4.20) gave persecuted Protestants almost no redress. They could neither rebel, nor participate in Roman Catholic worship, nor blame anyone else for their sad estate. It was God's punishment for their sins that placed such bad rulers over them.

The Scots Confession* (1560) summarized Reformed churches' teachings on the role of government (*BC* 3.24): Governments are appointed and ordained by God and are to serve "for the good and well being" of all. Those who rebel against duly established civil powers are both enemies to humanity and rebels against God's will. Those in authority are lieutenants of God who use the sword for the defense of the good and the punishment of evildoers. Such magistrates, whether kings or city magistrates, are appointed also to maintain true religion and suppress all religion that is idolatrous. David, Josiah, and others are examples. There is only a hint that rulers might be resisted in the oblique statement that no rebellion is allowable "so long as princes and rulers vigilantly fulfill their office." No doubt Calvin's admonition that such rebellion must be led by notable persons and only after grave provocation (*Inst.* 4.20.31) was being followed in this and all other sixteenth-century Reformed confessional statements.

Why, then, do historians call the Reformed branch of the Reformation the "revolutionary" branch? Why was it the Reformed who contributed to the revolt of the Netherlands against Spain, to the internal wars of religion* in France, to the Puritan* revolt against Charles I in England, and were the New England leaders in the revolt against England? Apparently for at least two reasons. First, there is a strong doctrine of lay empowerment in the Reformed understanding of the role of leadership. This led minor civic and regional leaders to assume strong opposition roles when it appeared that hereditary rulers were not ruling well. For example, John Knox's* friend James Stewart, later the Earl of Moray, bastard son of James V of Scotland, opposed his half-sister's mother and regent, Mary of Guise, on just such grounds and was supported in this by Knox and other ministers.

Second, while rebellion was almost unthinkable for Calvin, his high standards and expectations of rulers produced a nonquietistic relationship to government that contrasted with the subservient attitude inculcated in Luther's* laity or the clear Erastian* position of Anglicans. The smaller sectarian Protestants, on the other hand, took almost no interest in political rulers—provided they were left to practice their faith in peace.

Finally, it should be noted that, with the exception of Huldrych Zwingli,* all the great Reformed thinkers believed rulers were subject to the church in spiritual matters. The Second Book of Discipline* (1578) of the Scots Kirk said, "As ministers and others of the ecclesiastical estate are subject to the civil magistrate, so also the person of the magistrate is subject to the kirk spiritually and in ecclesiastical government." This was not the same as Pope Gregory VII's claim that all rule resided in Christ's earthly vicar. But in a world where magistrates owned church properties and many of the boundaries between church and state to which we are accustomed did not exist, this was certain to exacerbate church-state tensions. In Scotland and England these aggravations grew, until the Reformed contribution to theories of political revolution may have been as great as the "rights of man" doctrines usually ascribed to the great revolutions at the end of the eighteenth century. Undoubtedly the Reformed contributed to these theories.

W. F. Graham, *The Constructive Revolutionary* (1971); H. Höpfl, *The Christian Polity of John Calvin* (1982); J. T. McNeill, ed., *On God and Political Duty* (2nd ed. 1956).

W. FRED GRAHAM

Grace

Most broadly, "grace" describes both the nature of the triune God,* who is revealed in Jesus Christ as the sovereign Lord of all creation and thus God's activity in the world, and also what happens to the lives of those who receive God's grace—those called into God's covenant,* who are baptized* into the death and resurrection* of Jesus Christ. Baptized people are, by the grace of God, a "new creation," and grace describes how they come to life in Christ as well as the process whereby they are becoming a new creation in him. In the grammar of Christian theology, it is appropriate to speak both of "the grace of God" and "the Christian life of grace." The experiential reality of the latter is rooted in the ontological reality of the former. Grace, therefore, describes the human experience of God's free, gratuitous, salvific activity.

The grace of God is at the heart and center of most Christian theologies, including the Reformed tradition. Because grace is a thread running through the whole fabric of Christian theology, it is not always clearly defined and often appears not as a single theological topic but as an implicit presupposition in several, if not all, doctrines.*

History of Christian thought. Though the Greek word *charis* ("grace") is found frequently in the NT, it appears twice as often in the Pauline letters as in the rest of the NT. Paul writes frequently of the "grace of our God and the Lord Jesus Christ" (2 Thess. 1:12). For Paul, God's grace is God's special favor made known to the world in Jesus Christ. He sees God's grace made visible and tangible in the person of Jesus. It is not surprising, therefore, that Paul often closes his letters with words similar to these: "The grace of the Lord Jesus Christ, the love of God, and the communion of the Holy Spirit be with all of you" (2 Cor. 13:13). Jesus Christ is God's grace for the world because he is "Emmanuel"—"God with us."

When the church* has faced practical and theological issues similar to those which Paul confronted, it has returned to Paul's emphasis on God's grace. His distinction between the righteousness of the law* and the righteousness of faith* is based on his understanding of the nature of God's grace. Consequently, when the church has encountered those who emphasize the human capacity for goodness (and thus minimize the radical nature of human sin*), it has often been the Pauline theme of God's grace and God's grace alone which has been the basis of its response.

Four church history events illustrate the centrality of God's grace for the understanding and proclamation of the gospel. The first was the dispute between the British monk Pelagius and Augustine,* bishop of Hippo in the early fifth century.

Pelagius apparently argued that God would not have commanded humans to do something not possible for them to do. Hence, every person must have some capacity to choose good and evil, even after Adam's sin. In response, Augustine developed a doctrine of original sin* stating that sin is not simply a perverse act but also a state and condition into which all people are born. Humans are free, therefore, only to sin and by themselves can do nothing righteous. Nevertheless, they are responsible for the sin and deserve only God's judgment and wrath. Their only hope is God's grace which clothes them in the righteousness of Christ.

A second event was the sixteenth-century Protestant Reformation. In Paul's letters to the Romans and the Galatians, the Augustinian monk Martin Luther* discovered the true meaning of Christian freedom* for a soul tormented by the demands of God's law and a corrupt church which seemed to have turned its back on the gospel. Deeply dependent on Augustine and Luther, John Calvin* also found God's grace to be the basis for the Christian life and the doctrine of justification,* which he described as "the main hinge on which religion turns."

A third event was the debate between the followers of Jacobus Arminius and other theologians of the Dutch Reformed church in the early seventeenth century. Arminius and his followers rejected the notion that God saves some people and damns others, that Christ died only for the elect and not for the world, and that grace is irresistible. "Arminians"* did not deny that God's grace was necessary so a person could be saved, but they described that grace as an "assisting" grace. The Synod of Dort* (1618–19) declared that all people are conceived in sin and are children of wrath, "incapable of any saving good." God, however, "graciously softens the hearts of the elect . . . and inclines them to believe." But faith is not a human act God assists; rather, God "works in man both to will and to do, and indeed all things in all, produces both the will to believe and the act of believing also."

Finally, in Germany (1930s), a small group of Christians known as the Confessing Church rejected the claim by some "German Christians" that the life and history of the German people was a revelation* of God's Word and, consequently, that there were areas of human life where the authority of the state superseded that of the church. In the Theological Declaration of Barmen* (1934), the Confessing Church declared there are not many voices in life to which Christians must listen. Rather, "Jesus Christ, as he is attested for us in Holy Scripture, is the one Word of God which we have to hear and which we have to trust and obey in life and in death" (*BC*, 8.11). The freedom of the church "consists in delivering the message of the free grace of God to all people in Christ's stead" (*BC*, 8.26).

Grace of God. In most forms of Reformed theology, God's grace is understood as the foundation for all things. As Calvin put it, "We make the freely given promise of God the foundation of faith because upon it faith properly rests. . . . Faith properly begins with the promise, rests in it, and ends in it" (*Inst.* 3.2.29). Calvin describes God's grace as "the divine benevolence." Literally, God's grace, for Calvin, is God's good will made known in Jesus Christ. This strong sense of God's good will at work in individual lives and in the affairs of nations is the basis of Calvin's doctrine of election and his claim that goodness, wherever found, can be understood only as a gift of God's sovereign grace. The WCF* also interprets God's grace in terms of God's sovereign will, because God works "all things according to the counsel of his own immutable and most righteous will" (WCF, 2.1).

In contemporary Reformed theology, God's grace is understood not primarily as God's sovereign will but as God's suffering and sovereign love. The Confession of 1967* does not describe the grace of our Lord Jesus Christ in terms of God's "immutable and most righteous will," as does the WCF, but in terms of "God's sovereign love." The Brief Statement of Faith* declares that God created the world good "in sovereign love."

Christian life of grace. According to Calvin, those who partake of Jesus Christ, and by means of the power of the Holy Spirit* have their life in him, "receive a double grace: namely, that being reconciled to God through Christ's blamelessness, we may have in heaven instead of a Judge a gracious Father; and secondly, that sanctified by Christ's spirit we may cultivate blamelessness and purity of life" (*Inst.* 3.11.1). The significance of that statement for the Reformed tradition is threefold. First, Reformed theology since Calvin has understood the whole of the Christian life (both justification and sanctification*) to be a gift of God's grace in Jesus Christ. Second, there is no human goodness apart from God's grace; hence, all people are caught in a web of sin and estrangement from which they cannot extricate themselves. They live utterly in dependence on God's grace. Finally, the grace of God which saves them from their sin also compels those who live in Christ to express their gratitude to God in worship,* thanksgiving, and service in the world. Reformed Christians understand the grace of God to be that which frees them to witness to God in the world and participate in God's transformation of it.

GEORGE W. STROUP

Great Awakening

A series of loosely connected revivals* of evangelical (and largely Calvinistic) religion in the British North American colonies (approx. 1739–43). It was linked, through shared personalities and publications, to the Evangelical Revival in the Church of England and the organization of the Methodist societies; and, by its strongly "experimental" spirituality, to the larger context of eighteenth-century Pietism. In its effect, it combined "the impact of the civil rights demonstrations, the campus disturbances, and the urban riots of the 1960's" (Bushman, p. xi) and acted as the decisive shaping experience of American evangelicalism in general and American Calvinist theology and ecclesiology in particular.

Since many British North American colonies had been organized and peopled by dissenting Protestant sects, episodes of communal spiritual renewal became a necessary part of maintaining religious identity in the colonial setting. The general outburst of revival which became the Great Awakening began (1739) under the preaching of the Anglican Calvinist itinerant George Whitefield,* whose dramatic and confrontational appeals for conversion* touched off waves of excited revival and equally excited controversy. In New England, clergy sympathetic to Whitefield ("New Lights") began to imitate his tactics, with many resorting to aggressive itinerant preaching across parish boundaries. They found their most talented spokesman in Jonathan Edwards,* who justified the need for the Awakening in dignified but insistent terms. However, Charles Chauncy and James Dana, principal figures of the "Old Lights" in Massachusetts and Connecticut, replied by accusing the "New Lights" of antinomianism and invoked legal and ecclesiastical sanctions against them. Whitefield prompted similar confrontations among Presbyterians in Pennsylvania and New Jersey where "New Side" Presbyterians sympathetic to Whitefield were led by Gilbert Tennent* into secession from the "Old Side" Synod of Philadelphia (1741). Similar outbursts of revival continued to occur in the late 1740s and the 1750s in Virginia.

In New England, the Awakening pried open a number of cracks in Congregational* theology and ecclesiology. Many "Old Lights," disgusted with the "enthusiasm" of the Awakening and eager to accommodate the Enlightenment, moved into Unitarianism;* Jonathan Edwards and his followers Joseph Bellamy* and Samuel Hopkins* refashioned Calvinism* to accommodate the Awakening, while many other "Old Calvinists" were left struggling to hold a middle ground. The radical Awakeners survived briefly as a separate Congregational movement. In Pennsylvania, the "New Side" and "Old Side" Presbyterians were eventually reconciled (1758), but until then, Tennent and Jonathan Dickinson continued to promote "experimental" piety over confessional conformity, and continuing conflicts eventually produced a renewed schism (1837).

The Great Awakening was responsible for as many as 350 new churches and 50,000 converts and for the founding of several prominent colleges. Among its long-term effects, the Awakening made the dramatic genre of the public revival the major symbolic device in American evangelical culture. It was also a leading force in blunting the influence of the Enlightenment in America and in preserving the hegemony of Reformed theology in American Protestantism. For these reasons it remains problematic whether the Awakening contributed significantly to the American Revolution.

A. Alexander, ed., *The Log College* (1850); R. Bushman, ed., *The Great Awakening: Documents on the Revival of Religion* (1969); E. S. Gaustad, *The Great Awakening in New England* (1959); C. C. Goen, ed., *Works of Jonathan Edwards: The Great Awakening* (1972); J. Tracy, *The Great Awakening* (1842); L. J. Trinterud, *The Forming of an American Tradition* (1949).

ALLEN C. GUELZO

Groningen School

A moderate-romantic revision of Reformed theology that dominated Protestant thinking in the Netherlands in the middle third of the nineteenth century. Its chief proponent, Petrus Hofstede de Groot (1802–86), head theologian at the University of Groningen, expounded its claims in *Truth in Love: A Theological Journal for Cultured Christians* (1837ff.), which title aptly characterizes the movement's tone and clientele.

Groningen theology reacted against confessional orthodoxy and Enlightened rationalism by emphasizing historical development and human affect, especially in religion. It was Christocentric in every part, yet approximated a docetic view of Christ's nature and an Arian position on the Trinity.* Christ was the full revelation* of God* to humanity* and the full realization of human possibilities. By modeling a new moral law,* Christ appealed to the divine core of every human heart. The church* was to nurture that spark until the whole person was pervaded with a new sensibility, until the whole race had progressed into the kingdom that Christ had instituted, until each and all had matured into the full image of God.

For all his similarities to Friedrich Schleiermacher,* de Groot claimed actual inspiration from Herder, Lessing, and Benjamin Constant. His work stands in the general line of Christian Platonism and in the Dutch national tradition of Christian humanism. Repudiated as heterodox by confessionalists and as naive by modernists, Groningen theology nonetheless set the standard against which both reacted and informed the Dutch Protestant establishment for most of the century.

JAMES D. BRATT

Half-Way Covenant

A modification of church membership requirements in seventeenth-century New England Puritanism.* By 1636 Massachusetts Puritans had adopted the principle that only those persons who could testify to a conversion* experience would be admitted as church members. These "visible saints" were eligible for Baptism* and admission to the Lord's Supper* and had the right to vote in church matters.

Their children could also be baptized. But a problem arose when these children found themselves unable to narrate a conversion experience. They could not qualify for full membership, and sought baptism for their own children. The compromise, known as the Half-Way Covenant, allowed baptism of children of baptized but not fully confirmed parents if they acknowledged the discipline* of the church. Neither the parents nor the children were allowed to partake of the Lord's Supper.

The compromise was forged in two actions (1657; 1662) by ministers attempting to solve a pastoral problem. But in practice it was opposed by conservative laity. As late as the 1730s some churches refused to implement the policy, and it arose again as a controversy during the First Great Awakening.*

E. S. Morgan, *Visible Saints* (1963); R. S. Pope, *The Half-Way Covenant* (1969).

JOHN M. MULDER

Hampton Court Conference

A conference of bishops and Puritan ministers convened by James I (January 1604) to discuss the state and direction of the Church of England. Though the king conceded to a few Puritan reform desires, he rejected recommendations for polity* compromises between episcopacy and presbyterianism and for doctrinal revisions in a more explicitly Calvinist direction. Even some minor reforms that he agreed to were subsequently suppressed by the bishops, so the conference actually resulted in a setback for the Puritan cause and increasing polarization within the church. One major accomplishment was authorization for a new English translation of the Bible, fulfilled by the King James Version (1611).

Collinson, *EPM*; M. Curtis, "Hampton Court Conference and Its Aftermath," *History* 46 (1961): 1–16.

JOHN H. PRIMUS

Haroutunian, Joseph (1904–1968)

Presbyterian clergyman and theologian. Haroutunian was born in Marash, Turkey, son of a minister of the Armenian Evangelical Church. He attended the American University of Beirut and earned degrees at Columbia College (1926), Union Seminary (N.Y.; 1930), and Columbia University (Ph.D., 1932). He taught at Wellesley College (1932–40), McCormick Seminary (1940–62), and the University of Chicago Divinity School (1962–68).

Haroutunian's dissertation, *Piety Versus Moralism: The Passing of the New England Theology* (1932), was instrumental in recovering Jonathan Edwards* from decades of neglect. There he cast Edwards as a lonely defender of Calvin's* God,* with a piety,* intellect, and reverence for fact that towered over both his critics and his followers. In the 1930s Haroutunian wrote against liberal theology and early forms of neo-orthodoxy* in favor of a revitalized Reformed or, what he called, a "theocentric" Protestantism. *Wisdom and Folly in Religion* (1940) was a scathing critique of liberal Protestantism. With Louise P. Smith, Haroutunian edited and translated *Calvin: Commentaries* (1958). His last book, *God with Us: A Theology of Transpersonal Life* (1965), was a substantial theology of communion faithful to the Reformed tradition and cultural experiences of North American Christians.

S. D. Crocco, "Joseph Haroutunian: Neglected Theocentrist," *Journal of Religion* 68, no. 3 (1988): 411–25; J. Sittler, "Joseph Haroutunian: Total Theologian," *Journal of Religion* 50, no. 3 (1970): 215–28; and "A Selected Haroutunian Bibliography," *Journal of Religion* 50, no. 3 (1970): 323–26.

STEPHEN D. CROCCO

Hastings, James (1852–1922)

Editor of such massive reference works as the *Dictionary of the Bible* (4 vols. plus supplementary vols.; 1898–1904) and the *Encyclopedia of Religion and Ethics* (12 vols. plus index vol.; 1908–21), Hastings was also founder and editor (1889) of the *Expository Times*. He was born in Scotland, studied the classics at the University of Aberdeen, attended the Free Church Divinity College in Aberdeen, and was ordained a Free Church minister (1884). Much of his enormous editorial work was accomplished while he was a church pastor (retired 1911). His labors grew out of a twofold conviction: the importance of scholarship and its compatibility with essential Christian faith.

DONALD A. HAGNER

Healing Ministry

Healing was a prominent part of Jesus' ministry. He cured the sick in mind and body through a combination of divine power and natural means. The early church continued to heal in the name and power of Christ, through charisms of healing (1 Cor. 12) and/or sacramental ministry (James 5). After Augustine's* time, manifestations of divine healing power were no longer expected except at shrines or through the saints. The rite of anointing the sick became "extreme unction" for the dying. Bodily suffering was to be patiently endured and healing ministry transmuted into the "cure of souls" focusing on relationship with God.* The Reformed inherited these approaches. In Calvin's* Geneva there was Christian care for the sick and pastoral cure of souls. The "visible grace" of healing gifts seemed to be inactive. Bodily healing came through medical interventions or, rarely, by special providence* of God.

The split of healing ministry into medical care (physical) and pastoral care (spiritual) continued into the twentieth century. The dominant Reformed attitude is seen in "Of the Visitation of the Sick" in the Directories for Worship of the Presbyterian Church (1789–1960). Sickness was clearly the harbinger of death.* It was time for the sick to improve their relationship with God, examine their consciences,* repent,* and receive forgiveness* along with comforting words of Scripture* and prayer* to sustain them in their affliction.

A more holistic ministry to the sick person has been advocated in this century, through movements such as clinical pastoral education and individuals such as Paul Tournier and Granger Westberg. Charismatic gifts of healing were revived by Pentecostal groups and individuals such as Agnes Sanford. Alfred Price and the ecumenical Order of St. Luke restored services for healing to many churches.

The shift in Presbyterian thinking is reflected in the UPCUSA "Report on Relation of Christian Faith to Health" (1960). A whole person approach to health, sickness, and healing was embraced. A modern theology of healing ministry was sketched: (1) All healing is from God; (2) illness is an evil to be overcome; (3) faith is its own reward, not a means to an end; (4) prayer is efficacious for healing; (5) God has many therapies; and (6) human mortality points us to our relationship with God. Practical suggestions for ministry to the sick were outlined for pastors, church members, and physicians. A medical/pastoral team approach to healing was advocated, and fruits of psychological research were incorporated in a holistic understanding of pastoral ministry. Presbyterian Directory for Worship instructions for ministry to the sick changed to conform to these new views of ministry to the whole person, first after the merger to form the UPCUSA in 1958, then after the reunion to form the PC(USA) in 1983. The 1990 Directory includes a section on "Services for Wholeness." Increasingly, clergy and laypersons of the Reformed tradition are actively involved in either charismatic or liturgical forms of healing ministry today.

M. T. Kelsey, *Psychology, Medicine and Christian Healing* (1988); Presbyterian Directories for Worship (compare pre-1958 with 1970s and 1990).

BARBARA A. PURSEY

Health and Medicine

Beliefs and values shape the understandings and decisions that individuals make regarding their sexuality, birth, suffering, death, health, sanity, and many other matters of bodily and mental life. Religious heritage and present faith,* a primary source of beliefs and values, thus give rise to and sustain personal and communal commitments here. The Reformed tradition has been a powerful source of such individual and social values.

The sovereignty of God,* the reality of sin* and forgiveness,* the grace* of Christ, the gift and responsibility of life, the imperative to love and justice,* and the Lordship of God over nature, history,* and human destiny are themes that animate belief and value in the Reformed faith.

As the creating, sustaining, and consummating Being, God gives life, safeguards well-being, and receives death.* Recognizing this dependence yields dispositions of respect, stewardship,* and ultimate acquiescence to God's will as individuals live their lives, generate families, experience illness, and face death. Redeeming purpose and providence* are qualities of God's character that imprint one's existence. To succeed in life is to discern and accede to that plan and goodwill. Virtue or health is to advance that kingdom in all of one's action. In concerns of health and medicine, the doctrine of sovereignty has generated throughout history a curious blend of scientific and technical efforts to ameliorate the human condition and its ills and serene resignation in the face of deleterious forces, all the while confident of overriding purpose.

The Puritan ethic, for example, a cultural phenomenon in part created by Reformed faith, first articulated and propelled the medical value of prolonging life. At the same time, it developed a most exquisite theology of death anticipation, even celebration.

The Lordship of God* places parental and regal expectation on God's children, which expectation they have forsaken and from which possibility they have fallen short. Violating our designed nature and intended destiny we have sullied our native well-being. Sin allows disease to fester in our being, alienation to scar our emotional and relational lives, and death to cloud the horizon of our future. The drama of sin and grace punctuates our being most poignantly in disease and health.

"What is your only comfort, in life and in death? . . . My faithful Savior, Jesus Christ" (HC,* q. 1). With these words, a second motif of the Reformed faith bearing on health and disease is expressed. The grace of Christ overwhelms our boundedness to sin and death and renders possible the righteousness or health (salvation*) of God. In Christ we are heirs to the grace of life—which is health, love, marriage, progeny, longevity, and the good conscience of his service.

These existential doctrines of creation, fall, and redemption, especially given the tenor they develop within Calvinist history, activate a high sense of responsibility for life, health, and general welfare. Along with Jewish, Catholic, Lutheran, and Anglican communions, Presbyterians and Baptists found hospitals, medical schools and clinics, and send sons and daughters into the ministries of physical, mental, and spiritual health. Commitment is also inspired within this community to social justice as equity. Concern for the disadvantaged and charity are encouraged.

Finally, the Reformed faith proclaims God as the beginning, the center, and the end of our existence. We die, not to oblivion, but to God's presence. Death is the announcement that our work is done; we have completed our earth-side ministry. Though fighting disease and premature death is noble, our faith asks us to receive death as if we are entering a new life established by God who is faithful. As with Judaism, Reformed Christians honor life, health, the body, and longevity. In Christ we also receive pain, suffering, and death as the Lord's chastening, cleansing, and culminating will.

J. H. Smylie, "The Reformed Tradition, Health and Healing," in *Health Care and Its Costs*, ed. W. Wiest (1988); K. Vaux, *Health and Medicine in the Reformed Tradition* (1984).

KENNETH VAUX

Heaven

Heaven in Reformed understanding is a definite place. As God is creator of "all things visible and invisible," so heaven is the invisible portion of creation, that which is inaccessible to human beings. Heaven is God's dwelling place within creation,* the seat of the divine rule, that place in the created order where God's will is done. Because heaven is part of creation, however, God's presence transcends it: even the highest heavens cannot contain God. Heaven is also the dwelling place of God's "ministering spirits" (angels), the souls of the faithful departed, and the place from which the ascended Christ rules at the right hand of God.

The Reformed tradition consistently affirms that the souls of the faithful departed enter immediately into heaven to be with Christ. John Calvin* wrote his first major theological work, the *Psychopannychia* (1534), against the Anabaptist belief that the soul at death* enters into a state of unconscious slumber awaiting the final resurrection. In contrast to Roman Catholic doctrine of purgatory, the Reformed affirm that departed souls enter immediately into a state of heavenly bliss, though this bliss is perfected and consummated only at the final resurrection, as souls are reunited with their glorified bodies.

The bliss of souls in heaven is frequently associated with a final sabbath rest (cf. Heb. 4), though such rest is generally understood not as cessation from activity so much as relief from earthly burdens and afflictions and fullness of joy in the presence of God. The final resurrection* will also be accompanied by establishment of the kingdom of heaven on earth. Reformed theology tends to view this establishment as restoration rather than replacement of the world as we now know it.

Separation of heaven from earth is an important theme in the Reformed polemic against idolatry.* Because God's dwelling is a place apart, we are prevented from associating God with any earthly likeness or image. The separateness of heaven also figured prominently in debates with Lutherans over the presence of Christ's body in the Eucharist. Against Lutheran doctrine of the ubiquity* of Christ's body, the Reformed assert that Christ's human flesh remains in heaven, spatially removed from the sacramental elements.

Heaven also plays a central role in Reformed piety. Constant meditation upon the heavenly life to come frees believers from enslaving attachments to earthly things, helps them recognize thankfully the foretastes of divine glory given in this life, teaches them patiently to bear adversity, frees them from an immoderate fear of death, and spurs them to a life of faith and obedience. If this vision of the heavenly life "be taken away," says Calvin, "either our minds must become despondent or, to our destruction, be captivated with the empty solace of this world" (*Inst.* 3.9).

J. Baillie, *And the Life Everlasting* (1948); Barth, *CD* III/3, 369–76; R. Baxter, *The Saints' Everlasting Rest* (1650).

P. MARK ACHTEMEIER

Heidelberg Catechism

The catechism was occasioned by disputes among strict and moderate (followers of Philipp Melanchthon) Lutherans, Zwinglians, and Calvinists in the Palatinate (1550s), whose capital was Heidelberg. Elector Frederick III, the first German prince to accept the Reformed faith, commissioned Zacharias Ursinus* and Caspar Olevianus,* Reformed professors of theology at the University of Heidelberg, to write a standard of doctrine to bring peace and unite the regional churches. The work of these young second-generation reformers (both in their twenties) was adopted as a confession of faith, a guide to pastors and teachers, and a manual for the instruction of youth (1563). It became one of the most widely accepted and used of all confessional statements in Reformed churches throughout the world.

The catechism begins with two introductory questions announcing the three-part outline that follows the order of Paul's letter to the Romans. Part I (qq. 3–11) broadly describes human sin* and misery. Part II (qq. 12–85) deals with the redemption accomplished by Christ, explaining it with a Trinitarian exposition of the Apostles' Creed and a theology of the sacraments.* Part III (qq. 86–129) describes Christian life in response to God's grace,* summarizing it with an exposition of the Ten Commandments and the Lord's Prayer. Typically Reformed is its discussion of obedient Christian life under the title "Thankfulness."

The character and the tone of the catechism are revealed by its famous first question and answer:

Q. 1. What is your only comfort, in life and in death?

A. That I belong—body and soul, in life and in death—not to myself but to my faithful Savior, Jesus Christ, who at the cost of his own blood has fully paid for all my sins and has completely freed me from the dominion of the devil; that he protects me so well that without the will of my Father in heaven not a hair can fall from my head; indeed, that everything must fit his purpose for my salvation. Therefore, by his Holy Spirit, he also assures me of eternal life, and makes me wholeheartedly willing and ready from now on to live for him.

The catechism is a warm, personal, generally nonpolemical and ecumenical confession of evangelical faith, representing a moderate Calvinism* (there is no doctrine of double predestination) that appeals to the heart as well as to the mind, is unique among classical Reformed confessions in being expressed subjectively in the first person singular, and confesses Reformed faith and life as joyful, thankful, and free response to God's grace. It has been said to combine the intimacy of Luther, the charity of Melanchthon, and the fire of Calvin.

K. Barth, *The Heidelberg Catechism for Today* (1964); J. B. Rogers, *Presbyterian Creeds: A Guide to the Book of Confessions* (1985); Schaff, *Creeds*, vol. 1.

SHIRLEY C. GUTHRIE

Hell

The doctrine of hell in the Reformed tradition has rested on three theological tenets: God's justice, human depravity, and limited atonement.* God's justice demands the eternal damnation of all human beings. Only the elect will benefit from the atoning work of Christ and escape the terrible fires of hell. All others will be punished eternally.

Calvin's* understanding accords with this. He differs from later Reformed theologians on the nature of hell. Hell is real and terrible but a place of spiritual rather than physical torment. The biblical descriptions of bodily torture serve as metaphors for the sinner's experience of total abandonment by God and, further, divine displeasure.

Though sixteenth-century Reformed confessions assume eternal punishment, most mention the doctrine in passing. Early exceptions are the Basel Confession* (1534), which devotes a short article (art. 10) to it, and the First Helvetic Confession,* where salvation and damnation have a few sentences in a long paragraph on Christology* (art. 11). Significant elaboration is found only in the Belgic Confession* (1561; art. 37). Here eternal punishment is related to election, and the terrors of damnation and the delights of salvation* are juxtaposed. No doubt the bloody persecution of the churches of the Lowlands influenced the Confession's teaching; it promises that the elect "shall see the terrible vengeance which God shall execute on the wicked, who most cruelly persecuted, oppressed, and tormented them in this world."

Most theologians of Reformed orthodoxy* considered Calvin's passive spiritual view of eternal punishment inadequate. The Westminster Confession* (1647) holds that God does not merely withdraw from the damned but actively punishes them, though it does not specify whether the torment is physical as well as spiritual (ch. 33). Scholastic theologians would insist on both, distinguishing between *poena damni*, suffering caused by eternal separation from God, and *poena sensus*, pain of body and soul registered through the senses. The latter could occur only if hell were a place and not merely a state. The incorruptibility of the body permitted unremitting and endless torment, graded, some taught, according to the gravity of earthly sin. Both repentance* and annihilation were rejected. Puritan* preachers gave such teachings imaginative elaboration in sermons designed to convert people through vivid depictions of hell's terrors.

Nineteenth- and twentieth-century theologians present a variety of views of hell. Reformed orthodoxy has continued to defend the doctrine, though usually mitigating the harshness of earlier formulations. Friedrich Schleiermacher* taught universal salvation (universalism*), rejecting eternal punishment as inimical to Christianity. While many nineteenth-century Reformed thinkers followed his lead, neo-orthodox* theologians, recognizing that Scripture teaches both judgment and promise, found Schleiermacher's formulations unacceptable.

Perhaps the most creative reassessment has been made by Karl Barth,* who taught that Jesus Christ alone bears the world's damnation. Others, such as Hendrikus Berkhof,* have advanced a purgatorial view of hell. Of the doctrine of eternal punishment's three foundational tenets, modern Reformed theology has affirmed God's justice and the inability of humanity to save itself but questioned the proposition that atonement must be limited.

PAUL R. FRIES

Helvetic Confession, First

The *Confessio Helvetica prior*, or *Confessio Basiliensis posterior* (1536), was the first formula uniting Swiss Reformed cantons in common confession. Earlier documents, including the First Confession of Basel* (1534), were more local. Pope Paul III's call for a general council in Mantua (1537) persuaded the Swiss to gather their theologians and prepare a confession for the council. Theologians delegated by the magistrates of Zurich, Bern, Basel, Schaffhausen, St. Gall, Mühlhausen, and Biel gathered in Basel (February 1–4). Martin Bucer* and Wolfgang Capito* were present in their continuing effort to unite Lutherans and Zwinglians, a contributing reason for the conference.

Heinrich Bullinger* and Leo Jud of Zurich, Oswald Myconius* and Johann Grynaeus of Basel, and Kaspar Megander of Bern were named to prepare the document. It was signed by all the delegates on February 4 and published in Latin. Jud prepared the German translation, which is fuller than the Latin but of equal authority. Delegates of the town councils assembled on March 27 and adopted the document; Strassburg and Constance refused—Capito apparently preferred the Tetrapolitan Confession* as an instrument of reconciliation between Lutheran and Reformed.

Luther* received a copy through Bucer and made favorable response in letters (1537) to the burgomaster of Basel and Swiss cantons, promising to promote harmony. Bucer's Wittenberg Concord (May 1536) seemed hopeful but failed when the Swiss refused to sign.

The confession consists of twenty-eight brief articles (twenty-seven in the German, which combines arts. 13 and 14). It is comparable in content with the Second Helvetic Confession,* which Bullinger with Peter Martyr Vermigli* prepared (1561; publ. 1566) and which superseded it. Bullinger and Jud wished to add a caution against the binding authority of this or any confession that might compromise that of Scripture and Christian liberty, but their declaration was not included.

Arts. 1–5. The First Helvetic Confession begins with Scripture* (presenting the "most perfect and ancient Philosophy"), its interpretation (governing love and faith: Lat. *moderante*; Ger. *die Richtschnur*) and scope, or purpose (Lat. *scopus*; Ger. *Zweck*).

Arts. 6–11. God,* humanity,* sin,* free will,* salvation,* and Christ. Christ is our brother (*victor duxque*) in whom we are joined to God. The theme of union will pervade the Second Helvetic Confession. Article 11 and that on the Eucharist (art. 23) are the longest.

Arts. 12–14. The scope of evangelical teaching, office of the Christian (sanctification*), and faith* which is *substantia* and *assertio*.

Arts. 15–20. Church,* ministry,* ecclesiastical power, election of ministers, true pastors (*Christus . . . caput ac pastor solus est*), and office of ministry. Public gathering signifies the exalted Christ and his discipline.

Arts. 21–23. The crucial section on sacraments* is moderate and mediating: *signa* (Ger. *Zeichen*) are not nude or merely tokens (*tessera*) but symbols of divine grace,* offering what they signify by analogy: the "mystic meal" is fruitful, nourishing. Natural union of signs with signified is rejected, as well as local inclusion and carnal presence; the theme is thanksgiving (*gratiarum actio*; *Danksagung*).

Arts. 24–28. Church ordinances include media (*de mediis*—to be expanded in the Second Helvetic Confession), heresy* and schism, magistrates and marriage.*

H. A. Niemeyer, *Collectio confessionum* (1840), 105–22; Schaff, *Creeds*, vol. 3; cf. Schaff, *HCC*, vol. 8.

JOSEPH C. MCLELLAND

Helvetic Confession, Second

Authored by Heinrich Bullinger,* who succeeded Huldrych Zwingli* at Zurich, the Second Helvetic Confession was adopted by the cantons of the Swiss Reformation (1566) and many other Reformed lands.

Bullinger studied in the Netherlands and at the University of Cologne. Trained in medieval scholasticism, he was attracted to the church fathers, then to Luther* and Melanchthon, and was converted to the cause of reform (1522). He met Zwingli (1523), and they became fast friends. Bullinger taught the Bible as a lay professor in a Cistercian cloister, which he converted to the cause of reform. When Zwingli was killed on the battlefield of Kappel (1531), Bullinger (age twenty-seven) was called by the Council to take his place in Zurich.

Bullinger sought to unite the reforming parties of the Swiss cantons and the Germanies. With colleagues from Bern, Basel, Schaffhausen, St. Gall, Mühlhausen, and Strassburg he wrote the First Helvetic Confession,* seeking to effect such a union (1536). Initially, Luther spoke favorably of the document, but with the failure of the Swiss to accept the Wittenberg Concord, effected by Martin Bucer,* the First Helvetic Confession failed to have any lasting effect among Lutherans. It did, however, unify all German-speaking Switzerland and was the first Reformed creed of national authority.

The Second Helvetic Confession follows the first in its structure but is expanded, improved, and written solely by Bullinger. First composed when it received the personal approval of Bucer (1561), it was rewritten during a pestilence in which Bullinger expected to die (1562)—attaching the confession to his will as a final gift to Zurich.

This private testimony of faith became a public confession through the needs of the Swiss cantons and the Palatinate. Frederick III, elector of the Palatinate, who had only recently published the Heidelberg Catechism* (1563) to try to bring religious peace to his land, was now under attack by Lutherans who were considering charging him with heresy* at the Imperial Diet. Thus Frederick requested a full exposition of the Reformed faith of Bullinger (1565), who replied with a manuscript of his own recently completed confession. The Elector had it printed in Latin and German prior to the noble defense of his faith before the Imperial Diet, at which all charges were dropped.

The Swiss felt the need for a more ample description of their faith, the First Helvetic Confession being deemed too brief. Bullinger's was considered suitable, with a few changes to which he readily consented. The Second Helvetic Confession was printed at public expense in Zurich (March 1566) with agreement of all the Reformed cantons except Basel, which subsequently also accepted it. The same year Scotland gave its assent; a year later the Hungarian churches at the Synod of Debrecen (1567); four years later the French at the Synod of La Rochelle (1571); the Polish reformed in the same year, and again (1578). It was further used, albeit not officially received, in England and the Netherlands. Only the Heidelberg Catechism was more widely adopted among the Reformed.

The confession begins with the primary issue of church reform: authority.* Scripture* is the source of authority. With Luther, the preached word is the Word of God.* In ch. 2, against Rome the Holy Fathers, councils, and tradition are accepted only as they conform to the Word of God. Against Anabaptists, ch. 2 contains a hermeneutical guide which rejects a private interior interpretation by the Spirit in favor of one that is informed by the sense of Scripture, the original languages, and the testimony of the Fathers. In ch. 3, against the Socinians the Trinity* is affirmed.

The iconoclasm of Bullinger rests on the affirmation of Christ as our sole mediator for adoration, worship,* and invocation (ch. 5). The doctrines of providence,* creation,* the fall, and free will* follow (chs. 6–9). On free will (ch. 9), Bullinger is neither as optimistic as Erasmus* nor as hyperbolic as Luther. The *imago*, mind, and will are still present, but their ability to do good requires regeneration* which is the gift of God.

If regeneration is necessary to salvation* and is the gift of God, what determines that gift? Bullinger, with Paul, Augustine,* and Calvin,* posit the corollary of grace*: predestination.* Predestination is tightly tied to Christ as the means. At the same time, a holy life is to be proclaimed. Inquiry into one's election is only in the mirror of Christ: "By baptism* we are ingrafted into the body of Christ, and we are often fed in his Church* with his flesh and blood unto life eternal" (ch. 10).

The Anselmic doctrine of the atonement,* built on Chalcedon, is reaffirmed. Law* and gospel, justification* by faith,* and the role of good works are set forth with clarity and moderation, so that both Germans and Swiss might see their theology therein (chs. 11–16).

In the Lord's Supper* the faithful indeed receive the body and blood of Christ, yet not corporeally, but spiritually, but nonetheless "the very body and blood of our Lord Jesus" (ch. 21). Public worship receives much attention, including admonitions against "overlong" and tedious public prayers, the role of singing (ch. 23), holy days (ch. 24), catechizing (ch. 25), burials and purgatory (ch. 26) as well as admonitions concerning the patrimony of the church (now largely in the hands of the magistracy—for in the Reformation almost everywhere the civil government assumed the assets of the church in exchange for its reform and subsequent maintenance). Similarly, admonitions to the magistracy are to be read with the understanding that the church is financially dependent on the godly action of the state (ch. 30).

The Second Helvetic Confession is unique as written by a theologian whose career spanned the first and second generations of reformers, was the product of a single hand, and received the widest international reception of any Reformed confession. It is therefore the most authentic guide we have to the theological and pastoral ethos of the Swiss Reformation.

J. H. Leith, ed., *Creeds of the Churches* (3rd ed. 1982); J. B. Rogers, *Presbyterian Creeds: A Guide to the Book of Confessions* (1985); Schaff, *Creeds*, vol. 3; Istvban Tnokbes, *A Mbasodik helvbet hitvallbas magyarbazata, Commentarium in confessionem Helveticam Posteriorem*, 2 vols. (1968); and *Glauben und Bekennen: 400 Jahre Confessio Helvetica posterior* (1966).

DONALD J. BRUGGINK

Helvetic Consensus Formula

Late seventeenth-century theologians J. H. Heidegger, Lukas Gernler, Hummel, Johann Heinrich Ott, and Francis Turretin* wrote to each other of the need for a new confessional statement. Thus the diet of the four evangelical cantons (Zurich, Basel, Bern, and Schaffhausen) instructed their pastors to begin official correspondence (1674).

As completed, the twenty-six canons of the Consensus primarily reject the French Saumur Academy's teachings. Canons 1–3 reject the views of Louis Cappel, who questioned the authenticity of the Hebrew OT text as passed on to us. Canons 10–12 oppose Joshua de la Place because he rejected the immediate imputation of Adam's sin.* Canons 4–9 and 13–25 reject the view of Moïse Amyraut* on the universality of God's grace.*

The diet of the evangelical cantons accepted the Consensus (1675) and urged eight cities to adopt it. Some, such as Neuchâtel and Geneva after much delay and urging by other churches, adopted it as a sign of union with the other churches.

The Consensus was never widely used outside Switzerland. Since other statements dealt with the same theological controversies, and the theological climate soon shifted, its influence did not last long even in Swiss churches.

D. D. Grohman, "The Genevan Reactions to the Saumur Doctrine of Hypothetical Universalism: 1635–1685" (diss., Knox College, Toronto, 1971); J. H. Leith, ed., *Creeds of the Churches*, 3rd ed. (1982).

DONALD D. GROHMAN

Henry, Matthew (1662–1714)

English nonconformist* commentator. The son of an Anglican minister who had been ejected under the Act of Uniformity (1662), Henry became a Presbyterian* minister and served at Chester (1687–1712) and at Hackney north of London (1712–14). Biblical exposition in the Puritan* manner was his great priority. The lasting fruit was his multivolume *Exposition of the Old and New Testaments* (1708–10; to the end of Acts; others completed it). Numerous editions, abridgments, and adaptations attest the continuing appeal of its practical, devotional focus, simple piety, felicitous and even racy style, and wise common sense. Its precritical spiritualizing exegesis has long influenced evangelical religion.

Life by J. B. Williams (1828; 1865); and Life by C. Chapman (1859).

DAVID F. WRIGHT

Heppe, Heinrich Julius Ludwig (1820–1879)

German Reformed theologian and church historian who was a student (1839–43) and professor at the University of Marburg (1849–79). Against confessional Lutherans led by August Vilmar, Heppe argued that the Hessian church was originally "German Reformed," a unique and inclusive Melanchthonian (and Bucerian*) middle way between Lutheranism and Calvinism.* Though he published a widely used theological textbook of excerpts from orthodox Reformed divines (1861; ET

1950; *RD*), he was actually closer to Schleiermacher* and prepared the way for liberalism at Marburg.

E. W. Kennedy, "Reformed Orthodoxy Redivivus," *Reformed Review* (1980); L. Zuck, "Heinrich Heppe," *CH* 51, no. 4 (1982).

EARL WM. KENNEDY

Heresy

The rejection or distortion of a major element of Christian doctrine, particularly as defined in the church's creeds* and confessions.* John Calvin* cites Augustine's* distinction: "Heretics corrupt the purity of the faith with false dogmas, but schismatics, while sometimes of the very same faith, break the bond of communion" (*Inst.* 4.2.5). Heresy most appropriately denotes the deliberate and persistent denial by a professing Christian (thus distinguished from unbelief and apostasy) of a fundamental of the faith, especially a denial judged to put salvation itself at risk.

Major sixteenth-century Reformed theologians endorsed the ancient creeds and regarded the heresies that rejected creedal teaching, especially on the Trinity* and the person of Christ, as serious enough in some cases (cf. Michael Servetus* in Geneva) to merit capital punishment. The Reformers' own condemnations of false medieval doctrines (e.g., transubstantiation) were less precisely formalized but found lasting expression in Protestant church confessions.

Today, theological pluralism has made the concept of heresy of less practical value. Heresy trials have often hastened the relaxation of the terms of the churches' subscription to their confessions. Nevertheless the Theological Declaration of Barmen* (1934) stigmatized the "false doctrines" of the "German Christians," and in the 1980s the WARC* declared apartheid* a heresy. If in earlier generations the persecution of heretics shamefully disfigured Christianity, today a laissez-faire relativism is no less serious a danger. Universalism* may yet come to be seen as the distinctive twentieth-century heresy.

DAVID F. WRIGHT

History

The understanding of history articulated within the Reformed tradition agrees with the common Christian interpretation of history found in the church's ancient creeds. According to this view, the course of history begins with the divine creation of the world, continues with a human fall into sin,* proceeds toward the incarnation* of Jesus Christ as Savior, carries on with the church,* and culminates in the return of Christ and the beginning of life everlasting. The Reformed view of history differs from this common tradition by giving interpretive priority to the events and results of the Protestant Reformation in sixteenth-century Europe. The view is summarized in the titles given to the tradition: "Reformed" (past tense) and "the churches of the Reformation."

The churches founded during the Reformation enunciated their view of history in numerous new creeds. The French Confession of Faith* (1559), based on a draft by John Calvin,* stated the view clearly, saying that "it has been necessary for God to raise men in an extraordinary manner to restore the Church which was in ruin and desolation." This period of restoration succeeded two earlier periods: the primitive period of the ancient church and a long period of degeneration under the reign of the papacy. The period of the ancient church was a normative moment when the three creeds were adopted which the churches of the Reformation accepted as faithful to the Holy Scriptures—the Apostles', the Nicene, and the Athanasian. The period of the papal church which followed was regarded as a destructive time when the pure Word of God* was banished, the sacraments* were corrupted, and the faith was perverted into superstitions and idolatries. The period of restoration in the sixteenth century was meant to achieve the abolition of unwarranted "innovations" introduced by the Roman church as well as the reconnection of the church with the usages and customs of the primitive church. Calvin proclaimed to the king of France, when presenting the first edition of his *Institutes of the Christian Religion** (1536), that he and other faithful believers professed no novelty and no new gospel but merely wished to reassert the true religion of the Scriptures* as supported by the primitive Fathers.

The Reformed view of history expressed by this triad of periods was both cyclical and linear. On the one hand, the Reformation brought the church full cycle to the primitive period, claiming to renew ancient fidelity to the Scriptures. On the other, it moved the church onward in the course of history to what amounted to a new expression of the ancient faith. The Reformation creeds emerged from debates and struggles against what they took to be an awesome enemy unknown to the early church. In their linear expression, the new creeds, like the Belgic Confession* (1561) and the WCF* (1647), asserted the continuity of the one true church from the beginning of the world to the end of history. The creeds recited the history of the world from the creation and Adam, through Abraham and the prophets to Christ, onward to each national experience. The Scots Confession* (1560), for example, ran the story from Adam, Abel, and Cain to the true Church of Scotland associated with John Knox.* In their cyclic expression, these creeds identified a process of history punctuated by repeated reform, devout people arising as needed to recall the world to the true religion of God.* A Reformed church is always reforming.

A series of history books elaborated the Reformed interpretation of history found in the creeds. During the sixteenth century, Theodore Beza* wrote on the church reforms in France (1580), John Knox on the Reformation in Scotland (c. 1560s; 1570s), and John Foxe* on the English martyrs produced by the conflicts of Protestants against Rome (1563). In the nineteenth century, Jean Henri Merle d'Aubigné* enlightened a host of Reformed readers in Europe and North America about the Reformation of the sixteenth century, calling it the revolution that began the new world (5 vols.; 1838–53). A series of Reformed theological treatises from Calvin to Karl Barth* in the twentieth century discussed the common Christian doctrines of predestination* and free will* as well as providence.* These doctrines defined the interaction of divine, satanic, and human agency in history and depicted history as an ensuing struggle between the proponents and the enemies of the gospel. The Reformed tradition became widely associated with an emphasis on the acts of God who governs and directs all created things, disposes and ordains by a sovereign will all that happens in the course of history. In the twentieth century this traditional Reformed stress on God was counterbalanced by a new appreciation of human action. The idea of the cultural mandate given by God to humanity acknowledged that people were the actual caretakers of the creation* and the makers of history. As an expression of this idea, Herman Dooyeweerd* elaborated a Reformed philosophy of history that depicted history as the opening up of the creation by means of the ordinary re-creative acts of human beings (1953–57).

In the late twentieth century, Reformed churches still sought their identity in the events of the sixteenth century. The newer churches in Asia, Africa,* and Latin America experienced some discomfort with the linkage. Reformed theological curricula and scholarship still treated the Reformation as definitive and emphasized in their historical studies the prime role of the early church and the sixteenth century. In a new wave of creed making in the 1960s, 1970s, and 1980s, Reformed churches perpetuated both the cyclic and the linear features of the traditional view of history. The WARC,* in a message titled *Called to Witness to the Gospel Today* (1982), summarized the modern Reformed view of history. Reformed churches, the message affirmed, continued in the movement initiated by the sixteenth-century Reformers for the renewal of the church in their time, but they sought a new reform of the tradition by offering fresh responses to the Scriptures in the light of new experiences and new situations.

C. T. McIntire, ed., *God, History, and Historians* (1977).

C. T. MCINTIRE

Hodge, Archibald Alexander (1823–1886)

Successor to his father, Charles Hodge,* in the chair of didactic and polemic theology at Princeton Seminary. Hodge coauthored with B. B. Warfield* the article "Inspiration" (published in *Presbyterian Review,* April 1881) which crystallized the conservative Presbyterian position on the inerrancy of Scripture.* Educated at the college and seminary in Princeton, Hodge served for three years as a missionary in India and then held pastorates in Maryland, Virginia, and Pennsylvania. He became professor of theology at Western Seminary in Pittsburgh (1864).

Thirteen years later Hodge returned to Princeton as an associate to his father and acceded to the elder Hodge's chair (from 1878). Adhering closely to his father's theology, he made few alterations in the latter's intellectual legacy. His chief contribution was his ability to express that position with brevity, precision, and popular style. His major book, *Outlines of Theology* (1860; rev. 1879), struck the characteristic notes of the old Princeton Theology*: adherence to the Scottish common sense philosophy,* belief that theology was a science based on the data of Scripture,* confidence that theological conclusions could be rendered in propositional form, and assurance that these truths were fully consonant with other sciences. Hodge and Warfield's famous essay "Inspiration" asserted that God had superintended the writing of the original manuscripts (autographs) of the Bible so these were without error in all respects. This doctrine became a rallying cry for many conservatives both within and without the Presbyterian Church.

F. L. Patton, *A Discourse in Memory of Archibald Alexander Hodge* (1887).

JAMES H. MOORHEAD

Hodge, Charles (1797–1878)

Arguably America's premier Reformed theologian in the nineteenth century. Hodge taught at Princeton Seminary (1822–73). He edited the prestigious *Biblical Repertory and Princeton Review* (*BRPR*) and summarized much, though not all, of his theological formulae in the influential *Systematic Theology* (3 vols.; 1872–73). An informed student of science issues, erudite exegete of the NT, and acute commentator on ecclesiastical and political issues, Hodge shaped the Princeton Theology* in American Protestantism.

Son of a Scotch-Irish Philadelphia physician who died when Charles was seven months old, Hodge was raised by a widowed mother within Presbyterian communities in Philadelphia and, after 1812, in Princeton, New Jersey. His subscription to the Westminster Confession* came early, naturally, and without much questioning. While a student at the College of New Jersey (Princeton College), Hodge came under the pastoral and scholarly influence of Archibald Alexander,* founding professor of the new Presbyterian seminary in Princeton. Hodge often called Alexander his "spiritual father." After graduating from Princeton College (1815), Hodge enrolled at the Seminary (1816) and graduated (1819).

Hodge possessed a genius for making friends. That gift undoubtedly extended to Sarah Bache, a great-granddaughter of Benjamin Franklin. He married Sarah (1822), and together they parented and nurtured eight children, among whom were two theological professors, Archibald Alexander Hodge* (1823–86) and Caspar Wistar Hodge (1830–91). Sarah Hodge died (1849), leaving Hodge brokenhearted. He married Mary Stockton, a widow from a prominent Princeton family (1852). She outlived him by nearly two years.

Hodge's lifelong affections were focused on American Presbyterianism* and the Reformed tradition. These affections were rivaled only by his love for his family and circle of friends. Ordained by the Presbytery of New Brunswick (1821), Hodge found his preaching flat and uninspiring and accepted an invitation to teach biblical languages at the seminary. He was appointed professor of Oriental and biblical literature by the Presbyterian General Assembly (1822). Later (1840) he was named professor of exegetical and didactic theology.

Meanwhile (1826), Hodge was among the first American scholars to travel to the Continent for advanced studies. In France, Germany, and England he probed widely but selectively, studying Semitic languages with DeSacy (Paris) and W. Gesenius (Halle), theology with A. Tholuck (Halle), and biblical studies with W. Hengstenberg (Berlin). Along the way, he conversed with theologians such as Friedrich Schleiermacher,* historians like August Neander, scientists at Berlin's Royal Academy of Science, and biblical critics such as H. Ewald at Göttingen. Few Americans could rival such excellence in theological training. His letters home, many of which are unpublished and in French, reveal a lonely husband and father, a widening circle of scholarly acquaintances, heightened aesthetic sensitivities, and an expanding appreciation of his Reformed heritage.

From the moment of Hodge's return (fall 1828), Princeton Seminary became the focal point through which he interpreted the Reformed tradition to the young nation and beyond. He recast (1829) the fledgling journal he began (1825) and gave it a new name, *Biblical Repertory and Princeton Review*. By 1868, when he yielded his editorial responsibilities, it had emerged as one of America's most respected theological journals. Hodge himself contributed some 140 articles on diverse topics. These pieces are the best indicators of his ranging mind and stout confessionalism. They encompass virtually every significant issue in evangelical Protestantism: the perils and promises of German biblical scholarship; scholarly defenses of the Reformed doctrines of original sin* and atonement;* an advocacy of "doxological science" and Scottish common sense realism;* suspicion of Horace Bushnell's* romanticism and Schleiermacher's revisionism; revulsion toward Charles G. Finney's* revivalism,* Ralph Waldo Emerson's transcendentalism and Kantian philosophy; conservative views of slavery* in America and unusual opinions about race and America's racial relationships; an impatience with the "ultraist" mentality of some southern Calvinists, especially James Thornwell;* a Whig (and later, Republican) partisan in America's political controversies; a sustained advocacy of infant baptism;* irenic views toward Roman Catholicism;* and intractable skepticism about New School ecclesiology. Several masterful articles regarding the Civil War reveal Hodge's capacities as a political commentator, while his protracted debates with Edwards Amasa Park of Andover on the "Theology of Intellect and Feeling" are evidence of his polemical style and wit.

Hodge's articles in the *BRPR* were supplemented by other notable publications. His NT commentaries included Romans (1835; 1864), Ephesians (1856), and 1 and 2 Corinthians (1857). His *Constitutional History of the Presbyterian Church in the United States of America* (1840) was written to explain the continental and Scottish origins of American Presbyterianism following the denominational split (1837), and *Discussions in Church Polity* (1878) detailed his ecclesiology. His popular *The Way of Life* (1841), published by the American Sunday School Union, had sold over 35,000 copies by 1880 and was translated into Spanish and Hindustani. An impromptu speech given at the Evangelical Alliance in New York City (1873) later developed into a famous tract, *What Is Darwinism?* (1874). Ultimately, his three-volume *Systematic Theology* ensured his first-rank status as a Reformed theologian in nineteenth-century America. Its value, however, lies in what it summarized rather than in what it explored. One indispensable source for learning about Hodge's personal faith and piety is his *Conference Papers* (1879). Christianity, he once preached (1863), is that experience of Christ which "gains more and more complete control of the individual man and of human society, by controlling all forms of human thought, the inward character of men *and* their outward conduct."

Hodge left a legacy of influential scholarly works, taught over three thousand students, penned more than five thousand pages in the *BRPR*, served on many boards of denominational and interdenominational agencies, and was elected Moderator of the Presbyterian Church (Old School; 1846). His extant letters reveal voluminous correspondence with hundreds of different persons in America and abroad. Certainly few, if any, Reformed theologians in America were better known. A scholarly biography and appraisal of Hodge remains to be written.

A. A. Hodge, *The Life of Charles Hodge* (1880); F. L. Patton, "Charles Hodge,"

Presbyterian Review II (1881): 349–77; M. Noll, *Charles Hodge: The Way of Life* (1987).

JOHN W. STEWART

Hoekendijk, Johannes Christiaan (1912–1975)

The missiologist was born in Garut, Java, and died in New York City. He received a D.Theol. from the University of Amsterdam (1948) and served with the Dutch Student Christian Movement (1938–45); Mission Consul Dutch East Indies (1945–46); the Netherlands Missionary Council (1947–49); the WCC* (1949–52); and as professor at the University of Utrecht (1953–65) and Union Theological Seminary (N.Y.; 1965–75).

Hoekendijk's *The Church Inside Out* (1966) united the themes of his radical perspective and intense involvement in ecumenical evangelism* and mission. His dissertation "Church and Nation (*Volk*) in German Missiology" sharply critiqued the Christendom mentality in European mission. As WCC Evangelism Secretary, Hoekendijk wrote *Evangelism in France*, examining the secular dynamics of society in various nations and defining the evangelistic task with relation to them. This led to a series of ecumenical conferences at the Ecumenical Institute, Bossey, on evangelism in city and industry and later to the WCC-sponsored study "The Missionary Structure of the Congregation."

Theologically, Hoekendijk argued for the priority of mission over church.* The church happens "insofar as it actually proclaims the Kingdom to the world" (*The Church Inside Out* [1966], p. 42). All evangelism emphasis should therefore be on the proclamation of the judging and saving promise of God in Christ and the expression of this promise in communities of hope. With this he challenged both the saving of individual souls out of the world and Christianizing nations within the world as methods of Christian mission. "A church that knows that she is a function of the apostolate and that her very ground of existence lies in the proclamation of the Kingdom to the world does not engage in missions. She herself becomes mission, she becomes the living outreach of God to the world" (ibid., p. 43).

CHARLES C. WEST

Holy Spirit

The "third person" of the Trinity has been specially emphasized in various streams of Reformed theology since the sixteenth century. Fundamental for Reformed pneumatology is the witness of Scripture* to the presence and activity of the spirit of God in the world and among human persons, especially the testimony of the NT to the gift of the Spirit by the risen and ascended Jesus Christ and to the work of the Spirit as "the other Paraclete" who enables Christian faith, worship,* witness, and service. Reformed theology also follows the consensus of the early church articulated in the Niceno-Constantinopolitan Creed: the Holy Spirit is "the Lord, the Life-Giver, who proceeds from the Father, who with the Father and the Son is worshipped and glorified, who spoke by the prophets."

The term "Holy Spirit" is used in only two OT passages (Ps. 139; Isa. 63). But there is frequent mention of God's* *ruach* ("wind"); in later strands, human or divine "spirit." God's *ruach* is associated with creation and preservation of life, with outstanding gifts and capacities, with prophecy, and with the future hope of judgment and restoration. Several of these emphases are developed and modified in intertestamental literature—for example, in the messianic anticipations of Palestinian Judaism, in the "Two Spirits" dualism of Qumran, and in the association of *pneuma* (Gr.) with the divine wisdom in Hellenistic Judaism.

In the NT the Holy Spirit comes fully onstage as "the Spirit of your Father" (Matt. 10:20), "the Spirit of Christ" (Rom. 8:9), "the Spirit of life" (Rom 8:2), "the other Paraclete" (John 14:16), and so forth. The Messiah has come; the age of the Spirit has dawned; the Spirit is the power of the divine purpose and activity centered in Jesus Christ. The Synoptic Gospels and Acts emphasize the connection between Jesus and the Spirit and the presence of the Spirit in the church as manifested by charismatic signs and prophecy. More profound theological reflection is offered by Paul (e.g., 1

Cor. 12–14; the whole of Galatians, Romans, and the Corinthian letters) and John (esp. the Farewell Discourse, John 14–16).

The early church dogmatic consensus expressed in the Niceno-Constantinopolitan Creed (A.D. 381) issued out of hard debate that was provoked by the Arian controversy and led to the final rejection of previously widespread notions of the Spirit as an angel, creature, subordinate divine energy, or impersonal power—or as a charismatic dynamic entitling its bearers to cut loose from the historic Christian tradition. This recognition has paradigmatic significance for all subsequent Christian theology, for the old issues and questions continually resurface in plausible forms that nevertheless represent "old heresy warmed up." However, the fourth-century dogmatic consensus left open the question of the relation between the Holy Spirit and Jesus Christ as the incarnate Son and Word of God.* The Western church followed Augustine* in closing this gap by affirming (an expansion of the creed of Constantinople) that the Spirit "proceeds from the Father *and the Son*" (*filioque*). The Eastern Orthodox Church has more or less consistently rejected the *filioque* as an unauthorized Western interpolation, while Reformed churches have until recently generally followed the line inherited from the Western medieval tradition.

In classical Reformed theology of the sixteenth and seventeenth centuries, the Holy Spirit's activity was emphasized in three main respects. Together they contribute a distinctive profile to the Reformed tradition.

The combination of humanist historical, philological, and exegetical learning with the Reformation emphasis on the Word of God as the sole guide of faith* and life put the exegesis and preaching of the Bible in the center of the church's life. This led on the one hand to a tendency to make the Spirit the slave of the letter in the avowed interests of a high doctrine of the inspiration of Scripture;* on the other, to an opposed inclination to exalt the Spirit above the letter. The resulting tensions are already clearly diagnosed (*Inst.* 1.6–9) and have fermented in Reformed churches ever since.

The controversy between Zwingli* and Luther* over the real presence of the body and blood of Christ in the Lord's Supper* turned on pneumatological as well as christological* hinges. Reformed concern in the controversy was to emphasize the divinity of Christ, to block excessive adoration of the consecrated elements and insist that it is by the Holy Spirit that believers are united with Christ, not by any kind of transmutation of the physical elements or any "consubstantiation" of Christ's physical body and blood "in, with, and under" bread and wine. In this, a proper concern to distinguish between "spiritual" and "material" realities is recognized. Sometimes in the Reformed tradition, however, this has led to a denigration of the material which owes more to Hellenistic dualism or post-Enlightenment rationalism than to the biblical witness.

Classical Reformed theology, especially during the post-Reformation "orthodoxy"* period, came to be much exercised with tracing and defining the various actions of the Holy Spirit in individual lives along the lines of an "order of salvation" (*ordo salutis*). Thus the WCF* deals with effectual calling, justification,* adoption,* sanctification,* saving faith, repentance* unto life, good works, perseverance of the saints,* and assurance of grace* and salvation.* While this interest in the ongoing work of the Holy Spirit has its proper place, it is open in this form to the charge of artificial schematization (Barth, *CD* IV/2, 499–511). It also paved the way for a psychologizing reduction of the work of the Holy Spirit.

Three seminal nineteenth-century theological thinkers contributed especially to renewed reflection on the person and work of the Holy Spirit in Protestant theology.

Friedrich Schleiermacher* gave a new centrality to *human experience** in theology, distinguished *faith* alike from *scientific knowledge* and *ethical action*, and stressed "God-consciousness" as the core of religious self-awareness. So he defined the Spirit as "the union of the divine essence with human nature" which—fully realized in Jesus Christ—is now "the common Spirit which animates the corporate life of believers" (*CF*[2], sec. 123). In effect, this was a Protestant restatement of the classical Roman Catholic sense of the Holy Spirit as "the soul of the church" (*anima ecclesiae*).

Hegel's philosophical theology made *Geist* ("Spirit" or "Mind") its basic category and developed a vision of the entire history of the universe as the dialectical unfolding and return to itself of the divine Spirit: "Spirit" produces or posits "Nature" as its own opposite, through which it moves to return to itself, transfigured as "Absolute Spirit." While Hegel's system was virtually pantheistic, it represented a significant attempt to overcome deeply rooted dualisms in Western thinking—for example, between "spirit" and "matter" or "subject" and "object." It suggested new applications of trinitarian and incarnational models for theological reflection on the history of God with the created universe, and it pointed the way to a fresh understanding of "spirit" as a key to the nature of human existence.

Søren Kierkegaard ridiculed Hegel's system, inverted its method, and stressed the loneliness of the existence of the time-caught individual human person confronted with the overwhelming otherness of the eternal God. However, he also brought the notion of "spirit" into direct connection with his diagnosis of what it means to be human and developed a *relational* model of the human person: "Man is spirit. But what is spirit? Spirit is the self. But what is the self? The self is a relation which relates to its own self. . . . Man is a synthesis of the infinite and the finite, of the temporal and the eternal, of freedom and necessity" (*The Sickness Unto Death* [ET 1941], p. 17). Essential to this analysis is Kierkegaard's insistence that the self-relatedness constitutive of human existence is posited from without, by Another, that is, by God: "By relating itself to its own self and by willing to be itself the self is grounded transparently in the Power which posited it" (ibid., p. 19).

These three approaches—the romantic-ecclesiastical (Schleiermacher), the cosmic-pantheistic (Hegel), and the individual-existentialist (Kierkegaard)—have set the scene and defined terms of reference for much twentieth-century theological work on pneumatology. Fascinating and challenging though they are, however, they all reflect in one way or another a tendency to make ecclesial, cosmological, or anthropological reflection the basis of theology. In the process, the Spirit of God can all too easily be regarded merely as an institutional energy, a universal cosmic force, or a validator of human personality. That the Spirit has to do with all of these areas is not denied, but it is not reducible to any of them. It must be remembered that the Spirit is the *Spirit of God* and the *Spirit of Christ*: only a Trinitarian and christologically focused doctrine of God can give these perspectives their proper place in the overall scheme.

Twentieth-century theological work has been marked by a concern to achieve this correction, albeit along various paths. The two greatest Protestant systematic theologies of the post-liberal era, Barth's *Church Dogmatics* and Tillich's *Systematic Theology*, deserve special mention, as does the rise of "pentecostal" movements worldwide. Additionally, the new ecumenical climate of this century has encouraged Western rethinking of the *filioque* problem. Finally, the development of both the human and natural sciences has opened new perspectives on the relation of God, humankind, and the natural order, which may be expected to yield further fruits in the coming decades.

Guidelines for further reflection on the person and work of the Holy Spirit include:

God is Spirit and the Holy Spirit is God, nothing less.

God's Spirit is creator, ground, and goal of the human spirit, but not reducible to it.

God's Spirit may appropriately be seen as the immanent presence and action of God in the world and among human persons and communities but is not to be identified with the individual or social *psychē*, or "soul," as such.

God's Spirit "inspires" all kinds of gifts and activities but is not demonic or violent. Nor is it too quickly to be assimilated to this or that moral, political, or social program or claimed as their justification.

The abiding criterion of the presence and activity of God's Spirit is Jesus Christ, the unique receiver and giver of the Holy Spirit. He alone is the Lord of the church and Savior of the world; the Spirit of God is *his* Spirit, and none other.

As the crucifixion and resurrection* of Jesus Christ demonstrates, the Spirit of God is the fellow sufferer with all human sufferings and at the same time their Transfigurer and Transformer. This is promise and hope* for all Christian people.

A. I. C. Heron, *The Holy Spirit* (1983); H. I. Lederle, *Treasures Old and New: Interpretations of "Spirit-Baptism" in the Charismatic Renewal Movement* (1988); H. W. Robinson, *The Christian Experience of the Holy Spirit* (1928); T. A. Smail, *Reflected Glory: The Spirit in Christ and Christians* (1975); J. V. Taylor, *The Go-Between God: The Holy Spirit and the Christian Mission* (1972); L. Vischer, ed., *Spirit of God, Spirit of Christ* (1981).

ALASDAIR I. C. HERON

Hooker, Thomas (1586–1647)

Born in Markfield, Leicestershire, and educated in Queen's College and Emmanuel College, Cambridge University, Hooker advocated the Puritan view that conversion* and complete submission to God's will were the essential ingredients in true religion. He advanced these views as a cleric in Esher, Surrey, and as theological lecturer at St. Mary's church in Chelmsford, Essex. Just as Hooker's views reflected Puritanism,* they ran counter to Archbishop Laud's theological and ecclesiastical ideas. Hooker was silenced and summoned before the Court of High Commission (1630). He fled to Holland instead, where he became closely associated with the Puritan theologian William Ames.*

Hooker proceeded to Massachusetts Bay Colony (1633) and helped found Hartford, Connecticut (1636). As a colonial leader, he promoted the notion that magistrates should be appointed by the people and citizenship should not be limited to church members. He helped create Connecticut's "Fundamental Orders" (1638) and was instrumental in forming the New England Confederation (1643).

Given Hooker's strong emphasis on scholastic Calvinist views of grace* and predestination* (Lambeth Articles;* Canons of Dort;* Irish Articles of Religion*), he stressed godly sermons as the most complete means of grace. The sermon became the means by which the Holy Spirit* broke the human will, prepared individuals for grace, and converted people to the ways of God. In America also, Hooker became famous for his sermons which were a natural result of his theology.

Frank Shuffelton, *Thomas Hooker 1588–1647* (1977).

RONALD J. VANDERMOLEN

Hope

Hope as the inspiration and direction of Calvin's faith has been seen as preeminently central, as it was with his great example Augustine.* The eternal destiny of humanity* and the world was a major element of Calvin's faith* and reflection.

Immortality of the soul. Calvin's first theological writing, outlined before the *Institutes* (in 1534), was *Psychopannychia* ("the watchfulness of the soul"). It opposed Anabaptists, who believed the soul is sleeping during the intervening state between death* and the final resurrection. For Calvin, this was incompatible with the continuity and progress of the soul toward the vision of God.*

Calvin claimed the status of (bodiless) souls in the intermediate state to be "a provisional felicity" because "the progressive work of regeneration* must in no way be suspended by death" (*Psychopannychia* [1534], 55; 197). This notion of suspension returns in the *Institutes* with a different meaning: not suspended but not yet perfected and therefore still suspended "where in glad expectation they await the enjoyment of promised glory, and so all things are held in suspense until Christ the Redeemer appear" (*Inst.* 3.25.6). This concept bridges the second focus of Calvin's eschatological ellipse.

Growth of the church and the world to-

ward the end. For Calvin, not only does an individual go through different stages toward fulfillment (i.e., ethical progress; *Inst.* 3.6.5), but there is also "a sort of eschatological progress" (Quistorp, p. 84). Calvin brought close together secular history, church history, salvation history, and "the signs of the times" which announce the consummation. In contrast, Luther* emphasized the discontinuity between this world and the eschaton. This eschatological tension between the "not yet" and the "already," between suspension and progress, proves that "the Kingdom of God* through ongoing processes increases until the end of the world" (*Commentary* on Matt. 6:10; cf. sec. 12 on parables of growth). Or, "as the sun rises at heaven, so also the time of salvation* progresses toward its goal" (Berger, p. 100).

The progress paradigm is found also when Calvin speaks of the spread of the gospel or the great revival of the Reformation. It reaches its apex at the end of history,* where the signs of the millennium* and the Antichrist are found. Calvin is less interested in the first than the second because such a sudden and limited period of perfection is incompatible with his ideas of preliminary stages of suspended grace.* His refutation of chiliasm, however, is exegetically inaccurate.

On the Antichrist, Calvin mainly follows 2 Thess. 2:2–7 and sees the Antichrist as embracing several persons, groups, and generations. Many popes belong to those enemies of the Word; also Mohammed. The promise of v. 9 does not describe a sudden and short moment but a period of history including events like the revival and the Reformation, the mission of the church,* and the victory over its enemies. For Calvin, the saving of souls and the victory in history* are two sides of redemption.

H. Berger, *Calvins Geschichtsauffassung* (1955); H. Berkhof, *Well-founded Hope* (1969); I. J. Hesselink, "Calvin and Heilsgeschichte," *Oikonomia* (1967): 163–70; D. E. Holwerda, "Eschatology and History," in *Readings in Calvin's Theology*, ed. D. K. McKim (1984); J. Moltmann, *Theology of Hope* (1967); H. Quistorp, *Calvin's Doctrine of the Last Things* (1955); T. F. Torrance, *Kingdom and Church* (1956).

HENDRIKUS BERKHOF

Hopkins, Samuel (1721–1803)

Congregationalist* pastor in New England and a key architect of the "New Divinity" (New England Theology*), a theological system based on and amplifying the teachings of Jonathan Edwards.*

His theology is often called Hopkinsianism and was closely allied with the thought of his friend Joseph Bellamy.* Hopkins's emphasis was to reconcile the Calvinistic* doctrines of predestination,* election, and total depravity with evangelism* and moral reform. Hopkins defined sin* as "self-love," and there was no real distinction between "original sin" and "actual sin." Correspondingly, true virtue was "disinterested benevolence." Hopkins carefully distinguished in salvation* between "regeneration,"* which he saw as totally the work of the Holy Spirit,* and "conversion,"* the active, volitional exercise of the human will which leads to holiness. Thus one could be chosen by God and still play the major role in one's conversion.

The practical outworkings of Hopkins's theology were clearly demonstrated in his leadership in the anti-slavery* and temperance movements and in his call for American foreign missions.

S. E. Ahlstrom, ed., *Theology in America* (1967).

NATHAN P. FELDMETH

Horton, Walter Marshall (1895–1966)

Professor of theology at Oberlin College. Horton contributed to three significant movements in American Protestantism: neo-orthodoxy,* pastoral psychology, and ecumenism.* Trained at Harvard, Columbia, and Union Seminary (N.Y.) by teachers who generally espoused religious liberalism, Horton joined Reinhold Niebuhr* and others of their generation in mounting a thoroughgoing neo-orthodox critique of liberal theology. His *Realistic Theology* (1934) was a manifesto of the neo-orthodox movement, as it reverberated with the Reformed themes of human sinfulness,* divine transcendence, and salvation* by grace.* Even before his association with neo-orthodoxy, Horton was identified with the development of pastoral psychology. His *A Psychological Approach to Theology* (1931) was an early effort to examine the relationship between theology and psychology. Horton was also an active ecumenist. An ordained Baptist minister, he found parochial theology inadequate and therefore sought to construct an ecumenical theology.

W. M. Horton, "Between Liberalism and the New Orthodoxy," *The Christian Century* 56 (May 17, 1939): 637–40.

DENNIS N. VOSKUIL

Hromádka, Josef Lukl (1889–1969)

Professor of theology at the Jan Hus (Comenius) Theological Faculty in Prague (1920–39; 1947–68) and guest professor at Princeton Seminary (1939–47), Hromádka served on major WCC* committees (1948–61). He was founder and first president of the Christian Peace Conference (1958–69). He was ordained in the Evangelical Church of the Czech Brethren, which he helped form (1920), a union of Reformed and Lutheran congregations claiming the Hussite tradition. Among his translated English works are *Doom and Resurrection* (1945); *Theology Between Yesterday and Tomorrow* (1957); *Gospel for Atheists* (1958); *Impact of History on Theology* (1970); and *Looking History in the Face* (1982).

Born into a Protestant family in eastern Moravia, Hromádka was trained in Vienna, Basel, Heidelberg, and Aberdeen. He was a Reformation theologian, steeped in the spirit of free critical inquiry, political democracy, and personal response to the Word of God* in the church. Yet, with Slavic sympathy, he experienced the drama of Russian history as his own. He was drawn to Dostoevsky and accepted the Russian revolution as a judgment on Western Christendom's moral and spiritual failure. In him, East and West combined in a theology of crisis which, though like that of Karl Barth,* was distinctly his own.

Hromádka stressed the promised coming kingdom,* rooted in Christ's work, conquering the powers of darkness in this world, using the witness of a servant church,* a *communio viatorum*. Yet his deep appreciation of Roman Catholic piety constantly challenged his church and colleagues. He saw God's judgment both in and over the Communist revolution and took his place in the Marxist-Leninist society of Czechoslovakia after 1948. His friendship with, and ministry to, Communist leaders helped bring about the 1968 reforms. The destruction of those reforms and with it of "socialism with a human face" was for him a deep personal disappointment. His consolation and witness was not a human hope, but of the Christ: "His glory did not begin with his resurrection* and ascension.* His glory, His power, His victory are clear to the eye of faith* precisely in the places and moment of darkness and disability, curse and death" (*Das Evangelium auf dem Wege zum Menschen* [1961], p. 179).

CHARLES C. WEST

Huguenots

A name applied from about 1560 to members of the French Reformed Church and their exiled descendants. It may be a corruption of the Swiss *eidgenossen,* or "confederates," but (since sixteenth-century French Protestants often met at night) more likely refers to the nightwalking ghost of a legendary King Hugo.

The movement had been growing for almost fifty years, starting with revolutionary ideas on transubstantiation, justification,* and good works in the biblical commentaries of Jacques Lefèvre d'Etaples and their influence on his circle at Meaux. It received strong support from John Calvin,* whose *Institutes** was an effective handbook for French Protestant missionaries trained in Geneva. Despite persecution, around 1555 Calvinist congregations were being organized in France in defiance of the government.

At considerable risk, representatives of about fifty such churches gathered in Paris (1559) as a national synod formally organized the French Reformed Church. The synod adopted a confession* of faith and form of discipline.* Its polity* was a guardedly representative structure of ranked judicatories, including a local consistory, colloquy, provincial synod, and national synod (respectively comparable to a church session, presbytery, synod, and general assembly*).

By 1561 the church included 2,150 congregations and had grown into a formidable political, military, and ecclesiastical minority. It provoked bloody resistance from the Guises, which led to over thirty years (1562–94) of persistent civil war, thwarting efforts of Catherine de Médicis to achieve peace by negotiation and an edict of toleration.* The period's most notorious atrocity, the government-inspired St. Bartholomew's Day Massacre* (1572), when thirty thousand Protestants were slain, had little permanent effect on the balance of power but stimulated Huguenot political thought and publication advocating representative government and constitutional limitation on royal absolutism.

Religious civil war ended with the royal accession of a Protestant, Henry IV, who conciliated Catholics by personal conversion to Catholicism and the Huguenots through guarantees of civil and religious rights in the Edict of Nantes* (1598). These guarantees, enabling the Reformed Church in France to function as a fortified state within a state, were eliminated under Louis XIII. His successor, Louis XIV, mounted a program of persecution that forced thousands of Huguenots to accept Catholicism, but 400,000 fled to Holland, Switzerland, England, Germany, and North America, where they became assimilated within two or three generations.

In 1685 Louis XIV revoked the edict on the pretext that no Protestants remained. Nevertheless, throughout the eighteenth century a small remnant of the Reformed Church continued to exist without legal standing until 1802. Following a short period of Bourbon repression after 1815, it suffered no further restriction.

During the nineteenth century it grew and developed evangelical programs of education, mission, and Bible circulation. It has experienced both schism and reunion, and presently has over two million members, or about 2 percent of the population of France.

J. G. Gray, *The French Huguenots* (1981); G. A. Rothrock, *The Huguenots* (1979).

ROBERT M. HEALEY

Humanism

Historically the study of the humanities (distinguished from theology) in western Europe, said to have begun with Francesco Petrarch in the fourteenth century. The objectives of the humanists were: (1) restoration of correct and elegant usage of Latin (Lorenzo Valla); (2) recovery of the intellectual heritage of the classical world; and (3) improvement of the Christian community by making the results available to church and state through educational reform.

Beginning with the sixteenth century, the study of the "reborn" humanities generally became preparatory to professional higher education. Historians have distinguished *civic* (Leonardo Bruni, Bald, Castiglione, Thomas More) and *Christian* or *biblical* (Lefèvre d'Etaples, Erasmus*) humanism and also between Italian and northern humanism. After the first generations of the Reformation, the movement had a second flowering, known as late humanism (G. Sabinus, Johann Stigel, J. Lipsius, Joseph Scaliger). Humanists criticized medieval learning and education and their methods. The ideas of Plato partly as derived from late classical Neoplatonists (Plotinus) were introduced (Giovanni Pico della Mirandola, Marsilio Ficino), and new manuals for the education of children (Vittorino da Feltre, Juan Luis Vives, Erasmus) and dialectics (Rodolphus Agricola, Philipp Melanchthon) were written.

The humanists' motto, *Ad fontes!*, stimulated the search for classical writings in all subjects and thus became instrumental in the innovation of jurisprudence, medicine, and science. Through their editions of the Bible and the church fathers, the humanists facilitated the work of the Reformers whose program "by Scripture alone" now became more meaningful for an increasingly educated laity. Thus Erasmus was accused of having laid the egg that Luther* hatched, and Zwingli's* appreciation of Erasmus's NT is well known.

Begun in Italy where the ancient world was still present in Roman buildings and where manuscripts of classical authors were more readily available, humanism spread slowly across the Alps as Italian scholars traveled there (Petrarch, Aeneo Silvio) and northerners studied or visited (Agricola, Johannes Reuchlin, Willibald Pirckheimer, Erasmus) or invaded Italy (Charles VIII). The scathing criticisms of northern humanists for the schoolmen of northern universities in which to some extent they had been preceded by such devotionalist reformers as Geert Groote led to considerable opposition from these universities to humanist innovations. These had a better chance in newer foundations (Wittenberg, Alcalá) and when sponsored by the powerful (Francis I). Specifically, the schoolmen opposed Hebrew studies and attacked Reuchlin. The humanist response in the satirical *Letters of Obscure Men* (Ulrich von Hutten and others, 1515–17) is representative of the militancy of some humanists.

A. Goodman and A. McKay, eds., *The Impact of Humanism on Western Europe* (1990); H. Oberman and T. Brady, eds., *Iter Italicum* (1975); A. Rabil, Jr., ed., *Renaissance Humanism*, 3 vols. (1988).

DERK VISSER

Humanity

Traditionally the doctrine of humanity involves the nature of human being and the end or purpose (Gr. *telos*) of human life. These are articulated by humanity's status as created, fallen, and redeemed.

General. Two approaches to humanity characterize pre- and post-Enlightenment options in theological method. Classic Reformed faith from John Calvin* until the nineteenth-century "turn to the subject" is characterized by views of "man," but only as entailed in the biblically warranted doctrines about God* and the order of salvation.* That the earliest form of Reformed faith most certainly *did* offer important contributions to an understanding of humanity is suggested by Calvin's famous dictum on the necessary connection between God-knowledge and self-knowledge in the *Institutes.** This was simply not an approach allowing beliefs about humanity to create critical issues for revealed doctrines about God.

Only with the impact of modernity on theological reflection and the rise of historical consciousness and other critical disciplines might we properly speak of theological anthropology and mean the task of relating traditional convictions about theocentric human being to other, sometimes conflicting, knowledges of the human species. With this expansion, questions arise over what it means to define human being as religious being and how a Christian understanding is affected by cultural pluralism, gender, race, and other features of human difference. These explorations, in distinction from pre-Enlightenment approaches, bring alterations and conflicts over how theological authorities function allowing the doctrine of humanity more force in constructing other doctrine and practice.

Regardless of the approach or degree of reformation of the doctrine, three themes regularly appear in Reformed portraits of humanity as distinctive themes: (1) appreciation for the theocentric, or God-centered, nature of human being; (2) the central role of a lively piety* or account of religious affections evoked by a relation to the sovereign God who orders the world; and (3) a definition of that theocentric dependence which holds together the radical bondage of sin* with an equally strong conviction of accountability and call to activism in the world, a world ordered by that sovereign God.

Early boundaries. The recuperation of salvation* by grace* through faith* from dormancy in medieval Catholicism by the sixteenth-century Protestant Reformation created crucial definitional boundaries for Reformed thinking. The order of salvation (understood chronologically) was determinative of Calvin's and later Reformed understandings of humanity, providing categories of creation,* fall/redemption, and future consummation from which to define the nature and *telos* of human life. It was the lived dilemma of the life of faith, however, which proved most instructive for generating the distinctive claims.

Calvin put his stamp on a soteriological and ethical dilemma. On the one hand, he agreed with Lutheran reformers that salvation by grace through faith required denial that human actions merit salvation. God alone saves through Jesus Christ. On the other hand, Calvin was as clear that Christian life post-justification was shaped by a disciplined piety expressed as the rightly ordered response to the sovereign rule of this saving God, a God whose sovereignty extended to the ordering of the entirety of existence—individual, corporate, and societal.

Important implications from these boundaries for the image of God and the nature of sin followed. Sharing with Luther the conviction that the late-medieval Catholic account of post-fall human capacities for good were false to the human plight *coram Deo* ("before God"), Calvin set a precedent in Reformed faith for a distinctive account of sin's damage. To protect the need for salvation, Calvin claimed that the image of God and the will to fulfill God's law were destroyed. Human nature could be described as totally corrupt, not merely engaged in sinful acts, for creatures exist in a state of total depravity as a result of the primal parents' sin.

This dynamic is Reformed thought at its most pessimistic, but incomplete. The Second Helvetic Confession (1566) puts it correctly: "By sin we understand that innate corruption . . . by which we, immersed in perverse desires and averse to all good, are inclined to all evil" (ch. 8). This view alone, however, has given Calvinism* a reputation for harshness not entirely deserved. The other side of the reality of salvation by grace through faith is the conviction that humanity is created *imago Dei* for a vocation* of glorifying God (WLC, q. 1). Reformed faith has always included the view that humanity as the image of God is part of a world that reflected the glory of God. Thus boundaries against denigration and passivity implied by depravity are there to be drawn upon. From the perspective of God as creator-redeemer, human being is not a fated lump. Proper description of theocentric humanity requires that bondage to sin must be held together with accountability and enjoyment. Otherwise the vital piety that becomes a virtual Reformed vocation to reform whole societies cannot be understood.

Second- and third-generation developments. Another attempt to claim the human contribution to the drama of salvation came in response to second-generation developments of Reformed thought itself. Reaction against the forbidding logic of Calvinist orthodoxy's double predestination* created a controversy that culminated in the Synod of Dort* (1618–19). Dutch Reformed theologian Jacobus Arminius (1560–1609) and his followers, the Remonstrants,* resisted orthodox positions on double predestination from concern for a clearer preservation of free will along with the attribution of salvation to God alone. Their preferred position, called Arminianism,* proposed that persons could resist grace, that Christ died for all—not simply for the elect—and that persons' actions influenced their eternal destiny.

While the Arminians cut the nerve of the paradox of a Reformed understanding of theocentric human existence, the unpalatable theoretical resolution of the debate encoded the logic of double predestination in the Canons of Dort (1619). Its effect was to rescue God's priority in everything. However, it appeared to be a rescue made at the cost of obscuring how human life mattered. How a vital piety could be the distinguishing mark of a theocentric existence flattened out by the control of omnipotent,* omniscient, and mysterious divine will would remain unresolved in the canons. The later adoption of Arminianism by John Wesley (1703–91) distinguished the Reformed doctrine of humanity officially from Wesley's Methodist tradition.

A very different emphasis emerged in a context where other Reformed convictions gained ascendancy. In seventeenth-century Puritanism,* convictions about the goodness of creation, that human being is the pinnacle of creation's reflection of God's glory, and the purpose of human life in that glorifying is "to enjoy him forever," directed a unique understanding of humanity and its rightly directed powers of agency (WLC, q. 1). By this time the faith of two generations of Reformed believers had been tested in the continental persecutions, forging convictions of great mettle. That faith emerged in the broader context of the transition from feudalism to the modern age and created conditions ripe for new forms of participation in the creation of states and their alignments with religion.

In English Puritanism,* ideas such as Calvinist notions of vocation to worldly activity converged with changing ideas, both about the hierarchical nature of the body politic and about limits to resistance to unjust arrangements, to create a new theory of activity. The events associated with this brand of Puritanism culminating with the Cromwellian* Revolution represented first attempts of ordinary people to change government, to act out politically the desire to reform the entire social order. In view of this generation, the extension of reform to Calvin's Geneva was only the first indication of the move generated by Reformed faith away from the inward piety of Lutheranism.

The Reformed vision that emerged, though failing to establish Presbyterianism* in England, was a profound example of the noncontradiction between theocentric dependence at the heart of its piety and the life of disciplined obedience. The dependence implied by the theocentric doctrine of humanity proved congruent, even conducive, to creation of the first group of organized political revolutionaries in the West. The powerful combination of impetus for active corporate pilgrimage of faith together with the conviction that God alone is Lord which characterized this period fills out the meaning of depravity. In a real sense, predestination itself underwrote this activism. For the elect acted to "mirror" God's order for the world and therefore became agents over against the present order as it contradicted God's will. The work of redemption could create, then, not a world-denying piety but a world-transformative religious faith (Wolterstorff).

This faith proved open to the use of far more complex knowledges of the social networks of human life than Calvin could imagine. However, these would be explored in the later generations to discover the anthropological conditions for reform of a very different social order.

Post-Enlightenment shifts. With the post-Kantian turn to the subject in nineteenth-century theology, the press of other knowledges of the human began to affect the writing of theology, creating a new way to focus on human being. Theological anthropology in the hands of Friedrich Schleiermacher* was still constructed by a "grammar" of redemption, but the ground was laid for future challenges to traditional doctrine by his focus on the construction of the human self and its environs, environs that would eventually range from historical context to ideological and historical forces.

Schleiermacher, father of modern Protestantism, set theology to investigating the "Christian religious self-consciousness." He thus placed theocentric human being and religious affections or piety in the center of the theological task. Kant's challenge intended to protect religious faith by locating it in the moral or practical reason. Schleiermacher sought, importantly, to distinguish faith from scientific knowledge but refused to reduce it to morality. Reinvigorating the theocentric piety of the Reformed tradition, he developed an account of the religious affections as they were shaped by the order of salvation. Responding to historical criticism, however, Schleiermacher articulated the terms of salvation history in the modern form of structures of the religious self-consciousness rather than chronological moments in history. What he discovered in these affections was, true to his tradition, a radically theocentric human being, whose connection with God is one of "absolute dependence."

American theologian Jonathan Edwards* a full generation before distinctively contributed to Reformed anthropology in a different way by focusing on experiential piety. Responding to the experiential religion of the early eighteenth-century Great Awakening* and aided by John Locke's epistemological tools, Edwards underscored even as he redefined the centrality of the religious affections. He made important unifying connections between the emotions and rationality to reinfuse Puritan discipline into the emotional excess of revival religion. He also joined the emotions with rationality in profoundly new ways to resist dead piety. His conviction that the center of faith was a reasoning affectivity captured the unity of the self and the role of desire in the rightly ordered God-centered life.

Twentieth-century Reformed theologians continue to break new ground with familiar emphases. Karl Barth,* working with a more "objectivist" notion of revelation,* set himself as the antithesis of Schleiermacher but in fact reinforced theocentric dependence by a different route. Theologians of realism (H. Richard Niebuhr* and, less explicitly Reformed, Reinhold Niebuhr*) struggled with defining the structures of human life as historical, contingent, and yet ordered by God's providence,* adding a more tragic dimension to the paradox that has sometimes worked to protect God from the dark side of human existence.

In a more recent contrast of Reformed options, James Gustafson's theocentric ethics grants the God-centered strand of Reformed views of humanity such prominence that not only the christological* emphasis but also the humano-centrism of Calvin or Barth is contested. God's ordering of the cosmos, says Gustafson, cannot be centered around humanity, given late twentieth-century knowledge. Rightly ordered piety is, then, truly life lived to the glory of God. Whether these options will force difficult future choices is not clear. It may be that late modernity challenges Reformed piety to a new version of the call to be willing to be damned for the glory of God.

Additional future work for a Reformed understanding of humanity is created by the continued study of different cultures and effects of language and social location on the formation of persons. What began as a feminist concern with the power of language to contribute to the exclusion of women from church leadership has broadened into a major scholarly enterprise and issue of piety. Gender, and the concepts that name and place persons in relation to sexual difference, are now a significant analytical tool in the exploration of humanity, no longer conceivable as an undifferentiated "mankind." It is explored, along with race, class, and other variables of excluded and marginalized social groups, in its function in Christian teaching and practice. The century ends ironically—given modernity's turn to the subject—with a host of challenges to the very unity of something called human being.

Our Confessional Heritage (PCUS, 1978); J. Edwards, *Religious Affections* (repr. 1959); M. P. Engel, *John Calvin's Perspectival Anthropology* (1988); J. M. Gustafson, *Ethics from a Theocentric Perspective*, 2 vols. (1981–84); L. M. Russell, *Household of Freedom: Authority in Feminist Theology* (1987); Schleiermacher, *CF;* M. L. Walzer, *The Revolution of the Saints* (1965); N. Wolterstorff, *Until Justice and Peace Embrace* (1983).

MARY MCCLINTOCK FULKERSON

Hungary

The history of the Hungarian Reformed Church can be divided into the following seven periods: (1) The Reformation (1500–1608). (2) The Counter-Reformation (1608–1781). (3) The period of reform and renewal (1781–1849). (4) The Reformed Church in the Austro-Hungarian monarchy (1849–1918). (5) The church between the two world wars (1919–45). (6) The church in the socialist state (1945–48; 1948–89). (7) The new challenge: Reforms after stagnation (1989–).

In the late fifteenth century and the early sixteenth century, a "pre-reformation" movement spread throughout east-central Europe, with Hussitism, Paulicianism, the Franciscan movement, and the humanism* of Erasmus.* After 1517, Luther's teachings were first embraced by the citizens of the German-populated towns (at the Royal Court in Buda, in northern Hungary and Transylvania), principally the landowners. Some well-known preachers of the Lutheran faith were Mátyás Dévai-Bíró, Mihály Sztárai, and Gál Huszár.

The acceptance of the Helvetic or Reformed interpretation of the Reformation spread rapidly from the 1550s, mainly in the agricultural towns in the eastern and southern parts of Hungary. During this time the accepted dogma began to lean more in the Helvetic direction, under the influence of works by Huldrych Zwingli,* Heinrich Bullinger,* John Calvin,* and Theodore Beza.*

Three major leaders of the "Calvinist church" were Márton Kálmáncsehi-Sánta, Péter Meliusz-Juhász, and István Szegedi-Kis.

The first major confessions of those who espoused the Helvetic interpretation were the Confessio Debreceniensis (1562; in Hungary proper) and the Confessio of Tarcal-Torda (1563; in Transylvania). At the Constitutional Synod of Debrecen (1567), the Second Helvetic Confession* was accepted as the norm. During this time, the church was reorganized into bishoprics (church districts) and deaneries (church subdistricts). Colleges and schools were founded. The first Hungarian Bible was published by Gáspár Károlyi (1590). By the end of the sixteenth century, approximately 80 to 85 percent of the population (3 to 3½ million) had converted to Protestantism (first, Reformed; second, Lutheran). During the first half of the seventeenth century, Puritanism* spread through the country and revitalized the church. This resulted in the convocation of the National Synod of Szathmárnémeti which accepted the Heidelberg Catechism* in 1646.

By this time, the Counter-Reformation, which had begun at the end of the sixteenth century, was well under way. During the Thirty Years War the Reformed Princes Gabriel Bethlen and György Rákóczi I rose up against the violence of the Counter-Reformation and called for tolerance (1606; 1645). The years between 1671 and 1681, known as the "dark decade," were a period when pastors were persecuted and churches were occupied by the Hapsburgs' soldiers. The Reformed population decreased from 80 percent to only 30 percent during this period.

After the War of Independence (1703–11), the Hapsburgs adopted less violent means of persuasion. The Catholic clergy forced citizens of the Reformed faith to abandon positions of public office. It was only after the Edict of Toleration (1781) issued by the enlightened emperor Joseph II that the church could increase its activities (i.e., several hundred new churches and schools were built). After the unsuccessful War of Independence (1848–49), the Reformed Church was again the victim of suppression by the Hapsburgs.

The organization of the church was renewed by the United Synod meeting in Debrecen (1881). It established the General Conventus, which in turn was modeled on the Presbyterian system. Spiritual life was revitalized.

After World War I, as a direct result of the Treaty of Trianon, the Reformed church was forced to reorganize itself. Henceforth it had to exist in the four different successor states of Hungary, and with this one blow, it lost 60 percent of its membership. After World War II, the church in 1948 was faced with finding its role within the new socialist state. In the same year, the Reformed church reached an accord with the state. On the strength of this, the state was able rapidly to reduce the number of educational institutions under church supervision and home mission work. After the 1956 revolution as a theological grounding, the concept of a "theology of service" gradually evolved.

Today the Reformed church functions according to the synodical-Presbyterian form of government. The General Synod (half clergy; half laity) has a twelve-year mandate. There are four church districts, with bishops and lay curators. The number of baptized Reformed church members is approximately 1.8 million, with 1,250 independent parishes in four church districts and twenty-seven subdistricts.

R. J. Evans, "Calvinism in East Central Europe: Hungary and Her Neighbours," in *International Calvinism, 1541–1715*, ed. M. Prestwich (1985); E. Révész, *History of the Hungarian Reformed Church* (1956); E. Révész, S. Kováts, L. Ravasz, *Hungarian Protestantism* (1927); K. Tóth, "The Helvetic Reformation in Hungary," in *John Calvin: His Influence in the Western World,* ed. W. S. Reid, (1982); A. S. Unghvary, *The Hungarian Protestant Reformation in the Sixteenth Century Under the Ottoman Impact* (1989).

RICHARD HÖRCSIK

Huntingdon, Selina Hastings, Countess of (1707–1791)

Patroness of the Evangelical Revival. She married Theophilus Hastings, ninth earl of Huntingdon, and was converted under the influence of her husband's sister, Lady Margaret, who married (1741) the evangelist Benjamin Ingham (1712–72). She contacted the Wesleys and was an early member of their London society. Her residence became a center of evangelical activity and a haven for revival leaders.

After her husband died (1746), she left Donington Park. As a peeress she could appoint her personal chaplains. William Romaine (1714–95) and others served chapels attached to her residences in London, Brighton, Tunbridge Wells, and Bath. She believed she had a special mission to the aristocracy, and her naturally imperious manner brought many distinguished contemporaries to her "spiritual routs." The results were not impressive, and converts like William Legge (1731–1801), second earl of Dartmouth, were exceptions. She encouraged lay preachers and established a college at Trevecca in Breconshire (1768). It was the first nondenominational evangelical academy and had extensive influence. It moved to Cheshunt in Hertfordshire (1792) and to Cambridge (1902).

These activities were intended to serve the Church of England, but gradually the Countess developed her own organization—her "connexion." With George Whitefield* as her most illustrious chaplain (from 1748), she sided with the Calvinistic wing of the Evangelical Revival. Crisis came (1779) when her action in appointing and employing chaplains without local clergy consent was deemed illegal. She decided to license her chapels as Dissenting meetinghouses under the Toleration Act. Several of her leading chaplains withdrew in consequence. The first ordination under the Plan of Secession took place in 1783. In 1790 a Plan of Association ensured the Connexion's continuance.

The Countess was the most formidable woman among the leaders of the Evangelical Revival. She formed a comprehensive network of personal contacts that cut across the barriers of denomination and social class. The impact of her powerful personality and evangelical ardor influenced a surprisingly large number of people.

F. F. Bretherton, *The Countess of Huntingdon* (1940); J. B. Figgis, *The Countess of Huntingdon and Her Connexion* (c. 1892); G. F. Nuttall, *The Significance of Trevecca College 1768–91* (1969); [A. C. H. Seymour], *The Life and Times of Selina Countess of Huntingdon* (1839).

R. TUDUR JONES

Hymnody

For two centuries after the Reformation, followers of John Calvin* sang only scriptural songs, mostly metrical versions of the psalms.* Psalters began to be published in Geneva, at first incomplete (1542), with periodic updates, until a completed volume of 150 psalms and 125 tunes was published (1564). In England, faithful Calvinists produced *The Whole Booke of Psalmes, collected into Englysh metre,* by Thomas Sternhold and John Hopkins (1562) and subsequently *A New Version of the Psalmes of David fitted to the Tunes used in Churches* compiled by Nahum Tate and Nicholas Brady (1696). These English psalters also contained a few "hymns of human composition." Americans were using the *Ainsworth Psalter* until the publication of the Bay Psalm Book* (1640), the first book printed in North America. Entire volumes of hymns were published, including Wither's *Hymnes and Songs of the Church* (1623) and Thomas Ken's *Morning, Evening and Midnight Hymns* (1674).

John and Charles Wesley's collection, *Hymns and Sacred Poems* (1739), was instrumental in beginning a revival of hymn singing. Wesleyan congregations became noted for their singing, while their bishops mourned the state of psalmody.* The influence of the Wesleys went farther than the Church of England. Nonconformists* were split over the issues of hymnody and psalmody as were Congregationalists* and Presbyterians* in the Americas.

Isaac Watts,* English congregationalist, Christianized the psalms and wrote extensively on the need to modernize psalmody. He also challenged the strict use of psalms in worship,* citing the need for the church* to voice praise to God* in human language rather than in the language of God's revelation* to humanity.* In *Hymns and Spiritual Songs* (1707) he employed scriptural language and imagery adapted to the "mind of the living church." Strongly influenced by Watts was the young Congregationalist minister and hymn writer Philip Doddridge,* who was the first nonconformist to sympathize with the work of John Wesley and George Whitefield.*

Other hymn writers of note were two Calvinists, William Cowper (1731–1800) and John Newton (1725–1807). Together they published *Olney Hymns* (1779). In addition, the English Baptist John Rippon's *Selection of Hymns from the Best Authors* (1787) was intended to supplement Watts's materials.

Though Anglo-Catholic, John Mason Neale (1818–66) exercised significant influence over Presbyterians and their hymnody. His translations "Of the Father's Love Begotten," "O Come, O Come, Emmanuel," and "Christ Is Made the Sure Foundation," among others, are greatly revered within Reformed circles. Tractarians were encouraged to sing translations of Latin hymns to plainsong melodies, while others were singing from William Henry Havergal's *Old Church Psalmody* (1847) and Henry John Gauntlett's *Hymn and Tune Book* (1852). Peter Maurice introduced the German chorale in his *Choral Harmony* (1854).

These trends merged in *Hymns Ancient and Modern* (1861) which influenced European hymnody for the next forty years, though there were outcries about the inferior quality of some of the texts and tunes. Both *The English Hymnal* (1906) and *Songs of Praise* (1926) sought to correct the problems and provide less emotional fuel.

Joachim Neander (1650–80) was the pioneer of Reformed hymnody in Germany with his *Hymns of the Covenant* (1679). His hymns were intended for prayer meetings and home worship, not for the church. Catherine Winkworth's (1827–78) translation of his "Praise Ye the Lord, the Almighty, the King of Creation!" continues to be sung in churches today. Neander influenced not only the Reformed of Germany but also the Pietists and Lutherans.

Because of the political scene, the eighteenth-century Reformed people in Germany suffered terribly as did their worship. The Swiss-born Caspar Zollikofer von Altenklingen (1707–79) became one of the first to reform German hymnody with his *Neues Gesangbuch* (1766). It contained some four hundred hymns and only twenty-seven psalms. In 1773 the General Synod commended a psalter with hymnal supplement to the German Reformed Church. The Dutch Synod authorized a hymnal (1807), and two years later a hymnal was approved for use in Basel.

In the United States, Lowell Mason (1792–1872), heavily influenced by William Henry Havergal (1793–1870), feared that gospel music and folk tunes (what he considered "lighter music") would too much dominate Reformed worship. He published *Spiritual Songs for Social Worship* (1832), a collection not for church worship but for religious gatherings.

During the nineteenth century, hymnody took a romantic turn and many texts had a mission emphasis. The twentieth century's social gospel* movement brought a deeper concern for worship, social conscience, prayers for peace,* world community, environmental issues, ecology, and a deep yearning for the kingdom of God.* Henry van Dyke* (1852–1933), Harry Emerson Fosdick (1878–1969), Washington Gladden* (1836–1918), William Pierson Merrill (1867–1954), and Henry Hallam Tweedy (1868–1953) were among those influenced by the social gospel.

The earliest English-language psalm and hymnbook issued independently of the Lutherans by the German Reformed Church in the United States was *Psalms and Hymns* (1834), which went through thirty-nine editions in twenty years. Aside from the work of Philip Schaff,* American German Reformed hymnody depended largely on English, Scottish, and New England translators after the mid-nineteenth century. Schaff heavily influenced German-speaking Americans with his *Deutsches Gesangbuch* (1859).

He included Winkworth's work, Moravian hymns, and English translations as well as German translations of English hymns.

Within most Reformed churches, "gospel hymns" were confined to informal worship settings, as were African-American spirituals and other ethnic hymns. The political and social climate of the latter half of the twentieth century has forced the church to recognize the need to be more inclusive in its hymnody. Virtually every hymnal produced by Reformed communities in recent years has incorporated a broad spectrum of hymns to emphasize the diversity of the contemporary church. There is also a movement toward including more psalms. This perhaps attempts to balance the extremes of former centuries while highlighting contributions that Reformed faith has made to Christian hymnody.

The task of updating hymnody has been regularly undertaken. Each time, editors have to prune while trying to preserve worthwhile old favorites. In classic hymns they struggle to update archaic words, discriminatory language, and battlefield imagery while maintaining the essence of the original text. Most contemporary hymn writers have embraced inclusive language for humanity, but the debate over God language continues.

J. G. Davies, *The New Westminster Dictionary of Liturgy and Worship* (1986); H. Eskew and H. McElrath, *Sing with Understanding* (1980); J. Melton, *Presbyterian Worship in America* (1967); J. H. Nichols, *Corporate Worship in the Reformed Tradition* (1968); M. Patrick, *Four Centuries of Scottish Psalmody* (1949); D. G. Reid et al., eds., *Dictionary of Christianity in America* (1990); S. Sadie, ed., *The New Grove Dictionary of Music and Musicians*, 20 vols. (6th ed. 1980).

LINDAJO H. MCKIM

Hyper-Calvinism

An exaggerated, rationalist form of the Reformed faith that originated in English nonconformity* in the eighteenth century and is still found among Strict and Particular Baptists* as well as some Dutch-American Calvinist groups. It emphasizes the absolute sovereignty of God and God's eternal decrees.* Further, it deduces the duty of sinners toward God from the immanent acts of God (the eternal covenant* of grace,* eternal justification,* and adoption*). Thus the grace of God, as far as the elect are concerned, is irresistible and there is truly no need to offer the gospel to anyone. Thus there is no need for evangelism* but only to declare the truth so the Holy Spirit can use it to convert the elect sinners. This system encourages introspection to find out whether or not the sinner is truly of the elect.

The major proponent of hyper-Calvinism in the eighteenth century was John Gill* in his *A Body of Doctrinal Divinity* (1767). But he learned his system from Joseph Hussey of the Cambridge Congregational church. In modern times, Hussey's *God's Operations of Grace but No Offers of His Grace* (1707) has been reprinted in America. A modern theologian whose system is much like Gill's is Herman Hoeksema, whose *Reformed Dogmatics* (1966) places excessive emphasis on the sovereign grace of God.

The description of hyper-Calvinism is, of course, made from within central or classic Calvinism/Reformed theology. To people outside the Reformed faith it merely appears as a form of Calvinism, no better or worse than others.

C. D. Daniel, "Hyper Calvinism and John Gill" (diss., University of Edinburgh, 1983); D. Engelsma, *Hyper-Calvinism and the Call of the Gospel* (1980); P. Toon, *The Emergence of Hyper-Calvinism* (1967).

PETER TOON

Idolatry

A distinctive trait of Reformed theology has been its conception of God* as utterly transcendent and its eagerness to safeguard the spiritual dimension of worship* against materialist encroachments. During much of the early history of the Reformed tradition, this was expressed in a passionate struggle against idolatry, or false worship. It can be argued that the word "idolatry" itself became the Reformed shibboleth in the sixteenth and seventeenth centuries, the password through which the Reformed could be identified. In fact, the very name "Reformed" tradition alludes to how it opposed Roman Catholic* devotion and cleansed itself from all perceived traces of corruption in worship and piety,* in contrast to the more moderate and traditionalist reforms of the Lutheran and Anglican churches.

"Idolatry" is a polemical term presupposing a definition of what is true and what is false in religion. Most narrowly, it refers to worship of images constructed by human hands, or of false deities. More broadly, it means not simply worship of physical objects but any form of devotion judged incorrect. Reformed concern with idolatry extended far beyond use of painted or carved images in worship, and even beyond liturgical settings, to any devotional gesture displayed in public or private perceived as contrary to God's commands.

The Protestant Reformed attack on Roman Catholic piety had been foreshadowed in the Christian past by diverse protest movements, from the iconoclasts of eighth-century Byzantium to Lollards and Hussites of the fourteenth and fifteenth centuries. But its most evident immediate cause was the biblically centered reformist Christian humanism* impulse, principally through Erasmus.* Two of the most influential exponents of the Reformed theology of idolatry, Andreas Bodenstein von Karlstadt (1480–1541) and Huldrych Zwingli,* admitted their indebtedness to Erasmus.

Though Zwingli began publicly to criticize much of late-medieval piety in Zurich (1519), the Protestant attack on Roman Catholic "idolatry" began in earnest with Karlstadt in Wittenberg (1521) albeit abortively (Luther hurried home from his hiding place at the Wartburg to expel Karlstadt from Wittenberg and reverse his colleague's iconoclastic reforms). Karlstadt published the first Protestant treatise against idolatry, *On the Abolition of Images* (1522), a tract that made a substantial impact in Zwingli's Zurich.

It was in Zurich that the war against idolatry first triumphed (1524) when images were removed from all churches and the Roman Catholic Mass was replaced with a simplified (and "purified") liturgy. It was principally through a series of public challenges against images and the Mass that the Reformed movement managed to spread to Bern (1528), St. Gall (1528), Basel (1529), Neuchâtel (1530), and Geneva (1536). The Reformed theology of idolatry was further developed and refined by Zwingli, especially in his *Answer to Valentin Compar* (1525) and his larger *On the True and False Religion* (1525). Zwingli's successor at Zurich, Heinrich Bullinger,* would add a historical dimension to the Reformed argument against idolatry in his *On the Origin of Errors* (1528–29; rev. and enlarged, 1539). This inspired Martin Bucer* in Strassburg to take a more decisive stand and publish *That Any Kind of Images May Not Be Permitted* (1530).

Reformed Protestant polemic against idolatry reached its fullest and most enduring expression in the work of John Calvin.* He extended the struggle beyond Geneva to lands where Reformed congregations risked persecution, especially France, the Netherlands, and England. Unlike his predecessors, Calvin had to teach Protestants who did not have the power to overcome the "idolatrous" societies in which they lived. Though Calvin contributed much to the development of an anti-idolatrous theology in his *Institutes* and in lesser treatises such as *Inventory of Relics* (1543), it is principally in his struggle against the compromising attitude of the so-called Nicodemites* that he further sharpened the edge of the Reformed attack on Catholic piety. In opposition to the Nicodemites, who thought it permissible to partake in idolatrous worship as long as one's interior disposition was anti-idolatrous, Calvin argued that there could never be any compromise where worship was concerned and that any participation in Roman Catholic worship was sinful. In those cases where an open rejection of compromise raised the threat of persecution, Calvin allowed only two alternatives: exile or martyrdom.

After Calvin, another alternative began to be seriously considered by Reformed leaders: armed resistance to idolatrous rulers. In varying degrees, resistance,* and even revolution, would eventually be deemed proper and necessary. Important figures who argued in favor of resistance were Theodore Beza,* Pierre Viret,* Philippe Duplessis-Mornay (1549–1623), John Knox,* Christopher Goodman (c. 1520–1603), and John Ponet (1514–56).

In England, Reformed opposition to the "Romish" Anglican church and its idolatrous worship would lead to significant developments, not the least of which was creation of a Puritan separatist colony in Massachusetts (1620). Two decades later, the English Puritan struggle against idolatry would lead to civil war, regicide, and Oliver Cromwell's* Reformed commonwealth.

Since the end of the seventeenth-century religious wars, the word "idolatry" has gradually fallen into disuse among the Reformed; in our own ecumenically-minded age, it is no longer part of religious discourse. Nonetheless, the concepts signified by the earlier struggle against idolatry remain an integral part of the Reformed heritage.

C. C. Christensen, *Art and the Reformation in Germany* (1980); C. M. N. Eire, *War Against the Idols* (1986); C. A. Garside, Jr., *Zwingli and the Arts* (1966).

CARLOS M. N. EIRE

Incarnation

The biblical *locus classicus* for the doctrine* of the incarnation—that "the Word (Gr. *logos*) became flesh and dwelt among us"—is John 1:14. The doctrine gained new significance in the second century when Christian apologists such as Justin Martyr, influenced by Middle Platonic philosophy, used it to argue that Jesus was the manifestation of God's* eternal Reason (also *logos*). Irenaeus, writing against Gnostic Christology,* stressed the reality of the union of human and divine natures in the one person of Christ and argued that Christ became human so that human beings could become like God. For this apotheosis of humanity to occur, Christ had to be truly human and truly divine.

These early attempts to define the meaning of the incarnation led to many christological debates about the relationship between Jesus Christ and God the Father, and the relationship between the divine and human natures in the person of Christ. The orthodox teaching was promulgated at the Councils of Nicaea (A.D. 325) and Chalcedon (A.D. 451). The Chalcedonian Definition asserted that two distinct natures—divine and human—were inseparably united in the one person of Christ. To grasp fully the meaning of the doctrine of the incarnation, it would be necessary to examine the doctrines of creation,* revelation,* Christology,* and the sacraments.*

The Reformation did little to alter traditional teaching on the person and work of Christ. The Lutherans and the Reformed, however, in the context of sacramental debates, did arrive at somewhat different conceptions of the meaning of the incarnation for Christian faith. Martin Luther* argued that in the incarnation, the Second Person of the divine Trinity* willingly bound himself to the limits of human nature: a wonderful exchange took place in which humanity received the blessedness of Christ's divine being while Christ took up into himself the sinfulness and weakness of human nature. Through the *communicatio idiomatum* ("communication of properties") Luther argued, the divine nature in Christ shared properties of the human nature and vice versa. Thus the risen body of Christ is ubiquitous* and can be received in, with, and under the sacraments in all times and places. Luther believed that God must be sought exclusively in the person of Jesus. His Christology is reminiscent of Cyril of Alexandria's emphasis on the unity of the divine and the human in the one person of Jesus Christ.

The views of John Calvin* on the incarnation, on the other hand, tended to emphasize the distinction between the two natures in Christ. In the incarnation, Calvin argued, God was manifested in human flesh. However, because nothing finite can completely contain the infinite (*finitum non capax infiniti**), Christ is also active outside the flesh of Jesus. No less than Luther, Calvin insisted that God wills to be known only in Christ. But he did not believe this meant that God is revealed only in the incarnation: Christ, the eternal Word, also operates outside the work of Jesus. Lutheran critics of Calvin's Christology called this the *extra calvinisticum.** Calvin's emphasis on the distinction between the finite and the infinite had consequences for the way he conceived the relationship between the divine and the human nature in the person of Jesus. He understood the communication of properties as a figure of speech. The suggestion that there is an actual exchange of properties between the two natures sounded to Calvin dangerously like a mixture of the two, and any such mixture would compromise the reality of both natures of Christ. The body of Christ belongs to Christ's humanity and as such it cannot be ubiquitous. The union of the two natures is not so much a static union in the person as a dynamic union in the action of the Mediator—specifically in his threefold office (*munus triplex**) as prophet, priest, and king.

It would be misleading to overemphasize the distinction between Lutheran and Reformed theology on this point. As Karl Barth* pointed out, even Luther himself acknowledged that human limits could not enclose the divine. Calvin was no less insistent than Luther that we have no knowledge of God apart from Christ. Nevertheless, the distinction is not illusory: it becomes significant when one compares Reformed and Lutheran views on the sacraments.

Friedrich Schleiermacher* argued that John 1:14 is the basic text of all theology. Unlike Luther and Calvin, however, he conceived the incarnation not as the enfleshment of the Second Person of the divine Trinity but as the absolute immanence of God in the human consciousness of Jesus. Because Jesus' God-consciousness was without interruption and disturbance, it was a "veritable existence of God in him." Schleiermacher also understood a union of the divine and the human to be central to the meaning of justification* and sanctification.* In this sense, the process of redemption in individuals and the church* as a community is a progressive "incarnation" of the life of Christ.

In recent years, the logical status of incarnation language has been debated. A prominent British Presbyterian* theologian, John Hick, has argued that although incarnation is a fundamental theme in the Christian tradition, it is solely a metaphor and should not be converted to a metaphysical proposition or hypothesis. His criticisms of the traditional understanding, however, have themselves been debated.

Barth, *CD* I/2, 168–70; II/1, 487–90; Calvin, *Inst.* 2.12–14; M. Goulder, ed., *Incarnation and Myth: The Debate Continued* (1979); B. Hebblethwaite, *The Incarnation: Collected Essays in Christology* (1987); J. Hick, *The Myth of God Incarnate* (1976); Schleiermacher, *CF*, secs. 93–99; E. D. Willis, *Calvin's Catholic Christology: The Function of the So-called Extra Calvinisticum in Calvin's Theology* (1966).

DAWN DE VRIES

Independency *see* Nonconformity

Infralapsarianism

After the death of John Calvin,* Reformed theologians were concerned with "the order of the decrees of God." The two chief views of this order were infralapsarianism and supralapsarianism.*

Both views agreed that God brought all things to pass according to God's eternal plans or decrees.* They disagreed, however, on what precisely went on in the divine mind as God formulated these eternal plans. In the supralapsarian view, God's highest purpose was to glorify God in the salvation of certain human beings. To do this, God determined to create these people and permit them to fall into sin.* The eternal divine thought process was this ordered list of decrees: election-salvation,* creation,* permission of the fall.

The infralapsarians objected that this order made the fall an upward step to fulfilling God's redemptive purposes; thus it compromised the evil of sin. They posited a rival order rejecting attempts to explain the fall. This was: creation, permission of the fall, election-salvation. In this view, election is more clearly an election of fallen human beings.

Most Reformed theologians have been infralapsarian. Reformed confessions generally express themselves in infralapsarian ways without condemning the other position. More recently, some theologians, such as Herman Bavinck,* have refused to endorse either position. In this regard it may be argued that both views exaggerated their competence to read the divine mind and the most to be learned from Scripture is that each of God's thoughts takes each of the others into account. That is, God's purposes form a unity. Granted this premise, many "orders" are possible: God may do A for the sake of B and also B for the sake of A. Thus there may be truth in many suggested orders, and these may be mutually exclusive less often than theologians have thought.

J. M. Frame, *Doctrine of the Knowledge of God* (1987); R. A. Muller, *Christ and the Decree* (1986); B. B. Warfield, *The Plan of Salvation* (1942).

JOHN M. FRAME

Institutes of the Christian Religion

John Calvin's* *Institutes of the Christian Religion* is a summary of the Protestant approach to Christianity as understood by a French scholar of the sixteenth century.

First addressed to the French king, Francis I, Calvin's work was intended to win a favorable hearing for Protestantism at the French court. The first edition (Basel, 1536) was brief, clear, and scholarly. Claiming the authority of the Word of God* and support of the ancient church, it explained the Ten Commandments, the Apostles' Creed, the Lord's Prayer, and the sacraments* emphasizing a simple, classical approach not only to the doctrinal but also to the moral and liturgical aspects of Christianity. It was not intended primarily for theologians, yet it gave a masterful presentation of justification* by faith* and its significance for the Christian life. While it did not win over the French king, it made clear that Protestantism was an international religious movement rather than merely a religious expression of German nationalism.

The second edition of the *Institutes* (1539), published during Calvin's Strassburg pastorate, took a very different character. It was enlarged to serve as a textbook for theological students. Here Calvin began to give a full treatment of many traditional theological themes such as Trinity,* incarnation,* and atonement.* Though these subjects were not at issue for the Reformers, Petrus Caroli had denounced Calvin for a defective Christology (1537). This led Calvin to a meticulous study of both Greek and Latin Fathers. Calvin was a devoted classicist and always returned "to the sources." From then on, his Christology* had a distinctly patristic cast. With this edition, the doctrine of predestination* was fully thought out. Here as always, Calvin was, above all, concerned with being faithful to Scripture, yet the influence of patristic authors is also found. Calvin's predestination doctrine is both Pauline and Augustinian.* The matter was important, because ever since Luther* and Erasmus* debated the subject, it was clear that this was the issue that divided classical Protestantism from Renaissance humanism.*

Another feature of the 1539 edition is the section on the Christian life. Today this would be called a treatise on spirituality. But Calvin preferred the word "piety."* The Latin word *pietas* meant a way of life that respects authority. Calvin presented the Christian life as a humble and disciplined following of Christ. He rejected asceticism, teaching that God's gifts are to be appreciated and, with a sense of stewardship,* employed for the ends God intended. In the *Institutes,* piety is a primary theological concern.

After reorganizing the Genevan church, Calvin produced a third Latin edition (1543) and wrote into it large sections on the doctrine of the church* and the ministry.* As a trained lawyer, Calvin was interested in questions of church government and administration which in the Middle Ages were handled by canon lawyers rather than systematic theologians. Part of the genius of the *Institutes* is that it handles both. Several editions followed in which minor changes were made. But in 1559 Calvin produced an expanded final edition in which he completely rearranged the work, intending to make it a comprehensive statement of the Christian religion.

The 1559 *Institutes* is arranged in four books. Book 1 deals with our knowledge of God the Creator. Here Calvin works out his doctrine of revelation,* showing the authority of Scripture* both for a knowledge of God and of ourselves. He treats the doctrine of the Trinity, adding a considerable amount of polemical material against Michael Servetus.* The doctrine of creation* is addressed and finally the doctrine of providence* as the logical continuation of creation. Calvin carefully distinguishes the biblical understanding of providence from the philosophical concept of determinism.

Book 2 treats our knowledge of God the Redeemer. In Christ, crucified and risen, God is known as redeemer. While Book 2 speaks at length of the objective divine work of redemption, Book 3 treats the subjective experience. Now Calvin talks about salvation through election, justification, sanctification,* and glorification. Election is discussed in terms of the subjective experience of salvation. The point of this doctrine is that salvation is a divine gift rather than a human accomplishment. In Book 3, Calvin underlines the work of the Holy Spirit* in the human heart. While his emphasis on the Spirit only becomes clear in the 1559 edition, the doctrine of the Spirit had always been fundamental to his understanding of Scripture, prayer,* ordination,* and the sacraments.* The *Institutes* is characterized by an equal emphasis on the subjective and objective aspects of religion.

Book 4 is devoted to the external means by which God invites us into the society of Christ. Here too the doctrine of the Holy Spirit is prominent as Calvin discusses the church, the ministry, and sacraments. The *Institutes* presents a strong doctrine of church and ministry. For Calvin, the ministerial structure of the church is not indifferent but important to the church's faithfulness. These chapters are as theological as the earlier ones, even if they treat the more objective problems of polity* and worship.*

Calvin's treatment of the Lord's Supper* is an example. First he aimed at an approach that avoided making the sacrament into a sacrifice, thus compromising the unique sacrifice of Christ. For Calvin as for Luther, the chief problem with the Roman Mass was that it had been made a sacrifice. Second, Calvin wanted to recognize our union with Christ* at the Supper and yet avoid the scholastic* doctrine of transubstantiation. As Calvin saw it, Christ is present by means of the Spirit. The Spirit unites us to Christ in his death and resurrection through sharing the covenant meal. Calvin's approach was guided by the biblical concept of covenant* as well as the wisdom theology of John's Gospel which emphasized the real presence of the Word.

J. Calvin, *Institutes of the Christian Religion* (1559 ed.), ed. J. T. McNeill and trans. F. L. Battles (1960); *Institutes* (1536 ed.), trans. F. L. Battles (1986); H. T. Kerr, *Calvin's Institutes: A New Compend* (1989).

HUGHES OLIPHANT OLD

Iona Community

An ecumenical fellowship "seeking new and radical ways of living the Gospel in today's world." Though the historic island of Iona is its spiritual home, the Community mainly works in urban areas.

The Community was founded by George MacLeod* (1938) when he was minister of Govan Old Parish Church, Glasgow. Appalled by the church's lack of impact in working-class communities at a time of high unemployment, MacLeod left to launch an experiment on Iona—the Scottish Hebridean island on which St. Columba settled (A.D. 563). The Iona Community, consisting of ministers and craftsmen, began to rebuild the ruins of the living quarters of the medieval Benedictine abbey which had replaced the Celtic Columban foundation. MacLeod intended to train young ministers for work in industrial parishes of the inner-city and housing scheme areas of Scotland. He believed clergy should work alongside industrial workers and learn to live together in Christian community.

Today the Community has approximately 200 members, 800 Associates, and 2,500 Friends. Its members—ordained and lay, Protestant and Roman Catholic, men and women, married and celibate—share a fivefold rule of prayer, economic sharing, planning of time, meeting together, and work for justice and peace.

On Iona, the Community welcomes many people from all over the world as day visitors or to share in weekly programs of worship, work, recreation, healing, and study. Young people come to the MacLeod Centre—an international youth center completed during the Community's fiftieth anniversary (1988)—and to Camas, an adventure center on Mull. On mainland Britain, the Community has several "Columban houses"—experimental communities living out the Community's concerns—and staff members engaged in peace and justice work and in urban mission and worship renewal.

The Community organizes a training scheme—the Peregrini Scheme (after wandering Celtic monks)—in which young unemployed people are trained in theology and community leadership. It has a publication division, Wild Goose Publications, and its Wild Goose Worship Group promotes new forms of worship.

R. Ferguson, *Chasing the Wild Goose* (1988); and *George MacLeod* (1990); G. F. MacLeod, *We Shall Rebuild* (1944); T. R. Morton, *The Iona Community: Personal Impressions of the Early Years* (1977).

RONALD FERGUSON

Ireland

The Celtic church was assimilated into the Roman Catholic system and brought into line with the Church of England in the twelfth century. Sixteenth-century Reformation legislation of the Tudors was applied to Ireland. The reformed Church of Ireland retained an episcopal system and cathedrals and churches, but the Church of Rome retained its ministry and the loyalty of the great majority of people.

The Church of Ireland was marked by its use of the *BCP*, its claim to be in continuity from the early church, and its Protestantism which was much influenced by the Calvinist outlook of James Ussher.* This church has remained homogeneous in its doctrine and practice and its acceptance of the *Alternative Prayer Book* (1984).

Another reformed church order came to northern Ireland through the seventeenth-century plantation of Scots. By the patronage of landowners and assent of some bishops, Presbyterian* ministers were placed in parish churches. Under the Stuarts, demands for conformity to the episcopal system led to their ejection. They organized separate Presbyterian churches. The first presbytery was formed (1642). Under the limited toleration granted by William III and Mary, churches were founded over the country, mainly in the north. They were organized into the Synod of Ulster. A further family of Presbyterian churches related to the Scottish Seceders was organized into the Secession Synod.

Early in the nineteenth century, the Synod of Ulster split over subscription to the WCF.* Some ministers refused to subscribe, some adopting an Arian position. They and their supporters seceded and formed the Non-subscribing Presbyterian Church. In 1840 the Synod of Ulster and the Secession Synod united to form the Presbyterian Church in Ireland. The Bible is its "only infallible rule of faith and practice," and the WCF is the subordinate standard to which all ministers and elders must subscribe. The church's Rule of Faith states that the confession defines what the Bible teaches on "certain important points of doctrine and worship" and also affirms the right of private judgment and duty not to refuse light from any quarter. This latitude has allowed a variety of emphases within the unity of the church. The church was influenced by the 1859 Revival which has set the tone of much of its life and work. It maintains missions at home and abroad and many agencies to help its members and the community at large.

The Protestant community also includes the Reformed Presbyterian Church; Moravian, Methodist, Congregational, and Baptist churches; and churches of recent origin, including the Free Presbyterian Church and churches of American descent. The Church of the Brethren, the Society of Friends, and the Salvation Army maintain their forms of worship and witness.

Protestants form about one-fifth of Ireland's population. Most live in Northern Ireland, where they are almost two-thirds of the population. Their British loyalty and their fear of domination by the Roman Catholic Church have been potent factors in shaping the social and political structures of Northern Ireland and the Republic of Ireland.

R. F. G. Holmes, *Our Irish Presbyterian Heritage* (1985); T. J. Johnston et al., *A History of the Church of Ireland* (1953); R. B. Knox, *James Ussher, Archbishop of Armagh* (1967); R. B. McDowell, *The Church of Ireland, 1869–1969* (1975).

R. BUICK KNOX

Irish Articles of Religion

One hundred and four theological points adopted by the Irish Episcopal Church (1615) which incorporated the Calvinism* of the Lambeth Articles.* The Irish Articles were the church's doctrinal standard until 1635 when the Church of England's Thirty-nine Articles,* to which these are similar, were adopted. The Irish Articles were written by James Ussher,* professor of divinity in Dublin, and were a major influence on the WCF* which adopted the same order of topics, chapter headings, and phrasings at many points.

The articles cite the Nicene, Athanasian, and Apostles' creeds as scriptural (art. 7) while declaring that "the holy Scriptures contain all things necessary to salvation, and are able to instruct sufficiently in all points of faith that we are bound to believe, and all good duties that we are bound to practice" (art. 6). Only the "good pleasure of God" is the basis for predestination (art. 14) whereby God ordained "whatsoever in time should come to pass" (art. 11) and "some unto life, and reprobated some unto death" (art. 12). Election in Christ is to be "full of sweet, pleasant, and unspeakable comfort to godly persons" (art. 16). The articles maintain that God is not "the author of sin" (art. 28), and that "a true, lively, justifying faith and the sanctifying spirit of God is not extinguished nor vanished away in the regenerate, either finally or totally" (art. 38). The articles declare that it is lawful for Christians "at the commandment of the magistrate, to bear arms and to serve in just wars" (art. 62). General councils of the church "may err, and sometimes have erred, even in things pertaining to the rule of piety" (art. 76). The sacraments* are "not only badges or tokens" of Christian profession "but rather certain sure witnesses and effectual or powerful signs of grace* and God's good will towards us" (art. 85).

Schaff, *Creeds*, 3:526–44.

DONALD K. MCKIM

Irish Presbyterian Missions

In 1840 the first General Assembly of the newly formed Presbyterian Church in Ireland (PCI) commissioned James Glasgow and Alexander Kerr as missionaries to India. Thus mission has from the beginning been seen as integral to the work of this church. In the nineteenth and early twentieth centuries the main fields were Gujarat (India) and Manchuria (China). In addition, the church sponsored a strong Irish mission—aimed at the conversion* of Catholics to Protestantism—and a Jewish mission with active centers in Damascus and Hamburg.

The PCI's work has had a rapid geographic spread in the second half of the twentieth century—always in partnership with local churches in other parts of the world. As work in India and China has been localized, Jamaica and Malawi have become the major areas of Irish Presbyterian involvement. More recently, the PCI has sent missionaries to Kenya, Indonesia, Nepal, and Brazil and has begun to develop work in Israel, Malaya, Singapore, Spain, and France.

Throughout its history, the PCI has maintained a comprehensive view of mission which, while recognizing evangelization as a central force in mission motivation, has also accepted medicine, education, development work, and so forth, as valid expressions of Christian concern in specific contexts.

In addition to the official mission organs of the PCI, many Irish Presbyterians have traditionally expressed their missionary concern through service with, and support for, a number of independent, interdenominational mission societies, such as the China Inland Mission (now the Overseas Missionary Fellowship), the Qua Iboe Mission, and the Sudan Interior Mission.

J. Thompson, ed., *Into All the World: A History of the Overseas Work of the*

Presbyterian Church in Ireland, 1840–1990 (1990).

JACK THOMPSON

Irresistible Grace *see* Dort, Synod of

Irving, Edward (1792–1834)

Controversial Scottish minister. After years of schoolteaching and an assistantship under Thomas Chalmers* in Glasgow, Irving won massive acclaim as a preacher in the Caledonian Chapel, London. The crowds required a new sanctuary building and included many persons of social and cultural eminence. But Irving's teaching increasingly turned to prophetic and eschatological excesses, and the congregation split over tongue-speaking and other gifts of the Spirit.* Many followers reorganized in the new Catholic Apostolic Church.

Irving's notoriety was also in maintaining, somewhat like John McLeod Campbell,* that Christ's human nature was fallen or sinful. He was charged with heresy* and deposed from the Church of Scotland ministry (1833). But his Christology* found favor with Karl Barth* and T. F. Torrance.* Others hail him as a forerunner of Pentecostalism.

A. L. Drummond, *Edward Irving and His Circle* (1934); C. G. Strachan, *The Pentecostal Theology of Edward Irving* (1973).

DAVID F. WRIGHT

Jackson, Sheldon (1834–1909)

Presbyterian organizer and missionary, Jackson was educated at Union College and Princeton Seminary and ordained by the Presbytery of Albany (1858). He served as western superintendent for the Board of Home Missions, establishing churches in Montana, Utah, Wyoming, Colorado, New Mexico, and Arizona (1870–82).

Jackson was superintendent of Alaskan Missions (from 1884) and most of the time concurrently the U.S. Superintendent of Public Instruction for the territory. He imported reindeer, set up schools and churches, and sought assistance for the Eskimo populations and Anglo settlers in Alaska.

LOUIS B. WEEKS

Jesus Christ *see* Christology

Judgment *see* Hell

Judson, Adoniram (1788–1850)

Baptist missionary-translator in Burma (1812–50). Ordained a Congregationalist* minister, Judson was sent out under the American Board of Commissioners for Foreign Missions,* of which he was co-founder. En route to the field, he came to Baptist convictions on Baptism* and resigned from the Board, beginning Baptist missions in Africa.*

Judson's ministry and writings (e.g., his Burman liturgy, intended for missionaries and national assistants) indicate his alignment with the Calvinist* tradition on election in Christ, the atonement,* the work of the Spirit* in conversion,* and perseverance.*

F. Wayland, *Memoir of Adoniram Judson*, 2 vols. (1853).

STEPHEN R. SPENCER

Justice

Justice has a special place in Reformed understanding, particularly in Anglo-American Calvinist traditions. Calvin* emphasized justice by adding a third use to Luther's* two uses of the law.* For Luther, law convicted of sin* and, second, sought to limit human action and force. For Calvin, law could have a positive third role as teacher of the will of God* in human matters. Calvin learned from Plato and Aristotle, Augustine,* and Aquinas that justice is central to human interaction. Law can be a chief instrument for justice.

Plato and Aristotle posited justice as the virtue that gave content as well as form to human interactions wherein the other virtues of courage, prudence, and temperance could be evidenced. Augustine built his views of religion and society on two sorts of law and justice—the temporal (emphasizing love of self) and the eternal (characterized by love of God). He argued that justice is a universal norm. To do justice is to render proper due to each. Our duty to God is to love God. Hence justice can summarize Christian as well as more general ethics.

Calvinism* emphasized the continuing

validity and normativity of the Hebrew Scriptures for Christians. Old Testament emphases on justice and godly societal relations thus received important attention in Reformed theology.

A Renaissance scholar and trained lawyer before he became a pastor and a reformer, Calvin retained and practiced high regard for the magistrate's office as it seeks to govern justly. Subsequent Calvinists, such as the Rhinelanders, the Dutch, and John Knox,* continued this emphasis. The Puritan "revolution of the saints" (Michael Walzer) was centrally a Reformed movement. It brought parliamentary government to Anglo-Saxon lands. The Puritans* developed nascent bourgeois and contractual justice and society to replace the declining medieval order. That Reformed contribution continues to provide a major foundation for modern Western democratic social, political,* and economic* relations.

Biblical emphases. Biblical concerns for justice and society have been reemphasized in twentieth-century Reformed thinking. Before mid-century, Christian realism (cf. Reinhold Niebuhr*) utilized biblical understandings of humanity* and society to remind that human possibility for good makes democratic justice possible and that human proclivity for evil makes democracy necessary. The power of structures and systems caused realism to insist that Christian virtue and discipleship must have concrete expression in political and economic justice. In Europe, neo-orthodox* resistance to nazism was similarly grounded (cf. Karl Barth*).

After mid-century, liberation theology* reminded that both the Hebrew and early church Scriptures have social justice as a central emphasis. The Hebrew exodus from Egypt is seen as determinative for OT understanding. Not only the book of Exodus and the Prophets but the entire corpus was read in terms of God's overriding concern for justice in society and creation (cf. black and Latin American theology, José Miranda, Phyllis Trible, Walter Brueggemann, Paul Hanson). Where the KJV has usually read the Hebrew *mishpat* as (God's) "judgment," the better perspective sees God as creatively involved with and working for "justice."

Interpretation of early church Scripture was more mixed. In the early twentieth century, Walter Rauschenbusch and others saw Jesus as particularly concerned with social justice. After midcentury, the Lukan narrative became a seminal source for justice, since Jesus proclaims his ministry precisely as the establishment of justice in a broad social context (esp. Luke 4).

Attention to social settings of both the Hebrew and early church Scriptures proposes that social arrangements and the implied issues and norms of justice are central to NT understanding. Attention to justice and social context are important ways in which late-century theological inquiry engages pressing contemporary concerns.

Senses of justice. "Justice" is used in various ways. Four senses are often distinguished.

1. The Bible depicts *God as just and righteous.* These emphases have recently dominated. God's *mishpat* is viewed as justice rather than as judgment. That is, God works positively for just relationships rather than as one who principally chastises evil. Second, a strong emphasis on God as special friend of the poor and weak has emerged in the past decade (African-American and third-world liberation theology*). Third, the link between God's justice and human activity is seen especially as a call for godly people to do social justice with special regard for the poor and weak.

2. *Justice and society.* Biblical justice is thus closely linked to justice in the broader society and the political community. From Calvin and the Puritans to contemporary churches, a particular strength of Reformed Christians has been their emphasis on the interrelationship between Christian and general social norms. H. Richard Niebuhr* (*Christ and Culture* [1951]) termed this the "transformational" pattern. It has dominated expressions of Reformed theology in the United States and elsewhere, thus profoundly influencing U.S. and other history and theology.

Reflection on justice in the United States since Reinhold Niebuhr has been led by such social thinkers as John Rawls (*A Theory of Justice* [1971]) and Michael

Walzer (*The Spheres of Justice* [1983]). They both view justice as the "first virtue" of social arrangements. Both are committed to egalitarian principles and approve inequality only when it benefits the weak and needy.

For Rawls, justice in Western democracies preeminently requires *procedures* by which self-interest can be set aside in social decision making. For Walzer, justice requires communities that self-consciously and with sophisticated insight work to treat persons with respect in complex and differentiated social roles.

Given their histories and theologies, it is no accident that Reformed Christians and Jews are overrepresented in U.S. legislatures and in the legal profession. Like Calvin, Knox, the Puritans, and Barth, contemporary Reformed persons have unusual resources and opportunities to engage the broader culture.

In these roles, Christians participate in the authoritative allocation of values and address critical questions of social *distributive* and *commutative* justice. *Distributive justice* aims to distribute fairly a community's benefits and burdens (e.g., wealth, taxation, health care). Distributive justice is a seminal subject whether in liberation theologies or in works of Rawls ("Justice as Fairness") or Walzer (and a more social tradition). *Commutative justice* focuses more on direct interpersonal relations and thus deals with contracts (consent) and interpersonal crime and punishment. The great size, complexity, and pluralism of U.S. society make commutative justice much more perplexing than in earlier, simpler times.

3. *Justice and love.* Some Christian traditions separate and contrast justice and love. Such separation is easiest when both love and justice are caricatured: love is private, perfectionist, self-sacrificing, subjective, and so forth; justice is public, realistic, and objective.

If "justice" is a difficult and complicated concept, "love" has even more numerous and less precise meanings. The word "love" is often debased in contemporary thinking. The Greek word *agapē* (God's self-giving love) surely includes justice and no doubt goes beyond formal human justice categories. But justice often challenges and structures erotic love (*erōs*) and neighbor/brotherly love (*philia*). Justice puts higher standards than "All is fair in love and war."

A useful criterion is: "It is not Christian to get to love too soon." A danger of U.S. Protestant ethics is that of locating morality in the individual and one's subjective understanding. Love is particularly susceptible in this regard. When we interpret love from this perspective, we easily justify much in terms of self-interest. With love a debased concept, even married partners would do well to ask how to live justly with each other. That is, in order to know what it is to love, we must first understand what is just.

4. *Justice and character.* "Justice" is used to describe the character of a moral agent. God is preeminently the just One. It matters greatly, however, whether the emphasis is on God doing and bringing justice or whether God's justice is primarily ontological in God's self. Similarly, our overall theological and biblical understandings will control whether *mishpat* is rendered as God judging or God doing justice.

Some recent Protestant thought has emphasized the church as character-shaping community rather than as centrally concerned with teleology or public policy. Through the Holy Spirit* and by our living in the Christian community our character will be shaped toward virtues such as justice. Among the four classical virtues (justice, courage, prudence, and temperance), justice was supreme, ordering the others. To the classical virtues in Aristotle, Thomas Aquinas added the (higher—if more unusual) theological virtue of faith, hope, and love. In these terms, Christian character will be marked by justice ordering the virtues. Christian spirituality will result in justice as well as in courage, prudence, temperance, faith, hope, and love.

Disappointment at the failures of policies and actions that seek justice is partly offset by contemporary emphases on community and character. The disappearance of a U.S. Protestant moral consensus and the emergence not only of pluralism but of sharp cleavages over moral issues lead communities to emphasize the shaping of character (education and socialization). There is an easier and closer relationship between character shaping and current theologies of rhetoric or narrative* than between the latter and policy ethics. It is easier for Reformed church folks to think about "shaping Christian character" than to work for justice in the complexities of pluralistic public policy.

Recent studies suggest that genotype plays a major role in what we often term "character." Culture plays a major role in the definition and evaluation of virtue (bravery, prudence, temperance, justice). Character ethics and policy ethics are thus perhaps best linked in such phrases as "By their fruits you shall know them."

FRED O. BONKOVSKY

Justification

The doctrine of justification by grace* through faith* alone is central to the teaching of the Reformation. It stood as a key to Martin Luther's* own exegetical insight at the beginning and wellspring of the Reformation.

The importance of this biblical and doctrinal insight to both Lutheran and Calvinist forms of Protestantism can easily obscure the fact that the Reformation view of justification was not always the doctrinal view of the church and that neither the early church nor the medieval church recognized the principle of justification *sola fide*. Additionally, the patristic and medieval tradition, together with several of the first Reformers—notably Luther and Martin Bucer*—did not make an absolute distinction between justification and sanctification.* Bucer spoke of a double justification according to which believers were both counted and made righteous. Nonetheless it is the "*sola*," by faith *alone*, to the utter exclusion of works, that is the distinctive characteristic of the Protestant and Reformed teaching and the reason Luther, Calvin, and the later Protestant tradition affirmed categorically that justification is the *articulus stantis et cadentis ecclesiae*, the "article of the standing or falling of the church."

Luther's doctrine of justification by grace alone through faith rests on a view of faith as trusting or faithful apprehension of divine things, an utter trust in the grace of God* that sets aside all trust in worldly things and in salvation* attainable by human means. This faith itself is unattainable by human means and must be brought about by the work of the Holy Spirit* on the human heart. It is this faith alone that justifies. Luther insisted that the correct understanding of Rom. 3:28 requires the addition of *sola*, "alone," to the translation. Forgiveness* and righteousness are graciously imputed by God on the ground of this faith. Indeed, for Luther, faith itself justifies inasmuch as it is faith that apprehends Christ and appropriates his righteousness. This is not to say, however, that justification can be grounded even in part on Christian love or on works, as if faith were an act or choice of the individual. Sin* remains in the justified who, on the basis of their own acts, can never be worthy before God; and faith is an inward openness to God, a setting aside of our own merit, a negation of our insufficient moral striving. For Luther, as for all subsequent Lutheran and Reformed thinkers, the believer is *simul iustus et peccator*, "at once justified and a sinner."

Philipp Melanchthon's early systematization of Protestant theology was crucial to the development not only of Lutheran but also of Reformed doctrine. With Luther, he identified justification as the chief article of the Christian faith. Perhaps more consistently than Luther, Melanchthon regarded justification as a forensic act, but very much in the spirit of Luther he also insisted justification was intimately connected with the regenerative work of the Holy Spirit. The initial order of salvation proposed early on by Melanchthon moved from contrition or sorrow for sin to faith and, on the basis of faith, to the forgiveness of sins, understood forensically as justification, and the regeneration* of the believer. Faith, therefore, provides the ground both for the counting righteous and for the making righteous of believers—and it precedes both justification and regeneration or sanctification.

Calvin offers a clarification and codification of his predecessors' teachings. Like them, he was concerned to separate justification from any notion of works-righteousness but also to retain the connection between justification and the new life in Christ. He therefore spoke of a twofold grace (*duplex gratia*), by which believers are both reckoned righteous in Christ and sanctified by his Spirit (*Inst.* 3.11.1). Calvin insisted on the parallel and connection between the divine acts of counting the believer righteous and making the believer righteous: justification and sanctification are grasped together. But Calvin equally clearly removed all consideration of works and of personal righteousness from the basic calculus of justification, which is entirely forensic. A person is justified when counted righteous—"who, excluded from the righteousness of works, grasps the righteousness of Christ through faith" (*Inst.* 3.11.2). Faith therefore is not merely knowledge and assent. It is also a profound heartfelt or volitional acceptance of Christ that grounds the application of God's grace to believers.

Calvin's emphasis on faithful acceptance of Christ and his benefits as the basis of justification points toward the profound connection in his theology between justification and the substitutionary atonement* effected by Christ. Believers are counted righteous because of the righteousness of Christ who stands in their place and fulfills the righteousness and obedience required by God of human beings. Since individuals remain sinful after they are counted righteous through faith, Calvin can also argue a double justification—first of the sinner and then of the works of the justified sinner, which now are counted righteous insofar as they are offered to God in and through the grace of Christ.

Just as Calvin had offered a still clearer view of the utterly forensic character of justification than any of his predecessors, so the later Reformed tradition continued to sharpen the distinction between justification and sanctification. The development of Reformed orthodoxy* in the late sixteenth century saw the formulation of a more strict view of the order of salvation in which calling,* regeneration, faith, justification, sanctification, and glorification were understood not only as distinct moments in the order but also as strictly separate in significance and, to a somewhat greater degree than had been typical of the Reformers, were explained in terms of the fourfold Aristotelian causality. Nonetheless, Reformed orthodox dogmatics, notably the Leiden Synopsis* (1626), continued to follow Luther and Calvin in identifying justification as "foremost" and genuinely foundational doctrine of Protestantism. Justification is not, therefore, an infusion of righteousness but a judicial act of God that declares a believer righteous by grace apart from any personal merit. The orthodox declared that in this act God sits as a judge, but on "the throne of grace" rather than on "the throne of righteousness," inasmuch as the divine righteousness no longer stands over against human unworthiness as a ground of judgment.

Unlike Luther, but quite in the tradition of Calvin, the orthodox indicated it is not, strictly, faith that justifies but grace in Christ. Faith, defined as consisting not only in knowledge and assent but also and primarily as a faithful apprehension of Christ and of Christian truth by the whole person, provides the inward means of receiving God's grace. Since, moreover, faith itself is a gift of God's grace and not something initiated by the believer, there can be no confusion of faith with works. The efficient cause of justification is the grace of God, while the material cause is neither faith nor works but the righteousness of Christ applied against the case of the faithful but still sinful person. Righteousness remains inherent only in Christ and belongs to the believer by imputation.

Protestant orthodox writers also drew lines of connection between justification and other doctrines somewhat more clearly and pointedly than the Reformers. Thus, justification, as well as the faith on which it is grounded, is identified as a result of election and, in the theology of strict predestinarians* like Samuel Maresius (1599–1673), as an eternal forensic act executed in time. Similarly, the idea of double justification is connected more clearly and fully by the orthodox with the inward working of grace and the Spirit in believers, with the inherent but imperfect righteousness brought about in believers in their regeneration and sanctification, and with the freely given obedience of believers to the law* considered according to its third use.

After the orthodox codification of Reformed doctrine, the most notable discussion of the doctrine of justification in the Reformed tradition is Karl Barth's.* Barth attempted both to sum up the Reformed insights and to refashion them in the light of his own highly Christocentric model of theology. Barth's teaching builds on a conception of justification as a totally gracious temporal act of God in Christ rooted eternally in "God's freedom for man" as it is expressed in Jesus Christ. For Barth, justification must be understood as God's eternal decision for humanity in Christ who, in the cross and resurrection, is himself both elect and reprobate. Justification, therefore, remains a justification of the unrighteous, an acquittal by God opening for the sinner a new future grounded in faith. Thus, in his basic definition of the believer as "at once justified and a sinner" and in his insistence on justification as occurring by faith alone apart from all works, Barth remains faithful to the Reformed tradition. What is original to Barth is the way justification binds together time and eternity in Christ's own election and reprobation—granting that earlier Reformed theology understood election, but not reprobation, in Christ and viewed both decrees as directed toward human beings as individuals.

Barth, *CD* IV/1–2; G. C. Berkouwer, *Faith and Justification*, trans. L. B. Smedes (1954); J. Calvin, *Inst.* 3.1–4, 14–16; W. Dantine, *Justification of the Ungodly*, trans. E. W. and R. C. Gritsch (1968); H. Küng, *Justification: The Doctrine of Karl Barth and a Catholic Reflection* (1981); A. E. McGrath, *Iustitia Dei: A History of the Christian Doctrine of Justification*, 2 vols. (1986); A. Ritschl, *A Critical History of the Christian Doctrine of Justification and Reconciliation*, trans. J. S. Black (1872).

RICHARD A. MULLER

Kagawa, Toyohiko (1888–1960)

Kagawa Toyohiko (surname first) has been considered one of the twentieth century's greatest Christian workers. He was also one of the most creative persons in Japanese history in areas of social, economic, and political reform. More recent evaluations have noted flaws in his career, such as his apparent espousal of certain naive views current in the pre-World War I Western world regarding alleged connections between race and the character of persons. Yet these very few comments should not diminish Kagawa's stature or great contributions to the Christian church and the world.

Kagawa was born in Kobe, Japan (July 10, 1888), the son of an influential political leader and a concubine. After his parents' death, Kagawa (age four) was sent to live in the ancestral home on the island of Shikoku and be reared by his father's neglected wife and mother. The hostile atmosphere and abusive treatment here helped open him to the warm welcome, understanding, and sympathetic guidance he received from a Japanese Christian teacher and two missionaries of the PCUS, Drs. H. W. Myers and C. A. Logan.

In his deep personal suffering and tension, Kagawa experienced a profound conversion* to the God of Christian faith and came to express that faith with the ardent prayer: "O God, make me like Christ." This faith and his sufferings led Kagawa to a passionate concern for the weak, poor, and defeated of life.

Kagawa was trained in the Presbyterian-Reformed Meiji Gakuin Upper High School (Tokyo); he studied at the Presbyterian-related Kobe Seminary and at Princeton Seminary. Never losing touch with the faith and practice of this training, he later emerged as a broadly ecumenical and effective evangelist. Kagawa was the dynamic initiator and promoter of almost every movement for Japanese social reform for more than forty years. As a Christian, he informed the conscience of a largely non-Christian nation, probably more than any of his fellow citizens in the twentieth century. After his death (April 23, 1960), the emperor granted Kagawa one of the highest decorations open to a Japanese citizen.

RICHARD H. DRUMMOND

Kairos Document

The Kairos Document: Challenge to the Church (*KD*) was first published in South Africa (September 1985), with a revised second edition following a year later. The title indicates that the *KD* is a theological witness to reading "the signs of the times" in South Africa. It was drafted and signed by pastors and theologians, mainly but not exclusively black, seeking theological direction amidst the current South African political crisis. A significant number of the persons involved were members of denominations that belong to the Reformed family of churches, and the *KD* reflects several recurrent themes in the history of Reformed theology and confession.

The *KD* distinguishes between and critically examines three types of theology: "state," "church," and "prophetic." "State theology" supports and legitimates an unjust status quo on the basis of a false reading of Rom. 13:1–7, a confusion of justice* with law and order, as well as a conflation of Christianity and patriotism.

"Church theology" proposes reconciliation as the solution to apartheid* and advocates nonviolence as the only Christian means to social change. While both reconciliation and nonviolent action are grounded in the gospel, the way they are understood is based on faulty social analysis. The reconciliation proposed does not require justice as a condition, and the advocacy of nonviolence fails to deal with the violence of state and its structures of oppression.

"Prophetic theology" begins by analyzing the South African conflict in terms of the suffering of those who are oppressed. It proclaims that God is on the side of the oppressed and against the tyranny of the oppressors. On the basis of the biblical message of God's liberation, it provided grounds for hope, and in the light of that hope, it advocates concrete ways in which Christians and the church can participate in the struggle for justice in South Africa.

The *KD* is clearly influenced by liberation theology.* However, its critique of the idolatry of "state theology" and of the inadequacy of "church theology" to deal with the harsh reality of political oppression, and its espousal of a "prophetic theology" that is both iconoclastic and socially transformative, resonate well with prophetic trajectories within the Reformed tradition. Indeed, bringing together liberation and Reformed insights is indicative of a major contribution being made by South African theology to the ecumenical church and especially its social witness. This is seen in the worldwide responses to the *KD* and the subsequent *The Road to Damascus: Kairos and Conversion* (1989) prepared and signed by third-world Christians.

W. H. Logan, *The Kairos Covenant* (1988); and "Kairos Documentation," *Journal of Theology for Southern Africa*, nos. 55–60.

JOHN W. DE GRUCHY

Kingdom of God

"The Lord reigns," and the biblical symbol of the kingdom, is closely linked with God's* dominion over nature, history,* and every dimension of human life in the past, present, and future (Ps. 93:1; 97:1; 99:1; 1 Chron. 29:11; Dan. 4:3, 34–35). Many of the prophets look for the future consummation of God's reign in judgment and righteousness or a new age when nations shall be peaceably united by their willing obedience to the one true God of Israel (Isa. 2:1–5; 18:7; 59:20; Zeph. 3:9ff.; Zech. 14:9).

In the NT, Jesus proclaims and embodies the new age: "The time is fulfilled, and the kingdom of God has come near; repent, and believe in the good news" (Mark 1:15; Matt. 4:12–25; Luke 17:21; 21:31). The Sermon on the Mount may be read as proclamation of the possibility for a complete obedience that exemplifies what it means when God's kingdom breaks in. In John's Gospel, those who hear Jesus' words and have faith* already possess salvation* and eternal life, though the full gift comes only after Jesus' ministry through the resurrection (John 20:31). The Revelation to John envisions the future culmination of the kingdom in a new heaven and a new earth where nations walk by the light of God's glory and the lamp of Christ, the Lamb (Rev. 21).

Reformed theology typically understands the kingdom as God's sovereign and transformative reign of righteousness and truth in contest with the forces of Satan, chaos, and sin.* John Calvin* says that humanity* withdraws from God's kingdom in the fall and is therewith deprived of spiritual gifts, including faith,* love of God, and charity toward the neighbor—qualities restored only through the grace* of regeneration.* In Christ, God forgives our sins, corrects our inordinate desires, reshapes our obedience, and overcomes those powers and persons who stubbornly resist. Nevertheless, those who are thus returned to God's kingdom continue as pilgrims on earth until God is all in all. In the meantime, ecclesiastical constitutions are to order the church* under God alone, without entangling regenerate consciences in human inventions, encroachments, and ceremonies. Civil authority is not to command anything against God's law, and it provides for a public manifestation of true religion at the same time that it establishes civil justice* and outward morality (*Inst.* 1.14.15; 2.2.12; 3.19.15; 3.20.42; 4.10; 4.20.1, 32).

English Puritans, such as Thomas Cartwright* and William Perkins,* were more optimistic about the extent to which a new order might be realized here and now. They discussed an order where church patterns based on God's Word became the standard for social and political life. Puritans in New England such as Robert Winthrop and John Cotton* consciously attempted to fashion a new society under God's reign by framing constitutions and covenants based on revelation,* upholding the independence of the church in determining its own organization and discipline and supporting the limitation of human powers in every aspect of life (David Little, *Religion, Order, and Law* [1969], pp. 77, 81–131).

Albrecht Ritschl, a nineteenth-century Lutheran, understood the kingdom as the perfect moral fellowship or divinely ordained highest good. This final end, he said, is actualized in Jesus Christ and reflected Christian character; it also comprises the true motive for moral action and for the Christian's vocation in society (*The Christian Doctrine of Justification and Reconciliation*, vol. 3 [1874; ET 1900, repr. 1966], pp. 284–326). For Walter Rauschenbusch, an American Baptist who espoused the social gospel,* the kingdom is both present and future, task and gift; and it invites immediate action aimed at the redemptive transformation of society (*A Theology for the Social Gospel* [1917], pp. 131–45).

More recently, Wolfhart Pannenberg has argued that the coming kingdom, though now hidden, will fulfill the social destiny of humanity. Sharing in Christ's mission, the church provisionally anticipates the kingdom and calls present society to attend to God's promised future (*Jesus—God and Man* [ET 1968], pp. 373–75). The Confession of 1967 notes that the kingdom's final triumph cannot be identified with partial earthly achievements; yet it also insists that "with an urgency born of this hope the church applies itself to present tasks and strives for a better world" (*BC* 9.55–56; cf. 4.123; 7.102; 7.301).

H. R. Niebuhr, *The Kingdom of God in America* (1937).

DOUGLAS F. OTTATI

King's Confession

An appendix to the Scots Confession* (1560). It was also called the Second Scots Confession or Negative Confession. James VI of Scotland commissioned Rev. John Craig, a previous catechism writer, to compose it.

The Scots Confession is a Calvinist document portraying the faith of the Scottish reformers. From its publication to the production of the King's Confession (1581), there was great national fear of a resurgence of the Roman faith. It was believed the Scots Confession was signed by many secret papists, not because they agreed with its articles of faith, but with deceit in their hearts and perhaps even with a papal dispensation. There was a felt need for an appendix to the Scots Confession to root out hidden papists. With the king's signature and power for ecclesiastical authorities to prosecute all who refused to sign the King's Confession, it was widely circulated and all university graduates were required to subscribe to it. The King's Confession is a strongly worded litany of all that the

Scottish Protestants detested about the teachings and practices of the Roman Church.

G. D. Henderson, ed., *The Scots Confession, 1560* (1960).

RICHARD C. GAMBLE

Kirk, Kirk Session

"Kirk" is the Scottish (and northern English) equivalent of "church." Both derive from the Greek word *kyriakon*, "(house) of the Lord." It was the normal usage in the Scottish Reformation, but "church" became more common from the seventeenth century. "Kirk" is still a characteristic Scottish usage for the national Church of Scotland, in distinction from nonconformists such as Episcopalians, but also for other Presbyterian bodies, for example, the Free Church of Scotland.

"Kirk" survives in place-names and in compounds such as "kirkyard." Its only invariable use is in "kirk session" which in the Church of Scotland and similar Presbyterian churches is the governing body of the congregation, comprising the ruling elders* and the ordained minister (teaching elder).

J. T. Cox, ed., *Practice and Procedure in the Church of Scotland*, 6th ed., ed. D. F. M. MacDonald (1976).

DAVID F. WRIGHT

Knowledge of God

The category of knowledge functions as a major motif in Reformed theology. God* is viewed as the revealer and the human being as the knower. Accordingly, Reformed theology is preeminently a "theology of the Word," a theology which, following Calvin,* speaks of a twofold knowledge of God as creator and redeemer.

The exaltation of the category of knowledge is evident in the opening question and answer of the Geneva Catechism (1541): "*Teacher*: What is the principal end of human life? *Student*: It is to know God." Appropriately, the first two books of Calvin's *Institutes* (1559) are titled "The Knowledge of God the Creator" and "The Knowledge of God the Redeemer."

Normally the words for "knowledge" are the Latin *cognitio* and *notitia* and the Old French *cognoissance*. These terms do not denote a purely objective knowledge of God, a knowledge *that* (that God exists or that the gospel history is true) but a knowledge intensely personal in nature. Objectivity and personalism are held closely together, particularly in Calvin's theology (cf. Torrance).

Reformed theology has often been accused of overintellectualizing the Christian faith, and while admittedly the works of Reformed orthodoxy* betray this tendency, for Calvin knowledge was not simply a matter of the intellect but also of the heart and will. Calvin described faith as a kind of knowledge, not something that "flits about in our brains" without touching our hearts. It is "a firm and certain knowledge of God's benevolence toward us" which is "both revealed to our minds and sealed upon our hearts through the Holy Spirit" (*Inst.* 3.2.7). Moreover, it is intimately connected with the doing of God's will: "All right knowledge of God is born of obedience" (*Inst.* 1.6.2). Perhaps the closest modern equivalent of what Calvin meant by knowledge is "existential apprehension" (J. T. McNeill).

The Reformed understanding of the knowledge of God may be summarized:

1. Knowledge of God is the gift of God's grace.* All our knowledge of God arises because of God's gracious action. The prior act of all human knowing and speaking of God is God's gracious self-revelation.* If God had not freely chosen to be revealed, humanity* would know nothing at all about God. Knowledge of God is not of "what God is," that is, of God's essence, which remains incomprehensible to us, but only "of what sort God is," that is, of God's gracious giving of God's self to us.

2. Knowledge of God is accommodated knowledge. In God's revelation, God accommodates* himself to our weak human capacities. "God cannot be comprehended by us," says Calvin, "except as far as He accommodates (*attemperat*) Himself to our standards" (*Commentary* on Ezek 9:3, 4; *CO* 40, col. 196). God walks with a mother step, prattles to us as to a baby, and "lisps" in speaking so we

may understand. This accommodation is necessary for two reasons: first, because of the gap between creator and creature; second, because of the separation between a holy God and a sinful humanity. The twofold accommodation is seen supremely in Christ. As truly divine and truly human, Christ bridges the gulf between God and humanity and achieves our reconciliation "by the whole course of his obedience" (*Inst.* 2.16.5).

3. Knowledge of God is correlative knowledge. Calvin's opening sentence in the *Institutes* describes the bipolar character of knowledge: "Nearly all the wisdom we possess, that is to say, true and sound wisdom, consists of two parts: the knowledge of God and of ourselves" (*Inst.* 1.1.1). For Calvin, this was a fundamental principle: to know God is to know ourselves and to know ourselves aright is to be driven to look to God. Knowledge of God and knowledge of ourselves are so intimately related that all theological statements have their anthropological correlates and all anthropological statements their theological correlates.

4. Knowledge of God is twofold in character. Calvin also spoke, as did those who followed him, of a twofold knowledge of God (*duplex cognitio Dei*): the knowledge of God as creator and the knowledge of God as redeemer in and through Christ.

The sources of the knowledge of God as creator are:

a. Humanity itself. "There is within the human mind, and indeed by natural instinct, an awareness of divinity. . . . God himself has implanted in all men a certain understanding of his divine majesty" (*Inst.* 1.3.1). "Knowledge of God is naturally innate in the minds of all" (Vermigli, *Loci communes*, preface). This knowledge, however, is suppressed or corrupted by sin.* In Calvin's judgment, scarcely one person in a hundred acts on it rightly and there is not one in whom it grows to maturity. Humanity does not apprehend God aright. The human mind under the condition of sin is a veritable "factory of idols."

b. The fashioning of the universe and God's government of it. According to Calvin, God "daily discloses himself in the whole workmanship of the universe." Indeed, the universe is "a sort of mirror in which we can contemplate God, who is otherwise invisible" (*Inst.* 1.5.1). Calvin at times is lyrical in speaking of God's revelation in creation which he describes as "a dazzling theater" of God's glory. Though sufficient to render humanity inexcusable, because of human sinfulness the knowledge of God gained from creation is woefully inadequate: "If men were taught only by nature, they would hold to nothing certain or solid or clear-cut, but would be so tied to confused principles as to worship an unknown god" (*Inst.* 1.5.12). Interpreters of Calvin, however, have diverged sharply regarding the role and usefulness of natural theology* in Calvin's teachings.

On the basis of God's inward and outward revelation, Reformed orthodoxy distinguished between the natural knowledge of God, drawn discursively from the conscience* and created things, and revealed or saving knowledge which was the result of God's special revelation. While asserting the truth and usefulness of natural theology in rendering humanity inexcusable before God, Reformed theologians were virtually unanimous in asserting that natural knowledge is not saving knowledge.

Since the "seed of religion" in the human mind and the revelation in creation failed for their proper effect, God provided a self-revelation in the written Word as well as an inner testimony of the Holy Spirit* in the heart enabling sinful humanity to receive this revelation. By this conjoint divine action, objective and subjective, a true saving knowledge of God is communicated to sinful humanity. Calvin's formula is Word and Spirit. The work of the Spirit is not to supplement the revelation in Scripture* but to authenticate it in our hearts.

The knowledge of God as redeemer has only one source: *God's revelation in Jesus Christ embodied in Scripture and testified to by the Holy Spirit.*

The Enlightenment resulted in a fundamental shift in sensibility regarding the matter of the knowledge of God. Since Locke and Kant, modern theology has been faced with the question of justifying claims to the knowledge of God. Some Reformed theologians, such as Friedrich

Schleiermacher* adopted a foundational epistemological theory to justify the possibility of God's knowability. Schleiermacher understood revelation as supernatural and suprarational but believed it actualized a universal human possibility. Abraham Kuyper* and Herman Bavinck* strongly emphasized general revelation and common grace. Karl Barth* forcefully rejected the search for a foundational epistemological theory and every notion of a natural theology. According to him, there is no real knowledge of God apart from God's self-revelation in Jesus Christ. While denying the idea of a general revelation in nature and history, Barth granted, in the context of discussing the prophetic office of Christ, that there may be in creation* and history* "parables of the kingdom," lesser lights that reflect Jesus Christ, the Light of life (*CD*).

T. F. Torrance* has sought to establish both the uniqueness and the rationality of revelation in the intuitive self-evident nature of revelatory experience. Ronald Thiemann has given primacy to the paradigm of promise rather than knowledge. He believes we can still speak of revelation, not as a matter of God's knowability, but as narrated promise in which the doctrine of revelation is an account of God's identifiability.

E. A. Dowey, Jr., *The Knowledge of God in Calvin's Theology* (1952; repr. 1964); Heppe, *RD*; T. H. L. Parker, *Calvin's Doctrine of the Knowledge of God* (1959); R. F. Thiemann, *Revelation and Theology* (1985); T. F. Torrance, "Knowledge of God and Speech About Him According to John Calvin," in *Theology and Reconstruction* (1965); B. B. Warfield, "Calvin's Doctrine of the Knowledge of God," in *Calvin and Augustine* (1956); Weber, *FD*.

WILLIAM KLEMPA

Knox, John (c. 1514–1571)

Knox was born at Haddington, Scotland; was educated at St. Andrews, probably under the conciliarist John Major; and was ordained (1536). Thomas Guillaume converted him to Protestantism, and he subsequently came under the influence of John Rough and George Wishart.

Knox went to St. Andrews (1547), where he received a call as preacher. When the castle fell, he was sent to France and became a galley slave for nineteen months. During this period he wrote a summary of Henry Balnave's compendium of Protestant thought, a work in which Knox demonstrated his acceptance of Luther's* doctrine of justification.*

After his release (1549), Knox went to England, where he stayed until 1554. Here he was a preacher at Berwick and chaplain to Edward VI. While he criticized the details of English ecclesiastical policy, he generally approved of the religious climate of Edwardian England. The accession of a Catholic, Mary Tudor, to the English throne brought many changes. Within a few months, events drove Knox into exile (January 1554). From then until the deposition of Mary Stuart in Scotland some thirteen years later, he was primarily preoccupied with the problems of the "faithful Christian" confronted by "idolatry"* (i.e., Catholicism) and above all else by an "idolatrous" sovereign.

In exile, Knox spent time in Dieppe, Geneva, and Frankfurt and traveled to Scotland. He pastored exile congregations and wrote many works attacking Catholicism, setting forth the responsibilities of Protestants living in a Catholic land and urging the faithful to overthrow their idolatrous (Catholic) rulers.

The Protestant lords in Scotland sought Knox's return, and he arrived in May 1559. As a leader of the Reforming party, he devoted himself to preaching* and procuring money and troops from England. After the death of the regent Mary of Guise, Knox and others drew up the Scots Confession,* which Parliament approved. The authority of the pope was abolished and celebration of the Mass became illegal. Knox and five others also drafted the Book of Discipline (1560), which set forth a blueprint for the ideal Christian society. After Mary Stuart's return to Scotland (1561), Knox came into repeated conflicts with the queen over the question of having Mass celebrated for her as well as over the worldliness of her court. After her abdication, Knox became closely connected with the regent, the Earl of Moray.

Knox did not see himself as an academic theologian or a political theorist. His vocation* was to be a preacher of the gospel, not a writer or ecclesiastical official. Yet he did write in response to concrete problems, and from these writings his theology can be extracted.

Though Knox adhered to the basic principles of the Reformed tradition, he was a man of the OT. The main motifs of his thought are primary OT concepts. The religious abuses that Knox wished to correct were the "dregs of papistry," that is, the Catholic Mass and everything related to it. Essentially, he strove for a corporate return of Scottish religion to the ideal of spiritual Israel. He planned to use the "Christian Commonwealth" as the primary instrument for restoring the purity of Scottish religion. He regarded a "Christian Commonwealth" as a country in which both the civil and ecclesiastical powers cooperated in cultivating what he believed to be "true religion." He accepted the idea that government had a responsibility for establishing "true religion" and abolishing all contrary to it.

Knox's most distinctive positions concerned the purification of worship* and resistance to idolatrous rulers. For these notions he was indebted to many sources, but foremost is his method of interpreting Scripture, namely, an overemphasis on the OT and a pronounced literalness. Drawing from Deut. 12:32, he insisted that everything in worship be done according to the specifications of Scripture. If it was not, Knox regarded it as an idolatry to be resisted. His greatest anxiety was idolatry, which he equated with Catholicism; to be a Catholic was to be an idolater. The fight against the "idolatrous" Mass so dominated his thinking that virtually no major area of his thought was free from it. Increasingly, Knox developed his anti-idolatry theme in a political context and as a springboard to resistance against political authority.

J. Knox, *The Works of John Knox*, 6 vols. (1846–64); R. L. Greaves, *Theology and Revolution in the Scottish Reformation* (1980); R. G. Kyle, *The Mind of John Knox* (1984); W. S. Reid, *Trumpeter of God* (1974).

RICHARD G. KYLE

Kohlbruegge, Hermann Friedrich (1803–1875)

Born in Amsterdam, Kohlbruegge was raised in a pietistic Lutheran family that left the Reformed Church because of its rationalist and modernist tendencies. He became a candidate for the ministry in the Lutheran Church but was refused ordination while in graduate school because of theological controversy he stirred up regarding Christian anthropology and the meaning of sanctification.* His reading of John Calvin* and other early Reformed theologians led him to become the pastor of the independent Reformed church in Elberfeld, Germany, where he served (1847) until his death.

Kohlbruegge's place in the Reformed tradition is important as a catalyst and "irregular theologian" (Barth) who was widely read in Europe, especially among lay people. He provoked a spirit of resistance in the church which led to the Barmen* Synod and Confession and opposition to Hitler by the Confessing Church* (1930s). He was regarded by many as "the grandfather of Barmen." Barth* saw him as "the ray of hope" in nineteenth-century theology because he had faith and courage to "swim against the stream" (Barth). Kohlbruegge resisted the Evangelical State Church's ready submission to Bismarck and predicted that a compliant and conformist church was preparing the ground for a totalitarian state. This Protestant and reformist spirit in Kohlbruegge influenced such diverse figures as Abraham Kuyper* (with whom Kohlbruegge often disagreed), Dietrich Bonhoeffer, and Josef Hromádka.* His influence on churches in Germany, the Netherlands, Belgium, Czechoslovakia, Hungary, and the United States extended well into the twentieth century and is still felt in certain Reformed church circles, especially in eastern Europe.

Though he never mentions Karl Marx by name, it is evident that Kohlbruegge was aware of Marx's critique of religion. Marx lived in the region of Kohlbruegge's parish for nine years. Kohlbruegge regarded much of Marx's criticism as legitimate. He went so far as to have his congregation change the term *Gemeinde* ("congregation") in its title to *Gemeine* ("commons"). For Kohlbruegge, the local church was not merely a gathering of individuals, a congregation, but a shared life, a communion, a *Gemeine.*

Kohlbruegge took seriously both Marx's and Kierkegaard's criticisms of the church. He, however, rejected Marx's communism as an inadequate philosophical and political solution to social issues and rejected Kierkegaard's individualist existentialism as an inadequate perspective on the basic religious issues. Kohlbruegge's resistance to Marx, Kierkegaard, and Pietism was rooted in his understanding of the Bible and his reading of the Reformers, especially Calvin.

Kohlbruegge's theology was focused sharply on understanding the Word, and that in three primary forms: Christ as the Word, the Bible as the Word, and preaching* as the Word alive in the congregation. For this reason, Kohlbruegge could not separate theology from polity* and saw the congregation not simply as a gathering of saved and pious individuals but as a new community emerging in society for society. His preaching was therefore characterized by a passionate, prophetic note.

Because Kohlbruegge was a maverick and an "irregular" theologian, suspect in academic circles and not acceptable in the state church, he has received little attention in established circles. However, his insights have played a decisive role at key junctures of nineteenth- and twentieth-century European church history. He had minor influence in Reformed and Presbyterian circles in the midwestern United States in the first half of this century, especially in churches of German background in Wisconsin, Iowa, Minnesota, and the Dakotas.

Though over forty volumes of Kohlbruegge materials have been published in German and Dutch, his works are neither indexed nor translated and therefore inaccessible to most readers. He is, nevertheless, a significant figure in the Reformed tradition.

K. Barth, *Protestant Theology in the Nineteenth Century* (1972); G. C. Berkouwer, *Kohlbruegge in onze tijd* (1948); E. M. Huenemann, "H. F. Kohlbruegge: Servant of the Word by the Spirit and Grace of God" (diss., Princeton Seminary, 1961).

EDWARD M. HUENEMANN

Korea

South Korea, with perhaps 6½ million Presbyterians, is one of the five most Presbyterian and Reformed countries in the world, outranked in Presbyterian proportion (15.5%) of its population of 42 million only by Switzerland (40%), Scotland (38.5%), Holland (30%), and Hungary (19%). In sheer numbers of Presbyterians, however, by some counts South Korea may well now rank first, ahead of the United States, Indonesia, and South Africa.

But Korean Presbyterianism is very young, tracing back only to 1883/84. Its pioneer was a layman, So (Suh) Sang-Yoon, who was converted by Scottish missionaries in Manchuria and returned with Scripture portions to form a Christian group in his home village months before the first resident Protestant foreign missionary, Horace Allen, M.D., also a Presbyterian layman, landed (September 1884). The next year the first Presbyterian clergyman arrived, Horace G. Underwood, along with the first Methodist missionaries. Though public preaching of Christianity was forbidden, Allen's medical skill won him permission to open a hospital in 1885, the first legally permitted Christian institution in Korea. The next year Underwood performed the first baptism of a Protestant on Korean soil and organized the first Presbyterian church (1887).

The 1890s were years of expansion. Samuel A. Moffett opened up the northern interior, outside the treaty ports, to residential Protestant missionary presence, and by 1894/95 the first significant explosions of church growth were noted ("the fire in the northwest"). Emphasis was on evangelism,* but education was not neglected ("Plant a school with every church"). Presbyterian unity was considered a necessity. In 1893 the separate Presbyterian missions then at work (USA North and South, Australian, and, later, Canadian) formed a Presbyterian Council to override their imported differences and work for the formation of one Presbyterian Church of Korea. They agreed on a strategy of Korean self-support, self-government, and self-propagation, built on Bible study classes for all members (the Nevius method). In 1907 the first Korean presbytery was organized. It declared itself independent of foreign ecclesiastical connection and sent out its first Korean missionary. The first General Assembly was formed (1912) and sent its first missionaries to China.

The years of Japanese occupation (1905–45) were difficult, but the Great Korean Revival (1907–08) produced an inner Christian strength that survived persecution and produced the greatest Korean Christian leader of the period, Sun-Ju-Kiel, the first ordained and installed Presbyterian minister. He was not only the outstanding preacher of the revival but also became one of Korea's foremost spokesmen for national freedom in the Independence Movement (1919).

By 1934, when Presbyterians celebrated fifty years of mission in Korea, there were a total of 153,000 Presbyterians (communicants 103,000; baptized infants 24,000; catechumens 26,000) in a total population of twenty million. That is a percentage of less than 1 percent, but it was equal to the Roman Catholic* percentage and about five times as large as the Korean Methodist Church.

Now, half a century later (1990), the Reformed faith still dominates, but after the tragedy of the division of the country (1945) into a communist north and a democratic south, it is almost exclusively limited to the south. Before 1945 about two-thirds of Korea's Protestants (mostly Presbyterian) were in the north. Now North Korea is one of the most publicly non-Christian countries on earth. Only very recently has the communist government ended its unremitting persecution and provided two small churches in the capital, one Protestant and the other Catholic. According to some estimates there are also about 500 house churches surviving, with perhaps a total of ten thousand Christians.

In South Korea, membership figures are probably exaggerated, but the 6½ million Presbyterians are about three times more in number than the Roman Catholics, six times more than Methodists and Pentecostals, and nine times more than Korean Evangelical Holiness and Baptists. But since the Korean War they have been tragically divided into at least forty-five different Presbyterian denominations. Two are very large, with over a million and a half members each: the Presbyterian Church of Korea (T'ong-hap), which is ecumenical, and the Presbyterian Church of Korea (Hap-dong), which withdrew from the WCC* (1959). Two others report about half a million members each: Conservative Hap-dong and Reformed Presbyterian. Neither belongs to the WCC. Two more are smaller, the ecumenical Presbyterian Church of the Republic of Korea (300,000) and the Koryu Presbyterian (175,000) which is strongly Calvinistic but not in the WCC. The rest are smaller splinter groups. The larger ones have restored some sense of cooperation through a Presbyterian Council of leaders which meets irregularly.

All, however, are growing at a rate that continues to amaze. As with most third-world churches, their theology is conservative. Their spirit is an independent-minded connectionalism. The influence of Presbyterian schools and universities in society is pervasive. Commensurate with membership growth is the expansion of Korean Presbyterian missionaries around the world from Nepal to Brazil and from Africa to Los Angeles. How the parallel growth of Korean economic affluence will affect all of this remains to be seen.

SAMUEL HUGH MOFFETT

Kraemer, Hendrik (1888–1965)

Probably the most influential missiologist associated with twentieth-century dialectical theology* or neo-orthodoxy.* Though not an uncritical follower, Kraemer was the outstanding spokesman on Christian understanding of other world religions. He was born and educated in

Holland, serving for sixteen years in Indonesia as a lay missionary of the Netherlands Bible Society. He pioneered Christian work on Bali and became widely known for his ecumenical concerns and activity. He was first director of the WCC's* Ecumenical Institute in Bossey, Switzerland (1948–55). Kraemer wrote many books and emphasized the "discontinuity" between the Christian gospel and other religions.

RICHARD H. DRUMMOND

Kraus, Hans-Joachim (1918–)

Reformed theologian. Born in Essen, Kraus was OT professor in Bonn (1951–54) and Hamburg (1954–68) and professor of Reformed theology in Göttingen (1968–83). Well known as an OT scholar, Kraus has also written extensively on historical and systematic theology, particularly on John Calvin* and Karl Barth.* He has been concerned with the grounding of systematic theology in biblical theology, particularly the OT, the concept of "religion," and Jewish-Christian dialogue.

H.-J. Kraus, *Die biblische Theologie* (1970); *The Theology of the Psalms* (ET 1986); *Theologische Religionskritik* (1982); *Systematische Theologie in seiner biblischen-eschatologischen Kontext* (1983); and *Rückkehr zur Israel: Beiträge zum jüdisch-christlichen Dialog* (1990).

ROBERT R. REDMAN, JR.

Kreck, Walter (1908–)

Reformed theologian. Kreck taught at the Preachers' Seminary, Herborn (1945–52), and was professor of Reformed theology, Bonn (1952–73). A student of Karl Barth's,* he has been an articulate advocate of Barthian theology in the postwar era and was a forerunner in the eschatology* debates (1960s). Central features of his work have been his interactions with Barth's views and those of other contemporary systematic theologians, and the problem of ethics—particularly the role of Christians in socialist and capitalist societies.

W. Kreck, *Die Zukunft des Gekommenen* (1961); *Grundfragen der Dogmatik* (1970); *Grundfragen christlicher Ethik* (1974); *Grundfragen der Ekklesiologie* (1981); *Grundentscheidungen in Karl Barths Dogmatik* (1978); and *Kirche in der Krise der bürgerlichen Welt* (1980).

ROBERT R. REDMAN, JR.

Krummacher, Friedrich Wilhelm (1796–1868)

Leader of a revival among German Rhineland Reformed churches. Krummacher was called to Trinity Church, Berlin (1847), and was named preacher to the Prussian Court at Potsdam. His insightful expositions of Scripture* were sharply critical of the prevailing rationalism. In America he had considerable influence, especially among German settlers down the Ohio River and up the Missouri River but also through the Princeton theologians and his pupil Philip Schaff.* His sermon series *Elijah the Tishbite* (ET 1838) remains a classic.

Allgemeine deutsche Biographie, 17: 243–46.

HUGHES OLIPHANT OLD

Kuyper, Abraham (1837–1920)

The foremost leader of the neo-Calvinist movement that arose in the Netherlands around 1870 and left a deep imprint on Dutch life, especially its Reformed circles, for a hundred years thereafter. Kuyper not only formed the ideology of the movement but directed many of its institutions, serving in his lifetime (often simultaneously) as minister, journalist, politician, professor, philosopher, and indefatigable promoter.

Kuyper was born in a mildly conservative Reformed manse but showed liberal sentiments in his university years at Leiden (B.A. 1858; theology degree 1863). In his first, country parish, however, he converted to strict confessional orthodoxy. He assumed a popular—and populist—pulpit in Amsterdam (1870) from which he declaimed against the stodgy liberalism regnant in church and state. He gained a national forum in the daily newspaper *De Standaard* (founded 1872), which he edited until his death. Through it he shaped his cause, a devoted following, and his clear personal authority over both. Kuyper entered the Dutch Parliament (1873) only to collapse beneath his excessive workload. Thereafter he concentrated on organizing the three institutional networks that became the permanent foundation of neo-Calvinism: the Antirevolutionary* political party (1877), a national Christian day-school association (1878), and the Calvinistic Free University of Amsterdam* (1879). He chaired the first for forty years and taught at the last for twenty. Kuyper's most controversial actions caused a rupture in the National Reformed (*Hervormde*) Church (1886). He led his followers into union with the free church that had seceded (1834), forming the Gereformeerde Kerken (1892), which included about 10 percent of the Dutch population. Then Kuyper's attention returned to politics, and his pronounced democratic sympathies, particularly on labor issues, alienated many party conservatives. Nonetheless, his career soon peaked with the receipt of an honorary doctorate from Princeton (1898) and his elevation to the prime ministership (1901). Kuyper's term in office (through 1905) was complicated by a national railroad strike, and he remained rather embittered by his failure ever to get a second term. His last decade saw him chafing in the role of elder statesman, writing voluminously about the West's impending catastrophe which, he asserted, only a renewal of its Christian consciousness could avert.

All of Kuyper's labors cohere around an interlocking set of motives and convictions. First, he wanted to jar the orthodox Reformed from their pious slumbers into recovering, and sharply updating, the public and cultural dimensions of their Calvinist heritage. Second, he channeled the resulting energies against both religious and secular liberalism which were, he insisted, corrosive of justice and equity as much as of Christian faith. He further insisted, however, that this attack not be reactionary but rather encourage broad social differentiation and the full development of culture inherent in God's creation mandate. Instead of withdrawing from or dictating to public life, Christians were to enter a pluralistic landscape, their convictions anchored in a comprehensive worldview and coordinated by distinctive Christian organizations in every social sector. Kuyper's labors remain, in sum, an impressive example of Reformed Christianity in its social, political, and cultural witness, philosophically coherent, structurally concerned, and institutionally deployed.

A. Kuyper, *Principles of Sacred Theology* (ET 1898); and *The Work of the Holy Spirit* (ET 1900).

JAMES D. BRATT

Lambeth Articles

Originally composed by William Whitaker to oppose William Barrett's theology at Cambridge University, the Lambeth Articles (1595) were modified by Archbishop John Whitgift to reflect the scholastic Calvinist view of predestination.* Approved by Whitgift and ecclesiastical commissioners whom Whitgift had gathered were nine articles affirming: (1) Predestination* of some to life; reprobation of some to death. (2) Predestination to life is caused by God,* not by foreseen faith* or good works. (3) Predestination of a certain number. (4) Condemnation is based on sins. (5) Justifying faith "is not lost nor does it pass away either totally or finally in the elect." (6) True faith is accompanied by full assurance* of salvation* through Christ. (7) Saving grace* is not made available to all people. (8) Only those drawn to God by Christ actually come. (9) "It is not in the will or the power of each and every man to be saved."

The Lambeth Articles reflect opposition not only in Barrett but to Reformed and Lutheran theologians who viewed saving grace as applied to all people, gave a role in salvation to good works, made reprobation conditional, and temporized the idea that salvation was fixed eternally. At Cambridge the French Reformed thinker Peter Baro asserted many of the above ideas; and the issues became hotly contested in the Dutch Calvinist struggles over Arminianism.* Though the scholastic Calvinist view became the orthodox standard under Whitgift, the Elizabethan bishops, and the Heads of Cambridge's colleges, the Articles were not universally approved in England. In spite of Calvinist urgings, the Articles never became part of official Anglican church doctrine.

This failure was due to political opposition within the Elizabethan government and anti-Calvinism under James I (d. 1625) and Charles I (d. 1649). Politically, William Cecil and the queen opposed divisive public discussion of predestination. They also opposed the independent way Whitgift, the ecclesiastical commissioners, and Cambridge Heads had acted, for it seemed to imply an ecclesiastical freedom the Elizabethan state would not allow. Theologically, Baro and his followers immediately began to debate the Articles, largely from the viewpoint that people were created for salvation but lost it by rejecting God. Baro claimed that his views were identical with Augustine's before the conflict with Pelagius, many early church fathers, Philipp Melanchthon, and the Danish theologian Niels Hemmingson. In spite of his claims, Baro was forced to flee Cambridge.

After 1595, the Lambeth Articles remained the standard expression of English Calvinist orthodoxy; and some, such as Archbishop Ussher,* wanted to give the Articles confessional status. Others, such as Richard Neile and William Laud, attacked Calvinist orthodoxy and advanced notions of grace based on sacramental observances and on good works.

P. Lake, *Moderate Puritans and the Elizabethan Church* (1982); H. C. Porter, *Reformation and Reaction in Tudor Cambridge* (1958); N. Tyacke, *Anti-Calvinists* (1987).

RONALD J. VANDERMOLEN

Lang, John Dunmore (1799–1878)

Australian Presbyterian minister, politician, educator, and journalist. Born in Scotland, Lang was educated for the ministry at the University of Glasgow and earned an M.A. (1820). His formative life influences there were two leading Scottish evangelicals: his divinity professor Stevenson Macgill and his pastor, Thomas Chalmers.* His brother George in Sydney enticed him to emigrate to Australia, where he arrived in May 1823 and became the first Presbyterian minister in New South Wales (NSW). He received the D.D. from Glasgow (1825), and on another of his nine voyages to Great Britain (1831), he married Wilhelmina Mackie, with whom he had ten children.

Lang founded the Scots Church, Sydney, where he was the minister (1826–78). He was also founder and principal of Australia College (1831–54) and editor-publisher of the weekly papers *The Colonist* (1835–40), *The Colonial Observer* (1841–44), and the *Press* (1851). Embued with a Calvinist sense of social responsibility, he entered politics* and was elected to the Legislative Council of NSW (1843–47; 1850–51; 1854–56; 1859–69). A political liberal, he realized nearly all of his major goals: an end to penal transportation, separation of Victoria and Queensland from NSW, responsible government in the colony, radical land reform, national education, and abolition of state aid to religion. But he failed to win acceptance for his most radical idea: to make Australia a republic.

Less successful as a minister than a politician, he constantly quarreled with his co-religionists and established a breakaway synod of NSW (1850) which was reunited (1865) with the Synod of Australia for which he served as General Assembly* Moderator (1872). An evangelical in theology, Lang cooperated freely with other Protestants whom he perceived as biblically sound. However, his contentious nature, harsh criticism of the Roman Catholic* Church, controversial political beliefs, and propensity for litigation diluted his influence in the Australian religious community.

Lang's influence spread through innumerable sermons and lectures, three hundred books and pamphlets, thousands of newspaper articles, and his legislative activity. When he died, he was the most acclaimed and most denounced man of his time in Australia.

D. W. A. Baker, *Days of Wrath: A Life of John Dunmore Lang* (1986); K. Elford, "The Theology of Clerical Participation: John Dunmore Lang and Direct Clerical Representation in Politics," *Journal of Religious History* 5 (June 1969): 218–32.

ROBERT D. LINDER

Larger Catechism *see* **Westminster Confession of Faith**

Laski (a Lasco), Jan (1499–1560)

Reformed churchman. Born into an influential Polish ecclesiastical family, Lasco was originally intended for a career in the church, until his unexpected conversion to Protestantism. After a period in Basel living with Erasmus,* he went to Emden in northern Germany, where he was appointed superintendent of the East Frisian churches (1542). In this post, Lasco revealed a considerable talent for organization and attracted the notice of several leading reformers. Forced to leave Germany by the Augsburg Interim, Lasco came to England and was appointed superintendent of the new Dutch and French "stranger" churches (1550). He also attempted, through his friendship with John Hooper and Thomas Cranmer,* to influence the English church toward a more Reformed doctrine and practice. He went back to Emden (1553) but soon returned to his native Poland, where he died.

Throughout his career, Lasco showed a tireless enthusiasm for theological debate, capable of stirring controversy wherever he went. His theology was strongly oriented toward the Swiss Reformed tradition, though he was far from being an uncritical admirer of John Calvin* and Geneva. He adopted many features of Zurich polity* and doctrine* in his church orders which were his major achievement and monument.

O. Bartel, *Jan Laski* (1964); H. Dalton, *Johannes a Lasco* (1881); B. Hall, *John a Lasco: A Pole in Reformation England* (1971); R. Kruske, *Johannes a Lasco und der Sakramentsstreit* (repr. 1972).

ANDREW PETTEGREE

Lavater, Johann Caspar (1741–1801)

Often called "the genius of the heart," Lavater was the beloved pastor of St. Peter's Church, Zurich. Through his preaching, poetry, and essays he ranks with the literati of the Golden Age of German Literature. Though he was theologically orthodox and pious, he maintained a friendly attitude toward the contemporary intellectual currents. Several of his hymns are still used. He died from a bullet wound during the Napoleonic occupation of Switzerland. His works were edited by E. Stähelin (*Werke*, 4 vols. [1943]).

NSH 6:423–25.

HUGHES OLIPHANT OLD

Law

Third use of the law. A distinctive characteristic of the Reformed view of the law is its emphasis on the third use of the law. For John Calvin,* this function of the law as a norm and guide for the believer is its "proper and principal" use. Since Martin Luther* used the same words to describe the second use of the law (Lat. *usus elenchticus*)—for Calvin the first—whereby sinners come to know their sinfulness and need for grace,* it is assumed by some scholars (e.g., W. Elert) that this represents a polemic against Luther. This is doubtful, however, since Calvin nowhere alludes to Luther when treating this theme (*Inst.* 2.2.7ff.), and in their respective expositions of the Decalogue, Luther is even more extravagant than Calvin in praising the usefulness of God's commandments for the believer.

Yet it is true that Luther never formally taught a third use of the law. Calvin and he were one in their understandings of the first two uses of the law, the other being the political or civil use. They were also one in their views of grace, justification,* and Christian freedom* as well as in their opposition to any form of works-righteousness, on the one hand, or antinomianism, on the other. Their exegesis of key passages in their commentaries on Romans and Galatians is fundamentally the same.

Nevertheless, dogmatically, as over against exegetically, there is a basic difference between Luther and Calvin in approaching the law. For Luther it generally connotes something negative and hostile; hence his listing the law along with sin,* death,* and the devil. For Calvin, the law was viewed primarily as a positive expression of the will of God whereby God restores the image of God in humanity* and order in the fallen creation.* Calvin's view could be called Deuteronomic, for to him law and love are not antithetical but are correlates. Another way of describing the differing approaches of Luther and Calvin is to designate their exegetical understandings "denotative" and their broader, more dogmatic usage "connotative." Denotatively, Luther and Calvin were basically agreed; connotatively, they were worlds apart, due largely to their differing backgrounds and faith experiences. Accordingly, "for all the agreement on various designations of the law in these two theologies, and even that it is the law that curses and kills, there is a very different fundamental apprehension of law in Calvin which controls his usage and creates a very different connotative field of force whenever the law is mentioned with reference to the life of the believer" (Dowey, p. 151).

Outside the Lutheran-Reformed context, some form of the third use is generally recognized except by situationalist ethicists who recognize no rules or norms at all. Here Calvin and the Reformed tradition are closer to Wesley with his emphasis on sanctification* and the role of the law in that process.

Law and gospel or gospel and law? The question of the relation of law and gospel came to the forefront on the Continent again when Karl Barth* published his controversial *Gospel and Law* (1935). As a result of nineteenth-century Luther research, the order law-gospel had become a veritable dogma in Lutheran theology. By reversing the order and declaring that the gospel precedes the law, Barth was attacking a sacrosanct pillar of Lutheranism. Barth recognized a certain validity in that approach. But fundamentally, he maintained, we must begin with the promise (Gal. 3:17) and recognize that the law is "enclosed in the ark of the Covenant" (Barth, p. 71). The law is first of all a gift, an expression of God's grace, not a demand. Through sin, which deceives us, the law is seen and experienced as something hostile and negative and becomes "the law of sin and of death" (Rom. 8:2). In short, the law, according to its original purpose, is simply a form of the gospel.

Yet Barth recognized that law and gospel are not the same and must not be confused. "The gospel is not the law, just as the law is not the gospel; but because the law is in the gospel, comes from the gospel, and points to the gospel, we must first of all know about the gospel in order to know about the law, and not vice versa" (Barth, p. 72).

Many Lutherans assumed that this was simply an updated and radicalized variation of Calvin's position. There are similarities: Calvin, too, stressed the unity of the Word of God* and the covenantal* character of law. He also portrayed the law as a gift to God's chosen people and charter of their liberty subsequent to their redemption from bondage. However, the differences are significant. For example, contrary to Barth, Calvin also allowed for a significant role for the law of nature, however, inadequate, prior to the clearer version of God's will given to Moses and the Israelites in the Decalogue. Calvin also recognized that though the accusing, killing function of the law is "accidental," because of the fall, there is nevertheless something inherent in the law which results in an antithesis between law and gospel, narrowly conceived (*Commentary* on Gal. 3:10; 2 Cor. 3:7–8). Ultimately, the difference here goes back to their differing views of election and their different anthropologies.

Ethic of gratitude. One of Barth's concerns was to make theological ethics a part of dogmatics. A corollary is an ethic of gratitude. The believer strives to follow God's law not simply as an act of obedience but as a response of gratitude. This approach was already inherent in the classic answer to question 1 of the HC*: "What is your only comfort, in life and in death?" The answer includes not only the pellucid statement of the gospel: "That I belong—body and soul, in life and in death—not to myself but to my faithful Savior, Jesus Christ." It also includes its ethical corollary: "Therefore, by his Holy Spirit, . . . he makes me wholeheartedly willing and ready from now on to live for him."

Here we have "an ethics in embryo" (Niesel, p. 194). More precisely, we have in the HC an ethics of gratitude, for the Decalogue is treated in part III: "Thankfulness" (cf. WLC, q. 97). The first use of the law (*usus elenchticus*) is also there, but in the first part of the catechism which deals with human misery and sin, and here the form of the law is the two great commandments. The Decalogue, however, provides the basis for "the praise of works" which are done out of gratitude in response to the grace of God in Jesus Christ.

Barth, *CD* II/2, ch. 8; and "Gospel and Law," in *Community, State and Church* (1960); Calvin, *Inst.* 2.7–11; 3.6–7; 4.20; E. A. Dowey, Jr., "Law in Luther and Calvin," *Theology Today* 41, no. 2 (1984): 146–153; I. J. Hesselink, *Calvin's Concept of the Law* (1991); W. Niesel, *The Gospel and the Churches* (1962); Weber, *FD* 2:362ff.

I. JOHN HESSELINK

Lehmann, Paul L. (1906–)

Lehmann's ethic reflects three fundamental tenets of Reformed faith:

1. Christian ethics in the Reformed tradition focuses initially on God's activity and then, derivatively, on human activity. Though Lehmann's ethic emphasizes what it means to be "human," he never aligns himself with nontheological forms of humanism or theological traditions that *begin* with Christian anthropology. "Humanization" is a result of God's political activity in Jesus Christ, never a "natural" outgrowth of human activity.

2. Reformed thinking gives ethics a "contextual" rather than a prescriptive task. God's will is *not* mediated primarily by universal laws but by a contextual understanding of what God does "to make and to keep human life human." This does not mean that the circumstances of each situation alone dictate Christian behavior. Rather, divine activity creates the context for decision making and transforms human behavior. The response of human beings to God's activity becomes a living parable of God's action. The function of ethics is to *describe* divine action and human transformation and response.

3. The Reformers locate the point of departure of Christian ethics in the Christian *koinōnia.* In the *koinōnia,* the political activity of God and its humanizing effect are apprehended. While the individual is not lost in a corporate structure, individual identity and moral choices are played out in the context of the community of faith. Lehmann's ethic, grounded in the Reformed tradition, describes human relatedness which is created by God's action in Jesus Christ.

P. L. Lehmann, *Ethics in a Christian Context* (1963); and *The Transfiguration of Politics* (1975).

NANCY J. DUFF

Leiden Synopsis

The *Synopsis purioris theologiae* (1625), composed by Polyander, Walaeus, Thysius, and Rivetus, is an apologetic and polemic manual (880 pages) of Reformed doctrine as defined by the Synod of Dort.* With Scripture as its criterion, it surveys the history of doctrine. While it rejects idle speculation, traces of medieval scholasticism abound. Its physics is still pre-Copernican. Socinianism,* Anabaptism, Catholicism, and Lutheranism, but also Manichaeism, Pelagianism, Epicureanism, and anthropomorphism, are rejected.

H. Bavinck, ed., *Synopsis purioris theologiae* (1881); G. Itterzon, "De Synopsis Purioris Theologiae," *Nederlands Archief voor Kerkgeschiedenis* 23 (1930): 225–59.

DERK VISSER

Leigh, Edward (1602–1671)

English Puritan* theologian. Leigh was Oxford educated and a member of Parliament (1640–48). He served as a colonel in the parliamentary army during the English Civil War* and was a delegate to the Westminster Assembly.* Following his expulsion from Parliament (1648) for voting to accept the king's concessions, Leigh retired from public life and concentrated on writing. Among his many books on history, on biblical lexicography, and on theology was a major work on the covenant,* *A Treatise of the Divine Promises* (1633).

DNB 32:432–433.

LYLE D. BIERMA

Liberation Theology

A term applied to theologies that read the Bible and theological tradition from the perspective of poor and oppressed people and make liberation the central focus of Christian faith and life. Often used to refer to black, feminist, and third-world theologies, it refers more specifically to the Latin American theology that developed from an awakening of conscience to the poverty and suffering of the poor majority.

A Protestant movement, Church and Society in Latin America (ISAL), which began in the late 1950s, made a major contribution during the first stage of liberation theology's development. Led largely by Presbyterians and Methodists, it broke new ground in church circles by analyzing societal structures and patterns of dependency dominant in Latin America and emphasizing the need for systemic or revolutionary change. It dealt with social revolution as a theological problem, gradually moving from neoorthodox* theological categories to a theology of God's transforming action in history.* A Brazilian Presbyterian, Rubem Alves, gave creative expression to this approach in *A Theology of Human Hope* (1969).

Under the impact of Vatican II and the Medellín Conference of Latin American Bishops (1968), many Catholic priests, women religious, and laypersons moved toward the poor and began to read the Bible and rethink their faith in dialogue with them. This led them to use a new theological method and articulate a new theological paradigm.

Gustavo Gutiérrez, a Peruvian priest, laid out the main lines in *A Theology of Liberation* (1971). Authentic theological reflection must be grounded in faith and commitment to the struggle of the poor. It is "critical reflection on praxis in the light of the word of God"; reflection about God rising out of a shared experience of oppression, tested and transformed in effective participation in the struggle for justice.

Biblical faith is primarily concerned with liberation, which integrates three elements into one salvific process: liberation of the poor from oppressive economic, social, and political conditions; the ongoing historical process of creation of new human beings in a new society; and Christ's liberation of each person from sin, the ultimate root of all injustice and oppression, for communion with God.

In the last twenty years, growing numbers of theologians and biblical scholars, including a significant number of Protestants, have contributed to liberation theology's further development. Biblical study occupies a central place, giving particular attention to the centrality of the exodus in the Hebrew Scriptures, the focus of the prophets on social justice, and Jesus' message about the reign of God. Scholars emphasize the role of the poor as legitimate interpreters of the biblical message. They also use the "hermeneutical circle" in which interpretation is an ongoing process moving from experience to text and back again to experience. Many christological studies give greater importance to the historical Jesus and insist that following Jesus is a precondition for knowing Jesus. More recently, the spirituality of liberation has come to occupy a central place.

Liberation theology has a strong pastoral orientation, calling on the church to make a "preferential option for the poor" and working toward developing a new model of church, the Christian Base Communities. Focused on the transformation of human life in history, it uses the social sciences and categories of social analysis provided by Marxism. It also envisions a new economic order responding to the needs of the poor majority.

In developing their theology, Latin Americans have drawn on the work of European biblical scholars and theologians of the Reformed tradition. As Protestant participation grows, there is increasing recognition of elements in the Reformed heritage that are essentially liberationist or point in that direction: affirmation that truth is in order to goodness; the emphasis of John Calvin* on the sovereignty of God over all of life and history; his concern for the poor in Geneva and efforts to order the city's life by the Word of God.* Moreover, as liberation theology contributes to a new reformation today, it challenges Reformed churches to recover their vision of the *ecclesia reformata semper reformanda* ("the church reformed and always being reformed"), thus creating conditions for more dynamic ecumenical relationships.

M. RICHARD SHAULL

Liberty, Religious

Generally, the condition in which individuals or groups are permitted to adopt and, within limits, express and act upon beliefs concerning religious matters, free of interference or penalties imposed by outsiders, including the state. Leading members of the Reformed tradition have differed widely on the degree of latitude within which religious beliefs may permissibly be expressed or acted upon without the interference or restriction of human authorities. They have also differed over whether the church* or the state ought properly to decide the limits of religious expression and action.

For John Calvin,* the liberty or freedom to adhere to and put into practice the central tenets of religious faith is an essential implication of authentic belief. Just as compelled belief is no belief at all, human interference with legitimate belief is a grievous offense. This concern is focused particularly in Calvin's doctrine of the freedom of conscience.* The conscience is a special point of contact between human beings and God.* As such, it is "higher than all human judgments" and therefore not finally bound by any human laws, "whether made by magistrate or by church" (*Inst.* 4.10.5). By the same token, it is exempt from the coercive control of human authorities, "because [the power of the sword] is not exercised over consciences" (*Inst.* 4.11.8).

In addition, Calvin's preoccupation with organizational questions for both church and state is related to his concern for religious liberty. For example, his consistent opposition to monarchy, especially in church organization, and his preference for a "polyarchic" polity—a system combining aristocracy and democracy—was aimed at institutionalizing a greater opportunity for the free exercise of conscience on the part of believers.

There are grounds in Calvin's thinking, then, for a strongly libertarian theory of religious freedom, in which the state plays a very restricted role in regard to religious expression and practice. Such a theory eventually did emerge among radical seventeenth-century Reformed thinkers, particularly in England and America. At the same time, there are certain emphases in Calvin's thought that worked to inhibit that development. Having stressed that the inner forum of conscience and the outer forum of civil government are presided over by "different kings and different laws" (*Inst.* 3.19.15), and must therefore be considered separately, Calvin proceeded to assert that the civil government* must nevertheless "cherish and protect the outward worship of God" and "defend sound doctrine of piety and the position of the church" (*Inst.* 4.20.2). His apprehension, too, that democracy in church and state be tightly limited, lest it degenerate into anarchy and chaos, is an additional indication of the less radical side of Calvin's thought.

Whereas the reflections on freedom of conscience drive in the direction of sharply differentiating church and state, the concern civilly to establish uniform piety and worship modifies the distinction between the two spheres and considerably narrows the range within which religious beliefs may be expressed and practiced free of coercive restraint by civil authorities. Calvin's own practical policies in sixteenth-century Geneva were not notably libertarian. Expressions of idolatry* or blasphemy or attacks against what were regarded as "the essentials of the faith" were subject to civil punishment.

The ambiguity and the instability in Calvin's thought on religious liberty are reflected in the deep and complex tensions and conflicts within Reformed thinking, more broadly considered. For example, though Zwingli,* like Calvin, in practice favored the establishment of a uniform orthodoxy, he argued that it is the civil authority that is responsible to determine and supervise the "outward" aspects of religious life, namely, matters of ecclesiastical organization and discipline. Calvin, on the contrary, believed that such decisions were properly under the church's jurisdiction.

Some of Calvin's followers, like John Knox* in Scotland, Christopher Goodman and John Ponet in England, and Philippe Duplessis-Mornay and other Huguenots* in France, agreed with him that the church was ultimately responsible to impose authentic religious discipline* and worship* by means of civil enforcement. But, in attempting "to rescue consciences from the tyranny of men," as Calvin said (*Inst.* 4.10.5), and thereby to implement their version of religious liberty, they went farther than Calvin was usually willing to go. To his annoyance, they frequently called for open and armed rebellion against those whom they regarded as illicit rulers. The campaign against idolatry by people such as these inspired the revolutionary movements in northern Europe in the sixteenth century that are associated with Reformed Christianity.

However, in English and American Puritanism* in the late sixteenth and the seventeenth century the full range of ambiguities and tensions in Reformed thinking about religious liberty were most evident. In Elizabethan England, the Presbyterians, featuring the uniformist, establishmentarian side of Calvin's thought, were opposed by a "free church" separatist form of Congregationalism.* Inferring a more radical lesson from the Calvinist teachings of the Presbyterians, the separatist Congregationalists endeavored to widen substantially the range for the exercise of conscience by liberating religious expression and practice from "the civil forcing of men," in the words of Robert Browne,* father of the movement.

These same struggles within Puritanism were manifested again in the seventeenth century, both in England and in America. The question of religious liberty was at the center of the Puritan Revolution in England (1640–49). Once more, the Presbyterians sought to impose a uniform, civilly controlled religious system but were resisted by more moderate and radical Puritans who favored varying degrees of religious freedom. In colonial New England, conflicts between Reformed leaders like John Cotton* and the radical Calvinist Roger Williams were, at bottom, but another reformulation of the same contradictory religious liberty impulses.

In 1789 American Presbyterianism* reversed its attachment to the uniformist, establishmentarian side of the Reformed tradition in favor of a much more libertarian doctrine of religious liberty. Declaring that "God alone is Lord of the conscience," the church rejected the authority of the civil magistrate to punish heresy* or convene a church synod or, "in the least, [to] interfere in matters of faith."

DAVID LITTLE

Liturgy, Reformed

Reformed worship* glorifies God,* the holy God, whose gracious salvation* is a free, undeserved gift. Therefore Reformed worship can be described as "objective"; with awe it glorifies the sovereign God, yet it is essentially thankful.

If medieval worship had become an "office," a propitiatory work offered to God securing mercy, Reformation worship was responsive—like the biblical tenth leper who, healed, turned back to praise God. Thus Reformed liturgy is dialogic—we hear of God's graceful saving goodness and respond in gratitude, *charis* and *eucharistia.* Worship is neither a transactional sacrifice nor an awareness of religious experience. God acts, and, empty-handed, we respond to God's goodness in a "sacrifice of praise and thanksgiving."

The Reformers were scarcely innovative in liturgy. They inherited worship from Catholicism and, for the most part, retained the traditional shape of the liturgy. They were more concerned with theology. So they corrected theology, simplified forms, and restored proper congregational participation. But the basic movement of the Mass, from confessional rite to readings of Scripture* to prayers of the faithful to eucharistic celebration, was preserved.

Origins of Reformed worship. The history of Reformed liturgy is a tale of three cities: Strassburg, Geneva, and Zurich.

In 1524 Reformed worship began in Strassburg with the German mass of Diebold Schwartz. Within a few years Schwartz's vernacular Mass included a "common confession," psalms* for congregational singing, and sermons preached *lectio continua* from Scripture. Eucharist was celebrated by ministers behind the table, facing the people. Martin Bucer* further modified the service, adding intercessions and a didactic exhortation prior to the Supper. His *Grund und Ursach* (1524) became a "textbook" for worship in the Reformed tradition. He argued that worship must be founded on "clear and plain declarations of Holy Scripture" and should not attend the physical but be led by the Spirit who impresses God's Word on our hearts, urges prayers, and provides gifts for mutual service.

In 1524 Zurich was in turmoil. Huldrych Zwingli* had written *An Attack on the Canon of the Mass.* He considered the sacrificial Mass "full of Godlessness." Nevertheless Zwingli was liturgically conservative; he retained Latin, much ceremony, vestments, and the like. He did, however, add additional Latin prayers to the Canon. While conservatives in Zurich were uneasy, radical "Anabaptists" were appalled. Under pressure, Zwingli stripped churches of statuary, relics, and ornamentation. Walls were whitewashed and organs silenced so that worshipers could revere the Word of God alone. A year later, Zwingli urged abolition of the Mass in his *Commentary on True and False Religion* (1525). During Holy Week, a new service was introduced based on a medieval "Prone," including prayer, Scripture, and preaching.* Peculiarly, the service retained sung Ave Marias, and a Commemoration of the Dead, and it concluded with Confession of Sins.

Zwingli shaped a radical understanding of the Lord's Supper: Christians do *not* receive the substantial body and blood of Christ. Instead, the Holy Spirit* nourishes common faith* as congregations, aided only by symbols ("The flesh profiteth nothing"), recall redemption on Calvary. Zwingli's quarterly Communion was starkly simple; after Words of Institution, people passed wooden plates around in silence while portions of the Gospel of John were read. Through preaching, Scripture, and the action of the Supper, Christians realized and reaffirmed unity in the body of Christ.

Zwinglian tradition reached Geneva by way of the evangelical ministry of William Farel.* Farel prepared *La manière et fasson* (1524), a worship manual, based on Basel and Zurich practices. In Zwinglian fashion, he exalted the sermon and treated the Supper as a disconnected adjunct. Farel regarded the Eucharist as a testimony of faith and fellowship in the body of Christ. His service involved recital of the promises from God, an invitation to table, a call for self-examination, excommunication of the unworthy, the words of institution, plus an injunction to regard the risen Christ by faith rather than through "visible signs." Such was worship in Geneva when Calvin* visited (1536).

Under the influence of Calvin, "Articles Concerning the Organization of the Church and of Worship at Geneva" were drafted. The document called for a celebration of the Supper every Sunday and church discipline* to excommunicate those who manifestly did not belong to Christ. Calvin had to compromise, accepting monthly celebrations of the sacrament, because former Catholics, used to infrequent reception, bridled at the notion of weekly Eucharists. Reaction to discipline was sharper; Calvin was chased from the city.

Calvin served a French congregation in Strassburg (1538) and became acquainted with the liturgical revisions of Bucer. As a result, Calvin drew on Strassburg tradition in preparing liturgy and a metrical Psalter for his congregation. Thus Calvin's new liturgy incorporated the basic shape of the Mass, Word and Sacrament, rather than the stark "preachiness" of Farel's *La manière.* When the Eucharist was omitted, Calvin's service was an obvious Ante-Communion.

Calvin returned to Geneva bringing with him the Strassburg liturgy, published as *The Form of Prayers.* Once more Calvin urged a weekly Lord's Supper* instead of annual communication ("an invention of the devil"). Calvin was rebuffed when magistrates rejected his proposals, opting for quarterly celebrations. Until his death, Calvin pleaded for weekly observance of the Supper.

Ordering of worship. The structure of Calvin's Strassburg service was as follows:

Call to Worship: Psalm 124:8
Confession of Sin
Declaration of Pardon
Commandments sung with Kyrie Eleison
Prayer of Illumination
Scripture and Sermon
Offering
Intercessions
Paraphrased Lord's Prayer (omitted with Communion)
(When the Supper was omitted, a psalm was sung and people were dismissed with a Blessing.)

Apostles' Creed during Preparation of Elements
Eucharistic Prayer
Words of Institution
Fencing the Table
Recital of Promises
Sursum Corda
Communion
Psalm 138
Thanksgiving Prayer
Nunc Dimittis
Aaronic blessing

In Geneva the rite was abbreviated when people questioned a Declaration of Pardon and the Commandments. Initially the service was conducted at table except for the reading of Scripture and sermon.

Distinctive features of Calvin's order often found in Reformed liturgies may be noted. (1) The Confessional featured acknowledgment of corporate sinfulness, a bold Declaration of Pardon, and a recital of Commandments *following* absolution, expressing Calvin's "third use" of the law.* (2) Before the reading of Scripture, there was a Prayer of Illumination, dovetailing with Calvin's notion that Scripture is interpreted and applied by the Holy Spirit. (3) Eucharist was preceded by a fencing of the table, a reading of the Words of Institution as warrant for celebration, and an acknowledgment of the risen Christ joined to the "Lift up your hearts" of the Sursum Corda.

Character of Reformed liturgy. "No meeting of the church should take place without the Word, prayers, partaking of the Supper, and almsgiving" (*Inst.* 4.17.44). Preaching, prayers, Eucharist, and offering—the terms are an outline of Reformed worship.

Preaching. Reformed liturgy involved biblical preaching. In most congregations there were several Sunday sermons and weekday preaching as well. The Reformers did not separate Scripture and sermon in their thinking; together they were "The Word." They affirmed a "transubstantiation of the word," sure that when Scripture came into contemporary voice, human words became Christ's own word of mercy and command. Preachers often met for group Scripture study and sermon preparation.

Prayers. To Calvin, prayers* were said *and* sung. The true choir in worship *is* the congregation, he observed. So the people's part in worship was sung in melodies not unlike plain song. In particular, metrical psalms were used which Calvin understood as typologically related to Christ and appropriate for Christian praise. In addition, congregations sang Commandments, the Creed, and the Song of Simeon after Communion.

Other prayers in the service were prayers of the people—the Confession, Prayer of Illumination, Intercessions, and a usual Prayer of Thanksgiving.

Eucharist. For Calvin, Eucharist was union with Christ,* specifically with the glorified humanity of the risen Christ. In Communion, by Christ's choice we are joined to one another and to him by the mysterious bonding of the Holy Spirit. With Zwingli, Calvin affirmed that Christ is risen and therefore cannot be locally present in bread and wine. Likewise, with Zwingli, he saw the Supper as a public witness and rehearsal of the Christian life. But Calvin rejected Zwingli's "symbolic" understanding of the sacrament. Like Augustine,* Calvin used realist language for the Eucharist, but he was a "virtualist," affirming that through the Supper we receive saving benefits of Christ's sacrificial death which, in a way, *is* Christ himself for us. Thus, Calvinists* have repeatedly denounced the notion that Eucharistic elements are "bare and naked signs." Since he understood the Supper as union in faith with the risen Christ, Calvin installed preparation for the Lord's Supper, a time of self-examination and instruction, prior to Communions.

Offering. Though there was no presentation of offerings, lest propitiatory meanings attach to giving alms, offerings for the church and the poor were not slighted. Thanksgiving leads us into the world of neighbors in need—hungry, naked, and imprisoned. Offering was part of *eucharistia*—thanksgiving prompted by the self-giving of God in Christ.

J. J. von Allmen, *Worship, Its Theology and Practice* (1965); Y. T. Brilioth, *Eucharistic Faith and Practice* (1931); H. G. Hageman, *Pulpit and Table* (1962); A. I. C. Heron, *Table and Tradition* (1983); W. D. Maxwell, *An Outline of Christian Worship* (1936); *John Knox's Genevan Service Book* (1931); and *History of Worship in the Church of Scotland* (1955); K. McDonnell, *John Calvin, the Church and the Eucharist* (1967); J. Melton, *Presbyterian Worship in America* (1967); J. H. Nichols, *Corporate Worship in the Reformed Tradition* (1968); H. O. Old, *Worship That Is Reformed According to Scripture* (1984); F. Schmidt-Clausing, *Zwingli als Liturgiker* (1952); G. J. van de Poll, *Martin Bucer's Liturgical Ideas* (1954); R. S. Wallace, *Calvin's Doctrine of the Word and Sacrament* (1953).

DAVID G. BUTTRICK

Livingstone, David (1813–1873)

His family were members of an evangelical independent chapel. As a candidate for service with the London Missionary Society,* Livingstone began medical training at the Andersonian Medical School, Glasgow. He had prepared by going to night school while working in the mill. He completed his medical training in London and was sent to South Africa (1841). There he began work in close association with his future father-in-law, Robert Moffat.* He became fluent in Tswana and achieved an unusual intimacy with African people. He soon began to mount expeditions to the north, to find areas of dense population and African communities free from white pressure on their land.

In 1853 Livingstone thought he found this in the Zambesi valley and walked first to Loanda and then back across Africa to Mozambique to try to find an alternative entry route. His now extraordinary popularity gained him leadership of the government's Zambesi Expedition (1858). Tragically he found the area overrun by Portuguese and Arab slavers. The expedition was a failure and his prestige suffered greatly.

Livingstone returned to Africa (1866) obsessed with ending the slavers' work. In these last seven frustrating years and in his lonely death he gained more fame than ever but even less understanding of his beliefs about Africa and its peoples.

T. Jeal, *Livingstone* (1973); A. C. Ross, *Livingstone: Scot and Doctor* (1990).

ANDREW C. ROSS

Lloyd-Jones, David Martyn (1899–1981)

Having come to an explicit Christian commitment in the midst of a short but distinguished career in medicine, Lloyd-Jones assumed the lay pastorate of the Bethlehem Forward Movement Mission (Presbyterian in origin) in a slum of Sandfields, Aberavon, Wales (1927), amid a flurry of media publicity. He joined G. Campbell Morgan as co-pastor of the Westminster Chapel (Congregational*) in London (1939). Fourteen years later he assumed full responsibility for its leadership as it grew into an international congregation of several thousand, continuing there until his retirement (1968). Lloyd-Jones was best known as a rigorously Reformed evangelist, an intense preacher whose sermons were models of closely reasoned biblical exposition, a student of Puritan* theology, and leader within Inter-Varsity Fellowship, the International Fellowship of Evangelical Students, and the British evangelical movement.

C. Catherwood, ed., *Five Evangelical Leaders* (1985); and *Martyn Lloyd-Jones: Chosen by God* (1986); I. H. Murray, *David Martyn Lloyd-Jones: The First Forty Years (1899–1939)* (1982).

PHILIP W. BUTIN

London Conference *see* Baptists, Particular

London Missionary Society

Founded as the Missionary Society (1795), it declared that its basic purpose was to send to the heathen, not presbyterianism,* independency, episcopacy, or any other form of church order and government, but the glorious gospel of the blessed God. The name London Missionary Society was adopted in 1818. It became principally a society for English Congregationalists* and recently has been known as the Congregational Council for World Mission.

The first missionary enterprise began in Tahiti (1797), but little progress was made before the arrival of John Williams* (1817), a brilliant linguist whose Rarotongan NT was ready in 1834. He was killed and eaten by Erromangan natives (1839), apparently in revenge for earlier cruelties by an English crew. Despite this, it was claimed at the end of the nineteenth century that heathenism had practically disappeared from Polynesia.

A mission to Sierra Leone (1797–98) in cooperation with the Edinburgh and Glasgow Missionary Societies* was short-lived but missions to South Africa* prospered under John Philip* from Aberdeen. The most famous African missionaries were Robert Moffat* and David Livingstone.* Work was carried out at Bengal, Madras, Travancore, and the United Provinces of India (1804), and Robert Morrison* was the first missionary to enter China (1807).

N. Goodall, *A History of the London Missionary Society 1895–1945* (1954); R. Lovett, *History of the London Missionary Society 1795–1895*, 2 vols. (1899).

HENRY R. SEFTON

Lord's Supper

Definition. The preferred Reformation term for the sacrament or ordinance that Jesus instituted at the last supper. The Latin is *coena Domini*; the French, *sainte cène*; and the German, (*Heiliges*) *Abendmahl* or *Herrenmahl.* Zwingli* also liked "Eucharist" (the title of the First Helvetic Confession* art. 23 in Lat.), which expresses the element of gratitude (Gr. *eucharistia*) in response to grace* (*charis*). As another meaningful alternative, the Anglican Prayer Book and the Scots Confession* (art. 21; cf. Gallican [French]* Confession, art. 36) use "Holy Communion," that is, communion with Christ's body and blood (WCF,* 29.1) and also the communion of believers in Christ. The Reformers unanimously abandoned the medieval term "Mass" because of its intrinsic meaninglessness and dubious theological and practical associations.

The Supper is the second of the two dominical or evangelical sacraments, that is, sacraments that the Lord appointed and that have a sign, word, and gospel promise. The command "Do this" constitutes the appointment, the repeated "This is" forms the basic word, and the promise is that "with his crucified body and shed blood" Christ "feeds and nourishes my soul to everlasting life" (HC,* q. 75). The five observances that the medieval church added to produce seven sacraments are not in this sense "sacraments of the Gospel" (Anglican, art. 25), that is, "actions ordained by God himself . . . whereby he seals up his promises" (Second Helvetic Confession,* ch. 19). They may serve a profitable purpose, but they lack the features that give Baptism* and the Supper this distinctive rank.

Covenant. As Zwingli (see *Zwingli and Bullinger*, ed. G. W. Bromiley, LCC 24:131) and Calvin (*Inst.* 4.14.6) both say, the sacraments are covenant* signs. They resemble the covenant signs of the OT (LCC 24:138ff.). When God covenanted with Abraham and Israel, God gave them the symbolic actions of circumcision and the passover as perpetual pledges. The covenant contained both a promise and a command: "I will be your God and you shall be my people." The covenant signs thus testify to God's self-giving to his people and to his people's self-giving to God. Jesus fulfilled the covenant on both sides. The NT covenant is thus the same in substance, but the administration changes, and two new signs replace the old (WCF, 7.5ff.).

The NT itself supports the equation of the covenants. In Colossians 2, the thing signified in circumcision and Baptism is the same, and Jesus instituted the Supper in a passover setting. The most obvious difference explains the change. The OT signs involve blood-shedding, prefiguring Christ's death. The NT signs are bloodless, representing the blood that was shed once for all. "With the shedding of the precious blood of Christ the shedding of physical blood ceased." We now have "most friendly elements and signs" (LCC 24:132), "more firm and durable," but also "more simple, nothing so painful" (Second Helvetic, ch. 19). The substance, however, remains unchanged.

Reformed theology in the seventeenth century at times advocated an original covenant of works in Eden (WCF, 7.2). In some versions this also had two sacraments, the two trees. When disobedience annulled it, God set up the covenant of grace (WCF, 7.3). For the most part, however, churches have not pressed this speculative concept. The covenant of grace is the biblical covenant, promulgated in the OT and fulfilled in the NT. The common substance, as the Second Helvetic Confession perspicaciously observes, is Christ himself, "the only Mediator and Savior of the faithful" (ch. 19). The covenant is no abstraction. God fulfilled it in Christ. In token, God gave the prophetic signs of circumcision and the passover and the corresponding apostolic signs of Baptism and the Lord's Supper.

Visible Word. Word and Sacrament are two aspects of the one proclamation of the gospel. In Augustine's* phrase, the sacrament is a "visible word." It supplements the audible word as a sign and action that vividly illustrates what the spoken or written word proclaims.

As a visible word, the Supper is a divine accommodation* to human weakness. Zwingli called it a bridle to check the senses from dashing off in pursuit of their own desires (LCC 24:264). Calvin, who called the Word itself "God's baby talk," says that "because we are of flesh" we have it "under things of flesh . . . to instruct us according to our dull capacity" (*Inst.* 4.14.6). It is given "the better to present to our senses" what God "signifies to us by his word" and "works inwardly in our hearts" (Belgic Confession, art. 33).

The Supper engages all the senses, not hearing alone. Calvin stressed the visual side, a painted picture or reflection in a mirror (*Inst.* 4.14.6). Zwingli saw a larger involvement. We hear God's voice in the sacramental word, see the broken body and the shed blood in bread and wine, touch as we take in our hands, smell and taste as we receive. The Supper claims all the senses for the work of faith* (LCC 24:263–64). Indeed, we do more than perceive. We are caught up in an action. We enact our reception and self-commitment to God.

The visible and audible words belong together. Addition of the word makes the sacrament (Augustine). But the word must be more than mumbled and unintelligible repetition (*Inst.* 4.17.39). It must be clear and understandable proclamation which declares the meaning. By word and sign God gives himself objectivity in the sensory world to solve the problem of knowing divine things. If word and sign conceal, they also reveal, communicating the supersensory by the sensory.

Stress on the audible word and a learned ministry might seem to entail disparagement of the Supper, or its observance only for hallowed associations. Calvin, for all his Renaissance learning, disagreed. "So great is our native inability to know God," he stated, that by the sacraments God "attests his good will and love toward us more expressly than by word" (*Inst.* 4.14.6).

Sacrifice. The Supper graphically depicts Christ's self-offering for us. Bread and wine symbolize for Zwingli the reconciliation of God and the human race in and through Christ (LCC 24:263). The body was broken and the blood shed "as certainly as I see . . . the bread of the Lord broken for me, and the cup communicated to me" (HC, q. 75). The Supper is a seal "that the very body of the Lord was given up for us, and his blood shed for the remission of our sins" (Second Helvetic, ch. 19). Its function is to "offer and set forth Christ to us" (*Inst.* 4.14.17).

Exhibiting the unique self-sacrifice of Christ for sin,* the Supper is not itself an expiatory sacrifice (WCF, 29.2). The elements are not immolated, as medieval theology proposed, to remit the temporal penalties of post-baptismal sin. Christ's offering is the "perfect redemption, propitiation, and satisfaction, for all the sins of the whole world" (Anglican, art. 31). Priests are not "Mediators betwixt Christ and his Kirk" (Scots Confession, ch. 22). This belief, said Calvin, dishonors Christ, suppresses his cross and passion, and brings forgetfulness of his death and its benefits (*Inst.* 4.18.2–6).

The Supper, if it does not specifically re-present or plead Christ's sacrifice to God, undoubtedly represents it to us. It is also our own sacrifice of the praise and thanksgiving that we "both owe and render" to God (*Inst.* 4.18.13). It is "a spiritual oblation of all possible praise unto God" (WCF, 29.2). We thus pray God to "accept this our sacrifice of praise and thanksgiving." In so doing, we offer ourselves to God as "a reasonable, holy and living sacrifice," which is in fact our "bounden duty and service" (Anglican Prayer Book; cf. *Inst.* 4.18.16).

Presence. Beneath the medieval concept of a eucharistic sacrifice lay belief in the real presence of Christ in the elements. By consecration, it was held, the bread is substantially the body of Christ and the wine his blood. Naturally we still see, touch, taste, and smell bread and wine, for the so-called accidents remain intact. But the substance has supposedly changed (transubstantiation). Hence the priest offers Christ's body and blood on the altar, and communicants receive them by receiving the elements.

At the Reformation, Luther attempted a mediating view, rejecting a change of substance, but stating that Christ is substantially present in, with, and under the bread and wine. The Reformed, in contrast, rejected both those forms of presence. As Zwingli insisted, Christ in his humanity is now at the Father's right hand and will return only in his eschatological glory (LCC 24:214ff., 256ff.). Even at the first institution, when still present on earth, Jesus obviously was not present simultaneously both in person and in bread and wine.

This rejection does not imply Christ's absence from the Supper. The disagreement concerns only the mode. There is no need for a sham miracle by differentiation of substance and accidents. As Zwingli noted, Christ is present according to his omnipresent deity, which includes the humanity in virtue of the unity of the person (LCC 24:256ff.). More boldly, the Belgic Confession (art. 35) speaks of a partaking of "the proper natural body." The Scots Confession, too, refers to an eating and drinking of Christ's "flesh and blood" (art. 21), and the WCF states that Christ is "really, but spiritually present" (WCF, 29.7).

The secret lies in "the operation of the Holy Ghost" (Belgic, art. 35). As Calvin said, the power of the Spirit "towers above all our senses" (*Inst.* 4.14.10). The Spirit unites things separated in space, raising us up to Christ, and making bread and wine our spiritual food and drink. The mode of the presence is not that of the incarnation,* resurrection,* or return. It is that of presence by the Spirit. Himself in heaven, Christ feeds us "by the secret and incomprehensible power of his Spirit" (Gallican, art. 36).

The senses do not perceive the presence. It defies clear conceptualization. No one, said Calvin, "should measure its sublimity by the little measure of my childishness." We can only "break forth in wonder at this mystery, which plainly neither the mind is able to conceive nor the tongue to express" (*Inst.* 4.17.7). Yet the presence is real. It is the presence of the whole Christ, proclaiming his sacrifice, proffering fellowship with himself, and providing nourishment to eternal life.

Benefits. As a visible word, the Supper testifies to the historicity of Christ's crucifixion and resurrection (Zwingli; LCC 24:262). The material nature of the elements rules out false spiritualizing. Here is sensory historicity. The Word was made flesh. The Word takes bread and wine and hands them to us in attestation of the facticity of his saving person and work.

As this testimony, the Supper confirms and augments faith. Zwingli amended his initial rejection of this benefit (LCC 24:138, 263ff.). The confessions agreed that the sacraments are "sure witnesses . . . by the which" God "doth . . . strengthen and confirm our Faith in him" (Anglican, art. 25). For Calvin, it was the office of the sacraments to "sustain, nourish, confirm, and increase our faith" (*Inst.* 4.14.7). Does the Supper also "quicken faith" (Anglican, art. 25)? Is it a converting ordinance? Why not? Calvin stated that it might "beget faith" so long as the word is preached (4.14.4). Communion seasons can be great evangelistic occasions, as in the Scottish Highlands in the nineteenth century.

The Supper also grants fellowship with Christ. "Christ communicates himself with all his benefits to us" (Belgic, art. 35). In it we have "conjunction with Christ Jesus" (Scots, art. 21). Union with Christ* is the "special fruit" of the Supper (*Inst.* 4.17.2). There we are "one with Christ and Christ with us" (Anglican *BCP*).

This fellowship embraces spiritual nourishment, as the symbolism indicates. The HC expresses this beautifully: "With his crucified body and shed blood he himself feeds and nourishes my soul to everlasting life as certainly as I receive . . . and taste . . . the bread and cup of the Lord" (HC, q. 75). Christ is in fact the "substance" of the sacrament, so this is a "substantial eating" (*Inst.* 4.14.16). The nourishment is real, for "Christ himself . . . delivered up for us . . . is that special thing and substance of the Supper" (Second Helvetic, ch. 21).

Mutual Christian fellowship is a final benefit. "Godly souls" have here a "witness of our growth into one body with Christ" (*Inst.* 4.17.2). Distinctions vanish at the Lord's Table. Old and young, rich and poor, men and women, believers of all nations, races, or classes—all gather at the one table as members of the one body. Assured of God's forgiveness* and forgiving one another, they go out to live and work together as the one fellowship of reconciliation, anticipating the consummated fellowship of God's eternal kingdom.*

Efficacy. Medieval teaching deduced from Christ's presence by transubstantiation an automatic efficacy. In a valid celebration, all who receive the elements receive Christ, whether to blessing or, in the case of unabsolved mortal sin, to condemnation.

The Reformers did not deny sacramental efficacy. "God gives us really and in fact that which he there sets forth to us" (Gallican, art. 37; cf. Belgic, art. 35). But they rejected automatic efficacy. All receive the sign, not all the thing signified (Belgic, art. 35). Christ proffers himself to all, but he is received only to salvation. If some miss the benefits, it is because they do not receive Christ. Condemnation comes, not by receiving Christ unworthily, but by despising him (*Inst.* 4.17.33).

The efficacy of the Supper relates to the word. As there is no Supper apart from the word, "whatever benefit may come to us from the Supper requires the Word" (*Inst.* 4.17.39). Nor is the word merely the word of institution (WCF, 37.3). It is the "living preaching" which "reveals its effectiveness in the fulfillment of what it promises" (*Inst.* 4.17.39).

The efficacy relates to the Spirit (Gallican, art. 37). Partaking is dependent on the "power of the Spirit" (Belgic, art. 35). We are partakers "through the working of the Holy Ghost" (HC, q. 79). Sacramental efficacy implies the "inner grace of the Spirit" (*Inst.* 4.14.17). We seriously wrong the Spirit if we do not attribute partaking of Christ to his "incomprehensible power" (4.17.33).

Efficacy relates finally to faith. Christ offers spiritual food to all, but only "the faithful, in the right use of the Table," have fellowship with him (Scots, art. 31). Those who are "void of a lively faith" "press with their teeth" but "in no wise are they partakers of Christ" (Anglican, art. 29). Faith need not be perfect. It needs confirming and augmenting. The Supper is "medicine for the sick, solace for sinners" (*Inst.* 4.17.42). Yet without faith, we receive no more than the sign, doing "despite unto the death of Christ" (Second Helvetic, ch. 21).

In sum, the Lord's Supper means efficacious union with Christ* when it includes proclamation of the Word, is administered in the power of the Spirit, and is received with the faith of humility and obedience.

Administration. As a visible word, the Supper demands clear administration with open actions and in an understandable language. Elaborate ceremonial, though impressive, can hinder rather than help by obscuring the central event which is simple. As a meal, not a sacrifice, the Supper calls for a table rather than an altar. Bread and wine are the essentials, served in appropriate but not necessarily costly vessels. Essential too is rehearsal of the words of institution and proclamation of the associated gospel promises. A prayer of consecration and thanksgiving, a hymn or psalm, and a common confession of faith, also of sin, all belong suitably to the administration. Adoration and reservation of the consecrated elements, and their being carried in procession, have wrong theological implications and easily nurture superstition (Anglican, art. 28).

Properly, the Supper should be administered "very often, and at least once a week" (*Inst.* 4.17.43). Unhappily the medieval practice of weekly Mass but infrequent Communion still exerts a lingering influence. Non-communicating attendance makes no sense. Nor does the private Mass which supposedly reduces purgatorial pains (Anglican, art. 31; WCF, 29.4). It is a denial of communion (*Inst.* 4.18.8) and encourages cupidity (Second Helvetic, ch. 21) and error. By Christ's institution, all communicants receive the cup as well as the bread. Reasons given for its denial to the nonordained are flimsy (Scots, art. 21; *Inst.* 4.17.47ff.). Matters such as the time of administration may be arranged as is most convenient, and rules should not be imposed to cover personal practices, for example, the rule of fasting communion.

Since Christ himself is the host and true minister, the unworthiness of a human minister, though reprehensible, does not affect the sacrament's validity (Anglican, art. 26). Nevertheless, since faith is a prerequisite of efficacy, communicants should examine themselves, and obvious unbelievers and flagrant and impenitent offenders may be debarred (Scots, art. 23). Yet "fencing of the tables" must not be pressed too far in relation to either self or others. To wait until fully worthy, or to exclude for every offense, is to deprive the Supper of its evangelical purpose (*Inst.* 4.17.41–42). The Supper is not primarily a disciplinary tool. It is a means of grace. God has instituted it in grace, not judgment. In the power of God's Spirit, God uses it to build up the people of God in their new life in Christ and in a solidarity of fellowship and service.

GEOFFREY W. BROMILEY

Luther, Martin (1483–1546)

Though Luther was honored among the Reformed for his contributions to the theology and reformation of the church generally, the Reformed thought he did not go far or deep enough in his changes. The attack on indulgences and papal power, the assertion of justification* through faith* alone, and the authority of *sola Scriptura* have been applauded and affirmed by all Protestants. Equally supported by Calvinists was Luther's controversy with Erasmus* over bondage of the will where Luther asserted a position not far from Calvin's* double predestination* (though grounded differently for Luther in the "hidden God").

The initial point of dissension came with a dispute over the Lord's Supper*—first with Luther's colleague Andreas Bodenstein von Karlstadt and then with Huldrych Zwingli* and John Oecolampadius.* Disagreements focused on the bodily presence of Christ (whether in the bread and wine or in heaven) and the sacramental benefits (forgiveness,* life and salvation*—according to Luther). Attempts to heal the split began with the Marburg Colloquy* (1529), the Wittenberg Concord (1536), and the Zurich-Geneva Consensus Tigurinus* (1549).

Philipp Melanchthon's Augsburg Confession, to which Calvin subscribed while in Strassburg, was described as the only "confession" written in the sixteenth century: all the rest were church "constitutions" (G. Hendry). The growing ecumenical role of Melanchthon, Luther's colleague at the University of Wittenberg, brought him—with Luther's initial encouragement—into dialogue with Martin Bucer,* eventuating in the Wittenberg Concord and the Cologne Book (1543), the latter producing serious tension with Luther. Melanchthon's revision of the Augsburg Confession (1540; the *Variata*) and his work with Calvin at the Regensburg (Ratisbon) Colloquy (1541–42) brought Melanchthon to a more open position on the Lord's Supper. But Calvin was troubled by Melanchthon's more synergistic position on human bondage, his rejection of double predestination, and even Melanchthon's own "deterministic" position which he had affirmed in his *Loci communes* (1521; a book that Luther had suggested, with characteristic exaggeration, should be in the canon).

Differences over baptismal regeneration* (never a major controversy), predestination, the real presence and benefits of Christ in the Lord's Supper, along with certain christological* implications (bringing charges from Lutherans of Nestorianism and against Lutherans of Monophysitism), and the related issue of whether unbelievers receive Christ's body in the sacrament (*manducatio impiorum*) became hardened. In the Formula of Concord (1577) the Lutherans tried to settle their internal theological controversies and establish their own theological identity, in part by differentiating their positions over against the Reformed. Thus double predestination was rejected and single predestination affirmed. The "crypto-Calvinism"* with which Melanchthon was charged was met with the Formula's eucharistic Christology and the Lutheran shibboleth of Christ's body and blood "in, with, and under" the bread and wine. Ironically, John Williamson Nevin's* interpretation of Calvin's view of the real presence (*The Mystical Presence* [1846]) was characterized by a contemporary Princeton theologian as "crypto-Lutheran"! The publication of collected Lutheran confessional writings as *The Book of Concord* (1580) tended to reinforce the Lutheran-Reformed barriers as they shaped Lutheran identity.

Some Lutherans and Reformed were driven farther apart, even emigrating, because of their forced merger in the Prussian Union Church (1817). The experience of World War II, the fellowship of protest and suffering in the Confessing Church and its Barmen Declaration,* led after the war to the Arnoldshain Theses and the Leuenberg Agreement which has established intercommunion between most European Lutherans and Reformed. Dialogues in the United States since the 1960s are working toward such fellowship.

P. Althaus, *The Theology of Martin Luther* (1966); H. Oberman, *Luther: Man Between God and the Devil* (1989); H. Sasse, *This Is My Body* (1959); L. W. Spitz and W. Lohff, eds., *Discord, Dialogue, and Concord* (1977).

RALPH W. QUERE

Macartney, Clarence Edward Noble (1879–1957)

Descended from Scottish Covenanters,* Macartney was educated at the Universities of Denver and Wisconsin and at Princeton Seminary and Princeton University. Ordained in the Presbyterian Church in the U.S.A. (1905), he served in Paterson, New Jersey (1905–14), Philadelphia (1914–27), and Pittsburgh (1927–53). When elected to the chair of apologetics at Princeton Seminary (1925), he chose to remain in the pastorate.

In 1922 Macartney gained national recognition by leading the conservative response to Harry Emerson Fosdick's famous sermon, "Shall the Fundamentalists Win?" Convinced that orthodox Christianity was seriously imperiled by modernist inroads in the church, Macartney worked to ensure maintenance of traditional doctrinal standards. As Moderator of the 1924 Presbyterian General Assembly he furthered the fundamentalist cause.

Macartney sought to preserve orthodox Christianity in the church and maintain Christianity's influence on American culture. Deeply troubled by cultural and social changes that transformed America after World War I, he became an outspoken opponent of divorce, the decline of the family altar, Sabbath desecration, liquor, and the teaching of biological evolution.

After Princeton Seminary was reorganized (1929), Macartney supported the founding of Westminster Seminary to preserve the "Princeton tradition." Yet when his militant conservative ally, J. Gresham Machen,* left the church (1929), Macartney remained in the denomination. Macartney continued to try to further the conservative cause through preaching and lecturing, sermon publications, books and pamphlets, nurturing numerous assistant pastors, and leadership of the conservative "League of Faith."

C. Macartney, *The Making of a Minister* (1961); B. J. Longfield, *The Presbyterian Controversy: Fundamentalists, Modernists, and Moderates* (1991).

BRADLEY J. LONGFIELD

McCheyne, Robert Murray (1813–1843)

One of the most godly ministers and powerful preachers of the Church of Scotland, McCheyne was minister of St. Peter's, Dundee (1836). He went to Palestine with a Church of Scotland delegation along with his friend and biographer Andrew Bonar* (1839). While McCheyne was away, revival broke out in his church under William Burns. Upon his return, McCheyne threw himself into the work. This broke his health, and he died two months before the Disruption.*

A. A. Bonar, *Memoir and Remains of the Rev. Robert Murray M'Cheyne* (1844; new enl. ed. 1892; repr. 1966); A. Smellie, *Robert Murray McCheyne* (3rd ed. 1913); J. C. Smith, *Robert Murray M'Cheyne* (1910).

A. T. B. MCGOWAN

McCosh, James (1811–1894)

A leader of the Scottish Free Church movement, McCosh was parish minister in Brechin and Arbroath (1835–52), professor of logic and metaphysics at Queen's College, Belfast, Ireland (1852–68), and president of Princeton College (1868–88). Throughout his career, he tried to fortify an evangelical Protestantism rooted in the general tenets of Reformed theology.

McCosh was born in Patna, Scotland, and attended local parish schools and the University of Glasgow. Preparing for a ministerial career at the University of Edinburgh, McCosh came under the influence of Thomas Chalmers,* the most dynamic leader and important intellectual defender of the rising Scottish evangelical movement. As the Church of Scotland underwent a schism that sundered even local parishes, McCosh worked hard for the evangelical cause. His commitment grew from his sense that Scotland's age of Moderatism, of rational intellectual influences in the church and state control, had sapped the country's religious energy. When the Free Church of Scotland emerged (1843), McCosh marched with the procession that exited Edinburgh's St. Andrew's Church and declared its independence.

In his philosophical writings McCosh tried to define a middle position between intellectual movements he believed eroded authentic religious belief. He wished to resist the influence of French materialism and British empiricism and worked within the outlines of the common sense philosophy* of Thomas Reid* to defend an intuitional philosophy based on consciousness and introspection. Also, he wanted to secure Reid's doctrine of realism on a surer footing. Second, McCosh, as a late voice in the Scottish school, wished to undo the influence of Sir William Hamilton, a professor at the University of Edinburgh who influenced religious thinkers such as Henry Mansel. Hamilton's philosophy of the unconditioned had defined the absolute as an idea not apprehensible by human intellect—in short, a "negative" idea. McCosh associated Hamilton's position with certain dangerous trends in German thought, especially Kantianism. He believed these had encouraged speculative directions in religious thinking that insufficiently rooted ideas of God in realism. McCosh's resolution of this problem, and his contribution to the philosophical underpinnings of Reformed thinking, lay in his effort to ground the idea of the absolute in a positive notion of the mind, one that serves also to heighten a sense of human dependency on divine assistance.

At Princeton, McCosh worked to modernize the college curriculum and reinforce its evangelical purposes through student revivals. With his transatlantic connections he became an active organizer for the WARC* (1877).

J. D. Hoeveler, Jr., "Evangelical Ecumenicism: James McCosh and the Intellectual Origins of the World Alliance of Reformed Churches," *JPH* 55 (Spring 1977): 36–56; and *James McCosh and the Scottish Intellectual Tradition from Glasgow to Princeton* (1981).

J. DAVID HOEVELER, JR.

Maccovius, Johannes (1588–1644)

Polish nobleman, educated in Germany (under Bartholomäus Keckermann). Maccovius studied theology at Franeker (under Lubbertus), where he became professor of theology. He was a pioneer Reformed scholastic, censored at the Synod of Dort* for his extravagant use of scholasticism rather than for his theology. He was supralapsarian* and defended the *phrases duriores* (double predestination). Both his views and his methodology remained influential in the seventeenth century.

A. Kuyper, *Johannes Maccovius* (1899); J. Veenhof and F. Postma, "Disputen Omtrent de Predestinatie: Het Logisch denken van Johannes Maccovius (1588–1644)," in *Universiteit te Franeker, 1585–1611*, ed. G. T. Jensma et al. (1985), 249–63.

DERK VISSER

McGuffey, William Holmes (1800–1873)

Educator and author of children's readers. McGuffey was ordained to the Presbyterian ministry in frontier Ohio. He taught at Miami University (Ohio; 1820–36) until becoming president of Cincinnati College. He later moved to teach at the University of Virginia (1845–73). At Miami, McGuffey published the first of his graded *Eclectic Readers*, written to teach explicit moral purposes. The *Readers* sold over 122 million copies.

McGuffey demonstrates the evangelical desire to shape nineteenth-century American society and the realization that education's role was formative in building society's values.

RICK NUTT

Machen, J(ohn) Gresham (1881–1937)

Militant conservative Presbyterian educator and NT scholar Machen was the son of southern parents and was raised in a cultured and pious Old School Presbyterian home in Baltimore. He studied at Johns Hopkins University, Princeton Seminary, Princeton University, Marburg, and Göttingen.

In Germany, Machen found Wilhelm Herrmann's liberal theology extremely appealing and underwent a religious crisis. Nonetheless, he accepted a Princeton Seminary NT position (1906) and, influenced especially by B. B. Warfield,* gradually became a devout adherent of the Princeton Theology.* Machen was ordained in the Presbyterian Church in the U.S.A. (1914) and became assistant professor of NT at Princeton (1915). He published two major NT studies, *The Origin of Paul's Religion* (1921) and *The Virgin Birth of Christ* (1930), both of which reflected his allegiance to the Princeton tradition.

Machen is best known for defending the cause of conservative Christianity during the fundamentalist/modernist controversy* in the Presbyterian Church (1920s–1930s). After World War I, concerned about the increasing assertiveness of modernism in the Presbyterian Church and the growth of secularism in American culture, Machen published a landmark volume, *Christianity and Liberalism* (1923). He argued that liberalism or modernism was a completely different faith from Christianity and that liberals ought to admit their differences and withdraw from the church. Failing this, true Christians might be forced to secede. At the very least, he insisted, Christians should oppose modernism at every turn.

As controversy between liberals and militant conservatives grew in the Presbyterian Church (1920s), Machen emerged more fully as a fundamentalist party leader. In print and pulpit he worked to rally militant conservatives and oppose modernist efforts to win tolerance from the church.

When Princeton Seminary was reorganized to allow a more inclusive theological position (1929), Machen led in founding Westminster Seminary to preserve the "Old Princeton" tradition. Westminster was to train "specialists in the Bible" who would be willing to battle against the secularizing trends of the day.

Becoming ever more suspicious of modernist influences of the church's mission program, Machen founded the Independent Board for Presbyterian Foreign Missions (1933). Despite efforts of fundamentalist allies like Clarence Macartney* to convince him to moderate his stance, Machen refused to obey a General Assembly* injunction to sever connections with the rival mission board and was defrocked (1936). Soon he led in founding the Presbyterian Church of America (later the Orthodox Presbyterian Church). He died in Bismarck, North Dakota, while on a trip to encourage support for the fledgling denomination.

B. J. Longfield, *The Presbyterian Controversy: Fundamentalists, Modernists, and Moderates* (1991); N. Stonehouse, *J. Gresham Machen: A Biographical Memoir* (1954).

BRADLEY J. LONGFIELD

Mackay, John Alexander (1889–1983)

Presbyterian clergyman, missionary, educator, and ecumenist. Mackay was born in Inverness, Scotland, and graduated from Aberdeen (1912) and Princeton Seminary (1915). He spent 1915–16 at the University of Madrid with Miguel de Unamuno, the existentialist and mystic. He was ordained in the Free Church of Scotland and went to Peru as an educational missionary (1916), receiving a doctorate from the National University in Peru (1918) and becoming the first Protestant to occupy its chair of philosophy (1925). He then worked for the South American Federation of the YMCA (1926–32).

Robert E. Speer* encouraged Mackay to join the Presbyterian Church's Board of Foreign Missions as Secretary for Latin America and Africa (1932). Mackay was active in the 1937 Oxford Conference and the WCC.* Speer was also instrumental in Mackay's call to Princeton, where he served as president and professor of ecumenics (1936–1959). Mackay's Christocentric theology infused his irenic and egalitarian spirit to rebuild the faculty after the fundamentalist/liberal controversies* of the previous decade. His enthusiasm for ecumenical Christianity was contagious, and the seminary prospered.

In 1944 Mackay founded and edited *Theology Today*. He was Moderator of the General Assembly (1953) and president of the World Presbyterian Alliance (1954–59). Several of Mackay's thirteen books were written in Spanish.

T. Gillespie, "John Alexander Mackay: A Centennial Remembrance," *Princeton Seminary Bulletin* 10, no. 3 (1989): 171–81; E. Jurji, ed., *The Ecumenical Era in Church and Society* (1959).

STEPHEN D. CROCCO

Mackintosh, H. R. (1870–1936)

Professor of systematic theology at New College,* Edinburgh (from 1904). He is remembered as translator of the major works of Albrecht Ritschl and Friedrich Schleiermacher;* as an important interpreter of German theology; and, along with P. T. Forsyth,* as a "Barthian before Barth." He was one of the first Anglo-Saxon theologians to call attention to Barth. A student of Wilhelm Herrmann and Martin Kähler, Mackintosh steadily moved away from Ritschlian liberalism and sought to work out his own view which incorporated some Ritschlian insights with traditional and nineteenth-century Reformed perspectives, particularly in his Christology* and soteriology. His later theology strongly resembled the views of Calvin* and Knox,* as well as Barth, and was characterized by a concern for preaching* and evangelism.* His distinctive combination of exegetical, historical, and dogmatic interests prepared the way for the later contributions of his students, Donald Baillie,* George Hendry, and T. F. Torrance.*

H. R. Mackintosh, *The Doctrine of the Person of Jesus Christ* (1912); *The Christian Experience of Forgiveness* (1927); and *Types of Modern Theology* (1937); T. W. Gardiner, "A Tribute to Professor H. R. Mackintosh," *SJT* 5 (1952): 225–36; J. W. Leitch, *A Theology of Transition* (1952); R. R. Redman, Jr., "H. R. Mackintosh's Contribution to Christology and Soteriology in the Twentieth Century," *SJT* 41 (1988): 517–34; T. F. Torrance, "H. R. Mackintosh: A Theologian of the Cross," *Scottish Bulletin of Evangelical Theology* 5 (1987): 160–73.

ROBERT R. REDMAN, JR.

MacLeod, George Fielden (1895–1991)

Founder of the Iona Community.* MacLeod was born into a notable Scottish ecclesiastical dynasty and educated at Winchester, Oxford, and Edinburgh. After serving in World War I, he studied for the Church of Scotland ministry. He was called (1930) from the fashionable St. Cuthbert's Church in Edinburgh's west end to Govan Old Parish Church, Glasgow.

MacLeod became a pacifist and socialist (1930s) and an outstanding radio preacher. He founded the Iona Community (1938) and was the first Presbyterian to occupy the pulpit of St. Paul's Cathedral in London. He became the first Fosdick Visiting Professor at Union Seminary (N.Y.; 1954) and Moderator of the General Assembly* of the Church of Scotland (1957), the sixth of the MacLeod dynasty to be so honored. He was elevated to the House of Lords (1967), resigning as Iona Community leader, and became president of the International Fellowship of Reconciliation.

MacLeod won the Templeton International Prize for Progress in Religion and is one of the most influential and controversial British church leaders of this century. His Catholic sense of worship and radical political views brought early criticism, though he insisted he was reviving truly Reformed practices.

G. F. MacLeod, *Govan Calling* (1934); *We Shall Rebuild* (1944); and *Only One Way Left* (1956); R. Ferguson, *George MacLeod* (1990).

RONALD FERGUSON

Macleod, Norman (1812–1871)

Scottish Presbyterian clergyman, journalist, and zealous evangelical minister among the working classes of lowland Scotland. At the Disruption (1843), after a prolonged conflict between church and state over ecclesiastical patronage, Macleod remained in the establishment—working to revive its missionary outreach and making his Glasgow parish a model for urban ministry. Opposed to puritanism, including rigid Sabbatarianism,* Macleod helped shape the broad-church evangelicalism predominating in late Victorian Scottish Presbyterianism—especially as editor of the popular religious magazine *Good Words*.

D. Macleod, *Memoir of Norman Macleod* (1876).

STEWART J. BROWN

Makemie, Francis (1658?-1708)

Scots-Irish Presbyterian clergyman who came to New England (1683), Makemie is called "the father of the Presbyterian Church" in America primarily because of his successful itinerant ministry culminating in the first American presbytery (1706). He contributed significantly to colonial religious toleration. He was arrested by the governor of New York for unlicensed preaching and termed a "Disturber of Governments" (1707). Makemie's spirited defense of religious liberty resulted in his acquittal (he was forced to pay the expensive court costs) and enhanced the Presbyterian image among colonial dissenters.

R. DOUGLAS BRACKENRIDGE

Malan, [Henri-Abraham] César (1787–1864)

Genevan Reformed pastor, evangelist, and hymn writer. Malan was ordained in the Church of Geneva (1810) and taught in the Latin school (1809–18). Because of a conflict with the church, he opened his own "chapelle de Témoignage" (1820) where he followed a dogmatic Calvinism.* He traveled extensively and is responsible for over a thousand hymns, making him the founder of the hymn movement in French Reformed churches. He joined the Scottish Presbyterian Church, and the University of Edinburgh granted him an honorary D.D. (1826).

H. v. d. Goltz, *Genève religieuse* (1862); C. Malan (son), *The Life . . . C. Malan* (1869); Léon Maury, *Le réveil religieux*, 2 vols. (1892).

JOHN B. RONEY

Manton, Thomas (1620–1677)

An outstanding pulpit expositor, Manton studied at Oxford and began his ministry at Stoke-Newington (1644). He was clerk at the Westminster Assembly* and was called to St. Paul's Covent Garden (1656), one of London's leading Puritan pulpits. Strongly Presbyterian, Manton was ejected (1662) in spite of attempts of James II to win him for episcopacy. He continued to preach and was imprisoned. Twenty-two volumes of his works were published (1870–75), and his classic commentary on the Letter of James is still in print.

HUGHES OLIPHANT OLD

Marburg Colloquy

A conference between Luther,* Zwingli,* and other Reformation leaders to promote political unity and theological consensus among various Protestant parties. Convened by Landgrave Philip of Hesse at his castle in Marburg (1529), the meeting included Luther, Philipp Melanchthon, Justus Jonas, Johann Brenz, Kaspar Cruciger, and Andreas Osiander on the Lutheran side, and John Oecolampadius,* Wolfgang Capito,* Martin Bucer,* and Johnnes Sturm who, together with Zwingli, emphasized the symbolic significance of the Lord's Supper.* The two sides agreed on fourteen of the fifteen Marburg articles embracing such cardinal tenets as the Trinity,* person of Christ, justification* by faith,* and rejection of transubstantiation. On the nature of Christ's presence in the Supper, however, Luther and Zwingli sharply disagreed.

The breakdown at Marburg led to a widening rift between the Lutheran and Reformed churches. Luther continued to oppose any confessional alliance with "sacramentarians," as he called those who opposed his eucharistic theology. Zwingli defended his view that the controverted words of institution, *Hoc est corpus meum*, should be understood as "This signifies my body," since the literal body of Christ was in heaven at the right hand of the Father. Bucer, and later Calvin,* proposed a mediating position between the Lutheran and Zwinglian alternatives. Still, differences in eucharistic theology and practice remained a serious obstacle to Protestant unity long past the Reformation era.

T. George, *Theology of the Reformers* (1988); W. Köhler, *Zwingli und Luther: Ihr Streit über das Abendmahl nach seinen politischen und religiösen Beziehungen*, 2 vols. (1924–53); G. W. Locher, *Zwingli's Thought* (1981).

TIMOTHY GEORGE

Marguerite of Angoulême (1492–1549)

A gifted poetess, Marguerite was born a princess of the House of Valois and was famous for patronage of church reform. As Duchess of Alençon she had Guillaume Briçonnet named Bishop of Meaux, her duchy capital. There, assisted by Jacques Lefèvre d'Etaples and William Farel,* a brilliant attempt to reform the French church from within was made. Widowed (1525), she was forced to withdraw her support of the Meaux reform. She married Henry of Navarre (1527) and as Queen of Navarre protected Protestant refugees at her Nérac court.

NSH 7:177–79.

HUGHES OLIPHANT OLD

Marian Exiles

All the Marian exiles were Edwardian Protestants who fled from Mary Tudor's Catholic regime between 1553 and 1555. But their traditional image as religious radicals who returned to form a "Puritan party" has been totally discredited. The first to flee were Cambridge fellows, clergy and laypersons, involved in the defeated Northumberland conspiracy to subvert the succession. Others followed for political, religious, and academic reasons. They were never a homogeneous group. Of 472 adult males, 382 returned to England. Some, already distinguished, rejoined former associates among those Edwardians who constituted Queen Elizabeth's* necessarily Protestant entourage. Three were nominated to the original Privy Council, and five were court preachers. These presumably influenced policy formation. At least ten "exiles" sat in the 1559 Parliament, two of whom assisted the passage of the religious legislation. All are known to have been compliant government men.

The clerical "exiles" were predominantly middle-aged. Tempered by experience, they were embarrassed by the seditious extremism of John Knox* and Christopher Goodman. As members of an educated elite they were generally welcome in the nascent church. They dominated the ecclesiastical commissions (1559), which could absorb a modicum of evangelical zeal, and eventually occupied seventeen of twenty-five bishoprics. Thus, as individuals, a number of "exiles" played a leading role in the establishment of the Elizabethan church settlement,* a unique ecclesiastical compromise that did not correspond to any continental model.

N. M. SUTHERLAND

Marot, Clément (c.1497–1544)

French ballad singer, writer, and editor born in Cahors, France. Marot was educated there and in Paris. After a conversion* experience, he spent his energy metering the Psalms for singing. His *Aulcunes pseaulmes et cantiques mys en chant* (Strassburg, 1539) was carried to Geneva and authorized by Calvin* for worship* use. In 1542 Marot was charged with heresy* and forced to flee Paris after publishing his collection of thirty versified psalms. He went to Geneva, where Calvin enlisted him to produce both metrical psalms and worship aids for the Genevan Church. He died under mysterious circumstances and the work came to a halt until picked up by Theodore Beza* (1548).

LINDAJO H. MCKIM

Marprelate Tracts

A series of violent, unprecedented scurrilous Puritan* tracts attacking episcopacy issued under the pseudonym Martin Marprelate (1588–89). They reflect brilliant, humorous satirical prose that aroused hostility rather than sympathy for the Puritan cause. They were directed at prelates such as Archbishop John Whitgift, who decreed (1586) that all publications required proper ecclesiastical approval.

Suspected authors Job Throckmorton and John Udall denied the charges; John Penry was executed. Puritan sympathizer Robert Waldegrave printed the tracts sponsored by the Puritan patroness Elizabeth Crane. John Field* undoubtedly inspired their publication. The tracts were one of the first Puritan manifestoes to assume voluntarily the name "Puritan."

W. Pierce, *An Historical Introduction to the Marprelate Tracts* (1908); and ed., *The Marprelate Tracts* (1911); Collinson, *EPM*.

DAN G. DANNER

Marriage, Theology of

Reformed Christians have typically agreed that marriage is a life partnership analogous to the covenant* relationship between God* and God's people in Scripture.* They have disagreed about the implications of this analogy.

Following John Calvin,* Reformed Christians have traditionally believed that marriage faithful to the biblical norm is the relationship between the superior man whose role is to rule and the inferior woman whose role is to obey. However, they have also insisted that the husband is not to be a domineering tyrant or the wife a subservient slave but that marriage should be true companionship in which there is mutual giving and receiving, helping and being helped, caring and being cared for. Further developing the theology of Karl Barth* that began to move in this direction, many contemporary Reformed Christians reject the traditional hierarchical-patriarchal view and defend the full equality and mutual responsibility of husband and wife, each created in the image of God and called to love and serve the other.

Since the sixteenth century, Reformed theology has increasingly emphasized that Christian marriage is a partnership in which both parties freely and gladly decide to marry in order to establish a relationship that is good in itself and exists for its own sake, not just to "remedy sinful lust," produce children, or serve other personal, social, or economic goals.

There has also generally been increasing acknowledgment that though the full committed partnership of marriage is more than a relationship based on romantic-erotic love, such love is also included in it as the good gift of God who created us male and female, thus not only legitimating but blessing the physical-emotional-sexual side of marriage.

The Reformed tradition has consistently believed that marriage is ordained by God to be a permanent relationship. However, most Reformed Christians today acknowledge that divorce can be the legitimate recognition that human error and/or sin may prevent a marriage from becoming a true life partnership. When a marriage ends in divorce—as when it begins and continues—Christians count on the grace* of God that both forgives sinful people and enables them to make fresh starts (including the possibility of new marriage for divorced persons).

Rejecting the idea that marriage is a purely private arrangement between isolated individuals, the Reformed tradition has always insisted on the importance of an official wedding ceremony as the public confirmation of the broadening of two family circles, the couple's acceptance of their rights and responsibilities as members of a larger society, and (in the case of Christians) their desire for the blessing of God and declaration of their intention to live as members of the Christian community.

While Reformed Christians recognize marriage as a good gift of God, they realize too that those who never marry and those who lose their partner through divorce or death* may also live fully human lives as single people who have their own particular gifts and tasks from God.

Barth, *CD* III/4, 116ff.; E. Brunner, *The Divine Imperative* (1932; ET 1937); R. S. Wallace, *Calvin's Doctrine of the Christian Life* (1959).

SHIRLEY C. GUTHRIE

Marrow Controversy

A doctrinal controversy in the Church of Scotland (1718–23). As a result of Thomas Boston's* recommendation of *The Marrow of Modern Divinity* to a fellow minister, the *Marrow* (1st ed. 1645) was reprinted (1718) with a preface by James Hog. Written by Edward Fisher, a Presbyterian barber-surgeon, the *Marrow* was a work of popular divinity reflecting the orthodox Reformed opinions of its day.

The *Marrow* was attacked first verbally and then in print. Hog defended it, but a pamphlet war ensued when Principal Hadow (St. Andrews University) and James Hadow (a fiery, though ignorant country minister) attacked it in print. Hadow argued the *Marrow*'s use of phrases such as "Christ is dead for him" and "a deed of gift and grant" (taken respectively from the early seventeenth-century Puritans John Preston and Ezekiel Culverwell) demonstrated that the *Marrow* taught a universal redemption and, based upon it, an assurance* that was of the essence of saving faith.* Hog's defense was woefully inadequate and, after charges were drawn up by a Committee for Purity of Doctrine, the 1720 General Assembly* condemned the *Marrow*, both in terms of Hadow's charges and of charges of antinomianism brought by Adams. The act prohibited all ministers from recommending the book and required them to warn their people against it.

The Assembly's act drew national attention to a previously obscure book. It also stimulated a small group of ministers to defend the *Marrow*. Three of them (Boston, Ralph Erskine,* and Ebenezer Erskine*) are now widely remembered—though none of their opponents are—but at the same time, all but Hog were obscure country ministers. They submitted a *Representation and Petition* (1721), signed by twelve ministers, to the 1721 General Assembly, complaining that the 1720 General Assembly in condemning the *Marrow* had condemned gospel truth. Their complaint was not favorably received. After due consideration by the Assembly's Commission—all things considered, they had a fair hearing—the 1722 General Assembly confirmed the 1720 Assembly's act against the *Marrow*, vindicated it from the aspersions of the twelve Brethren, and rebuked them for erroneous doctrine and "injurious reflections" made against the Assembly. The submission of a Protest notwithstanding, the Assembly did not require them to subscribe the act and allowed the twelve to return to their parishes. But continuing prejudice in the church, against them and "Marrow doctrine," was such that it was an important consideration in the founding of the Associate Presbytery. The "Marrow" theology became that of the Secession churches.

Doctrinally, the controversy involved aspects of divine sovereignty and human responsibility in the work of salvation,* with the Marrow ministers emphasizing God's grace* and their opponents that which must be done to obtain salvation. The Brethren spoke of the covenant* of grace as a "testament," with promises of grace in Christ, who was to be freely offered to all. Assurance was in Christ and a believer's obedience a response of love and gratitude. Their opponents spoke of the covenant as a contract with mutual obligations, with the gospel offer made only to the "prepared" sinner. Assurance was based on a believer's good works, and obedience was obtained by threats of God's wrath.

In this the *Marrow* and its defenders were more in harmony with pre-1650 Reformed orthodoxy* and, on balance, the Westminster* Standards, while their opponents reflected the legalizing tendencies of late seventeenth-century Reformed theology rather than Reformed thought as a whole.

D. C. Lachman, *The Marrow Controversy* (1988).

DAVID C. LACHMAN

Marshall, Peter (1902–1949)

Pastor of the New York Avenue Presbyterian Church in Washington, D.C. (1937–49), and chaplain of the U.S. Senate (1947–49). Born in Coatbridge, Scotland, Marshall was called to the ministry following varied experience as a blue-collar laborer. His widespread popularity as a preacher stemmed from his straightforward emphasis on the relevance of the living Christ to the everyday concerns of ordinary Americans. Though he died suddenly at the age of forty-six, the enduring appeal of his Christian message and example is evident in the sales of over a million copies of a collection of his down-to-earth sermons, *Mr. Jones, Meet the Master* (1949), and over two million copies of his biography, *A Man Called Peter* (1951), written by his wife, Catherine, and successful as a feature film.

PHILIP W. BUTIN

Mary

The mother of Jesus. Surprisingly, Mary did not loom large in Reformation controversy. She rarely appears in Reformation confessions* or Protestant orthodoxy.* The Westminster Confession* names her only with the virgin birth. Yet early Protestantism criticized many forms of Marian devotion, and the Reformed tradition has paid little attention to her.

Medieval theologians debated about Mary's "immaculate conception" and "bodily assumption," but these were not defined as Catholic dogmas until later (1854; 1950). Before the Reformation the church's official beliefs were confined to her role in the virgin birth of Christ (strictly, her virginal conception) as "God-bearer" (Gr. *theotokos*, normally, misleadingly "mother of God") and her perpetual virginity—not only "before" but also "in" and "after" Jesus' birth. The Reformers mostly endorsed these teachings, with their own distinctive coloring. Luther* gloried in the paradox of the "mother of God" ("Mary suckles God with her breasts, bathes God, rocks him"). But Calvin* would not go beyond "mother of our Lord" (*Inst.* 2.14.4; Luke 1:43) and never explicitly affirmed *theotokos*. Different Christologies* determine their different presentations of Mary.

Calvin was likewise less clear-cut than Luther on Mary's perpetual virginity but undoubtedly favored it. Notes in the Geneva Bible* (Matt. 1:18, 25; Jesus' "brothers") defend it, as did Zwingli* and the English reformers, often on hazardous grounds (e.g., the established proof text of Ezek. 44:2, to rebut the charge of reliance on tradition instead of Scripture).

Yet the Reformers' high regard for Mary did not stop them from attacking her exaltation above Christ. On the Magnificat, Luther highlighted her medial position (Luke 1:48—not her meritorious "humility"), depicting her as a supreme example of God's unmerited mercy. The Reformers corrected the Vulgate's distortion of Luke 1:28 ("full of grace") and objected to prayers to the gentle Mary to intercede with her stern Son—or to mother Mary to influence her dependent baby Son.

Though Marian devotion was not rejected root and branch (e.g., Ave Maria might be retained in praise or congratulation, and some Marian festivals were kept in the Lutheran and Anglican calendars), Reformed faith has largely ignored her, no doubt reacting to the Marian extremism of modern Catholicism. Karl Barth* viewed Marian dogma as "the critical central dogma of the Roman Catholic Church, . . . the one heresy* . . .

which explains all the rest"—i.e., that of humanity cooperating in its own redemption (*CD* I/2, 138–46).

Though grass-roots Marianism still proliferates under papal patronage, Vatican II has affected Catholic Mariology. Mary has not yet been declared coredemptrix and is often portrayed not only as "mother of the church" but as the first and model believer (cf. Luke 1:38; M. Thurian, *Mary, Mother of the Lord, Figure of the Church* [ET 1964]). Feminist theology has encouraged the rediscovery of Mary, though her subservience has made her uncongenial to many feminists. Ecumenical discussions have still to grasp this issue.

R. E. Brown et al., eds., *Mary in the New Testament* (1978); G. Miegge, *The Virgin Mary* (1955); D. F. Wright, ed., *Chosen by God: Mary in Evangelical Perspective* (1989).

DAVID F. WRIGHT

Mather, Cotton (1663–1728)

The most celebrated preacher, prestigious scholar, and prolific writer of his day. In Boston, Mather exerted a major influence in reshaping the ecclesiology, spirituality, and missiology of New England Puritan Congregationalism,* redefining its concepts of covenant* preaching,* Christian history,* eschatology,* and the psychology of religious experience.* He worked tirelessly for spiritual renewal and prepared the way for the Great Awakening.* His voluntary religious and reform societies provided a foundation for the great missionary and reforming societies of the next two centuries.

The son of Increase Mather,* he held degrees from Harvard (1681, 1690) and the D.D. from the University of Glasgow (1710). He served with his father as preacher at Boston's Second Church. His books and sermons reflect a firm commitment to Westminster* theology, yet they also show such characteristic Puritan tendencies as the overloading of the conversion* experience and a hyper-Calvinistic* stress on inability and predestination.* He collected, practiced, and promoted spiritual disciplines drawn from many Christian traditions, some of which were incompatible with Reformed theology. His personal devotions were extremely intense, and he showed a fascination for mysticism, supernatural phenomena, divine providences,* angelic appearances, personal revelations, and witchcraft. He also had broad medical and scientific interest, holding membership in the Royal Society (1713). His most influential books include *Magnalia Christi Americana* (1702), *Manductio ad ministerium* (1726), and *Bonifacius* (1710).

D. Levin, *Cotton Mather* (1978); R. Lovelace, *The American Pietism of Cotton Mather* (1979); R. Middlekauff, *The Mathers: Three Generations of Puritan Intellectuals* (1971).

JAMES L. BREED

Mather, Increase (1639–1723)

A prominent preacher, scholar, church and political leader, and the most able statesman of seventeenth-century Massachusetts. Mather is regarded as the greatest native-born American Puritan.* The son of Richard Mather, Increase graduated from Harvard (1656), Trinity College, Dublin (M.A.; 1658), and served as Teacher of Boston's Second Church (1664–1723). He was president of Harvard (1685–1701), committed to Westminster* theology, and upheld the Half-Way Covenant.*

Cotton Mather, *Parentator* (1724); R. Middlekauff, *The Mathers: Three Generations of Puritan Intellectuals* (1971); K. B. Murdock, *Increase Mather* (1925).

JAMES L. BREED

Mayflower Compact

A civil covenant made by the Pilgrims on the ship *Mayflower* as it lay at anchor near Cape Cod, Massachusetts, on November 11, 1620. The Compact formed the basis for their colonial government. Modeled after the congregational* church covenants familiar to English Puritans* and Separatists,* it incorporated Puritan political theory, by which both a church and a civil government are held to be founded on a covenant* freely entered into by those confessing their faith and pledging their commitment.

See W. Bradford's history, *Of Plimoth Plantation* (various editions).

JAMES L. BREED

Melville, Andrew (1545–1622)

After study and teaching in France and Geneva, Melville returned to Scotland (1574), where he provided outstanding leadership for higher education and the Presbyterian church party. A brilliant student, able administrator, and galvanizing teacher, he revived the University of Glasgow and he upgraded curriculum, teaching methods, scholarship, administration, and discipline at St. Andrews University. He shared in framing the Second Book of Discipline* (1578) and (sometimes at serious personal risk) defended its principles against royal episcopal encroachment until he was imprisoned (1607) and later exiled by James VI (I of Great Britain). Recognized internationally as a great Latin poet, Melville died in exile.

ROBERT M. HEALEY

Mercersburg Theology

A gentle movement (1840–60) stressing the centrality of Jesus Christ and his presence in the Lord's Supper* that sought to correct perceived individualism and revival* excesses of Edwardsean* "new theology." From the Theological Seminary of the German Reformed Church and its Marshall College in Mercersburg, Pennsylvania, John W. Nevin,* a Presbyterian, led the movement with books such as *The History and Genius of the Heidelberg Catechism* (1841–42), *The Anxious Bench* (1843), and *The Mystical Presence* (1846). His faculty collaborator, Philip Schaff,* came to teach at Mercersburg from the University of Berlin, eager to share the richness of continental Reformed Christianity with American Christians.

In debates with other leaders of the German and Dutch Reformed, Lutheran, and Presbyterian Christians, Nevin and Schaff argued for a sense of the church* that emphasized the Catholic creedal affirmations of Nicaea and the Apostles' Creed. They stressed the importance of the Christian church through the ages and appreciated some Roman Catholic* contributions to doctrine* and ethics.* They looked forward to Christian development in the future.

Drawing on contemporary German theology, Nevin and Schaff criticized American sectarianism, loss of a sense of providence* in American dependence on revival techniques, and any Protestant "jump" straight from the Bible to the current situation. They urged on Reformed Christians especially a deep Christocentric piety,* dependence on the sacraments,* and an irenic disposition toward the rest of the Christian family.

J. H. Nichols, ed., *The Mercersburg Theology* (1966).

LOUIS B. WEEKS

Merle d'Aubigné, Jean Henri (1794–1872)

Genevan Reformed historian of Christianity. Merle d'Aubigné studied theology and was ordained in the Church of Geneva (1817). Robert Haldane, a traveling Scot, encouraged him to follow a more orthodox Calvinism* based on scriptural study. After study with August Neander in Berlin (1817), Merle d'Aubigné ministered in Reformed churches in Hamburg (1818–23) and Brussels (1823–31) before returning to Geneva to teach in the newly formed Evangelical School of Theology. The school was an organ of the Evangelical Society of Geneva which wanted to revive orthodox Calvinism within the established Church of Geneva but found much opposition there among the Socinian* leadership (Chenevière and J. I. S. Cellérier).

Merle d'Aubigné is well known for his *History of the Reformation in the Sixteenth Century* (5 vols.; Paris, 1835–53; Edinburgh, 1846–53) in which he attempted to recast the image of Calvin.* In contrast to the theocratic-dogmatic leader, he explained Calvin's religious experiences as spiritual and emotional struggles pointing to a man who deeply felt the presence of God.* He also noted the Reformation's importance as the foundation for nineteenth-century religion and society. He proposed construction of a "Salle de la Réformation" which became a museum and library in Geneva (1861). He published over eighty-five histories, letters, discourses, and sermons, receiving honorary degrees from Princeton (1838) and Berlin (1846), civic honors from Edinburgh (1856), and a Grand Medal of Gold for Science from Prussia (1853).

A. Biéler, *Un fils du refuge* (1934); J. B. Roney, "Jean Henri Merle d'Aubigné: Historian of Christianity in an Age of Revolution" (diss., University of Toronto, 1989); J. Winkler, *Der Kirchenhistoriker Jean Henri Merle d'Aubigné* (1968).

JOHN B. RONEY

Millenary Petition

Presented to James I of England at the beginning of his reign (1603) by the Puritan* party in the Church of England, in the name of a thousand (hence "millenary") ministers "all groaning as under one common burden of human rites and ceremonies." The petition called for a renewed reformation of the forms of worship in the Puritan sense and correction of common abuses, such as appointments of ministers who could not preach, absenteeism, and the holding of multiple benefices. In response, King James called the Hampton Court Conference.*

S. Babbage, *Puritanism and Richard Bancroft* (1962).

JOHN E. WILSON

Millennialism

Millennialism (Lat.), or chiliasm (Gr.), refers to a type of Christian eschatology* organized around the notion of a thousand-year reign of Christ at the close of history.* The idea is derived from Rev. 20:2–7, the only biblical occurrences of the expression.

Premillennialism holds that Christ's second coming is forewarned by biblically identified "signs of the times": catastrophes, widespread apostasy, appearance of the Antichrist, and a great tribulation for God's people. Upon his appearing, Christ will inaugurate his thousand-year reign, either in person or through his faithful. Deceased saints will be raised. Peace, general blessing, prosperity, and many conversions,* especially of Jewish people, will follow. At the close of the millennium, Satan will be briefly unleashed but then destroyed, the unbelieving dead raised and condemned eternally, and the saints welcomed into the new heaven and new earth. Irenaeus, Justin Martyr, and Tertullian advocated variations of this view. A few medieval thinkers and many modern evangelicals do.

A version of premillennialism is dispensationalism. It teaches that salvation* comes in different modes and periods during history, notably in the crucified and risen Christ during the era of the church, and especially in the reigning Christ during the millennium. As taught by John Nelson Darby (1800–1882), it defends a secret rapture of the church before the tribulation and return of Christ with his saints to establish his millennial rule. Cyrus Ingerson Scofield (1843–1921) spread dispensationalism through the notes of his widely used *The Scofield Reference Bible.*

Reformed theologians occasionally proposed premillennialism, particularly during times of political and social turmoil. Johann Heinrich Alsted (1588–1638) and Edward Irving* are examples.

Reformed emphases on the historical continuity of God's redemptive work, the unity of the Bible's two Testaments, God's covenant* of grace* with humanity,* the symbolic nature of apocalyptic and prophetic literature, and God's use of the means of grace have yielded a different eschatology. Through great outpourings of his Spirit,* effective preaching,* and his people's faithful service, Christ establishes his rule, converts the nations, and bestows spiritual and material blessings. Christ will visibly return, amidst such signs as the appearance of Antichrist, conversion of the Gentiles, and the regrafting of Israel into God's vine (Rom. 11:25–32). When he comes, the dead will be raised and the last judgment will occur.

The postmillennial variation within Reformed eschatology holds that the gospel's success rather than Christ's visible intervention will yield the millennium. Daniel Whitby (1638–1726) and Jonathan Edwards* were two proponents. A late twentieth-century mutant known as "theonomy" sees the substantial reintroduction of OT standards as essential to this era.

Many Reformed theologians, however, emphasize the continuous, simultaneous flourishing of God's kingdom and the kingdom of darkness until the end of history. Known as amillennialism, their position rejects the notion of a millennium. Here, "the thousand years" of Revelation 20 represents the entire period between Christ's resurrection and his return, between Satan's defeat and his destruction.

R. Clouse, ed., *The Meaning of the Millennium* (1977); A. Hoekema, *The Bible and the Future* (1979).

JAMES A. DE JONG

Miller, Samuel (1769–1850)

A major supporter of the founding of Princeton Seminary (1812) and the institution's second professor (1813), Miller taught church history and polity* until his death. A wide-ranging writer, he is remembered for his two-volume *A Brief Retrospect of the Eighteenth Century* (1803), one of the first American intellectual histories. Then Miller was somewhat tolerant of diverse interpretations of the Reformed faith; but in the 1830s he ardently defended the conservative Old School position in the controversies leading to the split of the Presbyterian Church in the U.S.A.

S. Miller, Jr., *The Life of Samuel Miller* (1869).

JAMES H. MOORHEAD

Milton, John (1608–1674)

An English Puritan* spokesman as a political figure in Oliver Cromwell's* government, writer of polemical prose on political and ecclesiastical issues, and poet. He gained international prominence as Secretary for Foreign Languages for the Council of State and defended the regicide of Charles I. His career as Latin secretary gave impetus to his polemical prose writing. He was neither a predestinarian nor a Puritan church-life leader, but his polemical prose remains a leading repository of seventeenth-century Reformed thought. The keynotes include a distrust of ceremonialism and episcopal church government, the authority of the Bible in matters of belief and conduct, the priesthood of all believers, and the covenantal basis of social institutions (including church, state, and family).

Milton is the supreme poet of the Reformation tradition. Next to Shakespeare the greatest English poet, Milton used the grandest resources of language and imagination to incarnate a Puritan view of life. His *Paradise Lost* (1667), *Paradise Regained* (1671), and *Samson Agonistes* (1671) express significant Reformation tenets—the importance of the Bible (a leading source for Milton's poems), the power of sin,* the redemptive grace* and sovereignty of God,* a providential* view of history,* and the doctrines of stewardship* and calling.* Milton's picture of paradisal life in *Paradise Lost* (bk. 4) and Samson's regeneration in *Samson Agonistes* are vintage Puritanism.

J. Milton, *Complete Prose Works*, 8 vols. (1953–82); G. B. Christopher, *Milton and the Science of the Saints* (1982); C. A. Patrides, *Milton and the Christian Tradition* (1979).

LELAND RYKEN

Ministry

The service of God* within the church and by the church to the world, which has its source, inspiration, and model in Jesus Christ, the suffering servant of God: for he who came from heaven to be the Word incarnate did not come to be served by people but rather to minister to humanity in its abject need and give his life sacrificially for all. He entered wholly into the pitiful and perverse condition of the human race as it exists before God, sharing its pain and estrangement; and he did so in order, by meek and personal service in doing good and offering healing and liberation, to bring reconciliation and peace between humanity and God. Thus finally as the climax of his diaconal ministry he offered himself as an atonement* for sin* at Calvary's cross to bring to a conclusion on earth his ministry. Now in heaven he ministers as priest through his intercession for his people.

In his earthly ministry Jesus created a community of the new covenant*: that is, a people called to minister by sharing in his ministry which began on earth and continues at the right hand of the Father in heaven. Each Christian finds the freedom to minister in the reality of being a slave/servant of Jesus Christ, who is both the Servant/Minister and the Lord and Master to his disciples. Ministry is therefore for the household of faith the humble service of God the Father and also in God's name and love the serving of fellow human beings in their sin, anxiety, degradation, need, and rebellion against God. Thus each and every baptized believer in his own situation is called to share daily in the diaconal ministry of Christ, yet is to do so not individualistically but rather as a member of the one body in fellowship with others.

Though ministry is primarily the vocation* of the whole people of God of the new covenant as it lives in fellowship with and in obedience to Jesus, some members are set apart as ordained ministers in order to facilitate the ministry of the whole. In the spirit of the NT, the offices are those of elder/presbyter and deacon. The historic threefold ministry of bishop, presbyter, and deacon was thereby reduced to two in the sixteenth-century Reformed churches. Of these, the presbyterial ministry is in essence that by which the Word and Sacraments* are dispensed to the people of God: presbyters act in the name of Christ as sent by him to proclaim his word of grace.* As servants of Jesus they are never to cease from administering the teaching and leading and from sharing wholly in the caring ministry of the whole people of God.

The diaconal ministry is that activity by and through which the responses of the people of God to God's saving grace are facilitated. Deacons* set an example of what is involved in being servants of God and together with teaching assist the congregations in the exercise of true *diakonia* (Gr.; ministry). In no other area have modern churches so failed as in the effective use of deacons to ensure the true *diakonia*/ministry of the whole body of Christ to the world. Deacons, female or male, are called to minister the mercy of God toward God's creatures: in particular they are to inspire and assist the intercessory prayer of churches for the world so that their prayers are united to those of Christ, the heavenly intercessor. Then also they are to lead the churches in witnessing for Christ by imitating him in his compassionate concern for humanity in its varying needs. This is not merely social service but concern for the whole person's relation to God as well as for relations with fellow humans. Such witness will usually involve suffering, for it will entail encountering the true face of evil and sin in the world. Then, also, they will seek to ensure that there is reconciliation and true unity both in the congregation and between congregations, so the people of the new covenant may exhibit to the world God's reconciliation in Christ.

The essential characteristic of all ministry/*diakonia* is that while it is to be undertaken in and by the love of Christ, it is also a service commanded by Christ and laid by him upon each and every member of the household of faith. There are no exceptions to this rule.

R. S. Anderson, ed., *Theological Foundations for Ministry* (1979); Barth, *CD* IV/3; R. S. Paul, *Ministry* (1965).

PETER TOON

Missionary Expansion

Gaspard de Coligny's Huguenot* mission to Brazil (1555), the initiative of the Netherlands* State Church in Formosa (1627), and the work of extraordinary individuals like John Eliot (d. 1690) in North America notwithstanding, Christianity in the early Reformed tradition was not seriously committed in practice to mission outside Europe. Though some Calvinist* theologians argued for missionary outreach as early as the mid-seventeenth century, this did not lead to any historically significant action. The only geographic expansion of the Reformed faith until the last decade of the eighteenth century was by emigration.

The rest of Protestantism fared no better, so the last decade of the eighteenth century is the critical period for all Protestantism. This is so despite some scholars' assertion of the essential missionary nature of both the Society for Promoting

Christian Knowledge (1698) and the Society for the Propagation of the Gospel (1701). It is historically confusing to assert that these societies were missionary societies in the same way that the London Missionary Society* (LMS; 1795) or the Netherlands Missionary Society (NMS; 1797) was to be, or as the Society of Jesus had been since 1542.

It was the First and Second Great Awakenings* in North America, the Evangelical Revival* in Great Britain, and its subsequent impact on the Netherlands, France, and Switzerland through the Réveil* that changed the situation. Though there were strong non-Reformed streams in this movement, many Calvinist thinkers like Jonathan Edwards,* Samuel Hopkins,* and George Whitefield* played important roles in shaping it. However, although eighteenth-century Deism scorned or was amused by the new enthusiasm, it was eighteenth-century scholastic Calvinism* that vigorously denounced and opposed the new movement.

Despite this, the LMS, the NMS, and the American Board of Commissioners for Foreign Missions* (1810), three of the most important missionary societies of the nineteenth century, were all firmly rooted in the Reformed tradition. It is also very significant for the approach of Reformed Christianity to mission that the first churches to establish "Foreign Mission" organizations were both Presbyterian—the Church of Scotland (1828) and the Presbyterian Church in the U.S.A. (1837).

Missionary expansion in the Reformed tradition has been characterized by four elements: (1) a view of the need to develop education to the highest level as a good in itself; (2) church-centeredness; (3) indigenization; and (4) an ability to create deep local loyalties.

From its very beginnings, Calvinism has emphasized the need both for an educated laity and for an educated ministry. By the beginning of the missionary expansion, this took the form of a belief in the Christian value of education in itself. John Philip* in South Africa* advocated it as an essential element in the missionary task. In his *Researches in South Africa* (2 vols.; 1828) he saw what he called "the awakening of the mind" of a people as an aspect of the redeeming power of the gospel. This commitment to educational development is found wherever the Reformed faith has spread, signaled by the foundation of Harvard so soon after the founding of Massachusetts. In South Africa, the Scots Presbyterians founded a high school and a teacher-training college at Lovedale (1841) while frontier wars still raged around it. In India, as soon as he arrived, Alexander Duff* began to build an institution of Western education which grew into Scots College, University of Calcutta. This was paralleled elsewhere in India by William Miller (1838–1923) in Madras, John Wilson (1804–75), first vice-chancellor of the University of Bombay, and many others.

In Japan, almost as soon as missionaries were allowed to operate freely within the country (1873), though they had been allowed to enter the country fourteen years earlier, Christian higher education was initiated. Jo Nijima (1843–90), a Japanese who had gone to America (1864) and become a Christian, returned as a missionary of the American Board. He began a Christian college in Kyoto, the Doshisa College, which gained university status the year he died (1890). Meanwhile, G. H. F. Verbeck (1830–98), a missionary of the Reformed Church in America, was called to head the new Imperial University in Tokyo (1869). He subsequently became an adviser to the emperor on relations with the European powers, though never ceasing to be a preacher and a teacher of theological students. In Korea,* the same pattern appeared. There Samuel A. Moffett (1864–1939), the father of Korean Presbyterianism, founded both Presbyterian Theological Seminary, the oldest theological institution in Korea, and Soongsil University. In China, there were parallel developments, though by the early twentieth century all the Protestant agencies appear to have been converted to higher education as an essential element in the missionary task. One of the more unusual developments in China was that of Moukden Medical College, founded by Dugald Christie (1855–1938), a product of the University of Edinburgh and missionary of the U.P. church. His home board would not take responsibility for the new institution which he opened, nonetheless (1912). Under Christie's leadership, Moukden became one of the leading medical schools in China and one of the most Chinese in staff and style.

The second characteristic of church-centeredness took two forms. The first was a concern that new Christians should form themselves into churches as fully and rapidly as possible. Rufus Anderson (1805–55) first articulated a clear church-centered theory of mission. The objective of missionary activity should be the creation of self-supporting, self-governing, and self-regulating churches. Though Reformed groups have not always lived up to this ideal, they often have, and only rarely have they continued to hold the local church simply as an adjunct of the mission. Two good examples are in Korea and Africa. Presbyterian missions began in Korea only in 1884, but a fully autonomous presbytery was formed (1907). Again, in Malawi, the first missionaries only arrived in 1875, but in 1901 the autonomous presbyteries of Livingstonia in the north and Blantyre in the south united to form the Church of Central Africa, Presbyterian.

The other form of church-centeredness was that Reformed missions were more the activities of the church in the sending country than of independent societies. Though three of the first missionary societies, the LMS, the NMS, and the American Board, were all rooted in the Reformed tradition, it was the Presbyterian churches in Scotland and the Reformed and Presbyterian churches in Canada and the United States that first made the work of mission an integral part of their ecclesiastical structures.

Though it would be wrong to claim a concern on the part of Reformed missions with what the last third of the twentieth century would understand by indigenization, yet in fundamental ways it was an aim despite much cultural blindness. This occurred by a combination of a determination to have the Bible in the vernacular together with a vernacular literature and a commitment to creating an educated ministry and laity. There is no way language can be studied without its cultural context also being studied. So David Clement Scott's *A Cyclopedic Dictionary of the Mang'anja Language* was also a massive contribution to the understanding of the culture of the people of eastern Zambia and parts of Mozambique as well as Malawi. Similarly, James Legge (1815–97), first head of the Anglo-Chinese College, Hong Kong, produced the first English translations of the Confucian and Daoist classic texts.

This combined emphasis on translation, developing education to the highest possible level, and creation of local church structures, was a distinctively Reformed contribution which encouraged indigenization of the faith whatever the original intentions of the missionaries. The extent and the depth of indigenization, however limited, are born out by the fourth characteristic, the creation of local loyalties. This is seen in many parts of the world where missionaries of the Reformed tradition have worked. These loyalties have been so deep that they have led, too often, to the existence of separate Reformed churches within the one state. This is clear in Indonesia, where the very success of Reformed missions in various parts of that country has led to a federal association of Reformed churches with strong local loyalties, for example, the Amboinese Church, rather than one Indonesian Church, and also in Kenya, where not all Gikuyu are Presbyterians but all Presbyterians are Gikuyu, including powerful kin groups like the family of the first president, Jomo Kenyatta. This has given the Presbyterian Church great strength in some ways, but its appearance to others as a Gikuyu institution has also limited its mission—a limitation it is only now beginning to cast off. Another example is the loyalty of certain Maya Indian groups in Mexico to their Presbyterian church where it has become a kind of mini-tribal nationalism. This is paralleled in South Africa, where the Reformed Presbyterian Church is a Nguni church and the Evangelical Presbyterian Church is a Tsonga church. This tendency is in sharp contrast with the way Methodist and Anglican churches have developed when they operate in the same countries.

ANDREW C. ROSS

Moderates

Though probably never outnumbering the Evangelicals in the Kirk as a whole, the Moderates began to achieve ascendancy in the General Assembly* (c. 1730) and dominated Scottish life and thought for almost a century thereafter.

As an administrative system, Moderatism stood for submission to authority, whether secular or spiritual. The law of the land must be obeyed, even when (as with patronage, imposed by Parliament [1712]) it was obnoxious to the Christian conscience.* The law of the church, laid down by the General Assembly, must not be flouted by "subordinate judicatories," however lofty their reasons. Such authoritarianism resulted in significant secessions (1733; 1752), though it could be claimed that it ultimately diverted church people's attention from controversial settlements to more important matters.

As an intellectual movement, Moderatism rose out of widespread disillusion with the controversies and persecutions of Covenanting times, and flourished in the "Age of Secular Interests" inaugurated by the Revolution (1688) and the Union (1707). Typical "Enlightenment" men, the Moderate clergy and their lay supporters were always strongest in Edinburgh and adjacent areas, but by 1800 they had virtually transformed the outlook of the entire country.

Salient among their characteristics were:

Zeal for liberal scholarship. Seventeenth-century churchmen sacrificed breadth to profundity. The Moderates, by contrast, compensated for theological superficiality with an impressive range of interests and achievements—literary, philosophical, historical, and scientific. Scotland's cultural flowering in the half-century after 1750 was due largely to them.

Hostility to Puritanical otherworldliness. While rightly accused of being more at home in city clubs and theaters than in praying societies, most Moderates displayed real pastoral concern. What they disliked was (arguably) simulated or misconceived piety,* not the genuine article. "It was of great importance," said one, "to discriminate between the artificial virtues and vices, formed by ignorance and superstition, and those which are real."

Aversion from Westminster Calvinism. Though seldom aggressively heretical, Moderates distrusted dogmatism and scholastic system making. Elevating conduct over creed, they favored a new type of preaching* that eschewed the traditionalists' weekly survey of "the scheme of salvation" and exchanged moral discourses, stylishly expressed, for eloquent proclamation of the mysterious and the supernatural. Opponents declared that their "moonlight" sermons, lacking awe and urgency, "ripened no harvest"; but the contrast with evangelical productions has perhaps been overdone. Where differences did exist, each type conceivably counterbalanced the other. The down-to-earth practicality of the Moderate homily no doubt had its attraction for hearers satiated with the abstruse and controversial harangues of former days.

By 1780, Moderatism's golden epoch was over, and the long decline began which finally ended in the evangelical resurgence of the age of Thomas Chalmers.*

I. D. L. Clark, "From Protest to Reaction: The Moderate Regime in the Church of Scotland, 1752–1805," in *Scotland in the Age of Improvement*, ed. N. T. Phillipson and R. Mitchison (1970); R. B. Sher, *Church and University in the Scottish Enlightenment* (1985).

ALEC C. CHEYNE

Moffat, Robert (1795–1883)

Trained as a gardener and sent to South Africa* by the London Missionary Society* (1816), Moffat worked nearly fifty years at Kuruman, Bechuanaland, among the southern Tswana. Though he had little formal education, he mastered the widely spoken Tswana language and produced the complete Tswana Bible (1857), a vital contribution to Christianity across all of southern Africa. Moffat encouraged his son-in-law, David Livingstone,* and was himself the pioneer in establishing relations with the conquering Amandebele of present-day Zimbabwe.

W. C. Northcott, *Robert Moffat* (1961).

ANDREW C. ROSS

Moffatt, James (1870–1944)

One of the leading NT scholars of the first half of the twentieth century, best known for his own translation of the Bible (NT, 1913; OT, 1924). Moffatt was born in Glasgow, studied classics at the University of Glasgow and theology at the Glasgow College of the Free Church of Scotland, and was ordained a Free Church minister (1896). He was appointed professor of Greek and NT exegesis at Mansfield College, Oxford (1911). Moffatt became professor of church history at Glasgow (1915) and took a similar chair at Union Seminary (N.Y.; 1927). The author of nearly forty books, he was a key figure in the production of the RSV.

DONALD A. HAGNER

Moltmann, Jürgen (1926–)

After Karl Barth,* Moltmann is perhaps the best known and most influential Reformed theologian of the twentieth century. A professor at University of Tübingen in Germany (from 1966), Moltmann was the primary founder of the "theology of hope." Many of the characteristics of mission theology, political theology, liberation* theology, and black theology can be traced to the new theological horizons opened by Moltmann's *Theology of Hope* (1964; ET 1967). This was followed by two other major books in a trilogy that established him as a major theologian of our time: *The Crucified God* (1974) and *The Church in the Power of the Spirit* (1977). Three volumes have been published in Moltmann's projected five-volume principal systematic work: *The Trinity and the Kingdom* (1982); *God in Creation* (1985); and *The Way of Jesus Christ: Christology in Messianic Dimensions* (1990).

Raised in the highly cultured but unbelieving family of a gymnasium classics teacher, Moltmann found himself on the front lines of World War II at age seventeen. After a short time in action he was captured and sent to a prisoner of war camp near Nottingham, England. There he underwent a conversion* and began theological studies. Upon his repatriation (1948) he took up the formal study of theology at the University of Göttingen, where his thought was shaped by his teachers, the Reformed theologian Otto Weber* and the "Reformed" Lutheran theologians Hans Joachim Iwand and Ernst Wolf. These three teachers were nurtured in the spirit of Barth, but none was an uncritical epigone. Rather, they inspired Moltmann to see precisely in the Calvinist tradition an eschatology* that opened up creative ways beyond Barth's theology. To be a good Calvinist in the modern world one had to be open to the best of the Lutheran tradition as well as the best of the left-wing Reformation. His teachers introduced Moltmann to Dutch federal theology* and to the urgency of ecumenical theology in the postwar world. There was also very early in Moltmann's shaping an openness to the church's world encounter with Marxism in the form of Marxist humanists, such as Ernst Bloch, with oppressed third-world peoples, other religions, and with impending ecological disaster. Calvinist theology, which some saw as being closed and narrow, has in Moltmann taken on its former world-open and catalytic character.

Working first as a historical theologian, Moltmann produced *Christoph Pezel (1539–1604) und der Calvinismus in Bremen* (1958), which studied the Calvinist theology that had developed in Moltmann's native Bremen region. Since then, his theology can be seen as a development of the doctrine of eschatology from Calvin's view of providence* and his ethics* as a steadfast interpretation of the Calvinist claim about the Lordship of Jesus Christ over all reality.

R. J. Bauckham, *Moltmann: Messianic Theology in the Making* (1987); M. D. Meeks, *Origins of the Theology of Hope* (1974); C. Morse, *The Logic of Promise in Moltmann's Theology* (1979).

M. DOUGLAS MEEKS

Morrison, Robert (1782–1834)

English missionary linguist trained for the Presbyterian ministry at Hoxton Academy who was appointed to China by the London Missionary Society.* No Protestant missionary had previously served there, since all but strictly commercial contact was forbidden and no facilities existed for learning Chinese. At the American trading post of Canton, Morrison acquired (from Roman Catholic works and local sources) so much Chinese that he was given legal status as a translator for the East India Company. He published a Chinese NT (1814) and with W. C. Milne's assistance had translated the whole Bible by 1819. His vast *Chinese Dictionary* (6 vols.; 1815–22) is also an encyclopedia of China. Morrison founded the Anglo-Chinese College at Malacca and an abortive London institute for Oriental studies. He died before official missionary work in China was possible.

Memoirs of the Life and Labours of Robert Morrison, compiled by his widow, 2 vols. (1839); K. S. Latourette, *A History of Christian Missions in China* (1929).

ANDREW F. WALLS

Munus triplex

In Reformed theology, Jesus Christ is often described as mediator, explicated by the *munus triplex*—the threefold office of prophet, priest, and king.

Though John Calvin* was not the first Christian theologian to use the *munus triplex* to describe Christ, his discussion (*Inst.* 2.15) is the basis for frequent use of the formula in many sixteenth- and seventeenth-century Reformed confessions. Martin Luther* and others had described Christ by the twofold office of priest and king; Calvin added the third office of prophet to interpret Christ's work as mediator.

In describing Christ as prophet, Calvin did not apparently think of Christ's announcement and enactment of the kingdom of God.* Rather, Christ is a teacher of "the perfect doctrine." The description of the Mediator as king refers to the eternal, spiritual reign of Christ over the church* and each individual in the church, a reign promising the church's perpetuity and protection. Because Christ is king, we pass through this miserable world "content with this one thing: that our King will never leave us destitute, but will provide for our needs until, our warfare ended, we are called to triumph" (*Inst.* 2.15.4). When he describes Christ as priest, Calvin refers to an everlasting intercessor who, by his death on the cross, "washed away our sins, sanctifies us and obtains for us that grace from which the uncleanness of our transgressions and vices debars us" (*Inst.* 2.15.6).

The *munus triplex* is in many classical Reformed confessions, such as the Heidelberg Catechism* (q. 31) and the WCF* (ch. 8). The Larger Catechism asks, "Why was our Mediator called Christ?" The answer is that Christ is the mediator because he was anointed by the Holy Spirit* and set apart "to execute the office of prophet, priest, and king of his Church, in the estate both of his humiliation and exaltation" (q. 42).

The *munus triplex* is not prominent in contemporary Reformed theology, though Karl Barth* and Emil Brunner* continued to discuss it in their interpretations of Christology.* Contemporary theologians worry that the *munus triplex* represents the imposition of a dogmatic structure on the biblical text and that Calvin's interpretation of the threefold office may not stand up under careful exegesis. Those who continue to use the *munus triplex* do so because it reflects the conviction that Jesus cannot be understood as Christ and mediator apart from the history of Israel's covenant* with God.

Barth, *CD* IV/3, pt. 1, 3–38; Heppe, *RD*; J. F. Jansen, *Calvin's Doctrine of the Work of Christ* (1956).

GEORGE W. STROUP

Murray, Andrew, Jr. (1828–1917)

Second son of Andrew Murray, Sr., leader of the Scots ministers who revitalized the Nederduitse Gereformeerde Kerk (Dutch Reformed Church), in South Africa.* Educated at the universities of Aberdeen and Utrecht, he was ordained (1849) and was a leader by 1860. For fifty years he dominated the life of the NGK, making it a missionary church. He shaped its warm evangelical piety which lasted through the first half of the twentieth century. He wrote two hundred and fifty theological and devotional books and pamphlets.

J. du Plessis, *The Life of Andrew Murray* (1919).

ANDREW C. ROSS

Murray, John (1898–1975)

Professor of theology at Westminster Seminary (1930–66), Murray was born in Scotland and graduated from Glasgow, Princeton Seminary, and Edinburgh. He taught at Princeton Seminary (1929), then began a long association with Westminster Seminary. John Calvin,* Charles Hodge,* and B. B. Warfield* influenced him theologically, though he did not slavishly repeat their formulations. Refining the work of Geerhardus Vos, he popularized Biblical Theology as a useful discipline for preaching* and indispensable to systematic theology. Important works include his two-volume commentary on Romans, *Redemption Accomplished and Applied* (1961), and *Principles of Conduct* (1957). His *Collected Writings* (4 vols.; 1976–83) were published posthumously.

THOMAS M. GREGORY

Musculus, Wolfgang (1497–1563)

Born near Strassburg, Musculus entered a Benedictine monastery at fifteen and studied theology and the classics. He was attracted to Luther's reform theology and was forced to leave (1527). He was appointed deacon of Strassburg cathedral (1529), where, mentored by Wolfgang Capito* and Martin Bucer,* he studied Hebrew and theology. Musculus pastored in Augsburg (1531–48) but was driven out by the Interim and became theology professor in Bern (from 1549). His most influential work was the *Loci communes sacrae theologiae* (1554).

L. Grote, *Wolfgang Musculus* (1855); P. Musculus, "Wolfgang Musculus en Lorraine et Alsace," *Bulletin de la Société de l'histoire du protestantisme français* (Oct.–Dec. 1931): 487–501; P. J. Schwab, *The Attitude of Wolfgang Musculus Toward Religious Tolerance* (1933).

RICHARD A. MULLER

Myconius, Oswald (1488–1552)

Born in Lucerne, Myconius studied at Basel, where he met both Zwingli* and Erasmus.* He taught in Zurich (1516–18) and preached in Lucerne (c. 1519–22). After his eviction, he returned to Zurich, lectured on the NT in German, and supported the reformatory work of Zwingli. He was called to preach in Basel (1531) and succeeded John Oecolampadius* as chief preacher and professor of theology. He was the primary author of the First Confession of Basel* (1534), based on an earlier work by Oecolampadius.

K. R. Hagenbach, *Leben Oecolampads und Myconius* (1859); and *Kritische Geschichte der Entstehung und der Schicksale der ersten Basler Confession* (1828); M. Kirchofer, *Oswald Myconius* (1813); Schaff, *Creeds*, vol. 1.

RICHARD A. MULLER

Mystical Union *see* **Union with Christ**

Nantes, Edict of

The last of a series of (religious) edicts of pacification in France (1598). As a recognition of deadlock, the Edict of Nantes represented both a maximum extortion and concessions. Its difficult gestation is reflected in its complex structure, being actually four separate documents of unequal juridical value. The Huguenots* remained an undefeated faction, hence the purpose of the Edict was to make peace and to regulate the relations between those of the two religions. Thus it was not simply a Calvinist charter but, by restoring Catholicism everywhere (art. 3), confirmed it as the dominant religion. Contrary to popular belief, the Edict did *not* establish a Protestant "state within the state." It conferred no political privileges whatsoever. Rather, it sought—and partially failed—to abolish that "state," illegally reconstituted (1594). It did, however, authorize a Presbyterian* ecclesiastical organization and the retention of about 150 towns, originally for eight years. Possessing a dangerous military capability, the Huguenots could exercise political leverage and remained an exploitable force. This accounts for their turbulent progression, through defiance and further war, to 1629, when the Edict was redefined. Its ultimate revocation remained a common aspiration. The Edict of Fontainebleau (1685) was merely the culmination of a long process of erosion that had produced juridical chaos.

R. M. Golden, ed., *The Huguenot Connection: The Edict of Nantes, Its Revocation, and Early French Migration to South Carolina* (1988).

N. M. SUTHERLAND

Narrative Theology

A loosely knit body of literature that first appeared in the last third of the twentieth century. The literature is "loosely knit" in that it spreads across both confessional boundaries and theological disciplines, and there is no consensus among those contributing to the literature concerning program or method. The one theme running throughout is the category of narrative. But there is little agreement on what genre narrative refers to and how it functions in theological reflection. Theologians, biblical scholars, ethicists, homileticians, Christian educators, and pastoral counselors have all used some form of narrative to rethink the nature and tasks of their disciplines.

Some theologians have asked how the doctrine of the Trinity* might be reinterpreted if it were understood not in terms of the metaphysics of being but as God's* narrative history. Others have tried to reinterpret Christology* by turning from the formulae of classical Christology and giving closer attention to the ways in which Jesus is described in the Gospels. Many biblical scholars have asked whether the theological voice in the Bible has not been muted in recent generations by an exclusive use of historical-critical methods and have turned to literary-critical methods of interpretation. Some Protestant ethicists have asked whether their discipline has emphasized principles, rules, and norms at the expense of equally important topics such as character, disposition, virtue, and vision.

Though the literature on narrative theology is relatively new, the role of narrative has long been present in Christian life and thought. Israel recites its history in its Scriptures by means of a story, and the church* proclaims its message about Jesus as the Christ by means of Gospels, which are, after all, stories about Jesus. Further, some of the most important theological documents in Western Christianity either make use of some form of narrative or presuppose it. The first nine books of Augustine's* *Confessions* are a reinterpretation of his life story from the perspective of Christian faith. Though Calvin's *Institutes* are not written in narrative form, the opening sentences make clear that Christian theology begins with the relation between knowledge of God* and knowledge of self. Christian narrative, therefore, might be understood as the result of an individual's or a community's interpretation of history* by means of the knowledge of God derived from biblical narrative.

Many important problems remain unanswered in narrative theology, such as the relation between narrative and history, the role of imagination in reading and interpreting narrative, and whether narrative is simply a useful introduction to theology or whether some form of it can and should be used to reinterpret Christian doctrine.*

Barth, *CD* IV/2, 154–264; H. Frei, *The Eclipse of Biblical Narrative* (1974); H. R. Niebuhr, *The Meaning of Revelation* (1941).

GEORGE W. STROUP

Native Americans

Historically, the indigenous people of North America maintained and practiced religious systems. Many tribes and individuals continue into the present day. Creation stories, after-life beliefs, sacred objects, symbols, and chants are all part of the Native American heritage. "Planting the flag and the cross," called the "Propagation of the Gospel," set the tone for impacting Native American beliefs to the extent of near cultural annihilation during the sixteenth- and seventeenth-century contact period.

A theology of foreboding permeated the teachings of Calvinists who preached throughout the thirteen colonies that "the mind of man is so entirely alienated from God that he cannot conceive, desire or design anything but which is wicked." Criticized and often prohibited were levity, excessive gift-giving, and dancing—all integral to and characteristic of Indian life. This understanding of Christianity was taught at the height of Great Britain's worldwide colonization when all charters contained a missionary clause.

Among important early events in Native American history are the following. In 1636 Roger Williams began preaching in the Indian language. In 1643 Thomas Mayhew became a missionary on Nantucket and Martha's Vineyard. In 1646 John Eliot, believing that converted Indians should be "sequestered from their heathen brethren," gathered four thousand Wampanoags into little communities of "praying Indians." By 1662, Eliot and Cockenoe de Long Island had translated the Bible into the Natick language.

At Mashpee, Cape Cod, among "shocking conditions resulting from the insatiable appetite for the remaining Indian lands" (Bingham), Richard Bourne openly recognized the injustice of expecting Indians to behave as Christians if their neighbors did not do likewise.

By 1740, Azariah Horton was working among Shinnecock and Montauk Indians, and in 1744 Peter John Cuffee, a Shinnecock, was ordained as a minister. In 1790, Peter John's grandson, "Priest Paul" Cuffee, also a Shinnecock, was ordained too. Shinnecocks slid their church over the ice on Shinnecock Bay to the Reservation.

Others who labored among the Indians were David Jewett, New London; James Davenport, Southold; Benjamin Pomeroy, Hebron; and Jonathan Parsons, Lyme.

A descendant of Uncas, the great Mohegan chief Samson Occom at nineteen was already a tribal leader and able to read English, having studied with Eleazar Wheelock. At twenty-five, Occom was ordained (August 30, 1759) by the Presbytery of Long Island. While he was "no more poorly educated than many a preacher of his day" (Blodgett, p. 35), he was "in eloquence, earnestness and simplicity, superior to most," having studied Hebrew, Greek, Latin, and French. Of his worship services, Occom said: "My method in our religious meeting was that on Sabbath mornings we assemble together about ten o'clock and begin with singing; we generally sang Dr. Watt's* Psalms or Hymns. I distinctly read the Psalms or Hymn first, and then put the meaning of it to them. After that we sing, pray, and sing again. Then I proceed to read some suitable portion of Scripture, speak in familiar discourse and apply it to them. We conclude with prayer and singing" (Blodgett, p. 46). David Fowler, of the Montauks and Brothertown Christian Indians, joined Occom at the Oneida mission.

In 1738 the Stockbridge, made up of Mahican, Housatonic, and Munsee tribes—all of whom had moved from their origins—voted to start a mission village. Beleaguered by "removals" of Indians and decimated by disease and the Revolutionary War, the Stockbridge/Munsee were finally granted land in Wisconsin under the Treaty of 1876 and were joined by Brothertown and Oneidas.

A. G. Bingham, *Mashpee, Land of the Wampanoags* (1970); H. G. Blodgett, *Samson Occom* (1935).

ELIZABETH BESS HAILE
AND HOLLY HAILE SMITH

Natural Theology

The attempt to know God* by reason* and experience* apart from any special revelation.* The Reformed view is basically that of Augustine,* who taught there is no "unaided" true knowledge of God. In the Reformed tradition the closest that one gets to natural theology is with such concepts as general revelation and common grace.* In the seventeenth century, Reformed theologians occasionally spoke of natural theology in contrast to revealed theology. But here natural theology at best served as a prolegomenon to revealed theology. An aspect of natural theology taught by John Calvin* and later Reformed theologians is natural law, but again with different presuppositions from those of advocates of natural theology.

The idea of a natural theology originated with Plato and the Stoics and received its classical formulation in

Thomas Aquinas, who distinguished natural and revealed theology, giving a significant place to the former. This is illustrated in Aquinas's five proofs for the existence of God. The official Roman Catholic position was stated at Vatican I (1870): "The Holy Mother Church holds and teaches that God . . . may certainly be known by the natural light of human reason, by means of created things." In Roman Catholicism, however, natural theology never suffices for a knowledge of the divine mysteries and hence must be augmented by divine revelation.

This is not so in the Enlightenment, where German scholars such as H. S. Reimarus and G. E. Lessing preferred reason and natural theology to faith* and revealed theology. Deists John Toland and Matthew Tindal also totally rejected special revelation. Thus understood, natural theology does not exist in Reformed theology. However, in a modified sense certain related concepts have played a minor role in the Reformed tradition beginning with the Swiss reformers.

John Calvin. One might begin with Huldrych Zwingli,* who, despite his clear views of the holiness of God, human sinfulness, and *sola gratia*, made a few exceptions with his favorite Greek philosophers. Despite the inability of sinful humanity* to know God aright, Zwingli believed that these philosophers were granted a sufficient, albeit dim, knowledge of God* which allowed them to join the saints in glory.

Zwingli never developed this notion, however, whereas the whole first book of Calvin's *Institutes* is devoted to the knowledge of God the creator. Here are echoes of what might appear to be traces of a natural theology with Calvin's appeal to a natural "awareness of divinity" (*sensus divinitatis*) and a "seed of religion" (*semen religionis*) in all people. He also follows the Roman Catholic understanding of Rom. 1:20–21 that in all humans the conviction of God's existence is "naturally inborn in all, and is fixed deep within [us], as it were in the very marrow" (*Inst.* 1.3.1, 3; 4.1).

However, Calvin proceeds to declare "this knowledge is either smothered or corrupted, partly by ignorance, partly by malice" (*Inst.*, title of ch. 4). He is only trying to establish humanity's* responsibility. In fact, this "primal and simple knowledge" of God was effectively lost in Adam's fall (*Inst.* 1.2.1). Like the Stoics and Aquinas, Calvin can appeal to the light of nature, for even "in man's perverted and degenerate nature some sparks still gleam" (*Inst.* 2.2.12). Moreover, in the realm of "earthly things," which do not pertain to the kingdom of God,* humans are by nature endowed with many natural gifts. However, when it comes to knowing God aright and the things that pertain to our salvation,* "the greatest geniuses are blinder than moles" (*Inst.* 2.2.18).

The idea that God endows all people with certain natural gifts has given rise to concepts of common grace or general revelation. Calvin uses the former phrase only once (*Inst.* 2.2.17), the latter not at all. But it came to be a key concept in Dutch and Dutch-American Calvinism in the late nineteenth and early twentieth centuries.

Reformed confessions. A trace of what has been labeled natural theology is found in certain Reformed confessions. In the opening articles of the French,* Belgic,* and Hungarian confessions, and in the WCF,* God is said to be known "first, in his works," and "secondly, and more clearly in his Word" (French Confession, art. 2). The Belgic Confession repeats this affirmation almost verbatim, whereas the WCF surprisingly is closer to Calvin: "Although the light of nature, and the works of creation* and providence,* do so far manifest the goodness, wisdom, and power of God, as to leave men inexcusable; yet they are not sufficient to give that knowledge of God, and of his will, which is necessary unto salvation" (WCF, 1.1).

Arthur Cochrane, following Barth, laments: "Having gained admission in the French Confession, the virus of natural theology quickly spread to the Belgic Confession of 1561, and thence to the Westminster Confession of Faith of 1643. Not until the Barmen Theological Declaration* of 1934 was natural theology categorically rejected in its first articles, and the original witness of the Reformed Confessions of the 16th century reaffirmed" (*Reformed Confessions of the*

16th Century [1966], p. 139). The question is, which sixteenth-century confessions? Moreover, this "virus of natural theology" has hardly had the destructive effects in the churches adhering to those confessions that Cochrane suggests. If there is a problem in these confessions, it is not the positing of a revelation in creation and the Word but rather the danger of assuming that one can appreciate God's revelation in creation and providence apart from the Word, a point Calvin stresses more clearly.

Neo-Calvinists and common grace. The two great theologians of the reform movement in the latter part of the nineteenth century in the Netherlands, Abraham Kuyper* and Herman Bavinck,* devoted much attention to the concept of common grace (*algemeene genade* or *gemeene gratie*). This concept, with slight variations, was also taught by Charles Hodge* and A. A. Hodge* of Princeton Seminary. As over against special grace which relates to salvation, common grace is extended to all people, believers and unbelievers, and is responsible for restraining evil and making life tolerable. Moreover, it also accounts for the natural gifts of humanity, social and civic justice, and makes possible the fruits of culture. As common grace is understood in Dutch Reformed theology, however, it does not mitigate human depravity or compromise the radical need for the special grace of God manifest in Jesus Christ. The goal, rather, is a world and life view (*Weltanschauung*) which acknowledges God's presence and activity in every sphere of creation. Though the Dutch neo-Calvinists would subordinate creation to redemption in order to fulfill their vision of the "cultural mandate," in the case of Kuyper it was combined with the idea of an antithesis between the church and the world. This "left Neo-Calvinism with ominous ideological strains" (J. D. Bratt, *Dutch Calvinism in Modern America* [1984], p. 18), but in no way did it result in a natural theology. For, similar to Calvin, whatever good non-Christians could accomplish was attributed not to human effort but to divine grace.*

Barth-Brunner debate. In the 1930s the question of natural theology came to a head in the famous dispute between Karl Barth* and Emil Brunner.* A key issue was whether there is a point of contact (Ger. *Anknüpfungspunkt*) for the gospel in so-called "natural man." Brunner challenged Barth's thoroughgoing Christocentrism and accused him of an unbiblical discontinuity between creation and grace. Barth replied with his sharp *Nein!* and attacked Brunner's use of the term *Offenbarungsmächtigkeit* (capacity for revelation). Brunner, no less than Barth, believed that God is truly known only by God's self-revelation in Jesus Christ as witnessed in Scripture.* At the same time, however, Brunner taught that God's general revelation could be seen in the creation, especially in orders (*Ordnungen*) of creation such as marriage* and the state, and in God's image in humanity, though defaced by the fall. "Its *form*, if not its *content,* remains our essential humanity, our personhood, our reason and our ethical responsibility" (A. I. C. Heron, *A Century of Protestant Theology* [1980], p. 87). Brunner appealed to the traditional interpretation of Rom. 1:19–20 and maintained that this interpretation was Calvin's. Barth also claimed Calvin for his position and was later defended in this regard by his brother Peter. Brunner, it is generally agreed, could lay better claim to having Calvin on his side, but various of his misleading statements made it possible for Barth, with some justification, to claim victory in this dispute.

For Barth this issue was more than academic. He regarded Brunner's "compromise" as a stab in the back in the midst of a life-and-death struggle against the "German Christians" who had succumbed to the wiles of Nazi ideology. Out of this struggle came the Barmen Declaration* (1934) with its forthright attack on the position of the "German Christians": "Jesus Christ, as he is attested for us in Holy Scripture, is the one Word of God which we have to hear and which we have to trust and obey in life and in death." This Declaration was adopted as one of the confessions of the UPCUSA (1967).

Conclusions. The threat of subtle forms of natural theology did not end with the demise of the "German Christians" at the end of World War II. Reformed churches are also susceptible to the temptation to let other gods in the form of false ideologies undermine "the faith once for all delivered to the saints." The unresolved question is whether there can be a legitimate understanding of creation, nature, or culture apart from a specific reference to Jesus Christ. Now that we are concerned about a theology of creation, which is quite different from a natural theology, it may be possible to praise the God of creation who is none other than the God and Father of our Lord Jesus Christ.

Barth, *CD* II/1, 10ff., 88ff.; K. Barth and E. Brunner, *Natural Theology* (1934); G. C. Berkouwer, *General Revelation* (1958); E. Brunner, *Revelation and Reason* (1946); Calvin, *Inst.* 1.1–8; 2.1–4.

I. JOHN HESSELINK

Neo-Orthodoxy

The term "neo-orthodoxy" describes the work of several twentieth-century European and North American theologians and, specifically, their approach to the task and substance of Christian theology. Like "scholasticism,"* neo-orthodoxy is a term of categorization usually referring to Karl Barth,* Emil Brunner,* the early Rudolf Bultmann and Friedrich Gogarten in Europe, and Reinhold Niebuhr* and H. Richard Niebuhr* in North America. Donald Baillie,* John Baillie,* and T. F. Torrance* of Scotland as well as the early Paul Tillich are also cited as neo-orthodox.

None of these theologians referred to their work by this term, which originated in the English-speaking world, nor by other terms like it: "theology of crisis," "Barthianism," "dialectical theology,"* and, in relation specifically to Reinhold Niebuhr, "Christian realism." The term, invented by critics, was never quite free of denigrative connotation. Though novel aspects were present in those theologies, such as the critical study of Scripture,* openness to other sciences and aversion to metaphysics or "natural theology,"* justifying the appellation "neo," critics meant to score what they believed to be the repristination of classic dogmatic loci of the Protestant Reformation. From this view, neo-orthodoxy reinstituted an orthodoxy that modern Christian theology in the West had long believed itself to have left behind.

The theologies to which neo-orthodoxy refers were worked out between the end of World War I and the height of the Cold War. This dating is not accidental. Many critics of neo-orthodoxy associate its rise with the disillusionment of a humanity failing its highest aspirations. In such times, the critics held, longing for firm ground turns to transcendentally legitimated authority, like that of Scripture in traditional Protestantism. Coupled with it is a pessimism about the potential of the spirit, will, and mind of humankind; the affirmation of God breeds an abnegation of the human and vice versa.

"Neo-orthodox" theologies share a strong repudiation of Western confidence in the abilities of goodwill and historical progress. Experiences of massive political and religious support of World War I (Barth), the actual fighting and its huge cost in human life (Tillich), the murderous exploitation of workers by the acquirers of capital (Reinhold Niebuhr and Barth), and the like, led to a loss of faith in social and cultural progress. Gone was confidence that the gospel proclaims God's reign as an optimistic and moral entity which can and ought to be realized by human beings, and this had shaken trust in the place and talk of church and theology. The reconstruction that neo-orthodoxy undertook sought to renew theology and church in continuity with the Reformation and its reliance on the Bible, the sole "authoritative" witness to the Word of God.* As this Word, the gospel tells the truth about the world, namely, that it is powerless to redeem itself and that every self-generated liberation leads eventually to new idolatry* and oppression.

Neo-orthodoxy is marked by Christocentricity. For example, Calvin's* teaching that the grace* of God's incarnation* in Christ granted to humans knowledge of God* gave structure to Barth's critique of liberal theology; Luther's* teaching on the work of Christ relating to sin* and justification* informed Reinhold Niebuhr's searing assessment of liberalism, particularly its efforts to "Christianize the social order." Their positive theological projects drew on the Reformation's incarnational Christologies in contradistinction from the liberal preoccupation with the "historical" Jesus. While the Christologies of neo-orthodoxy are not identical, they fueled discussion about Christology "from above" and "from below," the "human Jesus" and the "divine Christ." Neo-orthodoxy spoke decisively about the "Christ above us" who exceeds the liberal "Christ within us."

An antiliberal stance appeared in other features of neo-orthodox theology, accounting for much of its critics' reactions, both then and now. Neo-orthodox theologians stressed the otherness of God;* the discontinuity between the divine and the human. They replaced human religious experience* with divine self-revelation as the source of human knowledge of God. They interpreted God's reign and the meaning of history* in the light of biblical eschatology,* grounding it in God's action rather than in the progressive labors of humankind. They rejected the view that sin* was human ignorance and unwillingness to transcend what belongs to nature and that it was overcome by sound education. Sin was, rather, the desire to be godlike, a perversion of freedom,* which is undone entirely by God's forgiveness* alone.

Neo-orthodoxy held that God's truth is never direct and transparent but always indirect and dialectical; found in the tension between one truth and another. Because revelation* brings together eternity and time, revelation needs to be spoken of in terms of paradox, supremely in the paradox that Jesus Christ is both human and divine.

It was said that neo-orthodoxy succeeded in replacing the anthropocentrism of modernity with a theocentrism bordering on a supernaturalism which "bids us go back at a time when, if ever, we must go forward" (Edwin Lewis, *The Christian Century*, March 22, 1933). The perduring issue of critique is the "otherness of God," the insistence that God is wholly other and, as such, breaks in on the world from above. More often than not, this is taken to be a metaphysical assertion about God's being. Rather, it was a claim that the human experience of the God *of whom* the Bible speaks is wholly other from that of the God *of whom* modern theology spoke. For this reason the language of neo-orthodoxy about revelation sounded so different from liberalism.

Neo-orthodoxy has relatively little influence now in Europe and North America. Yet it is no mere stage in the history of theology. Its criticism of liberalism was valid and creative and responsive to the changing context. The theologies of Reformation churches and their ecumenical partners were influenced significantly by neo-orthodoxy, as is the thought of churches that are bearers of their people's liberation struggles; the work of A. A. Boesak* in South Africa and J. M. Bonino in South America come to mind. Neo-orthodoxy was ignored by theologians and churches at their peril, whether they understand it or not.

J. D. Godsey, "Neoorthodoxy," *The Encyclopedia of Religion*, vol. 10 (1987); P. L. Lehmann, "Crisis, The Theology of," *NSH Sup* 1:309–312.

H. MARTIN RUMSCHEIDT

Netherlands, The

The Synod of Dort* (1618–19) marked a significant turning point in the history of the Reformed faith in the Netherlands. It definitively established Calvinism,* over against Arminianism,* as the orthodox theology of the Reformed Church. Dort further established as doctrinal standards for the Dutch Reformed Church the Belgic Confession,* the Heidelberg Catechism,* and the Canons of Dort, the last representing the doctrinal deliverances of the Synod. Dort also clarified the polity* of the Reformed Church, though this polity—which gave the church greater independence in governance and discipline*—never enjoyed the full support or cooperation of the civil authorities. The Synod provided a new translation of the Bible into Dutch, which became the standard edition for the Reformed Church in the Netherlands. After Dort, the Reformed Church clearly enjoyed and benefited from its status as the privileged church in the Dutch Republic, though for much of the seventeenth century the Reformed Church never included a majority of the population.

In the seventeenth century both Pietism and scholasticism* exercised a significant influence on Dutch Calvinism. In the so-called "Further Reformation of the Seventeenth Century," a number of Dutch theologians, influenced by English Puritanism,* called for a revival of the practice of piety* within the church and placed a renewed emphasis on an experiential faith. William Teellinck* and William Brakel (1635–1711) were leaders in the Dutch pietist movement. The leading representative of Reformed scholasticism was Gisbert Voetius,* who was also deeply influenced by Pietism. He incorporated Aristotelian logic and method into his theology and became a champion of Reformed orthodoxy* and doctrinal purity. A strong defender of Calvinism against both Arminianism and a renewed Catholicism, Voetius also championed Aristotelianism in the face of Cartesianism and the growing influence of the scientific revolution. The seventeenth century also saw an increasing emphasis on foreign missions within the Reformed Church as the Netherlands became deeply involved in world trade.

In the eighteenth century the Reformed Church and its theology, like most of Dutch society, was influenced by the Enlightenment and the movement toward a tolerant and rational faith. However, Pietism never died out, and in the early nineteenth century the Reformed Church experienced a revival or awakening (the Réveil). It was a reaction against both the Enlightenment and the French Revolution, emphasizing the need for repentance,* conversion,* and practical Christian living, as well as faithfulness to the doctrinal and ecclesiastical standards of the Reformed Church. A division between the established church and those influenced by the Réveil led to a secession (the *Afscheiding*) by the latter and the establishment of a Seceder Church (1834). Another secession (the *Doleantie*), under the leadership of Abraham Kuyper,* occurred in the Reformed Church (1886), and in 1892 these two seceder groups joined to form the Reformed Churches of the Netherlands (GKN).

Kuyper was leader of a revival of orthodox Calvinism and the dominant figure in Dutch Calvinism (1870–1920). He was deeply involved in Dutch political life, developed the idea of Calvinism as a world and life view, and believed a revived Calvinism should confront liberalism and lead to Christian cultural engagement and political action. He became a leader in a Reformed political party (Antirevolutionary Party*) and helped found the Free University of Amsterdam,* a Calvinist institution of higher learning (1880s). Kuyper also edited a daily newspaper designed to promote a Reformed perspective on social and political issues and served as prime minister of the Netherlands (1901–5). The influence of Kuyper's Calvinism on religion, politics, and education was vast. In this same period, Herman Bavinck* offered a careful critique of modernism and promoted orthodox Calvinism.

In the twentieth century, Kuyper's spirit is seen in the work of Herman Dooyeweerd,* a philosopher and jurist who spent much of his life developing a Reformed philosophical system based on the idea of law. Kuyper also influenced the theology of G. C. Berkouwer,* longtime professor of dogmatics at the Free University. Twentieth-century Calvinism in the Netherlands has been influenced by the theology of Karl Barth,* and since World War II the various Reformed churches have struggled to find their place in an increasingly secular society.

O. de Jong, *Nederlandse Kerkafschiedenis* (1985).

MICHAEL A. HAKKENBERG

Nevin, John Williamson (1803–1886)

Born in Franklin County, Pennsylvania, Nevin graduated from Union College (1821) and Princeton Seminary (1826). After two years as an assistant at Princeton, he became professor of theology at the Presbyterian Seminary in Allegheny, Pennsylvania (1829). Nevin was called to the seminary of the German Reformed Church in Mercersburg (1840). There he taught until 1851, serving also as president of Marshall College (1843–53). From 1866 to 1876 he was president of Franklin and Marshall College in Lancaster, Pennsylvania, where he died.

With *The Anxious Bench* (1843), an attack on the prevalent revivalism, and *The Mystical Presence* (1846), a restatement of the eucharistic teaching of John Calvin,* Nevin laid the foundation for the Mercersburg Theology,* a task in which he was ably assisted by his colleague, the church historian Philip Schaff.* Mercersburg Theology sought to restore ecclesiological, sacramental, and liturgical elements to the Reformed tradition, especially the German Reformed Church. It was bitterly opposed in the Reformed tradition by evangelical revivalists as well as old-line Princeton* Calvinism.* Nevin's work, however, forced Reformed churches to reexamine their heritage and has been of lasting influence, especially in an ecumenical age, as is evidenced by recent reprints of his major works. He was clearly one of the major American theological figures of the nineteenth century.

HOWARD G. HAGEMAN

New College, Edinburgh

One of the leading centers of theological study in the Reformed tradition. It began (1846) on a prominent site overlooking Princes Street as the divinity hall of the Free Church of Scotland, with Thomas Chalmers* as its first principal. With church union in 1900 (between most of the Free Church and the United Presbyterians), it passed to the new United Free Church of Scotland. When most of the latter united with the national Church of Scotland (1929), it merged with the Divinity Faculty of the University of Edinburgh (whose history goes back to the university's foundation [1583]) in the New College building. It remains the seat of the University Faculty, now virtually the largest in Britain, while retaining a less obvious identity as a Church of Scotland college. The church appoints the principal and is represented in appointment to professorships. Both staff and students are thoroughly ecumenical and international, and New College trains men and women for ministry in other churches as well as for the national church. It has an outstanding library.

Notable teachers include the following: in the Free Church era (when it outshone the University Faculty), William Cunningham,* R. S. Candlish, James Buchanan, James Bannerman, A. B. Davidson, Robert Rainy,* and Alexander Duff;* in the United Free Church period, H. R. Mackintosh,* A. C. Welch, Alexander Whyte,* and Marcus Dods; and post-1929, John Baillie,* William Manson, James S. Stewart,* and T. F. Torrance.*

H. Watt, *New College Edinburgh: A Centenary History* (1846); "1583–1983" *New College Bulletin* 14 (1983).

DAVID F. WRIGHT

New England Theology

A rather standard Calvinistic theology came to New England with John Cotton,* Thomas Hooker,* Thomas Shepard,* and Peter Bulkeley. The Half-Way Covenant,* a distinct departure from traditional Calvinism* (which permitted Baptism* only for infants of communicant members), was adopted (1662). This led to Solomon Stoddard's opening of the Communion itself to persons with "historical faith" but not claiming conversion.* Jonathan Edwards's* objection to this led to his dismissal from the Northampton pastorate (1750).

Charles Hodge* contended that the senior Edwards deviated from Calvinism only on mediate imputation and metaphysical idealism, though he was disappointed also with Edwards's qualifications for admission to the Lord's Table.

What came to be called New England Theology was a more profound departure that could not call Edwards father, though his son, Jonathan Jr., Joseph Bellamy,* Samuel Hopkins,* and many others did so claim until its end with Andover Seminary and Edwards Amasa Park (1808–1900). B. B. Warfield* contended that Edwards, in spite of his activism, delayed the triumph of Arminianism* in New England a hundred years.

It is generally agreed that the *Concio ad Clerum* (1828) of N. W. Taylor* represented a clear break with Calvinism and Edwards, though this was not generally admitted by Yale's "New Divinity" or Taylorism. By 1837 a split in the Presbyterian Church between New School and Old School occurred.

At least six doctrines are commonly associated with the New England Theology:

the unconverted are by "natural ability" able to choose virtue but never do so of themselves; the governmental theory of the atonement;* inability does limit responsibility; disinterested benevolence; God in creation aims at humanity's* happiness; and "seeking" evangelism.*

JOHN H. GERSTNER

New Haven Theology

Initially propounded by Timothy Dwight,* this Reformed perspective made more room for the revivals which had been God's "surprising work" in colonial America. As Dwight, his student N. W. Taylor,* and others developed it, the New Haven Theology accentuated human agency more than had Jonathan Edwards's* theology. Original sin* here was seen as inevitable but not determined genetically. Humans are responsible for their sin and can overcome sinning. God's special care for the redeemed was accented over God's care for the whole creation. Christian life was largely a reasonable configuration of "duties."

In the New Haven Theology, Scottish common sense philosophy* prevailed over Edwards's Lockean grounding. It also "worked," as Dwight led a revival among Yale students (1818). Other New Haven revivalists joined in the prolonged Second Great Awakening.* Thus the theology provided a vehicle in the reconstruction of Calvinism* to appeal to a democratic American culture.

LOUIS B. WEEKS

Newbigin, Lesslie (1908–)

English missionary (Church of Scotland), ecumenist, and author who served in South India (1936–59; 1965–74). Active in forming the united Church of South India, by which he was consecrated bishop, Newbigin strongly defended it abroad. Appointed General Secretary of the International Missionary Council (1959–61), he assisted its integration with the WCC,* becoming an Associate General Secretary (1962–65). He taught at the Selly Oak Colleges, Birmingham (1974–83). An exponent of Biblical Theology, Newbigin stressed ecclesiology, notably the church's mission and unity.

L. Newbigin, *Unfinished Agenda: An Autobiography* (1985).

ROBERT S. BILHEIMER

Nicodemism

The term used by John Calvin* in the 1540s to describe evangelicals living in Roman Catholic territories who dissimulated, or kept quiet, their reforming beliefs, or even simulated Catholic beliefs by, for example, attending Mass. Claims that Nicodemism had a clear biblical base, and a European-wide network centered in Strassburg, are exaggerated. Named after Nicodemus (John 3), whose stealth was rewarded by Jesus' teaching about rebirth, it had leanings toward spiritualism and irenicism but also Libertinism. It had tactical attractions for Wolfgang Capito* and Martin Bucer* during the period of the religious colloquies and an appeal for individuals unhappy both with the old church and with emergent Protestantism. By insisting, however, that the honor of God demands a bodily as well as a spiritual witness against idolatry* and superstition, that the church of Christ must be visibly set apart from pollution and error, and that martyrdom or exile, not quietism, is the appropriate response to an ungodly ruler, Calvin enabled Protestantism to consolidate and survive in France and elsewhere.

C. Eire, "Calvin and Nicodemism: A Reappraisal," *SCJ* 10 (1979): 45–69; and "Prelude to Sedition? Calvin's Attack on Nicodemism," *ARH* 76 (1985): 120–43; P. C. Matheson, "Martyrdom or Mission? A Protestant Debate," *ARH* 80 (1989): 154–72.

P. C. MATHESON

Niebuhr, H. Richard (1894–1963)

Son of Gustav Niebuhr, an influential pastor in the German Evangelical Synod of North America, and younger brother of Reinhold Niebuhr,* H. Richard Niebuhr also became an acclaimed theologian and taught Christian ethics at Yale Divinity School (from 1931).

His writings treat the Protestant movement in America, dynamics of revelation and faith,* tasks of ministry,* and the role of the church* in the world. They also address critical issues, including the relationship between historical conditioning and Christian believing, the place of value theory in theology* and ethics,* the relation between devotion to God and culture's many commitments, and the interpretation of human agency. Prominent influences on Niebuhr's thinking include Augustine,* Jonathan Edwards,* Friedrich Schleiermacher,* Ernst Troeltsch, Karl Barth,* and Paul Tillich, as well as Josiah Royce's philosophy of loyalty and George Herbert Mead's pragmatic and social theory of the self. Niebuhr's theology was among the most original and creative of his generation. It emphasized the sovereignty of God* and the claim that Christian believing precipitates a transformation or revolution in ourselves that displaces lesser loyalties and moves us to respond in fitting ways to the entire community of being. His later works, *Radical Monotheism and Western Culture* (1960) and *The Responsible Self* (1963), indicate how thoroughly Niebuhr departed from the then-reigning dogmatic approaches among Protestant theologians and ethicists.

DOUGLAS F. OTTATI

Niebuhr, Reinhold (1892–1971)

Pastor, theologian, and social philosopher, Niebuhr was born in Missouri and grew up in the German Evangelical Synod of North America, an immigrant denomination loosely connected to the Church of the Prussian Union, created to combine key Lutheran and Reformed elements (1815). His degrees were from Elmhurst College (1910), Eden Seminary (1913), and Yale (1914; 1915).

From 1915 to 1928, Niebuhr's base for involvement in war, race, and labor issues was his pastorate at Bethel Evangelical Church in Henry Ford's Detroit. From background and training, Niebuhr came to the social gospel* naturally and embraced pacificism and socialism with enthusiasm.

Four years after he joined the faculty of Union Theological Seminary (N.Y.), he stunned liberals with *Moral Man and Immoral Society* (1932). By drawing a distinction between the moral possibilities of individuals and those of groups, Niebuhr deserted social theories based on a progression of love through moral suasion for theories based on the pursuit of justice,* which resorted to compromise and coercion informed by religious imagination.

In *An Interpretation of Christian Ethics* (1935), Niebuhr criticized liberals for thinking that Jesus' ethic could be directly implemented in political and economic matters. He also criticized orthodox Christians for denying any practical value to Jesus' ethic. Liberal and orthodox alike departed from prophetic religion by breaking a dialectic in which the law of love is the source of norms for implementing approximate justice and a corrective of these norms.

Niebuhr was associated with neo-orthodoxy* but sharply criticized Barth's positivistic view of revelation* and his inadequate social policy. Still, there was no mistaking that Niebuhr rediscovered the usefulness of the biblical and theological resources of Protestantism in the 1930s. Desiring the pessimistic Lutheran social morality of the Evangelical Synod to be modified by the transforming Calvinism of the Reformed Church in the United States, Niebuhr and his brother H. Richard,* advocated their merger (1934). The Evangelical and Reformed Church later became part of the United Church of Christ.

As World War II approached, Niebuhr abandoned the Socialist Party in favor of Roosevelt's New Deal policies. He remained a social activist, served on numerous committees, and wrote endlessly for magazines and newspapers on alternatives to Marxist and capitalist ideologies. He helped found Americans for Democratic Action and was founder and editor of *Christianity and Crisis.*

Of numerous books, the most important was perhaps his Gifford Lectures published as *The Nature and Destiny of Man* (2 vols.; 1941–43). There he presented a mature Protestant theology with robust doctrines of creation,* sin,* justification* by faith,* and eschatology* cast in service to political and social analysis.

Niebuhr was intensely interested in

planning the shape of the postwar world and was an early advocate of Zionism. In the 1950s he actively supported U.S. policies against Soviet expansionism, without the self-righteousness typical in the Cold War era. In the 1960s Niebuhr spoke out against American involvement in Vietnam, criticized Billy Graham for his close ties to Richard Nixon, and supported the civil rights movement.

R. Fox, *Reinhold Niebuhr* (1985); R. Harries, ed., *Reinhold Niebuhr and the Issues of Our Time* (1986); C. W. Kegley and R. W. Bretall, eds., *Reinhold Niebuhr* (1956); D. B. Robertson, *Reinhold Niebuhr's Works: A Bibliography*, rev. ed. (1983); R. H. Stone, *Reinhold Niebuhr: Prophet to Politicians* (1972).

STEPHEN D. CROCCO

Nonconformity

Nonconformists did not conform to the Church of England as by law established. Though by this definition Roman Catholics are nonconformists, the term generally denotes Protestants. Since the later nineteenth century, the term "Free Church" has often been preferred as more positively signifying persons whose freedom in Christ makes them free to be the church (i.e., "apart from the state").

The Toleration Act (1689) legalized the position of orthodox Dissenters and made it an offense to interfere with their worship and legitimate activities; but it left them in a sociopolitical ghetto for the next two centuries.

The oldest nonconformist groups with a continuing history are Congregationalists* and Baptists, whose roots are in Puritan* Separatism; Presbyterians* (from 1662; and subsequently tenuously until strengthened by influxes from Scotland, Ireland, and Wales); and Quakers (1668). The Methodists gradually came under the umbrella of nonconformity following separation from the Church of England. All these, together with some smaller bodies, are members of the Free Church Federal Council (FCFC; 1940), which is the descendant of the National Free Church Council (1892) and the Federal Council of Evangelical Free Churches (1919). Some nonconformist groups, including the Christian Brethren, do not belong to the FCFC.

The FCFC deals with chaplaincy matters and represents the Free Churches on certain official occasions. Its opinion is sought as appropriate by legislative and other bodies. It offers guidance to the churches on socioethical and educational matters. Here memory lingers of the struggle against the support of Anglican schools from rates paid by nonconformists, and the "nonconformist conscience," which erupted during the Irish question and embraced such matters as temperance and Sunday observance. It cannot be said, however, that the ecclesiological convictions that motivated historic Dissent command much attention today. Many feel that, the sociopolitical deprivations having been removed, the battle of Dissent is won. It may, however, be worthwhile to consider the possibility that in a post-Constantinian age the questions, Who are the church? and How are Christians to honor the rule of Christ in his church? press with renewed vigor. Moreover, since there exist Reformed and Lutheran establishments (of various kinds) as well as Anglican, the questions have some ecumenical significance.

D. W. Bebbington, *The Nonconformist Conscience* (1982); H. F. Lovell Cocks, *The Nonconformist Conscience* (1943); E. K. H. Jordan, *Free Church Unity* (1956); E. A. Payne, *Free Churchmen, Unrepentant and Repentant* (1965); A. P. F. Sell, "Dubious Establishment? A Neglected Ecclesiological Testimony," in *Dissenting Thought and the Life of the Churches* (1990).

ALAN P. F. SELL

Oecolampadius, John (1482–1531)

Born in Weinsberg, in the Palatinate, Johann Hüssgen or Hauschein ("candlestick") pursued the Christian humanists'* literary and historical studies at Heidelberg, Bologna, and Tübingen. Having mastered the classical languages, he grecized his name to Oecolampadius. Erasmus* recognized Oecolampadius's Hebrew competence and asked him to compile a philological index to his edition of Jerome's complete works. Oecolampadius was called to the pulpit of the Cathedral of Augsburg (1518), but by 1520 uncertainty about church reform led him to resign. Retiring from public life, he translated some of Chrysostom's writings, including his long series of Genesis sermons. These encouraged the Reformation to adopt the grammatical-historical exegesis of Scripture advocated by Chrysostom. Oecolampadius reappeared in Basel (1523) to preach through Isaiah as requested by the city council. He became pastor of St. Mark's Church and professor of Sacred Scripture at the university. Basel adopted his Reformation Act, which contributed much to the Reformed doctrine of the ministry* (1529). Though he supported Zwingli* at the Marburg Colloquy, his eucharistic theology had distinct mystical dimensions. Defending infant baptism* against the Anabaptists, he developed a strong covenantal* theology of worship.* Particularly significant is his definition of the concept "Reformed according to Scripture."

H.-R. Guggisberg, *RGG*[3] 4:1567–68; H. O. Old, "The Homiletics of John Oecolampadius and the Sermons of the Greek Fathers," in *Communio Sanctorum, Mélanges offerts à J.-J. von Allmen* (1982), ed. B. Bobrinskoy et al.; E. Stähelin, *Das theologische Lebenswerk Johannes Oekolampads* (1939).

HUGHES OLIPHANT OLD

Oldham, Joseph Houldsworth (1874–1969)

Born in India and educated in Britain, Oldham returned to India to work for the YMCA. At Oxford he was converted under Dwight L. Moody and became a protégé of John R. Mott. As secretary, he was the chief organizer of the World Missionary Conference in Edinburgh (1910) from which the modern missionary and ecumenical movements flowed. He was appointed Secretary of the Continuation Committee, became chief architect of the International Missionary Council, and was founder and first editor of the *International Review of Missions.*

Oldham rapidly became an ecumenical statesman who advised governments, coordinated international missionary efforts during World War I, and became an acknowledged authority on many aspects of colonial policy, particularly education. He was one of the founders of the WCC* and was appointed a president. He organized the Oxford Conference on Church, Community and State (1937) and established the Christian Frontier Council to help lay Christians "find out how the Christian faith bears on the questions which they have to deal with in their daily occupations."

Himself no mean intellect, Oldham organized (1940s and 1950s) a varied group of influential Christian thinkers which became known as "The Moot." These included T. S. Eliot, Michael Polanyi, John Baillie,* Donald Mackinnon, and Karl Mannheim, while Americans such as Reinhold Niebuhr* were occasional visitors. Oldham's intellectual influence was considerable but, despite a number of books (*Christianity and the Race Problem* [1924] and *Life Is Commitment* [1953] are probably the most important), it was quiet and inconspicuous and has not yet been properly assessed. Some saw Oldham as a prophet; he was called "a wily saint," and "the arch-intriguer for good." For others he is a pioneer of the ecumenical movement, or mission strategist, or turbulent priest (though he trained for the ministry of the United Free Church of Scotland, he was never ordained). He felt to the end that he was "still the missionary at heart," motivated by the evangelical faith he inherited and made his own.

DNB (1981); K. Bliss, "The Legacy of J. H. Oldham," *International Bulletin of Missionary Research*, Jan. 1984; K. Clements, biography in preparation.

DUNCAN B. FORRESTER

Olevianus, Caspar (1536–1587)

German Reformed pastor and theologian. Born in Trier, Olevianus studied law at the universities of Orléans and Bourges and theology with John Calvin* in Geneva. After unsuccessfully attempting (1559) to convert his hometown to Protestantism, he taught dogmatics at the University of Heidelberg for two years before becoming pastor of Heidelberg's Holy Spirit Church. During 1562 he served with Zacharias Ursinus* as an author of the Heidelberg Catechism* (1563), though his exact role in the project remains unclear. Forced to flee Heidelberg when the Lutherans came to power (1576), he spent his final years establishing Reformed churches in the Wetterau region of Germany and founding and teaching at the Herborn Academy (from 1584).

Olevianus's theological legacy lies largely in the area of the doctrine of the covenant, as his major works suggest (*De substantia foederis gratuiti* [1585]; *Der Gnadenbund Gottes* [1590]). Though neither the founder nor the final architect of Reformed covenant* theology, he was a key intermediary figure in its development. Not only was he the first to use the covenant of grace* as the leitmotif of a mature systematic theology, he was also the first to mention a pretemporal redemptive pact between the Father and the Son, an Adamic covenant with Satan at the fall, and a divine covenant with creatures for the protection of believers.

L. D. Bierma, *German Calvinism in the Confessional Age: The Covenant Theology of Caspar Olevian* (1991); K. Sudhoff, *C. Olevianus und Z. Ursinus* (1857).

LYLE D. BIERMA

Olivétan, Pierre-Robert (c. 1505–1538)

Early French reformer; translator of the French Bible (Neuchâtel, 1535), the Bible of the French Reformation,* many times revised. Information on Olivétan's life and activities is very sketchy. His true name was Louis Olivier, a cousin of Calvin, also born at Noyon in Picardy. Certainly he knew Calvin* well, since both their fathers worked for the bishop. Like Calvin, he studied at Paris and there, with William Farel* and others, joined the reform group inspired by Jacques Lefèvre d'Etaples. Theodore Beza,* who should know, says that Olivétan convinced Calvin to embrace the reform, apparently having accompanied him to Orléans (1528). He fled to Strassburg, where he studied with Martin Bucer* and Wolfgang Capito.*

By late 1529 Olivétan was an integral part of Farel's "missionary team" working to spread the reform message in the Vaud, Piedmont, and Geneva. Because of his training, he became a key player in Farel's strategy to control the educational enterprise; often we find him as "maître d'écoles" (Lausanne, 1529; Neuchâtel, 1531; Geneva, 1532). He also evangelized these areas, and especially the Piedmont. While there, he undertook Farel's longtime request of translating the Bible (entire year of 1534), completing it by February 1535. He came to Neuchâtel for the publication (by Pierre de Vingle), returned briefly to Piedmont, then went to Geneva (1536–April 1538) working with de Vingle's publishing venture, with Farel and Calvin, and preparing revised editions of the NT (1536; 1538). In late 1538, while evangelizing in Italy, he died, probably from poisoning.

G. Berthoud et al., *Aspects de la propagande* (1957); H. Delarue, "Olivétan et de Vingle," *Bibliothèque d'humanisme et renaissance* (1946): 105–18; H. Meylan, *Silhouettes du XVIe siècle* (1943).

BRIAN G. ARMSTRONG

Oman, John Wood (1860–1939)

British Presbyterian theologian, professor at Westminster College, Cambridge (1907–35), and principal (1922–35). Oman was Moderator of the General Assembly* of the Presbyterian Church of England (1931).

Oman's intensely personalistic theology was expressed in *Grace and Personality* (1917) and *The Natural and the Supernatural* (1931). The way of reverence is the path to freedom, and just as God graciously respects those whom God has made, so we must pursue moral nurture by moral (not authoritarian) means. Oman refers both to major Christian doctrines and to the Christian understanding of history.

DNB; G. Alexander and H. H. Farmer, "Memoir," in *Honest Religion*, J. W. Oman (posth. 1941); F. G. Healey, *Religion and Reality* (1965); F. R. Tennant, *Proceedings of the British Academy*, vol. 25 (1939).

ALAN P. F. SELL

Omnipotence

The affirmation that God is omnipotent has traditionally been taken to mean, "God can do all things." While widely held that God* is omnipotent, there is considerable disagreement on what this really entails. For John Calvin,* omnipotence was a central conviction understood to mean the effectual exercise of the divine personal will in accomplishing divine purposes. Closer study will reveal that Calvin's conception was complex, nuanced, and formed by diverse influences. He formed his view in conversation with (and over against) other perspectives available on his theological horizon.

In the medieval conversation about the scope of divine omnipotence, certain intractable problems were addressed. Does omnipotence mean that God can change the past? Can God create a square circle? Two significant limitations on the scope of omnipotence were proposed as a way of resolving such difficulties. In the interest of affirming the primacy and freedom of the divine will, Calvin refused both limitations.

The first limitation was to define omnipotence in terms of what is logically possible. The standard meaning came to be, "God can do whatever is doable." Calvin countered that it is in the freedom of the divine will to "determine" what is possible. The possibilities that are open to God are not limited by metaphysical necessities. God's personal will is what defines God's power. Therefore no external, metaphysical limitations can be placed upon divine power.

The second limitation employed in the Middle Ages involved a distinction between God's "absolute power" (divine power in itself) and God's "ordained power" (divine power in connection with divine willing). Calvin refused this distinction as well, saying that the concept of absolute power was an empty abstraction. God's power is not independent of God's moral character; rather, it expresses it. This power is not a neutral blind force of nature; it is the power of a free, personal will. Like the will of any person, God's will has a certain character—namely, the character of goodness which is part of the divine nature. While external, metaphysical limitations are to be refused, internal, moral limitations are to be admitted. God's power may be unlimited, but it is not arbitrary. Thus any abstract definition of omnipotence as "absolute power"—a definition that Duns Scotus was supporting—is to be rejected. This omnipotent power is displayed in the creation, governance, and final disposition of the world. The nature of its operation is as personal and particular care which works universally and continuously. By describing the operation of divine power in this way, Calvin found a middle way between the *necessitas* of the Stoics and the *fortuna* of the Epicureans.

Calvin vehemently and explicitly denied the accusation that he was a determinist. He saw two difficulties in the Stoic determinism of his day. First, a thoroughgoing determinism bound even God in its "fate," thereby denying God's freedom. Second, determinism had the effect of denying human freedom and responsibility. His insistence on omnipotence as expressed in personal and particular care excluded *necessitas* or "blind fate."

Calvin's quarrel with the Epicureans was that their system left things to chance. While he would admit it appears that some things are left to chance, this is only because God's purpose in them is hidden from our view (*Inst.* 1.16.9). God's power operates universally and continuously; nothing is outside its operation. Therefore nothing—not even the smallest detail—is left to chance. This is not just a general ordering in which God governs immanently through neutral laws of nature set up and left to function independently. God governs personally and directly. "Law of nature" is only a descriptive phrase connoting God's self-consistency in exercising power. What we call a "miracle" is not a special display of omnipotent power suspending "laws of nature." It is only one more example of God's unceasing (continuous) intervening activity. To multiply loaves and fishes is not qualitatively different from providing daily bread; it is just more calculated to strike the eye (Hunter, p. 57).

As Calvin articulated his understanding of the operation of divine omnipotence, his insistence on God's personal and particular care excluded necessity. His insistence that God's power is exercised universally and continuously excluded chance as well.

A. M. Hunter, *The Teaching of Calvin* (1950); C. B. Partee, *Calvin and Classical Philosophy* (1977); T. Rudavsky, ed., *Divine Omniscience and Omnipotence in Medieval Philosophy,* (1985); A. Verhey, "Calvin's Treatise 'Against the Libertines,' " *CTJ* (1980): 190–219; A. Case-Winters, *God's Power* (1991).

ANNA CASE-WINTERS

Orange Order

The Orange Institution, originating at the Diamond crossroads in County Armagh, Ireland, in September 1795, has been a major cultural and political focus for militant Protestantism, especially in the north of Ireland. Historical inspiration is found in the events of the late seventeenth century: the Glorious Revolution (1688), the siege of Londonderry (1689), and the Battle of the Boyne on July 1, 1690 (July 12, new style), the decisive victory by the Protestant William III over the deposed Catholic James II. Institutional beginnings lay, however, in sectarian disturbances in south Ulster in the late eighteenth century which led Protestants to form a permanent organization for self-defense and the maintenance of the Protestant Ascendancy and the Reformed religion.

The Order had a checkered history during the nineteenth century, suffering at times (1825; 1836) from proscription and dissolution but reviving in times of political crisis for the Protestant cause, as over Catholic Emancipation around 1829. From 1886 the Order took an important role in Protestant resistance to Home Rule in Ireland and, after the partition of Ulster (1921), became a powerful influence in Northern Ireland. Meanwhile, Orangeism spread extensively outside Ireland: to mainland Britain, Australia, New Zealand, Canada, and, on a limited scale, to the United States. In the early 1970s there were about 100,000 Orangemen in Ireland and a few thousand in other parts of the world. The Order is characterized by its hierarchical lodge structure of organization and its elaborate annual parades on July 12. Firm adherence to Protestantism is a prerequisite for membership.

M. W. Dewar, J. Brown, and S. E. Long, *Orangeism: A New Historical Appreciation* (1967); T. Gray, *The Orange Order* (1972); H. Senior, *Orangeism in Ireland and Britain,* 1795–1836 (1966); R. M. Sibbett, *Orangeism in Ireland and Throughout the Empire* (1914–15; 2nd ed. 1939).

JOHN WOLFFE

Ordination

Ordination is an act of the church* whereby persons are commissioned to a public ministry.* It intends to establish them in ministries of service and leadership by the authority of Jesus Christ. Reformed churches generally recognize three offices: ministry of the Word and Sacraments (pastor), governance (elder), and service (deacon). Terms used by other Christian bodies are variously appropriated to these three offices, for example, bishop to pastor. The ideals of a parity of ministry (no hierarchical order) and collegiality of ministry are reflected in the idea of calling* and the language of the rite itself. Recently many Reformed churches have been reshaping their rites to reflect more faithfully the general call to ministry that all Christians receive at their baptism.* This sets the particular ministry of leadership and service, for which ordination is the public sign, in the context of the universal ministry of the church. "We have gifts that differ according to the grace given to us" (Rom. 12:6).

Ordination to the ministry is enacted as part of the common worship* of the church: the proclamation of the Word of God,* celebration of the Gospel sacraments,* and the prayers of the people. The distinctive action is "the laying on of hands of the presbytery," a valuable precedent from the earliest Christian communities, and invocation of the Spirit of God by whose effectual power the ministry will be carried forth. By this act the gift of God is recognized and received, a link to the historic ordained ministry of the whole church is forged, and persons are established in the special ministries to which they have been called by inward persuasion, outward gifts, and public election. Additional practices, such as vesting the newly ordained, are optional.

Ordination is not a sacrament of the Gospel; it is a matter of good order for the health and fidelity of the churches. According to John Calvin,* God does not need ministers to do the work of the Spirit, but we do. God shows high regard for us by calling some among us to represent the divine will to the rest of us. We learn humility by being taught by another fallible human being and thus are nourished in a bond of love. The ordinand is set apart for this particular service within the company of the faithful. The ordained ministry depends on the ministry of the whole church, not the other way around. Although ordination is for life, it is not assumed that ordination conveys an "indelible character." The emphasis is on special responsibility for a lifetime of leadership and service.

Calvin, *Inst.* 4.3; T. F. Torrance, *Conflict and Agreement in the Church* (1960); H. J. Wotherspoon and J. M. Kirkpatrick, *A Manual of Church Doctrine According to the Church of Scotland* (1960).

THOMAS D. PARKER

Original Sin

The good creation* fell into sin. This is the story of original sin. We confess it but cannot explain it. For we must start where the Bible starts. It reveals the historical beginning of sin and evil but not its behind-the-scenes origin. Yet Christian thinkers struggle with this problem.

Two biblical presuppositions must govern such theological reflection. First, Scripture* affirms creation's pristine goodness. Sin and evil cannot claim creaturely status. They are not ontic realities. The Maker's handiwork was "very good" (Gen. 1:31). Second, is the Creator responsible for this downfall? No, for "in him is no darkness at all" (1 John 1:5). Reformation creeds echo this note: God is "by no means" and "in no sense" its cause. No third possibility exists. The originating sin remains an unfathomable mystery. This is the end of the matter. But no.

Three major theories have emerged, "explaining" original sin as the effect of some prior, deeper cause. Monist theories trace it back to the divine decrees.* As God acts "right-handedly" to do good, God is also involved "left-handedly" in evil. Both arise from an ultimate divine principle. Dualist theories trace it to two deities—the God of light and an anti-god of darkness. World history* is a power struggle between them. Demonic theories point an accusing finger at the devil. The devil becomes our "scapegoat."

All such "explanations" are exercises in futility. They only push the problem a step back into the hidden unknown. Every theodicy of sin ends in speculation. The biblical account is our only starting point: "In Adam's fall we sinned all" (*New England Primer;* Rom. 5:12–21).

The momentous event in Genesis 3 is our ultimate witness to the sin behind all sins. There Adam, with Eve, acting vicariously as covenant* head of humanity, failed the probationary test, broke the covenant, and brought God's judgment down upon every creature. We fell from the state of uprightness into condemnation. Our sinfulness is a settled issue. Adam's decision was also ours, made for us, but not apart from us. This is our existential predicament.

The transmission of guilt addresses the question, How are we implicated in that original sin? By imitation, Pelagius and his followers answer. Adam's act of disobedience set a bad example which all persons habitually emulate. By propagation, according to Augustinians.* Sin is transmitted by heredity from generation to generation. By imputation, Calvinists hold. Adam acted representatively for us. We now share vicariously in the righteousness of the last Adam as an atonement* for our vicarious participation in the unrighteousness of the first Adam. Contemporary views appeal to the theory of evolution, viewing sin and evil as remnants of a primitive stage in our development.

The effects of original sin are evident in personal and corporate rebellion against God, broken human relations, and abuse of the cosmos. As to legal status, we are guilty; as to condition, polluted. Our sinful nature issues in actual sins. Only in Christ is there now "no condemnation" (Rom. 8:1).

H. Berkhof, *CFI*; L. Berkhof, *Systematic Theology* (4th rev. and enl. ed. 1949); G. C. Berkouwer, *Sin* (1971); Weber, *FD*, vol. 1.

GORDON J. SPYKMAN

Orr, James (1844–1913)

Scottish theologian, professor of church history at the United Presbyterian Divinity Hall, Edinburgh, and then professor of apologetics and systematic theology at Trinity College, Glasgow. Born in Glasgow, Orr lost both his parents when a boy and was late in going to the university in his home city. He became minister of the East Bank United Presbyterian Church in Hawick (1874) and remained for seventeen years. He married and combined the work of pastor and theologian. One fruit of his studies was the Kerr Lectureship, published as *The Christian View of God and the World* (1893).

As a professor he read widely in the history and doctrine of the church and also in recent German theology. He became well known as a moderate defender of orthodoxy and an opponent of liberalism, especially Ritschlianism. Several of his books were first given as lectures in the United States, where he was often invited. *The Progress of Dogma* (1901) began as the Elliott Lectures at Western Seminary (Pittsburgh), *The Virgin Birth of Christ* (1907) as talks at the Fifth Avenue Presbyterian Church (New York City), and *God's Image in Man and Its Defacement* (1905) as the Stone Lectures at Princeton Seminary. He also contributed to *The Fundamentals* (1909–15) and was general editor of the prestigious *International Standard Bible Encyclopedia* (1915). His view of Scripture in *Revelation and Inspiration* (1910) rejected verbal inerrancy.

G. G. Scorgie, "A Call for Continuity: The Theological Contribution of James Orr" (diss., St. Andrews University, 1986).

PETER TOON

Orthodoxy, Reformed

The terms "orthodoxy," "scholasticism,"* "scholastic orthodoxy," and "confessional orthodoxy" refer to the post-Reformation theological development in the Reformed churches. It began in the late sixteenth century following the work of second-generation codifiers of the Reformation like John Calvin,* Heinrich Bullinger,* Wolfgang Musculus,* and Peter Martyr Vermigli* and extended into the eighteenth century. This theology is identified as orthodox or confessional because it attempted to codify and systematize "right teaching" within the bounds created by the great Reformed confessions of the sixteenth century. It is termed "scholastic" primarily because of the theological method it used in formulating its systems of doctrine.* The scholasticism of the late sixteenth and seventeenth centuries was facilitated by the increased openness of Protestant theology to the use of reason* and philosophy,* specifically to the revised Aristotelianism of the late Renaissance. In their attempt to create a genuinely Protestant, but also orthodox and essentially catholic or churchly, theological system, the Reformed thinkers of the post-Reformation era had recourse both to traditional models for theology, including the great medieval systems of Peter Lombard, Thomas Aquinas, Duns Scotus, Durandus, and others, and to the ongoing philosophical tradition, notably the thought of Francesco Zabarella and Francisco Suárez, that linked them to those systems. Granting the developments in logic, rhetoric, and metaphysics that had taken place in the fifteenth and sixteenth centuries, neither the method nor the philosophy of the Protestant scholastics was identical to that of the medieval thinkers.

The development of Reformed orthodoxy was paralleled by a similar development in the Lutheran church. This orthodox or scholastic Protestantism would be the dominant form of Protestant theology for nearly two hundred years. Within that two-century span, we can identify roughly four phases: early orthodoxy, high orthodoxy, the pietist and "transitional" phase, and the increasingly rationalistic phase of late orthodoxy and rational supernaturalism.

Origins of Protestant scholasticism and the early orthodox codification of system (c. 1565–1640). The initial codification of the theology of the Reformation in the era of Calvin, Bullinger, and the great national confessions* of the Reformed churches was a major theological development in itself. A transformation in style and method equally as profound as that witnessed in the transition from the writings of the first Reformers to the works of Calvin, Bullinger, Musculus, and Vermigli occurred in the years following 1560. Of these four representatives of the first great doctrinal formulation of Protestantism only one, Bullinger, lived past 1564 and his greatest systematic efforts had been completed by that date.

Several factors account for the transition from the theology of the Reformers to that of orthodoxy, not the least being the polemic with Rome. In the canons and decrees of the Council of Trent, called in December 1545 by Pope Paul III, the Reformation was answered and condemned by the best theological minds of the Roman Catholic Church; at the same time, the diverse strains of medieval theology, with the exception of the radical Augustinianism* that fed into the Reformation, were reconciled into a single, overarching confessional statement. After Trent, Protestant theology was subjected to the searching criticism of Cardinal Robert Bellarmine. Trent elicited several detailed Protestant rebuttals, notably from Calvin and the Lutheran theologian Martin Chemnitz (1522–86), and Bellarmine's polemic was answered in detail by a considerable number of early orthodox writers such as William Ames* and Festus Hommius (1576–1642). In the course of this polemic, Protestantism developed a more detailed synthesis of its own theological position.

A second factor was the demise of the first- and second-generation Protestant leaders and the third generation's need to state for themselves the meaning of the Reformation. This factor, together with a third, the interest among the successors of the Reformers in maintaining and emphasizing the catholicity of the Reformation in the light of the Christian tradition, may be viewed as a positive, internal impetus toward orthodox system. Also, the attempt to formulate a theological system for Protestantism on a large scale—far beyond that offered by the second-generation Reformers—necessitated the reintroduction of philosophical categories and, indeed, of metaphysical discussion, particularly in such areas of doctrine as the essence and attributes of God,* creation,* and providence.*

The early orthodox era, extending roughly from 1565 to 1640, is characterized by a certain newness and freshness of formulation and, in the cases of major formulators like Theodore Beza,* Zacharias Ursinus,* Caspar Olevianus,* Girolamo Zanchi,* and Franciscus Junius (1545–1641), a consistent wrestling with the problems of the organization and definition of theology* in the light of the interplay between exegesis, tradition,* and confessional synthesis. Zanchi was particularly important to the development, since he had been trained in Thomist theology at Padua before his conversion* to the Protestant cause and provided the model of a fully developed scholasticism for the next generation of Reformed theologians.

This was the age of the Heidelberg Catechism* (1563) and its exposition as system, of the Swiss Harmony of Reformed Confessions (1581), the Irish Articles of Religion (1615), and the Synod of Dort* (1618–19). The combined effect of well-defined dogmatic presuppositions on the confessional level, the need for more detailed positive doctrine and for a self-conscious theological methodology, and the ever-escalating polemic between Roman, Reformed, Lutheran, and the various sectarian theologies was to produce a more traditionally "scholastic" theology among Protestants, a theology open on the one side to the medieval tradition with its use of Aristotelian philosophy but on the other side ever aware of the Reformation mandate to allow no norm for doctrine equal to or higher than Scripture.*

The continuation of an "early orthodox" style can be identified well into the seventeenth century in the theologies of

Amandus Polanus,* William Perkins,* Bartholomäus Keckermann (1571–1609), Johann Heinrich Alsted (1588–1638), Franciscus Gomarus* (1563–1641), Johannes Maccovius,* John Downame,* and James Ussher.* Though the era of confessional formulation came to a close at Dort, at the very same time that the Thirty Years War was breaking out in Bohemia and the Palatinate, it was only after 1640 that the scholastic style of theology moved beyond that of writers like Polanus and Alsted, the great codifiers of the early orthodox system.

Corresponding roughly to the period of the Thirty Years War (1618–48) there is a phase of polemical formulation in which the various theological perspectives were still more clearly defined and full-scale polemical summa were written by theologians such as Johannes Cloppenburg (1592–1654) and Johannes Hoornbeek (1617–66). These theologians waged their own intellectual warfare, analyzing in purely polemical compendia the various doctrinal options—and, ultimately, by the end of the war, standardizing the attack, formalizing their victory, to the point that the "high orthodox" of the generation following the Peace of Westphalia could concentrate all the more on the internal elaboration of system.

High orthodoxy in the seventeenth century (c. 1640–1700). The era of "high orthodoxy" is by all accounts the great age of theological system, in which the theological task receives final definition down to the smallest, finest distinction at the hands of theologians like Markus Friedrich Wendelin (1584–1652) and Gisbert Voetius.* It was an age of considerable intellectual activity and genuine development in the fields of theology, linguistic study, and exegesis, the most notable achievement in the latter two fields being the great London Polyglot Bible (1654–57), edited by Brian Walton (1600–61), and its companion, the Lexicon heptaglotton (1669), by Walton's colleague, Edmund Castell (1606–85).

The internal Reformed controversies of the era, notably the debate over Cocceian federalism and the several controversies generated by the theologians of Saumur, were all debates over highly technical theological questions. Granting that the two theological systems of Johannes Cocceius* manifest all the organizational, logical, and indeed, metaphysical concerns typical of the works of his contemporaries and that the theology of his most bitter adversary, Voetius, manifests as much concern for piety and praxis as Cocceius's, the debate ought not to be viewed as often portrayed—as a debate between a biblical, covenantal theology and a predestinarian scholasticism. Rather, it was a debate between Reformed scholastics over the hermeneutical implications of the covenant* concept and, particularly over the implications of Cocceius's notion of a gradually abrogated covenant of works and a gradually inaugurated covenant of grace.*

The debate over the theology of Saumur extended from the end of the early orthodox era through the era of high orthodoxy and placed the theologians of that eminent French academy—Louis Cappel (1585–1658), Moïse Amyraut,* Claude Pajon (1626–85), and Joshua de la Place (Placaeus; 1606–55)—against a considerable array of French, German, and Swiss Reformed orthodox, including Pierre DuMoulin (1568–1658), Johannes Buxtorf, Sr. (1564–1629), Johannes Buxtorf, Jr. (1599–1664), Frédéric Spanheim (1600–1648), Francis Turretin* (1623–87), and J. H. Heidegger (1633–1698). Each of the debates manifests the difficulty experienced by orthodoxy in maintaining doctrinal continuity with the Reformation while also formulating a full theological system in an era of scholastic method, changing patterns in textual criticism and exegesis, and genuinely revolutionary development in science and philosophy. Cappel argued, against the elder Buxtorf, that the vowel points of the Hebrew text of the OT were invented by the Masoretes some six or seven centuries after Christ. This philological question was, at that time, inextricably linked with the doctrine of the authority of Scripture in its original languages. Since Cappel's views could be used to support Roman Catholic claims of the prior authority of the Vulgate, the orthodox opposed his findings. La Place held that the imputation of Adam's sin* to the human race was founded on the actual sinfulness of human beings and was therefore "mediate" or mediated by the facts of heredity. Against this, orthodoxy held an "immediate imputation of sin" on the grounds of no foreseen demerit in the progeny of Adam in order to maintain a strict parallel with the totally gratuitous imputation of Christ's righteousness to the faithful. In both cases, fine points of argument became tests of orthodoxy.

More important to the development and change of theology in the high orthodox era was the loss of the traditional Aristotelian synthesis of theology, philosophy, and science. Not only was the Aristotelian metaphysic now met by an equally powerful rationalist metaphysic but the Ptolemaic geocentric universe, to which the Aristotelian metaphysic and its theory of causes were bound, had been replaced by a new worldview, the Copernican. Orthodoxy began to feel the impact of Cartesian rationalism and, in England, of the natural theology* of early Deism. Toward the end of the era, the rationalistic systems of Spinoza, Leibniz, and Locke manifested even more clearly the changed philosophical climate. Spinoza and Leibniz, for all their positive interest in theology, constructed metaphysical systems inimical to orthodox dogmatics. At the same time, Arminian theology proved to be far more open to rationalism than the Reformed, moving first toward Cartesianism and then, in the thought of Philipp van Limborch (1633–1712), toward the Lockean epistemology and ethics.

Late orthodoxy and rationalism (c. 1700–1790). During the final decades of the seventeenth and throughout the eighteenth century, the phenomenon of theological orthodoxy and the companion phenomenon of a Protestant scholasticism entered an era of decline and stagnation. The spirit that produced a living orthodoxy and an energetically formulated scholasticism at the end of the sixteenth century and in the early decades of the seventeenth had long since dissipated, and even the essential intellectual strength of that initial formulation, which had carried Protestant orthodoxy in its several forms through the better part of the seventeenth century, had begun to wither. Orthodoxy and scholasticism such as remained after 1700 were transformed by the forces of Pietism, doctrinal indifferentism, and rationalism into forms radically different from those which dominated the seventeenth century.

Pietism offered a critique of scholastic theology from the perspective of the life of religion and the practical application of doctrine. Together with the so-called "indifferentist" theologians, the pietists were able to argue that orthodoxy had substituted detailed formulae for piety and conviction and had lost touch with the needs of the church. The impact of "indifferentism" to the fine doctrinal distinctions made by scholastic orthodoxy, or, as it is sometimes called, latitudinarianism, can be seen already in the ecumenical efforts and writings of William Chillingworth (1602–44), John Dury (d. c. 1675), and the Lutheran theologian Georg Calixtus (1586–1656), in the middle of the seventeenth century. These theologians tired of internecine Protestant polemic and searched for Protestant unity in the common affirmation of biblical truth beyond particularistic confessions. The impulse became stronger at the end of the century in the writings of continental theologians like Jean-Alphonse Turrettini (1671–1737) and Jean Frédéric Ostervald* (1663–1747) who experienced, far more than any of their predecessors, the difficulty of maintaining a scholastic and strictly confessional orthodoxy in the face of changing patterns of hermeneutics, philosophy, and science.

The late orthodox era, roughly from 1740 to 1790, begins with the victorious return of Christian von Wolff to the University of Halle, by imperial order, over the protest of the pietist theologians. After 1740, under the tutelage of the prolific Wolff, scholastic orthodoxy found its new philosophy, replacing Aristotle and ridding itself of the questionable Cartesian alternative by adopting as its intellectual underpinning the rationalism of Wolff and his associates. Among the Reformed theologians influenced by Wolffian philosophy were Daniel Wyttenbach (1706–79) and Johann Friedrich Stapfer (1708–75). Both systems assume that reason is the initial and necessary foundation for theology and that the truths of revelation* ought to be grounded on a foundation of natural theology.* By 1790 this rationalist phase of Protestant scholasticism had come to a close under the impact of Kant's critique of rationalist metaphysics.

The Age of Reason in England and France was as rationalist as the German Enlightenment but not nearly so congenial to traditional Christianity or to theological system. The Deists were particularly critical of the supernaturalistic assumptions of orthodoxy, and in England the development of a more or less Reformed theology was further complicated by the confessional and political disunity of the dissenting churches. Thus John Gill* defended the older orthodoxy in the name of a fully developed supralapsarian* determinism, while at the same time losing sight of the confessional bounds of the older Reformed theology. Thomas Ridgley's (1667–1734) massive exposition of the WLC manifests both the inroads of rationalism and, particularly in its modal approach to the doctrine of the Trinity,* the problem of adapting orthodox theological language to the new age. The theological system of the Anglican Thomas Stackhouse (1680–1752) evidences not only a rational supernaturalism in its approach to religion and revelation but also a willingness to accommodate theology to the findings of science in its doctrine of creation* and to rehearse the niceties of the debate with Arminianism* over predestination* in an almost objective style.

This "decline of orthodoxy" was not, of course, the end of the historical phenomenon of orthodox dogmatics. Orthodox Protestantism did not disappear under the critique of pietism and rationalism any more than in an earlier time did Thomism vanish under assaults of Scotism and Nominalism or, in a slightly later time, did rationalism pass out of existence following the critiques of Kant and the dawn of romanticism. Throughout the eighteenth and even the nineteenth and twentieth centuries, Protestant orthodoxy and Protestant scholasticism have remained alive in the theological work of writers like Heinrich Heppe,* Charles Hodge,* and Louis Berkhof.* It is also clear, however, that during the early eighteenth century, orthodoxy ceased to say anything new either to the culture or to itself. The eighteenth century, viewed as a positive age of intellectual growth, moved religious thought and the discipline of theology away from traditional orthodoxy and mounted a critique of facile dogmatism, such as the older orthodoxy had ultimately become.

B. G. Armstrong, *Calvinism and the Amyraut Heresy* (1969); I. A. Dorner, *History of Protestant Theology Particularly in Germany*, 2 vols. (ET 1871); Heppe, *RD*; R. A. Muller, *Christ and the Decree* (1986); and *Post-Reformation Reformed Dogmatics,* vol. 1: *Prolegomena to Theology* (1987); O. Ritschl, *Dogmengeschichte des Protestantismus: Grundlagen und Grundzüge der theologischen Gedanken und Lehrbildung in den protestantischen Kirchen*, 4 vols. (1908–27); H. E. Weber, *Die philosophische Scholastik des deutschen Protestantismus im Zeitalter der Orthodoxie* (1907); and *Reformation, Orthodoxie und Rationalismus*, 2 vols. (1937–51).

RICHARD A. MULLER

Ostervald, Jean Frédéric (1663–1747)

A native of Neuchâtel, Ostervald studied in Zurich, Saumur, and Paris before returning home and entering the ministry. Influenced by the Enlightenment and Pietism, he became a leading exponent of "moderatism," a more rational, ethical type of Christianity which emphasized Scripture but showed little interest in doctrine.* He advocated renewal of Protestant worship,* producing a translation of the French Bible as well as Christian hymns and a French Protestant prayer book. His prayer book was used by the Huguenot* church in Charleston, South Carolina.

NSH 8:283.

HUGHES OLIPHANT OLD

Owen, John (1616–1683)

Puritan divine of the Congregational Way and major adviser and participant in Oliver Cromwell's* religious settlement of England (1650s). After study at Oxford, Owen was episcopally ordained and served as a parish minister in Essex. In the Civil War,* he sided with Parliament and adopted the Congregational form of church government. He accompanied Cromwell on expeditions to Ireland and Scotland and soon afterward was appointed dean of Christ Church, Oxford, and vice-chancellor of the university. He labored to make this ancient seat of learning into a nursery of godliness through preaching, discipline, and reform of the statutes. He was a major influence in the Savoy Assembly* (1658), where Congregational principles were expounded. In 1660 he was forced to leave Christ Church and became the pastor of a small Congregational church in London.

Owen is best known as a theological writer. He expounded the great dogmas of the faith, defended them against Deism and Socinianism, and showed how they related to the practice of personal godliness. He also wrote on the doctrine of the church, its polity, worship, and vocation in the world. His collected *Works* are still in print and despite their Latinized style are carefully read. In his spiritual writings there is great warmth as well as a remarkable understanding of the work of the Holy Spirit* in the hearts of sinners.

J. Owen, *Works*, ed. W. H. Goold, 24 vols. (1850–55); S. B. Ferguson, *John Owen on the Christian Life* (1987); P. Toon, *God's Statesman* (1973).

PETER TOON

Paris Evangelical Missionary Society

The Réveil,* or awakening, among early nineteenth-century Francophone Protestants produced groups committed to prayer* and evangelical concern. Missionary enthusiasm in France led to the founding of the Société des missions évangéliques chez les peuples non chrétiens établie à Paris (1822). The sole aim (later expanded) was "to propagate the gospel among pagans and other non-Christian peoples." The Society was ecumenical from its origins, with Lutherans and Reformed participating; and it was international: its first missionary, Jonas King (sent to Palestine [1823]), was American, and much of its funds and personnel have always come from Francophone Switzerland.

Three Basel Mission* recruits became the nucleus of the "Maison des missions" for training missionaries (1824). After problems over ordination,* a mission was established in Tswana country in Southern Africa (1829). Of more permanent significance was the mission's association with Moshoeshoe I (from 1833) and its subsequent place in the history of Lesotho. This led to the Zambesi or "Barotse" (i.e., Lozi) mission (in modern Zambia) associated with François Coillard (1885).

The Society found a new role as French imperial pressures increasingly inhibited other Protestant missions. At the request of Krio Protestants, it went to Senegal (1863). It took over from the London Missionary Society* in the Loyalty Islands (1863) and New Caledonia (1922), and from the American Presbyterians* in Gabon (1892). It entered Madagascar (1892) to assist other missions and supplied the places of expelled German missionaries in Cameroun (1917) and Togo (1929). By 1964, nine autonomous churches had arisen from its work, leading the Society to a major rethinking of the relation of Western missions with resultant churches.

J. Bianquis, *Les origines de la Société des Missions Evangéliques de Paris, 1822–1829* (1930–35); C. Bonzon and J. Kotto, *Face à l'avenir* (1965); *Journal des missions évangéliques* (now *Mission*; 1826–).

ANDREW F. WALLS

Pastoral Care

In the Reformed tradition, pastoral care is one of the church's structured expressions of the means of grace.* Exercised by both clergy and laity, this care includes traditional tasks of general visitation, comfort of the grieving, help for the sick and needy, forgiveness for the guilty, and the "cure of souls" through discipline and forgiveness.* Or, pastoral care is a ministry* of the church to bring comfort and redirection to persons in need of renewal.

Pastoral care is not limited to theology* and ecclesiology for its content. From the Reformed belief that God* is active and present in all the world, there is a willingness to use knowledge from the human sciences of psychology, sociology, and anthropology. Informed by these multiple perspectives on God and human nature, pastoral care seeks the most effective means to carry out its tasks both for the sake of the recipients of the care and for the church.

The Reformed awareness of human finitude and sin* recognizes that special initiatives are often needed in the midst of life's difficulties. When death* occurs, for example, family members may become so bereft or angry with God that they fall away from the structured life and care of the congregation. The ministry of pastoral care takes the initiative to extend comfort, not only to offer sympathy but also to keep the deceased's family involved in the church's life, working actively to claim and affirm God's grace for them in times of suffering. Pastoral care in the Reformed tradition, then, consists of those acts designed and carried out by pastor and congregation which help persons interpret the significant events in their lives and which invite persons into involvement and growth in the life of the community of faith.

Historically there has been a disciplinary dimension to Reformed pastoral care as well. To persons who have "fallen away," care has been extended aggressively to return them to the community of faith where God's grace is openly acknowledged.

Pastoral care in the Reformed tradition is a ministry of nurture and support. Its forms of expression vary over time. Sometimes the reaching out has been done from a dogmatic, or authoritarian, posture; at other times with more gentleness and winsomeness. But whatever the form, the integrity of pastoral care in the Reformed tradition hinges on its purpose of maintaining an awareness of God's presence and activity in the world and interpreting that presence in people's lives. This in turn strengthens them to continue the pilgrimage to which God has called them in the world.

R. Baxter, *The Reformed Pastor* (1656; repr. 1963); D. S. Browning, *The Moral Context of Pastoral Care* (1983); W. A. Clebsch and C. A. Jaekle, *Pastoral Care in Historical Perspective* (1964; repr. 1983); E. B. Holifield, *A History of Pastoral Care in America* (1983); T. C. Oden, *Pastoral Theology* (1983).

WILLIAM V. ARNOLD

Pastoral Theology

As a special branch of practical theology concerned with the practice of ministry,* pastoral theology exists alongside historical and systematic theology, distinguished yet inseparable from them, with a particular responsibility for explaining the actual relationships between the Word of God* and the lives of God's people.

The discipline of pastoral theology today is difficult to define. Often associated with various psychological perspectives and psychotherapeutic techniques, pastoral care* has been cut adrift from clear theological foundations. Pastoral theology continues to be associated with the practical end of the curriculum, having acquired a functionalist and professionalized character. Much has been learned, but at the cost of a lost identity. Contemporary pastoral theology within the Reformed churches is not exempt from this condition.

Within Reformed faith, pastoral care has its place within theology* and the church. Pastoral care is ordered first of all by clear theological principle. John T. McNeill suggests that Calvin's* approach to pastoral care was ordered by his understanding of the doctrine of repentance.* What Calvin had in mind was regeneration* or sanctification,* the process by which a person grows in the obedience, holiness, and goodness that mark the restoration of the image of God. For Eduard Thurneysen, the theological heart of pastoral care is the proclamation of the forgiveness of sins.* In short, the theological focus of pastoral care within Reformed faith is the reconciliation of the believer with God.*

Pastoral care is, second, a discipline of

the church. The marks of the church are the preaching* and hearing of the Word of God and proper celebration of the sacraments.* Early in the history of Reformed faith, however, church discipline* was added (Scots Confession, art. 18). Today we would see this pastoral care, not, however, as a third mark of the church but the means of expression to the individual of the same gospel preached in sermon and celebrated in sacrament. Calvin wrote: "Christ did not ordain pastors on the principle that they only teach the Church in a general way on the public platform, but that they care for the individual sheep, bring back the wandering and scattered to the fold, bind up the broken and crippled, heal the sick, support the frail and weak" (*Commentary* on Acts 20:20). But note: under no circumstances could pastoral care have a content different from the content of sermon and sacrament.

Reformed pastoral theology is focused on the objectivity of God's grace* in Jesus Christ. "We have taught," wrote Calvin, "that the sinner does not dwell upon his own compunction or tears, but fixes both eyes upon the Lord's mercy alone" (*Inst.* 3.4.3). Like Luther,* Calvin was concerned to get people to look away from themselves to a gracious God who alone could bring them salvation,* healing, and peace. But one cannot look to God unless one first hears the voice of God. Therefore the Word of God is the center of all ministry. As Calvin noted, "It would not be sufficient for God to determine with himself what he would do for our safety, if he did not speak to us expressly by name. It is only when God makes us understand, by his own voice, that he will be gracious to us, that we can entertain the hope of salvation" (*Commentary* on Ps. 12:5).

It is uncertain yet whether we will see a significant recovery of a Reformed pastoral theology of the Word of God. Richard Baxter's* *The Reformed Pastor* (1656) is rarely read today, yet it remains a text awaiting rediscovery. Thurneysen's *A Theology of Pastoral Care* (ET 1962) is a modern classic of Reformed pastoral theology deserving wider recognition and more careful study than it has received in recent years.

J. Firet, *Dynamics in Pastoring* (1986); J. T. McNeill, *A History of the Cure of Souls* (1951); E. H. Peterson, *Five Smooth Stones for Pastoral Work* (1980); E. Thurneysen, *A Theology of Pastoral Care* (ET 1962); R. S. Wallace, *Calvin, Geneva and the Reformation* (1988).

ANDREW PURVES

Peace

Historically there are few discussions of peace in the Reformed tradition. An almost unanimous assumption of the just war theory has existed from John Calvin* to the present; only since World War II has there been a shift in the treatment of the subject.

Christian thought on the relationship of the Christian to war* has been dominated by Augustine's* just war theory. Many refinements have been made. For any war to be considered just and valid for Christian participation, it must be entered upon only after all other means of resolution are exhausted, be purely self-defensive, take measures to protect noncombatants, ensure the benefits of victory to outweigh the horror of war, and be declared by proper authorities. Just war theory assumes that war is wrong and forbidden to the believer until the conditions that justify the carnage are proven.

The Protestant Reformers embraced that tradition of the church.* Calvin argued against the pacifism of the Anabaptists and asserted the government's call to "defend by war the dominions entrusted to their safekeeping, if at any time they are under enemy attack." Scripture "declares such wars to be lawful" (*Inst.* 4.20.11). In the same vein, the WCF* declares that the civil magistracy has the right to "wage war upon just and necessary occasions" (ch. 23).

Adherence to the just war theory has produced two major results: support for efforts to promote peace (short of pacifism) and acquiescence to the justness of wars once a nation engages in them. Reformed bodies in the United States display both tendencies. Individuals, particularly Presbyterians* and Congregationalists* who held the New England

Theology,* were early supporters of the American Peace Society (1828). The movement that caught the imagination of many, however, was the drive for international arbitration of disputes between nations. The PCUS mounted a campaign for arbitration beginning in 1890. By 1898, 145 churches had signed petitions addressed to the governments of thirty-one nations. Reformed denominations supported the Presbyterian President Wilson's* call for a League of Nations at the end of World War I.

While seeking peace, Presbyterians went to war. In 1898 the UPCNA General Assembly argued that Spanish cruelty "justifies the interference of our government in the cause of humanity" in the Spanish-American War. The Allied cause in World War I was held to be God's cause, and prayers for the enemy's defeat were repeatedly invoked. Disillusioned with the results of the war and the failure of the peace, Presbyterians in the United States joined calls for disarmament (1920s; 1930s) and passed resolutions never again to "bless" war. Between world wars a pacifist witness against all war emerged within the Presbyterian Church in the U.S.A. in the form of the Presbyterian Peace Fellowship. The PCUS saw the formation of the Southern Presbyterian Peace Fellowship (1949). These bodies federated (1978) and were merged with reunion of the PCUS and UPCUSA (1983).

But the churches again "presented arms" with the onset of World War II, though in a more penitential and reserved spirit than during World War I. With the end of the war, Presbyterians again supported an international body for mediation of claims. Fearing communism, churches called for a strong defense and containment policy overseas but resisted efforts to militarize the nation (through universal military training and a peacetime draft) and abridgment of freedom in the form of McCarthyism. The PCUS said: "Communists often . . . make a strong appeal where inequalities, injustices and hunger prevail. But this does not mean that we have become communistic when we also speak out boldly for justice, equality and social welfare, for these are the basic standards of our Faith" ("The Christian Faith and Communism," General Assembly *Minutes* [1954]).

The Vietnam War proved to be a turning point in Presbyterian thought on peace and war. The churches, like the nation, were divided by the conflict. General Assemblies of the UPCUSA and PCUS questioned the war's morality, eventually declared it unjust, and called for U.S. withdrawal. At the same time, emphasis on whether war could be justified shifted to a positive theology of peace. This is seen in a number of General Assembly declarations and agency papers, perhaps most clearly in the UPCUSA's Confession of 1967* and the PCUS's A Declaration of Faith. Both stressed the horror of war, God's call to reconciliation and justice,* and those efforts which make for peace. There was no mention of a just war.

This trend resulted in the paper "Peacemaking: The Believer's Calling" (UPCUSA, 1980; PCUS, 1981) and the establishment of the Presbyterian Peacemaking Program. Peace was defined as the biblical *shalom* (wholeness, harmony, right relations). Far more than the absence of conflict, peace was held to entail active work to create justice for all people, understanding and reconciliation between communities and nations, and a mutual upbuilding at all levels of society. "We know that peace cannot be achieved by ending the arms race unless there is economic and political justice in the human family," the paper declared. The reconciling character of peacemaking made it central to discipleship. Though not embracing pacifism, the emphasis no longer fell on the right to war but on the necessity—indeed, the call of God—for true peace.

R. Abrams, *Preachers Present Arms* (1933); J. L. Brooks, "In Behalf of a Just and Durable Peace: The Attitudes of American Protestantism Toward War and Military-related Affairs Involving the United States, 1949–1953" (diss., Tulane University, 1977); A. C. Cochrane, *The Mystery of Peace* (1985); U. Mauser, "Peacemaking in a Militaristic Society," *JPH* 61 (Spring 1983): 118–26; R. Nutt, "To Witness for Christ as They Saw Him:

The Southern Presbyterian Peace Fellowship and Peace Work in the Presbyterian Church in the United States, 1949–1983" (diss., Vanderbilt University, 1986); R. Smylie, "A Presbyterian Witness on War and Peace: An Historical Interpretation" *JPH* 59 (Winter 1981): 498–516; "Peacemaking: The Believer's Calling," UPCUSA General Assembly *Minutes* (1980), PCUS (1981).

RICK NUTT

Peale, Norman Vincent (1898–)

Reformed Church in America minister and proponent of positive thinking. Peale was ordained by the Methodist Episcopal Church (1922) and served in Brooklyn and Syracuse. He was called to New York City's Marble Collegiate Church (1932), a Dutch Reformed congregation established in 1628. An inspiring preacher who regularly preached to thousands, Peale held this prestigious pulpit for over fifty years. Throughout, he proclaimed positive thinking—a blend of psychological theories, New Thought techniques, and Scriptural principles, packaged as a self-help prescription for anxious Americans seeking success, security, and happiness. His phenomenal best-seller, *The Power of Positive Thinking* (1952), brought Peale national prominence but also sharp criticism from theologians, especially from the Reformed tradition, who complained that positive thinking was a shallow religious form of American pragmatism and self-reliance.

A. Gordon, *Norman Vincent Peale* (1958); D. Meyer, *Positive Thinkers: Popular Religious Psychology from Mary Baker Eddy to Norman Vincent Peale and Ronald Reagan* (1988).

DENNIS N. VOSKUIL

Perkins, William (1558–1602)

Called "the principal architect of Elizabethan Puritanism" and "the most important Puritan writer," Perkins was the first theologian of the reformed English church to gain an international reputation. His preaching manual, *The Arte of Prophesying* (1592; ET 1606), is found on nearly every seventeenth-century New England book list.

Perkins graduated from Christ's College, Cambridge (1581), tutored by Laurence Chaderton, "the pope of Cambridge puritanism." He underwent a religious experience while completing his M.A. degree (1584) and began preaching in the jail. His skill led to an appointment as lecturer (preacher) at Great St. Andrew's Church (1584–1602), and he was also elected a Fellow of Christ's College (1584–95).

Perkins was a leader of Elizabethan Puritanism, though he himself never left the Church of England. He and other non-separating Puritans sought the church's spiritual renewal. His theology was Calvinistic, and he cited Calvin as well as Vermigli,* Beza,* Zanchi,* Olevianus,* and Junius. He also drew on Luther,* Melanchthon, Tyndale, Bradford, and Hooper. Among his major works were *A Golden Chaine* (1590); *Reformed Catholike* (1597); *Manner and Order of Predestination* (ET 1606); and *Whole Treatise of Cases of Conscience* (1606). Perkins's theological legacy extended through his Cambridge students, most prominently William Ames,* but also Baynes, Rogers, Taylor, and William Chappell, tutor of John Milton.*

Perkins's Calvinist theology was presented according to the logic and method of Peter Ramus.* Most of his works can be diagrammed as Ramist charts, and Ramean influences are found throughout. Particularly, Ramism helped Perkins maintain the unity of theology and ethics, provided an educational tool by streamlining logic, fostered plain-style preaching, enhanced the art of memory, provided a tool for biblical interpretation as well as supplying a secure philosophical base on which to build theology.

Perkins defined theology as "the science of living blessedly forever" (*Works*, 1:11). By definition this also included ethics, and Perkins always spelled out the practical "uses" of doctrines. He was concerned for the education of the church and that people "lay up the word of God in their heart as in a storehouse." Sermons were a primary communicative vehicle, and Perkins taught they should be "plaine and simple without affectation, and yet full of grace and maiestie" (*Works*, 2:55). His sermons followed a "doctrine/use" pattern. The "opening" of a Scripture text and its "analysis" according to (Ramist) "method" provided the way it could be impressed in memory for Perkins. Perkins wrote many biblical commentaries (e.g., Galatians; Heb. 11; the Lord's Prayer; the Sermon on the Mount) and believed that by uncovering the inner logic and connections of the biblical texts, the mind of the Holy Spirit would be known. This was grounded in his conviction that Scripture* is the Word of God.*

I. Breward, *The Work of William Perkins* (1970); W. Haller, *The Rise of Puritanism* (1938); D. K. McKim, *Ramism in William Perkins' Theology* (1987); P. Miller, *The New England Mind: The Seventeenth Century* (1939); R. A. Muller, *Christ and the Decree* (1986).

DONALD K. MCKIM

Perseverance of the Saints

The fifth of the so-called "five points of Calvinism," also known as preservation, eternal security, and the "once saved, always saved" doctrine, it is more properly designated as "Perseverance of God with the Saints." It asserts that whomever God* regenerates* will surely not be permitted to fall back into perdition but will be kept by the power of God unto eventual salvation.* This does not preclude the possibility of serious setbacks that may necessitate severe chastisements by God, as with David's monstrous sin "in the case of Uriah the Hittite" (1 Kings 15:5). This view is supported by many biblical passages, such as Matt. 24:24; John 5:24; 6:37, 39, 40, 44, 47, 51, 54, 56, 58; 10:3–5, 14, 27–29; 17:6, 9, 12, 24; Rom. 5:9–10; 6:4, 8; 8:11, 15–17, 30, 33, 35–39; 11:29; 14:4; 1 Cor. 1:8, 9; 2 Cor. 1:21–22; Eph. 1:13–14; 4:30; Phil. 1:6; Col. 3:3; 2 Thess. 3:3–4; 2 Tim. 1:12; 2:13; 4:18; Heb. 5:9; 6:9, 17–20; 7:25; 10:19–23; 1 Peter 1:3–5; 5:6–10; 1 John 2:19; 3:6–9; 5:18; and Jude 24. Since these emphasize God's action in safeguarding God's own children rather than human steadfastness in remaining attached to God, it is apposite to speak of God's perseverance with the saints rather than use the other terms. Perhaps the strongest of all passages is John 10:28, where it is clear that the hand of the shepherd will prevent anyone from snatching out any sheep and will not permit any sheep from withdrawing (they shall never perish!). A shepherd who would explain the loss of some sheep by the excuse, "They left of their own will," would be adjudged seriously delinquent!

Throughout the history of theology and interpretation there have been strong objections to this view, however, both because of the many Scriptures warning against apostasy and because some people who had given strong evidence of being born again turned away and appeared to close their life without repentance.* Augustine tied perseverance with election, not with regeneration, no doubt because his view of baptismal regeneration multiplied enormously the number of nonpersevering regenerates! The Remonstrants* indicated that the matter should be investigated anew, and Arminians* of all stripes have denied that regeneration ensures ultimate salvation. They have advanced in the main four arguments against this doctrine.

1. The warnings of Scripture against turning away from the path of life (Ezek. 33:12, 13, 18; Matt. 10:22; 18:32–34; 1 Cor. 9:27; 10:11–12; 15:2; 2 Cor. 11:3–4; 13:5; 1 Thess. 3:5; 1 Tim. 2:15; 4:15–16; 5:8; 6:11; Heb. 3:6, 14; 4:1, 11; 6:4–8; 10:26–29, 36, 38; James 1:12; 2 Peter 1:9–10; 2 John 8–9; Jude 20–21; Rev. 2:5, 16; 3:5, 11; 22:19).

These passages are interpreted by supporters of perseverance as providing the kind of exhortation by which God implements perseverance with those who also by God's grace do persevere. Hebrews 6:4–9 and 10:26–29 are seen as describing an external profession without an actual regeneration.

2. The examples of people like King Saul, Judas, Hymenaeus, and Alexander who, after being apparently renewed, turned away and "shipwrecked their faith" (cf. further Matt. 7:21–23; 18:32–34; 24:12; 25:12–13, 28–30; John 15:2, 6; Rom. 14:15; Gal. 5:4; Col. 2:19; 1 Tim. 1:6, 19–20; 4:1; 5:15; 6:9–10, 21; 2 Tim. 2:18; Heb. 10:29; 2 Peter 2:1; Rev. 3:16).

Such cases may be shown to be in harmony with perseverance by showing either that the people in view were never regenerated (Judas; John 15:2, 6) or that after a period of decline they returned to the faith.

3. God's certain safeguarding of God's own regenerate children is thought to be in conflict with the reality of human free will,* which demands that obedience or apostasy continue to be real possibilities.

Holders of perseverance indicate that this is a misunderstanding of the relation between the sovereign will of God and the reality of the power of decision in rational agents. The Arminian logic would destroy either free will in heaven* or the security of those who are redeemed in heaven and the holy angels.

4. A very harmful use of this doctrine is made by people who count firmly on their salvation while engaged in a course of willful disobedience to God. They say, "Once saved, always saved, so I can do whatever I please without endangering my salvation."

This is a drastic distortion of the doctrine, and if this type of reasoning is presented as one's life program, there is good reason to question that this person is at all regenerate. To invoke God's grace as an excuse for sinning is Satanic rather than regenerate (Rom. 6:1).

The doctrine of perseverance associated with the glorious assurance of salvation for obedient Christians was one of the great factors of strength in the whole Reformation movement (Lutheran, Anglican, and Reformed). The doctrine of assurance* separated from perseverance leaves the child of God subject to the constant fear that one's weakness may yet forfeit everything Christ has done for us!

Augustine, "On the Gift of Perseverance," *Post-Nicene Fathers*, 1st series, vol. 5; G. C. Berkouwer, *Faith and Perseverance* (1958); J. Owen, *The Doctrine of the Saints' Perseverance*: *Works of John Owen*, ed. W. Goold, vol. 11.

Against perseverance: I. H. Marshall, *Kept by the Power of God* (1969); R. L. Shank, *Life in the Son* (1960).

ROGER NICOLE

Philip, John (1775–1851)

Congregationalist minister converted during the Haldane revival. Philip was a warm supporter of the London Missionary Society* (LMS). He became its resident director in South Africa* (1819), leaving Aberdeen, where, for fifteen years, he had been the outstanding evangelical preacher. He reorganized LMS work and vigorously campaigned for removing all discriminatory laws in the colony. He persuaded the Paris Evangelical Mission and the American Board* to work in South Africa.

A. C. Ross, *John Philip* (1986).

ANDREW C. ROSS

Philosophy

Literally (Gr. and Lat.) "the love of wisdom and/or knowledge" (*philia-sophia*), philosophy crystallizes the supreme ambition of reason* and symbolizes the worthiest mode of existence. In Plato's *Republic*, dialectic or philosophy is called knowledge of beauty and goodness. In the heyday of scholasticism,* Thomas Aquinas, like Aristotle, characterized philosophy as knowledge of things through their causes (*Summa contra gentiles* [1258–60]). At the apogee of idealism, Hegel argued that philosophy was absolute science and true worship because it conceptually fathomed the true nature of things.

The contemplation of the totality of reality is the primary concern of philosophy. According to Francis Bacon, reality embraces God, nature, and humanity* (*Advancement of Learning* [1603]). As *sapientia humana*, philosophy investigates the essence of all things and addresses the fundamental issues regarding nature, humanity, and society. To define pure positions, draw general principles, frame a consistent, comprehensive, and meaningful system, and prescribe a way of living—together these constitute the philosophical task. As encyclopedic knowledge and rigorous quest for the highest truth, philosophy lays claim to universal science (*philosophia perennis*). Ordinarily its method of procedure is logical and rational. Despite topical affinities with religion and methodological congruences with the sciences, philosophy is irreducible to either. Exclusively dependent on reason and experience, philosophy as discipline repudiates the authority of supernatural revelation* and ecclesiastical tradition. Unlike any particular science, philosophy does not confine its concern to one particular area of reality.

Western philosophy was born in Greece in the sixth century B.C. At the crossroads of Euro-Asian trade, the confluence of Hellenic cosmogony with Middle Eastern wisdom, geometry, and astronomy created a psychocultural cradle in which philosophy and science (physics, mathematics) arose from religion concomitantly. Henceforward both remained closely related until the advent of nineteenth-century positivism (Auguste Comte) which sealed their divorce. The Milesian school initiated the crucial shift from mythological account (*mythos*) to conceptual-argumentative and universally verifiable explanation (*logos*), and the Eleatic school inaugurated metaphysics by differentiating the world of truth from the world of seeming.

The standard divisions of philosophy are logic, epistemology, anthropology, natural philosophy, metaphysics, ethics, and politics. There are three historical models of classification: hierarchical, symbiotic, and pedagogical.

In the hierarchical classification, Aristotle's *Prior Analytics* distributes the sciences into speculative (theology, mathematics, dialectic) and practical (mechanical arts, ethics). Descartes, the founder of modern metaphysics, compared philosophy to a tree whose roots are metaphysics and whose trunk and branches are the sciences (*Principia philosophiae* [1644]). Christian von Wolff, the rationalist, subsumed logic and metaphysics (theology, psychology, cosmology) under theoretical science, and ethics and politics under practical science (*Rational Thoughts* [1719–21]).

The symbiotic and pedagogical classifications were introduced by the Stoics, Platonists, and Neoplatonists and adopted by the Alexandrian school (Clement's *Stromateis* [A.D. 214]), Eusebius of Caesarea, Augustine (*The City of God* [A.D. 411]), and the Jesuits (*Ratio studiorum* [1580]). Their tripartite classification—physics, ethics, logic, or ethics, physics, epoptic—was associated with the triadic virtues, logos theology, and the Trinity.* Similarly, in Hegel's *Phenomenology of the Spirit* (1807) the Absolute Idea's dialectic triad unfolds into logic, philosophy of nature, and philosophy of the Spirit.

In modern times the following were prominent schools: rationalism; empiricism; criticism; idealism; romanticism; positivism; evolutionism; materialism; philosophy of existence; dialectical materialism; pragmatism; vitalism; neo-empiricism; neo-Kantianism; neo-Thomism; and phenomenology, whose epistemology treats the essences as acts of consciousness (Husserl's *Ideas* [1913]). Anchored in the belief in progress and in human rationality and sociability, one century, the eighteenth, earned the title "the philosophic age." The developing natural sciences and birth of the human and social sciences, which gradually disrupted the unity of philosophy, generated a wealth of topical theories: the philosophies of history, education, religion, art, science, and economics.

Generally, philosophy confronts Christian faith in matters of metaphysics and ethics, whereas Christian dogmatics needs philosophy either as propaedeutic or for its epistemology, anthropology, and rational elucidation. Natural theology* traditionally is where reason encounters faith. Historically, relations between philosophy and Christian theology took four patterns: (1) mutual noninterference, as recommended by Descartes and Pascal; (2) unrestricted belligerency to achieve complete supremacy, as advocated by irreligionists such as Spinoza, d'Holbach (*System of Nature* [1770]), and Nietzsche, as well as by foes of reason like Tatian, Bernard of Clairvaux, Luther* (*Conclusiones contra scholasticam theologiam* [1517]), and Barth;* (3) radical transformation by which either Christianity is reduced to a religion of humanity (Ludwig Feuerbach) or philosophy turned into a theology of the Word of God, the *philosophia christiana* of Rupert of Deutz, Erasmus,* and Calvin* (*Christianae religionis institutio* [1536]); and (4) expedient alliance either to Christianize natural reason (Kierkegaard) or enslave philosophy as the handmaiden of revealed theology (scholasticism, Schleiermacher,* neo-Protestantism).

After World War I, the philosophical scene was dominated by existentialism, analytical philosophy, logical positivism, language philosophy, Frankfurt social theorism and neo-Marxism, and recently by structuralism and deconstructionism. Ludwig Wittgenstein reduced the philosophical labor to the clarification of thoughts in his *Tractatus logico-philosophicus* (1921). It was as much the dawning of a new era as the pronouncement of a death sentence upon the perennial ambition of the *sapientia humana*.

JEAN-LOUP SEBAN

Pictet, Benedict (1655–1724)

Reformed minister, theologian, and hymn writer, Pictet is best known for his vigorous defense of orthodox Calvinism* in an age of theological transition. Born in Geneva, he was educated at the university, where he became professor of theology (1686). There he was a restraining influence on his colleagues, including his cousin, Jean-Alphonse Turrettini, who wanted to abrogate the Helvetic Consensus Formula* and institute other theological changes in the early years of the Enlightenment. A man of irenic spirit, Pictet authored two major theological works, published many books and pamphlets, wrote texts for numerous popular hymns, organized assistance for Huguenot* refugees following the Revocation of the Edict of Nantes* (1685), and promoted evangelism* in France.

E. de Budé, *Vie de Bénédict Pictet* (1874); J. I. Good, *History of the Swiss Reformed Church Since the Reformation* (1913); M. I. Klauber and G. Sunshine, "Jean-Alphonse Turrettini on Biblical Accommodation: Calvinist or Socinian?" *Calvin Theological Journal* 25 (April 1990): 7–27; F. Laplanche, *L'écriture, le sacré et l'histoire . . .* (1986).

ROBERT D. LINDER

Piety

Throughout the history of the Reformed faith, "piety" (often in the biblical phrase "practice of piety"), along with "devotion," "pilgrimage of the soul," "spiritual warfare," and "godly conversation," has denoted qualities and exercise of the Christian life today often associated with "spirituality." While in the nineteenth century the word tended to become debased to suggest merely "doing good," its broader meaning includes the cultivation of faith* and godly knowledge, religious experiences both intensely mystical and more routine, and the varieties of personal devotional and corporate worship* exercises that foster experiences of the divine.

Reformed piety has been characteristically evangelical, rooted in the biblical mandate to confess one's sinfulness and in the Gospel promise of forgiveness* and grace.* While in the thought of Martin Luther* the doctrine of justification* was paramount, Calvinists have stressed the experience of conversion* and growth in grace (sanctification*). From Huldrych Zwingli* and John Calvin* onward, Reformed spirituality has been characterized by its activism, both in family and church-centered religious life and in the world. The Reformed tradition embraced the concept of the covenant* developed by Calvin, Heinrich Bullinger,* Martin Bucer,* and other early theologians. Reforms of individuals, church, state, and society in general have been equal priorities. Outward effort directed toward godly ends has been deemed spiritual activity. This fusion of individual and social spiritual ideals in the Reformed tradition helped nurture the development of national identity, for weal or woe, in such places as Scotland, the United States, and South Africa.

Church organization, based on federal theology* and scrutiny of NT models, became an expression of Reformed piety's concern for fellowship (as in Congregationalism*) and orthodoxy (as in Presbyterianism*). Unlike more radical groups related to (as with Baptists) or just outside (as with Quakers) the Reformed tradition, it has always identified the church and its ministry* as indispensable "means of grace." This stance has at times opened Reformed pastors and theologians to the charge of "formalism" or "scholasticism" by more "Spirit-led" detractors. But personal piety, a yearning for a more immediate, powerful experience of Christ or the Holy Spirit,* continually resurfaces among the Reformed faithful.

Calvin's lifelong personal anxiety was shared by many of his heirs. The quest for "assurance* of salvation," exacerbated by the doctrine of predestination* of the elect and the damned, became a hallmark in the experience of Puritans* and other later Calvinists. Puritan spiritual writers analyzed the conversion process biblically and psychologically, with an extremely detailed, empirical approach. Individuals were urged to examine their lives against the standard of this *ordo salutis* laid down in sermons and theological tracts. This is not to say that those in the Reformed tradition did not find spiritual satisfaction. Spiritual "pilgrims" were expected to make "progress" on their way to heaven. The first question of the Heidelberg Catechism* (1563), for example, exudes personal assurance: "What is your only comfort, in life and in death? That I belong—body and soul, in life and in death—not to myself but to my faithful Savior, Jesus Christ." This text was revered next to the Bible by German and Dutch Calvinists on both sides of the Atlantic. English and American Puritans sought assurance through devotional Bible-reading, meditation, and "closet" prayer; family prayers and catechetical training; pastoral visitation; neighborhood devotional meetings; and in public worship. Devotional manuals (including directions for meditation and sample prayers), spiritual diary keeping, meditative poetry, and spiritual biography were widely used aids to the spiritual life. Many methods of meditation and prayer found in the Reformed tradition were quite similar to those characteristic of medieval and early-modern Catholicism. The personal writings of representative figures reveal that believers within the Reformed tradition were indeed blessed with powerful spiritual experiences. Despite Calvinism's tough-minded theology, many experienced God as gracious and Christ as bridegroom of the soul.

Reformed worship has traditionally centered on the reading of Scripture,* prayers (often freely conceived by the pastor), the singing of psalms (and, by the eighteenth century, hymns), and, most especially, the sermon. Reformed piety is intensely Bible-centered. The sacraments,* nevertheless, are also an integral part of this spiritual tradition. A doctrine of personal and corporate encounter with the real presence of Christ achieved high expression in America in seventeenth-century Puritanism and in the nineteenth-century German Reformed Church's Mercersburg* movement. Presbyterians in Scotland and in America's middle colonies participated in "sacramental seasons," in which thousands of members from many far-flung churches camped together for up to a week, devoting themselves to countless sermons, arduous prayer, Bible study, and self-scrutiny in preparation for massive and joyful celebrations of the Lord's Supper.* These traditional exercises, central to the spiritual and social lives of whole communities of people, issued in the revivalism* of the Great Awakenings.*

Reformed piety is distinctive among the various other families of Christian spirituality in its understanding that the personal experience of grace and salvation is inseparable from the corporate relationships of church, community, and world.

L. Bouyer, *Orthodox Spirituality and Protestant and Anglican Spirituality* (1965; vol. 3 of *A History of Christian Spirituality*); L. Dupré and D. E. Saliers, eds., *Christian Spirituality: Post-Reformation and Modern* (1989); C. E. Hambrick-Stowe, *The Practice of Piety: Puritan Devotional Disciplines in Seventeenth-Century New England* (1982); J. Riatt et al., eds., *Christian Spirituality: High Middle Ages and Reformation* (1987), 300–33, 454–63; L. E. Schmidt, *Holy Fairs: Scottish Communions and American Revivals in the Early Modern Period* (1989); D. D. Wallace, Jr., ed., *The Spirituality of the Later English Puritans* (1987); M. J. Westerkamp, *Triumph of the Laity: Scots-Irish Piety and the Great Awakening, 1625–1760* (1988).

CHARLES E. HAMBRICK-STOWE

Plantinga, Alvin (1932–)

The John A. O'Brien Professor of Philosophy at the University of Notre Dame was educated at Harvard University, Calvin College, University of Michigan, and Yale University. Plantinga has taught at

Yale, Wayne State University, and Calvin. Widely regarded as one of America's foremost analytic philosophers of religion, he has held many visiting professorships and prestigious fellowships and delivered the Gifford Lectures (1987).

Plantinga's significance for Reformed thought centers on three issues. His "Reformed epistemology" argues for the rational legitimacy of belief in God, even without evidence, because such belief is "properly basic" in the foundation of human knowledge. Plantinga does not show, however, that nontheistic religions could not make the same claim.

Plantinga's "free-will* defense" is an attempt to answer the charge that the existence of God is incompatible with the existence of evil. It rests on the claim that God could not both create significantly free humans and guarantee that these creatures would not choose to do evil. Some critics have contended that this emphasis on "freewill" is incompatible with his Calvinist* theology.

Plantinga's discussion of God's nature and its properties is reminiscent of the tradition of Reformed scholasticism* with its interest in identifying the attributes of God.

A. Plantinga, *God and Other Minds* (1967); *The Nature of Necessity* (1974); *God, Freedom and Evil* (1974); *Does God Have a Nature?* (1980); and co-editor with N. Wolterstorff, *Faith and Rationality* (1983); J. Tomberlin and P. van Inwagen, *Alvin Plantinga* (1985).

JAY M. VAN HOOK

Poissy, Colloquy of

Conference held by Catherine de Médicis (1561), regent during the minority of her son Charles IX, hoping to reconcile Catholics and the growing Protestant movement represented in France for a time by Anthony of Navarre and steadfastly by his wife, Jeanne d'Albret,* parents of the future Henry IV (reign 1589–1610). Theodore Beza* from Geneva and Peter Martyr Vermigli* from Zurich spoke for the Reformed church. The opposition included Diego Lainez, general of the Jesuit order.

The Colloquy's failure led to civil war and eventually to the St. Bartholomew's Day Massacre* (1572) in which about 70,000 Huguenots,* including the venerable Admiral Gaspard de Coligny, were killed. The Edict of Nantes* (1598), promulgated by Henry IV, brought a large measure of freedom, until its revocation (1685) under Louis XIV deprived French Protestants of all religious and civil liberties.

CHARLES PARTEE

Polanus, Amandus (1561–1610)

Professor of OT at Basel (from 1596), Polanus is an important figure in the beginnings of Reformed orthodoxy.* Though not an original thinker, he was a gifted consolidator and systematizer, giving to later generations a coherent, organized body of theology that would exert considerable influence by content and method. He also portrays the state of emerging Reformed orthodoxy* in the crucial years between Theodore Beza* and the Synod of Dort.*

Polanus wrote a number of biblical commentaries, including one on Romans, a treatise on predestination* against Bellarmine, and two major systematic works. These latter are prime examples of the emerging interest in an ordered and comprehensive exposition and defense of Reformed doctrine. *Partitiones theologiae* (1590) is a compendium of basic instruction in Christian doctrine.* It passed through several editions in Polanus's lifetime, including a number in English translation as *The Substance of Christian Religion.* His *Syntagma theologiae Christianae* (1609), structured virtually identically to the first, is many times larger and is an extended defense of the Reformed faith. Catholic opponents figure large, especially Bellarmine and Thomas Stapleton. The *Syntagma* is a far more polemical work, with an extended treatment of the developing Protestant doctrine of Scripture* set against its Catholic adversary.

Polanus's theology uses Aristotelian categories, including its fourfold causality and the syllogism. Yet more striking is the dominant presence of the methodology of Peter Ramus.* Ramist subdivision (usually dichotomous) abounds. The *Par-*

titiones is preceded by fifty-five pages of Ramist charts. Theology itself is subdivided into faith* and good works, giving ethics* a major significance for possibly the first time in Reformed dogmatics. The Ramist concern for praxis is very evident, for Polanus is concerned for the "use" of each doctrine he handles.

Polanus's most powerful single theme is the doctrine of God.* The whole outworking of creation,* human history,* and salvation* is dependent on the decree* of God in predestination and providence* and, behind that, the doctrine of God himself. However, these elements are balanced by Polanus's interest in the covenant.* Of importance in the development of federal theology,* he is one of the first to teach a pre-fall covenant of works. Equally, his predestinarianism is related closely to Christology* and soteriology. One would be mistaken to see him as dealing in logical or metaphysical speculation. He regarded Scripture as a higher authority than reason.*

Polanus is a bridge between the pristine Reformed teaching and orthodoxy, scholastic in constructing theology with academic precision and logical rigor but, with a strong doctrine of God, oriented to christological, soteriological, and practical concerns.

H. Faulenbach, *Die Struktur der Theologie des Amandus von Polansdorf* (1967); R. Letham, "Amandus Polanus: A Neglected Theologian?" *SCJ* 22 (1991); R. A. Muller, *Christ and the Decree* (1986); E. Stähelin, *Amandus Polanus von Polansdorf* (1955).

ROBERT LETHAM

Politics

Politics is the process by which groups of people make choices of their leaders and the use of their collective resources. Thus, John Calvin* was among the most political of theologians, for he relied for reformation of church and society, not upon individuals, "however high their social status or great their inspiration. He relied above all on organizations, and imparted to his followers an extraordinary organizational initiative and stamina. There have been few men in history who loved meetings more" (Walzer, p. 29).

Calvinists have paid extraordinary attention to politics in two spheres: church* and state. They have often influenced the second while trying chiefly to change the organization of the first. Yet in neither arena did they assume they could appeal to their own knowledge of absolute principles of how humans should organize themselves. Nothing was to rival the absoluteness—the sovereignty—of God* in Calvinist faith, worship,* and social life. All human authority and wisdom gets cut down to merely human size in this vision of God: kings like Charles I, forms of church government, particular human claimants to church leadership, one political party or another. The Calvinist vision of God was only indirectly "political"; but images of power, rule, order, and change dominate it. Sweeping political change emerged from those willing to live by those images.

As a people "astonished by the mercy of God" (J. T. McNeill), they were not easily astonished—or intimidated—by human politicians. This was a theology that "dignified the concrete, historical lives of ordinary people with the purposes of God" (Leith, p. 205). Puritans, nerved by such belief, identified with John Knox's* public defiance of a queen; Parliament's decision to execute a sovereign in the name of *the* Sovereign (God); new balances of power between parliament and kings; and a revolt of American colonists against all kings whatsoever.

If the political power of Calvinism stemmed from its vision of God, the political *practice* of the Calvinists was regularly shaped in the deliberations of their churches. For many, the congregation was "the school of democracy" (A. D. Lindsay). There, "the humblest member might hear, and join in, the debate, witness the discovery of the natural leader, and might participate in that curious process by which there emerges from the clash of many minds a vision clearer and a determination wiser than any single mind could achieve" (Woodhouse, p. 76). In the structure and processes of its church government, modern Presbyterianism* reflects these same political instincts.

The history of the influence of Reformed church politics on public secular politics is complex; historians will continue to argue over how much Calvinism* aided or hindered the rise of Western democracy. Virtually all agree, however, that this theological tradition—from John Calvin to Jonathan Edwards* to Reinhold Niebuhr*—sought with peculiar intensity to hold together in one system of thought and action a huge array of opposing human social ideas: liberty and equality, individual conscience and social restraint, church witness to society alongside separation of church and state, the universal sway of God and the limited local vocation* of humans, sinful* church and sinful society, holy church and holy community.

The Calvinist as righteous politician has been satirized; and modern disciples of "that Frenchman" of Geneva have to admit that the Calvinist concern for "liberty" has frequently conflicted with a "passionate zeal for positive reform, with the will, if necessary, to dragoon men into righteousness" (Woodhouse, p. 51). This phenomenon prompts a comparison of the spirit of Calvinism to the political spirit of Marxism, with the latter's tendency to dragoon whole societies into "justice"* (Walzer, p. 230). Ernst Troeltsch concluded that Calvinists, as rigorously as any Christian movement in history, embraced a vision of a "Holy Community," a church and an entire secular order reformed according to the will of God revealed in Scripture.* That the reach of this political-theological vision exceeded its historical grasp surprises no one, including Calvinists. That ever they had the courage thus to reach is the surprise.

The advantage of Calvinism over other politically minded faiths continues to be its capacity for recourse to the Transcendent, including new understandings of that Transcendent. "Perpetual revolution" in Calvinist political rhetoric entails perpetual repentance: intellectual, moral, and political repentance. Modern Calvinists may even need Karl Marx to enable them to remember, with modern theologies of liberation,* Calvin's own skepticism of wealth and power, his sense of the equality of all humans before God, and his expectation that God has no commitments to the defense of established human orders. The God who raised Jesus from the dead is sovereign over everything. Those with this faith can stand up when nations rage, human kingdoms totter, and God devises new political things for the world.

J. H. Leith, *An Introduction to the Reformed Tradition* (rev. ed. 1981); M. Walzer, *The Revolution of the Saints* (1965); A. S. P. Woodhouse, *Puritanism and Liberty* (1951).

DONALD W. SHRIVER, JR.

Polity

A particular form of government. The Latin and Greek roots of the word "polity" carry connotations of community, organization, and citizenship. There are three distinct types of church polity: episcopal, congregational, and presbyterian, each with distinguishing characteristics. Episcopal polity can be recognized by the presence of a singular leader (or bishop) as in Lutheran, Methodist, or Roman Catholic* communions. Congregational polity is characterized by the principle of one person, one vote of a pure democracy, as in Baptist polity. Presbyterian polity may be characterized as a representative democracy and is found in such communions as the Church of Scotland, the Presbyterian Church (U.S.A.), or the Reformed Church of Hungary. The origins of presbyterian polity are in the Reformation and Calvin's* understanding of church governance developed in his *Institutes* and practiced in Geneva.

Characteristics of Reformed polity.

Scriptural: Those who practice a presbyterian form of polity perceive its order to be derived from Scripture,* as understood by Reformed theology and expressed in the confessions of the Reformed faith. It expresses the principle that those of the Reformed faith must order their life together in accord with their faith* and as a witness to the demands of Scripture. Accordingly, the ministry* practiced in presbyterian polity preserves NT forms of ministry and is shared according to the gifts of its members: proclamation—ministers of Word and Sacrament; governance—elders; sympathy and service—deacons.*

The foundation stone of Reformed polity is the conviction that the church is "the body of Christ" (1 Cor. 12) and that all authority in the church belongs to Jesus Christ, head of the church.

Corporate: Therefore, decision making in presbyterian polity is always corporate, never individual. Decisions concerning the welfare of the church and all matters of theology and mission are made in governing bodies led by "moderators" and composed of elders and ministers of Word and Sacrament sitting in parity. At least two courts are always present in a Reformed polity. The most fundamental court of the church is the session. It governs the local church, is moderated by the pastor, and is comprised of elders elected by the congregation. Overseeing the session is the presbytery, in which the membership of all ministers of Word and Sacrament is lodged. The presbytery has oversight of its ministers, congregations, and sessions and is responsible for the ordination* of all ministers of Word and Sacrament.

Representative: Reformed polity is characterized by a representative form of government in which ministers of Word and Sacrament sit in deliberative assemblies with elders. The Greek word *presbyteros*, from which the polity derives its name, means "elder"—governance by elders who are representatives of the people.

Characteristics of American Reformed polity. The American Presbyterian Church has developed distinctive characteristics of its own because of its historical development in a frontier society and in a society that insists on the separation of church and state. The clearest exposition of the polity of the Presbyterian Church (U.S.A.) is in ch. 1 of the *Book of Order*, part of which, "The Historic Principles of Church Order," is believed to have been written by John Witherspoon* and adopted by the founding General Assembly* of the church (1789).

Constitutional: The polity of the PC (USA) is expressed in its Constitution which consists of four parts. The *Book of Confessions,* the first and determinative part, contains theological statements of churches of the Reformed faith. The remaining three parts of the Constitution are derived from, and express, these confessions. The Form of Government and the Directory for Worship detail how the members of the church shall live together, make their decisions, and worship. The Rules of Discipline make up the fourth part of the Constitution, which outlines procedures for discipline and judicial process within the church in a manner that emphasizes fairness, redemption, and mercy rather than retribution and punishment.

Ordered: The PC(USA) is governed by four interrelated governing bodies: session, presbytery, synod, and General Assembly. Each governing body makes its decisions by majority vote, the representatives of the larger part of the church having the power of review over governing bodies representing a smaller part of the church. The powers of each governing body are limited by the Constitution. They have no civil power. In the American church, the synod is a geographical entity composed of presbyteries under its jurisdiction. Its responsibilities are related primarily to enabling its presbyteries and to organizing mission within its geographic area. The synods also perform a crucial role in the judicial process of the church as a court of appeal. The General Assembly is the highest court of appeal in the church. It is responsible for national and international mission. The General Assembly, when it meets annually, speaks as prophet to the church, with no legislative power over the lower governing bodies; but, like the other governing bodies, it may legislate for itself.

Reformed and reforming: The PC(USA) claims not only to be a church in the "Reformed tradition" but to be a church that is constantly reforming. Reformation of the church's polity is continual and accomplished through amendment of the Constitution. The amendment process is illustrative of the interrelated nature of the governing bodies: any member of the Presbyterian Church may propose an amendment to the Constitution through the session; and the session, through the presbytery. Either a presbytery or a synod may propose an amendment directly to the General Assembly, which, by majority vote, may choose to recommend the amendment to the presbyteries. A majority of the presbyteries is required for a successful amendment to the Constitution. A two-thirds majority vote is necessary for an amendment to be made to the *Book of Confessions,* since the effect of such an amendment might be to change the theological foundations upon which all of the polity of the church rests.

MARIANNE L. WOLFE

Prayer, Practice of

The Reformation brought radical changes in the way Christians prayed. Yet it was in the century following that prayer disciplines of the Reformed church matured.

The Reformers' perception that the prayer life of the Middle Ages had broken down led to a thorough study of the scriptural disciplines of prayer. Rather than emphasizing the mental prayer which developed out of the Neoplatonism of late antiquity and monastic asceticism, the Reformers sought God in the frailties of the human condition. They understood Jesus to teach that we are creatures of need and in our hungering and thirsting we have communion with God (Matt. 5–7). Jesus, therefore, taught his disciples to pray about their common needs: relieving poverty and sickness, guidance in uncertainty, and patience to bear adversity. The Protestant catechisms* in explaining the Lord's Prayer all taught that daily prayer was essential to living by faith.

The Puritans developed a rich literature to guide Christians in the practice of prayer. Classics are John Preston's *The Saint's Daily Exercise* (1629); Thomas Watson's *The Lord's Prayer* (repr. 1960); Matthew Henry's* *Beginning and Ending the Day in Prayer*; and John Flavel's* *The Mystery of Divine Providence* (1678). Because of their strong belief in providence,* seventeenth-century Calvinists were particularly concerned in prayer to seek out their destiny from God's own hand.

Three characteristics of prayer in the Reformed tradition stand out.

Prayers of intercession. Early Reformed liturgies all devoted a large portion of public worship to intercessory prayer. It was understood as the priestly function of the assembled people of God to pray for the unity, sanctity, and apostolicity of the church (1 Peter 2:4–10; John 14–17). The church was to pray for the needs of humanity in general, the civil authority, the ministry of the church, the propagation of the gospel, and persons suffering various trials (1 Tim. 2:1–8; Eph. 6:18–20; Col. 4:2–4; Acts 4:23–31). This ministry of intercession regularly followed the preaching of the Word because in the hearing of the Word the church was guided to ever-new intercessory concerns.

Praying the Psalter. Early in the Reformation the Strassburg Psalter set the precedent for translating the Hebrew psalms into metrical poetry so they could be sung by the common people. Clément Marot* and Theodore Beza* provided the Genevan Psalter with superb metrical psalms which the Huguenots* have sung for centuries. The same was true in the Netherlands, Scotland, and New England. The psalms are prayers of the Holy Spirit, the songs God has given us to cry out in time of need, to assure us of the covenant* promises and to give us an intimation of our future (Ps. 42:8; 137:4; Acts 4:25). For Christians to pray the psalms is to pray with Christ. When Jesus prayed the psalms in his passion, he offered up the sorrows and the hopes that God's people have expressed through history.* In this priestly ministry he fulfilled the psalms; therefore Reformed psalmodists, such as Isaac Watts,* have often paraphrased the psalms in a Christian sense.

Family prayer. While the tradition of daily prayer was maintained by the Reformation, it soon became most frequently observed in the home rather than in the church. The Church of Scotland added a chapter to the Westminster Directory for Worship distinguishing family prayer from public worship on the one hand and "secret" or private prayer on the other (1646). Family prayer consisted of singing psalms, reading a chapter of Scripture,* and offering a full and comprehensive prayer including praise, confession, petition, intercession, and thanksgiving. It was to be held morning and evening each day. As Richard Baxter* put it, the family is a little church and therefore has the sacred privilege and duty to offer regular worship to God (*Christian Directory* [1673]).

C. E. Hambrick-Stowe, *The Practice of Piety: Puritan Devotional Disciplines in Seventeenth-Century New England* (1982); F. Heiler, *Prayer* (ET 1932); H. O. Old, "Daily Prayer in the Reformed Church of Strasbourg, 1523–1530," *Worship* 52 (1978): 121–38.

HUGHES OLIPHANT OLD

Prayer, Theology of

Prayer is human speech addressed to God.* It arises from a consciousness of the relation in which one stands to God and expresses the emotions, desires, and needs stemming from that consciousness. It includes adoration, thanksgiving, confession of sin,* submission, commitment, and petition. Within the Reformed tradition, there has been general agreement that petition is the central focus of prayer.

John Knox* defined prayer as "an earnest and familiar talking with God, to whom we declare our miseries, whose support and help we implore and desire in our adversities, and whom we laud and praise for our benefits received" (*Declaration of the True Nature and Object of Prayer* [1554]).

Prayer in the Reformed confessions. In the Reformed confessions, statements about prayer are generally brief and address Roman Catholic* beliefs and practices that are being rejected. Prayer is to be made through the intercession of Christ as the only mediator, so invocation of saints is forbidden. Prayers are not meritorious but express thankfulness for free grace.* In place of formality, there should be an orderly freedom. Prayer should be in the language of the people, not in an unknown tongue, so that it may be intelligible.

The Second Helvetic Confession* (1566), alone of the major confessions, devotes a separate chapter to prayer. It advocates brevity in public prayer, lest the people be wearied and so think the sermon to be overlong. The WCF* and the Confession of 1967* contain brief positive statements about prayer within the context of worship.

The Reformed catechisms on prayer. Since the early church, expositions of the Lord's Prayer have formed the basis of catechetical instruction. The catechisms* of the Reformation and post-Reformation eras follow the same procedure.

The HC* (1563) devotes questions 116–129 to prayer. Question 116 calls prayer "the chief part of the gratitude which God requires of us" as well as the means by which God gives his grace and Spirit. The WLC and the WSC (1648) treat prayer, along with the Word and Sacraments,* as a means of grace. A classic Reformed definition of prayer is obtained by collating the statements from the two catechisms: "Prayer is an offering up of our desires unto God, for things agreeable to his will, in the name of Christ, by the help of his Spirit, with confession of our sins, and thankful acknowledgment of his mercies" (WSC, q. 98; WLC, q. 178). The Larger Catechism asserts that the Lord's Prayer may be used as a form of prayer in public worship* as well as providing a framework for the composition of other prayers.

Prayer and Reformed theology. It is surprising that systematic theologians within the Reformed tradition do not give more attention to prayer. Heppe's *RD* has no section on prayer. Calvin is one exception. He treats prayer fully as "the chief exercise of faith, and by which we daily receive God's benefits" (*Inst.* 3.20.1). Calvin defends the necessity of prayer in relation to God's sovereignty. For proper prayer, one must have reverence, a sense of need, penitence, confidence that God will answer, and reliance on Jesus alone. Public prayer is to avoid ostentation and formality and be in the common language. While church buildings are not holy places, Christians are to pray in the appointed assemblies. When answers to prayer are delayed, perseverance is needed. Calvin includes a full exposition of the Lord's Prayer.

Charles Hodge* discusses prayer briefly as one of the means of grace (*Systematic Theology*, 3.20.20). He seeks to vindicate prayer by appealing to God's personhood and arguing for the occurrence of "spontaneous action" not limited by natural law.

Karl Barth* included prayer under ethics in his *CD* (III/4, sec. 53, par. 3). For Barth, the basis of prayer is human freedom before God, which is also God's gracious command. Since prayer is essentially petition, it is not meritorious. Those who pray do so as united with Jesus Christ and pray as representatives of the whole world. Barth repeats the Reformers' emphasis that true prayer is surely heard by God. In practical matters, prayer should be vocal, not silent; spontaneous, even though formulated; offered at regular times; and short.

The revitalization of prayer within the Reformed tradition would be furthered by recapturing Calvin's emphasis on true prayer as a response of faith* to the Word of God* found in Scripture.*

D. G. Bloesch, *The Struggle of Prayer* (1980); B. M. Palmer, *Theology of Prayer* (1894); W. R. Spear, *Theology of Prayer* (1979).

WAYNE R. SPEAR

Preaching, History of

Preaching is essential to the worship* of a covenant* community and has therefore throughout church history been one of the church's basic ministries. Very early, Israel's worship involved reading the Book of the Covenant and the promise to live by it (Ex. 24:3–11). From Deuteronomy, which contains much homiletical material, we learn that the teaching of the law* was an important priestly function even before the exile (Deut. 33:10). It was probably Ezra who introduced systematic reading of the sacred writings Sabbath by Sabbath, followed by explaining the text that had been read (Neh. 8:1–8). Synagogue liturgical preaching was expository preaching, a distinct genre characterized by its systematic interpretation of canonical* Scripture chapter by chapter. In addition to the priests, the prophets constantly exhorted the people of God to be faithful to the covenant (Jer. 7:1–15). Prophetic preaching is a distinct preaching genre that emphasized God's Word at a particular time and place. It was often, however, practiced outside traditional liturgical structures. Another genre of preaching, the catechetical, developed in the rabbinical schools, where the law was studied subject by subject.

Jesus came preaching the gospel (Mark 1:14), the good news of God's mighty acts of salvation.* This gospel radically changed preaching. While Jesus retained the form of the expository sermon developed in the synagogue, he used it to proclaim the gracious work of redemption that God was even then performing in his own ministry (Luke 4:16–30; John 6:25–59). This same kerygmatic emphasis is found in the apostles' preaching. The primitive church's evangelistic preaching emphasized that Jesus both suffered and was raised according to Scripture (1 Cor. 15:1–11). Therefore, the OT Scriptures continued to be read at the Lord's Day service, while the preaching interpreted the lessons in a Christian sense (Luke 24:44–48; 1 Tim. 4:13). Numerous passages suggest that the primitive church must also have had some sort of moral catechism* (Eph. 4:1–6:20; 1 Peter 2:12–5:11 and parallels). There was both preaching the gospel of salvation and teaching the commandments of Christ (Matt. 28:18–20).

The remarkable sermons of Origen provide the first good look at Christian preaching. While Origen's approach to allegory is exceptional for the period, his overall approach to preaching is typical. He preached through one book of the Bible after another, from both the OT and the NT, chapter by chapter, verse by verse. Most Christian preaching continued in this mold until well into the fifth century. The greatest preachers of the patristic period were Basil of Caesarea, John Chrysostom, and Gregory of Nazianzus. All three were well schooled in Greek rhetoric. While Gregory used his oratorical prowess to teach Christian doctrine,* Basil and Chrysostom were careful interpreters of Scripture,* reemphasizing the importance of grammatical-historical interpretation. Chrysostom's sermons are remarkable for their systematic coverage of the Bible, their moral application, and prophetic courage. In the West, Ambrose and Augustine* preached simple, practical, expository sermons that lacked the art of the Greek Fathers but nourished the church nevertheless. During the patristic period, the catechetical sermon developed as a major genre of Christian preaching. Drawn from the rabbinical tradition of moral instruction, it was designed to teach converts the Christian faith. The festal sermon, another homiletical genre developed during the patristic period, was based on the Greek panegyric. Rather than explaining a passage of Scripture, it attempts to explain what is being celebrated by the feast. With the last of the Latin Fathers, Popes Leo and Gregory the Great, festal preaching became increasingly important.

During the barbarian invasions, it became difficult to train preachers. Nevertheless the missionary monks, such as Patrick, Columba, Columbanus, Pirmin, and Boniface, developed the evangelistic genre of preaching. Still, for the average churchgoer during the Dark Ages there was not much preaching. It was Charlemagne who recaptured the vision of a sermon in every church every Lord's Day. To help priests become preachers, Alcuin was charged with drawing up a lectionary for all the feast days and all the Sundays of the year. Now that there was a required Scripture lesson for every service, sermon helps were provided by the homilary, a collection of model sermons based on these lessons. This system did not produce much inspired preaching but did improve the situation. In the twelfth century, Bernard of Clairvaux and Maurice of Sully raised the level of preaching considerably, but it was not until the founding of the Franciscan and Dominican orders that popular preaching really flourished. Dominic, Francis of Assisi, Anthony of Padua, Albert the Great, and Bonaventure were outstanding preachers. During the later Middle Ages, pietism dominated the pulpit. Advent and Lent with their penitential emphasis became the preaching seasons of the year. In Italy especially, the annual Lenten evangelistic crusade became a regular feature of church life. Among the great preachers of this period were Jean de Gerson, John Hus, Nicholas of Cusa, Johann Geiler, Bernardino of Siena, John of Capistrano, and Savonarola.

There was plenty of preaching when Protestantism appeared. For the Reformers the question was not whether there should be preaching but what kind of preaching there should be. Martin Luther* championed a recovery of expository preaching. A forceful public speaker, he had earned a doctorate in biblical interpretation. Huldrych Zwingli,* inspired by Chrysostom's example, began to preach through the Gospel of Matthew chapter by chapter, verse by verse, treating such diverse subjects as mercenary soldiering, clerical celibacy, superstitious religious practices, divine providence,* and justification* by faith.* John Oecolampadius,* also following Chrysostom, urged Protestant preachers to adopt grammatical-historical exegesis and abandon allegorical exegesis so popular in the Middle Ages. The Reformers generally did much to recover catechetical preaching. Johannes Zwick gave particular attention to catechetical preaching for children. John Calvin* was a master of the art of biblical interpretation and a skilled craftsman in word usage. His sermons are simple, clear, and informative.

The preaching culture of Great Britain lagged behind Germany and Italy at the beginning of the sixteenth century. While John Knox* was one of the exceptional preachers of history, it was not until the Puritan* movement began to have its effect that there was weekly preaching throughout Great Britain. By the beginning of the seventeenth century William Perkins,* John Preston, and Richard Sibbes had won a wide reputation for their plain-style preaching. The government felt threatened by the vision of a Christian commonwealth preached by the Puritans. Nevertheless, by the next generation England was teeming with outstanding preachers such as Richard Baxter,* Edmund Calamy, and Thomas Goodwin.* Some of the best English preachers, such as John Cotton,* Thomas Shepard,* and John Davenport, emigrated to America. With the Anglican ascendancy, other outstanding preachers, such as Thomas Watson, famous for his sermons on the WLC, Thomas Manton,* the master expositor, and John Flavel,* the sailor's evangelist, were forced into nonconformity.

The Netherlands* produced a number of outstanding preachers during the golden age of the Dutch Republic. Gisbert Voetius* was a doctrinal preacher, while Johannes Cocceius,* famous for his development of federal theology,* was a distinguished expositor. Lutheran Germany abounded in sound, learned preachers. Among the French Huguenots* the outstanding preacher of the seventeenth century was Jean Daillé,* but Pierre du Moulin and Jean Mestrezat also continued the Reformed tradition of both expository and catechetical preaching.

Influenced by classical rhetoric, the baroque period took a very different approach to preaching than did the Reformation. In England, Lancelot Andrewes and John Donne preached polished literary sermons supporting the Anglican state church and the divine right of the English monarchy. It was in Catholic France, however, that baroque preaching flowered. Jacques Bossuet, Louis Bourdaloue, and Jean Baptiste Massillon were greatly admired pulpit orators at the French court, where Louis XIV, though he lived a flagrantly immoral life, enjoyed hearing a good sermon. The influence of this homiletical school was great, even in Protestant circles.

Jacques Saurin* in the Netherlands and Jean Frédéric Ostervald* in Switzerland were two Reformed pastors who followed many of the baroque preaching trends, even though they remained Protestant, and maintained an enlightened orthodoxy in the face of eighteenth-century rationalism. In Scotland, Hugh Blair became the voice of Moderatism,* preaching with superb rhetoric a most genteel Christianity. Johann Lavater* in Zurich and Friedrich Schleiermacher* in Berlin conscientiously tried to interpret Reformed Christianity to an age that had largely embraced Deism.

Scandalized by the superficialities of baroque religion, Pietism began to take preaching in a different direction. Avoiding both doctrinal theology and biblical exegesis, Pietism focused its preaching on inward religious experience. This brought about a great revival in England, where John Wesley and George Whitefield* preached to coal miners and mill workers outside the church's institutional and liturgical structures. Unlike Wesley, Whitefield was a Calvinist,* even if his dramatic, extempore preaching style departed considerably from traditional Reformed pulpit practice. Coming to America (1739), Whitefield fanned the Great Awakening* along with Jonathan Edwards* and Gilbert Tennent,* who under the influence of Puritanism as well as Pietism had already begun preaching an experiential faith. These Americans tended to be more careful in their biblical exegesis and the doctrinal implications of their preaching than the pietists of Europe. The outstanding preacher of the Great Awakening was Virginia's Samuel Davies.

Nineteenth-century evangelicalism was represented by Scotland's Thomas Chalmers* and Thomas Guthrie. They were concerned not only with inner conversion* but with the outward conversion of society as well. Establishing a new congregation in the slums of Glasgow, Chalmers preached through the Gospel of John while organizing diaconal work with the poor. Alexander Whyte* maintained this tradition into the twentieth century. The biblical exposition of Friedrich Wilhelm Krummacher* did much to revitalize the Reformed churches of Germany, while in France Adolphe Monod's emphasis on classical Protestant teaching restored the Huguenot tradition. In Victorian England, Reformed preaching was represented largely by Congregationalists* and Baptists.

Alexander Maclaren, Joseph Parker, and Charles Haddon Spurgeon* spoke eloquently to the common people of God's power to transform human life. They drew their sermons from a careful and perceptive study of the Bible but largely ignored the problems raised by modern biblical research. Spurgeon, a staunch Calvinist, must be ranked as one of the greatest preachers of the Christian church.

In America, a distinct school of preaching developed. Inspired by evangelistic concern and prophetic zeal, it tended to neglect both expository and catechetical preaching. Charles G. Finney,* impatient with the theological disciplines of classical Protestantism but nevertheless deeply aware of the practical religious needs of the new nation, was typical of the frontier revivalist. Preaching conversion,* abolition of slavery,* and temperance, these homespun prophets preached a faith that was very real to the average American. While Horace Bushnell* and Henry Ward Beecher* developed this basic stance in the direction of liberal Protestantism, Dwight L. Moody, Billy Sunday, and George Truett increasingly devoted themselves to evangelism. A particularly lively variation of the American preaching tradition is found in the black churches. At the beginning of the twentieth century, Harry Emerson Fosdick, with his straightforward language, illustrations from everyday life, and his unbounded optimism, epitomized the American school of preaching. While outstanding representatives of this school were active well into the middle of this century, it seems finally to have exhausted itself.

E. G. Dargan, *A History of Preaching*, 2 vols. (1911); H. Dressler, "Preaching, I (History of)," *New Catholic Encyclopedia* (1967), 11:684–89; A. Niebergall, *Leiturgia* 2 (1955): 181–352; J. B. Schneyer, *Geschichte der katholischen Predigt* (1968); W. B. Sprague, *Annals of the American Pulpit*, 11 vols. (1857–69).

HUGHES OLIPHANT OLD

Preaching, Theology of

The Reformation did not invent preaching. Before Martin Luther* there were centuries of preaching: Clement and Origen, John Chrysostom, Augustine,* and Bernard of Clairvaux, not to mention preaching orders, Dominicans and Franciscans. Prior to the Reformation, preaching may have lost track of Scripture* and was sometimes given to droll rhetorical excess, but there were still faithful preachers: Wycliffe and the Lollards were both biblical and bold. In the late-medieval world, preaching may have become calculating, frivolous, or neglected, but it never died.

The Reformation ushered in a new era of biblical preaching, both in quality and in quantity. Most of the Reformers preached many times each week. Luther's sermons fill twenty volumes; Calvin's* forty; and Bullinger,* the successor of Zwingli,* preached the entire Bible in a little more than fifteen years. Most Reformers preached *lectio continua*, working their way through Scripture passage by passage. Though their sermons were biblical, they were, above all, gospel; according to the Reformers, they were preaching the "Word of God."*

The major Reformers (except for Philipp Melanchthon) were preachers, yet their understandings of preaching were scarcely monolithic. Luther, Zwingli, and Calvin differed in sacramental theology; they differed similarly over preaching as the "Word of God." If consubstantiation allowed Luther to affirm that bread and wine in Eucharist *are* Christ for us, so he insisted that when preachers preach, their voices *are* the voice of God! Luther's tendency toward Eutychian Christology* shows up analogously in his treatment of Word and Sacrament.* Similar parallels are in Zwingli and Calvin; they deal with Word and Sacrament in much the same way that they approach Christology. Luther and Zwingli represent somewhat antithetical positions on preaching, while Calvin, coming later, is often seen as a *via media*.

"The preaching of the Word of God is the Word of God." The issue dividing Luther and Zwingli was the relationship between Word and Spirit. In contrast to enthusiasts (*Schwärmer*), who supposed the Spirit was an immediate gift to the human soul quite independent of Word and Sacrament, Luther insisted that the Spirit was given by means of the Word: "The Word, I say, and only the Word is the vehicle of God's grace." Fearful of idolatry,* Zwingli demurred, rejecting Luther's binding of Word and Spirit. He edges close to the enthusiasts by insisting that preaching was a human witness to Christ, intended to prompt us to seek the true inner Word of God, given by the Spirit. Thus, Zwingli sharply distinguishes between the *verbum Dei externum*, which is human preaching, and the *verbum Dei internum*, which is the Holy Spirit.* He quotes the Gospel of John with approval: "No one can come to me unless the Father who sent me draws him" (John 6:44). Preaching might point to Christ, but only the Spirit draws.

Luther and Zwingli also differed in their view of Scripture. Luther appears to equate preaching and Scripture as "Word of God"; God's voice is heard in both. For Luther, the Word of God is the gospel, the free, soul-consoling message of justification* from pulpit or biblical page. In Zwingli's thought, Scripture is elevated above any human testimony. God the Spirit is the author of Bible and the only true interpreter of scriptural texts.

The man in the middle. Calvin's position may seem to occupy a middle ground. With Luther, Calvin affirms a kind of "transubstantiation of the Word." Though preachers are human, nevertheless preaching is the will of God for the church* and, *instigated by the Spirit*, is the mouth of God addressing us: "[God] deigns to consecrate to himself the mouths and tongues of men in order that his voice may resound in them" (*Inst.* 4.1.5). Of course, preaching is nothing apart from the Spirit who illumines our minds to hear. With Zwingli, Calvin stresses the biblical origin of preaching and the inward testimony of the Holy Spirit, but he insists that the Holy Spirit is given *in* preaching and is not waiting hidden in the heart.

The high and holy task of preaching. Calvin's confidence in the power of the Word is awesome: God's Word, never fruitless, does what it declares. Thus, if preaching declares absolution, then those who hear are truly absolved. In his *Commentary* on Isaiah, Calvin announces, "Nothing that has come out of God's holy mouth can fail in its effect." Of course, we must be quick to add that the power of preaching is by the Holy Spirit. If the Spirit is not with the Word, then sermons, no matter how eloquent, will be empty and altogether ineffective. Preaching is a human act having no intrinsic efficacy: sometimes God connects with preaching and sometimes separates from preaching. But when God chooses preaching, then it is surely the power of salvation.* Notice that Calvin links preaching to the purposes of God, namely, salvation.

Even when preaching is rejected, it is nonetheless efficacious. Preaching will either soften or harden the heart, save or condemn. The proper office of the gospel is salvific, but, because of human depravity, in an "accidental" way the gospel can harden and destroy. Though Calvin is blunt about the two-sided sword of the Word, preachers may not excuse themselves if the gospel is rejected; they must examine themselves and their preaching. Of course, ultimately Calvin links the acceptance or the rejection of the Word to God's election.

Preaching is crucial because Christ with all his saving graces comes to us through preaching. The means of our union with Christ* is the Word. So preaching is *revealing* and *saving* and *commanding*.

1. Though Calvin would insist there can be no further revelation* beyond God's self-disclosure in Christ Jesus, yet when preaching brings Christ to us in a contemporary context, revelation is "new" in its applications. Calvin's own preaching was never past-tense Bible study but was doctrine* applied to life.

2. Calvin stresses the gracious benefits we receive through preaching. Union with Christ is both our justification and our sanctification.* Forgiveness* is conferred through preaching, and holiness is shaped by preaching.

3. Preaching is the means by which Jesus Christ exercises authority.* The sovereign Lord claims rule in the church through preaching and, as the gospel is spoken evangelically by the church, claims Lordship in the world. Preaching establishes the kingdom of God* wherever the gospel is announced.

The mode of our union with Christ is faith, and faith is the product of the Holy Spirit. Though Calvin, with Luther, is fond of quoting Rom. 10:17, "Faith comes from hearing," and insists that without the Word faith is impossible, nevertheless faith is a gift of the Spirit who opens our ears truly to hear the promises of God. Faith,* for Calvin, is not passive; faith is active obedience. Through preaching, Christ establishes his rule, and therefore congregations must receive the Word with humble obedience. Among the Reformers, Calvin had more to say about a congregation's active, intelligent responsibility in attending sermons, even though hearing was a gift: "[Our Lord] will open our eyes and ears, and will not only give us intelligence but will also so form our hearts that we shall follow Him when He calls us" (*CR* 54, col. 114).

Preaching and Scripture. Calvin insisted that preaching is properly an explication and application of Scripture. Preachers should be schooled in the Bible, for Scripture is the Word of God provided by the Holy Spirit. Therefore Scripture is the source of the Word we preach and the norm by which we judge our gospel message. Yet the Holy Spirit is the true interpreter of Scripture and forms inner testimony of the Bible's truth. At times Calvin will speak of the "dictation" of the Spirit in the writing of Scripture, but he does not espouse a rigid theory of inspiration; he has an eye for error. Nevertheless Calvin is sure the message of Scripture is the saving truth of God and thus the source of proclamation. In many ways Calvin's understanding of Scripture seems to parallel his theology of preaching.

The preacher. What of the preacher? For Calvin, preachers are chosen by God to be ambassadors of the Word. Preachers ought to be holy, insightful, scholarly, and, above all, able teachers. Yet *the* qualification for the preaching office is God's choice and inner assurance of God's call formed by the Holy Spirit. The dignity of the preaching office is not based on character or position but on speaking the Word of God. While sinlessness is scarcely a criterion for ministry, preachers should seek to bring their lives under the Word they speak. All that preachers can do is to serve God as "ministers of the divine Word," praying, "Come, Holy Spirit!"

H. J. Forstman, *Word and Spirit: Calvin's Doctrine of Biblical Authority* (1962); G. W. Locher, *Zwingli's Thought* (1981); T. H. L. Parker, *The Oracles of God: An Introduction to the Preaching of John Calvin* (1947); R. Stauffer, *Dieu, la création et la providence dans la prédication de Calvin* (1978); W. P. Stephens, *The Theology of Huldrych Zwingli* (1986); R. S. Wallace, *Calvin's Doctrine of the Word and Sacrament* (1953).

DAVID G. BUTTRICK

Predestination

Election, or predestination, is the belief or doctrine* that God* has chosen some persons for the gift of salvation.* It is not to be confused with providence,* that is, God's governance of all things, nor with fate or philosophical determinism. An important teaching in Western Christianity, it has been especially emphasized in Reformed theology.

Predestination is rooted in the OT theme of God's choice of Israel and is based on many NT passages, especially in Paul (e.g., Rom. 8:29–30; 9:6–33). It was developed doctrinally by Augustine* against Pelagius, whom Augustine accused of teaching salvation by human effort. Augustine believed that out of the mass of sinful humanity God had chosen some to illustrate God's grace,* while passing by the remainder to illustrate God's justice. For Augustine, this was compatible with the will's freedom, understood not as choice but as free and willing assent to God's will (voluntary necessity). Moreover, since God was in eternity, not time, there was for God neither past nor future, so predestination was outside time. Augustine's teaching reappeared in such medieval anti-Pelagians as Thomas Bradwardine and John Wycliffe. Wycliffe used the doctrine to spiritualize the divine-human relationship and undermine priestly authority.

During the Reformation, Martin Luther* asserted predestination against Erasmus,* whom he accused of Pelagianism. But Lutheran theology eventually minimized it. Reformed church leaders, however, emphasized predestination to glorify God, instill humility and gratitude, insist against Roman Catholicism that salvation* was by God's grace alone and did not entail human merit, and to affirm that it was God's purpose to elect and sanctify a people to fulfill God's will in the world. Thus Huldrych Zwingli* taught predestination as part of the sovereignty and providence of God. His Zurich successor, Heinrich Bullinger,* described it as God's gracious choice of the undeserving. Martin Bucer* related predestination to the doctrine of salvation (it was "in Christ") and stressed election to holiness of life.

John Calvin* carried on Bucer's approach and also followed Augustine. He did not make predestination the center of his theology, nor did he treat it abstractly as an aspect of the doctrine of God, but he considered it in relation to soteriology and the Christian life: believers humbly and thankfully look back to their election as solely a gift of saving grace. Especially in later controversy, however, Calvin affirmed double predestination, or the reprobation of those not elected, though this was only because of their own sins. Like Augustine, he thought predestination harmonized with the will's freedom, since God never forced the will. The approach of Bucer and Calvin is reflected in the early Reformed confessions.*

The growth of scholastic* method in Reformed theology gave predestination more precise definition and more central theological placement than in Zwingli's programmatic writings and Calvin's exegetical ones. The Italian exile theologians Peter Martyr Vermigli* and Girolamo Zanchi* were significant in this process as they brought the logic of Aristotle and familiarity with medieval scholasticism to their versions of Reformed teaching. Zanchi followed medieval theologians in connecting predestination with the doctrine of God.* Scholastic method is also apparent in Calvin's Genevan successor, Theodore Beza,* who put God's decrees at the beginning of his system. Beza was also a supralapsarian,* holding that God's decrees of election and reprobation preceded God's decree of creation and permission of the fall. The doctrine of the earlier Reformed theologians had generally been infralapsarian,* with predestination subsequent to these things, but some later Reformed theologians further developed Beza's approach. In spite of these scholastic refinements, there remained an experiential core to belief in predestination, especially apparent among Puritan theologians such as William Perkins,* who emphasized its uses in giving hope and assurance to believers and stimulating good works: those who trust in Christ and strive to lead a holy life should consider themselves among the elect.

There was resistance to such a prominent, sharply defined, and sometimes supralapsarian doctrine of the double decree,* often deriving from the Erasmian* and humanist* elements of the early Reformation. Among the early Reformed, Theodor Bibliander was cautious about predestination. The seventeenth-century French theologian Moïse Amyraut* taught hypothetical universalism* which he said had been Calvin's view: the death of Christ was on behalf of all, even if effective only for the elect. This view became widespread among French Calvinists and was adopted by some of the English Presbyterians, including Richard Baxter.* More radically, Jacobus Arminius in the Netherlands maintained that God predestined on the basis of foreknowledge of who would believe. After bitter conflict, the Synod of Dort* (1618–19) condemned Arminius's opinion and affirmed unconditional election as necessary for the preservation of salvation by grace. The Westminster Confession* (1646) reflected the scholastic and anti-Arminian form of the doctrine but stopped short of supralapsarianism. In the following decades, Reformed scholastics such as John Owen* and Francis Turretin* continued to refute Arminians.*

The evangelical movements of the eighteenth century stressed God's grace, giving the doctrine of predestination renewed life, as in its defense by Jonathan Edwards* in New England. However, evangelicalism eventually led to a simplification of theology that eroded predestination, especially after its rejection by Wesleyan Methodism; the nineteenth-century American evangelist Charles G. Finney* denounced it as an impediment to revivals. Thereafter revivalism* tended to be Arminian, and many Presbyterians* and Congregationalists* in the United States abandoned belief in predestination, a process also abetted by the growth of theological liberalism. The Presbyterian Church in the U.S.A. added to the Westminster Confession a section stating it was God's desire that all be saved (1903). But scholastic predestinarian theology continued at Princeton Seminary with Charles Hodge.*

Liberals among continental Reformed theologians emphasized predestination. Friedrich Schleiermacher,* who said the essence of religion was the feeling of absolute dependence upon God, defended predestination as necessary for affirming that essence, though he rejected reprobation. Alexander Schweizer* argued that Schleiermacher had revitalized Reformed theology by emphasizing predestination, which Schweizer thought was the primary motif of Reformed theology. But Schweizer felt that the doctrine could be replaced by its distilled essence: dependence upon God.

The neo-orthodoxy* of the early twentieth century revived much in Reformation theology, reacting against liberalism. Emil Brunner,* however, criticized Zwingli for determinism and Calvin for the double decree. He held that election assures believers that a personal God calls from eternity those who, in the world of time, believe; there is no before or after, only grace.

Karl Barth* performed a more drastic recasting. For him, Jesus Christ is the object of predestination, and humanity is elected in him; thus the grace of God as the sole cause of salvation is preserved at the same time that the universality of this election removes the greatest obstacle to the doctrine: its invidious distinction of elect and non-elect.

Predestination is a difficult point for modern Christians. Yet it is an important guarantee of the gratuitousness of salvation, surely a central intention of Reformed theology. Also, when one considers that doctrinal formulations are human ways of understanding the mysteries of divine revelation, it may well be best to accept the intention of the doctrine: affirmation of God's gracious favor bestowed upon the undeserving, and set aside its negative implications as unbiblical. Further, it should be remembered that predestination rules out human merit, not freedom; God's will is exercised through secondary causes and does not compel the human will to any end to which it has not freely assented.

B. G. Armstrong, *Calvinism and the Amyraut Heresy* (1969); Barth, *CD* II/2; B. A. Gerrish, *Tradition and the Modern World* (1978); P. K. Jewett, *Election and Predestination* (1986); R. A. Muller, *Christ and the Decree* (1986); D. D. Wallace, Jr., *Puritans and Predestination* (1982).

DEWEY D. WALLACE, JR.

Presbyterianism in America

The Presbyterian churches in the United States, as elsewhere, are members of the historical Calvinist* stream of Christian communities, called Reformed in Europe (as in South Africa* and elsewhere), arising from the teachings of John Calvin.* Calvin expounded Scripture,* defined and defended a system of Christian doctrine,* and established a church order and relationship of religion to government in Geneva that was not only widely imitated but, in more fully evolved forms, powerfully influential in the formation of Western political and economic institutions.

"Presbyterian" describes the Calvinist churches in the English-speaking world (and mission areas served by English-speaking churches). It is from *presbyteros* (Gr.), meaning "elder." In modern usage it describes a form of church government by elders (the session) elected by members of a congregation and associated with elders and ministers of other congregations in a body called the presbytery. The uniqueness of Presbyterianism lies in the distinctive powers of the presbytery: to sponsor, ordain, and discipline the clergy; to establish, combine, and dissolve local congregations; to govern local churches where self-government has failed; to hold property on behalf of all member congregations; and to elect representatives to higher governing bodies of the Presbyterian churches: synods (regional associations of presbyteries) and the General Assembly* (national body). In judicial matters, a system of appeals ascends from presbytery through synod courts to the General Assembly, where final decision rests.

Nine distinct denominations in the United States call themselves Presbyterian in 1990. They may be divided into three groups: those originating in Europe which have resisted the mergers and modernizations that characterize the evolution of Christianity in America; bodies that are the product of those mergers and encompass the majority of American Presbyterians; and Presbyterian bodies produced in America by division and other organizational initiatives.

Origins of American Presbyterianism. The earliest European inhabitants of New England were English Puritans,* members of a religious and civil party that wished to "purify" the Church of England—to eliminate from its liturgy and doctrine elements it believed were the unbiblical residue of Roman Catholic belief and practice. Since the English monarch was also the "Supreme Governor of the Church," Puritanism was perforce also a political movement that desired to establish a monarchy substantially controlled by the Parliament, where Puritanism was strong.

The Puritan founders in America left England before the outbreak of the Civil War (1641), determined to establish before the whole world a community life totally responsive to the divine will. At first self-governing, their congregations began to form associations with varying degrees of power over the vital functions of the church: determination of orthodoxy in faith and practice, ordination,* and discipline.* As some of these associations achieved the powers described above as distinctive to Presbyterianism, notably those in the Connecticut River valley in Massachusetts led by the outstanding pastor Solomon Stoddard, Presbyterianism was defined in American history.

Under John Knox's* leadership, the Reformation in Scotland took an exclusively Calvinist direction, the more resolutely because Roman Catholic residues in the state-church of England intensified the traditional hostility of Scotland toward England.

The Presbyterianism that Knox established as the state-church in Scotland became a second major source of American Presbyterians with the emigration of Scots (those first transplanted to the northern colonies of Ireland are termed "Scotch-Irish") to North America, beginning in the seventeenth century but swelling to substantial numbers after 1714. While there were Scots in New England, great numbers landed on the shores of the Delaware and Chesapeake bays—New Jersey, Pennsylvania, Delaware, and Maryland. In these states the oldest Presbyterian congregations are found. In their quest for land, Scots moved west to the headwaters of the Ohio River and south through the Shenandoah Valley to the Carolinas.

In 1706 Presbyterianism in America achieved the form from which its history flowed continuously thereafter with the establishment of the Presbytery of Philadelphia. As the denomination grew, its organization changed, culminating in the establishment of a General Assembly (1788), which first met in July 1789.

Doctrinal and social development. Presbyterian congregations formed in the frontier settlements of Pennsylvania and elsewhere were the nuclei around which social development occurred. Records from the seventeenth and eighteenth centuries show that drunkenness was disciplined by local sessions, even when the culprits were not of the church. Academies were opened by the congregations and colleges were founded. Civil law drew on church models.

At the urging of Scotch-Irish elements in the church that feared for the orthodoxy of a body without a formal creedal commitment, the Synod of Philadelphia adopted the WCF* as the doctrinal standard of American Presbyterianism (1729). The controversies thereafter rarely disputed the articles themselves but had much to do with attitudes toward correct belief and uses of the confession in the church, the role of piety* in the Christian life and ministry,* evangelism,* attitudes toward the interpretation of the Bible, and the relative importance of doctrinal and social stances within the church. Presbyterianism always regarded the creeds of Nicaea-Constantinople (A.D. 325–381) and Chalcedon (A.D. 451) as its own and was willingly taught by the major sixteenth-century Reformed creeds,* notably the Geneva Catechism* (1541), the French Confession* (1559), the Scots Confession* (1560), the Heidelberg Catechism* (1563), and the Second Helvetic Confession* (1566). Today, three twentieth-century confessions are included in the *Book of Confessions* of the PCUSA: the Theological Declaration of Barmen,* the Confession of 1967,* and A Brief Statement of Faith.*

The new denomination established in 1706 fell into a controversy in the late 1720s that was to prove highly consequential. Gilbert Tennent* of New Brunswick, New Jersey, was orthodox by Westminster standards and troubled by his ineffectiveness in leading his people to renewed spiritual life. He resolved, he wrote, to "plead more faithfully for [God's] cause and take more earnest pains for the conversion* of souls." The response of his own people and other congregations that he subsequently addressed was immediate. Tennent was criticized for charging that the clergy had grown spiritually cold and that their strict subscription to orthodoxy did not move them to take seriously in actual experience the biblical warnings of human guilt and promises of grace* and forgiveness* upon repentance.* To him, the "unconverted" state of the ministry was the real enemy. By "unconverted," Tennent meant not that they held pagan doctrine but that neither their spiritual experience nor their behavior showed the impact of belief. From the small seminary, the celebrated "Log College" at Neshaminy, Pennsylvania, founded by his father, William, Sr., there now issued a stream of young men for a "converted" ministry.

The embittered quarrel that divided the preachers of the revival* (including George Whitefield,* James Davenport, and Jonathan Edwards*) from Presbyterians who entrusted the integrity of the church to its orthodoxy in belief, issued in division (1741) between Old Side and New Side. During these years the persuasive power of the two parties was put to the test, and preachers of the revival swept the field. Aggressively establishing new churches and producing a well-educated and effective clergy, the New Side demonstrated better understanding of the spiritual needs of people in a new land. From a sociological point of view, the revivalists were Americanizing the church, redirecting attention from attitudes and practices imported from Ireland and Scotland to the actual American environment. Henceforth mainstream Presbyterianism in America would incorporate a strong emphasis on sincere piety, describable Christian experience, and the expectation that theology and churchmanship be relevant to society.

The coming of the national period made new demands on Presbyterians. Loyal to the king until the Revolution actually broke out, Presbyterians supported it enthusiastically. John Witherspoon,* eminent pastor and educator, signed the Declaration of Independence. In 1787 the church adopted a declaration concerning religious freedom that still expresses the Presbyterian position: "God alone is Lord of the conscience and hath left it free from the doctrine and commandments of men, which are many times contrary to his Word. . . . Therefore they consider the rights of private judgment, in all matters that respect religion as universal and unalienable." Presbyterians in Virginia supported Thomas Jefferson's efforts to disestablish the Church of England in that colony before 1776 and his candidacy for the presidency, despite his known hostility to Calvinist theology. James Madison, who drove the Constitution of the new United States of America through the Constitutional Convention, had been Witherspoon's student at the College of New Jersey (Princeton University).

The emergence of presbytery-governed congregations in New England did not alienate the Congregational churches of that region, and as Americans streamed westward a cooperative plan for establishing new churches on the frontier was formulated, the Plan of Union (1801). During its operation, New England Calvinism's original institutions, notably Harvard College, abandoned the defining doctrines of its tradition and by 1830 Unitarianism* was fully formed. New England's evangelicals established Andover Seminary (1808) to train an orthodox clergy, but suspicion of the Plan of Union as a vehicle of the erosion of orthodoxy among Presbyterians, hostility to the creative theological spirit of Calvinist New England, a partisan power struggle, and other reasons created a complex controversy that ended in the division of the church (1837) into "Old School" (the critics of the Plan of Union) and "New School" (which continued cooperative mission work). Union Theological Seminary had been founded in New York City (1836) under the influence of the emerging New School. This institutionalized a historic polarity within Presbyterianism since Princeton Seminary, founded in 1812 through the separation of theological instruction of clergy candidates from the college curriculum and community, remained an Old School bastion.

Sociological elements in the eighteenth-century division underlay the new debates, principally that of adaptation to the changing American culture. To succeed on the frontier, churches required flexibility and decentralization, and Baptists and Methodists excelled. Conservative Presbyterians preferred an eastern educated clergy but could not meet the demands of the flourishing revival on the western frontier. The Presbytery of Cumberland, Kentucky, severed its ties with the General Assembly (1810) in order to ordain young men who had not met the formal educational requirements of the church but who possessed the necessary spiritual gifts. A kindred movement about this time produced also the Christian Church (Disciples of Christ) from among Presbyterians determined to meet the needs of the frontier. This group, however, was non-confessional and adopted congregational church government. So as such it left the Presbyterian family of churches.

The slavery* controversy exposed the differing attitudes of the Old and New Schools toward cultural change even more dramatically. In fashioning the 1837 division, northern Old School leadership agreed not to agitate the slavery issue in return for the adherence of the Presbyterian churches in the South. The New School in Ohio and elsewhere, by contrast, joined congregational institutions in frustrating the Fugitive Slave Law by assisting in the escape of slaves.

The secession of the Confederate States divided both Old School and New School, the former suffering more seriously because of the limited number of New School Presbyterians in the South. The Presbyterian Church of the Confederacy became the Presbyterian Church in the United States (PCUS; "southern Presbyterians") after 1865. A struggle to overcome the 1837 division succeeded and the Presbyterian Church in the United States of America (PCUSA) was reconstituted (1870).

Because of the defection of so many New England churches to Unitarianism* and New School ties with that region, doctrinal controversy was more pronounced in the nineteenth-century division than the earlier dispute between revivalists and conservatives. The New School never formally espoused a softened orthodoxy, but it was open to new currents of biblical scholarship, while former Old School leaders, particularly at Princeton Seminary, resisted the historical criticism of the Bible. Expanded into a debate on religious authority and oversimplified by the introduction of novel criteria of orthodoxy, a series of controversies divided Presbyterians in the first three decades of the new century, defining the new term "fundamentalist" and its opposite, "modernist." In 1936 some congregations under the leadership of J. Gresham Machen* of Princeton Seminary, having established an Independent Board of Foreign Missions, organized the Orthodox Presbyterian Church, a body more akin to the rationalist Calvinism of the seventeenth century than to American fundamentalism. Withdrawals of more typical fundamentalists from the Orthodox Presbyterian Church produced the Bible Presbyterian Church.

While the fundamentalist/modernist* controversies of the 1920s and 1930s caused no major decreases in the memberships of the principal Presbyterian denominations, they fostered distinct bodies of religious sentiment with differing, sometimes antagonistic concerns. Down to the present, the offspring of the New School tradition have concerned themselves with the church's confrontation with the increasingly secular society and spirit in America. Since 1900 the General Assemblies of the major Presbyterian bodies have issued many declarations on social matters covering a broad range of public concern: race relations, war and peace, national health policy, urban problems, church-state relations, women's rights, and the "life issues" such as population control, abortion, and capital punishment. More conservatively inclined Presbyterians have questioned the propriety of ecclesiastical activism and emphasized more individual religious concerns rooted in devotion to the Bible as opposed to its historical interpretation, personal piety,* and evangelism.* In recent years, these protean differences have been politicized and issued in a progressive dismantling of the action agencies of the General Assembly.

Immediately following World War II, American religious organizations experienced marked growth. Working jointly with other denominations, Presbyterians launched a comprehensive curriculum of Christian education* in their church schools; church-wide age group programs were encouraged; and the mission enterprise was refashioned to relate in a more egalitarian manner to the churches, formerly missions, in newly independent nations in Africa and elsewhere.

After the assassination of President John Kennedy (November 1963), social forces in the United States that still defy analysis broke into often chaotic activity. Among these was a growing popular distrust of church life, though the study of religion in secular university departments of religion attracted nonchurch youth in great numbers. The decline in Presbyterian church membership paralleled that in other mainline denominations and has not been arrested now. The power of the secular moral revolt to penetrate the minds and affect the behavior of church persons, including clergy, has produced a disintegration of traditional ethical standards. The new situation is at once more forbearing (e.g., the acceptance of divorce among clergy, previously taboo) and more troubling (e.g., increased incidence of sexual irresponsibility among clergy).

Theological education. In the eighteenth century the Presbyterian clergy in the United States was trained primarily through apprenticeship to respected pastors, in whose homes they resided and who supervised their reading and pastoral activity. Rudimentary institutions such as the Log College of William Tennent, Sr., grew into colleges at once civil and theological, such as the College of New Jersey, which had such eminent theologians as president Jonathan Edwards and professor John Witherspoon. Theological seminaries as we know them today—communal institutions separate from other degree programs, operating at a university level—took form throughout the nineteenth century.

Since church development tended to flourish in the vicinity of seminaries, many foundations were begun that could not survive once improved internal transportation brought them into competition with stronger schools. Presbyterian clergy today are educated in three main types of theological schools: denomination-sponsored (Pittsburgh, Princeton, Union [Richmond], Columbia, Austin, McCormick, Dubuque, San Francisco); those associated with universities but maintaining friendly relationships with denominations (e.g., Yale Divinity School); and nondenominational seminaries, many designed to supply clergy congenial to conservative Presbyterians (e.g., Fuller Seminary).

After World War II, Presbyterians provided funding for enlarged student bodies and the facilities to serve them. The recession in church life beginning in the 1960s progressively reduced the seminary system, while conservative independent seminaries grew.

In 1956 the PCUSA voted to ordain women as pastors and evangelists. The number of female candidates for the ministry has rapidly increased, and in 1990 some seminaries enroll nearly as many women as men. In recent years the broadening concept of the ministry has expanded the role of theological education, and many persons who are not candidates for ordination* are served by seminaries.

Ecumenical commitments. Before 1900, efforts to unify the scattered family of Presbyterian denominations were made, and in 1906 the PCUSA and the Cumberland Presbyterian Church rejoined, leaving a continuing Cumberland Church (1989 membership: 91,646). The division between North and South was overcome in the reunion of the UPCUSA and the PCUS (1983) after prolonged efforts. The present Presbyterian Church (U.S.A.) is a truly national denomination.

The United Presbyterian Church of North America (UPCNA) joined with the PCUSA to form the United Presbyterian Church in the United States of America (UPCUSA) in 1958. The UPCNA had itself been formed (1848) through the merger of the Associate Synod (founded [1753] by Covenanters*) and the Associate Reformed Synod (Seceders*). A continuing denomination refused the merger: the Associate Reformed Presbyterian Church (General Synod), based in the South (1989 membership: 37,585). A second continuing body, the Reformed Presbyterian Church of North America (Covenanters), had a 1989 membership of 5,114.

In addition to the Cumberland Presbyterian Church, the principal Presbyterian denominations originating in the United States are the Second Cumberland Presbyterian Church (black; founded 1869; 1989 membership: 15,000); the Orthodox Presbyterian Church (founded 1936; 1989 membership: 19,094); the Evangelical Presbyterian Church (founded 1981; 1989 membership: 33,000); the Presbyterian Church in America, formed by the withdrawal of fundamentalist type of congregations from the PCUS in and after 1973 (founded 1973; 1989 membership: 190,160); and the Korean Presbyterian Church in America (founded 1976; 1989 membership: 22,000).

The larger Presbyterian bodies in the United States have committed themselves to a variety of ecumenical bonds and ventures during the twentieth century. Membership in the National Council of the Churches of Christ in the United States of America (N.Y.), the most inclusive Protestant organization in the United States; the WCC* (Geneva, Switzerland), formed after World War II; and the WARC* (Geneva) are the principal organizations to which Presbyterian bodies have long belonged. Other ecumenical efforts take the form of multilateral conversations: the Consultation on Church Union, constituted in 1960 and embracing Presbyterians, Episcopalians, United Methodists, the United Church of Christ, the African Methodist Episcopal Church, and four other denominations, has fostered a range of collaborative efforts. Similarly, relationships with Lutherans, Roman Catholics,* and other Christians and with Jews have been cultivated through joint committee work on specific projects and timely declarations on public matters.

Current prospects. Interest in organizational union among Protestants has diminished in recent decades. Symbolically, in 1988 the PC(USA) removed its headquarters from New York City, where it was housed with the offices of many other denominations, to Louisville, Kentucky. The attenuation of the action agencies of the General Assembly expresses a trend toward religious introversion and parochialism and has sharply diminished the role of national leadership, both personal and organizational, within the church. Changing currency values and inflation have steadily increased the cost of overseas mission and reduced the number of fraternal workers. After a long period of stagnation, new church development has recommenced, but falling membership numbers have persisted. The combined membership of the UPCNA, the PCUSA, and the PCUS in 1958 was 3,798,234. In 1989, after the union of these bodies was consummated, membership in the PC(USA) was 2,967,781.

Aside from institutional problems, the quest among Presbyterians for renewal of faith* and spiritual understanding is earnest and widespread. The 1960s decade was marked by disappointment of hopes, frustration, and divisiveness. Yet it also opened new possibilities of renewal of spiritual life.

A historian is tempted to generalize this history by seeing long-term swings between Old Side–Old School and New Side–New School trends. In each of the three centuries of its history, the Presbyterian Church's broad parties have experienced their own internal changes. For example, fundamentalism did not take form until the twentieth century, and when it did, it sustained the New Side emphasis on conversionism at the side of a nominal orthodoxy well to the right of Old School Calvinism. Granting these substantial inward evolutions within each of the major streams of Presbyterianism, one may note that after the reunion of 1870, Presbyterians followed the New Side–New School impulse toward social ministry and adaptation to a developing America. Preoccupation with culture fostered this-worldly understandings of the kingdom of God* and a loss of the sense of the Transcendent, giving definition to modern "liberalism" in religion.

The Old Side–Old School tradition went through a prolonged struggle with issues of modernization and suffered much internal divisiveness but renewed its bid for the soul of Presbyterianism after the disappointment of activist Christianity beginning in the 1960s. The institutional decline of Union Seminary (N.Y.) compared to the sustained strength of Princeton Seminary; the decline of other denominational seminaries paralleled by sharp increases in numbers of Presbyterian clergy trained in recently founded evangelical and more fundamentalist institutions—these illustrate and reinforce a view that Presbyterianism in 1990 is experiencing a resurgence of Old Side–Old School churchmanship.

The membership decline since 1958 is attributed by some to neglect of spiritual religion in a church preoccupied with social action; in this same period, evangelical and fundamentalist churches have grown. Whether a revival of the Old Side–Old School tradition will prove able to do more than muffle the church's social witness and become an agent of spiritual renewal is a question for the new century.

M. Armstrong, L. A. Loetscher, and C. Anderson, eds., *The Presbyterian Enterprise* (1956); M. J Coalter, J. M. Mulder, L. B. Weeks, eds., The Presbyterian Presence series (1990–); L. A. Loetscher, *The Broadening Church* (1954); E. A. Smith, *The Presbyterian Church in American Culture: A Study in Changing Concepts, 1700–1900* (1962); W. W. Sweet, *Religion on the American Frontier, 1783–1840*, vol. 2: *The Presbyterians* (1964); E. T. Thompson, *Presbyterians in the South*, 3 vols. (1963–73); L. J. Trinterud, *The Forming of an American Tradition* (1949); *Yearbook of American and Canadian Churches* (1989).

ELWYN A. SMITH

Presbyterianism in Engand

During Mary Tudor's reign (1553–58), almost three hundred Protestants were martyred. Others found refuge in Frankfurt, Strassburg, Geneva, and other cities where they absorbed Calvin's teachings. On Elizabeth's accession (1558), they returned to England with a zeal for the purity of the church's doctrine,* worship,* organization, and moral teaching. Many became bishops, but their ardor was tempered by Archbishop Matthew Parker, who had not been in exile. On the whole, they carried out the royal policy of bringing all citizens to conform to the government and worship of the Church of England. Other returned exiles became parish ministers. Many organized "classes" for mutual study and the encouragement of preaching* based on the Bible. These "classes" had features of embryo presbyteries, the support of influential laity, and tacit approval from some bishops. Elizabeth saw them as a threat to church order and ordered their suppression. Parker's successor, Edmund Grindal, sympathized with the "classes" and opposed the queen's order. He was suspended from duty and confined to his palace. His successor, John Whitgift, supported the queen's policy. The "classes" were driven underground, but their influence persisted into the reigns of James I and Charles I.

Even more drastic programs for a presbyterian reform of the church had been issued by Thomas Cartwright* and Walter Travers* and were widely circulated. Ecclesiastical, political, legal, and financial grievances were aired in Parliament, in the church and in the country. These tensions led to the outbreak of the Civil War* (1642). Parliament sought aid from the Scots, who were also in revolt against royal policies and had replaced episcopal government with presbyterian government in their church. The Solemn League and Covenant* was approved (1643); in return for Scottish military help, the English agreed to a reform to bring the churches of England and Scotland into accord. The Scots were confident this would be along presbyterian lines. The English Parliament abolished the episcopal system and summoned an assembly of divines at Westminster* to draft a new system. Here the aim of the Scots was obstructed by Independent and Erastian* members who very reluctantly conceded that government by presbytery had a NT warrant. The Scot, Robert Baillie,* reported there had never been such obstruction since the Council of Trent but he held that the nearer approach of the Scottish armies would greatly assist the presbyterian arguments. Oliver Cromwell's* military prowess soon rendered Scottish help unnecessary. Cromwell refused to enforce the spread of a presbyterian system. The Restoration of the monarchy (1660) dashed presbyterian hopes. The new Parliament (1662) passed the Act of Uniformity under which all who would minister in the Church of England were required to have episcopal ordination* and also had to promise to use the *Book of Common Prayer.**

Over nineteen hundred ministers refused to conform and were ejected from their livings. About seventeen hundred were known to be supporters of a presbyterian system. Many of them ministered to clandestine congregations which had to be independent in their organization, though efforts were made to have at least a semblance of ordination by presbytery. These ministers endured many hardships, including imprisonment.

The 1688 revolution brought William and Mary to the throne. A limited toleration was accorded nonconforming ministers and congregations who secured licenses to meet. Over one thousand meetinghouses were erected in the next thirty years, but there was no general attempt to organize a presbyterian system. Presbyterian and Independent ministers met to draft a Happy Union and Concord that had some vestiges of a presbyterian system. This was soon shattered by controversies over the relation of law* and grace* and over the refusal of many presbyterian ministers to subscribe to Trinitarian doctrinal articles. Some presbyterian ministers became convinced or pragmatic Independents. Some moved to Unitarianism,* and they and their congregations retained their buildings (their successors are still found in the General Assembly of Unitarian and Free Christian Churches). Aspiring candidates for the nonconformist* ministry were trained in Dissenting Academies.*

Some congregations in the north of England retained their presbyterian outlook and secured ministers from Scotland. They formed the Presbytery of Northumberland (1783). A congregation in Stafford formed a connection with the General Synod of the Irish Presbyterians and secured a minister from Ireland.

Even more important for the renewal of Presbyterianism in England was the influx of Scots following the union of the Parliaments (1707). They came for parliamentary, legal, professional, and commercial reasons and founded presbyterian churches in London, Liverpool, Newcastle, and other centers. These churches wished to be organized into a synod of the Church of Scotland but its General Assembly* discouraged this and advised them to become an autonomous Presbyterian Church in England. This process began in 1836. Several of the native congregations in Northumberland were taken into the system which was completed with sixty-three congregations in six presbyteries (1842). A further group of about a hundred presbyterian churches was founded in connection with the Scottish Seceders who combined to form the United Presbyterian Church (1847). They were formed into an English Synod of the United Presbyterian Church (1863), and this church approved a petition from its English Synod to be allowed to unite with the Presbyterian Church in England which by then had 156 congregations (1876). The united church was called the Presbyterian Church of England. It had 260 congregations spread over ten presbyteries, with almost fifty thousand members.

Over the next century this church grew to 360 congregations with over sixty thousand members among whom were those of English birth and others from the Presbyterian Churches of Scotland, Ireland, Wales, the Commonwealth, and other countries. Ministers were called from Scotland, Ireland, and Wales, but the majority were trained in the church's own college, founded in London (1844) and transferred to Cambridge as Westminster College (1899). Among its teachers were notable scholars such as John Skinner, John Oman,* Charles Anderson Scott, Carnegie Simpson, W. A. L. Elmslie, and H. H. Farmer, who combined their loyalty to the Reformed tradition with understanding of other traditions and current movements of thought. The church founded and maintained missions in South China, Taiwan, and India. Many of its ministers and elders have been involved in movements toward Christian unity.

The Presbyterian Church united with the Congregational Church to form the United Reformed Church (1972). This church is Trinitarian in its doctrine. It affirms that "the Word of God in the Old and New Testaments, discerned under the guidance of the Holy Spirit, is the supreme authority for the faith and conduct of all God's people." The church's presbyterian background is reflected in its government where ministers and elders share in the work of all its councils. Twelve provincial moderators bring an element of personal oversight into the system, but their work is within and subject to the guidance of the General Assembly.

The Church of Scotland has a presbytery in England with nine congregations. The Presbyterian Church of Wales has fifty-two congregations in England, thirty-five of these being Welsh-speaking and seventeen English-speaking.

Annual Year Book and Reports of the Presbyterian Church in England (1876–1972); C. G. Bolan et al., *The English Presbyterians from Elizabethan Puritanism to Modern Unitarianism* (1968); Collinson, *EPM*; A. H. Drysdale, *History of the Presbyterians in England* (1889); R. T. Jones, *Congregationalism in England, 1662–1962* (1962); W. A. Shaw, *A History of the English Church During the Civil Wars and Under the Commonwealth, 1649–1660*, 2 vols. (1900); K. Slack, *The United Reformed Church* (1978).

R. BUICK KNOX

Presbyterianism in Scotland

From 1560 when the Scottish Parliament rejected papal authority, banned the Mass, and adopted a Calvinistic confession of faith (Scots Confession*), Scotland's national church was incontrovertibly Protestant and Reformed in theology,* worship,* piety,* understanding of church-state relations, and approach to social questions. Several generations were, however, to elapse before it became securely Presbyterian in government.

John Knox* and his reforming associates neither envisaged nor worked within an identifiably Presbyterian ordering of things, and their First Book of Discipline* (1560) outlines a system that has various differences from classical Presbyterianism. In addition to ministers, elders,* and deacons* (ministers to preach the Word,* administer the sacraments,* and tend the flock; elders to "assist the minister in all public affairs of the Kirk"; and deacons to manage parochial finances), other office-bearers are detailed. The serious lack of qualified pastors necessitated the recruitment of stop-gap "readers"* to conduct worship from the *Book of Common Order*, exhorters to undertake simple preaching duties as well, and—more strikingly—regional "superintendents"* to serve as pioneer missionaries in remoter areas, oversee the work of ministers, exhorters, and readers, and generally extend the organization and influence of the church (some historians have seen superintendents as resembling pre-Reformation bishops; but they were answerable to the General Assembly,* and certainly not regarded as belonging to a higher order of ministry).

Nor is the typically Presbyterian pattern of church courts clearly discernible in the First Book. There are kirk sessions, but they include deacons as well as elders and sometimes exercise authority over more than one congregation. Presbyteries do not appear, though ministers and others come together in "exercises" for Bible study and spiritual conference. Synods—"the superintendent and his council"—resemble a medieval bishop's entourage as much as a gathering of representatives from lower courts. Even the Knoxian General Assembly has sometimes been described as a religious session of Parliament rather than a purely ecclesiastical body.

In any case, the 1560 polity* did not last long. Its financial base proved insecure. It suffered gross interference from power-hungry politicians. Some ministers used it to exercise unacceptable "lordship" over their fellows. The survival of certain features of the pre-Reformation order generated confusion and possibilities of corruption. By the mid-1570s, Andrew Melville* and other radicals had become convinced of the superiority of the Presbyterian system, for which they claimed scriptural authority.

According to their Second Book of Discipline (1578), there are four essential offices in the church: deacon, elder, doctor, and minister. Deacons and elders are not greatly changed from the First Book, though the former become more exclusively financial officers, often without membership of the kirk session. The latter are now ordained for life rather than elected annually. The doctor (teacher) resembles today's schoolteacher or seminary professor. As for the minister, the Melvillians—alarmed by the apparent resurgence of episcopal power and pretensions, and believing there is only one essential ministry, that of Word and Sacraments—rejected any individual's claim to be a "pastor to pastors." "Oversight" (Gr. *episcopē*) has nothing to do with "lordship," and "bishop" is simply another designation for presbyter or pastor. The two-tier system of bishops and subordinate clergy which had begun to emerge in the 1570s is therefore unacceptable. So, indeed, is the First Book's four-tier system of superintendents, ministers, exhorters, and readers, from which only the minister survives.

In the overall government of the church, a new hierarchy of courts must replace the old hierarchy of individuals. The General Assembly stands supreme as the apex of the entire structure and chief agent of the Kirk in dealing with secular authority. Beneath it are ranged synods and kirk sessions. Presbyteries are not mentioned, though a court intermediate between synod and sessions, operating in an area smaller than the old diocese and taking over the functions previously exercised by superintendents or bishops, is clearly necessary. In the 1580s, that court (the presbytery) did at last materialize, and by 1592, when Parliament gave its approval to the new system, the Presbyterians had apparently triumphed.

But if organized presbytery may be dated from the 1570s, an equally well defined episcopacy began to emerge almost simultaneously. For more than a century thereafter the church was torn by conflict between the two systems. Sometimes, particularly in the Covenanting period (1638–60), the Presbyterian party or persuasion was dominant. At other times, power lay with its opponents (esp. 1600–38; 1660–88). Only at the Revolution Settlement (1688–89) did Presbyterianism finally capture the government of the state-supported church—thereby making it possible ever afterward for outside observers to treat "Scottish" and "Presbyterian" as well-nigh interchangeable terms.

Subsequent centuries have witnessed many changes in the national church as well as the emergence of dissenting Presbyterian churches embodying, in most cases, a broadly similar polity. The Kirk's General Assembly has increased in size from the small body (six ministers; thirty-five elders) of 1560 to a rather unwieldy aggregation of approximately twelve hundred commissioners. The twentieth century's representative elder is drawn from a much wider social background than eighteenth-century predecessors. The synod has slowly atrophied, and its days are almost certainly numbered. Presbyteries have altered little, but kirk sessions are probably more active than ever. Very significantly, all the traditional courts are now augmented, and sometimes overshadowed, by a multitude of committees centered in Edinburgh, often served by full-time secretaries and responsible for enterprises whose annual costs runs into many millions of pounds.

More revolutionary still, women were admitted to the eldership of the Kirk (1966) and to the ministry (1968), while in the 1980s the late-Victorian Order of Deaconesses was absorbed into a new diaconate of men and women which differed profoundly from the diaconate of Reformation times. Other innovations, such as the reintroduction of superintendents* or even a merger of the Presbyterian and Episcopalian systems, have been recommended but not as yet adopted. Less change is evident in the other Scottish Presbyterian churches, whose size and significance were vastly reduced by the church unions of 1900 and 1929.

J. K. Cameron, *The First Book of Discipline* (1972); J. T. Cox, ed., *Practice and Procedure in the Church of Scotland*, 6th ed., ed. D. F. M. MacDonald (1976); G.

D. Henderson, *Why We Are Presbyterians* (n.d.); J. Kirk, *The Second Book of Discipline* (1980).

ALEC C. CHEYNE

Presbytery *see* Polity

Priesthood of Believers

The doctrine (based on 1 Peter 2:9–10; Rev. 1:6; 5:10) that the whole people of God of the new covenant is a priesthood because it is in, with, and through Jesus Christ, the true and only priest (Heb. 3:1). This is a royal and holy priesthood with a corporate vocation.*

The doctrine has often been explained in popular teaching as pointing to the right of every individual believer to act in a priestly way—to pray to God for self and others and to teach God's ways to others. As such, it has been coupled with justification* by faith*—being "put right with God"—so that one may act as a priest. A better approach is to link the concept of priesthood with covenant* (as in the OT; Ex. 19:5–6) and see this doctrine as highlighting the corporate privilege and responsibility of the believing people of God of the new covenant. As a body, they offer spiritual sacrifice and prayers to God and commend God in Christ to the world. Thus each congregation of faithful believers is to act as a priesthood, being a microcosm of the whole church.*

There is no specific priesthood of the ordained minister, but ordained ministers do have the vocation of making the real priesthood of the whole people of God into a meaningful and workable reality.

This doctrine was clearly expounded by Luther* and Calvin.* But while Luther made some exaggerated claims and statements, Calvin's teaching is clear and balanced. Whether it has ever been truly grasped and put into full operation by a local church is doubtful. It remains that toward which the people of God are to move.

C. Eastwood, *The Priesthood of All Believers* (1960); J. H. Elliott, *The Elect and the Holy* (1966).

PETER TOON

Princeton Theology

An American expression of the Reformed Protestant tradition that emanated from a group of nineteenth-century Presbyterian theologians from Princeton Seminary. Three generations of scholars attuned to the WCF* shaped many of the theological discourses in America's Reformed communities. The first generation was comprised of Archibald Alexander* (1772–1851) of Virginia; Samuel Miller* (1769–1850) of Delaware and New York; and Charles Hodge* (1797–1878) of Philadelphia and Princeton. The second generation included Joseph Addison Alexander (1809–59), James Waddell Alexander (1804–59), Albert B. Dod (1805–45), and William Henry Green (1825–1900), while a third generation involved Archibald Alexander Hodge* (1823–86), B. B. Warfield* (1851–1921), Francis L. Patton (1843–1932), and J. Gresham Machen* (1881–1937).

Like sentinels, two major works stand at the front and back entrances in the theological territory occupied by these Old School Presbyterian theologians. At the beginning was Miller's influential *A Brief Retrospect of the Eighteenth Century* (2 vols.; 1803) which scrutinized encyclopedically the promises and perils of science, history, philosophy, literature, and religion. Charles Hodge's *Systematic Theology* (3 vols.; 1871–73) stands at the other end. It structured and summarized a vast array of theological issues from the "Didactic Enlightenment" to the waning impulses of romanticism. These multivolumed works addressed an unusual breadth of issues confronting Reformed communities in the emerging nation and simultaneously revealed reasoned, confessional discourses amidst the fluid commitments of nineteenth-century Protestantism.

Most of the Princeton theologians wrote voluminously. Among their most notable works were Archibald Alexander's *Thoughts on Religious Experience* (1841); Hodge's popular *The Way of Life* (1841); J. A. Alexander's internationally acclaimed commentary on Isaiah (2 vols; 1846–47); W. H. Green's *The Pentateuch Vindicated* (1863); and Warfield's *The Westminster Assembly and Its Work*

(1931). From 1825 to 1871 these theologians published a journal usually called the *Biblical Repertory and Princeton Review* which emerged as one of the premier Protestant journals in nineteenth-century America. Few issues of theology, philosophy, science, Protestant churches, or national politics escaped its comment. Hodge's masterful essays on the ecumenicity of the church,* slavery,* and the Civil War are only hints of these efforts to interpret the Reformed heritage to a splintered Protestantism, a divided nation, and an increasingly pluralistic culture.

Most estimates of these Princeton theologians are too narrow and polemical. A few recent historians, however, have noted an amalgam of commitments that characterized these Presbyterians' style and stance while doing Reformed theology. These include an unswerving commitment to the classical Calvinistic theism and the Westminster Standards; an informed commitment to the Bible's inspiration and authority and a skeptical response to German biblical criticism; the generous employment of Scottish common sense realism* and a revulsion for German idealism; an evangelical piety articulated in both personal and social terms; a sympathy for American Whig (and later Republican) political perspectives; a quest for credibility among the nation's scientific community; and an irenic ecclesiology both within Presbyterianism and the wider Christian church.

With the advent of the historical scholarship about the Bible, the impact of European liberal theology, the growing imperialism of scientific claims, and the faltering Protestant consensus in a pragmatic and democratized nation, the third generation of Princeton theologians narrowed their agendas. A. A. Hodge's *Outlines of Theology* (1878) operated safely within his father's orbit. Warfield and A. A. Hodge published a pivotal article on the Bible's inerrancy (1881), and Warfield's Inaugural Address at the seminary (1887) insisted that theology was essentially scientific. Two scholarly tasks—a quest to substantiate the tenets of the Princeton Theology by referencing the church's dogmatic heritage (see especially the essays by Warfield in his *Calvin and Augustine* [1956]) and an aggressive apologetical effort—displaced earlier emphases on religious experience, a breadth of societal interests, and an encounter with the frontier theological issues of the nineteenth century.

By the end of the century, however, the "golden days" of the old Princeton Theology had waned. Faced with an exhaustion of philosophical underpinnings, denominational conflict about biblical authority, and an increasingly secularized society, the heirs of the earlier Princeton theologians were confronted with at least two options. Either they could broaden their understanding of the Reformed heritage to include newer scholarship about the Bible, science, and the church's mission or they could regroup behind older formulae. Actually, the progeny of Miller, Alexander, and Hodge did both. But by the opening decade of the twentieth century, the original Princeton theologians' vision appeared blurred and their earlier inner cohesion, community, and accountability deteriorated.

A few historians have tried to show a linkage, however inadvertent, between the Princeton Theology and the emerging fundamentalism* of the twentieth century, while other students have noted the Princeton pedigree in various Reformed orthodox movements during the modern era. Most scholars of nineteenth-century American religious history agree, however, that the Princeton theologians were without peer in their efforts to communicate a Reformed confessionalism to the mind and manners of Victorian America.

A. A. Hodge, *The Life of Charles Hodge* (1880); A. Hoffecker, *Piety and the Princeton Theologians* (1981); L. A. Loetscher, *The Broadening Church* (1954); G. M. Marsden, *Fundamentalism and American Culture* (1980); M. Noll, ed., *The Princeton Theology, 1812–1921* (1983); A. Schorsch, "Samuel Miller, Renaissance Man," *AP* 66 (1988): 71–87; n.a., *Theological Essays: From the Princeton Review* (1846).

JOHN W. STEWART

Prophesyings

Originating in sixteenth-century Zurich, "prophesyings" (1 Cor. 14:29, 31) were "an academic exercise in the spirit of biblical humanism, replacing logical discourse as the principal discipline for the schooling of future ministers" (Collinson, p. 169). They were begun in Elizabethan England by "Puritan" clergy to provide "ministerial in-service training" (Morgan, p. 222) and featured the best-learned ministers expounding a text and conferring among themselves. Lesser-trained pastors listened, learned, and were examined. In places these became open to the public, and Elizabeth sought their suppression lest they become too clear a show of Puritan strength. Prophesyings reached their zenith under James I and represent Puritan concerns for "godly learning" and emphases on popular preaching.

Collinson, *EPM*; J. Morgan, *Godly Learning* (1986).

DONALD K. MCKIM

Protestant Ethic

The term is associated with Max Weber's *The Protestant Ethic and the Spirit of Capitalism* (1904–5; ET 1930; repr. 1958). Weber's thesis was that the teachings of John Calvin* contributed to the rise of capitalism. While this continues to be debated, evidence supports Weber's thesis among later Calvinists rather than in Calvin himself.

The seed for the "Protestant ethic" is lodged in Calvin's insistence that God* calls us to a life of holy living exhibiting self-denial and seeking God's will and destiny. Calvin emphasized strict adherence to the Ten Commandments and an uncompromised stance to follow God's will, not the will of the world. The Christian life was a struggle in the world, not a monastic separation from the world. Calvin's intraworldly quasi-asceticism was based on his theological convictions that (1) God holds absolute sovereignty over the totality of life; (2) humans are helpless and lost without the commandments to guide and exhort them; and (3) the reality of human sinfulness is overcome by God's grace* for our salvation* and forgiveness* of sins.

The ethics* derived from these convictions leads to a life of reverence and awe before God and to maintenance of chastity, sobriety, and frugality. Human life is a stewardship* and sacred trust before God. For Calvin, the "Protestant ethic" is characterized by a life of gratitude to God, the pursuit of the divine will in all things, and a life-style of discipline and productivity without conspicuous consumption. It also means giving to the poor and confronting wisely the sins of society through regulations, while never forgetting as good stewards to labor to God's glory.

A. Biéler, *The Social Humanism of Calvin* (1964); R. W. Green, ed., *Protestantism, Capitalism, and Social Science* (2nd ed. 1973); R. H. Stone, "The Reformed Economic Ethics of John Calvin," in *Reformed Faith and Economics*, ed. R. L. Stivers (1989), 33–48.

CARNEGIE SAMUEL CALIAN

Protestant Principle

A phrase popularized by Paul Tillich. It is a commentary on the first commandment: "You shall have no other gods before me," a protest against idolatry,* or the worship of "false gods." The human temptation is always to worship as absolute that which is only relative (political party, nation, church), thus rendering it a rival "god" to the true God.*

The principle is likewise embedded in the Hebrew prophets who inveighed consistently against the creation of idols or false gods. It is behind the rallying cry of the Protestant Reformers, *ecclesia semper reformanda* (the church always in process of being reformed), and it fueled their charge that the church of the time was demanding uncritical allegiance to its institutional forms and beliefs, thus substituting itself for the God it should have been proclaiming.

The Protestant principle, then, "contains the divine and human protest against any absolute claim made for a relative reality. . . . It is the prophetic judgment against religious pride, ecclesiastical arrogance, and secular self-sufficiency and their destructive consequences" (Tillich, *The Protestant Era*, p. 163).

But the principle is not exclusively negative. Tillich insists on wedding the "Protestant principle" to "Catholic substance," that is, affirming the basic Christian tradition in its wholeness or "catholicity" but always taking account of the dangers of idolatry.

P. Tillich, *Systematic Theology*, vol. 3 (1963); and *The Protestant Era* (1948).

ROBERT MCAFEE BROWN

Providence of God

Reformed theology has traditionally understood the providence of God* to embrace a threefold work: God's preservation of creation,* God's cooperation with all created entities, and God's guidance of all things toward God's ultimate purposes and their highest good. What this doctrine emphasizes is that the triune God, in goodness and power, preserves, accompanies, and directs God's entire universe. No facet of God's work is excluded from divine care.

This concept had been advanced and defended by many Reformed writers. Johannes Braunius notes: "The acts of the providence of God are three: (1) He preserves all things in their being and duration; (2) He moves all things to their action by concurrence, in fact by precurrence; (3) He steers and guides all things to the desired end to which they were appointed from eternity" (*Doctrina foederum* 1.12.2, in Heppe, *RD*, p. 256). Louis Berkhof* observed that "providence may be defined as that continued exercise of the divine energy whereby the Creator preserves all His creatures, is operative in all that comes to pass in the world, and directs all things to their appointed end" (*Systematic Theology*, p. 166). Similarly, Karl Barth* writes: "By 'providence' is meant the superior dealings of the Creator with His creation, the wisdom, omnipotence and goodness with which He maintains and governs in time this distinct reality according to the counsel of His own will" (*CD* III/3, 3).

Reformed theologians further maintain that this doctrine is explicitly taught in Scripture,* where God is portrayed as fulfilling this threefold activity, as outlined above. It is not a doctrine derived from general revelation; rather, it is a doctrine preserved and taught in Scripture.

First, the Reformed tradition understands the providence of God to be a work of *conservatio*, *sustentatio*, and *preservatio*. God actively preserves and upholds what God has created. God continues to see that the creation is maintained, that order prevails, and that life is sustained through, over, and above each species' divinely given power to propagate itself. As Calvin* explained: "We see the presence of divine power shining as much in the continuing state of the universe as in its inception" (*Inst.* 1.16.1).

God's preserving activity is a divine work in which the Son also participates. It exists for his glory (Rom. 11:36; Col. 1:17; Heb. 1:3). Christ is its principle of cohesion.

For Charles Hodge,* *preservatio* means (1) "that the universe as a whole does not continue in being of itself" and that (2) "all creatures, whether plants or animals, . . . are continued in existence not by any inherent principle of life, but by the will of God" (*Systematic Theology*, 1:575). For L. Berkhof, preservation entails "that continuous work of God by which He maintains the things which He created, together with the properties and powers with which He endowed them." For Emil Brunner,* God's conserving work is to be seen in the "constancy" of the "orders and forms of nature," which are expressions both of the divine will and of God's faithfulness to God's creation.

For Reformed theologians, however, it is not merely the preservation of the cosmos, or its orders, that Scripture emphasizes. God the Father through Christ the Son also preserves and upholds human life. This is accomplished both through God's commandment to the original couple (Gen. 1:28) and through the ineffable working of God's Spirit and God's divine loyalty to God's servants.

The Hebrew word *shamar* is central. It means "to keep, to preserve, to protect." It is the primary verb used to describe God's faithfulness to God's servants and is used in numerous passages (Gen. 28:15; Ex. 23:20; Num. 6:24; Josh. 24:17; Job 29:2; Ps. 16:1; 121:5).

Above all, the preserving activity of God is a divine work whose purpose is to sustain and uphold God's servant Israel and the church.* God's work of preservation cannot be separated from the covenant* and God's purposes of election in Jesus Christ. Neither the cosmos nor humankind possesses absolute value per se. The universe and human life exist for higher purposes than mere self-continuance, or self-affirmation, or propagation of the species. Both have been created and are sustained for the glory of God, who, in Jesus Christ, has resolved from eternity "to unite all things in him" (Eph. 1:10).

Second, Reformed theology has understood God's providential work as a divine cooperation with all creatures, or as a divine operation that accompanies the activity of all creatures. Orthodox dogmatics refers to this function as *concursus*. In L. Berkhof's view, *concursus* involves "the co-operation of the divine power with all subordinate powers, according to the preestablished laws of their operation, causing them to act and to act precisely as they do" (*Systematic Theology*, p. 170). Consequently, created powers do not act by themselves. Equally important, each power, as a second cause, is real and acts in accordance with its created powers. As such, it is accountable for its actions. Furthermore, second causes are voluntary, and not merely passive or involuntary instruments of God's will.

This distinction between active and passive, or between God's immanent accompaniment yet transcendent Lordliness, is viewed as a necessary qualification against pantheism on the one hand and Deism on the other. Nothing occurs aside from God's will. All things are allowed, foreseen, or caused by God. Yet second causes, in themselves, are accountable for their choices and actions.

As Calvin explained: "There is no random power, or agency, or motion in the creatures, who are so governed by the secret counsel of God that nothing happens but what he has knowingly and willingly decreed" (*Inst.* 1.16.3). Yet God cannot be blamed for human sin.* Rather, "in this way, while acting wickedly, we serve his righteous ordination, since in his boundless wisdom he will know how to use bad instruments for good purposes" (1.17.5).

Etienne Gilson identifies two further qualifications that are necessary to avoid extremes of "extrinsicism" and "intrinsicism." In "extrinsicism," God does it all by forcing God's will upon entities from without. In "intrinsicism," God does little or nothing, abandoning created beings to operate on their own. Neither extreme can be accepted without violating God's Lordship or humankind's uniqueness. Hence, God acts as a "total cause," conferring upon each being its unique capacities, while constituting the principal cause of all its interactions in the world.

Barth enthusiastically accepted the terminology of *cause* and *second causes* and believed it is a legitimate language for the theologian to use. He wrote, "The divine *causare* takes place in and with [our] *causare*."

Brunner is suspicious of such a doctrine. He considers it a "danger-zone" and warns that the church must renounce attempts to understand how human freedom and God's activity are interwoven. Barth, however, contends that if it is an error, it is an error meant to uphold the *maior Dei gloria* along with the Scripture's affirmation of the *minor gloria creaturae*.

Third, Reformed theology recognizes that the entire universe belongs to God and belongs to God to direct, both toward its immediate and its highest ends. This element is known as *gubernatio*, or steering. It has to do with the direction, purpose, and goal that God assigns to each entity as God directs the whole toward the accomplishment of God's divine purpose.

The Reformed tradition understands this work of *gubernatio* to pertain to nature, to all its sentient creatures, above all to humankind, and to history* itself. Intelligent creatures and voluntary things especially come under God's guidance. So too do nations and history. All is in God's hands, and God knows the ends toward which God steers it (Eph. 1:9–12; Phil. 2:9–11).

Modern theologians from Friedrich Schleiermacher* to the present (Rudolf Bultmann, Gordon Kaufman, and Langdon Gilkey) are quick to point up the inseparability of the nature-history nexus and the extent to which all things are caught up in a web of sociopolitical interconnections. Nonetheless, for Reformed theology, none of this erodes the central biblical conviction that the triune God, in goodness and power, is present preserving, accompanying, and guiding the entire universe toward God's highest will for it. Whatever aspects of self-determination God has conferred on voluntary creatures in no way detracts from God's power to forgive sin* or to call forth believers to participate in God's providential ordering of the world.

Barth, *CD* III; L. Berkhof, *Systematic Theology* (4th rev. and enl. ed. 1949); E. Brunner, *Dogmatics*, vol. 2 (1952); B. W. Farley, *The Providence of God* (1988); L. Gilkey, *Reaping the Whirlwind* (1976); E. Gilson, *The Christian Philosophy of St. Thomas Aquinas* (1961); Heppe, *RD*; C. Hodge, *Systematic Theology*, vol. 1 (1871).

BENJAMIN WIRT FARLEY

Psalmody

From its beginnings the Christian community continued the synagogue practice of singing psalms. Various methods of psalmody appear to have been used during the early years, including singing to the accompaniment of a stringed instrument, repeating each phrase sung by a soloist, completing a phrase begun by the cantor or by two halves of a trained choir singing antiphonally.

With the Reformation, metrical psalmody began to be sung by lay people in their own languages. This style originated with Clément Marot,* who as a poet in the court of King Francis I began translating psalms into French verse (1533). Popularized by the Catholic court, these metered psalms were quickly taken over by the Huguenots* and later by Calvin, who gave them their first formal place in worship.*

The practice of versifying the psalms swept Europe rapidly. Thomas Sternhold began the task at Edward VI's court in England. After Sternhold's death (1549), John Hopkins took up the work. Peter Dathenus translated the French Psalter into Dutch (1566) and Ambrosius Lobwasser into German (1573). The Scots (1564) and the Hungarians also developed psalters. Benedictine chanted psalms and metrical psalms—a unique characteristic of Reformed worship—stand as the two most important liturgical uses of the psalms in Christian history.

The metrical psalter became the precursor of modern hymnals. By the late nineteenth century many Reformed churches opted for hymnals rather than psalters. Today, there is renewed liturgical interest in psalmody, with many Reformed communions once again singing psalms.

LINDAJO H. MCKIM

Puritanism, American

To the extent that English Puritanism* considered itself a Calvinist* reform movement within the Church of England, it remained (1570s–1630s) in general conformity to the order and structures of the Church of England. However, this tacit conformity, concentrating on the promotion of preaching,* discipline,* "experimental piety,"* and Sabbatarianism* within sympathetic parishes, had meaning only so long as the theology of the Church of England remained basically Calvinistic.

But with the accession of Charles I (1625) and the promotion of William Laud to the see of Canterbury (1633), the Church of England was pulled toward an Arminian* soteriology, and harassment of the Puritans became increasingly savage. From 1629 until 1642, nearly 30,000 Puritans under the leadership of John Winthrop emigrated to New England, where eventually five separate colonial settlements were planted: Massachusetts, Connecticut, Plymouth, Rhode Island, and New Haven. Here all pretense of conformity to the Church of England was abandoned and a version of separatistic congregationalism* was erected as the standard. Full membership in the New England churches, by general consensus, became predicated on the capacity to give a "relation" of one's experience of grace;* worship* and church architecture* were simplified to the barest and most unadorned forms; and ecclesiastical authority, including the power to ordain and legislate, was located in the individual congregations and their lay elders.*

There was, nonetheless, substantial ambivalence on these points among the major Puritan divines who assisted in the planting of the New England Puritan colonies. In Massachusetts, Roger Williams and Anne Hutchinson gained prominence (1630s) from their radical calls for absolute separatism and claims of immediate revelation and antinomianism. Both were banished by Winthrop to Rhode Island as a danger to the political as well as the ecclesiastical balance of the community. On the other hand, the decision to establish congregationalism as the New England polity* was by no means accepted uniformly. Thomas Hooker* dissented from strict enforcement of the "relation" and founded the Connecticut colony at Hartford over the objections of the Massachusetts colony; Peter Hobart of Hingham, Massachusetts, organized his congregation along presbyterian* rather than congregational lines.

Further disagreements over Baptism,* ordination,* and church membership finally led to several important qualifications of the congregational pattern, first by calling a synod of clergy and elders to legislate a uniform pattern of discipline, the Cambridge Platform* (which was interpreted by bitter-enders as a compromise of pure congregational independence; 1646), and second by creating a category of "half-way" membership (1662) for baptized New Englanders who could not make a "relation" of grace. Solomon Stoddard of Northampton, Massachusetts, further disrupted the original pattern of congregationalism by opening all the privileges of church membership, and especially the Lord's Supper, to any baptized adult in his town (1677). In Connecticut, the shape of congregational government was altered even more toward presbyterianism in the Saybrook Platform (1708).

Puritanism in New England thus maintained its cohesiveness only by means of a general commitment to the structure of Calvinist soteriology, as expressed in Samuel Willard's two hundred and fifty lectures on the Westminster Shorter Catechism (published as *A Compleat Body of Divinity* [1726]), and by a generally (but not consistently) independent form of church government. By the 1740s, however, the contrary influences of continental Pietism (as represented by Cotton Mather*) and Enlightenment philosophy (as represented by Jonathan Mayhew) created still further tensions, until finally controversies sparked by the Great Awakening* wrecked what remained of the unity of the "New England Way" and rendered further use of the term "puritan" anachronistic.

American Puritanism produced comparatively few speculative or systematic theologians; only Jonathan Edwards* demonstrated sustained interest in abstract metaphysical inquiry. Puritan theological method, as mediated through Harvard (1636) and Yale College (1701), remained dominated by continental Protestant scholasticism until the eighteenth century, only to be succeeded in turn by various Protestant redactions of Cartesian logic. Puritan psychology was similarly dominated by intellectualist models of faculty psychology, which in New England encouraged the development of "preparationism" and gradualism in conversion,* and lay behind the movement toward "half-way" membership. However, the Puritan sympathy for "heart religion" inclined many others toward voluntarism and expectations of immediate volitional response to spiritual motives. The favorite Puritan genre was the sermon, based upon the Ramist* technique of "dichotomization," which taught the exposition of biblical texts according to a threefold division of doctrine, use, and application.

The term "puritan" has undergone various uses since the Great Awakening. In the nineteenth century, American historical writings, dominated by New England authors, lauded Puritanism as a movement of moral earnestness and liberty of conscience. Others, however, such as John Williamson Nevin,* used "puritan" as a synonym for "gnostic" and attacked "American puritanism" as the enemy of a genuinely catholic Christianity. In the early twentieth century, the moralism of puritan was lampooned as a symbol for bigotry and narrow-mindedness.

However, the publications of the "Harvard School" (Perry Miller, Samuel Eliot

Morison, Clifford Shipton) in the 1930s successfully revived the reputation of the New England Puritans as proto-modern intellectuals, struggling to balance piety and intellect. Substantial scholarly interest has been manifested in the 1970s and 1980s in Puritan millennialism and other forms of radical Puritanism, but compared to modern studies of English Puritanism, comparatively little work has been done on Puritan ritual structures and the relation of Puritanism and social change.

Collinson, *EPM*; N. Fiering, *Moral Philosophy at Seventeenth-Century Harvard* (1981); D. D. Hall, *The Faithful Shepherd* (1972); C. E. Hambrick-Stowe, *The Practice of Piety: Puritan Devotional Disciplines in Seventeenth-Century New England* (1982); E. B. Holifield, *The Covenant Sealed* (1974); P. Miller, *The New England Mind: The Seventeenth Century,* 2 vols. (1939; repr. 1961); P. Miller and T. Johnson, eds., *The Puritans* (1938); E. S. Morgan, *Visible Saints* (1963); H. E. Stout, *The New England Soul* (1986).

ALLEN C. GUELZO

Puritanism, English

A movement for further reform within the Reformation Church of England, beginning with the reign of Elizabeth I (1558) and continuing for more than a century as a force in the religious life of England. Puritanism was a militant version of the Reformed tradition; it was rooted in the work of early English Protestants who had been influenced by the Swiss Reformation such as William Tyndale and John Hooper. Nourished by the experiences of exiled English Protestants in the Reformed cities of Geneva and Zurich during the reign of Queen Mary (1553–58), it flowered in the vestiarian (vestments) controversy* (1560s), when "Puritans," as they were then first called, objected to some of the vestments and ceremonies required by the English Church. These "nonconformists,"* as they were also called, were usually university-educated clergy, drawn especially from Cambridge, though there were ardent laity among them. They thought the English Church should take as its pattern the Reformed churches on the Continent. They quarreled with bishops and eventually with monarchs (though supported in Parliament) over the pace and extent of reform; these conflicts contributed to the coming of civil war in the 1640s. Many Puritans supported the execution of Charles I (1648) and during the rule of Oliver Cromwell* had a moment of power. With the Restoration of the monarchy (1660), Charles II purged Puritans from the Church of England. However, though persecuted, they survived as "Dissenters" outside the state church and eventually formed Baptist, Congregationalist,* and Presbyterian* congregations. When the Glorious Revolution (1688) brought the more sympathetic William and Mary to the throne, they were granted toleration.*

Puritanism influenced the Reformed tradition in worship,* church government, ethics,* theology,* and spirituality (piety*). The original meaning of "Puritan" was purification of the church, as Puritans sought to discard elements of furnishing, liturgy, and ceremony that they considered not in accord with biblical simplicity and plainness (e.g., they objected to the sign of the cross in Baptism* and kneeling to receive the Eucharist). Instead of elaborate vestments, they preferred a black preaching gown, symbolizing the minister's character as a learned expositor of the Bible. They wanted every parish to have a resident minister able to preach, and to further that aim they formed "prophesyings,"* gatherings of ministers for sermons and pastoral advice, which Elizabeth I suppressed, fearful that they threatened her control of the church.

Thwarted by the bishops and committed to an ecclesiology that stressed the church as a covenanted fellowship, many Puritans rejected episcopacy. Thomas Cartwright* promoted presbyterianism, which would have put the control of the national church in the hands of the preaching clergy and their lay supporters, as its replacement. The more radical Robert Browne* (1582) advocated a congregational system, with ultimate authority in the local congregation, and also called for immediate separation from the "corrupt" Church of England. Some of his "Separatist" followers emigrated to the Netherlands to implement these principles. But more moderate Congregationalists, known as Independents, stopped short of Separatism. They influenced the Massachusetts Bay Puritans and became the main stream of English Congregationalism.* Other Puritans such as Richard Baxter* wanted a "reduced episcopacy" that combined presbyterian and episcopal features. All Puritans were wary of state interference and wanted church discipline to be controlled congregationally.

Puritans were not concerned only with a purified ritual and polity.* The whole body politic also needed purification, and, following Martin Bucer* and John Calvin,* they urged creation of a disciplined Christian society. They thought a whole nation could be in covenant with God for the realization of this ideal. Millennarian* hopes as well as the example of biblical Israel spurred them to their goal.

Theologically the Puritans were strict adherents of Reformed theology, which at first they shared with the Church of England as a whole (its Thirty-nine Articles* taught the Reformed doctrine of the Eucharist and asserted predestination*), but after many in the established church adopted a sacramentalist Arminianism* and attacked predestinarian theology (1620s), Puritans vigorously defended Calvinism* because of its uncompromising assertion of the unmerited grace* of God. Some Puritans, including William Perkins,* William Ames,* and John Owen,* were important in developing Reformed scholastic theology. A more distinct Puritan contribution was the development and articulation of the practical and affective side of religion. Richard Rogers, John Dod, and Richard Sibbes were fountainheads of a Puritan devotional movement; it especially flowered after the Restoration, with such great spiritual writers as Richard Baxter, Joseph Alleine, and John Flavel.* Puritans produced an enormous literature of the spiritual life, consisting of sermons, meditations, practical biblical expositions, aphorisms of spiritual counsel, exemplary biographies, and spiritual autobiographies. This literature stressed the search for assurance of salvation,* a personal experience of conversion,* regeneration* by the Holy Spirit,* the mystical union* of the soul with Christ, growth in holiness of life, and a devout frame of mind designated "heavenly-mindedness." The greatest product of this "affectionate divinity" was the allegory of John Bunyan,* *The Pilgrim's Progress*, which portrayed the Christian life as pilgrimage and spiritual warfare.

Collinson, *EPM*; G. R. Cragg, *Puritanism in the Period of the Great Persecution, 1660–1688* (1957); W. Haller, *The Rise of Puritanism* (1938); L. J. Trinterud, ed., *Elizabethan Puritanism* (1971); D. D. Wallace, Jr., ed., *The Spirituality of the Later English Puritans* (1987); B. R. White, *The English Separatist Tradition* (1971).

DEWEY D. WALLACE, JR.

Racism

Calvinism,* or the Reformed faith, is closely associated in origin and development with the modern world. It is not surprising therefore that it is intertwined with modern racism, a pattern of relation among groups and individuals that asserts that one group and its members are by divine creation* and nature superior to another and therefore deserving of greater power, privilege, and status. Modern racism had its beginning in the fifteenth century with European industrialization, conquest, and colonization of much of Africa and the Americas and its incursions into Asia. Modern racism consisted of doctrines of white supremacy rooted in beliefs about the divine creation and natural superiority of white groups and individuals and practices of discrimination and prejudice against nonwhite people because they were not white. The doctrine's function was to explain and justify the military, technological, and cultural dominance of white people. Calvinism contributed both to the achievements of European people and to their discrimination and prejudice against nonwhite people. The doctrine of God's* total sovereignty, equal creation of all people, and investment of persons with a special calling or vocation* not only motivated people to perceive themselves as sacred and their vocation as divinely given but also permitted them to see differences among people as divinely sanctioned. Whiteness gave birth to political, social, and economic superiority. Nonwhiteness was responsible for the absence of the Christian religion, civilization, and a just state. While the doctrine of God's total sovereignty and equal creation of all people suggested the oneness of the human family, the idea of different divinely approved vocations permitted Calvinism to understand social hierarchy and inequalities as God-ordained. Some people were destined by God's will to be slaves, to be incapable of participation in civil society and high culture, and to be without vote or representation in government. Calvinism in the Americas, in the West and East Indies, and in South Africa* affirmed these forms of racism. Within and without slavery they supported conceptions of white supremacy. Conception of stewardship* or duties owed slaves by masters mitigated but did not remove the idea and practice of white supremacy.

In North America this paternalistic idea of stewardship was widespread and sanctioned by an official statement (1787) by the forerunner of the General Assembly,* the Synod of New York and Philadelphia:

> The Synod of New York and Philadelphia do highly approve of the general principles in favor of universal liberty that prevail in America, and the interest which many of the States have taken in promoting the abolition of Slavery; yet, inasmuch as men, introduced from a servile state, to a participation of all the privileges of civil society without a proper education, and without previous habits of industry, may be in many respects dangerous to the community; therefore they earnestly recommend to all the members belonging to their communion to give those persons who are at present held in servitude, such good education as to prepare them for the better enjoyment of freedom; and they moreover recommend that masters, whenever they find servants disposed to make a just improvement of the privilege, would give them *a peculium*, or grant them sufficient time and sufficient means of procuring their own liberty, at a moderate rate; that thereby they may be brought into society with those habits of industry that may render them useful citizens and finally, they recommend it to all their people to use the most prudent measures consistent with the interests and the state of civil society, in the countries where they live, to procure eventually the final abolition of slavery in America.

The pattern outlined in the statement came to dominate American Calvinism whether or not the denomination favored the abolition of slavery,* and it persisted until the 1960s. Under its influence Calvinism established racially separate denominations, congregations, and units of governance and mission. They were in addition as a church passive in respect to social, political, and economic programs that advocated racial equality.

In the period following World War II and characterized by the demise of colonialism and the success of the civil rights revolution under the leadership of the Reverend Martin Luther King, Jr., and the Southern Christian Leadership Conference, these teachings and practices were changed. The Confession of 1967* recognized these changes:

> God has created the peoples of the earth to be one universal family. In his reconciling love he overcomes the barriers between brothers and breaks down every form of discrimination based on racial or ethnic difference, real or imaginary. The church is called to bring all men to receive and uphold one another as persons in all relationships of life: in employment, housing, education, leisure, marriage, family, church, and the exercise of political rights. Therefore the church labors for the abolition of all racial discrimination and ministers to those injured by it. Congregations, individuals, or groups of Christians who exclude, dominate, or patronize their fellowmen however subtly, resist the Spirit of God and bring contempt on the faith which they profess. (*BC* 9.44)

Following the adoption of the Confession of 1967, the church acted to define itself and its society in nonracial ways. In

1990 the Dutch Reformed Church of South Africa became the last Calvinist body to accept these teachings as doctrine. The abandonment of white supremacy as an official Calvinist teaching was due not only to cultural and political changes in western Europe and the United States but also to the initiatives of African, Asian, African American, and Latin American Calvinists who provided a new understanding of the temporal implications of the doctrines of God's total sovereignty and creation and the human person's obligations in respect to stewardship and covenantal community.

Having acknowledged their complicity in racism, Calvinistic people and churches are now pledged to rid themselves and their societies of racism. Racism has been defined as heresy,* because it denies the fundamental tenets of Christianity and the conceptions of human dignity and worth. The "Brief Statement of Faith"* of the Presbyterian Church (U.S.A.) says:

> We trust in God,
> whom Jesus called Abba, Father.
> In sovereign love God created the world good
> and makes everyone equally in God's image,
> male and female, of every race and people,
> to live as one community.

Differences among human people are no longer seen simply in terms of superior and inferior. Calvinism does not deny inequalities or social hierarchy. But it does assert that God employs differences among persons and groups to enrich human flourishing and community. God is to be obeyed in all domains of life and by all persons. God has not willed the superiority of any group or individual. God desires and enables all groups and individuals to live together without conflict, coercion, or violence. Relations among men and women of all groups are to embody mutuality and respect. Superior power where it exists, if it is just, is to be used in the interests of the common good and, where it is unjust, destroyed. Determination of human relationships on the basis of race is sinful and a violation of God's love for every human person. God's covenantal community is bonded by the image of God in persons and not language, culture, gender, and race. These natural bonds of association are to be transformed by one's loyalty to the totally sovereign Lord of creation and the universe.

W. D. Jordan, *White Over Black: American Attitudes Toward the Negro 1550–1812* (1968); A. Murray, *Presbyterians and the Negro: A History* (1966); A. J. Raboteau, *Slave Religion* (1978).

PRESTON N. WILLIAMS

Rainy, Robert (1826–1906)

Liberal Presbyterian scholar, teacher, and ecclesiastical politician, who led the Free Church of Scotland (1874–1906). Moved by the Disruption* (1843) to prepare for the ministry of the newly formed Free Church, Rainy was ordained (1851). He became professor of church history at New College,* Edinburgh (1862), and later principal (1874). Rainy worked to make the Free Church an intellectual as well as a spiritual force. He defended both evolutionary biology and freedom of inquiry in the teaching and study of Scripture.

Rainy also sought to restore the unity of Scottish Presbyterianism,* fragmented during the eighteenth and early nineteenth centuries. Convinced that the church-state connection was responsible for the divisions, he maintained that the disestablishment of the Church of Scotland must be the first step toward Presbyterian reunion. After 1874 he became leader of a national disestablishment campaign, which dominated Scottish religion and politics for over two decades.

Rainy's greatest achievement was the union of Scotland's two largest nonestablished Presbyterian denominations, the Free Church and the United Presbyterian Church (1900). Yet this was marred when a Free Church minority, mainly in the Highlands, refused to enter the United Free Church and successfully claimed all Free Church properties in a controversial legal decision (1905). An Act of Parliament provided an equitable division of property, but much ill-feeling remained. At his death, Rainy was exhausted by the lengthy legal proceedings.

P. C. Simpson, *Life of Principal Rainy* (1909).

STEWART J. BROWN

Ramus, Peter (1515–1572)

French philosopher-logician whose system of logic provided an alternative to prevailing Aristotelianism and was used by Puritan theologians as an intellectual basis for their thought.

Ramus sought a reform of logic (dialectic) and published *Dialecticae partitiones* (*The Structure of Dialectic* [1543]); *Dialecticae institutiones* (*Training in Dialectic* [1543]) and *Aristotelicae animadversiones* (*Remarks on Aristotle* [1543]) as the basis for his program. He sought a simplified, more practical orientation based on his commitment to humanism (*studia humanitatis*).

Ramus saw the logician's task as classification, arranging concepts to make them understandable and memorable according to "method," the orderly presentation of a subject. This usually proceeded through dichotomies so a skeletal system emerged that could be charted or mapped like a blueprint. All subject elements were divided and subdivided until each had its own location. The method of the reasoning process proceeded from the "general" to the "particular" and focused on self-authenticating axioms. Proper discourse emerged when axioms were arranged orderly and intelligibly.

A line of Cambridge University Puritan Ramists extended from Laurence Chaderton through William Perkins,* and his students, William Ames* to John Milton.* Ramism assisted Puritan emphases on the unity of theology and ethics,* religious education, plain-style preaching,* memory, and biblical interpretation. Philosophically, by developing *technometria* or "encyclopedia," Ramism offered a secure philosophical base (realism) which enabled theology to uncover the mind of God. The blend of "doctrine/life" is seen in Ramus's definition of theology as "the science of living blessedly for ever" (*Commentarium de religione Christiania* [1576], p. 6).

W. S. Howell, *Logic and Rhetoric in England, 1500–1700* (1956); D. K. McKim, *Ramism in William Perkins' Theology* (1987); P. Miller, *The New England Mind: The Seventeenth Century*(1939); W. J. Ong, *Ramus, Method, and the Decay of Dialogue* (1958).

DONALD K. MCKIM

Readers

A category of nonordained ministry. The title recalls the (ordained) lector of the early church, who read the biblical lections in worship.* In the Scottish Reformation, to remedy the shortage of ministers, readers were appointed to read the prayers and the Scriptures. They were often former ex-priests who with education would become ministers. The "reader's service" later might form a preliminary to the minister's role. Readers eventually disappeared after a 1581 decision to make no new appointments and the Westminster Assembly's* inability to justify them biblically.

Scarcity of ministers caused by World War I led to the reintroduction of readers in the Church of Scotland, but they have been largely restricted to emergency pulpit supply. By contrast, the Church of England makes important regular use of lay readers.

DAVID F. WRIGHT

Reason

The capacity in human beings by which universal judgments are made. "Reason" is sometimes used interchangeably with "understanding." It is the means by which one knows oneself and the surrounding world. But its principal use is to know God,* a goal it could attain before, but not after, the fall.

Rejecting the complex discussions of the philosophers, John Calvin* held that the human soul is an incorporeal substance, set in the body. It has two faculties, understanding and will, to which every other faculty is related. Understanding, "the leader and governor of the soul" (*Inst.* 1.15.7), distinguishes between things. The five senses, common sense, and the imagination supply materials about which reason forms universal judgments. What reason considers in a step-by-step analysis, understanding contemplates. The will strives toward those things which the understanding and reason present as good. According to Calvin, this simple account of these faculties suffices for godliness; those who desire more detail may study the philosophers.

Before the fall, the light of reason was sufficient, so that "his [humanity's] reason, understanding, prudence, and judgment not only sufficed for the direction of his earthly life, but by them men mounted up even to God and eternal bliss" (*Inst.* 1.15.8). The principal use of human understanding was to seek happiness, which consists in being united with God.

After the fall, a true knowledge of God is not possible through reason alone, for "his [humanity's] supernatural gifts were stripped from him" (*Inst.* 2.2.12). Faith, love of God, love of neighbor, and desire for holiness and righteousness were lost. There remains a natural instinct, an awareness of divinity (*divinitatis sensum*), which results in every person having the conviction that there is some God. This is the "seed of religion," but it now leads to superstition, denial of God, and false religion.

In the fall the "natural gifts" were corrupted. Reason's ability to understand was weakened, so it tends to focus on empty and worthless things, while paying too little attention to important matters. Still, with regard to its understanding "earthly things," such as government, household management, mechanical skills, and the liberal arts, the natural reason manifests considerable aptitude. Ability in the liberal and manual arts is a natural gift found among believers and unbelievers alike. The competence of secular writers, jurists, mathematicians, and natural scientists is praised by Calvin and seen as evidence that the minds of fallen persons are "sharp and penetrating in their investigation of inferior things" (*Inst.*2.2.15). Though the truth in them is not complete, it comes from the Spirit of God who is the source of all truth and so is not to be rejected or despised.

Human reason after the fall lacks spiritual insight, which is based on knowing God, God's way of salvation,* and how to live according to God's law.* On these matters, the philosophers grasp only an occasional truth but remain filled with error. True spiritual knowledge can be gained only through faith.*

Faith is a knowledge of God that is "revealed to our minds and sealed upon our hearts through the Holy Spirit"* (*Inst.* 3.2.7). In faith the understanding is raised beyond itself. In reasoning about ordinary things, the mind attains a comprehension which results in certitude about them. With faith, however, the mind becomes persuaded of what it does not comprehend. It has certitude even where it does not understand, because the knowledge of faith is founded on love. So believers are more "strengthened by the persuasion of divine truth than instructed by rational proof" (*Inst.* 3.2.14). Faith is like the certitude of a child who knows its parent's love but cannot explain it.

Because Calvin was only one among several theologians whose ideas gained acceptance in the Reformed churches, his conception of human reason was not the only one found in the Reformed tradition. Also, because Calvin gave a simplified account of reason and other faculties of the soul, Reformed thinkers have repeatedly found it necessary to supplement his ideas. Consequently, there has been no definitive Reformed view of the nature of reason. Calvinist views of reason have tended to reflect the influence of their age. Some Calvinists have been influenced by Cartesian, Lockean, Reidian,* Hegelian, neo-Kantian, and other positions. Many debates in the Reformed tradition on the nature and capacity of reason have had their origins in the divergences among these perspectives.

ARVIN VOS

Reformed Scholasticism *see* **Orthodoxy, Reformed**

Regeneration

While sometimes used of the cosmic renewal at the end of the age (Matt. 19:28; Acts 3:21), regeneration is more often used of the inner renewal of individuals by the Holy Spirit* (Titus 3:5). In this latter sense, it is a "new birth," or a "birth from above," caused by the sovereign action of the Spirit of God (John 3:3–5); and entry into God's kingdom* is dependent on this inner transformation within the soul.

This action of the Spirit was promised by the prophets (Jer. 31:31; 32:40) as belonging to entry into the new covenant.* Paul expounds it both in relation to the Spirit and to being "in Christ"—a coresurrection with Christ (Eph. 2:5; Col. 2:13); a new creation in Christ (2 Cor. 5:17; Gal. 6:15). Peter and James set out its connection with the gospel, for God "begets anew" (1 Peter 1:23) and "brings to birth" by the living word (James 1:18). While the duty of sinners is to receive the gospel by repenting of sin,* believing the promises of God and obeying the divine word, the work of God is to regenerate the soul so that the sinner can truly respond to the gospel.

In church history, regeneration as the act of God has been closely connected with the sacrament* of Baptism* because of the intimate NT relation of conversion* to God and baptism ("of water and the Spirit," John 3:5). Most baptismal liturgies of the early and medieval church proclaim an inseparable connection, so that regeneration is believed to occur at the time of baptism and God is thanked for having caused it. In fact, baptism was seen as conveying *ex opere operato** regeneration to all who did not obstruct the work of the Spirit. In Anglican and Lutheran baptismal liturgies, this close connection (with some ambiguity) is continued, so that baptismal regeneration can be claimed to be, in a minimal way, a Protestant as well as a Roman Catholic* and an Orthodox doctrine.

In Reformed theology, the close connection of the dominical sacrament of Baptism and the sovereign act of regeneration by the Spirit have been maintained but without any hint of *ex opere operato* teaching. This is because the Reformed doctrine of regeneration has emphasized that God implants a divine "seed" of life in the soul and, from this, true repentance* and faith spring and grow. Thus God may or may not implant this divine seed when an infant is baptized. An adult believer being baptized is presumed to be regenerate because one now believes the gospel and baptism is a sign and seal of this faith.

In Reformed theology the doctrine of regeneration is linked to other doctrines such as divine election (God only regenerates the elect), human sinfulness (God implants new life in a sinful soul), sanctification* (God provides internal renewal to produce holiness), and mortification (God gives strength to mortify the old nature). However, unlike other systems of theology, Reformed thought will not allow for any cooperation in the new birth by the Spirit. Regeneration is not caused by human effort or human cooperation. As God alone created the cosmos, so God alone is making the new creation and each act of regeneration in the human soul is totally and wholly the act of God. Yet by this act God unites the recipient not only with God in Christ but also to all others who are in Christ. So it is the beginning of everlasting life, holiness, and fellowship.

H. Burkhardt, *The Biblical Doctrine of Regeneration* (1978); B. Citron, *The New Birth* (1951); P. Toon, *Born Again: A Biblical and Theological Study of Regeneration* (1987).

PETER TOON

Reid, Thomas (1710–1796)

Scottish philosopher and principal author of the philosophy known as common sense realism.* Reid was a major influence in the Scottish Enlightenment, with an extensive following in the United States, where his ideas shaped academic thought and religious philosophy.

Reid was born in Strachan, where his father was parish minister. He studied in Aberdeen and became minister at New Machar (1737). He pursued interests in philosophy with the lively Aberdeen Philosophical Society and succeeded Adam Smith as moral philosopher at the University of Glasgow (1764). That year he published his *Inquiry Into the Mind on the Principles of Common Sense.* His later major works were *Essays on the Intellectual Powers of Man* (1785) and *Essays on the Active Powers of Man* (1788).

Reid was influenced by the inductive method of Francis Bacon and anxious to redirect philosophy from what he considered the excesses of speculation in David Hume. Though he was prominent as a Moderate* in the Church of Scotland, Reid nonetheless influenced Reformed thought in the United States. He secured a basis for certain religious ideas in intuition and appealed to an empiricist basis of thought in defending these. He also adhered to a dualism of material and spiritual reality that fortified religious notions of the soul and by implication doctrines of the afterlife. In an era of rising scientific influence, Reid's writings linked scientific habits of thinking and traditional religious notions.

R. D. Gallie, *Thomas Reid and "The Ways of Ideas"* (1989); K. Lehrer, *Thomas Reid* (1989); Rogers and McKim, *AIB*.

J. DAVID HOEVELER, JR.

Relief Church

Deposed by the Church of Scotland's General Assembly (1752) for defending a congregation's sole right to choose its minister, Thomas Gillespie joined Thomas Boston (the Younger) and Thomas Colier to constitute the Presbytery of Relief (1761). This became the Synod of Relief, numbering three presbyteries (60 congregations; 36,000 members). Presbytery exercised little authority over local congregations. The Synod had a liberal spirit, open to separation of church and state, hymn singing, and joint communion with other Protestant bodies. It merged (1847) with the United Secession Church to form Scotland's United Presbyterian Church.

ROBERT M. HEALEY

Remonstrants

"Arminians,"* followers of the Dutch Reformed theologian Jacobus Arminius, rejected certain teachings of orthodox Calvinism,* were condemned by the Synod of Dort* (1618–19), and established their own church, called the Remonstrant Brotherhood. After Arminius's death (1609), his followers, led by Johannes Uytenbogaert, drew up a *Remonstrance* (1610)—hence their name—which stated their view in the predestination* controversy with their Calvinist opponents.

Its five articles asserted the following: Election depends upon foreseen belief or unbelief; Christ died for all, though only believers are saved; people can do nothing good without regeneration;* grace* is not irresistible; and whether believers can fall from grace is uncertain. Later Remonstrants affirmed a possible fall from grace.

The controversy escalated and was complicated by political tensions between Prince Maurice of Orange and John Oldenbarnevelt, who supported the Remonstrants. Finally, the Synod of Dort summoned thirteen Remonstrants, led by Simon Episcopius, to examine their views but expelled them after procedural wrangling. It drew up the Canons of Dort which condemned Remonstrant views. More than two hundred Remonstrant ministers were deposed; about eighty were banished by the Dutch government.

In September 1619, exiled Remonstrant leaders met in Antwerp and established the Remonstrant Brotherhood. Persecution continued in the Netherlands until 1625 when the exiles could return and rebuild their congregations. The Remonstrants advocated religious liberty and toleration and later became allied with more liberal and rationalistic tendencies. Not until 1795 did the Remonstrant Brotherhood become officially recognized. It remains a small church communion in the Netherlands.*

A. W. Harrison, *Arminianism* (1937); Schaff, *Creeds*, 1:508–23.

DONALD SINNEMA

Repentance

The distinguishing characteristic of the doctrine of repentance in early Reformed theology is that true repentance is possible only through the work of the Holy Spirit* in a person's heart.

John Calvin* defined repentance as "the true turning of our life to God . . . and it consists in the mortification of our flesh . . . and in the vivification of the Spirit" (*Inst.* 3.3.5). He was explicit that repentance is not the cause of salvation but "a singular gift of God" (*Inst.* 3.3.21).

The seventeenth-century theologian

William Ames* stressed that repentance is not only a turning from evil but a "firm purpose to follow good." However, Ames says that insofar as repentance refers to the terror aroused by the law,* it precedes faith* and is found in the unregenerate. But repentance that is a true turning from sin depends on faith. So far, this accords with Calvin's thought. Then, however, Ames modifies Calvin's view when he speculates that repentance is likely to be known before faith, because one cannot be convinced that one is reconciled to God unless one turns from sin* (*Marrow*, 1.26.31–34).

Friedrich Schleiermacher's* concern to give proper attention to the human, subjective dimension of repentance led him initially to distinguish repentance and faith. Maintaining this separation would be to abandon the distinctive element of the Reformed view. However, he does eventually affirm the inseparable relationship between them when he writes that "true conversion-regret must always eventually arise out of the vision of the perfection of Christ." This means that the "beginning of regeneration must be due to Christ's redeeming activity. It is only on this view of repentance and faith that their interconnexion is clear, their origin thus being the same" (*CF*, sec. 108).

Karl Barth* devoted considerable attention to the themes of conversion, awakening, and repentance in his *Church Dogmatics* (ET 1936–69). He is faithful to the Reformed insight that repentance is the work of God, but he goes to great lengths to affirm that repentance involves the human heart, soul, and mind. A person's awakening is "both wholly creaturely and wholly divine." Barth is dependent on Calvin for many of his ideas but criticizes Calvin's treatment of repentance for neglecting the importance of "vivification" in the vivification-mortification distinction. Calvin dwells on mortification, while Barth wants to stress that repentance is liberation. "Vivification is God's proper work in repentance; mortification is God's alien work."

The distinction between remorse and repentance allows Reinhold Niebuhr* to maintain the Reformed understanding of repentance. If one recognizes only judgment, one will experience remorse. Niebuhr preserves one of Calvin's essential insights into the psychology of repentance when he writes that "without the knowledge of divine love, remorse cannot be transmuted into repentance." This is true because only the person who knows of God's love will rigorously examine one's self and be fully aware of sin's depths. In other words, the awareness of guilt in the repentant person is more profound than in the merely remorseful.

W. Ames, *Medulla theologiae* (1623 and 1627; ET *The Marrow of Sacred Divinity* [1643]); Barth, *CD* IV/2, 553ff.; Reinhold Niebuhr, *The Nature and Destiny of Man*, 2 vols. (1941–43), 1:241ff.

DAVID FOXGROVER

Reprobation *see* Hell

Resistance, Right of

Group of theories employed by Calvinist groups in the early modern period to justify their use of force against European rulers. Calvin* himself was initially extremely reluctant to sanction resistance to constituted authority either in theory or in practice. The final paragraph of the *Institutes** ambiguously commended the Spartan ephors' function of restraining the king. Toward the end of his life, the threatening civil war in France led Calvin to become more sympathetic to the constitutional justification for resistance and he permitted the princes of the blood to act against the French monarch. Such caution had already been abandoned by the exiles from Marian England in their revolutionary tracts: John Ponet, *Short Treatise of Politic Power* (1556); Christopher Goodman, *How Superior Powers Ought to Be Obeyed* (1558); and John Knox,* *The First Blast of the Trumpet Against the Monstrous Regiment of Women* (1558); and others. Later, George Buchanan* in *De jure regni apud Scotos* (1579) produced the most radical but least religious theory of resistance to explain the removal of Mary Queen of Scots from her throne. French Calvinists Theodore Beza,* *Du droit des magistrats* (1573), François Hotman, *Franco-gallia* (1573), and the author of *Vindiciae contra tyrannos* (1579), followed by their

Dutch co-religionists like Philipp Marnix de Sainte-Aldegonde, *Letter to William of Orange* (1580), argued for resistance to the ruler by the people's representatives. These ideas were also employed in seventeenth-century Britain, notably by the Scottish Covenanters, by Charles I's English opponents, and in the Glorious Revolution (1688–89).

Calvinist theorists drew heavily upon two types of Lutheran argument developed during the Schmalkaldic Wars: the religious and the legal/constitutional. The Calvinists expanded the idea of a religious duty to establish and defend the "true church" by force, especially against the agents of Antichrist (the papacy). They also adapted the legal/constitutional justification of resistance to the Holy Roman Emperor to fit circumstances elsewhere in Europe. The concept of "inferior magistrates" was broadened to include all the nobility and government officials. Greater emphasis was placed upon the historical/traditional theme of "liberties" and "Ancient Constitution" so strong in medieval thought. Roman law precedents were combined with covenant and contract ideas to explain the derivation and exercise of political authority. The resulting mix of arguments, strongly medieval and nontheological, was used to justify a right of resistance. This right, however, was not universal but confined to "public persons." Revolutionary in its own time and in its implications, it was eclipsed by the subsequent development of democratic thought.

J. Franklin, *Constitutionalism and Resistance in the Sixteenth Century* (1969); D. Kelley, *The Beginning of Ideology* (1981); Q. Skinner, *The Foundations of Modern Political Thought*, 2 vols. (1978), vol. 2; M. L. Walzer, *The Revolution of the Saints* (1965).

JANE DAWSON

Resurrection

No tenet of Christianity is more central than "the resurrection of the dead" (Apostles' Creed). Resurrection is at once the foundation of Christian faith and the focus of Christian hope.*

While the notion of resurrection is certainly not foreign to the OT, explicit references are few (e.g., Isa. 26:19; Dan. 12:2). These, however, reflect the much more pervasive conviction that Yahweh is the God of the living and, as the creator and source of life, will prevail over the power of death/Sheol (e.g., Ps. 16:10–11; 49:15). This conviction becomes dominant in the NT, now that Jesus has been raised from the dead. Inseparably connected with his death, such that the one is a "synecdoche" for the other (*Inst.* 2.16.13), Christ's resurrection is at the heart of the gospel (e.g., Rom. 10:9; 1 Cor. 15:3–5). Along with the promised restoration of the entire creation, the believer's own resurrection is the dominant hope of the gospel (e.g., Rom. 8:21–25; 1 Cor. 15).

In the history of doctrine,* the resurrection of Jesus has been relatively eclipsed—in Eastern Orthodoxy, where the accent has been on the incarnation* (salvation* as deification) and in Western Christianity (both Roman Catholic* and Protestant), where attention has been largely focused on the significance of the cross (the nature of the atonement*). The resurrection has been considered primarily for its apologetic worth, as the crowning evidence for Christ's deity and the truth of Christianity in general. In the modern period, especially since the Enlightenment, this apologetic value has been rendered increasingly problematic as the historicity of the resurrection has been questioned or denied. But for the NT, the gospel plainly stands or falls with the reality of the resurrection, understood, despite its uniqueness, as lying on the same plane of historical occurrence as his death.

Although a cardinal belief for all Christians, the resurrection has been given a distinctive emphasis in the Reformed tradition. For instance, in its christological* differences with Lutheranism the resurrection (not, in part, the descent into hell*) begins the state of exaltation. Similarly, rejecting the Lutheran notion of a ubiquitous human nature (the *extra calvinisticum**), the accent has been on the glorified human nature that Christ does not possess until his resurrection.

Based on NT teaching, Reformed theology has seen the significance of the resurrection along several interrelated lines. The resurrection of Jesus is the pivotal *eschatological* event. The resurrected Christ is "the first fruits of those who have fallen asleep" (1 Cor. 15:20, 23); his resurrection is the actual beginning of the general resurrection-"harvest" of believers. It is not simply a miracle, however stupendous, isolated in the past but forms an unbreakable unity with the resurrection of believers. It belongs to the future and anticipates the consummation of history; it (together with the ascension and Pentecost as a single event-complex) inaugurates the eschatological "age to come."

This eschatological dimension serves to reveal the *christological* and *pneumatological* and so the *soteriological* importance of the resurrection. At his resurrection, Christ received a glorified, "spiritual" body (1 Cor. 15:42ff.) and was constituted the glory image of God (2 Cor. 3:18; 4:4). This climactic transformation of his person, however, is not simply personal but corporate. All those united to Christ by faith* "have been raised with Christ" (Col. 2:12; 3:1); they share with him in the benefits of his resurrection. For them, resurrection is not only a future hope but a present experience. As resurrected, he is their sanctification* (1 Cor. 1:30), the image into which they are already being transformed (2 Cor. 3:18) and to which they will finally be conformed completely in their bodily resurrection (1 Cor. 15:49; Phil. 3:21). That will be as well the full realization of their adoption* (Rom. 8:23), so he might be "firstborn among many brothers" (v. 29). At the same time, the resurrection is the vindication of Christ in his suffering (1 Tim. 3:16). It reveals and seals the efficacy of his death for the forgiveness of sins (1 Cor. 15:14, 17); he "was raised for our justification" (Rom. 4:25).

At his resurrection, Christ, as "the last Adam," became "life-giving spirit" (1 Cor. 15:45). As resurrected, Christ is in such total and final possession of the Holy Spirit* that the two, without confusion or the obliteration of personal Trinitarian distinction, are one (cf. 2 Cor. 3:17) in the work of communicating eschatological, resurrection life; the activity of the Spirit in the church* is the activity of the resurrected Christ (Rom. 8:9–10). Primarily with Pentecost in view, the resurrected Christ tells his disciples, "I am with you always, to the end of the age" (Matt. 28:20). This forms the background for the Reformed understanding of the real, "spiritual" presence of Christ in the sacrament.*

The pneumatic factor also sheds light, with all the mystery that remains, on the much-discussed question of the nature of the resurrection body. What God has done for Christ, in raising him from the dead through the Spirit, God will also do for believers (Rom. 8:11). Their bodies, like Christ's, will be "spiritual" (1 Cor. 15:44), not in the sense of being adapted to the human spirit or composed of an ethereal, immaterial substance, but as transformed and made immortal by the power of the Holy Spirit.*

The resurrection of unbelievers for final judgment and eternal condemnation, though less prominent in Scripture* (e.g., Dan. 12:2; John 5:28–29; Acts 24:15), has received confessional status in both mainstreams of the Reformed tradition (e.g., Belgic Confession,* art. 37; Westminster Confession,* 32.2–3; 33.1–2).

G. C. Berkouwer, *The Work of Christ* (1965); Heppe, *RD*; G. Vos, *The Pauline Eschatology* (1930).

RICHARD B. GAFFIN, JR.

Réveil, Le

Nineteenth-century evangelical awakening which invigorated and enlarged Protestantism in France and Switzerland. In France, the century following 1685 brought terrible repression for Protestants. The respite granted by the extension of toleration (1787) vanished in the proscription of all Christian worship* in the revolutionary "terror" (1792–95). Submission by pastors, sometimes followed by demission of office, suggested a massive influx of Enlightenment thought. In France and its expanded territories, 1801–14 brought unprecedented government intervention in church affairs, allowing existence but discouraging expansion.

Signs of French resurgence were evident immediately after the "terror" but were very localized. In France and Switzerland, important preparatory work was carried out by agents of the United Brethren (Moravians) who evangelized widely and produced cells of the "awakened" within existing church structures, especially in the locales known as centers of Réveil activity (Lausanne, Geneva, Lyons, Bordeaux, Montpellier). British evangelicals also attempted to assist prior to the "terror" and in the brief peace (1802). Yet the extended hostilities largely limited them to the printing of Bibles and literature for French distribution.

The end of war (1815) opened the way for unrestrained commercial and ecclesiastical interaction between Britain and Europe. Joining this movement into Europe was the Scot Robert Haldane. He had been oriented to Europe by David Bogue (1750–1825), the Scots theological tutor and Independent* minister of Gosport, Hampshire. Haldane had also been a governor of the London Missionary Society* (1796–1804, the era from which its European interests dated) and promoter of itinerant evangelism prior to the rise of Scotland's Congregational Union. In 1808 he adopted Baptist views.

In 1816 in his Genevan lodgings Haldane began six months of exposition on the Letter to the Romans to divinity students and young ministers, assisted by two American Presbyterians. Though opposed by the city's theological faculty, he led many from Deism to vital Christian faith. He departed for Montauban, France (summer 1817), and left behind a following divided over whether to submit to ordination at the hands of the largely heterodox local company of pastors.

A similar blossoming of pietistic cells was proceeding at Lausanne, again with significant British influence. Participating divinity students who did not desist were barred from ordination even under that city's more orthodox regime. This sudden surfeit of unordained and unassigned theological students in the two centers provided a nucleus for an aggressive wider ministry. As the launching of independent Protestant churches within the cantons was highly problematic, given existing church-state relationships, efforts were focused on France (and eventually on Quebec). The independent "Bourg de Four" congregation at Geneva served as the major hub of this movement. The 1820s saw numerous Swiss from such independent connections working, where possible, with the French Protestant churches. British endeavors such as the Continental Society for the Diffusion of Religious Knowledge founded in London (1819) also employed such workers in itinerant evangelism and colportage. Greatest opportunities were found in regions beyond the catchment areas of large cities.

Orthodox theological graduates of Lausanne, Geneva, and Montauban were simultaneously propagating a similar evangelical message within their national Protestant churches and among the Huguenot* diaspora in Holland, Denmark, and Germany. Bible and mission societies proliferated, notably at Lausanne and Paris, often with British and American assistance. Important supporting periodicals such as *Archives du Christianisme au dix-neuvième siècle* were founded. By the 1830s, lay-directed societies at Paris and Geneva effectively assumed the supervision of itineration and colportage from foreign societies, while continuing to rely extensively on foreign funds. A theological college begun at Geneva (1831), with which the historian Jean Henri Merle d'Aubigné* and dogmatician Louis Gaussen* were long connected, provided pastors and evangelists (as did the sympathetic college at Montauban) and helped spread the Réveil to Belgium, Holland, Hungary, and northern Italy.

The impulse supplied (1830s) by private rather than ecclesiastical initiative contributed to the considerable estrangement of the Réveil from the established churches by the late 1840s. Success in colportage and evangelism led to the founding in France of self-consciously evangelical and Reformed congregations impatient with governmental intervention and creedal indecisiveness. Thus a French "free" church was founded (1849) in conscious solidarity with similar movements in Scotland, Holland, Geneva, and Lausanne.

While the Réveil impulse continued across church lines, the decade of the

1870s removed the last of the early leaders. Theologically, it had emphasized the deity of Christ, human depravity, justification* by faith,* and biblical authority* in an era when these were discounted. Historically, the movement revived interest in Calvinist* doctrine and heritage. Ecumenically, it brought French-Swiss evangelicalism into the orbit of the Evangelical Alliance (founded 1846). Yet in the theological upheaval of the late nineteenth century, the movement's influence was largely dissipated.

R. P. Evans, "The Contribution of Foreigners to the French Protestant 'Réveil' " (diss., University of Manchester, 1971); J. I. Good, *History of the Swiss Reformed Church Since the Reformation* (1913); A. Gretillat, "Movements of Theological Thought Among French-speaking Protestants from the Revival of 1820 to the End of 1891," *Presbyterian and Reformed Review* 3 (1892): 421–47; A. Haldane, *The Lives of Robert and J. A. Haldane* (1855); T. C. F. Stunt, "Geneva and the British Evangelicals in the Early Nineteenth Century," *Journal of Ecclesiastical History* 32 (1981): 35–46.

K. J. STEWART

Revelation

Sources. Christian theology teaches that we have access to God's* nature and purposes only through God's willful deeds of revelation, of which Jesus Christ is the center. These acts are not all we can say of God but are the basic ones on which other actions such as guidance, inspiration, and providence* are founded. In every Christian theology, revelation is fundamental. While apparently there are many similarities among traditions, there are also essential differences. The Roman Catholic concept of revelation, formulated mainly by Thomas Aquinas, centers around the duality of "nature and grace"; the Reformation concept centers around "sin and grace," the Lutheran more specifically around "law and gospel," whereas Calvin and his followers prefer to summarize God's revelation as a "twofold grace" (*duplex gratia*), that is, justification* and sanctification.* These seemingly minor differences create a different view of God, humanity,* sin,* revelation, and redemption but also affect social and political matters.

For Calvin and the other Reformers, the center of revelation is Jesus Christ who is himself the center of the Word of God* as incorporated in Scripture.* In his 1559 *Institutes,* Calvin does not start with the law or in classical medieval subjects and doctrines but with the believing subject (*Inst.* 1.2.2: "Knowledge of God involves trust and reverence"). Following, however, is a chapter titled "The knowledge of God has been naturally implanted in the minds of men" (*Inst.* 1.3; cf. 1.4, 5). These deal with "natural religion" or "natural theology,"* beginning with: "There is within the human mind, and indeed by natural instinct, an awareness of divinity." This is supported by quotations from Cicero and Plato. In *Inst.* 1.2.2, the person of Jesus Christ and his reconciling work is no more than superficially mentioned. Calvin wrote:

> I do not yet touch upon the sort of knowledge with which men, in themselves lost and accursed, apprehend God the Redeemer in Christ the Mediator; but I speak only of the primal and simple knowledge to which the very order of nature would have led us if Adam had remained upright. . . . It is one thing to feel that God as our Maker supports us by his power, governs us by his providence, nourishes us by his goodness, and attends us with all sorts of blessings—and another thing to embrace the grace of reconciliation offered to us in Christ. First, in the fashioning of the universe and in the general teaching of Scripture the Lord shows himself to be the Creator. . . . Of the resulting twofold knowledge of God we shall now discuss the first aspect; the second will be dealt with in its proper place. (*Inst.* 1.2.1)

Twofold knowledge of God (duplex cognitio Dei). This expression was added in the last edition of the *Institutes* and is "basic to the structure of the completed work" (LCC ed., p. 40 n. 3). The sharp division of the two kinds of knowledge, in spite of Calvin's repeated methodological warnings, often created confusions and misunderstandings. Calvin spoke of the "naturally implanted knowledge of

God" with so much ardor (*Inst.* 1.2, 3), in words like "fatherly care," "benefits," "love," "mercy," and so forth, that many who were acquainted with his earlier editions and catechisms must have been puzzled, if not shocked, by the novelty of a reasoning in which the door to the true God is opened not by notions such as Christ, Scripture, or reconciliation but by quotations from pagan philosophers.

This turn becomes more complicated because now the authority of Scripture itself functions in a twofold way: sometimes it means the message of God's salvation and reconciliation in Christ; at other times it testifies to God's work in creation, preservation, providence in nature and history, and in common blessings and judgments for humanity. On top of all, Calvin suddenly uses a conditional by-sentence about "the primal and simple knowledge to which the very order of nature would have led us if Adam had remained upright" (*si integer stetisset Adam; Inst.* 1.2.1). This seems to overthrow the whole preceding argument. One group of interpreters have seen it as a loose remark in a wrong context, others as the cornerstone in the whole argument which removes almost all that is said before. Calvin seemed to have wanted to express too many thoughts in too few words. *Institutes* 1.4 tries to bring them into a larger and more convincing cohesion (see Dowey). Calvin's wrestlings here are symptoms of his endeavor to combine what cannot be synthesized into a divine unity. This is why in Calvin so often there are ambiguities, tensions, or ambivalences. But these reflect the multicolored truth of God. Wilhelm Niesel characterized Calvin's method as *complexio oppositorum* ("composition of opposite viewpoints").

What, then, is the relation between the first and the second order, between God's work of redemption and that of God's action? Calvin deals with this (*Inst.* 1.6–18) through the famous image of the spectacles that people of limited visual faculty need for reading a book distinctly: "So Scripture, gathering up the otherwise confused knowledge of God, . . . shows us the true God" (*Inst.* 1.6.1). Even the OT patriarchs had to pass first through the general knowledge before that other inner knowledge was added (*Inst.* 1.6.1). Calvin passes from biblical and dogmatical arguments for the authority of Scripture to other revelatory sources: the witness of the Spirit, function of reason,* and "marks" to distinguish the true God from the idols. These arguments are not of equal weight and approach. The testimony of the Spirit is a major and indispensable source of revelation; the others are more secondary but must not be neglected if we seek true and pure knowledge about God.

*Witness of the Holy Spirit (Testimonium Spiritus Sancti).** The first half of the title of *Inst.* 1.7 reads: "Scripture must be confirmed by the witness of the Spirit. Thus may its authority be established as certain." We are used to concentrating, if not limiting, revelation in the Reformed tradition to Scripture alone (*sola Scriptura*). But Calvin says the authority of Scripture does not suffice in itself (*Inst.* 1.7.5; often overlooked). The Spirit points away from the Spirit to Jesus Christ and to Scripture. Inner and outer authority presuppose each other (cf. *Inst.* 3.1–24—a long description of the Spirit's work). Calvin is even characterized as "the theologian of the Holy Spirit" (B. B. Warfield). Calvin saw Word and Spirit as each other's presuppositions and instruments in the process of revelation.

Revelatory function of reason (fides quarens intellectum). Institutes 1.8 is titled: "So far as human reason goes, sufficiently firm proofs are at hand to establish the credibility of Scripture." Yet this holds only when one begins with the authority of Scripture, not vice versa. The arguments of reason—"not strong enough before to engraft and fix the certainty of Scripture in our minds—become very useful aids" (*Inst.* 1.8.1). Calvin thought of comparisons between the Bible and Greco-Roman literature, the profundity of Greek philosophy, or the antiquity of Egyptian culture. Ancient achievements in the arts and sciences Calvin called "most excellent benefits of the divine Spirit." If "the Lord has willed that we be helped in physics, dialectic, mathematics, and other like disciplines, by the work and ministry of the ungodly, let us use this assistance. For if we neglect God's gift freely offered in these arts, we ought to suffer just punishment for our sloths" (*Inst.* 2.2.16). Reason helps maintain and develop justice, law, and welfare for individual and societal benefit. All this is summarized as "general" or "common grace" (*Inst.* 2.2.12–17; LCC ed., p. 276 n. 63).

Calvin called all these blessings of the Spirit "earthly," separating them sharply from the "heavenly" ones. The first preserve and protect our temporal lives; the second pertain to the mysteries of the heavenly kingdom and the blessedness of future life (*Inst.* 2.2.13). Earthly blessings are strictly limited and in many respects corrupted by sin.* Both the blessings of common grace and their limitations by creation and by sin must be kept clearly in mind.

"Reason" is Calvin's general word for cultural gifts and achievements worked by the divine Spirit. As such, it is a great but ambivalent reality. It must constantly be judged according to the standards of God's creation as revealed in Scripture. While reason is a source of revelation, it is a secondary one.

Negative revelatory function of idolatry ("You shall not make yourself a graven image"). Ample space in these apologetic sections is reserved for the "antiquated" subject of polytheism (*Inst.* 1.9–14). Calvin taught that "every figurative representation of God contradicts his being" (*Inst.* 1.11.2). The starting point for Calvin's doctrine of revelation is God's transcendence, sovereignty, and uncomparability. Yet how can this God really be revealed to human creatures? Or, in reverse, how can God create man and woman "in his own image, after his own likeness" (Gen. 1:26)? For Calvin, "accommodation" is important.

Condescendent revelatory principle of accommodation ("I dwell in the high and holy place, and also with those who are contrite and humble in spirit" [Isa. 57:15]). Accommodation* can be considered the "central feature of the entire range of Calvin's theological work" (a "working principle," not as the topic of a separate locus; see Battles). Accommodation is the reverse of God's transcendent nature, and "at the center of God's accommodating Himself to human capacity however is His supreme act of condescension, the giving of His only Son to reconcile a fallen world to Himself" (Battles, p. 24). Calvin sees that, in order to bridge the gap of our ignorance and disobedience, God has accommodated God's self to the limits of human capacity and relates to humanity as a parent, teacher, and physician. These metaphors enable Calvin to introduce a flexibility in God's relations to human creatures in their advancing toward spiritual maturity.

Divine authority of the Bible (Dei loquentis persona). The main feature of the Reformed faith is the central position of the Bible as source, standard, and court of appeal of all divine truth. Nearly every page of Calvin's works testifies to this fact and function. His commentaries exhibit this, and his exegesis is still valuable today. But Calvin, like Luther, practiced the authority of the Bible in a rather "free" manner. Luther concentrated on justification by faith alone; Calvin, on the general and practical meaning of the text, without much interest in real or seeming contradictions within a passage or between several books. Many Calvin scholars interpret Calvin's words such as "dictate," "inspiration," "amanuensis," or "notary" as pointing to verbal inspiration. But, for Calvin, this would have contradicted his concept of accommodation or created an anachronism because the concept of literal dictation by mechanical means came up in the seventeenth century, the period of Reformed scholasticism. Calvin used synonymously mechanical, organical, and personal images. His pointed definition said: "The highest proof of Scripture derives in general from the fact that God in person speaks in it" (Lat. *Summa Scripturae probatio passim a Dei loquentis persona sumitur; Inst.* 1.7.4). By the mechanical images, Calvin wanted to stress the instrumentality and irresistibility of the process; by the personal images, the character of a person-to-person encounter or free will. The Reformed concept did not feel an either/or contrast, but two language fields that complemented each other, until new paradigms required a more precise and less analogous terminology, as later happened in the doctrine of "organic inspiration."

Barth, *CD* I/1; I/2; F. L. Battles, "God Was Accommodating Himself to Human Capacity," *Interpretation* 31, no. 1 (January 1977): 19–38; Berkhof, *CF*; E. A. Dowey, Jr., *The Knowledge of God in Calvin's Theology* (1952; repr. 1964); D. K. McKim, "Calvin's View of Scripture," in *Readings in Calvin's Theology* (1984); Rogers and McKim, *AIB*.

HENDRIKUS BERKHOF

Revivalism in America

A Christian emphasis on conversion* and renewal of religious commitment, especially in the context of large groups of people similarly engaged, has been part of American Reformed life from the beginning. Major times of revivals have centered around particularly charismatic evangelists, most of whom have been ministers in Reformed denominations.

At the same time, emphases on providence* and predestination* have led many Reformed leaders to resist revivalism. As a result of Reformed ambiguity, many Baptists actually moved out of Reformed theology. Communions other than those of the Reformed family have supported revivalism most fervently.

In America, the Great Awakening* (1730s) set the style for revivals to come. Jonathan Edwards,* in Northampton, Massachusetts, noticed a "surprising work of God" (1734), and enthusiasm of people for the gospel increased. He and George Whitefield* became the focal revivalists for a movement that extended through the middle colonies and affected Congregationalists,* Presbyterians,* Baptists, and evangelical Anglicans.

Scottish Sacramental Occasions, or Holy Fairs, and possibly religious festivals remembered by other European settlers, were recast in the pluralistic American environment. People would prepare with fasting and prayer, gather for sermons, fellowship, and especially for Communion, celebrated by ministers from several parishes. While this may have influenced the Great Awakening, it most certainly explains the Second Great Awakening (1800–10), in which frontier congregations sponsored sacramental occasions. Presbyterians James McGready and Barton Stone led great revivals, and Stone subsequently moved to form the Christian Church. The Cumberland Presbyterian Church also split, or rather was split, from the Presbyterian Church by this movement.

Revivals led by Charles G. Finney* also had a profound effect (1830–40s), as did prayer meetings (1857–60), right before the Civil War. Revival in these contexts meant both that new Christians would confess Christ and that those already in the faith would exercise deeper piety* and more maturity in Christian living.

Analysts speak of a third awakening beginning with the Dwight L. Moody revivals (late 1870s) and continued through World War I and the preaching of Billy Sunday. It is interesting that Finney and Sunday both served at the beginning of their ministry as Presbyterians.

Dwight L. Chapman and Rodney (Gipsy) Smith, also Presbyterians, led revivals early in the twentieth century. They linked evangelical messages to ethical prescriptions, as had their predecessors. By this time, however, great revivalists came also from the Southern Baptists, Holiness communions, and newer denominations, as the majority have since. In televangelism and megachurch institutions, emphasis on conversion has predominated over demands for Christians to become more engaged in ethical living, except on certain issues such as antiabortion stances and prayer in public schools.

Perhaps put off by the truncation of revivalism, or from more base motives, Presbyterians and other mainline Reformed Christians have depended less in recent decades on revivalism than in their past.

LOUIS B. WEEKS

Revivals (British Isles)

The word "Revival" covers a variety of movements—from local awakenings lasting a few weeks or months to national movements continuing for many years. An early widespread revival in the British Isles was the Puritan movement of the early seventeenth century. Puritanism* emphasized experiential religion, impassioned preaching,* the conversion* experience, and work of the Holy Spirit.* On the whole, Puritan worship* in England was quiet and orderly. Among Reformed churches in northern Ireland and southwest Scotland, however, there were local revivals accompanied by wild excitement, writhing, and moaning—as at Sixmilewater in Antrim (1620s) and at Stewarton and Shotts (1630s).

The next widespread revival movement began in the 1730s and was associated with the preaching of John Wesley and George Whitefield.* It was profoundly influenced by European Pietism and the Great Awakening* in the North American colonies. Many were affected and worked to convert the nation to evangelical piety. By the later eighteenth century, the "evangelical revival" was finding expression in social and political activity, including campaigns to reform prisons, extend popular education, and abolish slavery.*

In the early nineteenth century, the British Isles experienced the Great Revival, or Second Great Awakening, which had emerged about 1800 along the western U.S. frontier. Itinerant preachers from America brought a highly emotional preaching to the British Isles, together with open-air meetings modeled after American camp meetings where intense pressure was placed on sinners to convert. In the late 1830s and early 1840s, British and Irish churches were influenced by the "new measures" revivalism associated with the American Presbyterian* Charles G. Finney* and employing refined techniques for creating revivals, including protracted meetings, direct preaching to individuals, the "anxious bench" for unconverted sinners, public testimony of the conversion experience, and intense community pressure on individuals to convert. Many orthodox Calvinists opposed such "worked up" revivals and questioned the genuineness of the conversions achieved.

But others embraced the "new measures" revivalism.* Wales was shaken by the "Finney revival" (1839–43), and rural Scotland also experienced many revivals. The revival waves, which began in Ulster (1859) and spread through much of Britain (early 1860s), were also influenced by the "new measures" coming from America.

During the 1860s and 1870s, revivals assumed new forms in response to emerging mass urban society and the impact of secularization. One innovation was the perfectionist or "holiness" revivalism introduced by such American evangelists as Walter and Phoebe Palmer and Robert and Hannah Pearsall Smith. This movement used revivalistic methods to call Christians to a "second conversion," to be followed by total Christian commitment.

Another innovation was the emergence of the professional revivalist and mass revival campaign. This was associated with the American lay revivalists Dwight L. Moody and Ira D. Sankey, whose campaign (1873–75) set a new pattern for revivalist activity—including direct, conversionist preaching, "inquiry meetings," businesslike organization, gospel music, theatrical techniques, and interdenominational cooperation. Not all revivals, however, reflected the new patterns. In 1904–5 a revival of great intensity swept through the mining valleys and rural villages of Wales. The movement seemed a spontaneous expression of popular religion.

Following World War I, revivalist activity waned. Some revivalists, especially in the United Free Church of Scotland, endeavored to reach the largely unchurched working class through brief, intensive revivalist campaigns aimed at industrial districts (1920s). The results, however, were often disappointing.

Billy Graham helped restore the professional revivalist as a powerful religious force in the British Isles (1950s), with methods similar to those of Moody and Sankey. His campaigns, like those of revivalists of the past, have encouraged church growth and Christian commitment. Many Reformed Christians, however, continue to distrust the professional revivalist and the "worked up" revival, preferring the quieter work of the nurturing church.

R. Carwardine, *Trans-Atlantic Revivalism* (1978); W. Couper, *Scottish Revivals* (1918); J. Kent, *Holding the Fort: Studies in Victorian Revivalism* (1978); M. Westerkamp, *The Triumph of the Laity* (1988).

STEWART J. BROWN

Reynolds, Edward (1599–1676)
A prominent member of the Westminster Assembly* and later bishop of Norwich (1660). Educated at Oxford, Reynolds lectured at Lincoln's Inn, and was dean of Christ Church, Oxford, before and after John Owen.* He served on the committee that drafted the WCF.* He represented the Presbyterians* in negotiations with Charles II leading to the Restoration. In later life he was an advocate of toleration* in church and state.

E. Reynolds, *Whole Works*, 6 vols. (1826).

WAYNE R. SPEAR

Roberts, Evan John (1878–1951)
Welsh revivalist, born at Loughor, Glamorganshire, the son of Henry Roberts, a coal miner, and his wife Hanna. Roberts worked as a coal miner but became a candidate for the Calvinistic Methodist* ministry (May 1904). After a shattering spiritual experience (September 29, 1904), he conducted a series of revival campaigns until August 1906. Detailed press coverage of the 1904–5 revival made Roberts an internationally known figure. He retired from public life, later returned to Wales, and died at Cardiff.

E. Evans, *The Welsh Revival of 1904* (1969); R. T. Jones, *Ffydd ac Argyfwng Cenedl*, vol. 2 (1982), 122–227; D. M. Phillips, *Evan Roberts* (1905).

R. TUDUR JONES

Robinson, John (1575–1625)
English Separatist and pastor of the Pilgrims. Educated at Cambridge, Robinson served a small Separatist church near Gainsborough where he was associated with John Smyth. Exiled to Holland, Robinson's congregation moved to Leiden (1609), where he remained until his death. His *Justification of Separation from the Church of England* (1610) was the most extensive apology for Separatist ecclesiology in the seventeenth century. An expert theologian, Robinson was drawn into debates on predestination* and published a *Defense of the Doctrine Propounded by the Synod of Dort* (1624).

S. Brachlow, *The Communion of Saints* (1988); T. George, *John Robinson and the English Separatist Tradition* (1981).

TIMOTHY GEORGE

Rollock, Robert (c. 1555–1599)
Early Scottish advocate of covenant or federal, theology.* Rollock helped transmit to Scotland the double covenant concept associated with Caspar Olevianus.* Rollock's *De vocatione efficaci* (1597) and *Quaestiones et disputationes de foedere Dei* (1606) make the covenant,* in the form of works or of grace, central to theological reflection. He is credited with being the first to use the precise expression "covenant of works." A prolific theological writer and biblical commentator, and founding professor of the University of Edinburgh, he became its first principal (1585). When he was Moderator of the General Assembly* of the Church of Scotland (1597), his compliance in the face of royal church policy compromised his standing among Presbyterians.

DNB 49:171–73; Life, in *Select Works*, ed. W. M. Gunn (1849), vol. 1.

W. IAN A. HAZLETT

Roman Catholic Church
The ensemble of Christian believers who through their priests and bishops stand under the jurisdiction of, and in communion with, the bishop of Rome. It consists of over 700 million adherents worldwide. It is thus by far the largest ecclesiastical communion in Christendom.

The name Roman Catholic Church seems at first glance to be a contradiction in terms, though it is held by theologians of that communion to be only apparently so. The title, at least in its English form, seems to have first come into use in early nineteenth-century Britain, where there was a felt need among Anglicans and others to distinguish between different expressions of catholicism. Another term, Church of Rome, is also in general use, though, strictly speaking, this title refers only to the Roman diocese itself which is directly under the pope's jurisdiction in his role as its bishop. Indeed, the very notion of a "Roman Catholic Church" as one Christian body among many is a consequence of the multiplication of churches during and after the Reformation. Before that time it was usual simply to think of the Church of the West, in distinction from the Orthodox communions of the East. Prior to a series of events beginning in 1054, of course, there was but one church, despite differing interpretations of its governance, in both East and West.

The ecclesiological self-understanding of the Roman Catholic Church is of course deeply grounded in pre-Reformation thought and experience: in the thought particularly of Augustine* and Cyprian and in the work of the ecumenical councils. That ecclesiology began to be much more closely and juridically defined over against an emerging Protestantism at the Council of Trent (1545–63) and thereafter.

It was not the intent of the Reformers to found a new church. They desired to reaffirm the sole headship of Jesus Christ over the church, to hear and proclaim the message of the gospel as the one word of God.* Their aim was to reform the church in obedience to God's will revealed in God's Word, to "restore the true face of the church," and in pursuit of this aim to modify or eliminate many teachings, practices, and institutional structures that were held to have distorted the gospel and obscured the church's calling. A variety of circumstances in different places, including serious mutual misunderstandings, led to the establishment of ecclesiastical bodies not in communion with Rome. By the time of the opening of the Council of Trent the Reformers were persuaded that Rome did not intend to carry out the thoroughgoing reforms they demanded. Relations became marked by caricature and vituperative language on both sides, as, for example, in the words about the pope found in the original version of the Scots Confession* (1560).

In reassessments of this history by both Protestant and Roman Catholic scholars there is general agreement that the two sides repeatedly failed to understand each other's intentions. To the Catholics, "reform" in the church had to do with matters of discipline, pastoral concern, and practice; it was not grasped that the doctrinal concerns of Luther,* Calvin,* and others had to do with the integrity of the gospel in the church and therefore with reform at the deepest level. Roman Catholic authorities pursued their own practical reforms, while seeking to refute the Reformers' "doctrinal errors." Both sides, obviously, were stimulated to a new focus on ecclesiological issues. For Rome, ecclesiological awareness had to this time been largely confined to polemical and apologetical works dealing with church order. The Reformation challenge began to bring out assumptions that had been widely held but that had not before been formally expressed: that Christ founded the church, and the apostles he chose are the basis of a structure of episcopal authority in which the bishop of Rome has more than primacy of honor; that Christ promised unity for the church and therefore doctrinal consensus is a sign of Christ's presence and the Spirit's work; that the church was prior to Scripture and is the authoritative interpreter of the Word; that bishops hold primary responsibility for the governance of the church.

The Council of Trent was called to foster reforming movements in the Roman Catholic Church, to clarify matters of doctrine and discipline, and to refute doctrinal positions attributed to the Reformers. None of the latter are mentioned by name, but Luther's claim that the church taught a Pelagian doctrine of grace was taken with great seriousness, as were other doctrinal questions, particularly with respect to the sacraments.* More than any previous council, Trent emphasized the continuity of the church from the time of the apostles, ascribing apostolic authority to the development of tradition. This position prevented the council from taking seriously most of the changes being demanded by the Reformers on the basis of their reading of Scripture. While avoiding explicit statements about the ecclesiological disputes of the time, Trent took care to define the church as essentially a pastoral institution, and to see that bishops would in the future have a properly pastoral view of their office.

It is important to realize that reforming movements in sixteenth- and seventeenth-century Catholicism were not confined to initiatives flowing from Trent. New spiritualities, programs of catechesis, efforts at evangelization, and a fresh emphasis on preaching in connection with the sacraments are all to be seen in this period.

After Trent, Catholic claims were often presented in ways intended to refute Protestant views and reassure Catholics that theirs was the authentic "one, holy, catholic and apostolic church." Catholicism became increasingly juridical in approach, institutionally oriented, and papally centered. By the nineteenth century, partly in response to repeated attacks on the pope's spiritual and political authority, a hierarchical and juridical ecclesiology reached its zenith in the deliverances on papal authority of the First Vatican Council (1870). In fairness, it must be said the forced adjournment of Vatican I, caused by the outbreak of the Franco-Prussian War, prevented the development of broader ecclesiological themes. Owing to popular misconceptions, especially among Protestants, that "the pope is infallible," it is important to understand the teaching of Vatican I exactly. It is that the pope can, under carefully specified and limited circumstances, officially exercise the infallibility divinely given to the church as a whole in order to decide questions of faith and morals for the universal church.

By the dawn of the twentieth century, new influences were at work in the church: movements in biblical studies, liturgy, pastoral care, ecumenism, and other factors. These created the climate in which Pope John XXIII called the Second Vatican Council (1963–65). The most important document of Vatican II was no doubt the Dogmatic Constitution on the Church, known by its first words in Latin as *Lumen Gentium*. This document, significantly altered by the bishops from the draft offered at the outset, presents an ecclesiology notably different from the juridical and institutional stance of Vatican I and of other authoritative manuals. The "people of God" theme figures prominently, as does a vision of the church as "communion," alongside a presentation of the church as "mystical body." The collegiality and proper authority of the bishops in communion with the pope is set out at length. *Lumen Gentium* provided a capsule definition of the nature and mission of the church which has had great ecumenical influence. "By her relation to Christ, the church is a kind of sacrament or sign of intimate union with God, and of the unity of humankind. She is also an instrument for the achievement of that union and unity." Vatican II's Decree on Ecumenism, *Unitatis Redintegratio*, also went far to clarify relationships between the Roman Catholic Church and other Christians and ecclesiastical communities, declaring that a real, though imperfect communion exists between them because of their common baptism.

Since Vatican II, the Roman Catholic Church has become deeply involved in ecumenical affairs. In the wake of the Council, the Secretariat (now Pontifical Council) for Christian Unity was established. International and regional bilateral dialogues between the Roman Catholic Church and various world confessional bodies began and have continued. Though it has not joined the WCC,* and probably cannot, given the present configuration of the latter body, Roman Catholic scholars are active and influential in several divisions of the WCC, most notably the Commission on Faith and Order. A Joint Working Group meeting regularly links the WCC with the Pontifical Council for Christian Unity.

At the level of general theological scholarship, Roman Catholic writers today exercise immense influence in the Christian world. The names of Karl Rahner, David Tracy, Edward Schillebeeckx, Avery Dulles, Hans Küng, Leonardo Boff, Gustavo Gutiérrez, and many others are well known. Most of the important work in Latin American liberation theology* comes from Roman Catholic scholars, as do seminal works in fundamental theology, Christology,* ecclesiology, and many other fields. Christian theological scholarship today is one in a way that the churches are not yet.

Two series of world-level formal dialogues between representatives of the WARC* and of the Roman Catholic

Church have now taken place: the first in 1970–77 and the second in 1984–90. The first series published a report, *The Presence of Christ in Church and World*, and the second a document, *Towards a Common Understanding of the Church.* The latter document includes summaries of the history of relationships between the Roman Catholic Church and the Reformed churches and an analysis of the similarities and differences between the communions on the doctrine of the church as such. This last is no doubt the most current and definitive statement on the subject.

The basic ecclesiological difference between the Roman Catholic Church and Reformed churches, this bilateral document asserts, does not lie in such fundamentals as the origin of the church and its role in God's plan of salvation.* There is agreement today even on the centrality of justification* by grace* alone. The difference has to do with the forms of the church's historical existence. Both communions see themselves as belonging to the *Una Sancta* but differ in their understanding of that belonging. For the Reformed, the church is *creatura verbi divini*, the "creation of the Word of God." For Roman Catholics, the church is a "sacrament of grace." Further, there is disagreement concerning the continuity of the church through the ages and concerning the church's visibility and its ministerial orders. But these differences are not seen as sufficient to preclude steps to deepen relationships. The document recommends living for each other rather than against each other, further steps to affirm mutual recognition of Baptism, the attempt to reconcile historical memories, and the determination to bear common witness in the world. The time does not seem ripe for more. Unity in the Eucharist is not yet attainable, and discussion has hardly begun on the status and authority of the bishop of Rome.

W. M. Abbott, ed., *The Documents of Vatican II* (1966); *Towards a Common Understanding of the Church* (Reformed/Roman Catholic Dialogue: Second Phase, 1984–90); A. Dulles, *Models of the Church* (1974); and *The Reshaping of Catholicism* (1988); H. Küng, *The Council, Reform, and Reunion* (1962); H. Meyer and L. Vischer, *Growth in Agreement: Reports and Agreed Statements of Ecumenical Conversations on a World Level* (1984); E. Schillebeeckx, *The Church with a Human Face* (1987).

LEWIS S. MUDGE

Root and Branch Petition

Document presented to the English Parliament (December 1640) calling for the abolition of episcopal church government "with all its dependencies, roots and branches," to be replaced by "government according to God's word," that is, presbyterianism.* It was subscribed by 15,000 Londoners, and 1,500 supporters accompanied it to Westminster. The petition is composed of twenty-eight articles summarizing the evils practiced and grievances occasioned by the Arminian* prelates. It was debated and is a significant religious element in the events leading to the English Civil War.*

A. Fletcher, *The Outbreak of the English Civil War* (1981); H. Gee and W. J. Hardy, *Documents Illustrative of English Church History* (1921).

JOHN H. PRIMUS

Runner, H. Evan (1916–)

Graduate of Wheaton College, Westminster Seminary, and the Free University of Amsterdam,* Runner taught at Calvin College (1951–81). He enthusiastically represented the distinctively Christian philosophical thought and world and life view of his Dutch Calvinistic mentors Herman Dooyeweerd* (Philosophy of the Law-Idea) and Dirk Hendrik Theodoor Vollenhoven. Runner helped form the Association of Reformed Scientific Studies in Ontario (1956) and the Institute of Christian Studies in Toronto (1967). His greatest contribution is through his formative influence on the thought of his students, many of whom now teach in Christian colleges.

HENRY ZWAANSTRA

Rutherford, Samuel (1600–1661)

Leader of the Covenanters* in Scotland, Rutherford was banished for writing against Arminianism.* He was professor of theology at St. Andrews after the triumph of Presbyterianism* (1638) and a commissioner to the Westminster Assembly.* In *Lex rex* (1644) he rejected the divine right of kings and held that civil power is given by God* to the people, who are born free, and should choose and limit their rulers. In 1661, *Lex rex* was publicly burned. Rutherford died before being tried for treason. His letters are a devotional classic.

H. Bonar, *Letters of Samuel Rutherford* (1891).

WAYNE R. SPEAR

Sabbatarianism

The belief that the OT Sabbath commandment is natural, universal, and moral and continues to require that one specific day each week should be scrupulously devoted to rest and worship.* Most literal Sabbatarians are those who worship on Saturday, as in orthodox and conservative Judaism, and groups such as the Seventh-Day Adventists and the Seventh-Day Baptists.

In the Reformed/Presbyterian tradition the term is used primarily for English and American Puritans who were Sunday Sabbatarians, that is, who observed Sunday as the NT Sabbath but still in conscious obedience to the fourth commandment of the OT Decalogue. The beginnings of this Sunday Sabbatarianism were in the English Puritanism* of the last two decades of the sixteenth century when an unusual number of lengthy treatises on the fourth commandment appeared, and questions of Sabbath theology and Sabbath observance became matters of intense interest and debate in the Church of England.

An early Sabbath treatise was by Richard Greenham, pastor in Dry Drayton, one of the first Puritan parishes in England. But the classic statement and defense was by Greenham's stepson, Nicholas Bound, in *The Doctrine of the Sabbath* (1595) and *Sabbathum veteris* (1606). The latter is 459 pages in length. This Sabbatarianism had three components: a conviction that the fourth commandment is moral, universal, and perpetually binding; that Sunday is the Christian Sabbath established by divine appointment and not merely church tradition; and that the entire day must be set aside for public and private worship and Christian service, with complete abstention from work and recreation. Bound found support in several Reformed continental theologians, for example, Girolamo Zanchi* and Franciscus Junius. Bound's works may indicate that the desire to develop and refine the doctrinal basis for strict Sabbath observance was prompted by a religious situation where church attendance was spasmodic and behavior in worship services unruly and chaotic. Sabbatarianism, with its requirements for public and private worship, was also appealing because it correlated with the strong Puritan emphasis on preaching* and family piety.*

Many Sabbatarian treatises appeared in early seventeenth-century England along with others to refute the Sabbatarian position. King James's *Book of Sports* (1618), which encouraged Sunday recreation, fueled the controversy. It was officially burned (1643), and shortly thereafter Sabbatarian doctrine was incorporated into the WCF.* Strict Sabbath observance in England was enforced during the Interregnum.

In the American colonies, the Sabbath received heavy emphasis, especially in New England. Sabbatarianism led not only to ecclesiastical censure for Sabbath breaking but to civil laws forbidding Sunday work and recreation. Sunday legislation was universal throughout the colonies. It gradually gave way to forces of industrialization, urbanization, improved transportation, Sunday railway schedules, Sunday newspapers, and commercialized sports and recreation. Remnants of Sabbatarianism are still found in some smaller, more conservative denominations of the Reformed/Presbyterian tradition.

K. L. Parker, *The English Sabbath* (1988); J. H. Primus, "Calvin and the Puritan Sabbath," in *Exploring the Heritage of John Calvin* (1976); and *Holy Time* (1989); W. Solberg, *Redeem the Time* (1977).

JOHN H. PRIMUS

Sacraments

Visible holy signs and seals instituted by God* so that by their use God may make us understand more clearly the promise of the gospel and put God's seal on that promise. This is to grant us forgiveness* of sins* and eternal life, by grace* alone, because of the one sacrifice of Jesus Christ on the cross (HC,* q. 66).

The two sacraments set forth in the NT—Baptism* (Matt. 28:19; Acts 2:38) and the Lord's Supper* (Matt. 26:26–29)—were prefigured in the OT rites of circumcision (Gen. 17:11; Col. 2:11–12) and the passover (Ex. 12:7–8, 13; 23:14–17; 1 Cor. 5:7). All were intended to function as means of grace within the covenant* community, bringing its members into a closer walk with God. Baptism and the Lord's Supper had particular reference to redemption in Christ and communion with him through the Holy Spirit* (Acts 2:38; Rom. 6:3–5; Titus 3:5; 1 Cor. 11:23–27; John 6:53–58, 63; Col. 2:11–12). That the early church understood them this way seems clear (Mark 10:38–39; 1 Cor. 10:1–5). To the first Christians, the sacraments were not mere memorials of Christ's saving work but a representation of that work which became a means of grace through faith* and the power of the Holy Spirit. Baptism and the Lord's Supper, then, are dramatizations of the Word that is proclaimed, appealing to sight, touch, and taste as well as sound. It is possible to hear the Word of God* without the sacraments, but there are no sacraments apart from the Word which gives them meaning. It can even be said, with Luther,* that the Word is the one sacrament and that Baptism and the Lord's Supper are pictorial representations of it. By extended usage, a contemporary theologian, Edward Schillebeeckx, has called Christ "the sacrament of the encounter with God" in a book with that title (1963).

"Sacrament" derives from a Latin word that classically meant something sacred. In a lawsuit, money deposited by contending parties was *sacramentum*, for when forfeited it was used for a sacred purpose. The word was also used judicially and militarily; *sacramentum dicere* meant to swear an oath.

In the early church, *sacramentum* came to apply to many things sacred and to rites which had a hidden meaning. Thus it was used to describe religious ceremonies and was brought into connection with *mystērion* (Gr.), meaning "secret." In the Latin Vulgate, *sacramentum* is translated for *mystērion* (Eph. 1:9; 3:9; 5:32; Col. 1:27; 1 Tim. 3:16; Rev. 1:20; 17:7). Whereas Tertullian was the first theologian to use *sacramentum* with clear religious meaning, two centuries later Augustine* wrote that signs which "pertain to divine things are called sacraments." That broad meaning of the word continued into the Middle Ages. The sign of the cross, palms, ashes, anointing with oil, preaching, prayer, and visitation of the sick were all included. With sacrament conceived as a "sign of a sacred thing" (Peter Lombard), some theologians listed thirty. However, these "sacraments" were divided into classes, with Baptism and the Lord's Supper given prominence. In the thirteenth century, the number was set at seven.

The meaning given to sacraments was also an important development. Whereas Augustine had said they were visible signs of an invisible grace, they were later said to contain and confer grace. No mere channels, they were declared to be "efficient causes" of grace by a virtue inherent in themselves when properly administered. Thus Baptism regenerated,* and the Lord's Supper, by conversion of the bread and wine into the body, blood, soul, and divinity of Christ, was conceived as a propitiatory sacrifice to God for the remission of sins. The elements consecrated in transubstantiation could be reserved for later use and adored even as Christ himself (Council of Trent, Sess. 13, 22).

The Reformers swept aside these accretions to biblical teaching but disagreed among themselves as to the meaning and efficacy of the two sacraments they accepted. All rejected transubstantiation and the Mass as a propitiatory sacrifice, but Luther insisted on the real physical presence of Christ in the Supper. Acknowledging the mystery, he took literally Christ's words, "This is my body," and said that if we cannot believe Scripture here, we cannot believe it anywhere and are on the way to "the virtual denial of Christ, God, and everything" (*Works*, 37:29, 53).

Luther was protesting Zwingli's* view which denied any physical presence of Christ in the Supper and separated the sign from that which it signified to such an extent that he said we worship an "absent" Christ. Zwingli thought dualistically: The Word is both inward and outward, the church is visible and invisible, grace has an external form and is inward. No physical element can affect the soul but only God in sovereign grace. There must be no identification of the sign and that which it signifies; through the use of the sign we rise above the world of sense to God and the grace signified. By contrast, Luther held that God comes to us in the physical signs which sense apprehends. Zwingli held that the word "is" in the words of institution meant "signifies"; the bread signifies Christ's body. Thus Zwingli believed that in this instance "is" is similar to the other "I am" statements of Jesus. Luther's notion of the physical eating of Christ's body which was held to be "in, under, and with" the elements was repugnant to Zwingli and he believed that Luther's doctrine of the ubiquity* was nonsense.

Calvin* agreed with Zwingli in the latter's rejection of Luther's positions but denied Zwingli's claim that we worship an absent Christ. For then, Calvin reasoned, there would be no real communion, no real feeding on Christ in the Supper, and no reception of him. But communion with the crucified and risen Savior is what the Lord's Supper is all about. Thus Calvin took a position midway between the extremes of Luther and Zwingli. Learning from both, he held a doctrine truly his own.

The key to Calvin's understanding is his view of the Holy Spirit's role in communicating the benefits of Christ to believers. With Luther, he held that there is a reception of the body and blood of the Lord Jesus in the Supper but it occurs in a spiritual manner. The ascended* Christ, in heaven* with his body, gives himself to the faithful through the Holy Spirit. Nothing should be taken from Christ's "heavenly glory—as happens when he is brought under the corruptible elements of this world, or bound to any earthly creatures. . . . Nothing inappropriate to human nature [should] be ascribed to his body, as happens when it is said either to be infinite or to be put in a number of places at once" (*Inst.* 4.17, 19). Luther's "monstrous notion of ubiquity" (4.17.30) and the associated idea that Christ is corporeally (physically) received in the Supper were thus rejected along with Zwingli's mere "memorialism" in which the signs were conceived as representing that which is absent.

Reformation teaching on Baptism was less disputatious than on the Eucharist but followed similar lines of thought. In place of the baptismal regeneration of Rome, there was explicit emphasis on the Word, faith, and the Holy Spirit. Within Protestantism there were those who saw Baptism as little more than a badge indicating belief or sign of the covenant. But most Reformed people, including the Church of England, believed that Baptism was a real means of grace with multiple significance: the acknowledgment of sin, of cleansing through Christ, union with Christ,* the gift of the Holy Spirit, and Baptism as a sign of covenantal status. As a covenantal sign, it was seen as replacing circumcision (Col. 2:11–12). Because of Christ's redemption, it has a richer meaning than the OT ordinance. There was debate about the candidates for Baptism and the amount of water that was proper to use. But there was nothing like the acrimony which attended the "sacramentarian controversies" over the Lord's Supper.

The Reformed church generally followed Calvin in its confessional teaching about Baptism and the Lord's Supper. The sacraments are not "bare signs" (*signa nuda*) but are described as real means of grace with which the Holy Spirit nourishes believers. Signs and seals of God's promise of salvation,* they are made effective by God's Spirit who quickens and nourishes those within the covenant community who are united to Jesus Christ.

Thus the Reformed tradition, with most of the Christian church, believes it pleases God to use earthy materials—water, bread, the fruit of the vine—in the reconciliation of the world to God. Those Christians who depreciate the sacraments through disuse or by giving them minimum meaning because of their material nature, if consistent, might seek a word from God beyond the paper and ink of Scripture* or adopt a docetic Christology* in which the humanity of Christ, an earthy reality, is denied. In denigrating the sacraments, they reject a gift that God has given to God's people for the enrichment of their spiritual life and the strengthening of their faith.

There is also a "sacramental principle" discernible in life and universally utilized in natural religion. Though this is by no means the reason the church administers its divinely ordained sacraments, the presence of that principle is relevant to Christian theology as a witness to the reality of God's interaction with all people.

G. W. Bromiley, ed., *Zwingli and Bullinger*, LCC, vol. 24 (1953); J. Calvin, *Tracts Relating to the Reformation*, trans. H. Beveridge, 3 vols. (1844–51); O. Cullmann, *Baptism in the New Testament* (ET 1950); W. F. Flemington, *The New Testament Doctrine of Baptism* (1948); J. C. McLelland, *The Visible Words of God: An Exposition of the Sacramental Theology of Peter Martyr Vermigli A.D. 1500–1562* (1957).

M. EUGENE OSTERHAVEN

Salvation

The NT Greek terms translated "to save" and "salvation" are *sōzō* and *sōtēria*. They connote snatching others by force from serious peril. They may also mean saving from judicial condemnation or from an illness, hence curing. The Hebrew *yeshu'ah* has the sense of "deliverance." Fundamentally, the root means "to be broad" or "spacious." Thus to deliver is to set free from constraint, confinement, or oppression so the one delivered can develop unhindered. The OT story of Israel tells of God's mighty acts of deliverance and salvation. God's righteousness is manifest in saving the humble who cannot save themselves, the poor and the dispirited (Isa. 40:18–20; 44:9–20; 46:6–7). The phrase "God saves" could almost be likened to a primitive creed. The proper name "Jesus" has its root in this affirmation.

Christian tradition has many ways of imaging how our salvation is brought about in the work of Christ. All these NT images stand with no attempt to harmonize them, and the church* has not found it necessary to sanction exclusively any one view. The pluriform richness of these images may say there is more here than one model for understanding can carry. Each view in its own way sheds an illuminating cross light on what remains a profound mystery.

One view sees our predicament as a subjective sense of *guilt* for our sin* that causes us to turn from God and hide in shame. Salvation happens as God's love, which has *already forgiven*, is manifest in Christ.* Our hearts are stirred to repentance* and a response of love. Christ's life, which reveals both who God is and who we are (essentially, in union with God), becomes an "example" or "moral influence" for us. Abelard's view is of this type.

A second model draws upon images from the ancient Jewish sacrificial system. Here the priest is seen as the *mediator* between God and humanity, offering sacrifices to atone for sin. Blood is shed—in expiation, not propitiation—as a sign of the people's sorrow for their sin. In this model, Christ is presented as our great high priest (Hebrews) who lays down his own life as sacrifice in our behalf.

A third model draws upon military images. God and the devil are pictured as locked in combat over the destiny of humankind. Christ is the warrior of God who, after having been apparently defeated on the cross, by his death invades the realm of the evil one doing battle with sin and death and the devil. In the resurrection, Christ shows himself victorious (Christus Victor) and leads out of captivity those who had been carried off (Mark 3:23–27; 1 Cor. 15:24–28).

A financial image gives yet another angle of vision. Here the human condition is compared to slavery or imprisonment. We are in bondage or are held captive by the forces of evil. Christ offers his own life as our ransom. We are "redeemed" at great cost.

Yet another model, which has perhaps been the most prominent for Western Christianity, is the juridical model. In its early presentation developed in a feudal context (Anselm, *Cur Deus Homo?*), it portrayed God as an overlord against whom a vassal had committed a crime. The seriousness of a crime in feudal culture depended upon whom it was committed against. Since the crime was against God, an infinite guilt was incurred. Only an infinite restitution—which only God could provide—could satisfy the demands of justice. But it is the offender who must pay. Therefore only a human being could make restitution. Thus the only resolution possible would be restitution offered by one who was fully human and fully divine.

This "satisfaction" model was modified somewhat by Calvin's* day to a courtroom drama with God as the judge and human beings as lawbreakers. The verdict is "guilty," and the sentence is "death," but a righteous person stands in defense and offers "substitution," taking the punishment due to the offenders upon himself.

Calvin made use of all these images—even the subjective, "Christ as example" model. "Christ . . . has been set before us as an example, whose pattern we ought to express in our life" (*Inst.* 3.6.3). Calvin draws most frequently upon the mediator image (*Inst.* 3.11.9) as a way of thinking about Christ's reconciling work. Our primary predicament is alienation from God. We need one who can mediate and bring reconciliation. In this model, as all others, Calvin wants to show that the reconciling is God's work in Christ. He opposes and avoids any bifurcation that pictures God as wrathful and desirous of our destruction and Christ as merciful and desirous of our salvation—Christ over against God. "God was in Christ, reconciling the world" (2 Cor. 5:19).

The juridical model is also frequently employed by Calvin. It provides a way of articulating justification* and forgiveness* of sins which are central to Calvin's understanding of salvation. So prominent in the Reformation, this view of salvation was cast in the Pauline, juridical terms "justification by grace* through faith.*" Calvin follows Paul, but with interesting nuances.

For Calvin, the original sin was "unbelief"—not believing in God, turning to our own resources. We are, in Augustine's* words, *incurvatus in se.* That fundamental disorientation led to a corruption of our true relation to God and consequently a corruption of our true nature. This in turn is manifest in the multitude of "sins" imaged as "lawbreaking." The fundamental need is for reconciliation to God—a renewal of our relationship with God—and forgiveness of sins (which were the consequences of our disorientation from God).

If unbelief is the root sin, then it follows that "faith" is the locus of God's saving activity. This faith is God's gift to us. For Calvin, faith is engendered in us by God's Word (*Inst.* 3.2.6) and Spirit (*Inst.* 3.1.4), and it works to renew our relationship to God. Reversing the order that Luther* proposed, Calvin insists that faith precedes repentance, that repentance is in fact a consequence of faith (*Inst.* 3.3.1). Because we have received grace and the promise of salvation we are moved and enabled to repent. In a sense we are forgiven before we repent, by God's grace, on God's initiative— not our own. Salvation is not a matter of bringing external influences to bear in order to change God's mind about us. Faith is a firm and certain knowledge of God's benevolence toward us (*Inst.* 3.2.7) This knowledge provides a confidence and security that frees us from ourselves—from being *incurvatus in se.* We no longer live in unbelief, having continually to secure ourselves. We have faith in God and know ourselves to be ultimately secured.

Not only are we justified, we are also sanctified.* We experience a "double grace" of reconciliation and regeneration.* In true repentance, what happens is a "mortification" of the flesh (dying to the old self-preoccupied way of being) and a "vivification" by the Spirit. The regeneration the Spirit works in us restores the image of God that has been disfigured and all but obliterated. Calvin assumes that our justification will have real effects in our lives, that faith will issue in good works. Yet all good works are, like faith, not our own—a cause for boasting—they are a gift of God.

Calvin did not see this sanctification as a state of sinless perfection but as a process in which our hearts, minds, and wills come ever more into agreement with God's purposes for us. We become children of God, receiving the spirit of adoption.* "Christ is not outside us but dwells within us. . . . With a wonderful communion, day by day, he grows more and more into one body with us, until he becomes completely one with us" (*Inst.* 3.2.24). In this way of putting the matter, Calvin took a more modest line than Andreas Osiander, who claimed that Christ's righteousness is "infused" into us by our unity with God in Christ so we actually "are righteous." This essential righteousness enables God to justify us. Calvin countered that Christ's righteousness is "imputed" to us. One is justified when, excluded from the righteousness of works, one grasps the righteousness of Christ through faith and, clothed in it, appears to God not as a sinner but as righteous. There is both acquittal from guilt and imputation of righteousness (*Inst.* 3.3.10), but there is no hint of sinless perfection.

Calvin's third use of the law* is as a guide for life under the Spirit's ongoing work of sanctification. The main stress is on the positive nature of the "saved" life. As mentioned above, the term carries the sense of health and wholeness of the human being. It is not only "safety" but essential soundness or completeness—the fullest realization of human powers and values. The saved life is the fully human life—not lifted out of its finitude and creatureliness but "spacious" and "unhindered," authentic and spontaneous, no longer *incurvatus in se* but now set free for God and others.

ANNA CASE-WINTERS

Sanctification

The doctrine of sanctification has been a bone of contention in the church* through the ages. Among areas of controversy are the interdependence of sanctification and justification;* the relation of faith* and love; the interplay of grace* and works; the role of the Christian life in our salvation;* the tension between personal holiness and the righteousness of Christ; and the question of rewards.

Different understandings. The Roman Catholic view, developed by the mystics and the scholastic theologians, and formally articulated by the Council of Trent, tends to subordinate justification to sanctification. We are justified to the degree that we are sanctified. Justifying grace enables us to cooperate with the Spirit in living a sanctified life—a process often called deification or divinization. Faith by itself is deemed insufficient to justify us: faith must be formed or fulfilled by love. In Catholic mysticism, metaphors of the ladder and mountain were often used to illustrate the ascent of the believer to divinity, an ascent involving purgation and illumination and finally culminating in mystical union and ecstasy.

Luther's* emphasis was on the justification of the ungodly. God* comes to us while we are yet in our sins* and pronounces us just on the basis of the perfect righteousness of Jesus Christ. The mystical union with Christ,* already realized in faith, enables us to do works that glorify God. Faith in itself is passive, but it becomes active in obedience as the Spirit works within us. We are justified by grace alone through faith, and good works flow spontaneously and inevitably out of the commitment of faith.

Luther was emphatic that our justification and sanctification are based on the alien righteousness of Christ, which covers our sinfulness and makes us acceptable before God. He made a firm distinction between the righteousness of faith, which justifies us, and the righteousness of life, which attests our sanctification. The latter is a consequence and fruit of the former, but it is always incomplete, for the old nature is never entirely extirpated. Christians are righteous and sinners at the same time—righteous because our sin is covered by the perfect righteousness of Christ and sinful because in and of ourselves we are still prone to follow the cravings of the flesh.

Whenever Luther employed the ladder imagery of Christian mysticism, it expressed the descent of Christ to sinful humanity, not the ascent of the Christian to divinity. Instead of the Augustinian* synthesis of *caritas* (Lat.) in which grace makes possible the human ascent, Luther revived the NT motif of *agapē* (Gr.) in which God's love descends to the world of sin in order to serve and heal. Christians become instruments of divine love sent into the world to be servants of all. On the basis of faith we become sons and daughters of God, but through the power of love we become virtual gods, since we are now the hands by which God shapes a new world.

Luther also made use of the metaphor of the ship—representing baptism.* If we but stay aboard, we will finally arrive at our destination—glorification with Christ in heaven.* If we fall away from faith, we need simply to return to our baptism rather than seek a new means of grace such as penance or confirmation.*

Calvin,* like Luther, regarded justification as primarily a forensic act by which the holy and merciful God cancels our debts on the basis of the merits of Christ. He too viewed justification as the ground of our salvation, but Calvin tried to hold justification and sanctification in balance. Whereas justification is an event, sanctification is a gradual process. Justification is a change of status, sanctification a change in being. In justification we are covered by the righteousness of Christ; in sanctification (or regeneration*) we are engrafted into this righteousness. The basis of sanctification is justification; the goal of justification is our sanctification and glorification.

Whereas Luther portrayed the life of the Christian as moving forward but often slipping backward, Calvin's emphasis was on moving upward to Christian perfection through divine grace. Yet this is a broken ascent, because the old nature though dying continues to reassert itself. Paradoxically, it is also an ascent that is realized through a descent to the needs of an ailing and lost humanity.*

For Calvin, justification and sanctification are complementary, not parallel, terms. This is why he spoke of a twofold blessing. We are never justified apart from the blessing of regeneration. We are never recipients of faith without being motivated to practice love.

Yet even the works of the regenerate, Calvin insisted, are nondeserving of God's grace, accompanied as they always are by motives less than pure; at the same time, these works are not valueless. God crowns our works with God's grace and even rewards them. They are good because they are used by God to advance God's kingdom* and give glory to Christ.

The message of the Protestant Reformation was revived by Karl Barth* in the twentieth century but given a new thrust. For Barth, justification and sanctification are not successive acts of God but two moments in the one act of reconciliation in Christ. Our salvation was fully realized in its totality once and for all times, and for all humanity, in the sacrificial life and atoning death of Jesus Christ. In him we are justified, sanctified, and redeemed. Barth can even say that our conversion* takes place in Christ, since through Christ's death and resurrection the whole world was converted to him. Yet Barth also acknowledges the need for the subjective response to God's act of mercy and redemption; otherwise God's redeeming work would have no practical efficacy in our lives. Barth affirms that we are justified by faith and sanctified by love.

Barth accepts Luther's understanding that the Christian is both righteous and a sinner but insists that sin is now behind us whereas righteousness is before us. In Christ we cannot sin, for we are now rooted in perfect holiness. But the ontological impossibility of falling away from Christ happens again and again, and this is why the life of the Christian is a continuous returning to the fount and anchor of our faith—the cross of Calvary.

As Christians, Barth insists, we can do works that are pleasing to God—not meritorious, since they are performed by sinners, yet nevertheless pleasing to God because they are made possible by God's grace and declare God's righteousness and mercy. Good works are works in which our sin is recognized and confessed. Human righteousness is not divine righteousness but will in some way correspond to it.

The paradox of sanctification. Reformed theology holds that our sanctification is a secret work of the Spirit within us, yet it never occurs apart from human effort. The paradox of human striving and irresistible grace is certainly evident in Paul (cf. 1 Cor. 15:10; Phil. 2:12–13). The Christian life is both a crown to be won and a gift to be received. We are summoned to run the race and attain the prize but give all the glory to God, since it is God who makes us run and ensures that the prize will be ours.

The role of the Christian is not to procure or earn salvation but to witness to a salvation already accomplished and enacted in Jesus Christ. We are called to work out the implications of our salvation through a life of loving service. The Christian life is a consequence of salvation (Luther), a sign and witness of our salvation (Barth), and also the arena in which the work of salvation is carried forward (Calvin). We are not coredeemers but co-workers in making God's salvation known. We contribute not to the achievement of salvation but to its manifestation and demonstration. We also contribute to its extension (Calvin), since our works may well be used by the Spirit* of God to bring outsiders into the kingdom. We do not build the kingdom, but we can be instrumental in its advance.

Errors to be avoided. Among the errors that Reformed theologians have warned against are the following: confounding justification with sanctification, for then forgiveness* is not entirely gratuitous; viewing justification as wholly extrinsic, thereby denying or underplaying its mystical dimension; equating sanctification with works of purification, and so opening the door to legalism and moralism; reducing sanctification to special experiences, such as the second blessing—the error of experientialism and subjectivism; exaggerating the benefits of sanctification, which leads to perfectionism; minimizing the reality of sanctification, which fosters defeatism; and separating law* and gospel, which denies the law as a guide for the Christian life.

Reformed theology, as set forth by Calvin and Barth, contends for the unity of the law and gospel, seeing one covenant* in the Bible—a covenant of grace with two dimensions. The so-called covenant of works represents a misunderstanding, especially prominent in rabbinic Judaism. We are freed by grace for obedience to the law. But this is now the law seen in the light of grace—no longer a burden but a privilege, for, paradoxically, in our obedience we realize true freedom. In Reformed theology the second face of the gospel is the law and the second face of the law is the gospel. The law leads us to the gospel, and the gospel directs us back to the law—yet no longer as a legalistic code but now as the law of spirit and life, the law that equips us for service to God's glory.

D. G. Bloesch, *Essentials of Evangelical Theology*, 2 vols. (1978).

DONALD G. BLOESCH

Saurin, Jacques (1677–1730)

Born at Nîmes (southern France), Saurin was forced to flee France at the revocation of the Edict of Nantes* (1685). Settling in Geneva, he studied for the ministry. He became pastor of a French-speaking congregation in The Hague (from 1705), where he was highly popular with the intelligentsia of the Dutch court. Saurin mediated the eloquence of French oratory to the Protestant pulpit. A good example of Protestant "moderatism," he defended orthodoxy and yet preached a positive message to the Enlightenment.

A. Vinet, *Histoire de la prédication* (1860).

HUGHES OLIPHANT OLD

Savoy Declaration of Faith and Order

Some two hundred representatives of 120 Independent churches met at the Savoy Palace (September 29–October 12, 1658) to write this document. Participants included John Owen,* Philip Nye, Thomas Goodwin,* and William Bridge (the last three had been members of the Westminster Assembly* [1643–48]). They prepared a Preface, a Declaration of Faith, and the "Savoy Declaration of the Institution of Churches and the Order Appointed in Them by Jesus Christ."

The Preface affirms the freedom of the Spirit, who does not "whip men into belief . . . but gently leads them into all truth." The Declaration will answer the need for a clear articulation of gospel truth; demonstrate agreement with all who "hold fast the necessary foundations of faith and holiness"; and testify to "a great and special work of the holy Ghost," in that a large group of people completed it in only eleven days. Finally, it will prove that the ascended Christ "will . . . be with his own Institutions to the end of the world." The objective is humbly to give an account of their faith, "and not so much to instruct others, or convince gainsayers." (However, in presenting it to Richard Cromwell on October 14, 1658, Goodwin said the authors wished to contradict the "scandal . . . affixed upon us, viz., That Independentism (as they call it) is the sink of all Heresies and Schisms.")

Doctrinally and verbally the Declaration largely follows the Westminster Confession.* However, it strengthens Westminster's Trinitarianism, introduces the language of federal theology,* and speaks of Christ's active and passive obedience. It revises the Westminster's "Of Repentance Unto Life," adding "and Salvation" to the title. "Of the Gospel, and of the Extent of the Grace Thereof" (ch. 20) is entirely new. The power of the civil magistrate is curtailed compared with Westminster, and whereas the latter includes, Savoy omits the children of believers from the catholic church. Savoy adds a paragraph on the tranquillity the churches of Christ will enjoy in the latter days.

The concept of covenant* is present throughout the Declaration's thirty paragraphs on church polity,* but the term is not used. Particular churches are appointed by Christ's authority, and "Besides these particular Churches, there is not instituted by Christ any Church more extensive or Catholique. . . . " Such churches comprise pastors, teachers, elders,* and members, the officers being chosen by the members. The latter are "Saints by Calling," who "do willingly consent to walk together according to the appointment of Christ, giving up themselves to the Lord, and to one another by the will of God in professed subjection to the Ordinances of the Gospel." Church discipline is required, and "all Believers are bound to join themselves to particular Churches, when and where they have opportunity so to do." Provision is made for advisory synods comprising messengers sent by the churches (not comprising whole churches as advocated by Robert Browne*) and for the reception of members of other true churches as occasional communicants.

A. G. Matthew, ed., *The Savoy Declaration of Faith and Order* (1959); A. P. F. Sell, "Confessing the Faith in English Congregationalism," in *Dissenting Thought and the Life of the Churches* (1990).

ALAN P. F. SELL

Schaeffer, Francis A. (1912–1984)

A leader in churches formed by separation from the Presbyterian Church in the U.S.A., Schaeffer established the L'Abri center in Switzerland, where personal piety, biblical doctrine, and Christian social ethics were taught and practiced. Among his twenty-three books are *Escape from Reason* (1968), *The God Who Is There* (1968), and *He Is There and He Is Not Silent* (1972). These and a film, *How Shall We Then Live?* (also a book [1983]), show how the rise and decline of Western culture depended on the presence or absence of Reformed Christianity. Seven L'Abri centers and the Schaeffer Institute at Covenant Seminary (St. Louis) continue his work.

THOMAS M. GREGORY

Schaff, Philip (1819–1893)

Born in Chur, Switzerland, and educated in the universities of Tübingen, Halle, and Berlin, Schaff began his academic career at Berlin. He became (1844) professor of church history and biblical literature at the German Reformed Seminary in Mercersburg, Pennsylvania (now Lancaster Theological Seminary), and quickly came to understand and appreciate American church life. Schaff not only was able to bring to the American church a new appreciation of its catholic and European heritage but he also interpreted the American church to Europe.

Schaff moved to New York and became secretary of the New York Sabbath Committee (1863). He enthusiastically worked for a revised version of the Bible and was president of the American Committee. He was later active in trying to revise the creed of the Presbyterian Church. Schaff led in such ecumenical endeavors as the Evangelical Alliance and participated in the founding of the Alliance of Reformed Churches. The American Society of Church History was founded in his living room (1888). His own ecumenical attitude has been described as "evangelical catholicism."

Schaff made the best European scholarship, especially historical studies, available to the American churches. He developed a remarkable capacity to write clear, coherent English. His two most important works were *The Creeds of Christendom* (3 vols.; 1877) and the *History of the Christian Church* (12 vols.; 1883–93), both of which are continually reprinted.

JOHN H. LEITH

Schlatter, Adolf (1852–1938)

A leading twentieth-century exegete and theologian whose scientific study of the NT remained true to its message and thus went against the trends of his era. Schlatter was born in St. Gallen, Switzerland, and studied theology at Basel and Tübingen. Ordained by the Landeskirche (1875), he was a pastor for five years before being called to Bern, where he completed his *Habilitation* and became docent in NT. He became professor of NT in Greifswald (1888), of systematic theology in Berlin (1893), and of NT at Tübingen (1898), where he remained until his death. Schlatter's influence remains significant in contemporary German evangelical theology.

DONALD A. HAGNER

Schleiermacher, Friedrich Daniel Ernst (1768–1834)

German preacher, theologian, philologist, and philosopher. Born to a family of Reformed clergy on both the maternal and the paternal side and educated first among the Moravian pietists, then at the University of Halle, Schleiermacher was ordained to the ministry of the Reformed Church (1794). Two years later he was appointed to the Reformed chaplaincy of the Charité Hospital in Berlin. There he came in contact with some of the leading intellectuals of Prussian society, who encouraged him to write and publish his first book, *On Religion: Speeches to Its Cultured Despisers* (1799). During the same period, he embarked on two separate translation projects, the complete works of Plato (initially with Friedrich Schlegel) and the sermons of two British preachers, Joseph Fawcett and Hugh Blair. Schleiermacher served briefly as professor of theology and university preacher at the University of Halle but was forced to leave when Napoleon's troops occupied Halle and turned the university chapel into a storage warehouse. Returning to Berlin, Schleiermacher accepted the pastorate of Trinity Church (1809) and joined the faculty of the new university as professor of theology (1810).

The Evangelical Church of the Prussian Union, formed at the behest of the Prussian king Friedrich Wilhelm III (1817), united the Lutheran and Reformed churches. Schleiermacher participated actively in the discussions that paved the way for the union. For twenty-six years at Trinity Church he shared his pastoral appointment with a Lutheran colleague, Philipp Marheinecke. Later, when debates broke out regarding the liturgy for the Evangelical Church, he contributed his thoughts on the nature of liturgy in a united Lutheran and Reformed church. He also hoped for an eventual resolution of the opposition between Protestantism and Roman Catholicism, which he viewed in some respects simply as a different form of Christianity, not a corruption of it. In this sense, Schleiermacher may be seen as a forerunner of twentieth-century interest in ecumenical theology. Nevertheless, throughout his career Schleiermacher identified himself with what he called the Reformed "school," and he defended the doctrine of election against Lutheran criticisms of it.

Schleiermacher is often called "the father of modern theology" because of his seminal dogmatic work, *The Christian Faith* (1821–22; 2nd ed. 1831–32). Alexander Schweizer,* however, suggested that Schleiermacher is "the reviver of Reformed consciousness in the modern era." This title seems appropriate not least when one considers Schleiermacher's understanding of theological method as continual reformation of church doctrine.* He argued that dogmatic theology, along with exegesis and church history, is a part of historical theology, since doctrines are simply the expression of Christian faith in a particular church at a particular time (*Brief Outline on the Study of Theology*, sec. 85; *CF*, secs. 15–19). As such, doctrines are not themselves, nor are they the symbols of, eternally unchanging truths; rather, doctrines are historical products that must be subjected to constant criticism and revision. *CF* is Schleiermacher's own attempt to describe the Christian way of believing in the Evangelical Church of the Prussian Union and to criticize and reformulate the inherited theological language of his church. His thoroughgoing criticisms of traditional theological language about God, Christ, and eschatology* represent the first attempt to reconstruct the entire system of theology in a post-Enlightenment world.

But Schleiermacher was not simply an academic theologian. Throughout his life he continued to serve as pastor of a large congregation and thought of himself first and foremost as a preacher—a servant of the Word. His sermons, some of which were published during his lifetime, comprise ten of the thirty-one volumes in his collected works, and many more sermons exist in unpublished manuscripts. Schleiermacher preached homilies in the form of successive interpretations of individual biblical books (much like Calvin*) during the early Sunday service and topical sermons on theological, liturgical, or national themes at the main service. The sermons represent Schleiermacher's attempt to make biblical faith intelligible to Christians living in the modern world. It is in the proclaimed Word, he argued, that Christians today encounter the living Christ. With his emphasis on the sacramental word, Schleiermacher may also be seen as the reviver of the Reformed understanding of preaching.*

Schleiermacher's activity and influence, however, ranged even more widely. He was a significant biblical scholar; his critical work on the Synoptic Gospels and the pastoral epistles broke new ground in its own day. His lectures on the life of Jesus, a favorite theme of biblical reflection in the eighteenth and nineteenth centuries, were published posthumously. Schleiermacher is the father of modern hermeneutics, and his posthumously published lectures are still widely discussed.

Schleiermacher's right to a place in the Reformed tradition has come under question in this century, largely because of the criticisms of his theology voiced by Emil Brunner* and Karl Barth.* They argued that Schleiermacher's understanding of doctrine as the expression of Christian experience* substitutes subjective anthropology for the objective Word of God* and that his concern for making faith* intelligible in the modern world led him to abandon the central themes of Reformed theology. This discussion is by no means closed.

Schleiermacher's works (date of ET) include: *A Critical Essay on the Gospel of Luke* (1825); *CF* (1928); *Brief Outline on the Study of Theology* (1966); *Christmas Eve: Dialogue on the Incarnation* (1967); *The Life of Jesus* (1975); *Hermeneutics* (1977); *On the Glaubenslehre* (1981); *Servant of the Word: Selected Sermons of Friedrich Schleiermacher* (1987); *On Religion* (1988).

The standard reference work for writings by and about Schleiermacher is T. N. Tice, *Schleiermacher Bibliography* (1966; updated 1985); see also K. Barth, *The Theology of Schleiermacher* (1982); J. O. Duke and R. F. Streetman, eds., *Barth and Schleiermacher: Beyond the Impasse?* (1988); B. A. Gerrish, *A Prince of the Church* (1984); Richard R. Niebuhr, *Schleiermacher on Christ and Religion* (1964); M. Redeker, *Schleiermacher: Life and Thought* (1973).

DAWN DE VRIES

Schneckenburger, Matthias (1804–1848)

Though born in Switzerland, Schneckenburger was educated at Tübingen and Berlin. He was active as professor at the new university in Bern but through his German training was heavily influenced by Lutheran theology. He taught theology and NT exegesis and is primarily known for his analysis of Lutheran and Reformed confessions.

NSH 10:254f.; *RGG*[3] 5:1464.

RICHARD C. GAMBLE

Scholasticism

A term first used in a derogatory sense by humanists* in the sixteenth century. It is now applied to any theology in which concerns with logic and method are prominent, where theology is conceived as a type of science.

A scholastic movement flourished during the Middle Ages (1050–1500). Anselm, Abelard, Bonaventure, Thomas Aquinas, Duns Scotus, and William of Ockham were prominent figures. They also influenced later scholasticism. Reformed scholasticism of the last half of the sixteenth century and the seventeenth century had contemporary parallels in a Lutheran and a Catholic scholasticism. Reformed scholasticism has had a major influence on the development of the Reformed/Calvinist tradition.

Erasmus* popularized the negative image of the schoolmen as boring, tradition-bound professors who focused on useless subtleties. Calvin* also refers to the schoolmen in derogatory terms, though on occasion concedes the value of their careful analysis. Erasmus and Calvin were reacting to late-medieval scholasticism in which debates had often grown sterile. Both wished to return to a study of the Bible itself, a study directed by the liberal arts.

After Calvin, a new scholasticism was inevitable, for every great thinker has followers who teach and interpret his thought. The seeds of Reformed scholasticism were sown with the founding of the Geneva Academy.* Theodore Beza,* called by Calvin to teach there, is an early Reformed scholastic. In many ways, Beza's thought is simply a clear, consistent exposition of Calvin's position, but the systematizing and ordering, the further elaboration of difficult points regarding the inspiration of Scripture,* predestination,* and limited atonement,* modified Calvin's position in significant ways.

Reformed scholasticism is, however, more than just a simplifying and systematizing of Calvin's thought. Calvin was only one of a number of significant Reformed leaders. Huldrych Zwingli,* Martin Bucer,* and John Oecolampadius* preceded Calvin; and Peter Martyr Vermigli,* Girolamo Zanchi,* and Zacharias Ursinus,* as well as Beza, were contemporaries. Their contributions, along with Calvin's, became known as Reformed theology.*

While Calvin was most influenced by humanist attitudes and techniques, Vermigli and Zanchi, both Italians, were educated at Padua, the center of a great Aristotelian revival. In both, but especially in Zanchi, the influence of Aquinas is also evident. Like Beza, Vermigli and Zanchi order the doctrine of God* in terms of divine decrees,* resulting in predestination becoming a major point of contention. These three, more than Calvin, are responsible for the prominent place that predestination assumed in Reformed theology.

A notable example of Reformed scholasticism is the Synod of Dort.* Its formulation of Calvinism* was under five "heads of doctrine": total depravity, unconditional election, limited atonement, irresistible grace,* and perseverance* of the saints. The most prominent Reformed scholastics in the seventeenth century were Benedict Turretin and his son Francis.* Benedict supported the views of the orthodox party at the Synod of Dort and promoted them in Switzerland. His son Francis also defended the decrees of Dort and argued for the complete inerrancy of Scripture. His view is found in the Helvetic Consensus Formula* (1675) and is still influential today.

ARVIN VOS

Schuller, Robert Harold (1926–)

A minister of the Reformed Church in America, televangelist, and proponent of "possibility thinking." Nurtured in a Dutch Calvinist home in northwestern Iowa, Schuller attended Hope College and Western Seminary. Following a five-year pastorate near Chicago, he organized the Garden Grove Community Church in Orange County, California (1955). The church grew and completed a twenty-million-dollar glass and steel sanctuary designed by architect Philip Johnson (1980). The congregation is identified as the Crystal Cathedral of the RCA. Schuller's internationally televised "The Hour of Power" services (since 1970) feature upbeat music, famous guests, and Schuller's dramatic messages. He established an Institute for Successful Church Leadership (1969) and promotes "possibility thinking," the ideological drive wheel of his ministry. Closely related to the "positive thinking" of Norman Vincent Peale,* Schuller's message is an amalgam of therapeutic psychology, mind conditioning, and biblical prescriptions. Undergirding it is his "theology of self-esteem." Identifying the essential human problem as low self-esteem, Schuller claims that orthodox Calvinism* is negative and debilitating. His theological system stresses human goodness and potential rather than sin and limitation.

R. H. Schuller, *Self-Esteem: The New Reformation* (1982); D. N. Voskuil, *Mountains Into Goldmines: Robert Schuller and the Gospel of Success* (1983).

DENNIS N. VOSKUIL

Schweizer, Alexander (1808–1888)

Important contributor to Swiss Reformed theology, Schweizer was a prolific writer. His two-volume *Die protestantischen Centraldogmen in ihrer Entwicklung innerhalb der reformierten Kirche* (1854–56) is an excellent text source for sixteenth-century Swiss Reformed thought and its further development.

Schweizer became professor at Zurich (1840) and taught NT, practical, and systematic theology. He was the main preacher at the cathedral and believed that the living community of Christ and not dogmatics itself should be the starting point for theological thought.

NSH 10:283ff.; B. A. Gerrish, "Grace and the Limits of History: Alexander Schweizer on Predestination," *Tradition and the Modern World* (1978): 99–150; K. Otto, "Die Theologie der Predigt bei Alexander Schweizer und Alois Emanuel Biedermann," *TZ* 36 (1980): 26–39.

RICHARD C. GAMBLE

Science (Physical)

Physical science includes physics, chemistry, and the earth sciences (astronomy is treated separately under "Cosmology"). In the European West, physical science has progressed through four major phases: Aristotelian; post-Aristotelian (Paracelsus, Bacon, Descartes); Newtonian; and post-Newtonian (thermodynamics, field theory, and quantum mechanics).

Aristotelian philosophy dominated Western science from the thirteenth to the seventeenth century. It provided a comprehensive picture of the world as known without the aid of instruments that enhance human sense perception. John Calvin's* interest in Aristotelian physics is reflected in his sermons and commentaries. Like Martin Luther* and Huldrych Zwingli,* Calvin accepted the basic Aristotelian picture as a description of universal providence* but also appealed to phenomena like the elevation of mountains and the confinement of the seas as indications of particular providence. These "gaps" in Aristotelian science evidenced the continuous activity of God* in all of nature.

Calvin allowed a limited role for astrology in medical science but criticized what he saw as confusion of the natural and supernatural in Neoplatonism, Hermeticism, and alchemy. He wanted to affirm legitimate science as a vocation* but was sensitive to any indication of vainglory in eccentrics such as Agrippa and Paracelsus. English reformers like John Hooper and William Perkins* held similar views. However, Reformed physicians of the sixteenth century like William Turner and Oswald Croll revised the ideas of Paracelsus and helped pave the way for post-Aristotelian chemistry. Seventeenth-century chemists like Samuel Hartlib and Robert Boyle successfully combined alchemical skills with ideas of the newer mechanical philosophy.

In Elizabethan times, the strategy of finding gaps in physical science was shunned by churchmen like Thomas Cooper and Richard Hooker and by natural philosophers like Francis Bacon. God's activity in the present was limited to universal providence. Bacon also stressed the social utility of legitimate science and provided it with a Reformed ideology that was instrumental in the success of the Royal Society of London in the late seventeenth century. Christianity was to be seen in such deeds as the healing of disease and the subduing of the forces of nature as much as in words of faith* and forgiveness.*

Much of the seventeenth century was dominated by the philosophy of Descartes, which required a strict separation of physical science and theology. This tactic was stoutly resisted by Gisbert Voetius* at Utrecht but was defended by Johannes Cocceius* at Leiden and later accepted by Francis Turretin* of Geneva.

In the late seventeenth century, Isaac Newton revised the mechanical philosophy and combined the notion of inert matter with faith in a God who acts directly through space and force. In the eighteenth century, the son of a Swiss Reformed minister, Leonhard Euler, contributed to the foundations of mathematics and mechanics along more Cartesian lines. English Independent ministers who accepted the new science include Isaac Watts* and Joseph Priestley, the latter being partly responsible for the discovery of oxygen. The American Congregationalist minister Cotton Mather* and the son of a Dutch Reformed minister, Hermann Boerhaave, were able to combine the new physics with older ideas concerning the direct involvement of spirits in matter without any apparent sense of inconsistency. At a philosophical level, Jonathan Edwards* tried to bring out a more direct dependence of all matter on God.

In the nineteenth century, science became increasingly technical and professional, while Reformed theology was influenced by romanticism and revivalism.*

Some twentieth-century Reformed theologians who have treated scientific ideas seriously are Emil Brunner,* John Baillie,* T. F. Torrance,* and Harold Nebelsick.

J. Dillenberger, *Protestant Thought and Natural Science* (1960); C. B. Kaiser, *Creation and the History of Science* (1990); E. Klaaren, *Religious Origins of Modern Science* (1977); D. C. Lindberg and R. L. Numbers, *God and Nature* (1986); R. Westfall, *Science and Religion in Seventeenth-Century England* (1958).

CHRISTOPHER B. KAISER

Scopes Trial

John Scopes, a high school science teacher, was tried in Dayton, Tennessee, for teaching biological evolution contrary to state law (1925). Occurring at the height of the fundamentalist/modernist controversy,* the trial attracted widespread attention. Renowned Presbyterian fundamentalist William Jennings Bryan,* prosecution lawyer, debated Scopes's agnostic attorney Clarence Darrow. Scopes's conviction was later overturned on a technicality. But Dayton's country setting and ridicule of Bryan by the national press left the impression that fundamentalism was a rural phenomenon that would pass with the growth of an urban, sophisticated culture.

G. M. Marsden, *Fundamentalism and American Culture* (1980).

BRADLEY J. LONGFIELD

Scots Confession

The proclamation and testimony of faith of the Scottish reformers, accepted by Parliament and the reformed Church of Scotland (1560), accorded civil legal status in 1567. The confession belongs to the Reformed family of confessions and reflects the Geneva-Zurich doctrinal consensus. Militant, cordial, and evangelical in style, it became the chief subordinate doctrinal standard of the Scottish Church, presbyterian or episcopalian, until superseded by the Westminster Confession* (1647).

Decisive in the confession's composition and adoption was the intervention of Protestant England to help liberate Scotland from Catholic French interests. A companion text to the Book of Discipline,* the confession was drawn up by the "six Johns"—Knox,* Willock, Winram, Spottiswoode, Row, and Douglas.

The first ten of the confession's twenty-five articles embody the Catholic doctrinal traditions of the early church. The remainder reflect the characteristic controversial theology of the age, treating faith,* justification,* sanctification,*

Scripture,* the offices of Christ, the civil power, the church,* and sacraments.* Distinctive is the combination of systematic and biblical *heilsgeschichtliche* ("salvation history") theology. Notable also is the stress on ecclesiology, the sacramental eating of Christ's flesh and blood, and Christian ethics, the right to rebel against tyranny. Predestination* is not highlighted.

The voice of John Calvin* in the confession is clearly identifiable but less exclusive and authentic than usually assumed. A Latin translation was published (1572). Alongside the confession, the Scottish Church also sanctioned the Genevan English Confession,* the Second Helvetic Confession* (1566), and the acrimonious Negative Confession or King's Confession* (1581).

K. Barth, *The Knowledge of God and the Service of God According to the Teaching of the Reformation* (1938); A. C. Cochrane, ed., *Reformed Confessions of the 16th Century* (1966); W. I. A. Hazlett, "The Scots Confession: Context, Complexion and Critique," *ARH* 78 (1987): 287–320; G. D. Henderson, ed., *The Scots Confession, 1560* (1960); P. Jacobs, *Theologie reformierter Bekentnisschriften in Grundzügen* (1959); J. Knox, *History of the Reformation,* ed. W. C. Dickinson (1949); W. Niesel, ed., *Bekenntnisschriften und Kirchenordnungen* (1938); E. Routley, *Creeds and Confessions* (1962).

W. IAN A. HAZLETT

Scottish Missionary Society

Beginning its work in India (1823), the Scottish Missionary Society provided focus for foreign mission concern expressed in the preceding century by various evangelical efforts, including support for David and John Brainerd's mission to North American Indians by the Scottish Society for Promoting Christian Knowledge (est. 1709) and voluntary societies arising in Edinburgh, Glasgow, and other towns as of 1796. John Inglis, Moderate leader, having overcome earlier party hostility to foreign missions, persuaded the General Assembly* (1824) to appoint the Church of Scotland Foreign Mission Committee, of which he became the first Convener.

ROBERT M. HEALEY

Scottish Reformation

The Scottish Reformation as a formal event may be dated from 1560 when Parliament repudiated Rome, prohibited the celebration of Mass, and adopted a Protestant confession of faith. This legislation, which formed the basis of the religious settlement despite Queen Mary's failure to assent to it, was the work of an irregular gathering of the estates after the rebellion by the Protestant Lords of the Congregation* who resorted to revolution (1559) in defiance of the Crown's wishes. Yet, for over a generation before the Reformation Parliament approved these momentous changes, the politically assertive and progressive parts of the country had been receptive to reforming influences and propaganda.

Soon after Luther's revolt (1517), the Scottish Parliament had tried to ban (1525; 1535) the import of Lutheran literature, but it failed to stop the spread of Luther's teachings which east coast trading links facilitated. The bishop of Aberdeen (1525) complained of the circulation of Luther's books and beliefs within his diocese; at St. Andrews University, Luther's doctrine of justification* by faith* alone was debated (1520s); Patrick Hamilton, scholar of Paris, Louvain, St. Andrews, and Marburg, was burned at St. Andrews (1528) for affirming Lutheran tenets; and other prosecutions followed (1530s). By the 1540s, the circulation of pamphlets, books, broadsheets, ballads, and popular songs satirized and relentlessly exposed the shortcomings of the established church. Lutheran, Zwinglian, and Calvinist literature made their import among groups of nobles, lairds, lawyers, merchants, craftsmen, and farmers attracted by the message of the Reformation.

After Henry VIII's break with Rome, Scottish reformers were able to look to England as a potential ally, and England found it advantageous to encourage the reforming movement in Scotland with a view to detaching Scotland from the French alliance. The death of James V (1542) saw a struggle for power between

Cardinal Beaton, head of the pro-French, Romanist party and a foe of schismatic England, and the Earl of Arran, heir presumptive to the throne, who as governor attempted to follow a pro-English, reformist policy by promoting the circulation of Scriptures in the vernacular and favoring the betrothal of the infant Queen Mary to Henry VIII's son, Prince Edward of England. But Arran's resolution proved short-lived; he capitulated to the cardinal; legislation against heretics ensued, and Henry VII's failure by peaceful means to achieve the Scottish marriage resulted in English military action in Scotland—the "rough wooing" (1544–45).

Scottish Protestantism, still clandestine and unorganized, received fresh stimulus (1545) from the preaching mission of George Wishart, a Scottish student at Louvain and Cambridge, who helped popularize the ideas of the Swiss reformers. John Knox,* a renegade priest, associated himself with Wishart's work, serving as bodyguard, until Wishart's capture and execution, at the cardinal's behest (1546). A group of conspirators assassinated the cardinal and seized his castle in St. Andrews, and Knox, joining the insurgent "Castilians," accepted a call to enter the ministry. Yet any prospect of a successful Protestant revolt did not materialize. In the aftermath of Henry VIII's death, renewed English intervention came too late to save the rebels in St. Andrews who surrendered when French troops stormed the castle (July 1547) and consigned Knox with some associates to the galleys until 1549.

As a counterpoise to French influence, English occupation of Scotland (1547–49) helped sustain the hopes of a party pro-English in outlook and attached to the cause of reform. But with the departure of the English, Scottish Protestantism was again forced underground during the regime of Mary of Guise, the queen mother, who realized that, with the death of Edward VI, Scottish reformers could no longer seek support from England ruled by Mary Tudor. Yet the underground network of Protestants, who met in conventicles and "privy kirks" for worship, proved a formidable force. A program of Catholic reform promoted by Archbishop Hamilton and a series of provincial councils between 1549 and 1559 recognized the necessity for urgent action, but too little was done too late. In 1557 the Protestant Lords of the Congregation united in a covenant to set forward the Word of God,* defend true ministers, and renounce all superstition and idolatry.* By 1558 a program for Protestant worship and preaching had taken shape, and by January 1559 the "Beggars' Summons" had appeared on friary doors, threatening the friars with eviction.

During 1559 a reformed ministry* in many main towns became operative, supported by the magistrates. Knox was appointed minister of the capital (July 1559). When Mary of Guise outlawed some prominent preachers (May 1559), the Protestants gathered their forces. By October, they had deposed Mary of Guise from the regency and transferred power to a provisional government dominated by the Lords of the Congregation who still professed allegiance to Mary Queen of Scots in France. The changing political situation helped determine the timing of the Protestant revolution. The insurgents could justifiably appeal to patriotic resentment at French domination. Mary's marriage to Francis of France (1558) added weight to claims that Scotland might end up as a French province.

With Elizabeth's accession (1558), Scottish reformers were able to appeal for support to England. The intervention of the English fleet (1560) proved decisive in cutting communications with France. An English army then assisted Scottish forces besieging the French garrison at Leith, which ended when Mary of Guise died (June 1560). By July, the French and English agreed to withdraw from Scotland, and arrangements were made for summoning Parliament—the "Reformation Parliament"—whose proceedings sealed the outcome of the revolt.

Thereafter a report on polity and endowment, the Book of Discipline,* by Knox and five colleagues (1560), discarded the top-heavy medieval system, recognized the two dominical sacraments* of Baptism* and the Lord's Supper,* and focused attention on the needs of congregations, served by ministers and assistant exhorters and readers,* elected with congregational approval, governed by kirk sessions of ministers, elders,* and deacons,* and supervised by superintendent ministers for ten provinces. The Book of Discipline also laid claim to all parochial revenues to sustain the ministry, schools, and the poor, and episcopal property to support the universities and superintendents. In 1560, too, the General Assembly* met to direct the affairs of the reformed church. With startling success, the Reformation had overthrown the established church which had once commanded the allegiance of the nation.

G. Donaldson, *The Scottish Reformation* (1960); J. Kirk, *Patterns of Reform* (1990); and "The Scottish Reformation and Reign of James VI: A Select Critical Bibliography," in *Records of the Scottish Church History Society*, vol. 23, pt. 1 (1987), 113–55.

JAMES KIRK

Scougal, Henry (1650–1678)

Scottish divine, Scougal had a brief ministry at Auchterless, Aberdeenshire (1672–74), and taught philosophy and theology at King's College, Aberdeen (1668–72; 1674–78). He was the first in Scotland to teach Baconian philosophy, but his fame chiefly rests on his devotional classic, *The Life of God in the Soul of Man* (10th ed. 1769), published at the behest of Gilbert Burnet who wrote a preface. It has been frequently reprinted and translated into French. To it George Whitefield* ascribed "his first conviction of that doctrine of free salvation* which he afterwards made it the great object of his life to teach."

D. Butler, *Henry Scougal and the Oxford Methodists* (1899).

HENRY R. SEFTON

Scripture

The doctrine of Scripture has been prominent in the Reformed faith. Scripture is one aspect of the "Word of God"* and the medium through which God's self-revelation in Jesus Christ is made present by the witness of the Holy Spirit.*

Reformed confessions. Over against sixteenth-century Roman Catholicism,* the Scots Confession* maintained Scripture's authority "to be from God," not from the church which established the canon (*BC* 3.19). God communicates through Scripture which presents "the holy gospel" of Jesus Christ (HC, q. 19) received by faith,* whereby one accepts "as true all that God has revealed" in God's Word (HC, q. 21). "Scripture is the Word of God" (*BC* 5.003) where the church* has "the most complete exposition of all that pertains to a saving faith, and also to the framing of a life acceptable to God" (Second Helvetic Confession; *BC* 5.002). The Scriptures are the basis for the church's preaching: "The preaching of the Word of God is the Word of God" (*BC* 5.004). Preaching* is made effective by "the inward illumination of the Spirit" (*BC* 5.005); yet this "inward illumination does not eliminate external preaching" (*BC* 5.006).

The relationship of Scripture and the Holy Spirit (Word and Spirit) is developed more fully in the WCF* (*BC* 6.001–.005). There the canon of Scripture is identified as "the Word of God written" and all canonical books said to have been "given by inspiration of God, to be the rule of faith and life" (*BC* 6.002). This formulation focuses attention on Scripture's *scopus*, or purpose. God is said to be "the author" of Scripture, a way of stressing that Scripture "is to be received, because it is the Word of God" (*BC* 6.004). While many external considerations might move and induce people to esteem Scripture, "yet, notwithstanding, our full persuasion and assurance of the infallible truth and divine authority" of Scripture come from "the inward work of the Holy Spirit, bearing witness by and with the Word in our hearts" (*BC* 6.005). Scripture is to be interpreted in reliance on the Spirit, and while "all things in Scripture are not alike plain in themselves, . . . yet those things which are necessary to be known, believed, and observed, for salvation, are so clearly propounded and opened in some place of Scripture or other, that not only the learned, but the unlearned, in a due use of the ordinary means, may attain unto a sufficient understanding of them" (*BC* 6.007).

The Theological Declaration of Barmen* emphasizes that the church is built on "the gospel of Jesus Christ as it is attested for us in Holy Scripture" (*BC* 8.05). It is "Jesus Christ, as he is attested for us in Holy Scripture," who is "the one Word of God which we have to hear and which we have to trust and obey in life and in death" (*BC* 8.11). The Confession of 1967* indicates that Jesus Christ is known as the Holy Spirit "bears unique and authoritative witness through the Holy Scriptures, which are received and obeyed as the word of God written" (*BC* 9.27). While the Scriptures are given under the "guidance of the Holy Spirit," they are nevertheless human words "conditioned by the language, thought forms, and literary fashions of the places and times at which they were written" (*BC*, 9.29).

Theological formulations. Three emphases on Scripture have characterized various Reformed theologians. The Princeton Theology* of Charles Hodge,* B. B. Warfield,* and A. A. Hodge* saw Scripture as a book of inerrant facts. Scripture's inerrancy—its complete accuracy on all matters of science, history, or geography on which it teaches—was considered a crucial part of Scripture's authority since Scripture as "God's Word" shares in God's perfection of truth. This meant that Scripture was "verbally inspired" and was the source for all doctrinal* belief. Thus "the Scriptures are the word of God in such a sense that their words deliver the truth of God without error" (Warfield).

Karl Barth* stressed Scripture as the "witness to Jesus Christ" which "becomes" authoritative as a form of the Word of God as through it one encounters the living Christ by the work of the Holy Spirit. Because Scripture is written by humans who "witnessed" to God's revelation in Jesus Christ, the biblical texts are not to be perceived as "inerrant" in the sense of presenting unerring accounts, since they were written by fallible writers. Scripture was "inspired," for Barth, insofar as it witnesses to Scripture's special content: the Word of God, Jesus Christ.

Calvin, Reformed confessions, and theologians such as Abraham Kuyper,* Herman Bavinck,* and Gerrit C. Berkouwer* have emphasized Scripture as presenting a divine message in human thought forms. The purpose of Scripture is not to present inerrant facts; yet it is "infallible" in that it will not lie or deceive about what Scripture is intended to focus upon: God's salvation* in Jesus Christ. In this view, Scripture is seen in relation to its central purpose, the proclamation of the gospel (John 20:31). The Spirit witnesses to Scripture's content. Scripture is infallible in accomplishing its purpose.

Barth, *CD* I/1; I/2; G. C. Berkouwer, *Holy Scripture* (1975); D. K. McKim, *What Christians Believe About the Bible* (1985); Rogers and McKim, *AIB*; B. B. Warfield, *Inspiration and Authority of the Bible* (2nd ed. 1948).

DONALD K. MCKIM

Seceders, Original

Seceders in Scotland left the established church (1733). In subsequent divisions and unions, several bodies used the term "original" in their designations to indicate their adherence to the early positions of the Secession, especially strict subscription and the perpetual obligation of the Scottish Covenants.

The most prominent body was the Original Secession Church (1842). A majority united with the Church of Scotland (1852). In 1956 the surviving Original Secession congregations also joined the Church of Scotland.

C. G. McCrie, *The Church of Scotland* (1901).

WAYNE R. SPEAR

Sense of Divinity

Part of the theological attempt to understand the origin, condition, and value of the human aspiration toward God is the sense of divinity (*sensus divinitatis* or *deitatis*). In Western intellectual history this powerful yearning toward the Eternal is classically described with the concept of *erōs* by Plato in his dialogue *Symposium.*

For Christians, the doctrine of creation* includes the conviction that human beings are made in God's image

(Gen. 1:26) and that evidences of deity are manifest and can be known in the external world and within the created self. This natural theology* can be developed by the unaided human reason and differs from revealed theology based on God's revelation* in Scripture* and made effectual by the inner testimony of the Holy Spirit.* The sin* of humankind against God, as it affects this original and natural condition, is variously evaluated. Roman Catholic* theology, with its higher view of the capacities of human reason and will surviving the fall, distinguishes between natural and supernatural virtues. Likewise, the ability of natural reason* to demonstrate the existence of God is generally more esteemed in Catholicism than in Protestantism. In Reformed thought, the category of natural theology is smaller than in Roman Catholicism because the effect of sin is considered greater. Concerning the fall, Reformed theology teaches "total depravity." This does not mean that every human being is entirely evil but insists that reason and will can not be even relatively and successfully followed apart from God's guiding providence* and the necessity of the forgiveness* revealed in Jesus Christ. While vestiges of the original creation remain, sin results in complete, rather than partial, estrangement from God.

According to John Calvin,* in our estranged condition God is known in a twofold way as both creator and redeemer. The knowledge of God* the creator can be seen in creation and the knowledge of God the redeemer is seen in the face of Jesus Christ.* The sense of divinity, referring to the knowledge of God the creator, is universally and indelibly imprinted within created nature. Thus Paul (Rom. 1:19–24) is interpreted to teach that genuine knowledge of God the creator is objectively possible and valid but cannot produce salvation because human iniquity renders such natural knowledge inadequate and ineffective.

The Christian doctrine of God the creator as it has issued in a modest, but real, natural theology has led some Reformed thinkers to emphasize the doctrine of universal providence as a way of constructing a Calvinistic worldview (or philosophy) relatively independent of faith* on the basis of "sanctified reason." In recent times Karl Barth* leveled a severe criticism of all "natural theology."

E. A. Dowey, Jr., *The Knowledge of God in Calvin's Theology* (1952; repr. 1964); B. B. Warfield, *Calvin and Calvinism* (1931).

CHARLES PARTEE

Separatism *see* Nonconformity

Servetus, Michael (1511–1553)

The brilliant, multitalented Spanish physician who made significant contributions as a geographer and an anatomist and who also was one of the first to understand the circulation of blood. His interest in theology and the publication of two works on the Trinity* led to charges of heresy* by the Roman Catholic Inquisition and the Protestant Consistory of Geneva.*

Servetus, who went by the alias Villeneuve, maintained a secret correspondence with Calvin* and argued that the Holy Spirit* was a "power" of God, not a separate person, and that Jesus Christ* was not truly divine. Servetus also denied infant baptism.*

Though arrested by the Inquisition in Vienna, where he served the local archbishop as a personal physician, Servetus escaped and made his way to Geneva. There he was discovered and tried as a heretic. Calvin supplied evidence against him to both Roman Catholic and Protestant authorities. Servetus was burned at the stake in Geneva (October 27, 1553).

R. H. Bainton, *Hunted Heretic* (1953); E. M. Wilbur, ed. and trans., *Two Treatises on the Trinity* (1932).

NATHAN P. FELDMETH

Shedd, W(illiam) G(reenough) T(hayer) (1820–1894)

Shedd was born in Massachusetts and was educated at the University of Vermont and at Andover Seminary. He taught at the University of Vermont and at Andover Seminary before going to the Brick Presbyterian Church and Union Seminary (N.Y.). He demonstrated that a New England theologian was not necessarily an adherent of New England Theology.* He tended to be living proof that a New Englander could be Edwardsean* and Calvinistic.* He even served in both New England Congregational* and Old School Presbyterian churches.* It was as an orthodox Calvinist that he produced his greatest theological works, *Dogmatic Theology* (1889–94) and *A History of Christian Doctrine* (2 vols.; 1865; 10th ed. 1891).

His *The Doctrine of Endless Punishment* (1886) led Henry Ward Beecher* to call off a scheduled debate on that subject, being half persuaded himself by Shedd. His struggle with his Union Seminary colleague, Charles A. Briggs,* led to Briggs's dismissal and Union's separation from the Presbyterian denomination. Perhaps *Calvinism: Pure and Mixed: A Defense of the Westminster Standards*, written a year before his death, was the cue to his whole life. He said it was written to "promote the reaffirmation of the Westminster Standards pure and simple, precisely as they were adopted by both schools (Old and New School Presbyterian) in the reunion of 1870, instead of the reunion of them as now proposed." Little remembered today, Shedd's *Homiletics and Pastoral Theology* (1867) was in its tenth edition in 1891. His classical *Commentary on Romans* (1879) is still much discussed. He also did valuable contemporary service as a translator of H. E. F. Guericke's *Church History* (2 vols.; ET 1860–70) and commentator on Augustine's* *Confessions.*

JOHN H. GERSTNER

Shepard, Thomas (c. 1605–1649)

Puritan, educated at Cambridge and, after being forced to flee England (1634), the minister of the church at Cambridge, Massachusetts. He became one of New England's leading theologians and a bastion of Puritan* order and orthodoxy. Frequently cited by Jonathan Edwards,* Shepard's *Works* were republished (1853; 3 vols.; repr. 1967) with an account of his life and work. His spiritual autobiography was published as *God's Plot* (ed. Michael McGiffert, 1972).

JOHN E. WILSON

Shorter Catechism *see* Westminster Confession of Faith

Simonton, Ashbel Green (1833–1867)

First Presbyterian missionary to Brazil. Simonton felt called to foreign missionary service while a student at Princeton Seminary and was sent to Brazil (1859) by the Board of Foreign Missions of the Presbyterian Church in the U.S.A. He established a mission station in Rio de Janeiro and itinerated in Rio and São Paulo. He organized the first Presbyterian church (1862), church paper (1864), presbytery (1865), and seminary (1867). Simonton laid the foundation for the rapid growth of the Presbyterian church by emphasizing wide evangelistic itineration, the distribution of Scriptures, and preparation of strong national leadership.

M. RICHARD SHAULL

Sin

The Reformed tradition has always contained a virulent idea of sin. Having entered the human condition by "original sin,"* sin renders human existence both tragic and miserable and takes on a life of its own.

Most often the tradition regards sin as the human transgression of God's covenant* which represents God's active will for every human society and individual. Having sinned once, a person compounds the simple sin by rationalizing the behavior, typically: "I didn't do anything so bad; I'll do better next time." The first part fails to take God's will seriously. The second part fixes attention on doing more exactly what the covenant requires. Both parts gloss over the sin and its effects, justify the action, and set up a trap from which there is no human way out. Henceforth the sinner either sinks into gross and overt sins by ignoring the covenant altogether or becomes more sinful by trying to attain a self-sufficient goodness that comes from merely doing the works of the covenant. Attention to the covenant (and to the *sinner's* accomplishments) replaces attention to the covenant maker, God, and the harder a sinner tries to be good according to the covenant, the more sinful the person becomes.

A person's first sin makes the person a sinner. But the trap puts the sinner into a condition of sin that leads to constant sinning with every thought, word, and deed. The sinner is not all bad, just never all good; and sinners alone or in society cannot discern clearly which part is which, since the good and the bad are intermingled. Every action of the sinner is at least partially skewed, no matter how well intentioned—the doctrine of total depravity.

Such sin perverts the good things God provides, none of which are intrinsically evil. The most notable items perverted are the God-given covenant, the sinner's own thinking-willing-acting capacities, and the larger world of nature. As a perversion of the good, sin lodges in certain focal points of human outlook, behavior, and relationship. Most often mentioned are pride (self-worth turned to ambition, power, fame), desire (become self-serving in sex, money, self-indulgence), truth (turned to ideology or unreality), freedom (independence without relationship or responsibility), obedience (as blind loyalty, disobedience), and faith (as an end in itself, unbelief). The list could be lengthened indefinitely.

Surrounded by sin and sin's effects, the sinner takes sin to be normal and natural for human life. The awareness of sin comes to sinners when God's grace* breaks in, particular grace to particular people. Grace gives people the heart to see their lives as God sees them, loved and upheld by God but at the same time deformed and unworthy of love. Reformed piety* builds on this dynamic of grace and sin, sin and grace *beginning with* the move from grace to sin.

Different views of sin correspond with views of the atonement.* For the substitutionary atonement, wherein Jesus Christ on the cross takes upon himself the *punishment* due humans for their sins (forgives the debt, suffers the loss, pays the price), sin is disobedience, a moral misdeed, a violation of the covenant or some relational code. For the classical theory of atonement, wherein Jesus Christ *defeats death* by dying on the cross, occupying the space of death and transforming death into the gateway to life, sin in its extreme form is death* ("the last enemy to be defeated"; 1 Cor. 15:26; cf. 15:56; Heb. 2:14–15), both physical and spiritual. For the moral influence theory of atonement, wherein Jesus Christ taught *how to live a transformed life before God* and exemplified that life in his own full humanity, sin is an insufficient consciousness of God reflected in imperfect understanding, ignorance, bad attitudes, psychological maladjustments, and/or the breakdown of basic relationships.

The three views of sin suggest different levels of scope and concern. As imperfect God-consciousness, sin pertains to the inner, relational life of the human both individually and collectively. As moral misdeed, sin entails the behavior of the whole person outwardly and socially as well as inwardly and individually. As victory over death, sin involves the continuing problem and impact of evil, rooted in nature as well as in human life.

Calvin* and Barth* successfully blended all three views of sin and atonement. Other Reformed Christians, however, have compartmentalized sin in one view held singly, each one competing with the other two. In the late twentieth century, sin is regarded variously as individuals' private moral misdeeds (emphasis on substitutionary atonement; seventeenth to twentieth century), the realm of the inner person and one's damaged relationships (emphasis on moral influence atonement, nineteenth to twentieth centuries), and the sins of particular social contexts (the social dimension of the two previous items, notably in the twentieth century: the poor in relation to the rich, mixed races, women and men, the use and abuse of personal, corporate, and military power).

Additional questions deserve to be raised. In an era of advanced technology, can any human technological accomplishment be morally neutral without restructuring further the cycles of natural and human life? Have the structures and inequities of human society become so large and self-serving that they invariably oppress people and particular groups of people? Has the scale of evil in the twentieth century—world wars, the Holocaust, genocide, the threat of nuclear annihilation, apartheid,* unrelieved famines, the disruption of the environment, epidemics of substance abuse and AIDS—outstripped views of sin currently held singly? How have the varieties of people, ideologies, and ways of living complicated present attempts to identify and address what is sinful in particular situations and contexts?

Barth, *CD* III/3, 50; IV/1, 60; IV/2, 65; IV/3, 70; G. C. Berkouwer, *Sin* (1971); Calvin, *Inst.* 1.1–2; bk. 2; Heppe, *RD*, 301–70; Schleiermacher, *CF*.

MERWYN S. JOHNSON

Slavery

A state in which humans are held in involuntary servitude. Slavery has existed as a part of economic and social life throughout most recorded history. Slaves have been acquired by capture, purchase, indebtedness, punishment, inheritance, and birth. In Christian thought, slavery is used as a metaphor for the spiritual bondage of sin;* and deliverance from slavery, as a paradigm for salvation* (John 8:34; Rom. 6:6, 16–22; 7:14, 25).

In the ancient Near East, slavery was an accepted way of life. Because of the Mosaic legislation, a milder and more humane form of slavery existed among the Hebrews (Ex. 20:2; 21:20; 23:12; Lev. 25:39; Deut. 23:15). The NT did not attack slavery directly but recognized that God has special concern for the poor and oppressed, that master and slave were one in Christ, and that both were accountable to God (1 Cor. 12:13; Gal. 3:28; Eph. 6:5–9; Col. 3:11, 22–24; Paul's letter to Philemon urges a Christian master to treat his runaway slave as a brother).

The influence of Christianity has been to ameliorate and eventually suppress slavery. In medieval Europe, slavery was largely transformed into feudal serfdom, but the process was imperfect and gradual, for serfdom and slavery existed side by side for centuries. In England and northern Europe, slavery disappeared in and after the Renaissance. The slave trade never completely ceased. Commercial interests and strife between Christians and Muslims perpetuated it in the eastern Mediterranean. It was revived on a large scale with the discovery and colonization of the Americas. Native Americans and Africans were enslaved in Latin America, despite protests of some missionaries, particularly Dominicans, against their cruel treatment. The first African slaves in North America were sold into the English colony of Virginia (1619).

The Enlightenment and evangelical religion were two forces opposed to slavery. Quakers, Moravians, and Methodists were among the first voices of opposition. Efforts by leaders such as Thomas Clarkson, Granville Sharp, and William Wilberforce led to the prohibition of slave trade in Great Britain (1807) and the British Empire (1827). Then slavery was abolished (1833).

The importation of slaves ended in the United States (1808). Quakers, revivalists, and abolition societies opposed the institution. The Presbyterian General Assembly (1818) condemned slavery, insisting that Christians should work for its extinction. As cotton became more profitable to the South, ministers and statesmen increasingly defended the slave labor used to produce it. Notable attempts to evangelize slaves were carried out by the Methodist William Capers and the Presbyterian Charles Colcock Jones. Methodist and Baptist denominations divided over slavery (1845), as did New School Presbyterians (1857). The Old School Presbyterian General Assembly (1845) declared that slaveholding was no bar to church membership. Slavery was an indirect cause of the Civil War which divided the nation and Old School Presbyterians (1861). The Emancipation Proclamation was issued by Abraham Lincoln as a war measure (1863). After the war, the thirteenth amendment to the Constitution (1865) brought American slavery to an end. Slavery is said to exist in some parts of the world today and has been addressed by the United Nations.

G. H. Barnes, *The Antislavery Impulse, 1830–1844* (1933); J. K. Ingram, *A History of Slavery and Serfdom* (1895); W. S. Jenkins, *Pro-Slavery Thought in the Old South* (1935); I. S. Kull, "Presbyterian Attitudes Toward Slavery," *CH* 7 (1938): 101–14; R. Miller and J. Smith, eds., *Dictionary of Afro-American Slavery* (1988); A. E. Murray, *Presbyterians and the Ne-*

gro—A History (1966); K. M. Stampp, *The Peculiar Institution: Slavery in the Ante-Bellum South* (1956); C. D. Weatherford, *American Churches and the Negro* (1957).

ALBERT H. FREUNDT, JR.

Slessor, Mary Mitchell (1848–1915)

Raised in Dundee, Scotland, Mary worked as a weaver and early showed her lifelong charismatic ability to attract unbelievers. She was sent by the United Presbyterian Church to work at Calabar, Nigeria (1876). After her first tour, when her work was entirely conventional, she spent the rest of her life as a pioneer away from other missionaries. She gathered orphans around her who became her family as she went bareheaded and barefoot and lived in African-style houses at an African standard of living.

W. P. Livingston, *Mary Slessor of Calabar* (1916).

ANDREW C. ROSS

Smith, Henry Boynton (1815–1877)

Presbyterian theologian who studied at Andover and Bangor seminaries and in Halle and Berlin (1837–40). Smith taught Hebrew at Andover while a Congregational pastor (1842–46). He became professor of philosophy at Amherst College (1847) and professor of church history at Union Seminary (N.Y.; 1850), joining the New School Presbyterian Church.

Smith was recognized as his denomination's leading theologian and transferred to the chair of systematic theology (1855). His translations of German works introduced Americans to European evangelical scholarship. Smith mediated between New England and German theology and the extremes of New and Old School Presbyterian positions. He sought to make Christ the central point of all important doctrine and truth, exerting a conservative influence in New School Presbyterianism. He was moderator of the New School Assembly (1863) and the most powerful influence in the reunion of American Presbyterianism (1869), maintaining that the Westminster Confession* could be accepted in its integrity. Smith jointly edited the *Presbyterian Quarterly and Princeton Review* and was first chairman of the American executive committee of the Evangelical Alliance. His publications include *History of the Church of Christ in Chronological Tables* (1859); and, posthumously: *Faith and Philosophy* (1877); *Lectures on Apologetics* (1882); *Introduction to Christian Theology* (1883); and *System of Christian Theology* (1884).

G. M. Marsden, *The Evangelical Mind and the New School Presbyterian Experience* (1970); R. A. Muller, "Henry Boynton Smith: Christocentric Theologian," *JPH* 61 (1983): 429–44; Mrs. H. B. Smith, *Henry Boynton Smith: His Life and Work* (1880); L. F. Stearns, *Henry Boynton Smith* (1892).

ALBERT H. FREUNDT, JR.

Smith, Henry Preserved (1847–1927)

Presbyterian minister and respected biblical scholar, Smith taught OT at Lane Seminary (Cincinnati; 1877–93). He studied in Germany and embraced emerging critical theories. Smith's defense of Charles A. Briggs* led to his own heresy trial by the Presbytery of Cincinnati (1892) in which he was charged with denying the verbal inspiration and infallibility of Scripture.* He was found guilty and was suspended from the ministry. He resigned his position at Lane. The General Assembly (1894) sustained the presbytery's decision. Smith became chief librarian at Union Seminary (N.Y.; 1913–25) and professor of Hebrew (from 1917).

RICK NUTT

Smith, William Robertson (1846–1894)

Pioneering Scottish biblical critic. Smith was a genius whose intellectual interest and erudition were evident as a young scholar. From Aberdeen he went to New College,* Edinburgh, for theology and then to select German universities. He taught OT at the Free Church College, Aberdeen, but soon had trouble with some of the basics of the theology of the first generation of Free Kirk scholars and people. He rejected the propositional component in revelation,* the morality of substitution, and a faith he regarded as too cerebral and not sufficiently relational. His faith, which might have been called liberal evangelicalism, had implications for his major field of biblical studies as well.

Smith's views on Scripture appeared in an *Encyclopaedia Britannica* (1875) article on the Bible. He affirmed that the Mosaic legislation was promulgated, if not composed, during the exile, eliminated much of the prophetic element in the prophets, and denied the authorship of the Gospels to the evangelists whose names they bore. The ideas were not new, but were for many in Scotland, and were presented with brilliance and assurance. A five-year ecclesiastical trial began which ended in his removal from his chair (1881), from which he accepted an appointment to Cambridge.

Smith's books were models of scholarship, combining science, history, linguistics, and biblical studies. Though he was dismissed from a Free Church appointment, his views were soon held by many of the educated members of his own church and beyond.

T. O. Beidelmann, *W. Robertson Smith and the Sociological Study of Religion* (1974); J. S. Black and C. Chrystal, *The Life of William Robertson Smith* (1912); N. M. de S. Cameron, *Biblical Higher Criticism and the Defence of Infallibilism in 19th Century Britain* (1987); A. C. Cheyne, *The Transforming of the Kirk* (1983); R. A. Riesen, *Criticism and Faith in Late Victorian Scotland* (1985).

IAN S. RENNIE

Social Gospel

Though Presbyterians in Scotland, Canada, and the United States had interest in "the social gospel," the social gospel movement was primarily an American phenomenon (1870–1913). The term was coined during the 1870s as a few clergy began to respond to social ills related to industrialization, urbanization, and immigration. Social gospel leaders expressed concerns for labor problems, "workers," and the cities through sermons, lectures, books, and articles. Along with "progressives" and "muckrakers," they alerted the public to the excesses of laissez-faire capitalism.

Social gospel leaders were also concerned about political unrest and the possibility of class warfare. Theirs was a world where church members were unsettled by social and intellectual change, especially by talk of Darwinism and higher biblical criticism.

Strictly speaking, there was no social gospel among Presbyterians in America.* Social gospel leaders included two Baptists, Walter Rauschenbusch and William Newton Clarke, and two Congregationalists,* Washington Gladden* and Josiah Strong. Though Baptists and Congregationalists can be claimed as belonging to the Reformed family, it was differences in theology and polity* between Presbyterians, and Baptists and Congregationalists, that explain why there was no Presbyterian social gospel movement.

The Reformed is a tradition "especially of the word, elevating preaching, teaching (doctrine), and ethical practice to the forefront of its concerns. Thus confessional documents have always had a prominent place in its history, especially in the education and ordination* of ministers" (Purdy, p. 13). Social gospel leaders considered confessional statements and Calvinist theology a hindrance to social and moral progress. They were caught up in a "new" theology, one that adjusted the scorned "old" Calvinist theology to "present-day living." They preached a gospel calculated to inspire believers to emulate the life and character of Jesus so "the church" would lend moral force to the social progress they expected to usher in the kingdom of God* in America.

At a time when social gospel leaders were revising theology and their use of the Bible, Presbyterians reacted to the threat of higher biblical criticism with the heresy trial of David Swing, a Chicago pastor who was both a "modernist" and an "evangelical" (1874). Though Swing won the case, the point was clear: Presbyterians would continue to subscribe to the Westminster Standards.* This was the same decade in which the Baptist Clarke would decide that the ethical propositions of the NT "sweep away" the "ancient truth" of the OT.

Church historians usually relate Presbyterian failure to participate in the social gospel movement to class commitments. "The reasons for the relative conservatism of this denomination are obvious. Its members, especially the influential city elements, were traditionally of the upper social and economic groups. Through the important part played by elders* in Presbyterian church government, wealthy laymen had an especially influential role" (May, p. 193). Reformed polity's capacity to enforce doctrinal conformity also helps account for the extent to which the Princeton Theology*—which served the interests of the status quo—was dominant.

Presbyterians were not unaware of the plight of the lower class and labor problems. But the denomination took no formal action until the 1910 General Assembly* approved Thirteen Social Principles. Till then, most references to social problems were appeals to evangelism* to overcome threats of "Socialist anarchy." The Social Principles called for an end to child labor, a minimum wage, better working conditions, shorter working day, and the right to organize unions. This agenda was the work of "social gospel" leaders from other denominations.

Presbyterians established a Department of Church and Labor in the Board of Home Missions (1903). Approval of the Social Principles and the Labor Department were primarily the work of one man, Charles Stelzle. An ordained clergyman, Stelzle was the son of working class immigrants. When the controversial Labor Department he headed was discontinued (1913), he went into social work.

Stelzle belonged to a small minority of Presbyterians who wanted to "socialize" church teachings. Though Reformed piety* includes a sense of responsibility for the public good, Presbyterians in the United States have rarely expressed concern about economic issues. Members are encouraged to be informed citizens who vote. Education is the usual response to social and moral issues. The Presbyterian confessional stance did protect Reformed theology* from a naive social idealism that led to the demise of the social gospel (1913). But it also led to callous indifference to social injustice.

H. F. May, *Protestant Churches and Industrial America* (1949); J. C. Purdy, ed., *Always Being Reformed* (1985).

JANET F. FISHBURN

Socinianism

The religious movement named for Faustus Socinus (1539–1604). Socinus attempted to unify the various factions of Unitarianism. The chief symbol of the Socinians, the Racovian Catechism, was composed immediately after his death. The movement proceeded through Poland, Germany, the Netherlands, and Transylvania. It was frequently confronted with persecution.

Socinianism's unique teachings include the view that the doctrine of the Trinity was neither presented in nor deducible from Scripture. Socinians said the Holy Spirit is nowhere called God in Scripture. The preexistence of Christ was denied and the view that while Christ was on earth the divine and human natures could not be fully united; for certainly Christ could not have then died on the cross. Socinians generally held that a plurality of persons in one divine essence was not possible. Despite the ambiguity in Socinus's own teaching, Socinianism held to the total immersion of the adult believer and that Christians were not to use the sword.

J. H. S. Kent, "The Socinian Tradition," *Theology* (1975): 131–41; G. H. Williams, *The Radical Reformation* (1962).

RICHARD C. GAMBLE

Solemn League and Covenant

Agreement setting forth terms on which Scotland aided the Parliamentary forces in the English Civil War* (1643). It bound Scotland, England, and Ireland to the "preservation" of the reformed religion in Scotland (where a successful revolt against Charles I had occurred in 1638), and the "reformation" in the churches of England and Ireland of doctrine,* liturgy, government, and discipline,* according to the Word of God* and the example of the best reformed churches. As a political treaty, it pledged to preserve the rights and privileges of the Parliaments and the king's authority (provided he would preserve and defend the true religion). It voiced the Puritan* determination to "extirpate" popery and prelacy in Britain.

To implement the Covenant's pledge for religious uniformity, Scottish Commissioners were sent to participate in the deliberations of the Westminster Assembly,* already meeting in London. Their influence was such that the WCF* and the Shorter Catechism gained wide and lasting acceptance in Scotland.

Charles I and Oliver Cromwell* rejected the Solemn League. Charles II swore allegiance to it as a condition of his abortive coronation (1651). After the Restoration (1660), he renounced the Covenant and fiercely persecuted those faithful to it.

In later centuries, dissenting churches known as the Covenanters* and the Seceders were distinguished by making adherence to the Solemn League and Covenant, with the National Covenant (1638), conditions of membership.

R. S. Paul, *The Assembly of the Lord* (1985); D. Stevenson, *The Scottish Revolution* (1973).

WAYNE R. SPEAR

Soteriology *see* Salvation

South Africa

The creation of Cape Town by the Dutch East India Company (1652) was also the beginning of the Nederduitse Gereformeerde Kerk (NGK) in southern Africa. Under Company rules there was little formal missionary activity, but Christianity grew among slaves and Khoi (Hottentot) servants and the growing number of mixed-race families. In the nineteenth century these all merged to form the Afrikaans-speaking so-called Cape Coloured People.

After a brief occupation (1795–1803), the Cape became a British colony (1806), but the NGK continued to enjoy what amounted to establishment status. The Great Trek of Afrikaners from the Cape which led eventually to the creation of Natal, the Orange Free State, and Transvaal also led to two new Reformed churches: the Nederduitse Hervormde Kerk (NHK; 1856), the state church of the Transvaal when it was an independent republic but remains in existence today; and the Gereformeerde Kerk (1859; Doppers), a very conservative church with close relations to the Christian Reformed Chruch. In the Transvaal, the Free State, and Natal, as well as in Namibia later, churches in full communion with the NGK came into being. Their Synods remained autonomous until union with the Cape Synod in the General Synod (1963).

Initially the people who were later called "Coloureds" worshiped together with whites in the NGK. But because of a Synod decision (1859), separate congregations were formed which became the autonomous "NG Sendingkerk" (1915). The various black congregations that grew up throughout South Africa as a result of the missionary work inspired by Andrew Murray, Jr.,* became in the mid-twentieth century the "NGK in Afrika," and a separate Indian Reformed Church followed. Were all these churches one (they share the same confession of faith), they would be by far the largest denomination in Africa.

The London Missionary Society* began work in South Africa led by Johannes van der Kemp (1799). Its sister society, the American Board,* encouraged by John Philip arrived in 1835. The two Congregational Churches emerging from these mission works joined to form the United Congregational Church of Southern Africa (1963). The Glasgow Missionary Society* entered South Africa (1821), and its work, later supervised by the Free, then the United Free, then Church of Scotland, led to the creation of an African Church (formerly the Bantu Presbyterian Church), now the Reformed Presbyterian Church. Lovedale, central to the educational and spiritual development of nineteenth- and early twentieth-century Africans, is arguably this movement's greatest contribution to South Africa. A number of white congregations with some mission congregations formed the predominantly white Presbyterian Church of Southern Africa (1897). Very active missionary action has since made this church fully multiracial.

The last important church in the Reformed tradition grew out of the Mission Romande (1869). This church, originally called the Tsonga Presbyterian Church, has become the Evangelical Presbyterian Church. Like the Reformed Presbyterian Church, it is essentially an African church aided by a few expatriates and some white South Africans. However, all "black" Reformed and Presbyterian churches have encouraged white membership since the early 1970s in marked contrast with the attitude toward blacks by the NGK and NHK.

In the 1980s there have been powerful moves to create two major church unions, one involving all NGK churches and the other the Congregationalists and Presbyterians.

ANDREW C. ROSS

Speer, Robert Elliott (1867–1947)

Ecumenical pioneer and author. Born in Huntingdon, Pennsylvania, Speer attended Princeton University, where he became active in the Student Volunteer Movement and Dwight L. Moody's Northfield student conferences. He enrolled in Princeton Seminary (1890) but left (1891) to become Secretary of the Board of Foreign Missions of the Presbyterian Church in the U.S.A., where he remained for the next forty-six years.

As Secretary, Speer worked tirelessly in the cause of world evangelism. He greatly increased Presbyterian funding and mission recruitment, working closely with John R. Mott in the international movement. He became president of several missionary and ecumenical organizations and participated in the international conferences in Edinburgh, Geneva, Jerusalem, and Madras. Known for his powerful speeches, Speer carried on a voluminous correspondence, wrote numerous materials on foreign missions, and traveled to Presbyterian mission fields in Asia and South America.

To Speer, the missionary task was to "present Christ to the world." In "What Constitutes a Missionary Call," Speer gave his rationale for foreign missions. He was also associated with the controversial study *Re-thinking Missions* (1932), which argued that the task of foreign missions is to promote dialogue with other religions in a common quest for truth. Yet Speer rejected this syncretistic study, expounding his own beliefs in an extensive theological treatise, *The Finality of Jesus Christ* (1933).

W. R. Wheeler, *A Man Sent from God* (1956).

ROBERT BENEDETTO

Spirituality *see* Piety

Spring Resolutions

Following the secession of several southern states and the bombardment of Fort Sumter, two resolutions were introduced at the Philadelphia General Assembly (May 1861) of the Presbyterian Church in the U.S.A. (Old School) by Gardiner Spring of New York City. These sought to place the church under obligation to "promote and perpetuate . . . the integrity of these United States." The northern-dominated Assembly passed the resolutions that affirmed a commitment of loyalty to the United States, its federal government, and the Constitution. The one-sided vote culminated the process of North/South alienation which led to the formation of a separate Presbyterian Church in the Confederate States of America later that year.

E. T. Thompson, *Presbyterians in the South*, 3 vols. (1963–74), 1:551–71.

PHILIP W. BUTIN

Spurgeon, Charles Haddon (1834–1892)

English Baptist pastor and preacher. Born in Kelvedon, Essex, in a line of Congregationalist* ministers, Spurgeon was educated in a series of nonconformist schools. He was called to a Baptist church in Waterbeach (1851), a year after his conversion in a Primitive Methodist chapel and entrance into a Baptist congregation. Called to the New Park Street Baptist Church, London (1854), Spurgeon remained with this congregation until death, moving with them to the new, larger Metropolitan Tabernacle (1861). His widespread ministry included guest preaching, writing, and directing the numerous societies and missions he started (including a Pastors' College).

A staunch proponent of Calvinism* and lifelong student of the Puritans,* Spurgeon attempted to perpetuate that legacy in a decidedly non-Puritan age. Several major controversies marked his ministry. His early years at Park Street saw opposition from hyper-Calvinists* for his fervent evangelistic appeals but also from many others for his advocacy of Calvinistic views of election, sin,* and grace.* He challenged the Anglicans with teaching baptismal regeneration* and evangelicals with inconsistency in continuing their membership in the Anglican Church (1864). He ultimately withdrew from the Evangelical Alliance and left the Baptist Union (1887), citing growing influence of the "New Theology." The ensuing "Downgrade Controversy" occupied much of his remaining energies.

Autobiography, rev. ed.: *Spurgeon: The Early Years* (1962); and *Full Harvest* (1973); I. H. Murray, *The Forgotten Spurgeon* (1973).

STEPHEN R. SPENCER

Stewardship

The biblical term "steward" (Gr. *oikonomos*) describes the office of one who is entrusted with the properties of another. While there are twenty-six direct references to stewards and stewardship in Scripture, the concept was insufficiently developed in historical theology. In North America and other settings where the church could no longer count on public (state) support, stewardship practice as tithing or the donation of "time, talents, and treasures" to the church became an important aspect of ecclesiastical life. The deeper application of the biblical term as a symbolic expression for the whole Christian (and human) life has, however, only begun to inform theological discourse profoundly in our own time.

Biblical background. The OT usage confines itself to the technical meaning of the term but in doing so establishes the two dialectically related ideas that inform the more symbolic use of stewardship—accountability and responsibility. On the one hand, the steward is a servant (often a slave!) and strictly accountable to his master; on the other, he is given an exceptional range of freedom as one bearing high responsibility. Being accountable, he may be judged severely for the misuse of the trust placed in him (Isa. 22:15–16); yet this presupposes the honor of the office (e.g., Gen. 43; 44).

Some NT references are simple allusions to the office (Matt. 20:8; Luke 8:3; John 2:8); in others, a more explicitly theological connotation is present. Luke 12:42 links stewardship with "watchfulness" as a characteristic mark of Christ's true disciples. In 1 Cor. 4:1–2, Paul applies the concept of the steward explicitly to himself and implicitly to the church at large: "Think of us in this way, as servants of Christ and stewards of God's mysteries."

History. Despite its relative biblical prominence, stewardship did not achieve its potential for theological and anthropological significance in historical doctrine. Two factors contributed to its underdevelopment: (1) the spiritualization of Christian doctrine under the impact of Hellenistic thought and (2) the political establishment of the Christian religion from the fourth century onward. While there are of course exegetical references to the term in all periods, its capacity to transmit something of the worldly significance of Christian discipleship and function critically with respect to other "images of the human" was not explored. Though the Reformers advanced cognate ideas, only John Wycliffe made fairly extensive use of the steward metaphor as such.

With the loss of legal "establishment" in New World and other situations, Protestant churches found in stewardship a significant biblical basis for responsible financial and other support of the church's life and mission. This has kept the term alive, particularly in the North American context. At the same time, it has reduced its biblical profundity by applying it too exclusively to church giving.

Present status. Stimulated in part by secular appropriation of the metaphor, contemporary theology has begun to explore the potentiality of stewardship as a symbol of human vocation* and meaning. The three "great instabilities" of the age (injustice, war, and environmental deterioration) have inspired many to see in the ancient biblical concept an alternative on the one hand to human *mastery* (we are *accountable!*) and on the other to human *passivity* (we are *responsible!*). The symbol is used extensively in the Confession of Faith of the Reformed Church of Cuba and in numerous recent documents of Presbyterian and other Protestant denominations in the United States, Canada, and Europe. It was an integral component of the many documents that emerged from the WCC's* "Justice, Peace, and the Integrity of Creation" process.

D. J. Hall, *The Steward: A Biblical Symbol Come of Age* (1990); and *Imagining God: Dominion as Stewardship* (1986); T. S. Horvath, *Focus on Our Identity as Stewards* (1987); T. A. Kantonen, *A Theology for Christian Stewardship* (1956); J. van Klinken, *Diakonia: Mutual Helping with Justice and Compassion* (1989).

DOUGLAS JOHN HALL

Stewart, James Stuart (1896–1990)

A leading Church of Scotland scholar-preacher and Moderator of the General Assembly.* Stewart graduated from St. Andrews and New College,* Edinburgh. After service in World War I, he studied at the University of Bonn. He pastored churches in Aberdeen and Edinburgh for twenty-two years, establishing a reputation for outstanding preaching. He published several sermon volumes, a book on preaching (*Heralds of God* [1945]) and Pauline theology (*A Man in Christ* [1935]) before being appointed professor of NT (1946–66) at New College. Combining the preacher's zeal with sound scholarship and evangelical convictions, Stewart was made chaplain to the queen of Scotland (1952) and received the D.D. from St. Andrews (1945).

DONALD A. HAGNER

Strong, Augustus Hopkins (1836–1921)

A Baptist leader, Strong was also that tradition's most celebrated American theologian. He was born in Rochester, New York, and graduated from Rochester Seminary (1859). He later became president of the seminary (1872–1912). Strong's theological work is still being republished and widely read.

Though generally Calvinist,* Strong broke with the senior and the junior Edwards,* Archibald Alexander,* and Charles Hodge* on the necessity of volitions, while insisting on their certainty and on absolute divine foreknowledge.*

Never identifying himself with either the Edwardsean Calvinism* of Edwards senior mediated through Joseph Bellamy* and Samuel Hopkins* to Horace Bushnell,* or "Old Calvinism" from Charles Hodge to W. G. T. Shedd,* Strong surely was a mighty advocate of the Reformed faith. Yet he cited Calvin relatively little in his magnum opus, *Systematic Theology* (1886; 8th rev. ed., 3 vols., 1907–9), differed on the inerrant inspiration of Scripture* defended by his contemporary, B. B. Warfield,* and as a Baptist was sympathetic with the Congregationalism* of New England Theology* but against its infant baptism* and covenant* theology. Notably conservative in his general Calvinistic theology, he nevertheless staunchly defended his most famous student, Walter Rauschenbusch. Strong wrote what may be the most erudite Reformed systematic theology ever written enriched greatly by his love for, acquaintance with, and participation in contemporary poetry, *The Great Poets and Their Theology* (1897). His deep influence on Carl Henry, one of the leading Baptist advocates of the Reformed faith today, is quite evident.

G. Wacker, *Augustus H. Strong* (1985).

JOHN H. GERSTNER

Stuart, Moses (1780–1852)

One of the foremost American biblical scholars of his era, Stuart probably did more than any other person to introduce critical methods among orthodox Protestants. After graduating from Yale (1797), he taught school and read law but soon returned to Yale as a tutor. There he was converted in the revivals sweeping the college and read divinity with President Timothy Dwight.* He assumed the pastorate of New Haven's (Congregational) Center Church (1806). Stuart was inaugurated professor of sacred literature at Andover Seminary (1810), which had recently been created by orthodox Congregationalists* to combat the rise of Unitarianism* in New England.

Though limited in his knowledge of ancient languages at the time of his appointment, Stuart taught himself Hebrew and cognate Semitic languages. He mastered German by reading Johann Gottfried Eichhorn's *Introduction to the Old Testament* (1780–83) which opened modern critical scholarship to him. A prodigious worker, Stuart wrote or translated Hebrew and Greek grammars and authored six commentaries as well as numerous pamphlets and articles. His major work was *A Critical History and Defence of the Old Testament Canon* (1845). Stuart argued that the Bible ought to be interpreted as any other book, that is, according to historical-grammatical principles. He believed this approach would yield results consistent with orthodox faith; and despite his love of the method of the new biblical scholarship, he did not adopt its more radical conclusions. Stuart's work embodied the moderate Calvinism* of Andover.

J. W. Brown, *The Rise of Biblical Criticism in America* (1969); J. H. Giltner, *Moses Stuart* (1988).

JAMES H. MOORHEAD

Superintendents

Scotland's* First Book of Discipline* (1560), composed by Knox and five other reformers, provided for ten or twelve superintendents, one over each province into which the Kirk was to be divided, who would travel out from the major towns and plant congregations, erect churches, provide for instruction, and even refer heinous sinners to superintendents courts (Provisional Synods) or the General Assembly* for discipline. The Second Book of Discipline (1578) abolished the office, whose duties were taken over by presbyteries. An old argument persists as to whether superintendents were a continuing office, eventually to be Reformed bishops, supervised by General Assembly.

I. B. Cowan, *The Scottish Reformation* (1982); G. Donaldson, *The Scottish Reformation* (1960); J. Kirk, *The Second Book of Discipline* (1980); D. G. Mullan, *Episcopacy in Scotland* (1986).

W. FRED GRAHAM

Supralapsarianism

One of the two main positions on election after the death of John Calvin.* In dispute was the place of the fall in God's* electing purposes. As the term implies (*supra*, "above" or "before," and *lapsus*, "fall"), supralapsarianism affirmed that God decreed both election and reprobation from all eternity without respect to the merits or demerits of persons. It differed from infralapsarianism* (*infra*, "below" or "after," and *lapsus*, "fall"), which held that in predestination* God had in view sinful humanity,* of whom God elected some and passed by others. Expressed differently, the object of predestination in supralapsarianism was the human race as not yet created and not yet fallen (*homo creabilis et labilis*) and in infralapsarianism, the human race as already created and fallen (*creatus et lapsus*). For infralapsarianism, the temporal sequence of creation, fall, and salvation* was also the logical order, while for supralapsarianism, the logical and temporal orders of God's purpose were reversed.

The controversy was subtle yet theologically significant, fiercely debated but not fundamentally divisive. While infralapsarianism became the dominant confessional position of Reformed churches, theologians such as Theodore Beza,* Franciscus Gomarus,* Franz Burmann, and William Twisse subscribed to supralapsarianism. At the Synod of Dort,* infralapsarians were in the majority, and while the Canons do not exclude supralapsarianism, the bias is in favor of infralapsarianism. The same is true of the WCF.*

Though both positions were ultimately unsatisfactory—because the connection between election and the fall is inscrutable—supralapsarianism was more consistent, coherent, and comprehensive in scope. It viewed salvation* as God's primary purpose, while infralapsarianism was inclined to see salvation as God's reaction to sin,* that is, as a kind of emergency measure or redemptive repair work—"Plan B" after "Plan A" had failed. On the other hand, supralapsarianism tended to rationalize sin and evil by viewing them as necessary elements in God's plan, and it was accordingly accused of making God the author of sin. In the eyes of Roman Catholics, Lutherans, and even some Reformed theologians, the God of supralapsarianism took on the appearance of a demon who arbitrarily saved some and damned others, a God who created in order to condemn. By making both election and reprobation unconditional, it was less ethically satisfactory than infralapsarianism, which represented election as unconditional but regarded reprobation as conditional upon human sinfulness.

Attempts to reconcile supralapsarianism and infralapsarianism have not been successful. Karl Barth* sought to overcome their respective difficulties by arguing that supralapsarianism is relatively more nearly correct. If supralapsarianism is liberated from the dangerous presuppositions of an absolute decree and the symmetry of election and reprobation, and the doctrine of election is interpreted christologically, with Jesus Christ as the true object of predestination, then, according to Barth, supralapsarianism is preferable. So understood, election is solely and totally grace, "the sum of the gospel." Yet Barth's resolution of the problem is not without its own difficulties, especially with respect to reprobation and the ultimate force of the human creature's "no" to God. It appears that on the question of the place of the fall in the electing purposes of God a reverent agnosticism is advisable.

Barth, *CD* II/2, 127ff.; G. C. Berkouwer, *Divine Election* (1960); P. K. Jewett, *Election and Predestination* (1986).

WILLIAM KLEMPA

Synod *see* **Polity**

Taylor, Nathaniel William (1786–1858)

Connecticut Congregational preacher and theologian whose attenuated revivalist Calvinism,* "New Haven Theology,"* or Taylorism, contributed to American theological liberalism and evangelicalism.

After studying under Yale College's Timothy Dwight,* Taylor became pastor of New Haven's First (Center) Church (1812–22; when several revivals occurred) and then was Dwight Professor of Didactic Theology at Yale College (1822–57). He and his friend Lyman Beecher* successively attacked the current antirevivalist forces, especially Episcopalians, Unitarians, and conservative Calvinists. The last group, including Congregationalists* and Old School Presbyterians,* accused Taylor of Pelagianism, but his views spread in the Presbyterian Church and helped precipitate the Old School-New School schism (1837). He wrote no major work; some of his sermons, lectures, and essays were collectively published posthumously.

Whether Taylor was more Old Calvinist or more Edwardsean is still disputed. He used the Scottish common sense philosophy* to defend Calvinist theology's morality against Unitarian criticisms and develop a Calvinism consonant with revivalism.* He thereby abandoned the traditional doctrines of original sin* and regeneration,* teaching that humans are not born sinful but inevitably become sinners at their first moral act, that regeneration is their own act (albeit God's Spirit is also involved), and that their self-determining will has "power to the contrary" although their acts are "certain."

S. Mead, *Nathaniel William Taylor* (1942); E. Pope, *New England Calvinism and the Disruption of the Presbyterian Church* (1962; repr. 1987); R. C. Whittemore, *The Transformation of the New England Theology* (1987).

EARL WM. KENNEDY

Teellinck, Willem (1579–1629)

The earliest representative of the second reformation in England and Pietism in the Netherlands. Teellinck was educated in law at St. Andrews and Poitiers. His life abruptly changed after a visit to England, where he came in contact with Puritan* Calvinists influenced by William Whitaker, William Perkins,* and William Ames.* Their "practical godliness" impressed Teellinck. After studying theology at Leiden, he ministered to Reformed churches in Heemstede and

Bruges (1606) and Middelburg (1613). His further reformation was distinct from later Pietism, since it stood on Reformation foundations and addressed itself not only to individual but also to church* and public life. Teellinck's later works tend toward a mysticism similar to classic Christian mystics such as Bernard of Clairvaux and Jan van Ruysbroeck, emphasizing a spiritual union of believers with Christ.

HENRY ZWAANSTRA

Tennent, Gilbert (1703–1764)

Premier Presbyterian revivalist of the First Great Awakening,* Tennent preached a three-step conversion* adapted from the Dutch Reformed pietist Theodore Frelinghuysen.* Conversion involved "law work" or conviction of personal sin* through confrontation with the righteousness that biblical law defined, rebirth or the heart's reception of grace,* and the sincere practice of piety.* Speaking "in season" to where individuals lay on conversion's path, Tennent offered the biblical law's "terrors" to the self-righteous for repentance and Christian grace's "balm" to those already convicted for healing sin's wound. Sinners' self-righteousness represented the greatest obstacle to salvation,* but the major external barrier was unconverted clergy who knowing nothing of "new birth" preached free will and universal redemption.

M. J Coalter, Jr., *Gilbert Tennent, Son of Thunder* (1986).

MILTON J COALTER, JR.

Tennent, William, Sr. (1673–1746)

A Scotsman and ordained presbyter in the Church of Ireland for thirteen years before renouncing the Anglican system and joining Philadelphia Presbytery, Tennent established an informal seminary, the "Log College," in Neshaminy, Pennsylvania. Eighteen of his nineteen students became Presbyterian revivalists during the First Great Awakening.* These "New Light" ministers absorbed Tennent's stress on the individual heart's state over external observance of liturgical rites or mere rational assent to theological doctrines and his emphasis on Christians' "growth in grace" leading ultimately to a sincere practice of piety.*

M. J Coalter, Jr., *Gilbert Tennent, Son of Thunder* (1986); T. C. Pears, Jr., ed., *Documentary History of William Tennent and the Log College* (1940).

MILTON J COALTER, JR.

Tetrapolitan Confession

The oldest confession of faith by the Reformed church in Germany was written (1530), chiefly by Martin Bucer,* as a theological exposition of the views of four imperial cities: Strassburg, Constance, Memmingen, and Lindau.

The nascent Reformed church had hoped to effect a union with Lutherans and make common cause in opposition to Roman Catholicism.* To this end, Bucer and Zwingli* met with Luther* and Melanchthon at the Marburg Colloquy (1529). Since the attempt to form a single Protestant front failed, Reformed Christians were thereby excluded from the discussions between Lutherans and Catholics at the pivotal Diet of Augsburg (1530).

Nevertheless, Zwingli wrote a confession of faith for the Diet and the Tetrapolitan Confession was hastily prepared for presentation to the Holy Roman Emperor, Charles V. Later these four cities affirmed the Lutheran Confession and joined the Lutheran Smalcald League.

The irenic Tetrapolitan Confession contains twenty-three chapters. The first deals with the centrality of Holy Scripture* in the life of the church* and chapters 3 and 4 set forth the doctrine of salvation* by God's grace* through faith* and not by works of our own. Since it was on the doctrine of the Lord's Supper* that Luther most sharply disagreed with Zwingli, Bucer attempted in the Tetrapolitan Confession, and throughout his life, to find a compromise formula that would satisfy both Protestant sides—but without success.

CHARLES PARTEE

Theocracy

Apparently coined by Josephus (d. c. A.D. 100) to describe the government of Israel under Moses (Ex. 19:4–9; Deut. 17:14–20), the word "theocracy" literally means "the rule of God" (Gr. *theos*, "God"; *kratein*, "to rule"). Historically, the term has been used mainly to describe a form of government or state in which God* (or a deity) is regarded as the immediate and supreme ruler, while temporal power is in the hands of an individual or priestly order that claims divine sanction. Some have wrongly regarded Calvin's* Geneva, Cromwell's* England, and Puritan* New England as "theocratic." Calvin shared with theocrats the belief that in the ideal political system the secular authority should be responsible to God and that its goal should be the effectual operation of God's will. However, in Calvin's Geneva the clergy did not govern the state, church* and state were separate though interlocking, and prerogatives of the church were jealously guarded. Further, Calvin taught that the ideal form of government was a republic in which the rulers were chosen by the citizens from among "the best people," who were then responsible to both God and their subjects in the execution of God's will. Calvinists since Calvin, with few exceptions, have favored representative government and opposed various forms of absolutism.

R. Hancock, *Calvin and the Foundations of Modern Politics* (1989); H. Höpfl, *The Christian Polity of John Calvin* (1982); J. T. McNeill, *The History and Character of Calvinism* (1954); W. A. Mueller, *Church and State in Luther and Calvin* (1954).

ROBERT D. LINDER

Theological Education

Theological education refers to the education received by a minister or other professional church worker. Traditionally, this has included instruction in the Scriptures, systematic theology, and pastoral practice.

The intellectual history of the Reformed churches began in the Renaissance of the fifteenth and sixteenth centuries. Advocates of a European intellectual rebirth demanded that scholars set aside their compendia of familiar quotations and standard authorities. In place of these handbooks, Renaissance leaders suggested that scholars return to the original sources. Inspired by this ideal, intellectuals began systematic study of the Latin classics and initiated the study of Greek and Hebrew literature. Part of this rediscovery of ancient literature was the availability of the Bible and the church fathers to educated Europeans.

Huldrych Zwingli,* pastor of Zurich, was trained in the new methods of studying ancient texts at the Universities of Bern, Vienna, and Basel. Zwingli launched his reformation with a series of biblical studies and disputations that included an exposition of the complete book of Matthew. Once Zurich legally established the Reformation, Zwingli used small groups to retrain the existing ministry* in correct exegesis. In his essay *The Pastor*, Zwingli argued that the best ministry was one attentive to study. The faithful shepherd first learned and then taught.

In Geneva, John Calvin* conducted a similar Reformation. Before his conversion,* Calvin was a young humanist, author of a commentary on Seneca's essay *On Clemency*. After Calvin became a Protestant, he applied his hermeneutical skills to the interpretation of the Bible.

Exegesis was the nucleus of Reformed church life. The first Reformed ministers believed preaching* should be expository. A liturgical change further encouraged this style of preaching. Unlike Catholic and Lutheran churches, Reformed judicatories encouraged their elders* to select their own texts. While some texts could be expounded in a single sermon, many required several Sundays before the pastor finished the biblical passage. Many Reformed preachers followed Zwingli's and Calvin's example by preaching through different books of the Bible on successive Sundays.

The need for correct exegesis determined much of the early history of Reformed theological education. Under Calvin's leadership, Geneva required all children to attend school. The more able were to advance to Latin or grammar schools. In 1559 the City Council of Geneva completed the educational system. In that year, the town fathers invited instructors of the University of Lausanne to move to their city and reorganize as the Geneva Academy.* The new school required a heavy program of classical studies.

Few continental churches, however, had opportunity to begin new educational institutions. In most areas, Reformed churches inherited medieval universities. Though Reformed leaders modified these schools, they retained the basic outline of medieval theological studies, including dependence on Aristotle's logic.

By the seventeenth century, dogmatic theology had replaced biblical studies as the most important subject in many continental Reformed universities. Two motives underlay this change in educational focus. First, Reformed theologians needed to compete with the Catholic Counter-Reformation. Rejuvenated Catholicism presented its teachings in clear, concise, scholastic form. The Reformed had to answer in kind or risk losing the debate. Second, Reformed thinkers needed to answer such critiques of orthodoxy as that offered by the Dutch Arminians.* Despite this shift in focus, continental Reformed churches continued to require the classical languages and Hebrew before the study of theology proper.

England had a different educational pattern than the Continent. The Reformation marked the triumph of humanism* in the English universities. Though the scholastic programs—including theology—continued, instruction moved to the colleges. In the medieval period, the colleges were dining and residence halls. After the Reformation, college fellows and tutors assumed most of the teaching responsibilities. The tutors and fellows, often young men awaiting ecclesiastical preferment, drilled their charges in the classical languages. Strangely, the colleges neglected Hebrew, an important subject on the Continent.

In the American colonies, Reformed churches adopted various expedients. American Congregationalists* and Presbyterians* followed the English model. Harvard, Yale, and, later, the College of Rhode Island were modeled on English schools and followed established English patterns. Little theology was taught in the classrooms, even after the establishment of professorships in divinity.

The Great Awakening* apparently created a new demand for more formal theological study. Many candidates studied for a period of time (three months to three years) with an established pastor. In turn, those who completed this training, called "reading divinity," taught others. Unfortunately, many who participated in "reading" programs scrutinized the very convoluted speculative theology of the New Divinity or neo-Edwardseans.

The Dutch Reformed maintained the same standard for their colonial ministers as for continental pastors. Initially, Dutch Reformed churches used a two-leveled approach. Candidates for the ministry received their classical education in America, often attending Harvard or Yale, and then went to Holland, where they were trained in Reformed dogmatics. As ethnic distinctions became less important, the denomination created its own liberal arts school, Queens College, and appointed a professor to prepare young men for the preaching office. John Livingston (1746–1825) served as both theological instructor and college president.

In the early nineteenth century, the various American Reformed churches moved toward a different institution for the training of ministers: the seminary. The first seminary in the United States, Andover, opened in 1808. Other Reformed denominations quickly established similar institutions. The new seminaries had many similarities to the European faculties of theology, including a multiple faculty, a specialized library, and a confessional basis. But, unlike European theological schools, the new schools were private institutions organizationally separate from other institutions of higher learning.

Scottish theological arguments also contributed to the development of another type of theological institution. After the enactment of the Patronage Act (1712), the General Assembly* continually debated the role of presbytery in the appointment of ministers. Though a small group seceded from the Kirk in the eighteenth century, the most significant breach occurred in 1843. In this Great

Disruption,* approximately one-third of the ministers in the church withdrew. The new Free Church was numerous enough to establish its own educational foundations. New schools were founded at Aberdeen, Edinburgh, and Glasgow. These colleges combined the best features of Scotland's traditional university program with components borrowed from American seminary experience, such as boards of trustees.

By the beginning of the nineteenth century, more advanced scholars used the historical-critical method of biblical interpretation. The first notable Reformed thinker to struggle with the new approach was Friedrich Schleiermacher,* professor of theology at the University of Berlin. Schleiermacher argued that scholars had to interpret the Bible historically, and his own discussions of the pastoral epistles and the life of Jesus influenced later research. Yet Schleiermacher also believed that theology could not be chained to the results of any historical investigation. Hence he suggested that dogmatic theology needed to be grounded in the faith of the contemporary church.

For most contemporary Reformed churches, Schleiermacher's suggestions were too radical. In general, early nineteenth-century Reformed educators ignored the newer biblical studies. This policy of benign neglect, however, did not last long. Throughout the first half of the nineteenth century, scientific studies indicated that the earth was far older than Genesis indicated. Charles Darwin capped these arguments with his brilliant *On the Origin of Species* (1859). While scientists' findings did not directly concern biblical scholarship, they strongly suggested the Bible was not, as the Reformed tradition affirmed, an inerrant and infallible guide to all knowledge. If so, then the theological schools needed a new method of biblical study.

While the leaders of Reformed theological schools were reevaluating their programs, historical-critical study matured. In the hands of such scholars as Julius Wellhausen (1844–1918) and Wilhelm Wrede (1859–1906) the new method seemed to offer reasonable solutions to difficulties in the biblical text.

The new biblical study also contributed to several Reformed heresy* trials. In Scotland, William Robertson Smith* was tried for his articles on the Pentateuch in the *Encyclopaedia Britannica.* In 1881 the General Assembly of the Free Church convicted Smith and deprived him of his living. In the United States, Charles Briggs* of New York City's Union Theological Seminary was likewise tried and convicted for his understanding of the OT. However, Briggs's colleagues supported him. At the urging of the faculty, Union's trustees removed the school from the jurisdiction of the Presbyterian Church. Union became an ecumenical seminary. At Princeton Seminary, the leading conservative school, a 1929 decision to reorganize the school led J. Gresham Machen* and other fundamentalist* faculty members to establish Westminster Seminary in Philadelphia.

In Switzerland the universities gradually removed the requirement that members of university theological faculties pledge themselves to teach according to a set theological tradition. Though conservatives established separate theological schools in many cantons, few of the schools survive today. In Holland, the debate became so heated that the conservatives established the Free University of Amsterdam* (1880) to teach their point of view.

Though biblical conservatism has continued to influence Reformed theological education throughout the twentieth century, the neo-orthodox* theology of Karl Barth* and Emil Brunner* permitted many Reformed institutions to adjust to the new biblical studies. Both Barth and Brunner cut through the hermeneutical problem by separating the words of Scripture* from the revelation* that supported the text. Thus theologians could explore the historical world of the Bible as thoroughly as they wished without any substantial loss of theological substance. The American theologians H. Richard Niebuhr * and Reinhold Niebuhr* presented a similar solution to the biblical problem, and their neo-orthodoxy was more in line with the activism of the American Reformed tradition.

The most dramatic changes in Reformed theological education from 1965 to 1990 were in the composition of the institutions that trained pastors. In 1965 the schools were primarily male and most often white. Since then, significant numbers of women have completed their theological studies, and almost all Reformed schools have some female faculty members. Schools in Europe and North America have also enrolled students from third-world countries. This new openness to the world has led to an increasing interest in Reformed schools on such issues as the influence of race, economics,* and gender on theology.

G. T. Miller, *Piety and Intellect* (1990); and "Christian Theological Education," in *Encyclopedia of the American Religious Experience*, ed. C. H. Lippy and P. W. Williams, 3 vols. (1988), 3:1627–52.

GLENN T. MILLER

Theology, Reformed

All Protestant theology may be called "Reformed," but the name is appropriately applied to the theology originating from Huldrych Zwingli,* Heinrich Bullinger,* John Calvin,* Martin Bucer,* and others, to distinguish their thought from that of other Protestants. The Swiss reformers were more radical in emphasizing biblical authority than were the Lutherans, seeking to eliminate from the life of the church* not only what the Bible condemned but also all that did not receive confirmation in Scripture.* The background of the leading Swiss reformers, especially Zwingli and Calvin, was Christian humanism.* Erasmus* died a cardinal but spent his last years in Protestant Basel and exercised considerable influence over the Swiss theologians. Zwingli's and Calvin's intention, however, was not to create a unique theology but to proclaim the Christian (catholic) faith in the language and idiom of their time.

The seminal works of Reformed theology were all completed before Calvin's death (1564). The authors were preachers who directed their theological work to the edification of the church. The most important classical theologies include those of Zwingli, *On True and False Religion* (1525); Bullinger, *Fifty Godly and Learned Sermons, Divided Into Five Decades Containing the Chief and Principal Points of Christian Religion* (1549); Calvin, *Institutes of the Christian Religion** (editions 1536–59); Wolfgang Musculus,* *Commonplaces of Sacred Theology* (1560); and Peter Martyr Vermigli,* *Commonplaces* (posth. 1576).

The classic works of Reformed theology were followed by Reformed scholasticism.* School theologians, unlike the preacher theologians of the first generation, were concerned with precision and clarity of definition, coherence, and comprehensiveness. They sought to relate the Protestant theology to the old theology, as it had developed in the ancient church and medieval scholastic theology.

This development was as necessary as it was useful. In the generation after Calvin's death, Reformed theology had to be defined in the light of conflicts with Lutherans over the person of Christ and the Lord's Supper* as well as the carefully defined Catholic theology of the Council of Trent (1545–63). Within the Reformed community, disputes quickly arose over theological issues the Reformers had ignored or at least left open-ended. Jacobus Arminius* (1560–1609) raised questions about human responsibility over against the very vigorous doctrine of predestination* enunciated by Theodore Beza* and Franciscus Gomarus* (1563–1641). His theology also intensified the conflict over supralapsarianism* versus infralapsarianism,* a question Calvin did not really face—as to whether God* in election viewed people as creatable or fallen. Among the Saumur theologians, Moïse Amyraut* sought also to modify predestination. Joshua de la Place (Placaeus; 1606–1665) opposed the doctrine of the imputation of Adam's sin,* and Louis Cappel the younger (1585–1658) denied the Mosaic authorship of the Hebrew vowel points. Covenant* theologians, especially Johannes Cocceius* and Hermann Witsius (1636–1708) sought to organize theology around the various covenants, shifting the attention from the decrees of God* to the working out of the decrees in history,* modifying the arbitrariness of the divine activity and emphasizing human responsibility.

Covenant theology was the only modification of Reformed theology that became part of the official creedal life of the churches. The Synod of Dort* (1618–19) adopted a moderate Reformed position on predestination, insisting on unconditional election but denying that the decree to elect and the decree to reprobate were equal and parallel decrees. Furthermore, it was infralapsarian in its theological perspective. The WCF* included the doctrine of the covenants as one of the major organizing factors of its theology, but only alongside other theological rubrics.

Scholastic theology provided the Reformed community with a universal vocabulary that was carefully worked out and defined. It incorporated the accumulated wisdom of the church's theological tradition so that all theological questions were faced. Contemporary theologians may not agree with the answers the scholastics gave to theological questions, but they have to praise the theological acumen which lays out the issues so clearly and which, if used today, saves theologians much unnecessary work. Theologians as different as Karl Barth* and Paul Tillich have both paid tribute to the high theological competence of the Protestant scholastics.

Among the most important scholastic theologies were those of Beza, *Confession of the Christian Faith* (1558); Girolamo Zanchi,* *Commonplaces* (1617); Zacharias Ursinus,* *Commentary on the Heidelberg Catechism* (1584); William Perkins,* *A Golden Chaine* (1591); William Ames,* *A Marrow of Sacred Theology* (1623); Johannes Wollebius,* *Compendium of Christian Theology* (1626); James Ussher,* *A Body of Divinitie* (1645); and Francis Turretin,* *Institutio theologiae elencticae* (1679–85).

The works of Jonathan Edwards* were the most influential Reformed contribution to eighteenth-century theology. Edwards wrote his theology in the light of the emphasis of Isaac Newton (1642–1727) on an orderly world that left little place for God; of the insistence of John Locke (1632–1704) on the empirical basis of all knowledge and the reasonableness of Christian faith; and of the revivals that raised anew the problems of free will* and divine sovereignty. Edwards, who was unwilling to be called a Calvinist for the sake of distinction, wrote *A Treatise Concerning Religious Affections* (1746); *Freedom of the Will* (1754); *The End for Which God Created the World* (posth. 1765); and *A History of the Work of Redemption* (1739 sermons; publ. posth. 1774).

The Enlightenment and nineteenth-century intellectual and cultural events constitute one of the great divides—if not the greatest divide—in the history of Western culture. The churches' response generally was threefold: liberalism, which sought to incorporate the new wisdom into Christian faith sometimes at the expense of the faith; a conservative fundamentalism,* which in protecting the faith sometimes destroyed its intellectual vitality; and the social gospel,* to indicate how Christians should live in the new industrial society.

Some theologians in the Reformed tradition, such as Friedrich Schleiermacher,* sought to relate Christian faith to the new intellectual and cultural situation. In doing so, they raised the question of whether their theology should be distinguished as Reformed or characterized primarily as nineteenth-century liberalism. On the other extreme, theologians defied the nineteenth century and lost intellectual credibility. Reformed theologians generally found it easier to relate the Christian faith to the new social situation than to reach unanimity about theological concerns. This was the basis of the ecumenical slogan that doctrine divides but work unites. In recent years, however, work more radically divides the Christian community than doctrine, in part because work is based upon doctrine.

The most influential nineteenth-century Reformed theologians, however, cannot be classified as either liberal or fundamentalist. Heinrich Heppe's* *Reformed Dogmatics* (1861; ET 1950; repr. 1978) combined in one compendium much of the Reformed theological wisdom of various European traditions, proving to be an influential textbook which received Barth's commendation. In the United States, Charles Hodge's* *Systematic Theology* (3 vols.; 1871–73) was the most influential theological text of any school of thought. Hodge's theology built on the Reformed tradition and particularly on the seventeenth-century formulation of F. Turretin but united these traditions with the warmth of American revivalism.*

Reformed theologies after World War II moved beyond the peculiar problems of the Enlightenment and the nineteenth century. On the one hand, they sought to take the Enlightenment seriously; on the other, they intended to reaffirm in the idiom of a new day the classical Christian theology of the ancient catholic creeds and the classic Protestant Reformation. The most influential twentieth-century Reformed theological works include: Barth, *Church Dogmatics* (1936–69); Emil Brunner,* *Dogmatics* (3 vols.; 1946–60; ET 1950–62) and Otto Weber,* *The Foundations of Dogmatics* (2 vols.; 1955; ET 1982–83).

What are the distinguishing marks of Reformed theology? Reformed theology intended to be catholic but was formulated in such a way that it can be recognized even though its uniqueness cannot be defined with precision. In the nineteenth century, in discussions between Reformed and Lutheran communities in Germany, some insisted that Lutheranism was directed against Judaism or works-righteousness, while Reformed theology was directed against paganism or idolatry. Others pointed to Luther's* emphasis on the Christian's experience of grace* and Reformed emphasis on the activity of God. Still others sought to define the uniqueness of Calvin in terms of some central dogma from which his theology was deduced.

Emile Doumergue, the great Calvin biographer of the last century, emphasized the theocentric character of Calvin's theology, a quality shared with Zwingli. The Swiss reformers all thought of God as energy, activity, and moral purpose. God is the Lord of nature and of history.* They understood human history as the working out of God's purposes and the essence of human life as embodiment of the purposes of God. Calvin himself would insist, perhaps with a glance toward Luther, that salvation* of a human soul was subordinate to the glory of God.

The theocentrism of Calvin's theology, however, is strictly qualified. It is the theocentrism of the triune God who is made known to us in Jesus Christ. The theocentric character of Reformed theology involves a radical rejection of any form of unitarianism* as well as the exaltation of human concerns.

Reformed theology is distinguished by certain ways of doing theology:

1. It is always subordinate to the authority of the Bible as the Word of God* written. Theology is a coherent explication of Scripture in the language of ordinary discourse. The authority of Scripture is the norm of all theological thinking and speaking.

2. Reformed theology has always sought to illuminate experience* and the concreteness of the situation. Calvin subjected what he wrote theologically to the common sense wisdom of Christian experience. Revelation* may go beyond human experience, but it cannot and does not contradict the clear facts of human experience or common sense. Reformed theology is not an explication of Christian experience, but it never takes place apart from it and the demands of the concrete situation. It is not speculative.

3. Theology is a practical, not a theoretical, science. The purpose of theology is to glorify God, to save human souls, to transform human life and society. Calvin's "rhetorical theology," as William Bouwsma has indicated, is directed to practical results rather than a systematic theology intended for the ages.

4. Reformed theology is characterized by simplicity. At its best it is written without ostentation, with transparent clarity, and in the language of ordinary discourse. It rejects the pompous, the artificial, and the contrived.

Reformed theology is also distinguished by certain theological perspectives or decisions. It has always made a sharp distinction between creator and creature. It is Antiochene rather than Alexandrian. This emphasis on the distinction between creator and creature and the peculiar way of relating transcendence and immanence characterizes all of Calvin's doctrine from the person of Christ, to the presence of Christ in the sacraments,* to the nature of the church.

Reformed theology is also distinguished by an emphasis on the activity of God and particularly the prevenience of

God's grace.* Predestination may not be the unifying principle of Calvin's theology, but this emphasis upon the priority of the activity of God pervades every doctrine.

A third theological perspective is the way God the creator and God the redeemer are related to each other. Creation and redemption cannot be opposed. Yet they cannot be identified, for redemption is more than creation; not simply as its completion but, in the light of sin, as its transformer. The practical priority in Reformed theology is always on redemption. Calvin, for example, refused to discuss the possibility of whether the Word would have become flesh if human beings had not sinned.

The fourth characteristic perspective is the refusal to confuse or separate gospel and law,* justification* and sanctification.* Neither gospel and law nor justification and sanctification can be separated; for the gospel is in the law and the law is in the gospel. Salvation as God's mercy, justification by grace through faith, and salvation as God's power, sanctification, must never be separated or confused.

Reformed theology is also unified by a vision of the human community under the authority of God. Calvin, unlike Zwingli, wished to maintain the independence and distinction of church and state. Zwingli and Calvin were united, at least intentionally, in the sense that all society is under God's authority and should reflect God's glory. They sought to create the Christian community on earth. Hence, Reformed theology has never been satisfied with a pietistic definition of Christian faith.

No one distinguishing mark identifies any theology as Reformed. It is catholic in that it builds on the ancient creeds and protestant in its affirmation of Luther's writings (1520), as well as the early Swiss theses such as Bern (1528). However, any Reformed theology is distinguished by its emphasis upon God as energy, activity, and moral purpose, upon the Lordship of God over nature and history, upon the distinction between creator and creature, upon the refusal to separate, oppose, or confuse creation and redemption, law and gospel, justification and sanctification together with an emphasis on the life of the church in the world. Further, the style of Reformed theology is simple, and always in opposition to the pompous, the pretentious, and the ostentatious.

J. H. Leith, *An Introduction to the Reformed Tradition* (rev. ed. 1981); J. T. McNeill, *The History and Character of Calvinism* (1954).

JOHN H. LEITH

Thirty-nine Articles

The Thirty-nine Articles of Religion of the Church of England, which are substantially the same as Archbishop Cranmer's Forty-two Articles (1553), received their final form and authorization in 1571. Their purpose was "for the avoiding of diversities of opinions and for the establishing of consent touching true religion." They affirmed particularly the Reformed doctrine of Scripture,* salvation,* and sacraments* as a corrective to sixteenth-century Roman Catholic positions.

But not all the articles are polemical in this sense. The first five state briefly the historic faith regarding the Trinity* and Christology,* and the last three relate to certain civil and social matters, while the eighth declares acceptance of the classical creeds.

Articles 9–14 deal with original sin,* free will,* and justification,* proclaiming that "we are accounted righteous before God, only for the merit of our Lord and Saviour Jesus Christ by Faith,* and not for our own works or deservings" and that "Good Works, which are the fruits of Faith, and follow after Justification, . . . do spring out necessarily of a true and lively Faith." Article 17 states, "The godly consideration of Predestination,* and our Election in Christ, is full of sweet, pleasant, and unspeakable comfort to godly persons." Other articles condemn the doctrine of purgatory, issuing pardons or indulgences, adoration of images and relics, invocation of saints, and conduct of public worship* "in a tongue not understanded of the people" as "repugnant to the Word of God" (arts. 22; 24). Transubstantiation "cannot be proved by Holy Writ; but is repugnant to the plain words of Scripture, overthroweth the nature of a Sacrament, and hath given occasion to many superstitions" (art. 28).

The insistence on the sufficiency of Holy Scripture for salvation reflected adversely on the papal attribution to tradition* an authority equal with Scripture's (art. 6). It was not denied that there is a place for various traditions and ceremonies in the church, but only subject to the condition "that nothing be ordained against God's Word" (art. 34). Likewise, "the Church hath power to decree Rites or Ceremonies, and authority in Controversies of Faith," but "it is not lawful for the Church to ordain any thing that is contrary to God's Word written" (art. 20). Again, in article 21 on the authority of general councils, it is stated: "Things ordained by them as necessary to salvation have neither strength nor authority, unless it may be declared that they be taken out of holy Scripture." The hallmark of the articles is the insistence on the supreme authority of Holy Scripture over the church and its affairs.

In recent times, the Thirty-nine Articles have suffered neglect and met with contemptuous comment. Current signs of a renewal of interest and willingness to pay attention to the message they convey are welcome insofar as they carry hope of a recovery of strength for a weakened and confused church.

PHILIP E. HUGHES

Thornwell, James Henley (1812–1862)

American Presbyterian theologian. Thornwell excelled in the integration of philosophy* with theology,* the interpretation of Presbyterian church polity,* and the theological defense of slavery.* The PCUS originally revered him as its foremost thinker.

Of humble South Carolina parentage, Thornwell attracted notice as a child by his intellectual ability, and local planters provided for his education. He graduated from South Carolina College (1831) and—embracing Presbyterianism on doctrinal grounds—studied theology at Harvard and Andover (1834). He became a minister (1835), but except for brief pastorates he was for the next twenty years professor of moral philosophy at South Carolina College and its president from 1852 to 1855. He achieved prominence in the Old School Presbyterian Church, being Moderator of its General Assembly (1847). He became professor of systematics at Columbia Theological Seminary (1855). He played a leading role in the first General Assembly of the Presbyterian Church in the Confederate States of America (1861) and drafted its introductory "Address" to other churches.

Thornwell adhered to the Scottish common sense philosophy,* particularly as represented by Sir William Hamilton. His principal book, *Discourses on Truth* (1855), explored the ethics of veracity and attacked utilitarian moral theories. His pro-slavery writings also emphasized divine prescription and providential design and criticized contractual social thought.

Thornwell took a comprehensive view of the plan of salvation.* Like "New Divinity" theologians, he emphasized the "moral government" of God* and conceptualized it in juridical terms. But like many Old School thinkers, he pivoted it on the immediate imputation of Adam's sin,* and of Christ's righteousness, through federal covenant* headship.

Thornwell had most influence as a thinker about Presbyterian church government which he considered part of the revealed divine law. He questioned semiautonomous denominational "boards," insisting that church courts were the true mission agencies. He championed a high view of the ruling eldership, arguing that court quorums required attendance by elders* and elders should participate in imposing hands to ordain ministers. The PCUS and some other Reformed churches later adopted those rules. Thornwell was mistakenly credited with originating the PCUS rejection of all civil pronouncements by church courts.

J. H. Thornwell, *Collected Writings*, 4 vols. (1871–73); J. O. Farmer, Jr., *The Metaphysical Confederacy: James Henley Thornwell and the Synthesis of Southern Values* (1986); B. M. Palmer, *The Life and Letters of James Henley Thornwell* (1875).

JACK P. MADDEX, JR.

Toleration, Religious

Religious toleration took on a new dimension with the onset of the Reformation. The church had always been concerned about heresy,* but this became much more complex with the variety of Protestant dissent. Initially, toleration within the Reformed tradition was impeded by the corporate view of society where church and state were but different aspects of the Christian community. Thus, opinions other than the doctrines of the established church could not be tolerated. Toleration was realized within the Reformed tradition only in the eighteenth century.

Toleration was an issue from the very beginning of the Swiss Reformation. In early Reformed communities, dissenters were forced to conform, sometimes on pain of death, as with Felix Manz in Zurich and Michael Servetus* in Geneva. Basel, the one exception, became the most tolerant of Reformed cities by the mid-sixteenth century, allowing a group of refugee scholars, several of questionable orthodoxy, to gather at the university. The most prominent was Sebastian Castellio, whom Calvin* had forced out of Geneva.

Castellio began the open debate over toleration among the Reformed churches with *Whether Heretics Ought to Be Persecuted* (1554). Like Erasmus* and Sebastian Franck, who influenced him, Castellio argued that the civil magistrate had no authority over souls. Castellio responded to Calvin's *Defense of the Orthodox Faith,* in which Calvin argued that it was the magistrate's God-given duty to put heretics to death. Theodore Beza,* agreeing, wrote *Whether the Civil Magistrate Ought to Punish Heretics* (1554). For the next century, Castellio's descendants remained a small minority in the Reformed communities.

In the United Provinces, the toleration issue lay just below the surface of the Arminian*/orthodox Calvinist debates. The major Arminian spokesman for toleration was Simon Episcopius. While the established Reformed church produced no one who advocated complete toleration, Johannes Althusius, chief magistrate of Emden, did argue for and practice a limited toleration of Christian dissenters and Jews. Many other Reformed magistrates followed his lead, so the United Provinces were the most tolerant of all European states in the seventeenth century.

In Poland, Reformed, Lutherans, and Bohemian Brethren joined with the Catholics in signing the Confederation at Warsaw (1573) to establish toleration in Poland for nearly a century. A practical toleration existed in Poland since the mid-sixteenth century, when the anti-Trinitarians broke with the Reformed Church. Faustus Socinus was the greatest toleration spokesman in eastern Europe.

In England, both Presbyterian Puritans* and Separatists opposed the established Anglican Church, but neither advocated religious toleration. No Reformed advocated toleration until the Congregationalist* John Owen,* who argued for toleration of all dissenters (1649). Owen advocated toleration until his death (1683) and influenced John Locke in his *Essay on Toleration* (1689).

Among the American colonies, the basis for future U.S. religious liberty* was set in Virginia. The toleration struggle that had begun in the mid-seventeenth century was carried on by the Presbyterians, among others. The resultant Act for the Establishment of Religious Freedom (1786) was the basis for the clause on religion in the First Amendment to the Constitution (1791).

S. H. Cobb, *The Rise of Religious Liberty in America* (1902; repr. 1978); H. R. Guggisberg, *Basel in the Sixteenth Century* (1982); W. K. Jordan, *The Development of Religious Toleration in England,* 4 vols. (1932–40); J. Lecler, *Toleration and the Reformation* (1960).

J. WAYNE BAKER

Toplady, Augustus Montague (1740–1778)

Church of England minister and hymn writer. Toplady was educated at Trinity College, Dublin, and served parishes. He was converted through a sermon by the Wesleyan James Morris. He was further converted to staunch Calvinism* (1758) and wrote *The Church of England Vindicated from the Charge of Arminianism* (2 vols.; 1769) and *The Historic Proof of the Doctrinal Calvinism of the Church of En-*

gland (1774). When John Wesley ridiculed Toplady's 1796 translation of Girolamo Zanchi,* pamphlet war broke out between the "old fox" and the "exquisite coxcomb," where serious discussion of the Calvinist-Arminian* issue was clouded by misrepresentation and marred by mutual invective.

Toplady's most famous hymn, "Rock of Ages," appeared in *The Gospel Magazine* (October 1775). Following this, he published *A Collection of Hymns* (1776) and *Works* (1794).

DNB; J. Julian, ed., *A Dictionary of Hymnology* (1907; repr. 1957); T. Row, "Memoir" in A. M. Toplady, *Works*, 6 vols. (1794), 1:25; A. P. F. Sell, *The Great Debate* (1982); T. Wright, *The Life of Augustus M. Toplady* (1911).

ALAN P. F. SELL

Torrance, Thomas F. (1913–)

Born in China of missionary parents and educated at Edinburgh and Basel, Torrance is Professor Emeritus of Christian Dogmatics which he taught at Edinburgh (1952–79). He has served the Reformed tradition as theologian, churchman, ecumenist, and evangelist. Along with several honorary degrees, he received an M.B.E., the Collins Award for Theological Science (1969), and the Templeton Prize (1978). He is also a Fellow of the Royal Society of Edinburgh and the British Academy.

Torrance has especially served Reformed theology as teacher and producer of positive (revealed) theology, historian, and editor. Out of a deeply Trinitarian and Christocentric perspective, shaped particularly by Athanasius, John Calvin,* and Karl Barth,* he seeks to reform theology out of obedience to the Word of God* and openness to the new science/physics (*Theology and Reconstruction* [1965]; *Space, Time, and Resurrection* [1977]; and *The Mediation of Christ* [1983]). His historical studies have focused on Nicene theology (*The Trinitarian Faith* [1988]); Reformation studies (*The Hermeneutics of John Calvin* [1988]); and twentieth-century theology (*Karl Barth: An Introduction to His Early Theology, 1910–1931* [1962]). In addition to translating and editing sermons by Robert Bruce and catechisms* of the Reformed Church, he has co-edited Calvin's New Testament Commentaries, Barth's *Church Dogmatics*, and the *Scottish Journal of Theology*.

As minister in the Church of Scotland he served two parishes, published sermons (*When Christ Comes and Comes Again* [1957]), was chaplain in World War II and Moderator of the Church of Scotland (1976–77). As Reformed churchman, Torrance has also furthered oneness within the catholic church through ecumenical* activity based on Christ's atoning work (*Theology in Reconciliation* [1975]). He worked on the Faith and Order Commission of the WCC,* contributed to reunion talks between the Church of England and the Church of Scotland (*Royal Priesthood* [1955]), supported closer understanding between Lutheran and Reformed churches (*Kingdom and Church* [1956]), and promoted conversation between Reformed and Orthodox Churches (editing *Theological Dialogue Between Orthodox and Reformed Churches* [1985]). For Torrance, fostering genuine oneness requires deep devotion to the triune God* and overcoming problematical dualisms within modern culture.

As a Reformed evangelist to the natural scientific community, he owes much to classical Greek theology and to Clerk Maxwell, Albert Einstein, and Michael Polanyi. He calls for a dialogue where theology provides fundamental ideas and answers to ultimate questions, while natural science provides a deeper understanding of the contingent spatio-temporal creation in which God's gracious acts occur. His contribution to such integration includes *The Ground and Grammar of Theology* (1980) and *Transformation and Convergence in the Frame of Knowledge* (1984); the book series he is editing, Theology and Science at the Frontiers of Knowledge, for which he wrote the first volume; and his work with the Center of Theological Inquiry at Princeton.

T. F. Torrance, *The Christian Frame of Mind* (1989); R. McKinney, ed., *Creation, Christ and Culture* (1976), 307–21; R. J. Palma, "Thomas F. Torrance: Reformed Theologian," *Reformed Review* 38, no. 1 (1984).

ROBERT J. PALMA

Total Depravity *see* Sin

Tradition

From the Latin word *tradere* ("to hand over"). It primarily refers to an action or a process of transmission and reception. Most broadly, tradition is whatever the past gives to the present and the present receives from the past. Tradition includes, among other things, beliefs, documents, institutions, and rituals as well as ways of seeing, hearing, believing, doing, reading, writing, speaking, thinking, and acting. The word itself is neutral. It does not suggest anything normative about the past or about what we have received from it. In the NT, adhering to "tradition" (*paradosis*) is sometimes criticized: "Thus making void the word of God through your tradition that you have handed on" (Mark 7:13); or affirmed, as when Paul commends the Corinthians because they "maintain the traditions just as I handed them on to you" (1 Cor. 11:2). The verb "to hand over," in English, Greek, or Latin, means both to deliver and to betray. Scripture* is ambivalent about tradition.

In Christianity's early centuries, tradition came to be considered "the deposit of faith." It became normative in the degree to which it was understood as coming from the apostles. Hence, the NT canon* was received as consisting of authentic apostolic writings and teachings. In the fifth century, Vincent of Lérins argued that the "true faith" is to be determined from the authority of the biblical canon and from tradition of the church.* In terms of contents, the biblical canon was sufficient; but its proper interpretation required the guidance of tradition. Therefore he proposed that "we hold to that which has been believed everywhere, always, and by all." His norms—which themselves became traditional—were universality, antiquity, and consensus. In principle, with the emphasis on antiquity, the norms were conservative. In practice, however, the norms were used ever more frequently to legitimate the recent and novel. The criterion was no longer antiquity of source but became universality of acceptance. Some began to claim that, under the Spirit's* impulse, through the church's teachings, the apostolic tradition may continue to unfold, even to grow and enlarge.

Increasingly in the Middle Ages, attention shifted from the distinction between text and interpretation, between source and unfolding, to that between the *written* traditions (in Scripture and the creeds) and the *unwritten* traditions, supposedly transmitted, from apostolic times, orally and secretly. Thus many came to believe that divine revelation* flowed through two streams: Scripture* and tradition. This notion was reinforced by the Council of Trent (1546), which "receives and venerates with the same piety and reverence all the books of both Old and New Testaments—for God is the author of both—together with all traditions concerning faith and morals."

Among the Reformers, Calvin* was critical of Trent, arguing that it compromised the normative character of Scripture not only by mixing it with tradition but also by deciding that in the use of Scripture the traditional (but unreliable!) Vulgate version was to be the standard. Thus, while Calvin was quite open to using nonbiblical language in theology, and suggested that Christianity was truer in the early centuries, centuries that were a "purer" time, a sort of "golden" age, for him, only Scripture contains the authentic, reliable, and normative tradition in the truest sense (cf. *Inst.*, "Prefatory Address"). At the same time, within the Reformed tradition, there has been a willingness to use traditional theological language of the Trinity and Chalcedonian Christology* as well as traditional documents such as the Nicene Creed. Further, the Reformers themselves clearly did not always recognize the measure to which they were the unwitting inheritors and practitioners of many quite recent traditions.

A significant statement of Reformed understanding appears in the Second Helvetic Confession* (1566), "Of Interpreting the Holy Scriptures; and of Fathers, Councils, and Traditions" (ch. 2). Here, while the Fathers and the councils may be instructive in Scripture's interpretation, Scripture remains the norm; and "we reject human traditions, even if they be adorned with high-sounding titles, as though they were divine and apostolical . . . which, when compared with the Scriptures, disagree with them." The WCF* affirmed that the conscience is "free from the doctrines and commandments of men which are in anything contrary to his Word, or beside it in matters of faith or worship" (20.2).

Y. M.-J. Congar, *Tradition and Traditions* (1966); E. Shils, *Tradition* (1981).

JOHN E. BURKHART

Travers, Walter (c. 1548–1625)

Educated in Christ's College, Cambridge, and friend of Theodore Beza,* Travers strongly advocated more extensive church reform than was allowed in the Elizabethan church. He called for more intense church discipline* through presbyterian church polity* (1574) and advocated liturgical changes (1584). Though satisfied that Church of England doctrines were biblical, Travers attacked Richard Hooker's advocacy of the established church but himself became a target of Archbishop Whitgift's campaign to enforce ecclesiastical conformity. He was prohibited from preaching (1591) but became provost of Trinity College, Dublin. His views were used by the Westminster Assembly* (1644).

S. J. Knox, *Walter Travers* (1962).

RONALD J. VANDERMOLEN

Triers, The

A commission instituted in England by Parliament (March 20, 1654) to examine and approve or reject candidates for vacant ecclesiastical benefices and sequester the income of legally contested benefices until they could be lawfully supplied. Including Presbyterians, Independents, and Baptists, it was not an ordaining body but was empowered to admit to pastoral office a candidate whom, "for the grace of God in him, his holy and unblamable conversation, as also for his knowledge and utterance," it judged to be an able and faithful preacher and to exclude "weak, scandalous, popish, and ill-affected persons."

ROBERT M. HEALEY

Trinity

The doctrine of the Trinity affirms that the one and only God is the threefold reality of Father, Son, and Holy Spirit.* While classical Reformed theologians made no substantive contributions to traditional doctrinal formulae of the patristic era, contemporary Reformed theologians have contributed significantly to understanding the triunity of God as a "community" of divine being.

The principal elements of the doctrine of the Trinity were settled during fourth- and fifth-century Trinitarian controversies under the leadership of the Cappadocian Fathers and Augustine.* Then the "grammar" of the doctrine was fixed, though the terminology took different forms in the Greek East and the Latin West. Eastern theologians referred to God as one essence in three hypostases, while Western writers said that God is one substance in three Persons. For some time this terminology caused considerable confusion because the Greek *hypostasis* was often translated by the Latin *substantia.*

As time went on, East and West divided over the way the relations among the Persons was described. The East preferred to speak of the Trinity as having one Source (or Font) and two issues: that is, the Father is the One who begets the Son and from whom the Spirit proceeds. The West attempted to reinforce its reading of the biblical references to the Spirit as the Spirit *of Christ.* Thus the custom developed in the Latin-speaking church of adding the word *filioque* to the Niceno-Constantinopolitan Creed (the Spirit proceeds from the Father *and the Son*). This problem (and the authority by which the addition was made) led to the 1054 schism and has been a principal cause of East-West division ever since.

Among the most significant contributions to Trinitarian doctrine was Augustine's *On the Trinity* (c. 425). He intended to explain and defend Nicene orthodoxy, while also expounding the view of the relations among the Persons that led to the inclusion of the *filioque.* Augustine considered numerous analogies. Some are taken from nature (fire, heat, and light); some are social (parents and child). One extensively discussed is the psychological analogy to the operation of the human mind: God's triunity is compared to the relations between memory, understanding, and will. In the end, Augustine expounded the analogy of Lover, the Beloved, and Love which binds them together as the best description of the internal life of God.

Augustine's work and the defenders of Nicene orthodoxy laid the foundation for Reformation consideration of the Trinity. Few reformers questioned the Trinity's centrality, and its outlines were restated by the confessions* and catechisms.* Calvin* defended Trinitarian orthodoxy primarily by emphasizing the divinity of Christ and Christ's centrality for the work of salvation.*

Within the Reformed family, very little substantive discussion of the Trinity occurred until Karl Barth* made this doctrine the theme both of his consideration of revelation* and of his theological anthropology. He opened his *Church Dogmatics* by contending that the fact of God's self-disclosure makes clear that God *is* ("in unimpaired unity yet also in unimpaired distinction") Revealer, Revelation, and Revealedness. The revelation that stands behind Scripture* is the God who is at the same time: *who* is revealed, *what* is revealed, and *how* revelation is effected. The doctrine of the Trinity is thus not an exercise in abstract theological speculation. It is the church's* reflection on its experience of God who makes God's self known in the revelation that both *is* and is contained *in* the Bible (*CD* I/1, pt. 1).

In interpreting the event of revelation, the church discerns that God is an "indissoluble subject" who reveals God's self in three distinctive "modes of being" (Ger. *Seinsweisen*). These ways of God being God subsist in their mutual relations as Father, Son, and Holy Spirit. Though it is from the one essence of God that the threeness of God occurs, yet the unity of God "is not to be confused with singularity or isolation" (*CD* I/1, 354). God's way of being one Subject is to be in real, internal relationship within God's self. It is in part to preserve this dynamic quality that Barth prefers the term "triunity" (*Dreieinigkeit*) in describing divine relatedness.

Because the triunity of God is reflection on God's self-disclosure which is the history of revelation as recorded in Scripture, we discover that at the heart of God is the event of election. God's free choice to love and redeem humanity* is far more than an act of God directed outward; election is not simply an act of God taken in response to humanity's fall into sin.* Election is an act of God's eternal self-determination, for it entails a decision as to how God intends to be related to God's self, and, through that decision, how God intends to relate to all humanity. In the classical language, election is not one of the *opera ad extra*; election takes place first of all within the divine being. In election, God decides to be both the Elector and the Elected One. Thus choosing and being chosen, redeeming and being redeemed, are ways in which the divine subject is self-related and has been from all eternity.

What Barth hopes to accomplish with this unusual description of God's triunity is to explain how the radically transcendent God can be really related to creation* and to humanity. His solution to this dilemma is that creation is the external form of the covenant relationship which inheres in the being of God. The redemption of humanity is the repetition *ad extra* of the electing love with which the Father loves the Son and with which the Son responds in obedience to the Father.

A most interesting sidelight to Barth's consideration of the Trinity is how it functions in his anthropology. He begins from the premise that God is a subject distinguished by real relationships. The history of revelation shows that God is a being in correspondence or confrontation with itself. Using Martin Buber's language, there is within God "I and Thou." This means that "God Himself is not solitary, that although He is one in essence He is not alone, but that primarily and properly He is in connexion and fellowship" (*CD* III/2, 324).

The move from Trinitarian doctrine to anthropology centers on the exegesis of

Gen. 1:26–27: Humanity as created in the "image and likeness" of God. Barth argues that the point of correspondence between God and humanity is in the fact and form of human relatedness. As the human being is created to be God's partner, so the essence of humanity is found in partnership (or the relationship of I and Thou) among humans. The essential form this partnership takes is the relation of man to woman. In their relationship (in general and not simply in the covenant of marriage*), male and female correspond to the relatedness that is at the heart of God. A curious implication of this is that their relationship thus takes the form of that between the Elector and the Elected One. Thus Barth concludes that there is always between male and female a structure in which male precedes and female follows; in which male initiates and female responds. Barth admits that this is a structure of superordination and subordination but denies that this infringes on the equality of the male and the female any more than a similar structure of superordination and subordination threatens the unity and equality of the Persons of the Godhead.

While Barth has clearly made a significant contribution to the discussion by linking the structure of the divine being both to God's self-disclosure and to the human created in God's image, many have questioned the way the analogy is made to work. Feminist* theologians argue that "subordination," no matter how carefully defined, cannot be separated from the notion of inherent inequality between any superordinate and subordinate. They resist the idea that male and female are anything but created equally in God's image. It is also fair to suggest that Barth has, by defining God's primary internal relation as that of election, introduced a structure of superordination and subordination into the Godhead that stands at odds with the entire orthodox tradition. The difficulty with Barth's proposal is not that humanity reflects the divine relatedness (several modern Reformed authors have found this useful). The difficulty is in the way in which the divine relatedness is defined, for example, as command and obedience.

Several contemporary Reformed theologians have proceeded from Barth's foundation and continued the discussion of the triunity of God as a community of real relatedness in the one Godhead. Eberhard Jüngel* has confronted various philosophical arguments about the impossibility of speaking about God in the modern world by a further exposition of Barth's thought. The doctrine of the Trinity leads us to see that God is "a being structured as a relationship" (Jüngel, p. 25).

Jürgen Moltmann's* work is more extensive as he takes over Barth's notion that the work of redemption occurs first of all within God's own being. Moltmann makes a significant alteration, however, suggesting that what takes place with the Godhead is not election but crucifixion. To describe how God can be really related to human suffering, he concludes that the suffering of Christ is not an event that takes place in the life of the human Jesus and "outside" the Godhead. The love of God (which is compassionate and suffering love) can be understood only if the cross and suffering of Christ are at the heart of God's own experience and existence. Moltmann is so convinced of the need to affirm God's active sympathy with human suffering that he is willing to claim that God "suffers" not only through the human nature of the Son but in the Godhead itself. Thus he claims that patripassianism (that the Father suffers along with the Son) should never have been declared heretical.*

Two things are striking here: first, the way in which Moltmann follows Barth's suggestion that real relatedness is what characterizes the being of God; and second, the distinctive way in which Moltmann defines the nature of that relationship. No longer are Father and Son related as Elector and Elected One (the One who commands and the One who is obedient). Now they are the One who hears the cry of abandonment and the One who is abandoned.

Moltmann moves on from this discussion of suffering love at the heart of God to discuss ways in which the divine community can serve as a model for human community. Here again, Moltmann follows Barth's form but with distinctive content. Rather than focus on the relationship of male and female as the primary form of human relatedness, Moltmann's concern is for humans in broader community. He suggests that the free self-giving and compassionate love manifested in triune relatedness can serve as a model for human life in community (both political and ecclesiastical). God's self-revelation of love is the history of freedom.* The "kingdom of God"* is the condition where humans share with one another in the community of God's free love for all creation.

Another Reformed theologian who reflects on the significance of triune relatedness for human relationship is Letty Russell. She suggests that the doctrine of the Trinity contributes to our understanding of "partnership." The Christian message is that we are set free to live as partners not only with one another but with God in the ongoing work of creation. Thus, "the partnership of God in the persons of the Trinity also provides an image of mutuality, reciprocity, and a totally shared life. The characteristics of partnership, or *koinōnia*, may be discovered in their perfection in the Trinity, where there is a focus of relationship in mutual love between the persons and toward creation" (Russell, p. 35).

Among feminist theologians, both within and outside the Reformed tradition, considerable discussion has been given to the status of the triune formula. Many argue that naming the triune God "Father, Son, and Holy Spirit" (and using masculine pronouns for all three) reinforces the incorrect notion that God is male and that only masculine language is strictly appropriate when speaking about God. Various proposals for alternative formulae have been made, the most common being the identification of the Persons by their function: for example, Creator, Redeemer, and Sustainer; or Creator, Christ, and Spirit.

While having the advantage of removing exclusively masculine terms, these alternatives raise another difficulty. Early church theologians argued that the Persons should not be distinguished by specific acts or functions, because this leads inevitably to a modalism (the threefold nature of God is found in the *roles* God plays toward us). In fact, they argued, the act of one is the act of all. Thus the Creed says that God the Father is "Maker of heaven and earth," God the Son is the One "by whom all things were made," and God the Spirit is "the Lord and Giver of Life."

Others object to renaming the Persons of the Godhead because they hold that the triune formula "Father, Son, and Spirit" is in fact God's self-disclosed, *proper* name (cf. Bloesch). This view, however, seems contrary to the ancient notion that the triune names signified the relations between the Persons rather than the essences of the Persons themselves.

This discussion of how the triune Persons are to be named is likely to continue with significant contributions from those who wish to eliminate any confusion that God "is" male as well as from those who are concerned about the vast ecumenical significance of the triune formula, especially as Christians from East and West find themselves in closer theological as well as ecclesial relations.

D. G. Bloesch, *The Battle for the Trinity* (1985); C. M. Campbell, " 'Imago Trinitatis': An Appraisal of Karl Barth's Doctrine of the 'Imago Dei' in Light of His Doctrine of the Trinity" (diss., Southern Methodist University, 1981); E. Jüngel, *The Doctrine of the Trinity* (1976); J. Moltmann, *The Crucified God* (1974); and *The Trinity and the Kingdom* (1982); L. M. Russell, *The Future of Partnership* (1979).

CYNTHIA M. CAMPBELL

Turretin, Francis (1623–1687)

In 1612, Francis's father, Benedict, completed his studies in Geneva and became the professor of theology at the Geneva Academy* and pastor of the Genevan Italian congregation. Francis studied theology at Geneva under Giovanni Diodati, Théodore Tronchin, Frédéric Spanheim, and Alexandre Morus. He later studied in Leiden, Paris, and Nîmes and became acquainted with Moïse Amyraut,* Joshua de la Place, and Louis Cappel while he was in Saumur.

Francis Turretin, along with Diodati, Tronchin, and Spanheim, resisted the introduction of new teachings in Geneva, especially the doctrine of hypothetical universalism. This doctrine, widely accepted in the Reformed Church of France, teaches that God* has both a universal and a particular mercy. By God's universal mercy, God wills the salvation* of all people on the condition of faith.* Since sin* makes faith impossible, God, by particular mercy, efficaciously wills the salvation of some particular people.

The Company of Pastors* and the Small Council debated with Morus and with each other (1641–49). Morus was charged mainly with teaching the nonimputation of Adam's sin and hypothetical universalism. Morus and the Company of Pastors finally signed theses (1649), became Geneva's definitive statement on these issues. In later controversies, Turretin was a prominent leader, maintaining that the position of the 1649 theses should be sustained. When Charles Maurice was admitted to the Company (1669), the 1649 theses were reaffirmed over protests of seven members of the Company. When Jean-Robert Chouet came to Geneva as a philosopher he was excused from signing the theses. Pierre Mussard wanted to come as a pastor but refused to sign the theses and was never admitted to the Company. The Genevan adoption (1678) of the strongly anti-Saumurian Helvetic Consensus Formula* was anticlimactic, since Geneva's theological position on these topics had been definitively stated (1649) and reaffirmed and officially sanctioned (1669). Ironically, it was largely through efforts of Turretin's son, Jean-Alphonse, that Geneva revoked the Consensus (1706).

Turretin's major theological work, *Institutio theologiae elencticae* (1679–85), is the most important systematic theological work written in Geneva during the seventeenth century. In it he rejects hypothetical universalism by arguing that (1) God's decretive will cannot be divided into antecedent and consequent, efficacious and inefficacious, or conditional and absolute; (2) God did not intend a universal mercy; (3) the decree to send Christ must follow the decree of election; (4) the covenant of grace* is not universal; and (5) God does not call the reprobates with the intention of saving them.

Francis Turretin's *Institutio* was used as a theological text at Princeton Seminary in the nineteenth century, and his influence there continued into the early twentieth century.

J. W. Beardslee III, "Theological Development at Geneva Under Francis and Jean-Alphonse Turretin (1648–1737)" (diss., Yale University, 1957); D. D. Grohman, "The Genevan Reactions to the Saumur Doctrine of Hypothetical Universalism: 1635–1685" (diss., Knox College, Toronto, 1971); G. Keizer, *François Turrettini: Sa vie et ses oeuvres et le consensus* (1900); R. A. Muller, "Scholasticism Protestant and Catholic: Francis Turretin on the Object and Principles of Theology," *CH* 55, no. 2 (1986): 193–205.

DONALD D. GROHMAN

Ubiquity

Reformed and Lutheran theologians agreed that Christ is everywhere according to his divine nature. The main controversy rose over whether Christ's presence in the Lord's Supper* necessarily implies, as some Lutherans insisted, that Christ is everywhere bodily.

Calvin* insisted that Christ* be confessed to be "really," not just "sacramentally," present in the Lord's Supper. Calvin (e.g., 1563 Dedicatory Letter to Frederick, *CO* 20, col. 75) was content to rely on Peter Lombard's distinction (*Sentences* III, d. 22, 3) to hold that the whole Christ, but not everything that belonged to Christ ("*totus Christus sed non totum*"), is really present by the power of the Holy Spirit.* To go farther and argue that Christ's body had communicated to it the divine property of ubiquity was, according to Calvin, to threaten Christ's true humanity on which, no less than on his true divinity, our salvation* depends.

Subsequent Reformed orthodoxy* distinguished among several senses in which the communication of the divine and human properties in the incarnation* can be understood. Heppe (*RD*, pp. 432–47) identifies three main senses considered by representatives of Reformed orthodoxy. In the first (*genus idiomaticum*), the attributes of each nature are ascribed to the entire Person; according to the second (*genus apotelesmaticum*), the redemptive acts proper to the whole Person are ascribed to one of the natures; and according to the third (*genus majestaticum*), the human nature is magnified by the properties of the divine nature. Reformed theologians affirmed the first and second senses but insisted that holding to the third sense, as many of their Lutheran opponents did, argued for Christ's bodily ubiquity at the expense of the true humanity of the one Person.

Barth, *CD* II/1, 484–90, 515–45; E. Bizer, "Ubiquität," *Evangelisches Kirchenlexikon: Kirchlich-theologisches Handwörterbuch* 3 (1959): 1530–31; H. Chavannes, "La présence réelle chez St. Thomas et chez Calvin," *Verbum Caro* 13 (1959): 149–70; P. Jacobs, "Pneumatische Realpräsenz bei Calvin," *Revue d'histoire et de philosophie religieuse* 44 (1964): 389–401; K.-H. zur Mühlen, "Jesus Christus, IV: Reformationszeit," *TRE* 14:759–72; J. Städke, "Abendmahl, III, 3: Reformationszeit," *TRE* 1: 106–22; D. Willis, "Calvin's Use of Substantia," in *Calvinus Ecclesiae Genevensis Custos*, ed. W. H. Neuser (1984), 289–301.

DAVID WILLIS-WATKINS

Udall, John (c. 1560–1592)

English Puritan theologian educated at Cambridge, condemned to death (1590) for publishing a work against episcopacy and in favor of a Reformed church order. He was not executed but held in prison until death. Though he died quite young, he was a respected Hebraist and preacher. His most famous works are the ones for which he was condemned: *A Demonstration of the Truth of That Discipline Which Christ Hath Prescribed for the Government of His Church* (1588) and *The State of the Church of England* (1588). His *Commentary Upon the Lamentations of Jeremy* (1593) is an important source for the study of the use of Scripture in Puritan theology.

JOHN E. WILSON

Uniformity, Acts of

British parliamentary decisions, primarily in the mid-sixteenth century, enforcing the use of the *BCP** in the newly protestantized Church of England. Under Edward VI, the first Prayer Book was composed largely by Thomas Cranmer* (1548), and Parliament enjoined its national use (January 1549) by the first Act of Uniformity. The original Prayer Book retained a number of elements of medieval worship, however, and was not acceptable to the reforming party in the church. So a second Prayer Book and a second Act of Uniformity enforcing its use were adopted (1552). This act also made church attendance on Sundays and holy days obligatory. A third act was adopted (1559) upon the ascendance of Queen Elizabeth following the Marian Catholic interlude. This act reestablished usage of the second Prayer Book (with a few amendments), instituted more stringent penalties for failure to use it and for absence from church, and included an "ornaments rubric" requiring the clergy to wear the vestments used during the second year of Edward's reign. This rubric was resisted, especially by the Marian exiles* who had been exposed to some of the "best Reformed churches on the continent." The ensuing vestments controversy* (1560s) reveals the significance of nascent puritanism in the origins of the Church of England. Another Act of Uniformity was later adopted (1662), reestablishing use of the Prayer Book from the time of the Restoration following the Cromwellian* interlude.

H. Gee and W. J. Hardy, *Documents Illustrative of English Church History* (1921).

JOHN H. PRIMUS

Union with Christ (Mystical Union)

Mystical union in Reformed understanding is that personal engrafting of believers into Christ which constitutes the foundation of the Christian life. As branches are joined with the vine, their source (John 15), or members of a body with their head (Eph. 4), so the elect are united with Christ. This ingrafting does not entail dissolution of the believer's individuality in the divine, nor does it stand as the goal of a process of spiritual development. It is, rather, that work of the Holy Spirit* which engenders faith* and enables individuals to share in the fruits of Christ's saving work. Baptism* is the sign and seal of this union; the Lord's Supper* nourishes and sustains it.

Calvin* sees personal union with Christ as the means by which we appropriate Christ's benefits: in this union Christ takes our sin as his own and we take his obedience as our own. Some Reformed theologians speak of a federal or judicial union in which God declares believers joined to Christ, the Second Adam, as their representative head. Karl Barth* has emphasized union with Christ as the goal of Christian vocation.*

Barth, *CD* IV/3, pt. 2, 520–54; L. Berkhof, *Systematic Theology* (4th rev. and enl. ed. 1949); A. A. Hodge, *Outlines of Theology* (1878); L. Smedes, *Union with Christ* (1983); R. S. Wallace, *Calvin's Doctrine of the Christian Life* (1959).

P. MARK ACHTEMEIER

Unitarianism

The name for those who reject Trinitarian theology to stress the oneness of the Father. Though there were precursors in the early church, the term is usually used for a variant of the Reformation with roots in Italian humanism* and radical biblicism. Significant churches emerged in Poland, Lithuania, and Transylvania, where leaders like Fausto Sozzini, George Blandrata, and Francis David insisted that divinity was to be ascribed to the Father alone and that traditional theology of incarnation* and atonement* should be rejected. David rejected prayer to Jesus. The Unitarian Church was given legal standing, along with other confessions, by John Sigismund of Transylvania (1568), but similar groups in Poland were crushed by 1658. Small churches still exist in Romania and Hungary, but the main strength of the movement is in Britain and the United States.

In Britain, the movement stemmed from criticism of Calvinism,* the influence of Arian emphases and aspects of Deism. One of the pioneers was John Biddle, who wrote anti-Trinitarian tracts and was imprisoned. Such ideas spread widely among Presbyterian* chapels during the eighteenth century where traditional Calvinism was steadily replaced by more rational theology which stressed the humanity of Jesus and rejected miracles and original sin.* Ministers like Richard Price and Joseph Priestley were influential, but the first to take the name Unitarian was Theophilus Lindsey, who left the Church of England (1774).

In the American colonies, similar trends were gaining momentum in congregations where traditional Puritanism* and modern revivalism* were seen as retrogressions from true Christianity. King's Chapel in Boston adopted a Unitarian liturgy (1785). One of the most eloquent statements of the trend was William Ellery Channing's "Unitarian Christianity" (1819). His influence was reinforced by Ralph Waldo Emerson and Theodore Parker, and the new views won control of the Harvard Divinity faculty. The American Unitarian Association was formed (1825), but the congregational polity of most congregations was zealously cherished. A National Conference was formed (1865).

In England, penal acts against Unitarians lasted until 1813, and there were many disputes over property until settled by Parliament (1844). The British and Foreign Unitarian Association (1825) and the Hibbert Trust (1853) and leaders like James and Harriet Martineau exerted wide influence beyond their own denomination by their emphases on the ethical element in Christianity. In Ireland, controversies among Presbyterians about confessional subscription led to the formation of groups sympathetic to Unitarian influences. In the twentieth century, various strands of the movement have united in both Britain and the United States. There are about 140,000 members in the United States, many of whom are sympathetic to humanism and theism and partnership with world religions.*

C. G. Bolam, *English Presbyterianism* (1968); J. L. M. Haire, *Challenge and Conflict* (1981); R. Miller, *The Larger Hope*, 2 vols. (1979–86); D. M. Robinson, *The Unitarians and Universalists* (1985); D. Scott, *The Halfway House to Infidelity* (1980); E. M. Wilbur, *A History of Unitarianism* (1952); G. H. Williams, *The Polish Brethren* (1980); C. C. Wright, *The Beginnings of Unitarianism in*

America (1955); and *A Stream of Light* (1971).

IAN BREWARD

United Secession Church

Denomination formed in Scotland (1820) by 280 Presbyterian congregations having roots in the Associate Presbytery (organized 1733; later Associate Synod). During the eighteenth century, questions posed by liberalizing theology, state establishment, patronage, and ecclesiastical authority over individual conscience that had originally provoked separation from the national church subsequently divided the synod into four groups: "Old Light Burghers," "New Light Burghers," "Old Light Antiburghers," and "New Light Antiburghers." The 1820 reunion, however, proved stable. It joined with the Relief Synod to form the United Presbyterian Church of Scotland (1847).

ROBERT M. HEALEY

Universalism

Universalism affirms the salvation* of all humanity and rejects the Christian doctrine of eternal punishment. Hints of it are found in Gnostic writings. The Greek theologians Clement of Alexandria, Origen, and Gregory of Nyssa taught it, while Augustine* and the medieval tradition strongly opposed it. Sixteenth-century Anabaptist writers Hans Denck and Hans Hut promoted it, though their tradition has largely distanced itself from universal salvation. Martin Luther* and John Calvin* opposed it.

During the European Enlightenment the view found new favor in a variety of theological streams. The pietist mystic Jakob Boehme, the Puritan Philadelphians, the Wesleyans James Relly and his disciple John Murray, liberal Congregationalists Jonathan Mayhew and Charles Chauncy, and ex-Baptist Elhanan Winchester all promoted universalism during the seventeenth or eighteenth century.

Attempts to unite universalists through common publications and doctrinal statements have occurred in the United States. Doctrinal compatibility with Unitarianism* yielded formation of the Unitarian Universalist Association (1961). However, many with universalist inclinations remained outside this movement.

Karl Barth* represents a latent or implied universalism through his emphasis on Christ as simultaneously elected and rejected by the Father. Since Christ is the covenant* head of all humanity,* like him all are simultaneously elect and reprobate. Barth refrains, however, from speculating on the eternal consequences of this position.

Some Roman Catholic* emphases on Christ's hidden presence in non-Christian religions and Protestant ecumenism's* theory of dialogue with other faiths suggest a universalism incompatible with historic Reformed teaching.

JAMES A. DE JONG

Ursinus, Zacharias (1534–1583)

Born in Breslau (Wroclaw), Silesia; died in Neustadtan der Haardt. Ursinus studied at Wittenberg (1550–57) and Zurich (1560–61). He taught in Breslau (1558–60) and was called by the elector Frederick III to help in the reformation of the Palatinate. He became *Loci* professor at Heidelberg (1561–68), rector of the Collegium Sapientiae (the seminary; 1561–76), and lectured at Neustadt, mostly on Isaiah (1577–83).

Ursinus was primary author of the Heidelberg Catechism* (1563). He wrote its defense against Lutheran attacks (*Bekanntnuss*, 1564) and the *Admonitio* (1581). His great influence on Reformed theology came from his lectures on the Heidelberg Catechism, collected by his pupil and successor David Pareus in the *Explicatio catecheseos*. The catechism was officially approved at the Synod in Dort* and Ursinus's *Explicatio* used in Reformed seminaries and universities. Ursinus's method in this work is scholastic; his theology, Calvinist. Questions 12–18 of the Heidelberg Catechism caused Ursinus to introduce much of Anselm's *Cur Deus Homo?* (but see W. Metz).

Zachariae Ursini Opera Omnia (1612); F. Klooster, "Ursinus' Primacy in the Composition of the Heidelberg Catechism," in *The Reformation and the Palatinate, 1559–1583* (1986); W. Metz, *Necessitas Satisfactionis* (1970); E. K. Sturm, *Der junge Zacharias Ursin* (1972); D. Visser, *Zacharias Ursinus: The Reluctant Re-*

former (1983); and "St. Anselm's *Cur Deus Homo* and the Heidelberg Catechism," *Anselm Studies* 2 (1988): 607–34.

DERK VISSER

Ussher, James (1581–1656)

Educated at Trinity College, Dublin, Ussher was an ardent student of ecclesiastical history. He advocated theological ideas that Puritans promoted, without accepting Puritan criticisms of Church of England polity and ceremonies. His main focus was anti-Roman Catholicism, which he strongly maintained as chancellor of Trinity College (1605), Dublin's professor of divinity (1606), and archbishop of Armagh (1621). Because he accepted the Church of England as a replica of early Christianity, Ussher refused to support Puritan criticisms or Roman Catholicism. He promoted some changes in episcopacy but rejected radical alterations. Ussher's chronology of universal history became widely accepted within early modern Christianity.

R. B. Knox, *James Ussher: Archbishop of Armagh* (1967).

RONALD J. VANDERMOLEN

Van Dusen, Henry Pitney (1897–1975)

Presbyterian educator, theologian, and ecumenist. Van Dusen was educated at Princeton University (1919), Union Seminary (N.Y.; 1924), and the University of Edinburgh (1932). An advocate of liberal theology and the social gospel,* he entered the ministry of the Presbyterian Church in the U.S.A. (1924) and served as secretary of the YMCA. He held various positions at Union Seminary (N.Y.; from 1926), becoming Roosevelt Professor of Systematic Theology (1936) and president (1945–63).

Under Van Dusen's leadership, Union Seminary expanded its faculty and student body while growing in commitment to ecumenics.* World-renowned theologians such as Reinhold Niebuhr* and Paul Tillich increased the seminary's stature as an international theological leader in education.

Van Dusen became a prominent ecumenical statesman, playing a major role in forming the WCC* (1948) and following WCC meetings in Evanston (1954) and New Delhi (1961). He was active in the National Council of Churches and served as vice-president of the Board of Foreign Missions of the Presbyterian Church.

Van Dusen published numerous works championing liberal theology and ecumenism. He served on the editorial boards of *Christendom*, *Christianity and Crisis*, and the *Ecumenical Review*. He was awarded more than fifteen honorary doctorates.

R. Handy, *A History of Union Theological Seminary in New York* (1987); *New York Times*, Feb. 14, 1975, p. 40; D. K. Thompson, "Henry Pitney Van Dusen: Ecumenical Statesman" (diss., Union Theological Seminary, Va., 1974); *Time*, April 19, 1954, pp. 62–66.

BRADLEY J. LONGFIELD

van Dyke, Henry (1852–1933)

Presbyterian minister and literary scholar. Van Dyke received degrees from Princeton University (1873; 1876) and Princeton Seminary (1877) and studied at the University of Berlin prior to ordination (1879). He served as pastor of the Brick Church in New York City (1883–1900), after which he became professor of English literature at Princeton University. There he befriended Woodrow Wilson,* the university's president. He was elected Moderator of the General Assembly of the Presbyterian Church in the U.S.A. (1902).

In 1913, now President of the United States, Wilson appointed van Dyke as minister to the Netherlands and Luxembourg, a position he held until 1917. After the United States entered World War I, van Dyke volunteered for active duty, becoming a lieutenant commander in the Naval Chaplain Corps. In 1923 he retired to his beloved Princeton home Avalon, devoting the remainder of his life to literary endeavors.

Van Dyke was considered one of the greatest preachers and literary leaders of his generation. His gift for language is well documented through his work as editor of the Committee on Revision of *The Book of Common Worship** (1905). His motion at the General Assembly* (1928) led to the further revision of 1931. He also served on the advisory committee on *The Hymnal* (1933).

Recognized worldwide as a great scholar and writer, van Dyke wrote more than twenty-five books, among which are *The Reality of Religion* (1884); *The Poetry of Tennyson* (1889); *The Story of the Other Wise Man* (1896); and *The Gospel for an Age of Doubt* (1896). Van Dyke received many honorary degrees, including Doctor of Civil Law from Oxford University.

LINDAJO H. MCKIM

Van Mastricht, Petrus (1630–1706)

Professor of theology who studied in Utrecht, Leiden, and Heidelberg. Mastricht was pastor in Xanten and Glückstadt and taught practical theology in Frankfurt an der Oder, Duisburg, and Utrecht, succeeding Gisbert Voetius.* Mastricht polemicized against Johannes Cocceius* and Cartesianism in *Novitatum Cartesianarum gangraena . . . seu theologia Cartesiana detecta* (1677). His major work was *Theoretica-practica theologia* (2 vols.; 1655). This work, reprinted several times, reflects Mastricht's pastoral experience and the Voetian emphasis on pastoral as opposed to a primarily systematic theology. No modern treatment of Mastricht exists.

J. J. Herzog, *Realencyklopädie*, vol. 18 (1906), 757.

DERK VISSER

van Ruler, A. A. (1908–1970)

Born in Apeldoorn, the Netherlands, Arnold Albert van Ruler was a minister of the Dutch Reformed Church and taught at the University of Utrecht (from 1947). He developed an original and experimental Reformed theology of culture. Seeking a truly trinitarian method, he "fenced" the Christology* of Reformed orthodoxy* with pneumatology. The Spirit extends messianic salvation* into every area of temporal existence, thus forming Christian culture. The OT and creation* assume primary importance, though soteriology and ecclesiology also receive significant treatment. His writings, particularly on the Holy Spirit* and creation, continue to influence continental theologians.

PAUL R. FRIES

Van Til, Cornelius (1895–1987)

Prolific writer in defense of the Reformed faith, Van Til was professor of apologetics at Westminster Seminary for over forty years. He was born in the Netherlands, and his family emigrated to America (1905). Called to the ministry, he studied at Calvin College and Calvin Seminary and completed his degrees at Princeton. There the exhilarating interaction of two vigorous streams of Calvinistic thought, those of Abraham Kuyper* and B. B. Warfield,* fired his thought. Van Til saw their strong family resemblances but basic methodological differences in apologetics.* To effect a creative synthesis of these two Reformed traditions became his life's work. He began teaching at Princeton Seminary (1928) but then left with J. Gresham Machen* for Westminster (1929).

Van Til claimed that the source of all his thought was the Bible. It reveals the counsel of a self-attesting God* and presents the self-attesting Christ who becomes the authority for accepting what is derived "analogically" from Scripture* (and nature). Asked how he knew the Scriptures are true, he replied that to ask this question is to shift ground from the Bible to another starting point. In his thinking, testing the Bible's authority arises out of autonomous human thought and violates God's sovereignty, compromises God's revelation,* and misunderstands the supreme purpose of Scripture as a divinely given instrument for "the gathering of Christ's people unto himself, not through rational argument as such, but through meeting the Christ of Scripture" (*Jerusalem and Athens*, ed. E. R. Geehan [1971], p. 171; cf. Van Til's "My Credo," pp. 3–21).

Van Til also presented a philosophical account of the antithesis between Christian and non-Christian thought. Both viewpoints ultimately begin with mutually exclusive presuppositions about the nature of reality: the Christian assumes a God who has revealed his comprehensive plan for the universe once for all in Scripture; the non-Christian presupposes an ultimate which is the consequence of an ongoing philosophical dialogue about regularities and facts "found" in nature. Christianity has a privileged position that makes its truth the necessary foundation for attempting to prove anything at all.

Criticisms of Van Til's thought are rife, and he was graciously diligent to answer them. Perhaps the most astute criticism, never fully answered, was by Gordon Clark, who argued that when the truths of Scripture are not analogous to the truth in the mind of God in at least one univocal proposition, then the truth of God in Scripture is unknowable at best and not amenable to the law of contradiction at worst.

Criticism notwithstanding, Van Til remains a stimulating defender of Reformed thought and action. His writings have occasioned considerable creative effort toward finding the meaning of the unknowable truth of God by an asymptotic approach which uses the instrumental methods of ordinary language philosophy and literary analysis.

C. Van Til, *The Defense of the Faith* (1955); *Christianity and Barthianism* (1962); *A Christian Theory of Knowledge* (1969); *The Reformed Pastor and Modern Thought* (1971).

THOMAS M. GREGORY

Vermigli, Peter Martyr (1500–1562)

The greatest of the Italian reformers is best known for his biblical commentaries and sacramental theology. Born in Florence and named after St. Peter Martyr of Verona, Vermigli entered the Lateran Congregation of Augustinian Friars Regular in Fiesole (1514). At the University of Padua (1518–26) he studied Aristotle, learning Greek and scholastic* theology. As an ordained priest and doctor of divinity, he was elected public preacher. He was vicar at Bologna (where he learned Hebrew), abbot of Spoleto and then of St. Peter *ad aram* in Naples, where he belonged to the circle around Juan de Valdés.

Vermigli became suspect on the question of purgatory; the Theatines procured his suspension from preaching, but his friends Cardinals Gasparo Contarini and Reginald Pole had the ban lifted. He became one of his congregation's four visitors (1540), then prior of S. Frediano at Lucca, where he is said to have exercised quasi-episcopal authority. He gathered a brilliant group of teachers and students, introducing monastery and congregation to reforming doctrine. Under Inquisition pressure, he was summoned before his order at Genoa but went to Florence, where Bernardino Ochino also sought refuge. They fled northward in August 1542.

Vermigli went to Zurich, then to Basel; in December, sponsored by Heinrich Bullinger,* he joined Martin Bucer* in Strassburg, lecturing on the OT in the College of St. Thomas. He married Catherine Dammartin, who died in Oxford (1553). He remarried (1559) but had no surviving children.

Thomas Cranmer* invited continental reformers to form a "godly synod" in England; Ochino and Vermigli went together in December 1547 and Bucer in 1548. Vermigli wintered with Cranmer, becoming Regius Professor of Divinity at Oxford (1548) and canon of Christ Church, where his wife was the first woman resident. He lectured on 1 Corinthians and Romans. Most significant is the public Disputation on the manner of Christ's presence in the Eucharist (1549). He argued that "the body and blood of Christ is sacramentally joined to the bread and wine." He somewhat influenced Cranmer's 1552 Prayer Book, the Forty-two Articles (1553), and abortive ecclesiastical law reforms. After Mary's accession, the imprisoned Cranmer named Vermigli partner in defending the "whole doctrine and religious order established" under Edward VI.

Returning to Strassburg (1553), Vermigli lectured on the Book of Judges and on Aristotle's *Nicomachean Ethics* and commenced the large *Defensio adv. Gardinerum* which Cranmer had planned. The Lutheran-Reformed "supper-strife" precipitated Vermigli's debate with Johann Brenz on ubiquity.* He moved to Zurich as professor of Hebrew (1556).

Vermigli's last years included lectures on Samuel and Kings, debate with Theodor Bibliander (and support of Girolamo Zanchi*) on predestination,* and participation with Theodore Beza* in the Colloquy of Poissy* (1561). He died in Bullinger's presence on November 12, 1562.

J. P. Donnelly, *Bibliography of the Writings of Peter Martyr Vermigli* (1990); and *Calvinism and Scholasticism in Vermigli's Doctrine of Man and Grace* (1976); J. C. McLelland, *The Visible Words of God: An Exposition of the Sacramental Theology of Peter Martyr Vermigli A.D. 1500–1562* (1957); P. McNair, *Peter Martyr in Italy* (1967).

JOSEPH C. MCLELLAND

Vestarian Controversy *see* **Vestments Controversy**

Vestments Controversy

A sixteenth-century dispute about official clerical attire in the newly protestantized Church of England. Vestments especially disputed were those specified by the Ornaments Rubric in the Act of Uniformity* (1559), though even earlier under Edward VI, John Hooper and others had resisted use of the alb, cope, stole, and surplice, regarding these as "popish" remnants of Roman Catholicism.* The controversy is significant for showing in the earliest stages of the protestant Church of England two conflicting parties: conformists and more radical reformers or "puritans."*

J. H. Primus, *The Vestments Controversy* (1960).

JOHN H. PRIMUS

Vinet, Alexandre (1797–1847)

Often considered the most remarkable French-speaking Calvinist theologian since John Calvin,* Vinet was the guiding spirit in the modern European Reformed effort to establish religious liberty* and separation of church* and state on Christian grounds. A quiet man best known for his writings, Vinet taught French literature (Basel), then practical theology (Lausanne), until the church-state conflict led him to withdraw from the state church and help found the Free Church of Vaud, Switzerland (1847).

Vinet's most important book is *Essai sur la manifestation des convictions religieuses et sur la séparation de l'église et de l'état envisagée comme conséquence et comme garantie du principe* (1842; ET 1843). Its essence is: To be a mature person, to create a morally healthy society, every individual must grapple with truth. Christians recognize the obligation to know and witness to truth in the example of Christ, but every person must seek and practice truth. To pursue truth, each person must be free to develop and express these (religious) convictions, subject only to humility, justice, and charity. For this pursuit, separation of church and state is a necessary condition, though not a guarantee against apathy. When the government of the Vaud, by fiat, stripped the established church of any confession on the grounds the church is a spiritual democracy and the majority no longer believed the creed, Vinet acted on his convictions.

E. A. McKee, "Alexandre Vinet on Religious Liberty and Separation of Church and State," *Journal of Church and State* (1986): 95–106.

ELSIE ANNE MCKEE

Viret, Pierre (1511–1571)

Reformed minister and popular preacher in Switzerland and France during the first generation of the Reformation. Born in Orbe, not far from Lausanne, Switzerland, Viret was one of three sons of the local tailor. He was introduced both to humanism* and to Reformation doctrines by his teachers in the Orbe schools and enrolled in the Collège Montaigu at the University of Paris to study theology (1528) at approximately the same time that Calvin* and Ignatius Loyola were students. He experienced an evangelical conversion* to Christ there and embraced Protestantism.

Returning to Orbe (1530), Viret met William Farel,* who urged him to become a minister of the gospel. Viret preached first at Orbe, then at Payerne and Neuchâtel before joining Farel again at Geneva (1534). Viret assisted Farel in preaching salvation* and reform, celebrated the first Genevan baptism* according to evangelical forms, survived an assassination attempt, took part with

Farel in a disputation to abolish the Mass, aided in the Genevan struggle for independence from Savoy, and witnessed the decision of a majority of Genevans to become evangelicals.

Viret moved to Lausanne (1536), where in an October public disputation, along with Farel and Calvin, he helped establish the Reformation in that city. He eventually became chief pastor of the Church of Lausanne (1536–59), with several interludes in Geneva to help with various crises, including the period of Calvin's homecoming (1541–42). At Lausanne, Viret also established, supervised, and taught in the academy before running afoul of the Bernese authorities who controlled the area politically and who objected to his attempt to establish a Geneva style of discipline in the Lausanne church. Exiled, he spent 1559–61 as a minister of the Church of Geneva and as a professor in the city's academy. For reasons of health (1561), he moved to southern France. There he was a pastor, evangelist, church administrator, religious adviser to the Queen of Navarre, and peace negotiator between Catholics and Protestants. In particular, he helped introduce the Reformation in Lyons and presided over a Reformed national synod there (1563). He died at Pau.

Viret's reputation and influence rested largely on his preaching and writing. An eloquent pulpiteer, he often addressed crowds numbering in the thousands, as at Nîmes (1561) where he regularly preached to eight thousand people. More than fifty of Viret's works appeared in at least seven different languages, with many of his books going through numerous printings.

Generally speaking, Viret's theology was similar to Calvin's. However, in terms of the Lord's Supper,* Viret originally was closer to Zwingli* than was Calvin, and Viret's view eventually was reflected in the Consensus Tigurinus* (Zurich Agreement; 1549). Viret also favored more lay participation in church government than did most of his Reformed contemporaries, including Calvin and Beza.* However, Viret's main contributions to early Calvinist thought were in the political realm, where he advocated religious tolerance and a church separate and independent of the state. He also provided the earliest known exposition of a Calvinist resistance* theory when he wrote that believers, when led by duly constituted inferior magistrates, had the right to resist the state for reasons of both religious and political tyranny (1547).

P. Viret, *Instruction chrestienne*, 2 vols. (1564); J. Barnaud, *Pierre Viret, sa vie et son oeuvre* (1911); R. D. Linder, *The Political Ideas of Pierre Viret* (1964); "Pierre Viret and the Sixteenth-Century French Protestant Revolutionary Tradition," *Journal of Modern History* 38 (June 1966): 125–37; and "Pierre Viret's Concept of a Just War," *Andrews University Seminary Studies* 22 (Summer 1984): 213–30; H. Vuilleumier, *Histoire de l'Eglise Réformée du Pays de Vaud sous le régime Bernois*, 4 vols. (1927–28).

ROBERT D. LINDER

Visser 't Hooft, Willem A. (1900–1985)

Born into the Netherlands Reformed Church, Visser 't Hooft received the D.Theol. from the University of Leiden and various D.D. degrees. A resident of Geneva (1925–85), he was ordained by the Reformed Church of Switzerland.

Visser 't Hooft held positions as Boys' Work Secretary, World's Committee of the YMCAs (1924–28); Secretary, World's Student Christian Federation (1928–32), and General Secretary (1932–38); Secretary and General Secretary, the Provisional Committee of the WCC* in Process of Formation (1938–48); General Secretary, WCC (1948–65); and Honorary President (1965–85). He exhibited talents as theologian, analyst of world social trends, administrator, editor (*Student World*; *Ecumenical Review*), and author. Three elements of his faith were crucial: the supremacy of God,* the uniqueness of Christ, and the common calling of the world's churches to renewal in their life, especially as expressed in their unity, evangelism,* and social witness.

Visser 't Hooft's principal achievement was to lead the provisional WCC during wartime and postwar circumstances to its founding (1948) and thereafter guide its growth. He wrote: "The worst thing that could happen to the council would be that it should come to be considered as just another cog in the ecclesiastical machinery. My role was not to invent brand-new ideas, but to discover the most forward-looking initiatives in the life of the churches and to seek to make them fruitful for the whole ecumenical family" (*Memoirs*, p. 345).

W. A. Visser 't Hooft, *Memoirs* (1973).

ROBERT S. BILHEIMER

Vocation

The affirmation that each person in society is called by God* to a specific vocation or function is a hallmark of the Reformed tradition. This conviction undergirds and strengthens those who perform even the lowliest daily tasks. Both Martin Luther* and John Calvin* developed a doctrine of vocation.

Calvin uses "calling" (Lat. *vocatio* "vocation") for the choosing of the elect but specifically in relation to God's appointing human beings to certain occupational or family positions. He writes: "The Lord bids each one of us in all life's actions to look to his calling. For he knows with what great restlessness human nature flames, with what fickleness it is borne hither and thither, how its ambition longs to embrace various things at once. Therefore, lest through our stupidity and rashness everything be turned topsy-turvy, he has appointed duties for every man in his particular way of life. And that no one may thoughtlessly transgress his limits, he has named these various kinds of living 'callings' " (*Inst.* 3.10.6).

That each person receives a calling from God was not the pre-Reformation understanding of "vocation." Calvin stood in direct opposition to those who withdrew from business and entered the contemplative life on the ground that they alone received a call. "On the contrary," he observes, "we know that men were created for the express purpose of being employed in labor of various kinds, and that no sacrifice is more pleasing to God than when every man applies diligently to his own calling, and endeavors to live in such a manner as to contribute to the general advantage" (*Commentary on a Harmony of the Evangelists* 2:143).

The conviction that one is called gave courage to people in a society in dramatic flux. In sixteenth-century Geneva, structures from medieval society had broken down, peasants were given new powers, refugees streamed into the city fleeing persecution, and a feeling of uncertainty pervaded the changing order. In such rootlessness, the knowledge that God calls people provides the ingredient necessary for a fulfilled life, namely, courage: "Nothing can fill us with courage more than the knowledge that we have been called by God. For from that we may infer that our labor, which is under God's direction, and in which He stretches out His hand to us, will not be in vain. Thus it would be a very serious accusation against us to have rejected God's call. It should, however, be the strongest encouragement to us to be told, 'God hath called thee to eternal life. Beware of being distracted by anything else or of falling short in any way, before thou hast obtained it.' " (*Commentary* on 1 Tim. 6:12).

Moreover, whether a person is president or slave, no labor is too high or low that it is not blessed by God. "From this will arise also a singular consolation: that no task will be so sordid and base, provided you obey your calling in it, that it will not shine and be reckoned very precious in God's sight" (*Inst.* 3.10.6).

When each person fulfills the function or occupation to which he or she has been called, a certain orderliness in society results. It is incumbent upon each person who has received a calling to "keep within the limits" of that calling, thus preventing confusion and disorder. Peace is the result: "The best way, therefore, to maintain a peaceful life is when each one is intent upon the duties of his own calling, carries out the commands which the Lord has given, and devotes himself to these tasks; when the farmer is busy with the work of cultivation, the workman carries on his trade, and in this way each keeps within his proper limits. As soon as men turn aside from this, everything is thrown into confusion and disorder" (*Commentary* on 1 Thess. 4:11). Such an injunction, however, was not offered as a means of control but so that society as well as the inner self might be at peace. If we "claim more for ourselves than we ought," care and worry are the result. Work, therefore, should not be carried to excess but be kept under control. A sense of calling counters our restlessness and anxiety. "Immoderate care is condemned for two reasons: either because in so doing men tease and vex themselves to no purpose, by carrying their anxiety farther than is proper or than their calling demands; or because they claim more for themselves than they have a right to do, and place such a reliance on their own industry, that they neglect to call upon God" (*Commentary* on Matt. 6:25).

But Calvin does not insist that a person born in one station or calling in life must never seek to change it. Commenting on Paul's advice, "Let each one abide in that calling," Calvin says: "But at this point someone is asking if Paul wishes to impose something binding on people, for what he says may seem to suggest that each one is tied to his calling, and must not give it up. But it would be asking far too much if a tailor were not permitted to learn another trade, or a merchant to change to farming." The doctrine of vocation attacks the "restlessness which prevents individuals from remaining contentedly as they are" (*Commentary* on 1 Cor. 7:20).

The doctrine of vocation, God's calling, affirms all work,* for it is the work of God. Our work has meaning because, seen as God's calling, it is the very work of God in human society.

A. Biéler, *The Social Humanism of Calvin* (1964); W. J. Bouwsma, *John Calvin: A Sixteenth-Century Portrait* (1988); R. S. Wallace, *Calvin's Doctrine of the Christian Life* (1959).

JOHN R. WALCHENBACH

Voetius, Gisbert (1589–1676)

Dutch Reformed scholastic theologian. Educated at the University of Leiden, Voetius served two pastorates (1611–34) and became theology professor at the academy in Utrecht (1634–76). He was a delegate to the Synod of Dort (1618–19) and thereafter bitterly contested not only with Arminians* but also with Johannes Cocceius, Descartes, Jansen, and Jean de Labadie. Though a zealous defender of Calvinist orthodoxy, he also became a leading supporter of Dutch "Precisianism," a proto-pietist movement that stressed spiritual discipline and purity of life.

A. C. Duker, *Gisbertus Voetius*, 3 vols. (1897–1914).

LYLE D. BIERMA

Waldenses

Since the late twelfth century, "Waldenses" has denoted several groups of similar and possibly related "heretics." Since the Reformation, it has referred more specifically to some communities in the Alps of Piedmont-Savoy that adopted the creedal forms and church structures of Genevan Calvinism* (c. 1560). At present, the Chiesa Evangelica Valdese constitutes the Italian-speaking Protestant Reformed church.

The first medieval Waldenses took their name from a rich Lyons citizen called Valdensis or Valdesius (Peter Waldo) who was converted to a life of apostolic poverty (c. 1170). He was in trouble with church authorities when he and his followers insisted on preaching without permission. They were excommunicated and expelled from Lyons (1182–83) and condemned along with other heretical sects at the Council of Verona (1184). In the early thirteenth century the Waldenses spread and possibly absorbed other heretics in areas as far apart as southern France, Lombardy, and the Holy Roman Empire. The first Catholic treatises were written against them at this period. These ascribed to the Waldenses distrust of the ministry of sinful priests, an almost complete rejection of the Catholic sacraments, denial of the belief in purgatory, and objections to civil oaths and judicial homicide.

The Waldensian communities of one specific area, the southwestern Alps between the Dauphiné and the duchy of Savoy, were absorbed into the Calvinist movement while retaining their own name and identity. These groups were apparently discovered as late as the 1290s. Inquisitorial records from the mid-fourteenth century onward describe their beliefs, rites, and sufferings (as for other similar groups in northeastern Germany and Austria). The late-medieval Waldenses did not "anticipate" the Protestant Reformation in any detailed way. They doubted the value of prayers for the dead and church rites but took the Catholic sacraments nonetheless. They confessed their sins to traveling, celibate pastors (called "Brethren" in Germany and "Barbes" in the Alps) every few years.

The early German reformers, Luther* included, usually confused the Waldenses with the Bohemian (also known as "Waldensian") brethren in eastern Europe. However, the Waldenses of the southwestern Alps (along with their colonies in Provence and southern Italy) were converted to the Reformation by French-speaking missionaries based in Switzerland. Antoine Saunier and Pierre-Robert Olivétan,* associates of William Farel,* visited them (1530s); the Waldenses helped pay for Olivétan's sumptuous French Bible (1535). These heretic* communities became ordered, public churches only when resident pastors were sent from Geneva by Calvin* to settle among them after 1555. Between 1558 and 1564 they adopted a version of the French Reformed Confession of Faith* and an adaptation of the Genevan Ecclesiastical Ordinances.* Following a successful uprising against the Duke of Savoy (1560–61), they were given limited toleration* within their districts. The persecutions they suffered (1655; 1686–89) aroused great sympathy and solidarity from the European Reformed churches. They acquired full civil rights in Piedmont-Savoy (1848).

The present-day Waldensian church includes some 20,000 to 30,000 members in the Alps, Turin, Florence, and Rome as well as émigré communities in South America. An annual conference, or Tavola, is held at Torre Pèllice. The Facoltà valdese di teologia (from 1855) is based in Rome. The Società di Studi Valdesi publishes an annual scholarly bulletin on the movement.

A. Molnár, A. A. Hugon, and V. Vinay, *Storia dei Valdesi*, 3 vols. (1974–80); E. Cameron, *The Reformation of the Heretics: The Waldenses of the Alps 1480–1580* (1984).

EUAN CAMERON

War

Few issues have divided Christians more than the question of war. Three major historical positions have emerged.

1. Pacifism. The unwillingness of its members to participate in war characterized the early church and created some of the earliest "church-state" conflicts.

2. The just war theory provided criteria for determining whether or not a war was just, for example, declared by a legitimate authority, fought with a right intention, undertaken only as a last resort, waged with respect for the principle of proportionality (the end to be gained must outweigh the evil means employed), offering a reasonable chance of success, and waged with the greatest possible moderation. If all the criteria could be met, Christians could participate.

3. The holy war or crusade in which the moral stakes were considered so high that any action necessary to bring victory was legitimate, particularly if the war was between God's partisans and the "infidels."

The Protestant Reformers had little use for pacifism, but its tradition was kept alive by many "left-wing sectarians" (Quakers, Anabaptists, etc.). De facto, the major Reformation groups implicitly affirmed the just war theory, convinced that wars often had to be fought to support the right and oppose the wrong. But the line between a "just war" and a "crusade" was often blurred, and excesses of violence marked the "wars of religion" that raged in the wake of a divided church.

The duty to obey the state is frequently invoked as a reason for Christians to bear arms, though Calvin provided a tiny loophole at the end of the *Institutes* (4.20.32) in which "lesser magistrates" were encouraged to rebel if the cause of the king was clearly against God's will. Today most churches support the right of "conscientious objectors" to war to be excused from military service.

In the nuclear era, terms of the discussion have shifted, for wars can no longer be limited in scope or so waged that only professional soldiers are killed. Everyone is now a target. Entire villages can be exterminated with a single bomb, and the possibility of a chain reaction that would destroy the planet is real. As a result, a new position, "nuclear pacifism," has emerged, claiming that no "good" coming out of a nuclear war could justify the destruction involved.

War is now interrelated to all other issues; the ruinous cost of arms means lack of revenue for social services; the possession of nuclear weapons as "deterrents" threatens to escalate into use; large nations not wanting to risk global war turn to "low-intensity conflict" as a way of controlling the destinies of small nations at an "acceptable" cost.

As the social and human costs of modern war become less and less acceptable, the ancient biblical vision assumes new relevance: "Nation shall not lift up sword against nation, neither shall they learn war any more" (Isa. 2:4).

R. H. Bainton, *Christian Attitudes Toward War and Peace* (1960); A. Marrin, ed., *War and the Christian Conscience* (1971); J. Nelson-Pallmeyer, *War Against the Poor* (1989).

ROBERT MCAFEE BROWN

Warfield, Benjamin Breckinridge (1851–1921)

Major proponent of the Princeton Theology,* Warfield was born near Lexington, Kentucky. His father was a well-to-do farmer who specialized in breeding shorthorn cattle. His mother was the daughter of Robert Breckinridge, a learned Presbyterian pastor who wrote a two-volume systematic theology and was known for his anti-slavery* views.

After brilliant studies at Princeton University and in Europe, Warfield entered Princeton Seminary, where Charles Hodge* was still active, assisted by his son, A. A. Hodge.* Upon graduation (1876), Warfield married Annie Pearce Kinkead. During their honeymoon, she was struck by lightning in the Harz Mountains and was a permanent invalid. Warfield was wonderfully considerate of her to the day of her death (1915), hardly ever leaving their home for more than two hours at a time and carrying her up and down the stairs with exquisite tenderness.

After a short stage as assistant pastor in Baltimore, Warfield accepted a call to teach NT at Western Theological Seminary in Allegheny, Pennsylania (1878). There he distinguished himself in the study of the recently rediscovered *Didache*. With A. A. Hodge, he published an important article, "Inspiration," in the *Presbyterian Review* (April 1881). This set the tone for one of the major emphases of his career as a theologian. A small work, *Introduction to the Textual Criticism of the New Testament* (1886), was found so useful that it appeared in nine editions on both sides of the Atlantic.

Warfield accepted a call to succeed A. A. Hodge in the chair of didactic and polemic theology at Princeton Seminary (1887), where he remained active until his death on February 16, 1921. He taught his classes that very day.

Warfield's influence was exercised through his classes in the largest seminary of the Presbyterian Church, his impact on his colleagues, his editorship of the *Presbyterian and Reformed Review* (1890–1902) and later the *Princeton Theological Journal* (from 1903), and through a great stream of articles. This heritage was secured for posterity in ten substantial volumes in which many of his most important articles were reproduced, grouped by subjects (1927–32; repr. 1983). Another, briefer collection appeared in five volumes (1948–58), supplemented by two volumes of his *Shorter Writings*, not previously published and often very elusive (1970; 1973).

Warfield contended resolutely against proposed revisions of the WCF.* These were offered to soften the particularism of the confession and to assert a universal divine saving will for all humanity. In the late 1880s the General Assembly rejected the revisions, but in 1903 they were endorsed and incorporated into the church's Constitution, much to Warfield's chagrin. This and the union with the Cumberland Presbyterian Church spelled a certain waning of Warfield's influence in the Presbyterian Church U.S.A.

Though the range of Warfield's interests and articles was extremely broad, it is not difficult to pinpoint areas of specialization in his scholarship: Augustine,* Calvin,* and the Westminster Assembly.* The subjects to which his major concentration was given were the inspiration of Scripture,* predestination* and God's decrees,* the person and work of Christ, and perfectionism. Foremost among these is undoubtedly the defense of the plenary inspiration and inerrancy of Scripture, a topic to which Warfield devoted no fewer than eighty-three distinct printed contributions and in connection with which his name is justly famous.

One could probably state that no more accomplished scholar in the modern age has arisen to vindicate against all dissenters that the Bible is the very Word of God,* inerrant in the autographs and authoritative in all it asserts or requires, and that this is the teaching of the Bible itself and of the church universal until the nineteenth century.

ROGER NICOLE

Wars of Religion (French)

Eight civil wars for Huguenot* freedom of worship complicated by noble rivalries (Guise, Montmorency, Bourbon, Châtillon), international involvement (English, Swiss, papal, Netherlandish), and war with Spain (1562–98). Despite persecution under Henry II (1547–59) and Francis II (1559–60), Reformed Christianity grew and sought recognition. Catherine de Médicis, regent queen mother of Charles II (1560–74), issued a toleration edict (January 1562) unacceptable to the Guises, who massacred Huguenots at Vassy (March 1), leading to war. Louis de Condé's peace (March 1563) achieved limited toleration* but pleased few. Second and third wars (September 1567–March 1568; October 1568–August 1570) gained four fortified Huguenot towns. Gaspard de Coligny sought French support for international Protestantism in the Netherlands. He was massacred in Paris with other Huguenots on St. Bartholomew's Day* (August 24, 1572), renewing war (1572–73; 1574–76). Protestant resistance* theories flourished. Catholic Politiques opposed war and Spain. Peace (1576) allowed Huguenots worship everywhere except Paris and seats in the Parlements (courts). A militant Catholic League formed, and war recommenced (1577; 1580). The League resisted Henry of Navarre's succession to Henry III (1574–89), assassinated in the "War of the Three Henries" (1585–89). Henry IV (1589–1610) continued fighting Leaguers and the Duke of Parma, then reconciled Catholics by converting (July 25, 1593). War with Spain (1595–98) ending, he issued the Edict of Nantes,* granting Huguenots limited freedom of worship, fortified cities, and rights to office and justice.

N. M. Sutherland, *The Huguenot Struggle for Recognition* (1980).

JEANNINE E. OLSON

Watts, Isaac (1674–1748)

The father of English hymnody. Refusing an offer to be educated at Oxford that would have required him to become Anglican, Watts attended the nonconformist academy at Stoke Newington for eight years. He became pastor of Mark Lane Independent Chapel in London (1701) but soon thereafter became quite ill and an assistant was hired for most of the work. Watts remained a semi-invalid for life. He was a noted writer of books on grammar, pedagogy, ethics, and psychology; three volumes of sermons; and twenty-nine treatises on theology—fifty-two works in all, plus over six hundred hymns.

Watts was fifteen years old when he wrote his first hymn. This began a musical revolution in Reformed worship.* Hymns of human composition were thus introduced to the Anglican and Dissenting Churches of England. While Watts was not the first to write hymns, he was the first to have a method for doing so. Watts believed our songs are a human offering of praise to God.* Therefore the words should be our own. The psalms, if sung, should be Christianized and modernized. Thus Watts wrote two types of hymns, those of human composure and those based on psalms in which he used his imagination. Among his most popular hymns are "Joy to the World!" "When I Survey the Wondrous Cross," "Our God, Our Help in Ages Past," and "From All That Dwell Below the Skies."

Monuments to Watts are in Abney Park, Southampton Park, and Westminster Abbey. A memorial wall and a museum are on the site of his birthplace.

LINDAJO H. MCKIM

Weber, Otto (1902–1966)

Reformed theologian. Weber taught at the Theological Seminary, Elberfeld (1928–34), and was professor of Reformed theology at Göttingen (1934–66). He joined the Nazi party and the "German Christians" (1933) and was appointed by Reich Bishop Müller to the three-member Geistliche Ministerium as the Reformed Church representative. After the war he publicly renounced nazism and, thanks to Karl Barth's* recommendation, was allowed to continue teaching.

Weber is best known as a Calvin* scholar, Barth interpreter, and systematic theologian. A translator of Calvin's works, including the *Institutes* and commentaries, he also wrote extensively on Calvin's theology. His "Introductory Report" on Barth's *Church Dogmatics* remains a standard companion to Barth, while his own two-volume dogmatics has been widely hailed as an accessible introduction to Barthian systematic theology.

Weber's theology is characterized by dogmatics as the church's* response (*Antwort*) to the Word (*Wort*) of God* which is closely related to proclamation. Dogmatics follows, leads, and accompanies preaching;* there can be no preaching without dogmatics, but neither can there be dogmatics without preaching. The emphasis on the faithfulness of God in history* is a recurring theme for Weber. God's faithfulness, named and realized in Jesus Christ, is the foundation of Christian faith and life. Originally an OT scholar, Weber made considerable use of exegetical scholarship and historical theology in his systematic reflections.

O. Weber, *FD; Gesammelte Aufsätze,* 2 vols. (1967–68); *Karl Barth's Church Dogmatics: An Introductory Report* (ET 1953); and *Versammelte Gemeinde* (1949).

ROBERT R. REDMAN, JR.

Welsh Calvinistic Methodism

The Calvinistic Methodist Church of Wales began as a reform movement in the Church of England in eighteenth-century Wales. It was initiated by "Methodists" Griffith Jones (1683–1761), Howel Harris (1714–73), and Daniel Rowlands (1713–90) and influenced by the Calvinistic theology of George Whitefield.* Calvinistic Methodists founded churches among the Welsh settlers in New York, Pennsylvania, and Ohio. These churches organized a General Assembly (1869) and united with the Presbyterian Church in the U.S.A. (1920). The Church of Wales (68,585 members; 1989) belongs to the WARC.*

ROBERT BENEDETTO

Westminster Assembly

An assembly of 121 divines, assisted by lay assessors and Scottish commissioners, charged by the "Puritan" Long Parliament with making proposals for the reform of the Church of England, to make it "more agreeable to the Word of God." The meetings were held in Westminster Abbey—thus the name. However, the Assembly was not a synod or a church court but an advisory council summoned by the Parliament at a time when it was in open conflict with the monarch, Charles I, who was committed to the episcopal polity of the national church.

Its sessions (1643–48) were held during the Civil War,* and its work went much farther than originally intended. Work on the reform of the Thirty-nine Articles of Religion* led to the production of a Confession of Faith (Westminster Confession*), the Larger and Shorter Catechisms, the Directory for Public Worship, and the Form of Church Government. Further, Francis Rous's metrical version of the psalms was approved and commended for use by the churches.

Not England but Scotland, and churches related to the Church of Scotland, benefited from the Assembly. The Scottish Kirk and other Presbyterian churches adopted the Westminster documents. In England, where Independents had come to the fore through the war, the documents were not used. With the Restoration of the monarchy and episcopal government (1660), they were forgotten.

S. W. Carruthers, *The Everyday Work of the Westminster Assembly* (1943); J. H. Leith, *Assembly at Westminster* (1973); A. F. Mitchell and J. B. Struthers, eds., *Minutes of the Sessions of the Westminster Assembly* (1890); R. S. Paul, *The Assembly of the Lord* (1985); B. B. Warfield, *The Westminster Assembly and Its Work* (1931).

PETER TOON

Westminster Confession of Faith

The work of an English assembly and Scottish commissioners (1647), the WCF was a fair summary of the theological consensus among British Protestants. But it never played a significant role in the future of Protestantism in England.

Yet the confession did become the most influential and, for centuries, the sole confessional authority among most English-speaking Presbyterians. This remarkable influence of a confession written under the authority of an assembly called by an English Parliament is due to the high technical competence of the confession itself and its success in embodying a consensus of Reformed theology* as modified by English Puritanism.* It unites the work of the classical Reformed theologians such as Zwingli,* Bullinger,* and Calvin* with the ancient Augustinian* tradition in England as well as the prolific theological work of the Puritans.

The confession embodies the theological achievements of Protestant scholasticism* that produced in the seventeenth century a universal Reformed vocabulary along with clearly defined theological terms and carefully analyzed theological issues. The scholastics, in seeking clarity and precision, became increasingly abstract, and the WCF lacks the historical qualities of the Scots Confession (1560) or the experiential emphasis of the Heidelberg Catechism* or even the Second Helvetic Confession.*

The opening chapter, "Of the Holy Scripture," is an introduction to the confession's theology, laying out the sources of theology and directing how the theologian moves from sources to theological confession, that is, to what must be said in a particular time on the basis of what is said in the Bible. The confession's authors were sure God was revealed through "the light of nature," a revelation of God implanted in the human heart as well as in the created order. The confession did not denigrate this revelation, but insisted it was not sufficient for human salvation.* The Scriptures* are indispensable, and they are the norm of all theological work. The chapter predates historical criticism but is so carefully done that it does not require revision in the light of what is known as the critical study of the Scriptures today.

A second characteristic of the confession is the emphasis upon the Lordship and sovereignty of God. When the writers attempted to say who God is, they declared their belief in the "one only living and true God . . . working all things according to the counsel of his own immutable and most righteous will." When they spoke of God's eternal decree, that is, God's eternal purpose, they declared that "God from all eternity did by the most wise and holy counsel of his own will, freely and unchangeably ordain whatsoever comes to pass." The ease with which the confession speaks of the decree of God* creates a difficulty for contemporary Christians. But when "purpose" is substituted for decree, the writers' intention becomes clear. The confession emphasizes throughout the personal activity of God in the created order.

The most striking innovation in seventeenth-century Reformed theology was the development of covenant* theology. Along with election, covenant is a preeminent expression of God's saving activity among human beings. Biblical faith can be reduced to neither election nor covenant. The WCF remarkably unites election and covenant without making either one the single dominating, unifying principle of the theology. Covenant theologians focused attention away from the decrees of God abstractly considered to the working out of those decrees in human history,* and they related the decree of God to the responsible action of human beings.

A fourth characteristic of the confession is an emphasis on the Christian life.

The writers knew that the end of Christian faith is not forgiveness* but the sanctification of the forgiven person, the transformation of the sinner into the image of Christ. The confession's emphasis on sanctification,* adoption,* and finally glorification—the completion of the transformation of human life in the kingdom of God*—is supplemented by the extensive treatment of the commandments in the Westminster Larger Catechism and Shorter Catechism. Two-thirds of the confession is devoted to an analytical description of the Christian life and its practices and responsibilities in the world. The primary purpose of the Christian life is the glory of God, not the realization of human identity or potential or even the service of human beings.

The confession fully reflects its origin in the struggles of English society (1643–47). Its statements about church and state are very dated. But even in the midst of these most dated sections, there are remarkable affirmations: "God alone is Lord of the conscience, and hath left it free from the doctrines and commandments of men which are in anything contrary to his Word, or beside it in matters of faith or worship. So that to believe such doctrines, or to obey such commandments out of conscience, is to betray true liberty of conscience; and the requiring an implicit faith, and an absolute and blind obedience, is to destroy liberty of conscience, and reason also" (*BC*, 6.109).

A. I. C. Heron, ed., *The Westminster Confession in the Church Today* (1982); J. H. Leith, *Assembly at Westminster* (1973); A. F. Mitchell, *The Westminster Assembly: Its History and Standards* (1883); A. F. Mitchell and J. B. Struthers, eds., *Minutes of the Sessions of the Westminster Divines* (1984).

JOHN H. LEITH

Westminster Standards *see* Westminster Confession of Faith

Whitefield, George (1714–1770)

The "Grand Itinerant" of the American Great Awakening* made a greater impact on evangelical Christianity in the eighteenth century than any other single colonial preacher. His tireless regimen of preaching ten sermons a week led him to every colony, where his powerful orations brought significant growth to every English-speaking Protestant group of Reformed leanings.

Whitefield was born in Gloucester, England, where he was raised by his widowed mother. Despite poor eyesight and financial hardships, he proved to be an apt student and matriculated at Pembroke College, Oxford University. At Oxford he met John and Charles Wesley and joined the Holy Club, a serious group of students who met regularly for prayer and Bible study.

A conversion* experience (1735) propelled Whitefield into open-air evangelism* and early fame as a preacher. Three years later he sailed for Georgia and established "Bethesda," an orphanage for the poor children of that colony. In order to raise money for this project Whitefield began a series of speaking tours which took him to England, Wales, Scotland, and Ireland. Seven times he sailed to America.

His preaching was emotional and extemporaneous. He emphasized the "new birth" which led to assurance of salvation* and progress in sanctification.* His contact with Presbyterian* ministers and evangelists led him to move away from Wesley's Arminian theology to a clearly Calvinistic* position. While holding to predestination* and personal election, Whitefield nevertheless offered Christ's salvation* to all. His approach led to criticism from university professors as well as the nonrevival party of the Presbyterian ministers. He died of asthma while on a Massachusetts preaching tour.

G. Whitefield, *Works*, 7 vols., ed. J. K. Gillies (1771–72); A. A. Dallimore, *George Whitefield*, 2 vols. (1970–80).

NATHAN P. FELDMETH

Whyte, Alexander (1836–1921)

Late-Victorian Scotland's greatest preacher, Whyte was minister of Free (later United Free) St. George's, Edinburgh (1870–1916), and principal of New College (1909–18). An evangelical of evangelicals, Calvinist* in theology and Puritan in piety,* he expounded human sinfulness and divine grace* with exceptional eloquence, imagination, and psychological insight. Irenic and open-minded, he published discerning appreciations of Christians as diverse as Dante, St. Theresa, Bunyan,* Law, and Newman, and—influentially—welcomed both the new science of biblical criticism and the beginnings of the ecumenical movement ("Edinburgh, 1910").

G. F. Barbour, *The Life of Alexander Whyte* (1924).

A. C. CHEYNE

Williams, John (1796–1839)

Missionary born in Tottenham, London, who served an apprenticeship as an ironmonger. Converted through a Calvinistic Independent congregation, Williams volunteered with the London Missionary Society* (1816). Though only age twenty and little educated, he was accepted for stationing in the Pacific. Until 1827 he was based in the Society Islands, mainly Raiatéa. He purchased a ship and identified Rarotonga (in the Cook Islands). He built his own ship and ranged widely, evangelizing through Polynesian missionaries. He also translated and stimulated local technology. In Britain (1835–38) he moved audiences nationwide and wrote one of the earliest missionary best-sellers. He went to Samoa (1838) and was killed endeavoring to introduce the gospel in Erromanga (in Vanuatu).

J. Williams, *A Narrative of Missionary Enterprise in the South Sea Islands* (1839); J. Campbell, *The Martyr of Erromanga* (1842); J. Garrett, *To Live Among the Stars* (1982); E. Prout, *Memoirs of John Williams* (1842).

ANDREW F. WALLS

Williams, William (1717–1791)

Welsh evangelical clergyman, author, and hymn writer. Williams was born at Llanfair-ar-y-bryn, Carmarthenshire, son of John and Dorothy Williams. He was educated at Llwyn-llwyd Academy and while there was converted under the preaching of Howel Harris. Though a Congregationalist, he was ordained deacon in the Anglican Church (1740) and served as a curate until 1743 when he was refused ordination as a priest. Thereafter he worked with the Methodists, becoming one of their foremost leaders. After his marriage to Mary Francis (1748), he lived at Pantycelyn, hence his sobriquet "Williams Pantycelyn."

Williams published over ninety titles—poetry and prose—in Welsh and English. He was a sensitive protagonist of Reformed orthodoxy* in the idiom of covenant* theology which he expounded with rare existential warmth. Thus his epic poem, "Golwg ar Deyrnas Crist" ("View of Christ's Kingdom"), celebrates the objective and cosmic significance of God's mighty works, while its companion, "Theomemphus," analyzes the subjective impact of redemption. But his greatest contribution was his hymns. He composed 893 in Welsh and 123 in English. These place him in the front rank of Christian hymn writers.

DNB; Dictionary of Welsh Biography; Glyn Tegai Hughes, *William Pantycelyn* (1983), Derec Llwyd Morgan, *The Great Awakening in Wales* (1988).

R. TUDUR JONES

Willison, John (1680–1750)

A minister of the Church of Scotland, Willison wrote extensively on the classical Reformed approach to worship* and piety.* As pastor of South Church, Dundee, he won wide respect for his thoughtful catechetical instruction and reverent conduct of worship. His *Sanctification of the Lord's Day* (1713) is a good treatise on the theology of worship, while his Communion sermons and *Sacramental Directory* (1846) portray the traditional Scottish Communion season. His *Sacramental Meditations* (1761) was very popular for several generations in both Scotland and America.

DNB 21:498ff.

HUGHES OLIPHANT OLD

Wilson, Woodrow (1856–1924)

Wilson was born in a Presbyterian manse in Staunton, Virginia. His father, Joseph Ruggles Wilson, was a pastor and seminary professor and for nearly forty years Stated Clerk of the General Assembly* of the PCUS. His mother, Janet (or Jessie)

Woodrow, came from a distinguished family of ministers, including James Woodrow (1828–1917), a prominent southern Presbyterian theologian.

After a brief and unhappy period of practicing law, Wilson became a professor at Bryn Mawr, Wesleyan, and Princeton and was elected president of Princeton University (1902). He became governor of New Jersey (1910) and won election as President of the United States (1912; 1916).

Wilson voiced his "unspeakable joy" at being raised in a minister's family and testified often to the importance of faith* in his life. "My life would not be worth living," he declared, "if it were not for the driving power of religion, for *faith*, pure and simple." Biographers have also stressed the centrality of religion in understanding Wilson's personality and politics. Calvinism* influenced his understanding of both his personal and the nation's identity and mission.

A. S. Link, *The Higher Realism of Woodrow Wilson* (1971); J. Mulder, *Woodrow Wilson: The Years of Preparation* (1978).

JOHN M. MULDER

Wishart, George (c. 1513–1546)

Martyr and forerunner of the Scottish Reformation.* Wishart was Louvain-educated, and his apparent humanist* background may have facilitated his conversion* to Protestantism. Charged with heresy* both in Scotland and in England (1538–39), possibly for Anabaptism, he fled to Germany and Switzerland. In Switzerland he was influenced by moderate Zwinglianism and translated the First Helvetic Confession* into English. On his return to Scotland (1543), he preached for three years before being executed for heresy. He is reputed to have influenced the conversion of John Knox.* Wishart helped both to mediate the Zurich theology to Scotland and to popularize the notion of the church* as the gathered congregation of believers.

DNB 62:248–51; J. Knox, *History of the Reformation in Scotland*, ed. W. C. Dickinson (repr. 1949); P. Lorimer, *The Scottish Reformation* (1860).

W. IAN A. HAZLETT

Witherspoon, John (1723–1794)

After serving two parishes in the Church of Scotland, Witherspoon emigrated to America (1768) to become president of the College of New Jersey (Princeton University). He was a leader in the American Presbyterian Church,* a statesman who served in the New Jersey state legislature and the Continental Congress, and the only clergyman to sign the Declaration of Independence (1776).

Witherspoon was educated at the University of Edinburgh in arts and divinity. After ordination (1745), he soon acquired national renown as an evangelical preacher and leader of the Popularist party within the Scottish Church. In America he denounced Berkeleian idealistic philosophy while instructing his Princeton students in Scottish common sense realism,* which was to become increasingly influential in the nineteenth century. Education should lead to public service, he taught, and set a memorable personal example. His graduates included one U.S. President (Madison), one Vice-President, twenty senators, twenty-three representatives, and three Supreme Court justices.

In the church, he held fast to the Westminster Standards, customarily preaching strong biblical sermons on WCF* themes. While recognizing the need for American denominations to coexist peaceably, he worked actively to form a national Presbyterian Church and was named convening Moderator of its first General Assembly* (1789).

Witherspoon's *Works* contained his preeminent college course, "Lectures on Moral Philosophy," political essays, "Lectures on Divinity," and numerous sermons (4 vols.; 1800–1801). The definitive biography remains that of Varnum L. Collins, *President Witherspoon* (2 vols., 1925; repr. 1969).

L. GORDON TAIT

Witness of the Holy Spirit

The witness of the Holy Spirit (*testimonium Spiritus Sancti*) enables Christians to know the truth of reality and the reality of truth. In opposition to the Roman Catholic Church, John Calvin* stressed the importance of this teaching. Scripture's believability is based not on the (authority of the) church* but on the Spirit's external witness in Scripture* and internal witness in Christians. Although Scripture is *autopistic*, that is, carries its own credibility and evokes respect for its inherent majesty, it does not seriously affect believers until the testimony of the Spirit seals it upon their hearts (*Inst.* 1.7.5). Through this internal witness, Christian believers obtain the faith* necessary to acknowledge, with indubitable certainty, the *theopneustic* (inspired) character of Scripture (2 Tim. 3:16; 1 Peter 1:21) and its divine authority.

Through this witness, Christians not only accept Scripture as God's Word but also acknowledge (John 15:26; 16:13; Rom. 8:16) the entire revelation of salvation,* that is, the promises of the gospel, the grace* of God, their election in Christ, and their acceptance as God's children.

The inner testimony of the Holy Spirit is not a separate, isolated, or additional revelation, nor is it a proof based on psychic experience or rational proof. According to the WCF,* it is a power that convicts and assures Christians of the infallible truth and divine authority of Scripture.

This witness of the Spirit is important not only for personal faith but also for ecclesiastical acceptance of Scripture as canon.* Believers accept "without a doubt all things contained in Scripture—not so much because the church receives or approves them as such but because the Holy Spirit testifies in our hearts that they are from God" (Belgic Confession, art. 5).

Herman Bavinck* stated that the basis for acknowledging the canon of Scripture lies in Scripture itself as the Spirit's *external* witness and that Christians actually recognize this canon of the written Word through the Spirit's *internal* witness in their hearts. Although not the basis, this inner testimony (*testimonium internum*) of the Spirit is the deepest reason for the faith of Christians (Acts 16:14; 1 Cor. 2:14).

Calvin rejected the intellectualism inherent in medieval scholasticism.* Knowing does not precede the witness of the Spirit, nor does it merely confirm in the heart what is already known in the head. Revelation is not rational, nor is faith intellectual. Believers are not first rationally convinced by the formal credibility of Scripture and only afterward convicted in their hearts by the internal witness of the Spirit concerning the message of the written Word.

The *autopistic* character of Scripture is not isolated from and preparatory to the Spirit's witness. Unlike the theologians of Protestant scholasticism,* Calvin did not think of reason* and Spirit's witness as constituting two forms of faith, Scripture and Spirit as providing two sources of knowledge, or Scripture (as external object) and witness of the Spirit (as internal subject) producing two kinds of witness.

Scripture is not prior to and complemented by the internal witness of the Spirit. The Spirit's witness continues and completes the witness of Scripture. Though not identical, these two forms of witness are intimately related to each other. Believing Scripture is impossible without believing in Jesus Christ, and believing in Jesus Christ is impossible without believing Scripture (Luke 24:27). Believing Scripture presupposes and expresses itself in believing in Christ. Scripture is not something rational apart from the Spirit, nor is the Spirit something mystical apart from Scripture. The inner testimony of the Holy Spirit is the basic reason for and essence of Scripture's pointing to Christ.

By being grounded in Christ through the Spirit's witness, Christians appropriate the truth of Scripture. It prevents them from separating Scripture and Christ and from succumbing to three dangers—namely, *spiritualism*, which separates Jesus and Spirit from Scripture and creation;* *secularism*, which ignores the Spirit's witness and Scripture; and *biblicism*, which relativizes general revelation and the witness of the Spirit and places ultimate certainty in a set of rationally accessible teachings. The Spirit that causes Scripture to be inspired by its authors also causes it to be accepted by its readers. Not of themselves, but through this testimony of the Holy Spirit,

Christians are immediately convinced of Scripture's divine authority (1 Cor. 2:14).

H. Bavinck, *Gereformeerde Dogmatiek* (1928[4]), 1:552ff.; H. Berkhof, *The Doctrine of the Holy Spirit* (1967); E. Doumergue, *Jean Calvin*, vol. 4 (1910); S. Greijdanus, "Karakter van het Testimonium Spiritus Sancti volgens Calvijn," *Gereformeerd Theologische Tijdschrift* 14 (1914): 519–43; A. Kuyper, *The Work of the Holy Spirit* (1900); T. Preiss, *Das innere Zeugnis des Heiligen Geistes* (1947); G. Vandervelde, ed., *The Holy Spirit: Renewing and Empowering Presence* (1989).

JOHN C. VANDER STELT

Wollebius, Johannes (1586–1629)

German Swiss Reformed author of a popular theological textbook. A lifelong Basel resident, Wollebius studied theology under Amandus Polanus,* took a pastorate (1611), and became cathedral preacher and professor of OT (1618). His *Compendium theologiae Christianae* (*Compendium of Christian Theology*; 1626), representative of the Dortian* era, was quickly reprinted several times and translated into English and Dutch because of its clarity, conciseness, organization, and orthodoxy. It was infralapsarian* on predestination* and influenced the Westminster* catechisms, for example, in bifurcating theology into the knowledge of God* and the service of God.

J. W. Beardslee III, ed. and trans., *Reformed Dogmatics* (1965).

EARL WM. KENNEDY

Women in the Reformed Tradition (16th–18th Centuries)

Reformed leaders, inspired by the writings of John Calvin,* regarded marriage,* sexuality, and women much more positively than did their medieval predecessors. Yet their views did little to alter women's subordinate position in Western culture, though they did initiate beneficial changes in marriage laws and educational opportunities. While it is unclear why they were motivated by such changes, many women, particularly of noble birth, were active in promoting Calvinism* in Europe. Calvinist beliefs and practices also had an impact on the status of women in the North American colonies through the New England Puritans.*

Reformed leaders agreed that marriage had been depreciated unjustifiably by the medieval church which had mistakenly concluded that celibacy earned great merit in the eyes of God.* On the basis of Jesus' words and OT examples, marriage was regarded as blessed by God and the norm for all Christians. Calvin did concede that God sometimes gave Christians a temporary gift of celibacy but that it was rare and was bestowed only to facilitate God's work. Closely linked to the Reformed claims about marriage was the insistence that sexual union in this relationship was honorable and holy. Marriage was certainly described as God's provision for the orderly satisfaction of lust as well as for the creation and rearing of children. But the Reformed leaders gradually enlarged their understanding. Marriage came to be spoken of as a union of souls, a close companionship, and an opportunity for the growth of faith.*

Though the Reformed tradition exalted marriage over celibacy, it removed marriage from its status as a sacrament.* There was no biblical warrant for considering it as such. This meant that divorce became an option where the Reformed tradition dominated, though it was not encouraged. Grounds for divorce included adultery and desertion, and in some places laws were enacted enabling women as well as men to sue for divorce.

Reformed leaders agreed with their Lutheran counterparts that women and men were spiritual equals. Just as Adam and Eve shared responsibility for the first sin,* so their descendants were equally prone to evil and equally redeemed by the work of Christ. Yet while the Calvinists shunned the misogynism of the medieval period, they did continue to teach that the principle of supremacy and subordination be applied to all male/female relationships. Calvin shaped the Reformed position in claiming that in God's original creation, the female was created as the helper and inferior of the male. The tradition backed up this biblical claim by noting that women had certain physical and intellectual weaknesses which made them unfit for leadership in church and state. Thus, both Calvin and Knox* could speak out against female monarchs, though Calvin was forced to conclude that God sometimes placed women in unnatural positions of leadership to reproach men.

A great deal of attention was given particularly to the operation of the principle of subordination in the home. Wives were to be obedient to their husbands, even when suffering abuse. Yet the Reformed pastors gave new prestige to married women who bore children and managed a household. Their work was called a vocation,* a noble enterprise ordained by God. Their domestic sphere was the preeminent locus for the nurturing faith in old and young alike. Their responsibility especially to teach the Bible and the tenets of the Reformed tradition led to some efforts to see that women received an education. In imitation of the Genevan example, schools for girls were established in many Reformed communities to teach reading, writing, needlework, and pious and submissive behavior. Humanism* had already promoted female education among the economic elite; the Reformation promoted it among middle- and lower-class women.

Reformed leaders affirmed Luther's* doctrine of the priesthood of all believers, giving women a role equal to men's in nurturing faith in others. This activity was always circumscribed, however, by what the community accepted as decent and orderly conduct. For Calvinists, this meant that women were excluded from the public ministry of Word and Sacrament as well as governance of churches. Even attempts by some Reformed churches to introduce the position of deaconess for women to institutionalize their work in charity and nursing were discouraged. Calvin, however, makes an interesting distinction between fundamental doctrines that were true for all time and church practices that could vary from culture to culture. He classifies the silence of women in the latter category.

The ideas and practices of European Calvinism were transported to North America primarily by English and Scots Presbyterians* and by English Congregationalists* and Baptists. Woman as Jezebel and spiritual inferior to man is an image present in some early Puritan writings and provides a context for the persecution of nonconformist women such as Anne Hutchinson and Mary Dyer. Gradually, however, the major themes of European Reformed thought dominate colonial literature. Women are accorded honor as submissive wives and mothers but kept firmly in subordinate roles in home, church, and colony. They do not teach, preach, or celebrate the sacraments* as was the practice occasionally in European congregations. They were sometimes seated separately from men and received the Lord's Supper* after them.

Many women contributed to the spread of Calvinism in Europe. Most did so indirectly as spouses of Reformed leaders. Among the noble classes, however, opportunities for obeying Calvin's mandate that Christians create a holy society were significant. Women with property and political influence, such as Madelein Mailly, comtesse de Roye and Renée de France, duchess of Ferrara, gave refuge to Reformed preachers, financed schools, and sponsored public debates. Particularly in France, they used their powers of persuasion and position to win converts to Calvinism and tolerance* for its churches. A similar pattern can be detected among Puritan women in England.

In the New England colonies, power was exercised by women in some alternative manners. Women persuaded town councils to provide churches and ministers, had a hand in shaping ministerial reputations in the community, and became adept at writing and speaking on behalf of their faith. The conversion* experience of the eighteenth-century awakenings provided an additional context in which women could step over prescribed gender boundaries. They formed prayer and discussion groups and, like Sarah Edwards, discovered that the ecstasy of grace* made them more anxious to please God than man.

J. D. Douglass, *Women, Freedom, and Calvin* (1985); R. L. Greaves, ed., *Triumph Over Silence: Women in Protestant*

History (1985); B. J. MacHaffie, *Her Story: Women in Christian Tradition* (1986); R. R. Ruether, ed., *Religion and Sexism* (1974); L. T. Ulrich, *Good Wives: Image and Reality in the Lives of Women in Northern New England 1650–1750* (1980).

BARBARA J. MACHAFFIE

Women in the Reformed Tradition (19th–20th Centuries)

Traditionally the Reformed position on women's authority in the church* followed an interpretation of Scripture* which held that God created women to be subordinate to men and silent in the church. In the nineteenth and twentieth centuries, however, women in the Reformed tradition assumed influential financial and programmatic responsibilities in the areas of missions and education. They also sought a reinterpretation of the definition of women's role and ultimately secured the right to equal status through ordination.*

Early Reformed theologians acknowledged that women were "religiously inclined" but insisted that the Bible, the order of nature, and propriety mandated the exclusion of females from governing or ministerial roles. This explication, largely based on their interpretation of the position of John Calvin* regarding women in church and society, supported the argument undergirding women's ecclesiastical role well into the twentieth century, even with changing cultural, social, and theological patterns.

Subordinate, silent, and submissive in the nineteenth-century church, many women assumed a position responsible for the nurture of the family. Some women, however, became interested in the varied nonsectarian male organizations devoted to societal reform, missions, colportage, education, and publication that proliferated in the first half of the century and themselves established their own small praying, cent, and sewing societies. In the United States, for example, the experiences of these modest groups foreshadowed in the latter part of the century the development of large regional and national women's organizations that emphasized "woman's work for women and children" and financially supported mission, health and education, and church extension projects. Such involvement, as well as the availability to women of church vocations not requiring ordination, increased their participation in church endeavors.

Women's influence and financial support did not hide their disenfranchisement in church courts and congregations. In the early twentieth century, several issues—including a dissatisfaction with procedures among active churchwomen, decline of interest and membership among younger women, and public discussion of theological issues concerning women's rights in the church—motivated a political struggle to secure full equality. At differing times, denominations in the Reformed tradition amended their constitutions to permit women to be elected deacons,* then elders.* Much slower to be enacted was the right of women to serve as ordained clergy.

The discussion of the role of women was replicated in other groups, such as the WCC* (1948). In 1952 Kathleen Bliss prepared a study, *The Service and Status of Women in the Churches*, the first worldwide study of its kind that gathered and interpreted information regarding women from fifty-eight countries. Two years later, the WCC created the Department of Cooperation of Men and Women in Church and Society, which would promote the recognition of women in the total life of the church. Similarly, the WARC* urged the approval of women delegates to the all-male assembly (1953). Hugh T. Kerr presented a paper to the Alliance on "The Place and Status of Women in the Reformed Tradition" in which he noted that "it is a sobering and humiliating fact that the various movements in modern times for the emancipation of women have owed more to sociological and secular forces than to the witness or impact of the Christian Church." The Alliance admitted women delegates (1954), but since delegates had to be either ministers or elders, the number of women eligible was very small.

In terms of women's ordination, the United Reformed Church in England ordained Maude Warden in 1917. The United Church of Canada ordained Lydia Gruchy (1936), while the Presbyterian Church in Canada authorized women's ordination in 1968. The French Reformed Church ordained Elisabeth Schmidt (1949), though it was 1965 before women in general were permitted ordination. In Japan, women's ordination, begun by the Presbyterians (1933), continued with the establishment of the United Church of Christ in Japan. In the United States, Louisa Woosley was ordained in the Cumberland Presbyterian Church (1889), though the ordination was revoked a few years later. Margaret Towner became the first woman minister in the Presbyterian Church in the U.S.A. (1956). Rachel Henderlite was the first woman ordained in the PCUS (1965). In 1979 the General Synod of the Reformed Church in America voted to ordain women.

Legislating equality did not mandate attitudinal approval of women deacons, elders, and clergy. In terms of the parish ministry, women seminary graduates found first calls elusive and upward mobility limited. Advocacy groups seeking to improve acceptance of women clergy are reporting improvement, particularly as more congregations experience the ministry of women pastors.

Even with the history of restricted access to ordination and participation in decision making in the Reformed tradition, many women have distinguished themselves as ministers, administrators, teachers, missionaries, evangelists, and philanthropists. Wives of ministers and missionaries have had a significant impact on the developing role of women in the church. Above all, female members, often comprising a majority of the congregational memberships, have supported the churches by their gifts, service, and attendance throughout the nineteenth and twentieth centuries.

M. K. Bennett, *Status of Women in the Presbyterian Church in the U.S.A. with References to Other Denominations* (c. 1929); L. A. Boyd and R. D. Brackenridge, *Presbyterian Women in America: Two Centuries of a Quest for Status* (1983); C. J. Blaisdell, "The Matrix of Reform: Women in the Lutheran and Calvinist Movements," in *Triumph Over Silence: Women in Protestant History*, ed. R. L. Greaves (1985); J. D. Douglass, *Women, Freedom, and Calvin* (1985); R. Tucker and W. Liefeld, *Daughters of the Church: Women and Ministry from New Testament Times to the Present* (1987).

LOIS A. BOYD

Word of God

The Word of God is God's eternal Wisdom, itself fully divine, which subsists eternally as the Second Person of the triune being of the Godhead. Directed outward toward the world, this Word becomes the active instrument of God's creative and redemptive power: The Word is the active agent in creation (Gen. 1) and the embodiment of God's redeeming power in history (Isa. 55:10–11).

The Word of God revealed. The Word functions as the vehicle of God's self-disclosure. It came in "many and various ways" to the patriarchs and prophets of old and appears finally incarnate* in human flesh in the person of Jesus (John 1:1–14; Heb. 1:1–2). The distinctiveness of the Reformed doctrine of the Word lies less in any novel conception and more in the doctrine's centrality both in theology and in the life of the church. Though Reformed theologians differ over the extent to which a natural knowledge of God* is theoretically attainable within the created order, most agree that the only effective means for sinners to attain a saving knowledge is through God's self-disclosure in the Word. The attempts of fallen human beings to reach upward to God are ultimately futile, whether the point of contact with the divine is conceived as nature, history,* reason,* tradition,* experience,* or even religion itself. Access to the one true God is given in the form of a divine initiative, a sovereign Word which comes to us from One who is other than ourselves. As such, it is a gift of divine grace, utterly beyond the reach of human striving and wholly beyond human control.

Attentiveness to this revealed Word thus becomes the central focus of life and worship* among the Reformed: Their churches are reformed "according to the Word of God" and sustained by it; their worship centers around the proclamation of the Word; their sacraments are understood as inseparable in principle from the Word.

The Word of God written. Reformed theologians affirm that the Word of God is contained in the Scriptures* of the OT and NT, though the sense in which this is the case is subject to varying interpretations. Barth speaks for much of the recent tradition in describing Scripture as authoritative testimony to the Word of God which was given directly only to the prophets and apostles. Another strand of the tradition, typified by the so-called high orthodoxy* of the late seventeenth century, posits a more mechanical theory of inspiration in which the text of Scripture is dictated word for word by the Holy Spirit, with the biblical writers acting as little more than recording secretaries. Both strands claim Calvin as a forebear, and one can indeed find isolated passages in the *Institutes* that appear to support either view (see McNeill).

Reformed understandings of Scripture are characterized by an emphasis on the essential unity of OT and NT. Christ, the incarnate Word, is the unifying content of both, though the manner of his presentation differs from one to the other: the OT foreshadows Christ under signs and types; the NT presents him directly.

The Word of God proclaimed. The Word of God manifests itself in the church's proclamation. The Second Helvetic Confession states: "The preaching of the Word of God is the Word of God" (ch. 1). Human language, however, whether the biblical text or the church's proclamation, becomes the bearer of God's Word only by the active power of the Holy Spirit. Calvin insists (*Inst.* 1.9.3) that the Word of God in Scripture and proclamation is joined inseparably with the work of the Holy Spirit*: God's Word comes to us effectively through these human media only as the dead letter of the text is vivified by the life-giving Spirit. Thus the Spirit causes believers to hear and respond to God's authoritative address in the human words of Scripture and preaching;* and these words in turn give positive content to the inward testimony of the Spirit.

Barth, *CD* I/1–2; J. T. McNeill, "The Significance of the Word of God for Calvin," *CH* 28 (June 1959): 131–46; R. S. Wallace, *Calvin's Doctrine of the Word and Sacrament* (1953); U. Zwingli, "Of the Clarity and Certainty of the Word of God," in *Zwingli and Bullinger*, ed. G. W. Bromiley, LCC, vol. 21 (1953).

P. MARK ACHTEMEIER

Work

In the Reformed tradition, work is viewed positively as part of everyone's call to serve and glorify God. Worshiping God, however, rather than work is our ultimate purpose in life. The creation of the Sabbath as the day of rest was intended to put the meaning of work in perspective. Work is an expression of our stewardship;* worship* is the culmination of our vocation.* Whenever work is separated from worship, the former loses its purpose and becomes the curse that alienates and dehumanizes us (Eccl. 2:4–11, 20–22; Luke 12:16–21). Work that becomes an end in itself is a form of idolatry.*

This is why Calvin* insisted that a person's work be seen as one's calling. We were created and called to be stewards of God's creation;* we live by grace* and our response daily ought to be one of thanksgiving and gratitude. To those who do not work, the biblical charge is clear: "Anyone unwilling to work should not eat" (2 Thess. 3:10). Such a biblical admonition was taken seriously by the Reformers, for they saw work as both a duty and a discipline under God.

However, in contrast to an earlier agrarian society, the realities in our technologically oriented world may make this admonition to work more difficult to fulfill. Is there sufficient and meaningful work today for everyone? Should work be understood as a basic human right? These are some of the perplexing theological and ethical questions confronting us as we seek to understand the future meaning of work while remaining faithful to our biblical heritage.

All work, to be meaningful, must not only fulfill the human search to be needed but also contribute an added value to society. Work must reflect and uphold the intrinsic worth of persons, lest individuals become treated as commodities. Also, the worker must realize that work is created to meet the real need of society and not simply work for the sake of work.

All work should come with some sense of "calling." This understanding of Christian vocation* has always been a significant theme in Reformed thought. Along with the sense of calling for whatever work one does, the worker also brings a dimension of creativity to the situation. Creativity with a sense of calling is what makes work meaningful. We were created to create, and there can be no creation without a God-given sense of calling, no matter how modest that contribution may be. In short, the Reformed understanding of work celebrates every worker who labors to God's glory.

G. Baum, "Toward a Theology of Work," *The Ecumenist*, Sept.–Oct. 1989; R. A. Calhoun, *God and the Day's Work* (1943); J. Moltmann, *Creating a Just Future* (1989); J. C. Raines and D. Day-Lower, *Modern Work and Human Meaning* (1986); A. Richardson, *The Biblical Doctrine of Work* (1952).

CARNEGIE SAMUEL CALIAN

World Alliance of Reformed Churches

The Alliance (WARC) results from the 1970 union of the World Presbyterian Alliance (1875; WPA) with the International Congregational Council (1891; ICC). James MacGregor and James McCosh,* among others (1860s), proposed convening an international council of Presbyterians for fellowship and testimony. Philip Schaff* and William Garden Blaikie promoted this, the latter becoming the first president of the WPA (1888–92). Thus was born the oldest modern Christian world communion.

History. In 1874, Hastings Ross published "An Ecumenical Council of Congregational Churches"—a suggestion also espoused by Henry Martyn Dexter and Alexander Hannay. Robert W. Dale* presided over the ICC's first meeting.

The WPA held 19 Councils prior to the 1970 union; the ICC, 10. The Centennial Consultation (1977) was followed by the twenty-second Council in Ottawa (1982) and the twenty-third in Seoul (1989). The Alliance currently has 172 member churches from more than eighty countries, embracing some seventy million Christians.

Whether the WPA should prepare one confessional statement for all member churches was debated twice prior to 1930. Such a statement was never devised by the WPA, however, partly because some argued that the attempt at a universally acceptable form of words would result in division and partly because the WPA, as an instrument of fellowship and not a churchly body as such, had no need for a confession of its own.

Membership of the Alliance is open to applicant churches and unions that meet the requirements of the Constitution (amended 1982): "Any Church which accepts Jesus Christ as Lord and Saviour; holds the Word of God given in the Scriptures of the Old and New Testaments to be the supreme authority in matters of faith and life; acknowledges the need for continuing reformation of the Church catholic; whose position in faith and evangelism is in general agreement with that of the historic Reformed confessions, recognizing that the Reformed tradition is a biblical, evangelical and doctrinal ethos, rather than any narrow and exclusive definition of faith and order, shall be eligible for membership."

Under this rubric a diverse family has gathered. Member churches differ historically, ecclesiologically, theologically, culturally, linguistically, and economically. Some look to such "Reformers before the Reformation" as Peter Waldo and John Hus; many have yet to reach their centenary. Most are presbyterian* in polity,* some congregational,* emphasizing the nature of the church as at once gathered and catholic. About sixteen are transconfessional products of twentieth-century ecumenism. Concerning doctrine, some member churches are more, others less formally committed to subordinate standards; and, though the terms are "slippery," it may be said some are as a whole more conservative theologically than others. Some feel called to adopt a prophetic societal role, some cannot; and while most are, technically, voluntary societies, a few are, in different ways, established churches in their respective states.

Probably none are utterly cold toward ecumenism,* though a few are distinctly chilly, and not many are really hot. The several churches live among many cultures and language groups; some are in affluent societies, most are not—and members in the West will have to realize they themselves no longer account for the majority of Alliance membership.

The Alliance has sponsored a European Committee and Council and a Caribbean and North American Area Council (CANAAC). In 1988 Southern African member churches held a consultation in Botswana and formed a Southern Africa Regional Committee of the Alliance. An Executive Committee meets normally annually, and a General Council is held every five to seven years.

The offices of the Alliance are in the Ecumenical Centre, Geneva, the departments being the General Secretariat, Theology (1959), and Co-operation and Witness (1965).

Theological contributions. The WPA and the ICC were concerned with articulating major Christian doctrines and, especially, examining what their respective traditions had to offer to the wider Christian world. Neither body intended to become an exclusive confessional bloc. They also addressed socioethical issues. Some issues, such as war and peace, recur throughout the history; some, like temperance and Sabbath observance, virtually disappeared from the agenda after World War I; others, notably apartheid,* have been major concerns in recent years. In 1982, the Alliance declared at its General Council that "apartheid . . . is a sin, held that the moral and theological justification of it is . . . a theological heresy." For almost the first half of its life, the Alliance's parent bodies offered critical comment on the current philosophico-intellectual scene, but this waned sharply after 1920—a commentary, perhaps, on developments in both philosophy and theology.

The constituting of the Department of Theology (1959) enabled more continuous theological work to be undertaken. Numerous individuals and groups of scholars, appointed to specific tasks, have reported since that time. On occasion the Department (comprising one-third of the members of the Executive Committee, together with a Moderator and a Secretary) has undertaken projects, as have the European Committee and CANAAC.

The range of topics is evident from the titles of the publications: *Profile of the Eldership* (1974); *Theological Basis of Human Rights* (1976); *Theology of Marriage and the Problems of Mixed Marriages* (1977; with the Lutheran World Federation and the Secretariat for Promoting Christian Unity of the Roman Catholic Church); *Reformed Theology and the Jewish People* (1986); *Living Among Muslims* (1987; with the John Knox International Reformed Centre); and *Covenanting for Peace and Justice* (1989). From the European Committee have come: *Living in the Covenant Fellowship* (1980); *Sola Scriptura* (1986); and *Bible—Witness—Europe* (1987). CANAAC has produced *Reconciliation in Today's World* (1970); *A Covenant Challenge to Our Broken World* (1982); and *Peace, War and God's Justice* (1989).

The question of Christian unity was raised in the WPA and the ICC from the outset and, more particularly, in the periods following the Edinburgh (1910) and Lambeth (1920) Conferences. As time went on, an increasing number of member churches of both bodies entered into union with others, but the merger of the WPA with the ICC was the first (and still the only) union of its kind at the international level. A series of international bilateral dialogues was inaugurated when it became clear that the ecumenical contribution of the WCC* (1948) called for complementary activity on the part of the several Christian world communions and as a response to the ecumenical overtures of the post-Vatican II Roman Catholic Church.

The Presence of Christ in Church and World (1977) reports on conversations with the Roman Catholic Church. Christ's relationship to the church, the teaching authority of the church, Christ's presence in the world, the Eucharist, and the ministry were discussed. Many ecclesiological questions were left on the table, and some have been addressed in a second phase of dialogue (1984–88), the report of which is awaited. The sole mediatorship of Jesus Christ has been emphasized, and the question, "Is there a God-given structure of the Church?" has been discussed. The booklet *Reformed and Roman Catholic in Dialogue* (1988) surveys the results of national conversations. In these, CANAAC has been especially active.

Conversations between the Reformed and the Orthodox have occurred in many countries, and in 1973 the conclusion of a three-year dialogue between representatives of the North American Area of the Alliance and the Standing Conference of Canonical Orthodox Bishops in America was marked by publication of *The New Man*. Following preliminary conversations (1979; 1981; 1983) with the Ecumenical Patriarchate of Constantinople (T. F. Torrance, ed., *Theological Dialogue Between Orthodox and Reformed Churches* [Edinburgh, 1985]), a full-scale dialogue between the Orthodox Churches and the Alliance began (1988) on "The doctrine of the Trinity in the light of the Nicene-Constantinopolitan Creed."

As expected, the most practical recommendations toward manifesting the God-given unity of the church are in the dialogue reports between the Alliance and communions which in various ways understand themselves as sharing a common Reformation heritage. Thus, the Anglican-Reformed international dialogue report (*God's Reign and Our Unity* [1984]) recommends: "Where churches of our two communions are committed to going forward to seek visible unity, a measure of *reciprocal* communion should be made possible; for communion is not only a sign of unity achieved, but also a means by which God brings it about." This report notably discusses the ordering of the church in relation to the church's mission and the reign of God. Questions of women's ordination, and of establishment, are raised but not resolved.

Conversations between the Alliance and the Baptist World Alliance (1973–77) resulted in *Baptists and Reformed in Dialogue* (1984). The dialogue moved toward a comprehensive understanding of Christian initiation, implying that "those who focus the initiatory process in a composite rite of confession, baptism with water, admission to the Lord's Table at a specific point of time and those who relate the significant elements of this process by way of a temporal differentiation between its successive acts and phases may jointly recognize and agree that, in either case, by the grace of God and the work of the Spirit, the result is actual membership in the church of Christ. . . . But the question remains how theological theory and ecclesial practice can be held together." Thirteen years later, it is unclear how widely that question has been discussed by member churches of either Alliance, or what, if any, the results may have been.

Following a service of reconciliation in Zurich Cathedral (March 5, 1983), during which sixteenth-century Reformed persecutions of Anabaptists were confessed and repudiated, an Alliance and Mennonite World Conference dialogue was inaugurated (1984; *Mennonites and Reformed in Dialogue* [1986]). The two families introduced themselves to one another and paid further attention to historic anathemas. The peace question is raised in appendixes. Clearly, a more detailed study was needed of three "neuralgic" topics. Hence a second set of conversations were held (1989), and a report, *Baptism, Peace and the State in the Reformed and Mennonite Traditions*, is soon to be published.

In 1985 a preliminary consultation was held between the Alliance and the Disciples Ecumenical Consultative Council. The booklet *Reformed and Disciples of Christ in Dialogue* (1985) was well received, and a full-scale consultation took place (1987), the report of the latter, *Towards Closer Fellowship* (1988), declaring, "There are no theological or ecclesiastical issues which need to divide us as churches," and urging that Reformed–Disciples unity be expressed at all foci of church life—local to international.

Acknowledging that in many parts of the world those of the Reformed and Methodist heritages have already entered into church unions, a preliminary consultation was held (1985) between the Alliance and the World Methodist Council to assess the current situation. Traditional doctrinal and ecclesiological obstacles were identified and given detailed consideration at a major consultation (1987). The findings (*Reformed and Methodists in Dialogue* [1988]) affirm that "historic differences of theological perspective and practice still maintain their influence, but are not of sufficient weight to divide us. . . . In particular, we have found that the classical doctrinal issues which we were asked to review ought not to be seen as obstacles to unity between Methodists and Reformed." Thus the report poses questions to the two communions in their local, regional, and international aspects.

The international dialogue commission of the Alliance and the Lutheran World Federation (1985–88; LWF) produced *Toward Closer Fellowship* (1989). The commission built on European work which had resulted in the Leuenberg Agreement (1973) and on twenty years of North American consultations between CANAAC and its Lutheran partners, the most recent report being *An Invitation to Action* (1984). The international commission found that "nothing stands in the way of church fellowship" and urges member churches of WARC and LWF to establish "full pulpit and altar/table fellowship, with the necessary mutual recognition of ministers ordained for word and sacrament."

The nagging question persists: "With whom are the Alliance's dialogue partners in conversation?" We thus come full circle to the diversity of the Alliance family. Leaving on one side that the Alliance family is not coextensive with the Reformed family, since a number of Reformed churches are not members of the Alliance, and some belong to other small international Reformed organizations, we may ask (and others persistently ask): "How do Alliance members understand catholicity?" This was the subject of a study encapsulated by the first Theological Secretary of the Alliance, Lewis S. Mudge, in *One Church: Catholic and Reformed* (1963).

Again, "How far are Alliance member churches truly united with one another?" Different missions planted Reformed churches in the same country, and separation continues to this day; Presbyterians and Congregationalists live side by side; and the Reformed propensity for secession (as well as, paradoxically, for union) leaves its train of separate churchly bodies. This is discussed in the consultation report on "Unity and Union in the Reformed Family" (1985).

Yet again, "What do the member churches of the Alliance confess?" Encouragement toward answers is provided by the study program *Called to Witness to the Gospel Today* (1982) and the booklet *Confessions and Confessing in the Reformed Tradition Today* (1982). In 1986 a major consultation was held on "Confessing the Faith Today," and the subject was further pursued at the General Council (1989).

Finally, "How much do Alliance member churches know about one another?" "The Ordination of Women" (1985), "The Lord"s Supper" (1986), and *Saints: Visible, Orderly and Catholic. The Congregational Idea of the Church* (1986) were Alliance publications to acquaint its members with features of its tradition and current practice. With its booklet *Responding to "Baptism, Eucharist and Ministry": A Word to the Reformed Churches* (1984), the Alliance encouraged members to respond to the WCC's study, *Baptism, Eucharist and Ministry*. Reformed responses to this text were published (1986).

The desire to work for a unified Reformed communion is understandable—indeed, such unity is essential if the ecumenical work of the Alliance is to advance. There is, however, something paradoxical about this quest. Undue concern for Reformed identity would not be a truly Reformed concern! The Reformers sought the re-formation of the Church catholic. Accordingly, the question of how the Alliance is to balance confessional and ecumenical interests, and caution against inner-family sectarian trends, is perennial. It presses more urgently in a post-Constantinian age when many non-Western theological voices need to be heard, and the matter of relations with those of other faiths and of none cannot responsibly be shelved. The least (and perhaps most?) that a voluntary body claiming moral authority can do is press the question relentlessly, hoping its members will pay heed.

It is a fact (and a lament) that many

theological and dialogical seeds have been sown under Alliance auspices that have not as yet been harvested by member churches. Perhaps what is most needed is a grateful and obediential reappropriation of the gospel of God's grace by which we have been made one in Christ—whether we like it or not.

WARC Constitution (1970/1982); WPA, ICC, and WARC Council Proceedings; *The Reformed World* (and predecessor journals); *World Congregationalism* (1959–65); *Congregational Studies* (1965–70); A. Peel and D. Horton, *International Congregationalism* (1949); M. Pradervand, *A Century of Service* (1975); A. P. F. Sell, *A Reformed, Evangelical, Catholic Theology* (1991).

ALAN P. F. SELL

World Council of Churches

"The World Council of Churches is a fellowship of churches which confess the Lord Jesus Christ as God and Saviour according to the scriptures and therefore seek to fulfill together their common calling to the glory of the one God, Father, Son and Holy Spirit." Thus defined in its basis, the first article of its constitution, the WCC was constituted at its First Assembly in Amsterdam (August 23, 1948), by vote of official delegates from 145 churches belonging to the Anglican, Eastern Orthodox, and Protestant traditions. By 1989 membership had increased to over 300 churches in 108 countries. Among these were 46 Reformed member churches, not counting those United Churches which contain former Reformed churches.

The WCC's founding expressed the ecumenical* concern of the twentieth century, a new element in the history of Christianity, as well as the vision of notable church leadership during World War II and the postwar period. In the Reformed tradition alone, this leadership is attested by such names as John Baillie,* Roswell Barnes, Madeleine Barot,* Marc Boegner,* Emil Brunner,* Samuel Cavert, Josef Hromádka,* Alphonse Koechlin, Hendrik Kraemer,* John Mackay,* Reinhold* and H. Richard Niebuhr,* Henry P. Van Dusen,* and W. A. Visser 't Hooft.* Similar lists could be compiled from other traditions. Moreover, Reformed emphasis upon biblical theology and Reformed ecclesiology have contributed significantly to WCC identity, policy, and effectiveness.

With the member churches composing the basic element of the WCC, its structure consists of six parts.

1. The Assembly is the WCC's highest authority and broadest forum. Seven have been held: Amsterdam (1948), Evanston (1954), New Delhi (1961), Uppsala (1968), Nairobi (1975), Vancouver (1983), and Canberra (1991).

Assemblies have two functions: (*a*) They provide focus upon the ecumenical calling of the member churches. Using varied forms, Assemblies formulate ecumenical thought on the churches' search for unity and upon pressing aspects of their witness in the contemporary world. (*b*) Assemblies conduct business of the WCC. This includes formulating policy upon recommendation of the Central Committee and receiving reports from the Central Committee, the General Secretary, and the varied program units. The Assembly elects the presidents of the WCC and the Central Committee of 150 members.

Assemblies are composed of one delegate from each church, with additional delegates for larger churches in numbers determined by the Central Committee; and youth delegates, consultants, fraternal delegates, observers, and accredited visitors and press representatives named by the Central Committee.

2. The Central Committee, which meets annually, is composed of 150 members elected by the Assembly to govern between Assemblies. This includes appointing the General Secretary and staff, initiating and reviewing programs, authorizing and reviewing budgets and seeking funds. The Central Committee also addresses issues of world or church concern, either in private discussion or in public debate. An Executive Committee meets twice a year.

3. The Program Units, supervised by appropriate committees and served by employed staff, incorporate major WCC interests.

Program Unit 1, "Faith and Witness," addresses problems of church unity in faith and order; concerns in the pursuit of Christian world mission and evangelism; issues of worldwide import for the churches' task in society; and matters concerning dialogue with people of living faiths.

Program Unit 2, "Justice and Service," includes assistance to the churches' participation in development; to their witness concerning international affairs and peace; to their efforts to combat racism; to their programs of interchurch aid, refugee and world service; and Christian medical concerns.

Program Unit 3, "Education and Renewal," provides assistance to churches concerning education, including theological education; youth; the situation of women in church and society; and church renewal and congregational life.

4. The Ecumenical Institute (Bossey) receives younger and older scholars who come for substantial periods of study and research on topics of ecumenical concern. It is host, upon invitation, to important smaller ecumenical meetings.

5. Further elements of program are a substantial ecumenical library, a communications office, and the official journal (quarterly) of the WCC, the *Ecumenical Review* (1948–).

6. Relations between the WCC and the Roman Catholic Church are maintained and developed under the aegis of the Joint Working Committee, appointed jointly by the Vatican and the WCC. Created under the impetus of the Second Vatican Council (1965), this committee meets annually, is the principal formal instrument of Roman Catholic and WCC collaboration, and reports to the WCC Assembly.

The WCC has been served by four General Secretaries: W. A. Visser 't Hooft, Reformed Church of the Netherlands (1938–48, Provisional Committee; 1948–65); Eugene Carson Blake, Presbyterian Church in the U.S.A. (1966–72); Philip Potter, Methodist Church, West Indies (1972–84); Emilio Castro, Methodist Church, Uruguay (1985–).

R. S. Bilheimer, *Breakthrough: The Emergence of the Ecumenical Tradition* (1989); *History of the Ecumenical Movement*, vol. 1: *1517–1948*, ed. R. Rouse and S. C. Neill (1967); vol. 2: *1948–1968*, ed. H. E. Fey (1970).

ROBERT S. BILHEIMER

World Religions

It is difficult to discuss views of other religions within the context of the Reformed faith and its history. This is because both circumstances and perspectives in the early years of that history were so different from those more recent, as well as different from those of the early church.

Differently from the Mediterranean orientation and increasing access to the wider world of Roman Catholic lands after the Reformation, central European Protestants had little or no existential knowledge of the great non-Christian world of their time. Luther* had evidently read Theodor Bibliander's Latin translation of the Qur'an, at least in part, and deemed it an "accursed, shameful and desperate book." Calvin,* on the basis that the name of the one God was everywhere known, concluded that "the heathen, to a man, by their own vanity either were dragged or slipped back into false inventions" and were therefore without excuse (*Inst.* 1.10.3).

Neither Calvin nor Luther, however, in the widely eclectic scholarly as well as religious world of the sixteenth century was fully consistent in his perceptions or views. This was also the time of "spiritual" writers like Sebastian Franck, who wrote, "God is no respecter of persons but instead is to the Greeks as to the barbarian and the Turk, to the lord as to the servant, as long as they retain the light which has shined upon them and gives their heart an eternal glow" (G. H. Williams, *Spiritual and Anabaptist Writers* [1957], p. 150). Above all, the whole range of Protestant Reformers drank deeply from and contributed to the cultural humanism* of their day. Thus Calvin saw the liberal arts, the contents of whose studies were very largely of non-Christian origin, as gifts of God and felt free to borrow from any source he could regard as having come from God. He believed that philosophers in all times and places had been stimulated by God, "that they might enlighten the world in knowledge of the truth" (*Inst.* 1.3.1). Calvin had some genuine respect for the religious insights of persons everywhere, of "even the most remote peoples." At the same time, he was careful to discriminate, regarding the religion of the Greeks as qualitatively superior to that of the Egyptians or the Romans.

The way out and up from the limitations of common Reformation thinking has been long and even tortuous. Within the specifically Reformed tradition we may note the Dutch Arminian* Remonstrants* of the second half of the seventeenth century. Like the Cambridge Platonists in England with their emphasis on "inner illumination," the Dutch Remonstrants, who had long and close associations with the English Platonists, showed a "general courtesy and politeness, . . . reasonableness and breadth of view" in their personal and theological posture. This tradition of profound spirituality, relatively conservative biblical scholarship, and religious understanding open to the data of natural science,* minority a view as it was in its time, came to be the attitudinal foundation for broader understanding in the following centuries. Protestant foreign mission activity, in which Reformed churches played an increasingly important role, contributed greatly to larger perspectives. Often missionaries who left their homelands believing that non-Christian religions were simply the work of Satan were forced by their field experiences to modify these views. As early as 1710 the German pietist missionary in India, Bartholomäus Ziegenbalg, wrote that he did not reject everything taught by the Hindus but, rather, rejoiced that for them "long ago a small light of the Gospel began to shine" and that "one will find here and there such teachings and passages in their writings which are not only according to human reason but also according to God's Word" (W. R. Hogg, "Edinburgh 1910—Perspective 1980," *Occasional Bulletin of Missionary Research* 4, no. 4 [Oct. 1980]: 149).

At the present time a rather weighty consensus among Reformed theologians regarding world religions is emerging from renewed studies of the early church and recent biblical studies. The biblical covenants* that played a central role in the faith life of both Israel and the Christian church are seen to begin with universal covenants. Some scholars hold that the divinely initiated covenants begin with creation itself. Others prefer to see the first biblical covenant in the promise of God to Eve (Gen. 3:15–16). All agree that the divine covenant with Noah and his family includes not only all humanity but also "every living creature of all flesh" (Gen. 9:8–17). These covenants are now seen as both revelatory and salvific in meaning and as constituting the framework of the entire biblical story.

We now see that the mainstream of theologians in the early church shared in this perception of the "wider work of God in the world." The Logos theology of Justin Martyr (100–165) with its view of a "seed" (Gr. *sperma*) of the Logos given to every human being long before the manifestation in Jesus of Nazareth made it possible for Justin and other early Christians to recognize some qualities of the Logos—seen perfectly in Jesus—in noble pagans. Justin dared identify as worthy of the name Christian pre-Christian philosophers of Greece like Socrates or Heraclitus. Irenaeus (fl. 185) taught that God is one and the same to all humans and has aided the human race from its beginning by various economies or arrangements (Lat. *variis dispositionibus*). Clement of Alexandria (150–215) wrote that "all authentic understanding or wisdom is sent by God and that the true teacher of the Egyptians, the Indians, the Babylonians and the Persians, indeed of all created beings, is the first-begotten Son, the Fellow-counselor of God. . . . Many are the different covenants of God with men" (*Stromateis* 6. 7).

A major contemporary responsibility of Reformed churches is to combine these wider perceptions of the presence and work of the triune God throughout human history with a renewed and Reformed commitment to the Christian world mission. To realize that no human being is a blank sheet of paper before our Maker and that a wise missionary is prepared to learn from as well as to teach persons of other backgrounds does not call for the abolition of that mission but for its purification in both motive and practice.

RICHARD H. DRUMMOND

Worship

In Reformed churches, worship is the service of God's glory. This service is in Jesus Christ, continuing his preaching* of the gospel, his acts of mercy, his ministry of prayer,* and celebration of the sacraments* he instituted. It is both in Christ's name and in the fellowship of his body. Finally, worship is a divine work initiated, inspired, and constantly supported by the Holy Spirit* at work in the individual human heart and the assembled congregation.

The Reformed approach to worship is most easily understood from certain key Scripture passages. A fundamental principle of Reformed theology is that worship must be formed and constantly reformed according to Scripture.* That worship be according to God's Word* follows from the perception that it is God's work. Our worship is at Christ's bidding and therefore bears the promise of his presence (Matt. 28:20). In working this out, the Reformers—notably John Oecolampadius*—intended to steer a middle course between the strict principle that what is not commanded by Scripture is forbidden and the lax principle that what is not forbidden is permitted. By the end of the sixteenth century this had become a major plank in the Puritan* program for liturgical reform as in the Admonition to Parliament* (1572). William Ames* affirmed the principle of Augustine* and Calvin* that nothing glorifies God quite so much as that which comes from God—that is, our worship should reflect God's glory. A most balanced statement of this principle is in the Westminster Confession* (1.6).

Already in the first tablet of the law of Moses, Israel is called to serve God's glory. This service is to be to the one true God and no other. Neither idols, which could confuse God's nature, nor magical formulas, which would profane God's name, are to be used. Rather, God's people are to gather each Sabbath in remembrance of God's mighty acts of creation and redemption. For a Reformed theology of worship a Christian understanding of the first four commandments has always been fundamental (cf. Zacharias Ursinus* on the Heidelberg Catechism* [qq. 93–103]). As Calvin said, the first tablet of the law was summed up by Jesus as the first and greatest commandment, the commandment to love God. Worship is, therefore, in terms of the love relationship between God and the people of God (*Inst.* 2.8.11–34). Paul treats several liturgical questions in 1 Corinthians 10–14 in terms of this covenant love. For this reason, many Reformed preachers, such as New England's Thomas Shepard,* Scotland's John Willison,* and New Jersey's Gilbert Tennent,* often preached on the wedding feast of the Lamb at Communion. They understood worship in terms of covenant love.

When Martin Bucer* set down the program of liturgical reform of the Church of Strassburg in his *Grund und Ursach* (1524), he drew from Acts 2:42 that worship should consist of (1) reading and teaching the Scriptures; (2) fellowship, expressed especially in giving alms; (3) celebration of the sacraments of Baptism* and the Lord's Supper*; and (4) the service of daily prayer. Strassburg developed a very full diet of prayer, including the singing of psalms and hymns, prayers of confession and supplication, prayers of intercession, thanksgivings, and benedictions. Place was given both to set forms of prayer and to extempore prayer. Bucer, as the Reformed tradition generally, was not so concerned for the sequence of these elements as that they all be included.

The Reformed approach to worship can be explained in terms of several dimensions of worship. First there is the kerygmatic dimension. Jesus came preaching the gospel of the kingdom.* The preaching of the gospel is worship because it proclaims God's rule and witnesses to God's sovereignty. In the worship of the Temple many of the psalms were acclamations of God's sovereign presence (e.g., Ps. 93; 96–99), not only in regard to Israel but all nations. In the same way evangelism* glorifies God by proclaiming the Lordship of Christ over all nations and cultures. The missionary and evangelistic preaching of the nineteenth and twentieth centuries understood well the kerygmatic dimension of worship. Just as many of the ancient psalms were kerygmatic, so many Christian hymns* are kerygmatic. One thinks of Isaac Watts's* paraphrase of Psalm 72: "Jesus Shall Reign Where'er the Sun," or of Joachim Neander's "Praise to the Lord, the Almighty, the King of Creation." Much church music is kerygmatic. Organ preludes and postludes emphasize the kerygmatic dimension of Christian worship just as the sounding of the shofar and the blowing of trumpets announced the Sabbaths of ancient Israel.

Worship has an epicletic dimension; it calls on God's name for our help and salvation. An epiclesis is a prayer calling upon or invoking God. Just as it was important for OT worship not to use God's name in vain, so it was important for NT worship to hallow God's name. God is worshiped when the faithful call upon God in time of need. Many psalms are lamentations, supplications, and confessions of sin (e.g., Ps. 22; 42; 51; 102; 130). Jesus prayed them in his own worship, and in the Lord's Prayer he taught his disciples to pray for the forgiveness of their sins, for the supplying of their daily bread, for deliverance from evil, and for the coming of the kingdom. Reformed worship gives great attention to the invocation of God's name at the beginning of worship and the invocation of the Holy Spirit before the reading and preaching of the Scriptures. In the celebration of both Baptism and Communion, God the Father is called upon to send the Holy Spirit so that what is signified in the sacramental action becomes a reality in the lives of those who receive it.

Worship has a prophetic dimension. Jesus and the apostles no less than the prophets insisted that while God's glory is obscured by injustice and immorality, it is magnified when the worshiping community reflects God's holiness (Micah 6:6–8; Amos 5:21–24; Isa. 6:3–8). The service of God's glory entails the service of mercy toward the neighbor (Matt. 22:36–39; Rom. 12). The collection of tithes and alms, therefore, has a place in worship. It is in the diaconal ministry that the service of mercy and the service of worship are tied together. Theodor Fliedner and the German Reformed deaconesses developed this in a notable way. From this prophetic dimension of worship Reformed churches have developed a simple, orderly worship and have avoided sumptuous liturgical forms. As Calvin put it, "Humility is the beginning of worship" (*Commentary* on Micah 6:8).

The wisdom tradition of the Old and New Testaments shows us yet another dimension of worship. The wisdom tradition delighted in the Word of God (Ps. 1:2–3). In studying the Word, memorizing it, teaching it, preaching it, and living it, God was glorified. As in Psalm 19, the law, God's Word, glorifies God in the same way as the order of creation. In fact, God delights in wisdom (Prov. 8:30). In Johannine Logos Christology* we find how the wisdom tradition approached worship (John 1:14–18; 2:1–11; 6:25–69; 20:29–31). The wisdom dimension helps us understand the importance of preaching in Reformed worship. Sermons of Huldrych Zwingli,* Thomas Goodwin,* or Charles H. Spurgeon* delight in Scripture. Thomas Manton's* 190 sermons on Psalm 119 can best be appreciated in terms of this delight.

Finally, there is a covenantal dimension. This is found in the worship described in Exodus 24. The Book of the Covenant is read, and with the making of vows of faith, the covenant is sealed both by the sprinkling of the blood of the covenant and by the sharing of a meal. Early in the Reformation, Heinrich Bullinger* developed a covenantal understanding of the sacraments. Ever since, Reformed theologians encouraged by 1 Cor. 11:25 have seen these covenantal assemblies of the OT as types of Christian worship where the breaking of bread and the sharing of the cup unite Christians in the new and eternal covenant. So also with Baptism, which, because it was a sign of the covenant as was circumcision, was appropriately given to the children of the covenant community. From this baptismal understanding, Horace Bushnell* derived his ideas on Christian nurture. One place where this covenantal dimension is seen most clearly is in the Scottish Communion season. There the vows of faith were made and renewed. From New England's Jonathan Edwards* and Virginia's Samuel Davies, it was clear that those who came to faith during the Great Awakening* formally professed that faith at Communion.

E. B. Holifield, *The Covenant Sealed* (1974); J. H. Nichols, *Corporate Worship in the Reformed Tradition* (1968); H. O. Old, *Worship That Is Reformed According to Scripture* (1984).

HUGHES OLIPHANT OLD

Zanchi, Girolamo (1516–1590)

A pivotal figure in the formation of Reformed scholasticism.* Trained as a Thomist, Zanchi converted to Calvinism* under Peter Martyr Vermigli.* Targeted by the Inquisition, he was forced to live in exile. In October 1551, Zanchi left Italy for the Italian community in Geneva. He lived there for nine months while attending Calvin's* sermons and lectures. After teaching in the humanist academy at Strassburg (1553–63), he pastored a Reformed congregation of Italian refugees in Chiavenna until 1567. He contended with the ultra-Lutheranism of Johann Marbach of Strassburg, articulating a Reformed view on Christology,* the Eucharist, and the perseverance of the saints.* Zanchi's eucharistic and christological interests converge in his *De coniugio spirituali* (posth., 1591), where he insisted on the human finitude of the Lord's body against Lutheran notions of ubiquity.* A radical Augustinianism underlies Zanchi's doctrine of perseverance: divine sovereignty and immutability ensure that those who are elected to eternal life can never lose it. In response to rising anti-Trinitarianism at Chiavenna and the University of Heidelberg (where he taught from 1568 until 1577), Zanchi wrote *De tribus Elohim* (1572) and *De natura Dei* (1577), presenting a thoroughly Chalcedonian orthodoxy. After the death of Zanchi's patron, the elector Frederick III, Ludwig VI's Lutheran sympathies necessitated Zanchi's leaving Heidelberg to spend his final years as a professor of biblical theology at the Casimiranum in Neustadt an der Haardt.

Zanchi's primary contribution to the development of the Reformed tradition lies in his blend of Thomism and Calvinism, providing a crucial linkage between the Reformed faith and the heritage of medieval Catholicism. Zanchi demonstrated the fruitfulness of deploying Aristotelian and scholastic resources in support of a systematic exposition and defense of Reformed doctrine. Though this led him to theological controversy, his tone is not entirely polemical. His approach reveals a remarkable warmth and generosity, finding its fullest expression in his vision of a Reformed Christianity that is nonpartisan and ecumenical.

Operum theologicorum D. Hieronymi Zanchii (1613), vols. 1–8; C. J. Burchill, "Girolamo Zanchi: Portrait of a Reformed Theologian and His Work," *SCJ* 15, no. 2 (1984): 185–207; J. P. Donnelly, "Calvinist Thomism," *Viator* 7 (1976): 441–55; O. Gründler, *Die Gotteslehre Girolami Zanchis* (1965); J. Moltmann, *Predestination und Perseveranz* (1961); D. Schmidt, "Girolamo Zanchi," *Theologische Studien und Kritiken* 32 (1859): 625–708; N. Shepherd, "Zanchius on Saving Faith," *WTJ* 36 (1973): 31–47; J. N. Tylenda, "Girolamo Zanchi and John Calvin: A Study in Discipleship as Seen Through Their Correspondence," *CTJ* 10, no. 2 (1975): 101–41.

JOHN L. FARTHING

Zell, Katharina Schütz (1497/98–1562)

A reformer, writer, and religious activist in Strassburg through the first four decades of the Protestant Reformation. Katharina was the daughter of a cabinetmaker and received a good middle-class girl's education. Though she never mastered Latin, she wrote German fluently, as her five published treatises demonstrate.

Katharina has traditionally been remembered as "the wife of Matthew Zell," one of the four major Strassburg reformers. She clearly regarded her marriage to the former Roman Catholic priest as a religious vocation* to advance the cause of the gospel and save Matthew's soul and the souls of others led astray by the impossibility of adhering to clerical celibacy. Katharina entered vigorously into the new role of pastor's helpmeet, convinced this calling was a partnership in service even should it lead to shared martyrdom. As a Protestant pastor's wife, she welcomed visiting reformers and refugees alike, sometimes (e.g., during the Peasants' War) organizing food and shelter for scores of people.

According to her understanding of the priesthood of believers,* however, Katharina did not confine her calling to the household, or even to the service of the poor, sick, or refugees. Because she had no living children of her own, her energies were freed for a more active public—and occasionally controversial—role. Among strangers whom Katharina welcomed were people whose religious views were increasingly unwelcome in Strassburg, especially after the new church regulations (1533) and the Interim (1548). Katharina continued to defend such friends as Kaspar Schwenckfeld; among her last acts was that of presiding at the burial of one of his followers whom the city clergy considered heretical (1562). Katharina's civic sense was of a piece with her religious activism, as her complaints to the magistracy about hospital malpractice illustrates.

Katharina also disturbed the peace by her publications which were unusual in scope and time span for a woman or layperson. The first pamphlet (1524) was a letter of consolation to women separated from their husbands for the Protestant faith. The same year, Katharina entered the religious controversy over clerical marriage, addressing a lively treatise to the bishop. A decade later (1534–36) came four little booklets of hymns with a preface by Katharina. More polemic in defense of the Reformation appeared in an autobiographical exchange of letters with a Lutheran pastor (1557), and pastoral concerns prompted Katharina's final publication (1558) of devotional meditations on certain psalms and two of the traditional catechetical* loci (the Lord's Prayer and Creed). A manuscript sermon preached at her husband's death (1548) also survives. Katharina's writings, full of biblical allusions and vivid metaphors, confront the reader with a dynamic, independent character of conviction, faith, and humor.

R. H. Bainton, *Women of the Reformation in Germany and Italy* (1971); E. A. McKee, *Katharina Schütz Zell: The Life, Writings, and Theology of a Sixteenth-Century Reformer* (1992).

ELSIE ANNE MCKEE

Zwingli, Huldrych (1484–1531)

Huldrych (Ulrich) Zwingli, not John Calvin,* was the father of the reformed Reformation in Switzerland. Though allied to the Swiss Confederacy, Geneva never became a part of Switzerland until after 1815, and despite the harmony present in the First* (1536) and in the Second Helvetic Confession* (1566), which appeared after Calvin's death (1564), Calvin had surprisingly little influence on the German Swiss cantons that accepted the Reformation. Indeed, the Swiss reformed cantons viewed Calvin's conception of the church* and the Geneva Consistory's* infrequent and restrained use of excommunication with great suspicion.

Zwingli was born in the village of Wildhaus in the duchy of the Toggenburg, a part of the Swiss Confederacy. His father was the local bailiff, and his family had long been involved in the local government. Zwingli inherited a keen sense for the problems of government and later identified his reform program with the interests of Zurich's two ruling councils. His willingness to work with the government to introduce church reform caused a split among his own followers and led to the founding of a church that practiced believer's baptism, rejected Zwingli's alliance between clergy and magistracy (1525), and was crushed by the Zurich magistracy. Modern scholars still puzzle over the causes of the rift between Zwingli and certain of his followers.

Educated for a clerical career, Zwingli attended school at Basel and Bern, studied at the University of Vienna, where he was influenced by the humanist* and cultural nationalist Conradus Celtis. He received his B.A. (1504) and M.A. (1506) from the University of Basel. At Basel the theology of Thomas Aquinas and Duns Scotus ("the ancient way"), which later played a role in the development of his theology, interested him more than Occam's "modern way."

Ordained on September 29, 1506, Zwingli was appointed to the parish of

Glarus in the canton of Glarus. While he was there, his friend Glarean introduced him to the humanist circle at Basel led by Erasmus.* Erasmus brought Zwingli to study the church fathers and the Bible and caused him to be critical of scholastic* methodology. Zwingli never abandoned Erasmus's conception of church reform, though he synthesized it with other influences from Marsilius of Padua, Origen, Luther,* and, through Luther, Augustine.*

From his humanist studies and experience as a military chaplain in Italy (1513; 1515), Zwingli rejected the sale of mercenaries to foreign powers. His opposition to the mercenary treaty with France (1516) forced him to leave Glarus and become people's priest at the cloister of Einsiedeln, where he continued to preach church reform and had a liaison with a local woman.

Despite the opposition of some of the canons who disliked Erasmian reformers and were involved in the sale of mercenaries to France, Zwingli was chosen people's priest at the Zurich Great Church (late 1518). On January 1, 1519, he began a series of sermons on the Gospel of Matthew which marked the beginning of the Zurich reformation.

Between 1519 and 1528 Zwingli introduced church reform to the urban cantons of Zurich, Bern, Basel, and Schaffhausen and to parts of the rural cantons of Appenzell and Glarus. His reformation was less successful in the forest cantons which were goaded into war by the aggressive tactics of the Zwinglian cantons. The defeat of the Zwinglians and Zwingli's death in the second battle of Kappel ended the spread of Zwinglianism in the Swiss Confederacy and freed Zurich's ally, Bern, to continue its westward expansion which opened the way for the introduction of the reform movement at Geneva under Calvin's guidance.

Zwingli's theology. Zwingli's reformed Protestantism was characterized by its moral rigorism, simplicity of worship*—pictures, statues, stained-glass windows, and organs were removed from the churches—and emphasis on the sovereignty of God* which led Zwingli to assert that God had elected some to eternal salvation* before the creation of the world (*supralapsarianismus*; supralapsarianism*). Zwingli never discussed the fate of the others and cannot be called a double predestinarian. He believed the sermon was the center of worship and followed Luther in saying that when the gospel was preached, the congregation heard the living Word of God.* Baptism* and the Lord's Supper* were the two sacraments* accepted as biblical and valid. Baptism served as a sign of membership both in the civil community and in the visible church which was coterminus with the city republic and whose worldly affairs, including decisions about excommunication, were under the control of the magistracy.

Though he spoke of a "spiritual eating," Zwingli denied that Christ was physically present in the bread and the wine of the Lord's Supper. He argued that the sacrament was a joyous celebration of the memory of Christ's death, but he was no mere memorialist. Zwingli believed that Christ was spiritually present and united the congregation as his body. His interpretation caused a prolonged conflict with Luther which prevented both a theological consensus and a military alliance between the Lutherans and the Reformed (Marburg Colloquy,* 1529). The failure of the Marburg Colloquy left the Swiss Protestant cantons isolated and contributed to their defeat (1531).

E. J. Furcha and H. W. Pipkin, eds., *Prophet, Pastor, Protestant: The Work of Huldrych Zwingli After Five Hundred Years* (1984); U. Gäbler, *Huldrych Zwingli: His Life and Work* (1986); J. V. Pollet, *Huldrych Zwingli et le Zwinglianisme* (1988); R. C. Walton, "Zwingli: Founding Father of the Reformed Churches," in *Leaders of the Reformation*, ed. R. DeMolen (1984); and *Zwingli's Theocracy* (1967).

ROBERT C. WALTON